Canadian Communications

Issues in Contemporary Media and Culture

Second Edition

Edited by

Bohdan Szuchewycz
Brock University

and

Jeannette Sloniowski
Brock University

Prentice Hall

For Tomas, Kieran, and Jane.
–Bohdan

To my parents, Alfred and Kitty Neal.
–Jeannette

Canadian Cataloguing in Publication Data

Main entry under title:

Canadian communications : issues in contemporary media and culture

2nd ed.
ISBN 0-13-090584-4

1. Mass Media — Social aspects — Canada. 2. Canada — Cultural policy. 3. Cultural industries — Canada. I. Szuchewycz, Bohdan George, 1954–   . II. Sloniowski, Jeannette Marie, 1946–   .

P92.C3C28 2002   302.23'0971   C2001-930584-4

ISBN 0-13-090584-4

Vice-President, Editorial Director: Michael Young
Editor-in-Chief: David Stover
Acquisitions Editor: Andrew Wellner
Executive Marketing Manager: Christine Cozens
Associate Editor: Tammy Scherer
Production Editor: Joe Zingrone
Copy Editor: Alex Moore
Production Coordinator: Patricia Ciardullo
Page Layout: Heidi Palfrey
Permissions Research: Susan Wallace-Cox
Art Director: Julia Hall
Cover/Interior Design: Amy Harnden
Cover Image: Comstock

1 2 3 4 5   05 04 03 02

Printed and Bound in Canada.

Contents

Chapter 23: Public Relations: The Canadian Spin   372

Chapter 24: History for Sale: Let the Buyer Beware   388

Preface

Books on issues in Canadian culture and communications require regular revision because of the vitality and rapid rate of change in both of these areas. We have responded here not only to our own sense of what is new and exciting on the cultural landscape, but also to comments elicited from instructors using the text, our teaching assistants and students, and the outside reviewers and editors at Pearson Education Canada. We thank all of them for their insightful and useful suggestions.

The second edition, although it retains the same format as the first, is considerably different. Our authors, old and new, are well informed, passionate about their subjects, and opinionated enough to generate discussion among readers. We have chosen people who have something to say—even if we do not agree with them. They are all part of the vital and ongoing debate about Canada and Canadians.

We have retained the issues we felt to be important, and have updated the articles in most chapters. Some new chapters, like *Canadian Identity* and *Youth Culture*, have been added. We have blended in other chapters, like those on the Internet, in order to allow technology to figure more prominently throughout the book. Certain issues, like the Teale/Homolka news ban, have been dropped in favour of a chapter on the wider issue of censorship across a range of media. Other issues, like the Into the Heart of Africa exhibition at the Royal Ontario Museum, have been retained because the controversy created there retains a profound and chilling effect upon art galleries and museums, both in Canada and elsewhere. Each chapter has more Weblinks and some new questions. We have also added suggestions for further reading to many chapters where excellent and up-to-date theoretical sources exist.

The book is divided into six sections:

Language

Cultural Forms

The News

Representations

Policy and Regulation

Advertising

Each section contains chapters about important political and cultural debates.

We have put together a book of accessible writing on Canadian media and culture. It is our hope that instructors will provide a wider theoretical framework that will enable students to understand the issues at stake behind particular chapters.

Acknowledgments

We would like to thank Will Webster, Dean of Social Science, for his continuing support of this project. Our teaching assistants Caroline Stikkelbroeck, Stephanie Clayton, and Elizabeth Cecci gave us invaluable insight into which issues resonated with students and which did not. Briget Cahill, the administrative assistant in the Department of Communications, Popular Culture and Film, was a great help in getting the final manuscript out.

We would like to give a special word of thanks to faculty who reviewed the manuscript and made many valuable suggestions about how it might be improved. They are: Seth Feldman, York University; Gary Genosko, Lakehead University; Keith Hampson, Ryerson Polytechnic University; and Grant Havers, Trinity Western University. Useful feedback was also provided by Paul Attallah, Carleton University; J. Gillies, Ryerson Polytechnic University; and Michael Monty, Seneca College.

We would also like to thank our authors for their passionate, intelligent, and occasionally grumpy essays. Their writing demonstrates, in no uncertain terms, that debate about Canada is alive and well.

chapter one

Language Laws:

Speaking of the Distinct Society

INTRODUCTION

Choice of code is one of the fundamental aspects of all acts of communication, and the consequences of that choice at both the individual and societal levels reflect profound issues of personal and national identity, issues of power and prestige, and issues of individual and collective rights.

This section opens with a speech by Maxwell Yalden in which he outlines (1) the link between human rights and language rights in Canadian and international law, (2) the relationship between multicultural minority rights and multilingualism, and (3) how Canadian policy in particular might be seen in terms of its position with respect to a unicultural/unilingual multicultural/multilingual continuum.

While Yalden clearly favours a multicultural/multilingual approach to language policy in Canada, Ray Conlogue presents the unicultural/unilingual position and the argument that language policy be based on recognizing only the dominant majority language of a specific territory or jurisdiction. In other words, a person must expect to learn and, in official contexts, to be served only in the majority language of the area.

Against this broad background on language rights and human rights, the following pieces deal specifically with the question of the Quebec language laws—laws that make French the required language of commerce in Quebec.

John Fraser's piece, although it focuses only on one historical source, *Saturday Night* magazine, provides a valuable historical lesson on anglophone arrogance towards francophones in Canada and thus helps contextualize the contemporary situation with respect to the French language in Quebec.

The final two short pieces reflect a recent controversy involving the application of Bill 101 to commercial Web sites originating from businesses within Quebec. The OLF's (Office de la langue française) official statement on the issue is reproduced along with a list of frequently asked questions concerning the application of the law. The final selection, an editorial from the *Gazette* (Montreal), questions the role of government in determining how businesses can advertise their services on the Web.

LANGUAGE, HUMAN RIGHTS AND THE NEW WORLD ORDER

Maxwell Yalden *(Canadian Speeches: Issues of the Day)*

I am honoured to have been asked to speak to you about multilingualism in an interdependent world.

The subject is one that concerns me deeply and one to which I have devoted some years of professional effort. It is not, I need hardly add, a matter that loses any of its significance with the passing of the years.

Linguistic Pluralism and Human Rights

Given my own background and present duties, my immediate aim this evening will be to relate our overall topic to some of the issues surrounding linguistic pluralism and human rights.

In summary form, I think that task involves, first, establishing a connection between language and human rights; second, an examination of the relationship between multiculturalism (minority rights) and multilingualism (language rights); and, third, an attempt to situate Canada on the spectrum between what one might call uniculturalism and unilingualism on the one hand and pluriculturalism and pluralism on the other. An attempt, so to say, to borrow an expression from our neighbours to the south, to balance the "pluribus" and the "unum."

First, as to the matter of language and human rights. So far as the law of Canada is concerned, we have it from no less an authority than the former chief justice of the Supreme Court of Canada, Brian Dickson, that "language rights are a well-known species of human rights and should be approached accordingly." This dictum also reflects the position in international law, where, for example, the International Convenant on Civil and Political Rights asserts (article 27) that: "In those States in which ethnic, religious or linguistic minorities exist, persons belonging to such minorities shall not be denied the right, in community with other members of their group, to enjoy their own culture, to profess and practice their own religion, or to use their own language."

In other words, in both domestic and international law, language rights are recognized and language is treated as a forbidden ground of discrimination. So far so good. However, there is clearly a distinction to be made between a bare-bones approach to language rights

Maxwell Yalden. 1993. Language, human rights and the new world order. *Canadian Speeches: Issues of the Day* 7(6), 9-13. (Speech to a conference on "Multilingualism in an interdependent world," sponsored by the Ontario Institute for Studies in Education and the Goethe Institute, Toronto, September 9, 1993.)

qua human rights and a full blown scheme of multiculturalism-multilingualism, let alone "in an interdependent world." It is to these latter questions that I would like principally to address myself this evening.

What I would like to do is to consider with you how Canada has in the past attempted and should in the future attempt to cultivate what is best and most productive in our linguistic inheritance while at the same time trying to reconcile within the spirit of our human rights commitments those conflicts that inevitably arise. In doing so, I hope, we will be able to acknowledge and accept those differences that must sometimes exist among languages, and to do so with an eye on the experience of other countries and the exigencies of an interdependent world.

Canadian Public Policy Position

Before trying to outline what may be "the best," or at least "a better" mix of public policies, we would do well to remind ourselves how we arrived at our present configuration of linguistic and cultural policies. They are, I would suggest, an attempt to reflect the political and cultural history of Canada in ways that do some sort of justice to the unique blending of peoples and interests that makes up both our past and our present experience as a country.

After a decidedly checkered history of tolerance and intolerance, Canada has over the last 20 years or so espoused an official policy of bilingualism and multiculturalism. This, as many of you will know, represents a compromise position that arose from the experience of the Royal Commission on Bilingualism and Biculturalism.

The government of the day, in responding to the Commission's recommendations, came to the conclusion in 1971 that it could not sustain a bicultural policy, based upon a two-founding-nations theory. If that thesis had ever made any sense, it was their conclusion that it could not do so any longer as we moved in to the last decades of the 20th century.

Even looking backwards, if there were only "two founding peoples," what was the role of European immigrant populations—non-English and non-French—in founding western Canada? And if there were only "two founding peoples," what of the others from all corners of the globe who increasingly make up the contemporary Canadian family? And what of our first peoples who were left almost entirely out of this calculation?

Whatever the answer to these questions, for better or for worse, there was born a new doctrine of two official languages, but no official cultures, as it was then described. Or multiculturalism, for short. What multiculturalism means for Canadians today, and what benefits derive from that official policy, is no doubt a matter of one's personal history and perspective. It has a different practical resonance not only for Canadians of English, French or aboriginal backgrounds, but also for third-generation Europeans or first-generation Asian or African Canadians.

Multiculturalism and Multilingualism

It also has consequences for multilingualism which are rather less clear. For there has never been and there is not today a direct linkage between the two concepts: multiculturalism and multilingualism. If for no other reason than that, in law, in Canada, they are different: two languages occupy a privileged situation as languages of public discourse, for example; no culture can pretend to that situation, at least not in law.

And law aside, two languages, and more particularly one of them, occupy a situation of power that no others can match. Or as Joshua Fishman reminded a colloquium on language planning in Ottawa some years ago, the human rights principle that "all languages are equal" runs smack up against the fact that, in practice, "languages are mainfestly unequal in social utility and therefore, in social power."

Canada's policy of multiculturalism cannot alter that fact. It can however, do either more or less to temper its consequences for Canadians who do not have either English or French as a mother tongue. The question is precisely where the policy I have been describing leaves the many other languages spoken in Canada vis-à-vis their official treatment and support.

Leaving aside their rather marginal rights of public usage in the courts or with the federal, provincial or municipal bureaucracies, what one may loosely call the immigrant languages of Canada clearly enjoy the following rights:

- they may be freely used for purposes of domestic or community communication;
- they can be and are quite widely used in media communications or for creative purposes; and
- they may be used as either languages of instruction or as subjects of study in the education system.

By and large, and speaking from a human rights perspective, the first two areas of social utility are neither more nor less than what may be enjoyed by many languages in many countries around the globe. More critical is the degree of official encouragement these languages receive at the educational level.

Canada's multiculturalism policy has always given support to the retention and use of heritage languages within its various linguistic communities. The proper form and extent of public support to heritage languages within the school curriculum has, however, been a source of controversy. To put the matter bluntly, we have never been very clear where we stand on the scale that runs from maximum tolerance for linguistic and cultural differences to an official investment in what some critics consider to be a new Tower of Babel.

By the very nature of our public policies, it is clear that all Canadians are expected to achieve some fluency in English, French or both. What is less clear is how that ties in with either the transitional use, the maintenance or the acquisition of any other language spoken in Canada, from Arabic to Zulu. What is more, the experience of other countries, in this interdependent world of ours, while intriguing, does not always provide the sort of clear sign posts we might hope to find.

For example, as I understand it, every European state, with the sole exception of Iceland, has minority language populations, and each tries to deal with them in its own way. But would one wish to take lessons from France, say, with its Breton, Basque, Corsican and other minorities? Or from Italy in the Alto Adige or the Val d'Aoste? Or Great Britain with respect to Welsh or Scots Gaelic? And are these situations truly relevant to the Canadian experience in any case? For are we not looking there at indigenous populations whose languages have moved to a minority status with demographic change and shifting frontiers, rather than at the Canadian experiment with essentially immigrant languages?

Perhaps the languages of the Gastarbeiter, or other migrants such as the Maghrebi in France are more apt illustrations. And there is no doubt that much useful work has been done in Europe, and that there is much to be learned from that source. About language teaching, that is, and the integration of minority groups; but less I think about the sort of policy Canada should adopt as to its overall placement on the unilingual-multilingual spectrum.

Nor is the United States, that never-ending source of fascination for Canadians, a much more enlightening source of policy leads. In some respects, Americans have come a long way since Willa Cather questioned what she called the "rooted conviction" of "legislation that a boy can be a better American if he speaks only one language than if he speaks two." But the long-running battle between the proponents of "English Only" and the advocates of linguistic pluralism has not necessarily led to victory for the latter.

The bilingualism or multilingualism that began as a transitional educational program to enable minority-language students, mostly Spanish-speaking, to fully enjoy their constitutional entitlements to public education has assumed a much broader aspect in the wake of the civil rights decision in the Lau case. The result has been—in theory—to give broader rights to a wide spectrum of immigrant languages, particularly in California.

As some observers see it, this could have the effect not only of swamping or distorting access to public services but—in the longer run—of working to the detriment even of such languages as Spanish or Chinese, which, in that context, might be thought to have a historical and demographic title to recognition that is not like that of Korean or Vietnamese.

At all events, once again, we must consider whether this experience is in any way comparable to that which we are living through or are likely to live through in Canada. Is it at all clear that, because there is reason to question whether the schools have been able to handle the problem adequately in Los Angeles we will not be up to it in Vancouver, Toronto or Montreal?

Here we return to the heart of the human rights dilemma. The nature of modern societies—let alone the exigencies of an interdependent world—make it impossible to put all languages on a completely equal footing from the standpoint of public policy. Nor, I might add, is it likely that, if the political authorities totally vacated the language field and let nature take its course, the results would be any more equal in human rights terms.

Like it or not, the vast majority of contemporary societies find themselves having to make distinctions among languages while at the same time trying to limit the discriminatory effects of the distinctions. I do not think it can be denied that these official policies and practices, though they may be forced upon us by a kind of linguistic realpolitik, place a constant strain upon our parallel commitment to ensure that everyone can enjoy the same basic rights and freedoms and equal protection of the law.

The task that faces modern states, therefore, is to provide as much scope as possible for linguistic pluralism without either fostering politically unhealthy divisions or imposing crippling administrative burdens.

Placing Canada on the "Pluribus-Unum" Spectrum

In that regard, it seems to me that Canada, when viewed against the larger international backdrop, has succeeded better than most in finding a workable line between the humanistic counsels of perfection and the practical complexities of keeping the linguistic peace among its different language communities.

But what we have to ask ourselves now is whether we are doing enough to maximize the enjoyment of linguistic and cultural freedoms while also taking account both of our ideals of fair play and our competitive prospects in an increasingly interdependent world. This leads us in turn to re-examine the public policy rationale for supporting the use of those minority languages; to try to decide what is the proper scope of such public support; and finally, to ask how we should mediate competing claims of various language groups, given the inescapable limits of public funding.

For my part, I see no persuasive reasons to question the three fundamental pillars of the existing rationale that I have already alluded to: our common human rights interest in favouring cultural diversity; the need to facilitate the integration of new Canadians within the national community in ways that are both sensitive and helpful; and the desirability, in an interdependent world, of cultivating a broad range of linguistic resources for both cultural and commercial reasons.

In the perpetual debate between bluntly assimilationist and broadly pluralistic approaches to language policy, I believe Canada has now squarely taken its stand on the latter. We have, it is true, legitimized a two-tier linguistic system that gives pride of place to English and French. Within that general framework, the state has an interest in enabling all new Canadians to acquire or perfect their official language skills. But it has also declared its intention to encourage them to maintain their mother-tongue skills, as a way of expressing their particular cultural identities, while providing good second and third language education so as to foster awareness of other cultures and give value to our own store of languages.

When we ask ourselves how well we may be doing in any of these areas, we can certainly find room for improvement. The availability of official language training for immigrant women, for example, is still less than adequate. Heritage language schooling, whether as a transitional program or for cultural maintenance remains something of a lottery, even in our major centres. And the quality of second and third language education in Canada, English and French aside, is relatively modest considering the advantages at our disposal.

On the other hand, I believe we are now showing a greater disposition than formerly to use the other person's tongue—if we can—either to provide an institutional service or as a matter of personal courtesy. It may be in other words that the ever-increasing exposure to less familiar cultures that comes with new immigration patterns and new commercial challenges in a more interdependent world is finally teaching us new lessons in practical civility. Possibly. But we cannot take this for granted.

Even in the best climate imaginable, however, there are many who would argue that the extent of immigrant language use is destined inevitably to decline over time. If so, one might ask, in conclusion, and whatever the merits of the considerations I have outlined, whether there is any real point to a multilingual policy, either in Canada or elsewhere. Are we not being either improvident or hypocritical, or both, in seeming to sustain what may well be languages in decline? What does multilingualism hope to achieve?

There are several ways in which one might respond to that charge. In essence, they come down to this: given the world we have to live in, there is more to multilingualism than either linguistic viability or economic advantage. The symbolic value of any language, for speakers of that language, goes far beyond questions of public utility or commercial strategy.

In the end, we are motivated to underwrite the phenomenon of multilingualism because of the value we attach to human diversity in general and because of the quality and fulfillment it can bring to a multitude of individual lives. If our country can also tap into the fact of its own multilingualism as a source of pride, and as a counter to cultural prejudice, this is clearly a bonus for all of us.

It is too easy, I think, merely to suggest that a policy of linguistic pluralism presents us with practical opportunities in an interdependent world. It will only do so if we are clear about our motives for fostering multilingualism; if those motives are genuinely pluralistic; and if we provide ourselves with public policies that can be seen to be fair, reasonable, useful and adequately funded.

As Vaclav Havel pointed out last April in a speech at George Washington University: "We live in a world in which our destinies are tied to each other more closely than they have ever been before. It is a world with a single planetary civilization, yet it contains many cultures that, with increasing vigor and single-mindedness, resist cultural unification, reject mutual understanding and exist in what amounts to latent confrontation. It is a deeply dangerous state of affairs and it must be changed."

As Havel points out elsewhere in that speech, the resurgence of all kinds of ethnic nationalism within the former Soviet Bloc is no doubt an understandable reaction to "the tendency of communism to make everything the same." The greatest enemy of communism was always, as he says, "individuality, variety, difference—in a word, freedom."

But as we know to our cost, the collapse of Soviet-style communism has not led to an outburst of universal freedom and respect for difference. If anything, its first fruits have been an egoistical re-assertion of tribal identities. Nor is this a phenomenon that either Western Europeans or Americans can safely observe from the sidelines; the proliferation of petty hatreds impinges on all of us.

Thus, in advocating a policy of linguistic pluralism and respect for human rights in Canada, we will do well to keep in mind the alternatives. Linguistic and cultural differences do not in themselves make for a simpler or a quieter life. Nevertheless, the worst thing we can do, either directly or indirectly, is to suppress them. If, instead, we genuinely give them room to express themselves and make them part of the larger national vision, we can, I trust, avoid the worst dangers of xenophobic rivalries and at the same time harness our variety to the general good.

The interdependence of Village Earth does not make this any easier with time. And the homogenization that is implicit in the term "an interdependent world" is evidently not in itself a friend to linguistic diversity. As a result we owe it to ourselves not just to stand up for multilingualism but to show how it can be brought into a healthy and workable relationship with the respect for difference that is so central to human rights. We must continue to learn, continue to mediate differences, and continue to make our case. I hope this conference will help us to do all three.

ARRÊT! YOU ARE ENTERING A FRENCH-SPEAKING AREA

Ray Conlogue *(Arrêt!)*

Quebec's close brush with secession has prompted a good deal of soul-searching in think tanks and in the halls of power about renewing the Canadian federation.

Language is a prominent issue. In spite of modest progress in the past 30 years, francophones have little faith in current policies. A 1995 survey by André Blais at the

Ray Conlogue. *Arrêt!* You are entering a French-speaking area. *The Globe and Mail,* March 22, 1997, D3. (Reprinted with permission from *The Globe and Mail.*)

University of Montreal, for example, showed that a majority of Quebec's francophones believe their language would be more secure in an independent Quebec.

For this reason, the C.D. Howe Institute recently published a proposal by Simon Fraser University economist John Richards on a new approach to language policy. He advocates replacing our current bilingualism, where language rights attach to the individual citizen, with territorially-based language rights modelled on those used in such countries as Belgium and Switzerland.

Lying behind these models are two opposed ideas of how to protect a minority language in a modern democracy. Canada's policy, as articulated in the 1969 Official Languages Act, is called "personality bilingualism." It calls for services in both official languages throughout the country. English speakers are also encouraged to become bilingual, so that speakers of the minority language feel they are accepted as equals.

Advocates of "territorial bilingualism" argue that it is idealistic and even naive to think that majority language speakers can be persuaded to view minority speakers as equals. They point out that John Stuart Mill, the father of liberalism, said that minority languages were especially unwelcome in democracies because they impede communication among citizens.

The answer, say the "territorial" people, is to separate the two languages geographically, as most countries already do. Canada is alone in building a language policy mainly on the "personality" principle.

Professor Richards contends that a switch to a territorial model would be relatively simple because most French speakers in Canada are concentrated in one province. He believes a constitutional amendment giving Quebec broad power over the public use of language would largely do the job. By arresting possible future inroads by the English language, such an amendment would assuage the concerns of "Joe Lunchbucket in Trois Rivières [who] votes for the Oui," he said in a recent interview.

"I'm a pragmatist. I don't think we need major monkeying about with our institutions. We just have to look at where we've got it wrong." In his view, language—rather than vague notions like "distinct society"—is the key.

A problem is that English Canadians have largely accepted the American-style model of individual rights enshrined in the 1982 Charter of Rights and Freedoms. French Canadians, on the other hand, bristle at the notion that language is an individual rather than a collective concern—and Prof. Richards agrees: "Language can't be left to individual choice because the spillover effects of one person's language choice affect the value of other people's language."

He argues that a minimum population of about four million people is required to produce a full range of "language goods" (the cultural products, from books to television, necessary to a modern society). In our current system, which he castigates as a form of "linguistic free trade," majority and minority speakers compete freely throughout the country—and the minority language loses. Once it drops below a critical mass, it may collapse altogether.

Quebec's response has been a series of "collectivist" laws, of which the most controversial is Bill 101, the Charter of the French language. Passed in 1977, it established French as the obligatory language in the Quebec workplace and obliged most immigrants to educate their children in French. It was one of the irritants that led to the passing of the Canadian Charter of Rights and Freedoms five years later. Prof. Richards likens the subsequent conflict between these two charters to a "chronic disease" in the Canadian political system.

In its pure form, territorial bilingualism solves the problem by creating a zone where the majority language has no status whatever. In Switzerland, for example, a citizen who moves from Zurich (in the German zone) to Lausanne (in the French zone) is obliged to function in French. His children must go immediately to a French school. He shouldn't expect to find anything, not even a train schedule, printed in two languages.

Prof. Richards is not advocating this hard-line model for Canada. But he feels that the core idea of a guaranteed zone for the minority language is essential, and he observes that "the Quebec government has *de facto* insisted that this principle apply to Canada" since the early 1970s.

Although it is not widely remembered today, the members of the Royal Commission on Bilingualism and Biculturalism (the Bi-Bi Commission) debated the merits of these approaches in the mid-1960s. Territorial bilingualism made more sense, but it left "local minorities" (in Canada's case, the English in Quebec and the French outside it) without legal protection. Unwilling to face this awkward consequence, the commissioners chose the personality principle.

Why does Prof. Richards believe it has failed? "I start with my personal experience," he explains from his home in Vancouver. "My wife is *pure laine* French and our daughter attends a French school. But it is almost impossible to get her to speak the language." His daughter reflects what he feels is a prevailing attitude that French makes little sense in British Columbia. "You shouldn't try to introduce more political unity than people really want."

In his view, the rough-and-tumble political deals of Canadian history, from the Quebec Act of 1774 through to the British North America Act of 1867, recognized this reality in a common-sense way. A territorial division of language rights would make sense in this tradition.

But the 1982 Charter upset the apple cart by suggesting that freedom of language could be a fundamental human right. This was a radical extension of what is usually thought of as human rights, but a lot of English Canadians bought into it. Now, for the first time, an anglophone in Vancouver could feel *personally* affronted if the language "rights" of an anglophone in Montreal were infringed upon. "Michael Walker of the Fraser Institute bluntly says he sees 101 as an affront to individual rights," notes Prof. Richards with some dismay. The Supreme Court reinforced this impression by attacking the bill in 1988 and striking down some of its restrictions on the English language.

Francophones, even federal Minister of Intergovernmental Affairs Stéphane Dion, will never accept such attacks. Mr. Dion has called Bill 101 "a great Canadian law" because it frees francophones from feeling "constantly obliged to justify their survival in North America."

Specialists like University of Toronto political scientist David Cameron increasingly feel that it was a mistake in the charter to marry "language and culture issues to the language of human rights." But not all agree with Prof. Richards' solution.

Alan Cairns, a charter defender who teaches constitutional law at the University of Saskatchewan, says the charter is more flexible than Prof. Richards thinks. It's true the Supreme Court used it to attack Bill 101, but much of Bill 101 survived and is now reluctantly accepted by Quebec's anglophones.

Kenneth McCrae of Carleton University worked with the Bi-Bi Commission and has studied territorial bilingualism in Switzerland, Belgium and Finland. He feels that Prof. Richards is "trying to put an end to the endless litigation"—which ranges from the Bill 101 case to challenges of unilingual parking tickets—"but I'm not sure his plan is very realistic." Prof. McCrae agrees that Canada should use the territorial principle, but adds that it is not a cure-all. "These things don't get settled ultimately. You manage conflict, and it's always changing."

While the debate continues, Canada seems to be heading for territorial bilingualism whether we like it or not. Francophones outside Quebec are now being assimilated at the head-spinning rate of between 40 percent (in Manitoba) and 74 percent (in British Columbia) with each generation. In Quebec, anglophones have declined from 13 percent of Quebec's population in 1961 to less than 9.5 percent today, and migration of English speakers from elsewhere in Canada has virtually stopped.

This leads demographers like Charles Castonguay at the University of Ottawa to argue that "personality" bilingualism can no longer be defended honestly. "Sheila Copps recently appeared before a House of Commons committee and claimed that the assimilation of francophones outside of Quebec has been halted," says Prof. Castonguay. "The gap between reality and the fiction described by the Heritage Minister is becoming larger."

Territorial bilingualism may describe reality better, but it also deprives majority-language speakers who happen to live in the minority zone (read: English Quebeckers) of legal protection. It may increase the pressure on them to assimilate or leave. But, says Prof. Richards, "there is no escape from making explicit choices about winners and losers in linguistically contested regions." In Quebec, French has the "better moral claim."

Not surprisingly, prominent Quebec anglophones take a dim view of this. Jack Jedwab, Quebec director of the Canadian Jewish Congress who has recently written a book called *English in Montreal*, agrees that Quebec's anglophones are "experiencing a loss of vitality" while francophones outside Quebec are in a state of crisis. But instead of writing off both groups, he feels that the present policy of bilingualism should be more vigorously enforced.

Prof. Richards answers that his plan allows for anglo-Quebeckers to retain their current status if they agree not to expand their presence. This also disturbs Mr. Jedwab, who says he has "trouble with the idea of French having a better moral claim."

He points to "excesses" of Bill 101, such as forcing anglophones who move to Quebec from other provinces to educate their children in French (struck down by the courts), as proof that anglophones can't be abandoned to negotiate alone with the Quebec government.

However, Dermod Travis, a 36-year-old Vancouverite who moved to Quebec five years ago and has organized a group called Forum Quebec to mediate between French and English, feels that "you could devolve language and cultural power to Quebec with the proviso that it be subject to Quebec's own charter of rights" even though Quebec's charter is not a Constitution. He feels that younger anglophones, comfortable in French, have a greater trust in the good intentions of francophones.

McGill University chancellor Gretta Chambers is distressed at the idea of entrenching territorial bilingualism in the Constitution. But she agrees that Quebec must assume authority over language. "Anglos here must stop saying [as a negotiating tactic] that they are part of Canada and Canada is going to save them," she says.

In her view, Bill 101 is legitimate in its attempt to sustain the French population by compelling immigrants to become francophones. "Anglophones are starting to accept that their population cannot grow in Quebec. But they want to save their institutions and have a communal life."

Prof. Richards argues that there would be a better chance of that happening if the rest of Canada would get off Quebec's back. He admits that under his system the English in

Quebec "would become more clearly a minority group. But I believe a majority of [francophone] Québecois are as tolerant as the rest of the country."

The fact that Prof. Richards sees even a modest future for English and French minority communities means that he is quite a distance from hardline territorial bilingualism. But Prof. McCrae, the Canadian authority on the subject, feels that this is wise. "We need a made-in-Canada solution, a multiple solution. I'm less optimistic than I was 20 years ago about uniform solutions for whole countries."

Prof. McCrae feels the Richards plan would have the symbolic merit of completing the unfinished work of the Bi and Bi Commission, which dissolved in acrimony after writing only six of its 10 proposals. "The other four parts would have addressed the question of the two majorities," he recalls.

Prof. Richards calls this inability to find a solution for the two majorities a case of Canadian "moral failure." By "retreating into liberal discussions about free choice," we have avoided difficult "moral arguments about language policy." But he believes that there is fresh support for change—particularly in the West.

> More and more people have a view of the federation that isn't incompatible with that of moderate Quebec nationalists. On cultural matters, there's more acceptance of the rationale of what I'm saying among government officials in Edmonton than in Ottawa.

WHY CAN'T QUEBEC LISTEN TO SENSE?

John Fraser *(Saturday Night)*

In Canada, the politics of language is invariably divisive. This is not because the difference between "yes" and "oui" is worth dying for but because the language debate has always been the outer dress of the twin solitudes that identify the Canadian soul. Now, a generation that thought it had bridged the essential linguistic and social contradictions of the nation has had to come to the realization that it simply met the necessities of its own era. We are still only a controversy or a court decision away from the familiar sense of self-destruction.

This is the main reason sensible politicians try to avoid the issue of language and would do almost anything—waffle, circumscribe, fudge, even hyperventilate—rather than tackle it. To embrace squarely anything that so risks inflaming French-English passions in this beloved aberration of a country is to flirt with the devil. There is always a price to be paid.

Journalists and academics are less sensible than most politicians. Ever since . . . Premier Robert Bourassa announced Quebec's intention to retain—despite a ruling by the Supreme Court of Canada—many of the particulars of its controversial Bill 101 affecting the use of French on public signs in the province, we've been for it in both official languages. A prominent and persuasive western journalist, for example, has argued that Quebec has played the separatist card once too often. "The whole prospect of Quebec's departure," wrote Ted Byfield, founder of the influential *Alberta Report*, "far from being an unthinkable disaster, has become in many minds a rather tantalizing possibility." Conrad Black, the proprietor of this magazine and a staunch defender of the French-Canadian reality, nevertheless wrote in his column in *The Financial Post* that Quebec has come very close to forfeiting its right to receive further transfer payments by treating the English-speaking minority so shabbily. In

John Fraser. Why can't Quebec listen to sense? *Saturday Night* 104(4), April, 1989. 13–16.

his nationally syndicated column, Allan Fotheringham—guru to the ungrateful and seer to the masses—journeyed to Regina, of all places, in order to heap scorn and disgust on Premier Bourassa for taking so long to denounce the torching of the Alliance Quebec offices in Montreal and for stating that the English-speaking minority in Quebec was privileged in comparison to French-speaking minorities in the rest of Canada.

The dateline of Fotheringham's column was the capital of the same province that nine months earlier had—like Quebec—declined to uphold its own national linguistic responsibilities. Hypocrisies abound whenever provincial politicians feel the need to march to local drummers. That Gary Filmon, a Conservative premier of Manitoba, should turn out to have had the biggest stick with which to beat Quebec is both fitting and ironic. The controversial "notwithstanding" clause invoked by Mr. Bourassa and denounced by Mr. Filmon was, of course, forced into the constitution—to safeguard parliamentary supremacy—by Filmon's predecessor as Tory premier of Manitoba, Sterling Lyon.

Perhaps a spirited debate on the language issue, or a larger one on the perpetual French-English divide, is just what we need. Somehow I doubt it. At *Saturday Night*, for example, we have been sending tart, remedial messages to French Canada for the past hundred years, all to no seeming avail. We have *nearly* got it into our heads that there is a society and culture in Quebec that ignores the sensible editorial postures of English Canada. But judge for yourself. Here, for a start, is a genial little prescription from the magazine's founding editor, the redoubtable Edmund E. Sheppard, after he'd learned that the federal Parliament had voted in June, 1891, to have a short recess in the honour of St. John the Baptist, patron saint of Quebec.

> [English-Canadian politicians] are not [in Ottawa] to loaf around on saints' days; they are down there to attend to our business, and I imagine that if they quit this queer work and told some of the greasy haired Jean Baptistes to go and take a bath, there would be less of public money spent, both directly and indirectly, than now is being squandered on keeping some very unimportant people quiet.

Moving smartly on to the tolerant twentieth century, we find the fortunes of *Saturday Night* prospering and the first mention in the magazine (May, 1909) of the bizarre notion of a bilingual Quebec:

> A bill has just been passed by the Quebec Legislature which, if it stands the test of the high courts of the Empire, will force all common carriers, telegraph companies, etc., to have their waybills, contracts, tickets, in fact all documents with which the public come in contact . . . printed in French as well as in English. The business of the Province of Quebec so far as regards corporations is, of course, overwhelmingly English. The railways, the telegraph companies, the telephone companies, the shipping corporations, the manufacturing concerns and the large wholesale houses are, with very few exceptions, dominated by English-Canadians. The French language is utilized when business necessities arise, but not otherwise. Now, however, a certain section of ultra French-Canadians will have it a provision of law that the French language be placed on an equal footing with the English upon all documents issued by common carriers and corporations of like nature. Naturally the railways and business men are up in arms against it, and the chances are that the bill will find itself eventually in the cellar along with a lot of other fool legislation which is attempted at Quebec from time to time.

Three years later, in July, 1912, *Saturday Night* told Quebec that it was an inevitable consequence of progress and demographic reality that "the use of French should gradually disappear from the Parliaments and Courts of Canada," adding, "There is hardly one man in a hundred of the citizens of Ontario and the West who gives a thought to Quebec except at election time."

The conscription crisis during the First World War, lest we forget, made the foregoing almost benign:

"This protest by French-Canadians against French-Canadians fighting the battles of Britain," editorialized *Saturday Night* in August, 1915, "is the result of insular, bigoted upbringing, combined with dense ignorance. The French-Canadian of the type who marches and riots as a protest against recruiting is perhaps more to be pitied than blamed. He is ignorant and he is narrow, and so he will remain just so long as his schools refuse him facilities for a liberal education. He knows nothing beyond his Province, and he cares less. All Jean Baptiste wants is to be left alone."

The following year, as English-Canadian anger over Quebeckers' intransigence on conscription continued to gather momentum, some of the warning calls we still hear today begin to emerge:

> The Province of Quebec must either go into the discard as a political factor or continue to be catered to and pampered by both parties as in the past. If catered to, conscription flies out of the window. The question is whether the present Government is big enough and strong enough, and sufficiently awake to the trend of public opinion in this country, to grasp the fact that Quebec is no longer essential to a successful political party.

By 1925, the magazine was striking a more positive—if paternalistic—note, undoubtedly induced by a few years of quietude. Readers were offered this cheery word sketch that could have captioned a painting by Krieghoff:

> It is pointed out that between 1911 and 1921 Northern Ontario's Population of French origin grew from 45,000 to 63,000, out of a total population of 267,000. There is nothing surprising and nothing perilous as some would like us to believe in this migration of French-Canadians to the "back of the beyond." The French-Canadian is an ideal pioneer. Simple in tastes, industrious, ready and willing to put up with what we would consider considerable hardship, he is the man who fits naturally into our open spaces. He minds his business, does not join any Bolshevik clubs, behaves himself and brings up a large family, all good Canadians, who are in future generations likely to stick to the land, in place of decamping to the United States or gathering in our cities.

When the corrosive issue of conscription emerged once again during the Second World War to haunt the nation, a terse tone of minimal civility replaced the previous hysterics, but—as always—the underlying incomprehension and exasperation remained perfectly intact:

"We may as well be frank about these matters," wrote B.K. Sandwell in March, 1942. Sandwell is still rightly regarded as one of the great editors of *Saturday Night*, and is remembered particularly for his steely judiciousness in opposition to the internment of Japanese Canadians during the war. On the subject of the perfidious French Canadian, however, Sandwell's judiciousness was tested to its limits:

> We may as well be frank about these matters. Active service against the enemies of Canada involves the risk of death. The unequal distribution of that risk among the different racial elements which make up Canada is the chief cause of the friction and bitterness that are developing over the question of conscription for service outside Canada. . . . There is among English-speaking Canadians a widespread feeling that the real motive of the French-Canadian attitude toward conscription is the desire to improve the numerical strength of that element in the Canadian population, by avoiding its full proportional share in the casualties.

In 1970, following the October Crisis during which federalist Quebeckers were pitted against what was perceived as the ultimate separatist threat, another great editor, Robert Fulford, lamented the demise of a mythic peaceable kingdom where the various races had learned how to live together without violence. "Perhaps what we had before was based on illusion or stupidity," wrote Fulford, "but it was nevertheless important to us. It was our national dream—and what dream isn't based on illusion?"

The voices grow more tolerant in our pages, travelling from bigotry to elegy, yet they are united in being exclusively reactive. Quebec pushes, we deplore—or lament, wheedle, legislate, lecture, set up royal commissions, call out the troops.

And now, once again, dream and illusion in English Canada have collided with French-Canadian reality. Once again, Quebec appears to be changing the rules of the game. Once again, Quebec wants everything her own way. Once again, Quebec does not appreciate that English Canadians will take only so much. Once again, the solitudes have been reinforced. Once again, once again. . . . Like some long-married couple grown strange and crabby even as the partners cling to each other for warmth and protection, French and English Canada seem locked in a pattern of mutually irritating sufferance and unappreciated compromise.

Pierre Trudeau's creative new twist to our dilemma—that French Canadians should embrace federalism and break out of the traditional stockade of Quebec—has been so thoroughly assimilated that it's either taken for granted or enduringly resented. To some extent, in the reaction to the Supreme Court ruling on Quebec's Bill 101, and in the reaction to Quebec's response to that ruling, we are witnessing the long-delayed shakedown of the Trudeau era. Premier Bourassa's actions—which, despite the hue and cry in English Canada, have actually brought some bilingual relief from the earlier Parti Québécois sign-law legislation—simply return us to the rhetoric of the old impasse so familiar to *Saturday Night* centenarians.

If it is tedious, once again, for English Canada to have to react to an unacceptable action by Quebec, it is equally tedious to have to remind all Canadians that we have an obligation to come up with new solutions to maintain the central reality of our distinctiveness. Pro-free-traders in the West who resent the encroachments of bilingualism nevertheless are beholden to Quebec for making the difference in the free-trade vote. Anti-free-traders in Ontario who resent the spoiling factor inside Quebec nevertheless have to cling to the French fact of Canada as the most incontestable sign of our cultural originality. On and on it goes—the pluses are cancelled out by the minuses, and vice versa.

There is always the possibility of embracing a different logic, of creating an alternative script. It would be one that for English Canada begins with an understanding that not only is official bilingualism the glue that holds the philosophical and illusory notion of this nation together but that French language rights have not been something we bestowed on an ungrateful Quebec; rather, they have been prised out of the English-speaking majority at some cost.

Then we might understand that Mr. Bourassa's "unacceptable" legislation is no more unacceptable than a dozen pieces of unacceptable federal and provincial legislation enacted to counter the passions of the day. Pierre Trudeau is no longer around as a public lightning rod to attract all the sullen anger against federal bilingualism; for those many other English-speaking Canadians who felt a programme of comprehensive federal bilingualism should be sufficient to render Quebec "a province just like the others," the latest developments are equally repugnant. Quebec remains a special case, is undeniably different, and continues to seek protection for that difference.

Perhaps, in the 122nd year of Confederation, the vigour and consistency of the French-Canadian attempt to assert language rights could be acknowledged. Despite the engaged rhetoric, the essential defensiveness of Premier Bourassa's decision can be easily perceived. For much of the history of this land since the Conquest of 1759, French has survived in Quebec not because it has been the will of the majority of Canadians but because the speakers of French in Quebec have declined to relinquish their mother tongue. For some English Canadians, today as throughout our history, the whole notion of the French language's surviving in North America is absurd. The assumption is that it will eventually die out and become a quaint relic just as it has in Louisiana. If you want to discover the engine that drives separatism in Quebec, that drove every reaction to federal or imperial incursions into the province in the past, it is here in the fear of the "ordinary common sense" in English Canada and the logic of the cultural trends in North America.

Let us find a different common sense. Let us for example, concede that, during the past several decades of debate about the cost of Confederation, the territory of English-Canadian culture has been steadily expanding in quality and quantity. And who in English Canada has ever thought of rejoicing that our mother tongue is under no threat or that we can operate easily throughout most of the country in that language, even in those parts of it where bilingualism may always be a dirty word—like Calgary, or Quebec City, or Bai d'Espoir in Newfoundland. (That's Baie d'Espoir pronounced Bay Despair.)

Let us do it now, before we fall into the danger, once again, of turning the people of Quebec and their leaders into scapegoats—this time for all the festering, messily articulated misgivings so many of us in English-speaking Canada continue to have about the Meech Lake accord and whatever future it holds for the nation. Meanwhile, here at *Saturday Night*, we promise to sustain our century-old tradition of *evolving* towards civilized communication.

THE CHARTER OF THE FRENCH LANGUAGE AND WEB SITES (REVISED AUGUST 12, 1997)

Office de la langue française.

It is standard procedure for the Office de la langue française to follow up on complaints regarding non-compliance with various provisions of the Charter of the French language. The Office thus decided to intervene in the case of complaints with respect to commercial advertising on the Internet.

Commercial advertising, as a whole, is dealt with in the Charter regardless of the medium used. The Office thus considers that commercial advertising posted on a Web site, as well as advertising material sent by fax or electronic mail, fall under section 52, which means that the use of French is compulsory. A translation may be provided as long as French is given equal prominence. Section 52 applies to all advertising documentation made available to the public by a firm which has a place of business in Québec. Non-commercial messages or those of a political or ideological nature are consequently excluded.

The Office considers that a firm which has an address in Québec falls under section 52. Under the law, commercial advertising posted on the Web pages of firms must include a French translation. Let us remember that, in Québec, consumers have a right to be informed and served in French.

Office de la langue française. The Charter of the French Language and Web Sites (Revised August 12, 1997).

The Office applies to Web sites the same rules and exceptions as those concerning commercial advertising. English media Web sites could thus use English exclusively without violating the Charter. In addition, products of a cultural or educative nature may be advertised exclusively in the language of the product, without a French version.

Aware of the fact that the Internet is now used by companies as a means of advertising products on the global market, products which are often destined only for exportation, the Office de la langue française will apply a simple rule: a French version must be provided only in the case of advertisements posted on the Web site of a company located in Québec for products available in Québec.

It is noteworthy to specify that "cyber-inspectors" will not be surfing the Net for possible language violations. The Office does not have the time nor the resources to dedicate to such task. In practice, OLF almost exclusively follows up on complaints received from the public.

We have set up a FAQ section whereby we try to answer some of the questions raised as regards the application of the above rule.

FAQ

Is there a law requiring the use of French on a business Web page?

Commercial advertising, as a whole, is dealt with in the Charter of the French language, whichever medium may be used. The law does not mention the word "Internet," nor does it mention the word "fax" or the expression "electronic mail." Those advertising media nevertheless fall under the general provisions of the Charter. In concrete terms, the Office de la langue française considers that commercial advertising posted on a Web site is subject to section 52 which provides that French is compulsory, but may be accompanied with a text drafted in any other language. This applies to advertising material made available to the public by a Québec-based company.

Is there a law requiring the use of French on a personal home page?

No. The law is not aimed at non-commercial messages. For instance, Web sites dealing with political or ideological matters are entirely exempted.

How does the Office go about enforcing the rules?

The Office considers that any company with an address in Québec falls under section 52. It is thus accountable for any commercial information posted on its Web site. Moreover, firms employing fifty or more persons must comply with the requirements of a francization programme which includes the use of French in information technologies. Consequently, the absence of French on the Web site of those firms could result in the cancellation or suspension of their francization certificate.

How does the Office determine which Web pages to go after? Will it force all of the competition in a particular area to translate their Web pages into French as well?

The Office may decide to act on its own initiative. In practice, it almost exclusively follows up on complaints from the public. Complaints could be lodged both against a company and its competitors, but the Office could also evaluate the usefulness of systematically patrolling the Net for violations in that particular sector.

What are the penalties provided for in the law?

For a first offence, fines now range from $500 to $1400 in the case of a business firm, and from $250 to $700 in the case of individuals.

What if a company's head office is located in Ontario and its Web pages are designed there?

A company which does not have its head office in Québec or/and a place of business or an address in Québec, cannot be compelled under Québec laws to use French on its Web site.

What if a person, unrelated to a company, sets up a Web page usurping the name of that company?

It goes without saying that, prior to taking any action, the Office verifies all circumstances and the identity of the company which advertises on a Web site. A company could not be held responsible for sites it has not itself set up, which fact should be brought to the Office's attention in case of an investigation.

Who is exempt from the obligation to use French? Are English newspapers, radio stations and TV channels obliged to advertise in French?

All exceptions which apply to commercial advertising also apply to Web sites. English newspapers, radio stations and TV channels Web sites may, under those exceptions, use English exclusively without violating the language law. Moreover, cultural and educational products may be advertised exclusively in the language used in those products, without a French version.

Is the Québec government well aware of the fact that the Internet is used by most companies as an inexpensive means of advertising on the global market and not necessarily on the Québec market?

The Office is indeed well aware of that fact. Québec companies may advertise their products on the global market. In fact, some Québec companies only manufacture products for exportation, in which case neither the packaging nor related inscriptions are subject to the Charter. This is taken into account when such companies advertise their products on a Web site. In view of the above, the Office de la langue française applies a simple rule whereby products available in Québec stores must be advertised in French on the Web site of a company or a dealer which has a place of business or an address in Québec. It is quite obvious that a Québec computer store which advertises its weekly specials is subject to the above rule.

MS. BEAUDOIN SURFS THE NET (Montreal *Gazette*)

Louise Beaudoin, the Quebec minister responsible for language, seems alarmingly impervious to ridicule. No imagined, perceived, or even stupidly real infraction of the French Language Charter is too small or insignificant for her department to prosecute.

Once again, her department has threatened to fine a Quebec-based company for failure to give equal visibility to French in a Web site.

Two years ago, the Office de la langue francaise threatened to fine a Pointe Claire store, Micro-Bytes Logiciels, unless it removed its English-only Web site—even though it was in the process of developing a bilingual Web site. This time, the Office has gone after

Ms. Beaudoin surfs the Net. *The Montreal Gazette*, Wednesday, June 9, 1999. www.efc.ca/pages/media/gazette.09jun99.html (Reprinted with permission from *The Montreal Gazette*.)

a photography studio in Chomedey, ordering www.michaelsphoto.com off the Internet for its failure to provide a French version.

Allowing the Office to behave like some sort of demented Ewok and chase off into cyberspace at the sight of an English-language Web site verges on irresponsible.

As a minister of Quebec's government, here is something that Ms. Beaudoin should keep in mind and use to guide her future actions: the United States is the world's top-performing economy, the wealthiest, the most competitive.

How does it continue to be No. 1 in the world year after year? According to a comparative study this year out of Switzerland, the core of U.S. competitiveness is a unique ability to grow using innovations. Right now, it is riding the Internet and E-commerce wave with more vitality than any other economy.

Quebec needs to be on that wave, riding it into a strong economy and the creation of high-technology jobs. Technology is creating a global economy that is in a phase of amazing growth. Information and capital move around the world virtually unimpeded by regulatory forces.

In Canada, even such a normally meddlesome agency as the Canadian Radio-television and Telecommunications Commission has declared the Internet a regulatory-free zone—aside, of course, from existing laws on pornography, hate literature, fraud, and money-laundering. No government or agency can claim ownership of the Internet. Why, then, should a Quebec Web site owner's obligations include having to present a French face to the world?

Inside the physical world of Quebec, the government, through the French Language Charter, has ruled that all Quebec-based catalogues, brochures, commercial directories, and similar publications must be in French and it is now pretending that Web sites fall under the same legislation.

But cyberspace is not confined to a specific physical place. That is the source of its immense freedom. Everyone the world over has access to it, in any language they choose to use, and at the same time nothing is imposed. Quebecers would have to seek www.michaelsphoto.com out of literally millions of Web sites to feel offended at the lack of French.

Smart businesses operating in Quebec will, if they can afford it, see the value of a bilingual Web site in attracting customers. But that should be their choice, not the government's.

DISCUSSION QUESTIONS

1. Evaluate the OLF's statement in terms of its relative position on Yalden's unicultural/unilingual multicultural/multilingual continuum.

2. Speculate on the economic and political consequences of attaching official status to a particular language or languages and not to others.

3. Discuss the following statement: It is up to individual speakers to preserve their language, not the state.

4. Do you think that the rapid development of the Internet, which thus far has been an overwhelmingly English medium, poses a threat to the future of other languages?

WEBLINKS

L'Office de la langue française
www.olf.gouv.qc.ca/

Alliance Quebec (Quebec English Rights Group)
www.aq.qc.ca/

Office of the Commissioner of Official Languages: Your Language Rights
ocol-clo.gc.ca/5e.htm

The Department of Canadian Heritage: Official Languages Support Program
www.pch.gc.ca/OFFLANGOFF/english/index.htm

Canadian Government: French on the Internet
www.ocol-clo.gc.ca/answer.htm

Provinces and Official Language Minorities
www.pch.gc.ca/OFFLANGOFF/perspectives/english/languages/prov.html

Minority Language Educational Rights
www.constitutional-law.net/language1.html

chapter two

Language and Ideology:
Newspeak and Bafflegab

INTRODUCTION

There has been a long history of debate on the relationship between language and thought. The Sapir-Whorf hypothesis, for example, suggested that the language spoken by members of a social group determines in a profound way the cultural patterns and behaviours of members of that group. Language did this in part by imposing a set of labels and classificatory structures upon its speakers, which directly influenced their perceptions of the world. These shared perceptions in turn shaped the behaviours, and hence the culture, of the group.

While most would now reject a strong deterministic version of the Sapir-Whorf hypothesis, the influence of language on perception and behaviour continues to generate interest. Instead of focusing on the structural differences between different languages and their cultural impact, recent work has focused on the varied resources within a particular language—English, for example—and how their use may reflect and/or influence perceptions, ideologies, and behaviour.

The three pieces included in this section all concern the use of English, while focusing on very different aspects of the language. David Smith articulates the basic argument that language influences our conceptual thinking, while focusing specifically upon the role of militaristic metaphors in structuring our conceptions of non-militaristic contexts.

He also argues that developing a critical awareness of metaphorical language is an essential aspect of a good education.

Clive Thompson examines the recent trend in business and political rhetoric to use the language, imagery, and conventions of apocalyptic genres. The millennium, Thompson argues, provides the convenient context and cultural authority to those who use this "apocalypse" script to avoid discussing the real ideological motives and consequences of their social and political decisions. It is a powerful rhetorical device because it gets "people on side" easily by precluding any logical objections or alternate solutions they may have. Perhaps more importantly, it removes from consideration "the fact that a society evolves mostly because of the decisions made by people in power, and not according to the immutable forces of nature and time."

The final piece provides an analysis of the language of the government and banks that holds students hostage with huge student loans. Christy Ann Conlin was not amused by the religious metaphor used when the Ministry of Education and Training decided to send her bank a "forgiveness payment" on her student loan. Conlin goes on to discuss the use of language to make indebtedness and poverty into sins, with banks and governments empowered to give out miserly "grace" periods and "forgiveness." She argues that the emphasis in the language is on sin and redemption, and not where it should be—on high tuition rates, and lack of access to higher education for low income earners.

DE-MILITARIZING LANGUAGE

David C. Smith *(Peace)*

Linguistic research over the last quarter century has exposed the influence of language on our thinking patterns and processes. We are seldom aware that the kind of language we use affects our behaviour in significant ways. One example of these revelations is the militarization of English over a long period of time. The result is that our conceptual and higher-level thinking is shaped in ways that we might not consciously wish it to be, and that the language we use in some cases may actually prevent us from attaining our goals.

The History of Military Metaphors

Military metaphors have become part of our language over hundreds of years. This has been a normal process, since people tend naturally to draw upon experiences in one area of life in order to give fresh insight and understanding to experiences in another. Think of the language that sailors have brought from the sea to the land ("to know the ropes"), that urban dwellers have adapted from farms ("to put the cart before the horse"), or that people have brought home from their places of work ("to strike while the iron is hot").

Soldiers have had vivid, sometimes traumatic, experiences during military duty that they have then applied to non-military situations. Today, we may ask someone to "spearhead the discussion" or to "get off your high horse." From marching, someone may "get off on the wrong foot" or "mark time"; from strategy, we might "close ranks" or "beat a hasty retreat";

David C. Smith. De-militarizing language. *Peace* 13(4), 1997. 6-18.

from weapons, we can "cross swords" with an adversary or "look daggers." From the military hierarchy, we refer to "the top brass" or "the rank and file." There are literally hundreds of military metaphors used in everyday speech and writing.

One might well argue that at the relatively shallow level of vocabulary, or even of metaphorical expression, the use of militaristic language is harmless, and serves to make our communication more colourful, more precise and perhaps, as Aristotle claimed, to convey fresh meaning or perspective. Indeed, there are words in use which we do not link at all to their origins with the military establishment (such as "harbinger," someone who went before an army to find accommodation, especially for officers). If no violence or military meaning is associated with the word, surely its use is innocuous. But is the use of military language in our society cause for concern at a deeper level?

Metacognitive Thinking

What has concerned some linguists and philosophers is not the use of military language per se, but patterns of metaphorical thinking at the metacognitive level. In their book, *Metaphors We Live By*, Lakoff and Johnson(f.1) give clear examples of such metaphorical thinking. They assert that in English-speaking society we conceive of "argument as war" as shown by the following set of conceptual metaphors:

"Your claims are indefensible."

"He attacked every point in my argument."

"I have lots of ammunition in my arsenal."

"His criticisms were right on target."

"I demolished his argument."

"If you use that strategy, she'll wipe you out."

"You disagree? OK. Shoot."

"He shot down all my arguments."

While there are many alternative metaphors, we may often think of "love as war":

"She fought for him, but his mistress won out."

"He is slowly gaining ground with her."

"He won her hand in marriage."

"She is besieged by suitors."

"She has to fend them off."

"He made an ally out of her mother."

"He is known for his many conquests."

Both of the overriding ideas that "argument is war" and "love is war" consist of coherent and consistent sets of metaphorical expressions. Such related clusters are referred to as structural metaphors, and it is these metaphors that may become part of our generally unarticulated belief system.

In order to explore these ideas further over the past year, I have been reading and analyzing a variety of newspaper and magazine articles mainly in the areas of politics, economics, environment and health. My analysis has involved the identification of structural metaphors and their supporting evidence. Perhaps I can give one example from the recent federal election campaign, as reported in the *Montreal Gazette* of February 24. Under the headline, "Charest broadsides Liberals" we find the following:

"Charest made a blistering attack on the Liberal record."

"He's not targeting the Bloc."

"He has a shot at becoming prime minister."

"Federalist forces could easily rally against separatists."

"He has been an underdog, fighting to keep the politicians in Ottawa honest."

"They played the song, 'Another One Bites the Dust.'"

"He devoted his entire speech to attacking the Liberals."

In all, there were 13 military metaphors which supported the structural metaphor, "electoral campaigning as war." In the same article there were three conceptual metaphors supporting the structural metaphor "election campaigning is a race." The dominant metaphor was clearly that of war.

Analysis of articles such as these yields an interesting variety of structural metaphors. However, the dominant theme of war emerges repeatedly: "Politics is war," "Electoral reform is war," "Improvement of the economy is a battle," "Marketing is war," "Environmental protection is a battle," "Medical progress is a battle," etc.

In their book, *Language and Peace*, Schaffner and Wenden (f.2) assert that structural metaphors like these do not exist in our belief systems as separate ideas, but are related to one another and systematically organized into metaphors at an even higher, ideological level. The metaphor "Life is a (an uphill) battle" would be one such ideological metaphor. In presenting the research of linguists and philosophers over the past ten years, the authors arrive at a number of sobering conclusions.

They conclude that the language of journalists and diplomats frequently represents ideological stances that accept and promote war as a legitimate way of regulating international relations and settling inter-group conflict (legitimization); that language unquestioningly promotes values, sustains attitudes and encourages actions that create conditions that can lead to war (propagation); and that language itself creates the kind of enemy image essential to provoking and maintaining hostility that can help justify war (justification).

Critical Language Education

Recognition of the kind of metaphor contained in the language we use should become part of the education of every person. Schaffner and Wenden write about the need for critical language education in *Language and Peace*. The elements of such education might include the following:

1. Develop an awareness of metaphorical language. The study of metaphor could be introduced at the elementary level, beginning with simple examples (such as White Tiger Kung Fu, Blockbuster Video, Arrow Taxi, Check-Mate Investigations), and proceeding to more sophisticated ones at the secondary and tertiary levels. We already study metaphor in poetry and novels; to study its use in political and other discourse would create an understanding of the way in which language reflects ideologies and can influence the exercise of power.

2. Develop skills in decoding metaphorical language. One model of formal analysis is to identify conceptual and structural metaphors and "map" the latter by showing the intended parallels between the structural metaphor and the issues under discussion. This can then provide the basis for a critical summary of the mode of metaphorical reasoning.(f.3)

3. Recognize the limitations of metaphors. Sure, metaphors are helpful in enlarging our understanding of something we may already be familiar with, yet the system that allows us to comprehend one aspect of a concept in terms of another (for example, argument in terms of war) will necessarily hide some aspects of the concept. There may well be aspects of argument that are inconsistent with war. We may lose sight of the opportunities for cooperation in an argument, of sharing viewpoints that do not support our own position, or of learning from the points raised by the other person.

4. Become more self-critical to enhance communication skills. Many kinds of discourse use metaphorical language that is inconsistent with the purpose of the speakers or writers. A simple example is the one-page article on influenza that includes 13 conceptual metaphors to support the structural metaphor, "preventing flu is war."(f.4) The mental set of the person who accepts the article is to fight the flu. However, the article concludes with the contrary advice, "Finally, remember to be a nice person; studies have shown that feelings of hostility reduce immune system levels, while being at peace with your world will actually increase your body's ability to resist infection." We need to ensure that the language we use is consistent with the message we wish to convey.

5. Encourage creativity through the use of alternative metaphors. Suppose instead of thinking about argument in terms of war, we were to think of argument as a pleasing, graceful dance.(f.5) How would such a metaphor cause us to conceptualize argument in a different way? It is initially difficult for us to accept such a creative challenge, because the present cultural metaphor gets in the way of conceiving argument in terms other than war. We may even conclude that thinking of argument in terms of dance produces a concept that is not argument at all. That is precisely the power of metaphors to control and limit our thinking; yet it is also their power to create a breakthrough (military metaphor intended) to renew and reconstruct.

Footnotes

(f.1) G. Lakoff and M. Johnson, *Metaphors We Live By*, University of Chicago Press, Chicago, 1980.

(f.2) Christina Schaffner and Anita Wenden (Editors), *Language and Peace*, Dartmouth Publishing Company, Aldershot: 1995.

(f.3) Tim Adamson, Greg Johnson, Tim Rohrer and Howard Lam, "Metaphors We Ought Not Live By: Rush Limbaugh in the Age of Cognitive Science," paper distributed publicly over the Internet, University of Oregon, Department of Philosophy, 1997. metaphor.uoregon.edu/rush.htm

(f.4) Kerry Campbell, "Beat the Flu Bug: Get Vaccinated," *We Care Home Health Services News*, Vol. 8, No. 1, 1996.

(f.5) Lakoff and Johnson, ibid.

APOCALYPSE NOW

Clive Thompson *(This Magazine)*

As the year 2000 approaches, politicians and business leaders are getting ready for the end of the world. Things have never looked better.

This all started when I accidentally got lost in the business section of my local bookstore. I had been searching for an obscure book of poetry and didn't notice where I was walking until I looked up and found myself in an aisle crammed with management self-help books. Vaguely panicked, I had turned to leave, when I noticed a book called *Liberation Management*.

My curiosity was piqued by the title, which is a cryptic nod to the left-leaning Liberation Theology of South American radicals. I soon found myself flipping through the dense, 834-page book. Written by futurist Tom Peters, it was described in the cover promo blurb as "The bestselling guide to economic excellence in the 1990s."

And what a guide it is.

In a tone that mixes wide-eyed giddiness with outright terror, Peters declares that the age of reason in business is over—and that it's time to embrace chaos. A new world is dawning, he says, in which the old link between hard work and success will be severed, luck will be the law of the land, and self-destruction will be the only possible response to an insane world. "Things are moving too fast for us to sort out logically what's going on," Peters writes. "Our understanding of cause and effect is hopelessly incomplete, frightfully misleading, and getting worse by the day." His solution? "Destroy your corporation before a competitor does! Disorganize! And keep disorganizing!"

I plowed on. Peters became steadily more psychotic. "The essence and engine of a market is failure," he writes. He advocates "blasting the violent winds of the marketplace into every nook and cranny in the firm," producing "The Transformation of Positively Everything" (a chapter title). He praises a Swedish firm for laying off 95 percent of its staff; he lauds the "staff destruction" of "visionary companies."

Peters, as it turns out, is just the tip of the iceberg. I started walking around the business section and found myself staring at a panorama of global riot and corporate dread, bookshelves full of authors prophesying similarly imminent and devastating changes to society and global finance. Most were nervously fixated on the year 2000—books such as *Waves of Change*, *Managing for the Future*, *Future Tense*, and *The Manager's Guide to the Millennium* (which advises the alert executive that "Doing nothing is just not an option. Get ready now!"). Or the baldly anarchic *Stop Paddling and Start Rocking the Boat!*, and *If It Ain't Broke . . . Break It!*

"What the heck is up with this stuff?" I asked the clerk as I purchased a copy of *Liberation Management*. "What's everyone so freaked about?"

"I don't know," he said, squinting at the price and punching the cash register. "The future?"

In most world cultures, there's a story about the end of the world, and in very broad strokes it goes like this: greed or sin or vice build up and up and up until society is no longer able to survive. Prophets warn the people to shape up, but nobody listens. Chaos builds as sin is rewarded and virtue is punished.

Then the apocalypse arrives. It's a time of horrible violence: riot and misrule, fire and explosions, women and children screaming, dead bodies flying through the air. But ulti-

Clive Thompson. Apocalypse now. *This Magazine* 29(5), January, 1996. 30-33. (Clive Thompson is technology columnist for *Newsday* in New York. He can be reached at clive@bway.net.)

mately it ends, producing a magnificent, cleansed new world, infinitely better and more beautiful than the one before.

This is a powerful story in Western thought—so much so that as we get closer to the end of the millennium, it's increasingly taking over pop culture, arguably the collective unconscious of our times. It's there in movies such as *Strange Days*, which paints a picture of America in full hedonist millennial bloat, a massive den of iniquity where law is falling apart and gangs run the world. You can also see it in "The X-Files," with its continually looming, terrifying "truth" about the paranormal. Apocalyptic ideas range from the utterly mainstream—such as the yuppie self-actualization bible *The Celestine Prophecy*—to the loopy political margins, such as *The Turner Diaries*, a favourite book of white-supremacist conspiracy theorists, in which patriotic whites rise up to kill Jews, blacks and government officials at the close of the 20th century.

To a certain extent, you could say these movies and novels are a healthy artistic impulse, a way of helping us explain powers beyond our control. It's a way of shaping our fears, and our desire for transformation. That's part of what art is for, after all—it helps us deal with our irrational side.

But that's art. What is far more disturbing these days is how millennial fever has swept into the twin worlds of business and politics.

In the last few years, invoking the millennium has become a favourite technique for business leaders and politicians to justify the blood sport of "downsizing." What was once a purely spiritual and artistic concept is now being tossed around the boardroom and the legislature—and, in the process, wrecking people's lives. Everyone from Tom Peters to Ralph Klein has discovered that doomsaying is a strangely compelling message.

At first blush, it makes sense; the apocalyptic story perfectly suits the world of conservative realpolitik. There are the sins of Canadian society: a generous social-safety system that has caused a massive deficit, minorities with too many rights, and unions that have gotten way out of hand. And now we've got the inevitable payback: a wrenching, unstoppable change that will destroy Canada as we know it. If we can just tough out the hard times, the story goes, we'll produce a new, leaner, more virtuous country.

If nowhere else, this trend has been glaringly obvious in the endless stream of books and speeches predicting massive social upheaval in "the 21st century." In her book *A Matter of Survival: Canada in the 21st Century*, Diane Francis, the *Financial Post* editor, paints a gruesome picture of our impending penance. "Sometime in the 1990s, a Canadian crisis of monumental proportions will occur," she writes. "This is not speculation. It will happen . . . Some tough choices await us before the century turns. While the prospect is unpleasant, we cannot indulge in self-pity."

CIBC chair Al Flood may have managed to top even that level of rhetoric when he addressed his Halifax customers last fall. "Our quality of life is at risk unless we control and cure our fiscal cancer," he said glumly. "The answer is spending cuts. Large cuts. More immediate cuts. . . . We stand on the edge of the precipice with an entirely unjustified optimism that somehow we will inch ourselves back to safety."

Sensing the power of this rhetoric, Canadian politicians have rushed to set the millennium as a deadline for deficit and debt reduction. Federal finance minister Paul Martin announced that he'd balance the budget by the year 2000, a promise that was later matched by Ontario's new Tories. "The status quo, doing nothing, will be a disaster for the finances of the province," Ontario Premier Mike Harris said as he laid out the timeline.

Even at the municipal level, politicians can't escape the mystique of the millennium. When Pierre Bourque won the mayoralty race in Montreal this year, his acceptance speech was laced with the rhetoric of salvation: "We have to end the decline of Montreal and give new dynamism to the city," he said. "If Montreal is to stand as a shining example in the year 2000 . . . not just in our imaginations but in reality, then we must begin our work immediately." Glowing words—and his first task was to push for $100-million in cuts to the city's social services.

In the business world, it's equally panicky—so much so that it's become rare for a powerful CEO to talk about the year 2000 without simultaneously announcing that the company is about to axe a platoon of employees. Dofasco CEO John Mayberry once explained his decision to scrap 750 jobs while enjoying a $62-million third-quarter profit by arguing that "We have repositioned ourselves for the year 2000."

The examples could go on and on, but what's interesting here isn't so much the individual scorched-earth policies. There are internally consistent—if horribly misguided—ideological reasons for balancing your budget on the backs of the powerless. You don't need to invoke the apocalypse to justify it. And it's debatable whether any business leader or politician actually believes there is a definable deadline for the apocalypse.

No, what's more interesting is that business and political leaders implicitly understand that apocalyptic rhetoric is very convincing—because it's not logical at all. It doesn't try to argue. As the popularity of millennial pop culture shows us, it's a good narrative device. Having thousands of years of Judeo-Christian tradition behind it doesn't hurt either. Invoking the apocalypse becomes a way of avoiding discussing your real, ideological motives. No matter how rational your political deadlines might seem, invoking the year 2000 is like a supra-rational trump card. End of world, end of argument.

In an even creepier way, it's also about feeling ecstatic about the carnage.

Millennial thought always carries an element of frenetic, nigh-erotic energy—the sense that, yeah, well, maybe things are falling to pieces, but it's exciting as hell!! Canadian poet Maggie Helwig once wrote an essay about apocalyptic trends in pop music and noted this very element, most evident in the songs of Prince. In "1999," for example, he lays out a scene of "people runnin' everywhere . . . from the destruction," and yet decides the joint is rockin': "2000 zero zero party over oops out of time / So tonight I'm gonna party like it's 1999."

Maybe this is why W.H. Auden once famously prohibited artists from becoming involved in politics—they're too attracted to destruction. "All poets adore explosions, thunderstorms, conflagrations, ruins, scenes of spectacular carnage," he wrote, dryly concluding that "The poetic imagination is not at all a desirable quality in a statesman."

That same giddy delight is front-and-centre in the new millennial corporate panic. On the far end, you've got Tom Peters and his chaos-surfing way kewl approach to loving the insanity: "Instead of the frantic pursuit of total comprehension," he writes, "let's revel in our very lack of comprehension!" With his worship of chaos and ruin, you could argue that Peters is really just trying to add a sexy, dynamic edge to the free market, partly to perpetuate the myth that Western markets really are free, and partly to re-romanticize the profit motive, making it seem newly heroic. He throws in a kind of zen-like guru mystique to his message by tossing off aphorisms that openly contradict each other, such as his "Rules for Luck": "#18. Listen to everyone. Ideas come from anywhere. #19. Don't listen to anyone. Trust your inner ear."

Canada even has its own deep-dish futurist, Frank Ogden, who became famous for writing *The Last Book You'll Ever Read*. In it, he prophesies the "tumultuous change" that will destroy government in the millennium, and the amazing world of plenty that this will open up: "It is my belief that when the turbulence of transition finally settles down in the Communications Age, the wealth of the planet will have increased another hundred-fold . . . We can all do much more now with less. Success is just an idea away."

You could dismiss this as fairly transparent lunacy (or maybe not that transparent; both books were on the best-seller lists for many weeks). But Ogden and Peters aren't that different from Alberta's Ralph Klein or Ontario's Mike Harris, who have found that blindingly fast cuts to social programs can produce a strange, sexy energy in modern politics. On the part of those doing the cutting, there's the feeling of acting decisively and heroically. On the part of their activist opponents, there's almost a kind of relief—it's like the gloves are off, so the Armageddon can begin in earnest.

But again, it's the emotionalism of apocalyptic thought that's so spooky. The purging and the healing, the destroying and the building, the fear and the glee—they're all mixed up together. Eventually we're faced with bald paradox: the only way to save welfare is to end it. We've got to close these hospitals to maintain health care. If this company wants to grow, it's going to have to axe half its staff.

No way! Way.

In 1979, at the peak of the Cold War, the *Toronto Star* published a two-page map of Toronto showing the effects of a nuclear bomb on the city. It had a bunch of concentric rings radiating from City Hall out to the suburbs, so you could locate your house and find out what damage would occur. I was in Grade 6 at the time, and as I recall, my neighbourhood was in for "heavy radiation poisoning," "uncontrollable vomiting," "hair loss," and "lingering death."

Needless to say, I didn't sleep for weeks.

That map was one of a number of things, I think, that built public support for a ban on nuclear testing and a general end to nuclear terror. It got people on side with opponents of nuclear weapons. God knows, it got me and my class to write a letter to Pierre Trudeau.

It's the same with the new millennial rhetoric of politics and business. Presenting things in an apocalyptic light makes it a lot easier to get people on side, to convince them to let go of their logical objections and believe that you truly represent the inevitable. It obscures the fact that a society evolves mostly because of the decisions made by people in power, and not according to the immutable forces of nature and time. More importantly, it obscures the alternatives to those decisions.

And there are alternatives. A number of executives are discovering now that the corporate purges and hair-shirt fever of the last 10 years may have been the worst thing to do for the economy—and for the companies themselves. Business pundits Gary Hamel and C.K. Prahalad note in their book *Competing for the Future* that going "lean and mean" to pump short-term profits has doomed many firms to shoddy morale, institutional amnesia, and even more limited investment potential. "Although perhaps inescapable and in many cases commendable," they say, "the resulting restructuring has destroyed lives, homes, and communities—to what end?" Even the *Report on Business Magazine* has acknowledged this: in a January 1995 article, outplacement specialist Robert Evans slammed short-sighted downsizing for producing "a demoralized, disloyal and dysfunctional workforce. People [are] working their buns off with the justifiable fear that their efforts and loyalty don't count for much . . . As long as it is a mere code for ruthless cutting, talk about 'organization renewal' is largely meaningless."

In the land of politics, the alternatives to the panicked hacking of social programs are similarly thriving, if ignored. There's the annual alternative budget produced by activists across Canada, with tons of constructive suggestions for cuts to non-essential government services and handouts. There's the long-unexamined possibility of turning our unwieldy welfare system into a guaranteed annual income. There's economist James Tobin's tax proposal to smooth out—and generate revenue from—reckless currency trading by taxing each transaction. Hell, while we're at it, how about a return to the social censure of greed? Not all of these ideas completely hold water, of course, but neither does every cut proposed by Harris, Klein or federal Finance Minister Paul Martin.

As usual, the hardest thing is just to deprogram yourself. And in the megawatt culture of millennial panic, where "X-Files" TV dread bleeds over into real-life hatred of government, deprogramming is a full-time job—not the least because feeling excited and creeped-out about the future is a perfectly normal human emotion, even if it isn't much of a basis for public policy.

To get a bit futuristic here, imagine how we'll feel once the year 2000 actually comes, and millennial rhetoric isn't possible anymore. The rhetoric of apocalypse and purgatory may well become a new kind of optimism, as a friend recently suggested to me over lunch.

"Think about it," he said. "There won't be any big deadline looming. Nobody will be able to talk about getting ready for the 21st century. This feeling of claustrophobia will turn into a sense of boundlessness. Or even better, it'll be a type of movie remake—*Twentieth Century: The Sequel. This time we get to do it right.*"

I laughed. "I've got a book you gotta read."

MY BANKER, MY PRIEST

Christy Ann Conlin *(This Magazine)*

Last Christmas, I received a gracious letter from my bank. Issued by the Loan Forgiveness Department, it declared that the Ministry of Education and Training had "forgiven" a portion of my student loan. Apparently the Ministry would send the bank a "forgiveness payment," thus reducing my "indebtedness."

I didn't know what to feel: the touch of grace or the burn of shame? If forgiveness is offered—by a financial institution, in the moral language of a church—there must be a sin. What was mine? Student debt? Then I had my epiphany. But of course: commerce and spirituality have "consolidated their resources," merged to form a new religion. It's the theology of economics. We are, after all, a money-worshipping civilization, in our private and public lives. The bankers and politicians, our clergy, lay out the tenets of the faith while we (the laity), work to achieve a state of (financial) grace, avoiding poverty and debt, the new original sin.

Politicians on both left and right speak of the national debt as an "evil," one so great that we are called on to make "sacrifices." We suffer and pay taxes (offerings) in order to exorcize this evil from society. Purging the national debt becomes the focus of the nation while homelessness, environmental woes, illiteracy and the erosion of health care become lesser evils, dwarfed by the über-shame of debt.

As for the citizens, the debt-free and those able to amortize are blessed with credit. Those unable to, fall from grace as they lose their credit rating and are cast out like apostates. Excommunicated from the economy, they are pursued by none other than the Dark Master himself, ensconced in his new realm, the collection agency.

Christy Ann Conlin. My banker, my priest. *This Magazine* 32(5), March/April, 1999. 4.

As Noam Chomsky points out, consent is manufactured by the powerful for their policies; language is their tool. Strategically named programs such as *The Canadian Opportunities Strategy* and *Student Debt Management* provide, for example, "loan forgiveness" and "grace periods." Unemployment with reduced benefits masquerades as "economic adjustment." The language keeps us from examining the real issues: Why have student debts become so enormous? Why are there so many obstructions for low-income people seeking university educations? Why are there so few jobs for young people? Heretical thoughts.

Fidel Castro said in his 1999 address to the Cuban people, "The most fanatical ... believers in the market have converted it into a new religion. This is how the theology of the market emerged. Its academics, more than scientists, are theologians; for them it is a question of faith." On a global scale, banks, lender nations and the International Monetary Fund (IMF) march into needy countries with this faith, just as missionaries once came bringing food and medicine. They proselytize with offers of huge loans if people will adopt their economic beliefs. And when debt and enormous interest rates retard the development of these countries, "loan forgiveness" is piously considered.

Church and state? Forget it. After all, the elite clergy of bankers and bureaucrats make policy that benefits themselves—while their spin doctors, writers of the new sacred texts, sell us false dreams of future financial freedom. Well, I'd rather be damned. Or maybe, with other degenerates, I'll start a Reformation. Like Martin Luther, who challenged the corrupt Church by nailing a declaration to its door, we can paste our own declarations of rebellion on the glass doors of banks, constituency offices and ATMs until our voices are heard.

DISCUSSION QUESTIONS

1. What are some other examples of the extension of the militaristic metaphor into non-militaristic contexts? How does the metaphor help structure your ways of perceiving and talking about that other context?

2. Other culturally powerful genres (e.g. hero tales, fairy tales, creation myths) are frequently used to characterize events in the media and politics. Identify some examples of this rhetorical practice and discuss how our common knowledge of the genres' conventions help to structure our understanding of the specific event.

3. Discuss whether it is possible to communicate with language in an ideologically free manner, i.e., in a manner that does not reflect and encourage particular perceptions over others.

4. Select a current PR Newswire release (see link below) or a recent government announcement and discuss how the writer's choice of language reflects the vested interests of the company or government.

WEBLINKS

American Newspeak (a satirical e-zine of political doublespeak)
www.scn.org/news/newspeak/

Propaganda Analysis Home Page
carmen.artsci.washington.edu/propaganda/home.htm

PR Newswire Service
www.prnewswire.com/

chapter three

PC on Campus:
The War over Words

INTRODUCTION

Political correctness is a "hot-button" topic on campus; so heated is this debate that even the name "political correctness" has become problematic because both sides of the debate use the term differently and for vastly different purposes. Rick Salutin argues that the phrase began in Canada as a joke that the left wing made about itself, but it has become the mantra of a very potent attack on the left by conservative groups—a case of a rather innocent phrase being co-opted by a strong political lobby group and turned to different, and frequently misleading, uses.

Salutin gives an overview of how the term has been used, and notes that extreme groups on both sides of the debate have done disservice to the worthy causes that it was meant to support: women's rights, anti-racism, and anti-discriminatory practices. Salutin makes a very strong argument about the poor quality of media research into supposed acts of repression by the "politically correct." The media in general has tended to repeat questionable anecdotal, but attention-grabbing, evidence of repressive acts of "political correctness" rather than well-researched examinations of the issue.

Salutin's position echoes that of American scholar and lawyer Stanley Fish in *There's No Such Thing as Free Speech ... and It's a Good Thing Too* (New York: Oxford University Press, 1994). In that book, Fish pointed to the media and its creation of what Lawrence

Grossberg has called "affective plagues" which tabloidize and encourage artificial panics about poorly understood issues such as free speech and political correctness. Rational argument and evidence frequently fly out of the window in the face of these emotional issues.

P.A. Sullivan articulates the position of the Society for Academic Freedom and Scholarship (SAFS) with respect to the issue of political correctness and academic freedom. He argues that in the context of the university, evidence of the impact of "political correctness" can be seen in the establishment of speech code policies, in academic hirings, and in the evaluation of the teaching and research of faculty. Sullivan stresses that responsible and unconstrained debate and the rational evaluation of fact remain at the core of academic freedom, and that this freedom is currently under serious threat from "political correctness" and what he describes as the "widespread acceptance of the doctrine of postmodernism."

Krishna Rau and Clive Thompson do an analysis of the politics and research of some of the members of the Society for Academic Freedom and Scholarship. They note that the research of several of the prominent members of the Society is supported by extremist groups who have disturbing political agendas around issues like race, gender, and employment equity. Arguing that Canada needs a strong group to fight for academic freedom, Rau and Thompson propose a more open and intelligently researched discussion of this issue.

David MacFarlane concludes this chapter by questioning, as did Salutin, whether there is any evidence of political correctness actually acting as a moderating, let alone "shackling," force in contemporary culture. Though humorous in tone, his brief commentary succeeds in casting the debate in a new light.

LOOSE CANONS

Rick Salutin *(Saturday Night)*

The first time I heard the phrase was in a Chinese restaurant during the late 1960s, after a political meeting or protest march. Those things built an appetite. Someone always has to take charge when you're ordering Chinese food, and someone did. She listed a number of dishes and asked if it sounded okay. "I don't know," somebody else said, "whether that's a politically correct order." It got a little laugh, as a touch of slightly self-conscious left-wing humour. But it worked because the cuisine was Chinese, and Maoism was then the most popular fare on the left's ideological menu.

Around the same time, a comic strip called Korrect Line Komix appeared in the alternative press along with the Fabulous Furry Freak Brothers. A chubby little Mao face in the corner of each panel said things like, "Where do correct ideas come from?" Next panel he'd ask, "Do they fall from the sky?" Then some guy would get bonked on the head by a falling idea and Mao would chirp, "Nope!" A nice send-up. It's a shame really: people on the left concoct a phrase that pokes fun at themselves—a healthy instinct—and more than twenty years later every mass medium in the triumphant capitalist West is using it to pummel whatever spirit of opposition remains in the post-Cold War world.

The media frenzy over political correctness, or PC, has consumed most of 1991. It started before the Gulf War and outlasted it. It must be trying to tell us something. To me the best way to treat the subject is to start with that media reaction before going back to have a look at the thing itself. I'm not saying the object of all the attention doesn't exist; it does,

Rick Salutin. Loose canons. *Saturday Night* 106(10), December, 1991. 20-24, 74-75.

and I'll get to it. But the reality of political correctness is minuscule compared to the orgy of media attention—the overkill—launched in its name. I mean, how big should a story be to rate cover or feature treatment in *Newsweek, New York, Time, The Atlantic, The New Republic*, and (wait for it, because you had to) *Maclean's*? We're talking about World War III or the fall of the Berlin Wall. At least you'd think so.

The first cover story showed up like a grim Christmas present in the December 24, 1990, issue of *Newsweek*, wrapped in the words, "Watch What You Say: THOUGHT POLICE." The story centred on universities, where, as *Time* later put it, "a troubling number of teachers, at all levels, regard the bulk of American history and heritage as racist, sexist, and classist and believe their purpose is to bring about social change." The evidence was mainly anecdotal. Check that: entirely anecdotal. In fact, *all* the coverage has revealed nothing more than a batch of scary tales: some students or professors being criticized or harassed for using certain language; some changes in curriculum to de-emphasize certain authors and stress others. No statistics to show how widespread the phenomenon is, no studies or surveys, no coherent theory to explain the thing and put it in perspective. (One of the few stats I did find said 100 to 200 U.S. colleges and universities—out of 3,600—had tried to restrict speech on PC grounds, and a number of those restrictions had now been withdrawn.) Even the anecdotes were often feeble. "If I was at lunch [in the dorm]," a Stanford student told *Newsweek*, "and we started talking about something like civil rights, I'd get up and leave. . . . I knew they didn't want to hear what I had to say." Now, into each life a little rain must fall, but for these stories, newsmagazine correspondents all over America are asked to submit reports, which are exhaustively culled by editors at head office—and *this* tale made the cut?

There was also some light analysis in *Newsweek*. Like: "PC is, strictly speaking, a totalitarian philosophy." Huh? Where is it taught? Name a single thinker or book that expounds this philosophy. Elsewhere, PC was called a "movement." So what are its organizational structures or publications or membership? For Pete's sake, "Star Trek" is more of a movement than PC. It makes better sense to call racism a movement or philosophy; you could name spokesmen, institutions, guiding thoughts, and thinkers. *Newsweek* also struggled to uncloak the obscure literary technique called deconstruction, seen as a deadly weapon in the PC armament, and expose its threat to, gasp, The Canon. Some of this gets pretty unreal. The foes of PC are furious over challenges to the list of literary and philosophical classics taught as the Western "canon" and the attempts to add on, say, "testimonials written by oppressed Guatemalan women"—as Ray Conlogue of *The Globe and Mail* put it in a fine show of Western open-mindedness. They're terrified that Shakespeare and, of all things, Rabelais will be tossed out with the morning garbage. Yet even the notion of canonization in its original sense—establishing the text of the Bible—is controversial: the Catholic canon differs from the Protestant, which differs from the Jewish. The revered canon of Western literature wasn't even set until the 1930s, in the case of its British component; and until the 1950s, for the American. I don't mean there's not a lot of good stuff in there —I'm partial to Shakespeare myself, though I doubt he'd be peeing his pants over whether he made the canon—but there's mediocrity, too: did you ever try reading *The Pilgrim's Progress*?

The whole investigation by *Newsweek* had a thumb-sucking quality, a sulky sense of grievance that anyone would dare challenge the prevailing value system in the West, and especially "the single most compelling idea in human history, individual liberty, which as it happens is just now sweeping the entire world." *Hey, we're number one, our product is wiping the competition, how come they're raining on our parade*? Still, *Newsweek* wasn't entirely one-sided. It ran an interview with a prof who supported curriculum change, and an account from someone who'd worked on a campus programme to combat traditional prejudices. In retrospect, *Newsweek* starts to look good.

New York magazine's January 21, 1991, cover showed a bespectacled white fellow tortured by the question "Are You Politically Correct?" There were photographs of Hitler Youths burning books in the 1930s, along with student guidelines handed out by Smith University, and washroom graffiti at Brown. Imagine how swamped you'd be if you decided to go after racism or sexism on the basis of such "evidence"? *Time's* long essay on April 1 agreed that universities should be "centers for the critical examination of Western beliefs," but said this had now taken a "strident turn" —as if upping the volume were cause for declaring a national emergency. It singled out an assistant professor who teaches a course on white male writers; she argues that since there are courses on women writers and black writers, why not one on white men? Personally, I don't see the fallacy. In *The New Republic*, historian Eugene Genovese called the PC people "storm troopers" and demanded counterterror in response. Others referred to PC as "fascism of the left" and "the new McCarthyism." A little overstated, perhaps, since, unlike German, Italian, or Japanese fascism, or the original McCarthyism, the PC movement has no government representing it, no money behind it, no mass media or propaganda presence, no paramilitary forces. What would fascism have amounted to with so little support? Something like the PC "movement"—maybe. The *Atlantic's* March cover story, by a former Reagan staffer, Dinesh D'Souza, quoted a teacher at Duke University who hopes "to create a Marxist culture in this country, to make Marxism an unavoidable presence in American social, cultural and intellectual life." A man and his dream, to be sure, but enough to make an entire society tremble? At a time when even the Soviet Communist Party had ditched Uncle Karl? The worst, though, was yet to come.

In late May, "Canada's Weekly Newsmagazine" became the last on its block to get a PC cover. It showed a young white couple in graduation garb with gags over their mouths and hurt expressions. The title was "The Silencers." In his note to readers, *Maclean's* editor, Kevin Doyle, condemned the "vociferous intolerance" of what he called "the Nons." Though he found many practices they were protesting (racism, sexism, fascism) "distasteful"—"in the extreme," actually—he said their own actions represented "a far more insidious evil." Doyle relied for backup, as did the cover story, on what he called "a recent, little-noticed speech" by George Bush [Senior]. The speech was about as little-noticed as the heart scare Bush had later the same day he gave it. It was valuable in one way though: it summed up the shallowness and hypocrisy of much of the assault against PC.

Bush criticized political correctness for declaring off limits certain topics, expressions, "and even certain gestures." Yet he himself had run against Michael Dukakis on the issue of the pledge of allegiance, and had tried to introduce a constitutional amendment forbidding gestures demeaning the U.S. flag. Bush attacked those who'd set "citizens against one another on the basis of their class or race"—after using mug shots of the convicted black killer Willie Horton to create white anxiety about Dukakis. He denounced "the temptation to assign bad motives to people who disagree with us," yet had called Saddam Hussein *worse* than Hitler and the war against him a simple case of good versus evil. Bush warned of "the growing tendency to use intimidation rather than reason in settling disputes," but rejected sanctions against Iraq despite evidence that they were working. And he praised the freedom to speak one's mind as "the most fundamental and deeply revered of all liberties," after attacking Dukakis as a "card-carrying member" of the American Civil Liberties Union. Bush, just like Kevin Doyle, found the desire to combat racism and sexism "laudable," apparently forgetting that after his 1988 television debate with Geraldine Ferraro he had told the world that he'd "kicked some feminist ass." Bush's speech was normal political pap. What's remarkable is the deference with which Doyle and *Maclean's*—alone in all of journalism—treated it. Two weeks later, even *Maclean's* own American columnist, Fred Bruning, ridiculed the speech.

The text of the *Maclean's* cover story was mostly a rehash, larded with weasel words ("many academics," "some feminists," "some social commentators," "critics say," "lots of people") to hide the absence of specifics. A psychology prof at the University of Western Ontario grumbled "I have to measure my words carefully" —which doesn't sound like such a horrid burden for a teacher and scholar. Besides Bush, the piece peddled one other U.S. authority, an employee of the National Association of Scholars, which is an anti-PC organization funded by several seriously right-wing American foundations. *Maclean's* quoted him seven times in two pages, and included his photo. Speaking of pictures, one could do a little deconstruction of the juxtaposition of George and Barbara Bush at a graduation, waving and smiling with open hands, set across the page from a sea of mostly black graduates raising clenched fists. Then, there was one of those joyous generalizations only *Maclean's* has the staff to research: "From Vancouver to Miami, people say that they are constantly being harangued or induced to change." I'd love to see the transcripts. Historian Michael Bliss lamented that, these days, "You're not allowed to sin against ethnic equality, you're not allowed to sin against gender equality." Pity. But as the mag assured us, in another breathtaking *aperçu*, "off-color and ethnic jokes are now as rare in mixed company as the three-martini lunch." If you think you've heard the odd such joke lately, well, you probably just drank too much at lunch.

What's a touch hard to take is how distressed Doyle and his employees get about "The Silencers" when they've been known to practise some, let's say, restraint themselves. Merely on the level of editing, *Maclean's*, as Robert Fulford has said, "is the most rigidly edited magazine in Canadian history." Or have you never wondered why all those reporters write in exactly the same style? One former correspondent says any time he proudly reported anything that hadn't appeared elsewhere, the editors would say, "Good. We'll cut that." Or there was the time *Maclean's* airbrushed the genitals out of a painting by Attila Richard Lukacs, after Doyle had warned the art department to stay alert for "objectionable details." In fact, *Maclean's* own employees have formed an "Editorial Integrity Committee" evincing a certain lack of confidence in their leader. A survey taken in-house by that committee showed widespread alarm over "lack of balance" in the political-correctness cover story itself. For another case of "Stifling," as the subhead on the cover put it, consider Kevin Doyle's own, ah, alteration to an exclusive interview with President Bush himself in the summer of 1990. Bush referred to a dinner he'd had with Brian Mulroney, "and a couple of drinks, I might add"—an interesting reference since there'd been much speculation at that time about whether Mulroney had returned to his old drinking habits because of Meech and Oka. Then Bush added, "Oh, I hope I'm not getting the prime minister into trouble," or words to that effect. It showed an impressive awareness of Mulroney's medical and political problems, but Doyle cut the line from the story.

And for a sample of political correctness of a different sort, just glance at *Maclean's* cover two weeks later. "The Private Prime Minister" featured seven pages of exclusive photos of a day in the life of Brian. It came in the wake of this year's spate of rumours and reports about the PM, which centred on marital breakdown. Strangely enough, nine of the twenty-eight pictures included Mila or the kids—with lots of kissyface and popping in unexpectedly on hubby at the office. The shots were taken by a *Maclean's* photo editor who happened to have been Mulroney's official photographer during his first year in office.

There's been some other Canadian comment on PC. "How long might it take to repair the damage wrought by the PC movement?" fretted Conlogue in *The Globe and Mail*, neatly assuming a devastation of the campuses that had nowhere been established. On CTV's "W5," the regular political panel also grumped about the subject. The New Democrats' Gerry Caplan was sure they all regretted that everybody on their panel was a white man in a suit, but no-one volunteered to step down and improve the balance. In an impassioned column, Dalton Camp said he could remember "when it was considered politically correct for anyone to say anything that came to mind and when outrageous opinion was not only indulged, but encouraged." Funny, I don't. He never said when that happened, but you got the impression he was thinking of the *fifties*.

All those poor fellows in suits with columns and tenure are twitching frantically about a lost golden age that never was, except maybe for them; and about a new McCarthyism, or worse, for which there's only meagre evidence. Sure there are some students and profs making demands. Ranged against them are the entire mass media, most of the academic establishment, and politicians starting at the level of the president of the U.S. You get the idea the anti-PCs might manage to hold their own. Could that really be what it's all about: a bunch of guys sitting there in their bastions of privilege, at the *Globe* or the university, with tenure or a by-line they've worked and schemed to acquire, and feeling so incredibly insecure they go wild to protect that privilege against—not even a threat but a mild and fairly marginal challenge?

You don't hear much from these same people about a different threat to university independence: the invasion of business influence, for which there's lots of evidence—joint academic-corporate councils and forums, grants to encourage research that will increase profits, "joint-venture discovery parks" on campus just like the industrial parks cities build to compete for business, deals profs negotiate with companies on patents and discoveries, university-business liaison, and real-estate officers alongside the deans and registrars. You could say there are signs of a threat to academic independence there—but no magazine covers.

And finally, there's the mainstream media's own version of PC, though they never call it that. As Thomas Walkom of the *Toronto Star* wrote, "This year's most telling examples of political correctness come not from the dispossessed but from the powerful: the media jingos who treated any criticism of the Gulf War as treasonous; and the business lobbies that—regardless of the circumstances—rail against government deficits."

So, having established that the entire media offensive against the so-called PC movement is overblown, dishonest, and hypocritical, I'd like to turn to the phenomenon itself. Personally and politically, I find it a pain in the ass.

It can be irksome and picky, for starters, especially concerning language: doing search-and-destroy missions on phrases like "a nip in the air," or "a chink in the armour," or words like "blackmail." And I can't get comfortable with the phrase "people of colour." It sounds prissy and self-congratulatory to me. I feel like the San Francisco writer who was upbraided for dumping on the term, and said he didn't want to discuss it until he'd had his coffee of morning.

It gets more serious though. People or groups with rigid, "politically correct" attitudes and demands on matters like racism and sexism really can be a threat—but *not* to pillars of the establishment like *Newsweek*, *Maclean's*, and George Bush, who've been responding to them with the equivalent of the war against Iraq. The politically correct people are generally pretty marginal and powerless, striving for a toehold in the curriculum or hiring policy, or just to be noticed. They pose no serious danger to the right, or the establishment; but they can be a real problem for the left, and for efforts actually to combat forces like racism and sexism. They muddy the water, set people of goodwill against each other, create disunity, and present a version of their causes that alienates potential allies and provides a big fat target for their enemies.

This is an old story. It happened to Maoism, to go back to where we started. Just twenty years ago, it didn't look all that implausible, in China or elsewhere. But the mindless and parodic versions of it mouthed by students and others during the Cultural Revolution made it impossible to ever take seriously again. Mao himself, who had a sense of humour—just read some of his unofficial speeches—wondered if there wasn't a plot to make his ideas look ridiculous.

The PC mind-set is just a phoney nuisance for the establishment, but it can make trouble for serious movements of social change. Consider for instance the battle of the Women's Press, a small feminist publisher painstakingly created over a period of sixteen years. A few years ago it nearly died in a virtual blood bath of political correctness about who was racist. There were demands for public confessions, stacked meetings, and the lock on the door got changed. In the end eight women who'd put their life's effort into building a useful feminist institution were driven out, and the bitterness and infighting are still going on. Not exactly the way you build an alternative movement to challenge the status quo.

Then there's the case of June Callwood, who until the end of 1989 was a rare voice of social conscience at the new, Darwinian *Globe and Mail*. Publisher Roy Megarry had been trying to ditch her for years, unsuccessfully. Then, outside a writers' convention, the black author Marlene Nourbese Philip harangued Callwood for racism—a ludicrous charge. In frustration, Callwood told Philip to "fuck off," which was duly reported, re-reported, and editorialized about in our newspaper of record. The upshot was that Callwood left the paper, not really a great victory for the cause of reform—though Marlene Philip was the subject of a flattering profile in the paper a few days after Callwood departed.

Or take even the case of the playwright Joanna Glass, a person of talent and goodwill, but little experience of political action, who attended a Women Playrights Conference in Toronto recently. She was so alienated by the posturing and bullying that went on concerning colour, and men, and the "correct" views on women in the arts that she "came away from it deploring (for a change) not man's inhumanity to man, but women's inhumanity to women." My own feeling is that so much needs changing in this society—and the larger world society too—and the forces in power are so cocky and entrenched that it's sheer idiocy to drive away potential supporters like Joanna Glass, while creating deep divisions among those already committed.

The scariest part of all is who you find yourself agreeing or disagreeing with—for instance, when the well-meaning advisers to York University on the status of women, and race and ethnic relations, write, in the style of an encyclical, "White males cannot be victims of racism or sexism. Discrimination results from systemic oppression." Sorry, but racism and sexism are more flexible than that, which is what makes them hard to eradicate. Oppression can be practised by victims; in fact, victims are powerfully motivated to victimize others in turn—if they can get away with it. On the other hand, I reluctantly nod my head to Lorrie Goldstein, in the odious (and often racist and sexist) *Toronto Sun*, when he says, "Political correctness isn't just good liberal intentions run amok. . . . It is racism and, for that matter, sexism. . . . Accept that only blacks can teach African history or that only men can be sexist and you are not very far from accepting that blacks have rhythm, that women make lousy drivers, and that Jews are good with money." Ouch. The *Toronto Sun* gets it right?

So a pox on both their houses, both the media hysterics of the mainstream and the self-righteous crusaders of PC. It will, however, require a considerably larger pox to deal with the former than with the latter.

ACADEMIC FREE SPEECH NEEDS CONTINUAL DEFENCE

P. A. Sullivan *(SAFS Newsletter)*

In an increasingly complex civilization, universities play a vital role in promoting scholarship: the preservation, dissemination and expansion of knowledge. Crucial to that role is academic freedom.

This is the right of unfettered debate on contentious issues according to the principles of responsible scholarship: rational argument applied to factual evidence. But this right is both hard-won and continually attacked by individuals, groups and governments taking offense for religious, political, or commercial reasons.

In Western democracies these attacks usually come from conservative forces external to the university; current examples are attempts by corporations to suppress information discovered by university researchers on harmful side effects of drugs. Such threats are well understood, but the last 30 years have witnessed attacks from other, more subtle, sources. Activists assert that, being dominated by white heterosexual males, universities need reform to eliminate racism and sexism.

The incident initiating this development occurred at Cornell University a generation ago. In 1963, Black students rioted and held several hostages, claiming that a professor's evaluation of the economic performance of several African countries was "racist." Setting terrible precedents, Cornell met the students' demands for an academic program having an explicit political mission, and forced the professor to apologize.

There have since been many similar assaults on academic freedom, with administrations routinely botching their resolution. In Canada, one of the worst occurred at McGill in 1993 when feminists disrupted a lecture by a U.S. psychologist arguing that recovered memories of sexual abuse are implanted by the therapists. McGill failed to discipline the offenders or to provide redress to the speaker.

These failures reflect widespread acceptance of the doctrine of postmodernism, which displaces the idea that facts and evidence count with the idea that everything reduces to subjective interests and perspectives. Postmodernism politicizes scholarship and legitimizes tactics such as discrediting an argument by pointing to the proponent's race or sex. Typically, "chilly climate" investigations of the political science departments at the Universities of Victoria and British Columbia portrayed critiques of feminist scholarship as sexual harassment.

Postmodernism has also fostered the adoption of speech codes and racial and sexual harassment criteria having subjective definitions of "offence." Furthermore, in academic appointment and promotion practices, when an individual's excellence—however imperfectly evaluated—should be the predominant criterion, postmodernism accentuates [inappropriate] group membership criteria.

P. A. Sullivan. Academic free speech needs continual defence. *SAFS Newsletter* #21 (March 1999).

The Society for Academic Freedom and Scholarship was formed in 1992 following both attacks on controversial professors and the ensnarement of others in absurd harassment proceedings. The Society does not deny the problems that speech codes and harassment policies address. It argues that experience has confirmed early critics' predictions: the codes and policies have created secretive, self-justifying bureaucracies, and unfair investigative practices prone to abuse by individuals bearing grudges. Furthermore, by creating a climate of uncertainty, they assault academic freedom.

Speech codes have been especially troublesome; indeed, political scientist Abigail Thernstrom depicts U.S. universities as "islands of repression in a sea of freedom." In Canada, Ontario's NDP government introduced a draconian code which civil liberties lawyer Alan Borovoy described as "making one person's free speech contingent on another person's thin skin." This code is still in force.

As the recent swimming coach case at Simon Fraser University illustrates, harassment policies have also been problem-ridden, with administrations repeatedly bungling their implementation. Although few in number, such debacles have serious legal consequences, lead to agonized policy revisions, and polarize campus communities.

The Society believes that speech codes and harassment policies have proved to be unnecessary, costly, divisive failures. For example, the harassment uppermost in the public mind, "sex for grades," was a serious academic offense long before harassment codes were introduced, so that these codes focus on trivial cases such as leering or the ideologically offended.

Typically, this February, in granting the appeal of a Waterloo sociology professor against his conviction for offending a student by savagely criticizing employment equity, the adjudicator commented on the flawed nature of the university's policy, and on the absurdity of forcing insincere written public apologies. [Also, this May, when a few students in a University of Massachusetts biology class objected to a professor's factual description of an abortion drug, a bureaucrat declared it harassment warranting replacement of the professor with someone more "sensitive."] Given evidence such as this, it is time for detached and open reappraisal of these policies.

Critics such as the *Toronto Star*'s Thomas Walkom portray the Society as defending only certain views. But it speaks out on all attacks on academic free speech, regardless of the ideological content. In the recent past we have defended a conservative Muslim, a feminist scholar, a leftist homosexual, as well as academics who discussed sex and race differences in human groups in ways that may have been uncomfortable for some but which were consistent with the academic mission of the university, which is the search for truth through reasoned argument.

HATE 101

Krishna Rau and Clive Thompson *(This Magazine)*

The document is a slim seven pages, but it drives John Furedy nuts. Standing in his office, he waves a copy of York University's proposed race relations policy. His lobby group, the Society for Academic Freedom and Scholarship (SAFS), has been fighting to quash the policy, which the university hopes will reduce racial harassment on campus.

Krishna Rau and Clive Thompson. Hate 101. *This Magazine* 28(7), March/April, 1995. 18–24.

Furedy's motley crew of academics thinks the policy will stifle free speech. But so far, all they've been able to do is delay it until spring.

It isn't much of a victory, and it's left Furedy in his most sarcastic mode. "I think now it's more like the concentration camp at Dachau, rather than Auschwitz," he says. "No gas ovens."

Heavy words, but the overblown rhetoric is typical of the University of Toronto psychology professor's style. As president of the Canada-wide SAFS, Furedy—who himself lost family members in the Holocaust—leads what he sees as a battalion against the modern-day forces of totalitarianism: speech codes, affirmative-action hiring, and political correctness. Unqualified women and minorities are getting hired over hard-working white men, he says, and thought police are clamping down on free speech. "Intellectual discourse," Furedy wrote in a recent article, "has thereby become the slave of ideology."

But the war Furedy is fighting isn't only about free speech. While on the surface the SAFS says it's just defending hard work and merit, at the root of its leaders' angry opposition to equity policies are some explosive scientific theories. In a modern-day twist on social Darwinism, the SAFS leaders discussed in this article believe that people really *aren't* born equal and should not be equally represented in the academe. If white men are at the top of the heap at universities, they say, it's simply because they're the best equipped biologically to be there. For several key members of the group, inequality isn't just a matter of opinion, it's a cold, hard fact supported by their own research. Founding president Doreen Kimura and early member Philippe Rushton, for example, have built their careers on studies linking intelligence and aptitude to race or gender. Kimura argues that women are inherently worse than men at math and spatial reasoning; Rushton claims blacks have lower IQs and higher criminal tendencies than whites. Others SAFS leaders have even led attacks on students with learning disabilities, arguing that they have no place in institutions of higher learning.

It's theories like these which make one question just who is pulling the strings in the SAFS's "academic freedom" debate—and why. This question becomes even more worrisome in the face of evidence that several prominent members have quietly developed extensive funding, publishing or membership ties to racist groups with white supremacist ties, at least one of which spends millions of dollars funding academic research. That group is the Pioneer Fund. Its incorporation papers state that it funds research into "problems of race betterment" and "problems of heredity and eugenics in the human race." It financed a good chunk of the research cited in the recent American bestseller *The Bell Curve*, including studies by Rushton. Like some SAFS members, *The Bell Curve* authors argue that there are links between race and intelligence. And they openly call for those results to be used in formulating public policy and restructuring society.

While keeping such links quiet, the SAFS has won power and influence, particularly on campuses hit by genuine examples of over-the-top political censorship. Since its founding three years ago, the group's membership has grown to 375 professors across Canada, many of whom hold influential positions at their own institutions. Last fall, the SAFS was given a $210,000 grant by the Canadian Donner Foundation. And, as one of Canada's few free-speech groups, the SAFS has been adopted by the likes of journalist Robert Fulford, who devoted a column in *The Globe and Mail* to praising its defense of academic excellence. A generous assessment of people whose ideas about excellence are considerably less generous toward much of the world's population.

It should come as no surprise that the SAFS has roots in notions of racial and gender inequality—the group was formed around Philippe Rushton. When Rushton presented a paper entitled "Evolutionary Biology and Heritable Traits" at a January, 1989 science conference, few realized the far-reaching political effects of his seemingly fringe ideas. Rushton's paper was the first public outline of his theory that people of Asian descent have larger brains and greater intelligence than Caucasians, who in turn have larger brains and more intelligence than blacks. The University of Western Ontario psychology professor also argued that there is an inverse relationship between brain size and the size of men's sexual organs, and that blacks—having the smallest brains and largest penises—are more promiscuous and criminally-minded.

Rushton's paper generated an immediate firestorm of protest from students and fellow academics. Even then Ontario premier David Peterson called for Rushton's dismissal, and demonstrations at Western led administrators to order the professor to teach some classes via videotape.

But while the media spotlight focused on Rushton, several like-minded colleagues were getting worried. They saw the attacks as a trend towards intolerance of controversial research. Over lunch-time discussions, Furedy and Western professors Kimura, Davison Ankney, and Douglas Jackson—all of whom have done research on gender differences or genetic determinism—laid the groundwork for what in 1991 would become the Society for Academic Freedom and Scholarship.

Detractors tried to dismiss the SAFS as the "Rushton Defence Society," and while the founders still resent the label, they agree that Rushton was their main stimulus. "Here was a case where what he said was disturbing to many people, especially in the case of the term 'racism' being thrown around," Furedy says. "There have always been attacks on free speech, especially in the universities, but the attacks had always come from outside . . . so the contrast in the Rushton case was very strong."

Their timing was perfect. Since the late-eighties, campuses had become increasingly politicized and divided. The Rushton protests were only the tip of the iceberg. Activists had aggressively attacked professorial power, making ideas such as academic excellence and free speech seem naive and old-fashioned.

Sometimes campus activists did indeed go over-board. A few of the examples the SAFS raises can't—and shouldn't—be dismissed. Kimura often cites the case of Jeanne Cannizzo, who curated "Into the Heart of Africa," an exhibit of colonial artifacts at the Royal Ontario Museum. Protestors claimed the show depicted Africans as ignorant and backward. When she was hired to teach African anthropology at U of T, several non-students verbally abused her in her classroom and even at her home. She eventually fled the university and the country.

"That was just appalling," Kimura says, shaking her head. "It's amazing how few people would actually speak up and say anything, and how hard it was to get reasonable attention for a different point of view."

Into this morass of campus politics the SAFS brought simple answers and bold stances. While other groups on both sides of the debate fought over the arcane details of issues like gender-neutral language, the SAFS outlined its purposes in two terse phrases: "1) Maintaining freedom in teaching, research and scholarship. 2) Maintaining standards of excellence in hiring and promotion of university faculty."

The group also had political wiles to match their sound bites. Acknowledging the danger of looking like self-interested male academics, they elected Doreen Kimura as their president. Few female scientists come more high-powered than Kimura, a world-renowned psychologist with media savvy and a healthy sense of the absurd (she is probably the only white-haired Canadian academic with a Guns 'N Roses poster in her office). Her hard-nosed stances on academic freedom, as well as her research on female mental ability, have splashed her photo everywhere from the slick pages of *Psychology Today* to the local *London Free Press*.

With an accomplished older woman at the helm of the SAFS, Kimura notes with amusement, it was harder to say the group was merely anti-feminist. Ironically, though, feminism became more of a target than ever—with Kimura leading the charge. "Recently, university administrations in Canada have begun a campaign that can only be described as discrimination against men, and particularly Caucasian men," she told a crowd of 150 academics at the SAFS's first conference in 1993. Employment equity was a popular target among the men she was addressing.

But as often happens with anti-PC arguments, the emotions seem to overwhelm the facts. If you look at the statistics, it's hard to believe that unqualified women are storming the barricades. According to Statistics Canada, women comprised only 7 percent of all full professors in 1989. Since they were 4 percent in 1961, that's an increase of a measly one-tenth of 1 percent per year. In engineering and applied sciences, the numbers are even grimmer—from 0.9 percent to 2.9 percent over the same 28 years.

The SAFS's rhetoric, in contrast, relies mostly on anecdotal evidence and word of mouth. Furedy can cite a few examples of politically driven hiring decisions: a Dalhousie University chair of black studies job that was restricted to black applicants and a University of Manitoba professorship that reportedly went to a woman who didn't have a doctorate. But he freely admits that he doesn't have any numbers. "That's very difficult to gather, because the administration doesn't want to let you know about that," he says. "We're very handicapped because most of us are amateurs, and we can't do that research."

But many of the group's leaders do conduct research of a different kind—research they don't like to talk about when they're wearing their SAFS hats. As the extensive footnoting in *The Bell Curve* shows, a startling number of academics around the world are engaged in research linking intellectual ability to gender or race. And few Canadians realize how many have congregated at Western—and how many are active in the SAFS. When you line up the scientific work of the group's founders, it forms an interesting flip side to their activism.

When we called Kimura for an interview about the SAFS, we unwittingly found ourselves in the middle of a media frenzy. Her secretary was running interference big-time: to deal with the onslaught of reporters, she said, Kimura was requiring everyone to submit a faxed list of questions. Only then would she agree to talk about the fingerprints. The fingerprints?

As it turns out, Kimura had released a study linking fingerprint patterns to male homosexuality. The press, of course, was going wild—did this mean homosexuality was genetic? Would there be testing?

This wasn't the first brouhaha over Kimura's work. She has built her reputation on research into intellectual differences between men and women, with equally controversial findings. In 1988, she made international headlines when she published a study arguing that hormonal changes in women affect their cognitive abilities, making it harder to engage in spatial reasoning. Kimura went on to claim that hormonal differences between the sexes from birth lead to different aptitudes—with men winning out in the maths and sciences.

Kimura and Rushton are the most prominent SAFS members with interests in these hot-button topics, but they're not the only ones. Ankney, a zoology professor and founding SAFS board member, is another gender-intelligence researcher, and probably the most unusual. For most of his career, he stuck to publishing papers on waterfowl. But in 1992, he turned his attention to human beings. After studying data from a series of autopsies, he concluded that women have smaller brains than men, even after body size is taken into account, and thus are less adept at mathematics and spatial relations.

"Others with 'politically correct' agendas . . . can ignore or even deny the existence of these fascinating aspects of human biology and behaviour," he argued later in defence of his idea. "They cannot, however, make them disappear."

Douglas Jackson, another psychology professor and the SAFS's founding secretary-treasurer, has done extensive research into "vocational interest," looking at relationships between personalities and aptitudes. In 1985, predating the SAFS's concerns, Jackson teamed up with Rushton to try to define the traits of the productive university researcher, organizing a conference and editing a book on "scientific excellence." Although one essay actually slams universities for systematically sealing out women, Rushton's study pulls out his infamous genetic arguments, suggesting that research abilities "appear to have substantial heritabilities associated with them."

Of the group's leaders, Furedy alone isn't directly involved in intelligence research, although he supports the findings wholeheartedly, and cites them often. He even wrote a highly positive review in the *Toronto Star* of both *The Bell Curve* and Rushton's latest book, *Race, Evolution and Behavior*.

Publicly, though, its leaders' intelligence research about race and gender isn't something the SAFS wears on its sleeve. Furedy, in his *Star* review, identified himself only as a psychology professor, never mentioning his SAFS presidency. And in the grant proposal to the Donner Foundation, Furedy describes the SAFS as the only campus group with no political agenda. He even goes so far as to invoke Socrates: "The Socratic principle of disinterestedness underlies all modern democratic societies, and is exemplified by an insistence that any committee . . . have 'no axe to grind'" (a serious omission of the fact that SAFS leaders' research presents a very clear political agenda on issues of race and gender).

In interviews, the founders echo this "non-politicized" line. Kimura says she was leery of accepting the position of president, fearing conflict-of-interest charges. "I had this nagging concern that people would see this as mixing my research interests and my political interests."

No wonder. Internal documents show that the SAFS routinely mixes its members' genetic research findings with the group's political goals—particularly when it comes to equity hiring. After Kimura attended a 1992 conference on "Women in Engineering, Science and Technology," she wrote a withering report in the SAFS newsletter, dismissing arguments that science and engineering faculties can be hostile environments for women. Instead, she explained the low participation rate of women by citing "actual intrinsic ability differences between the sexes in areas which impinge on science and math requirements," and "women's native preference for work that is people-oriented as compared to object-oriented."

At the 1993 SAFS conference, Kimura drew an explicit connection between these beliefs and her attacks on equity policies. "No mention is made [in the policies] of group preference for certain kinds of work or group suitability," she said.

Outside the supportive atmosphere of Society conferences, however, getting SAFS members to talk openly about the social implications of their research isn't easy. When the topic was raised during interviews, they waffled, clearly aware that the subject is a touchy one. It took repeated questioning before Kimura admitted that her research is mixed liberally with her activism.

"I try to keep the roles separate, but I probably don't always succeed—and maybe one shouldn't," she says. "That is, maybe part of the point of this is to have some applications where it's appropriate to say 'look, there are certain expectations that you can have about representation of men and women in different occupations that are, not totally, but substantially biologically based.'"

It's not surprising that the SAFS shies away from openly using its members' research as a political tool—the research itself has won scorn from many scientists. It is hardly accepted enough to act as the basis for forming university hiring policies. One of the most prominent opponents to this type of research is Harvard paleontologist Stephen Jay Gould, who argues that people who link intelligence to genetics are too quick to dismiss upbringing and environment. It's not surprising, he writes, that rich, well-looked-after kids are smart, or that girls who own "math-class-is-tough" Barbies wind up opting for English over engineering. Everyone from white-power population-control nuts to opponents of welfare have used genetic arguments, he notes in *The Mismeasure of Man*: "Determinist arguments for ranking people according to a single scale of intelligence . . . have recorded little more than social prejudice."

The group's Darwinian bent has brought the SAFS to some startling extremes. At Western, for instance, the group has fought to strip students with learning disabilities of special consideration like extra time on exams.

"It is especially absurd to have someone who's unqualified in the academic discipline tell a professor how much extra time he should give," Furedy says. "For a math professor to have some ignorant idiot—and I use the term advisedly—come around and tell him that certain students have to be given twice as much time, it's a gross interference. If someone's learning disabled, I don't want to make special allowances for him in university."

Christopher Essex, a Western math professor and coordinator of the SAFS's London chapter, says the issue is also one of power—professors aren't shown documents to prove the students' disabilities. He also claims that non-disabled students have taken to making false claims.

But much of the opposition comes from a basic belief that many learning disabilities simply don't exist. Ankney is willing to grant the existence of dyslexia, but believes that most other cases are mere stupidity. "We've gone from a well-known problem like dyslexia to the situation where maybe there's nothing more than what used to be called genuine low IQ."

The SAFS's attacks on equality have not happened in a void. They have been developed by academics who happily walk arm in arm with openly racist organizations. Nowhere is this more evident than in the case of Kenneth Hilborn, a Western history professor who last year led the SAFS in a successful bid to drastically water down his university's racial harassment policy.

Hilborn posed it as a question of academic freedom: he said the policy stifled professors' ability to discuss race. In particular, he cited the example of Marjorie Ratcliffe, a Western Spanish professor who was charged with racial harassment after a student claimed she had made a derogatory comment in class about Iranians.

"A lot of people thought Phil Rushton asked for it—going on talk shows, he seemed to be really enjoying himself," Hilborn says. "Whereas Ratcliffe was just teaching her course, and everyone thought, 'this could happen to me.'"

Hilborn was well positioned to lead the attack. As a member of both the university's senate and its faculty association executive, he's an academic power broker. And when he called on SAFS members to stack a crucial faculty association meeting, they came out in force. When the dust had settled, central parts of the policy had been gutted—the time allowed to file a complaint had been cut from nine months to six weeks, and students who made what Hilborn calls "vexatious complaints" were no longer protected from reprisal.

On the surface, it seemed like a clear-cut case of an SAFS member acting on solid academic freedom principles. But a closer look reveals ultra-right-wing connections that bring Hilborn's motives into question. A member of the Reform Party, Hilborn has published five books with Citizens for Foreign Aid Reform (C-FAR), a group run by Paul Fromm, which has also published Rushton's *Race, Evolution and AIDS*. Hilborn's books fulminate against Canadian foreign policy toward South Africa; he attacked sanctions and supported the former white apartheid government. His latest book, *The Cult of the Victim*, is a study of "victim mentality" recommended in an SAFS newsletter.

Hilborn's publisher Paul Fromm, who has a long history with racist groups, used to be a high-school teacher in Mississauga. But after the Canadian Jewish Congress obtained a videotape of his address to a 1990 Heritage Front meeting, he was reassigned to adult education. In the video, Fromm spoke from a stage decorated with swastikas and KKK flags, to a crowd giving Nazi salutes and shouting "White Power" and "Sieg Heil."

But this doesn't faze Hilborn. "Paul Fromm is someone I've known for years," he says. "He's never said anything to me I consider racist. When he's spoken to racist groups, as he has, it's been in defense of their right to speak, not their ideas."

Hilborn and Fromm's work has not gone unappreciated. In 1991, the Northern Foundation—a group closely linked with the Heritage Front—honoured both men "as thinkers and activists who are working for freedom."

Hilborn and Fromm are also members of the World Anti-Communist League. According to the 1986 book *Inside the League*, its membership has included Latin American death squads, East European fascists, Nazi collaborators, and eugenicists. Hilborn, however, insists WACL isn't racist because its leaders are "Orientals." ("Right-wing Orientals, mind you," he jokes. Hilborn, in fact, preserves a sense of humour about his associations, calling himself "one of the notorious Cold Warriors.") We called the Reform Party to ask about its members' extremist connections. An interview with the party's Ontario manager produced a panicked call from Troy Tait, the party's national policy coordinator, desperate to stress how repugnant Hilborn's associations were to Reformers. "We do not put up with this type of behaviour," he said. "That's not compatible with what the party stands for." The party has referred Hilborn's membership to a committee, which will decide whether to expel him.

To the SAFS, however, Hilborn's connections are irrelevant. Kimura says the only measure of SAFS members is their belief in its policies. "Our concern has to be whether the people who become members are really dedicated to the principles of the SAFS, which are freedom of inquiry and the merit principle in hiring and promotion," she says, clearly annoyed at having to slog through another discussion about racist ties. "If you meet those, I think that's really all we can require."

But Hilborn is only the tip of the iceberg. Several other prominent SAFS members have funding and publishing ties with a wide network of racist groups—especially the Pioneer Fund, the U.S.-based foundation for "race betterment."

The Pioneer Fund was incorporated in 1937 by two American scientists, Harry Laughlin, who received an honourary doctorate from the University of Heidelberg for contributions to Nazi eugenics, and Frederic Osborn, who wrote that the Nazi sterilization law was "the most exciting experiment that had ever been tried."

SAFS member Rushton has received over $500,000 from the Pioneer Fund. Douglas Jackson, a friend and defender of Rushton, says the fund cannot be racist because several members were decorated during the Second World War, and that Rushton had no choice but to accept its money. "There are certain areas, as you know, that government funding sources will simply not investigate."

The Pioneer Fund has also given $1 million to University of California psychologist Arthur Jensen, one of the most prominent eugenicists in the U.S. and a board member of *Intelligence*, the journal that published Ankney's paper on brain size, as well as a similar paper by Rushton. Jensen and Rushton also publish in *Mankind Quarterly*, another Pioneer Fund-financed publication devoted to "race science." It is edited by Roger Pearson, a psychologist who wrote the book *Eugenics and Race*, founded the neo-Nazi Northern League in 1958, and is a past president of the World Anti-Communist League. A Rushton graduate student, Maria T. Phelps, published an article in *Mankind Quarterly* in 1994 arguing that Natives perform poorly on IQ tests because of inferior genetic stock.

Perhaps what's most disappointing about SAFS is that it is a missed opportunity. Canada needs a committed group to fight for academic freedom. There's no doubt that the late 1980s and early 1990s have ushered in many wrong-minded policies and intolerance of political difference. You only have to look at the Ontario government's "zero tolerance" policy toward sexual and racial harassment, which was so heavy-handed that even campus harassment officers called it ludicrous. And while there's no shortage of rhetoric about "white male privilege," there's no real debate over the complexities of hiring equity—how to address historical wrongs while maintaining everyday fairness.

This debate isn't happening, even though the SAFS seems to be convincing many that they're the calm moderates ready to talk. The facts don't back up their contention. It's hard to imagine a reasoned debate between people who think historic discrimination can be addressed with high-pitched slogans and intimidation—like the opponents of professor Jeanne Cannizzo—and those who say there's no real discrimination, just biological fact.

WHAT SHACKLES OF POLITICAL CORRECTNESS?

David MacFarlane *(The Globe and Mail)*

Whenever I hear people say that it's time to free ourselves from the shackles of political correctness, I find myself idly wondering what political correctness?

But not just idly. Wondering silently and politely and respectfully, of course, so as not to give any possible offence to anyone at all—but wondering all the same: what planet are these people from? I don't want to be irreverent, and I have nothing but the highest respect for all those who I happen to think are dead wrong about absolutely everything, but I can't help but ask: exactly how long have they been unconscious?

Because it does seem to me—so I must say in all candour—that we live in what must surely be the least politically correct age since the sack of Rome. Perhaps those who would free us from our PC shackles haven't spent a lot of time yet on the Internet. Perhaps they haven't heard of the *Alberta Report* or Don Cherry or David Frum or the National Citizens Coalition or the Fraser Institute. Or the editorial pages of every newspaper in the land. Maybe they haven't had a chance to notice the triumph of the right.

David MacFarlane. What shackles of political correctness? *The Globe and Mail*, Monday, November 13, 2000, R3.

It may just be me. In fact, since I am, at the moment sitting here alone writing this, we can safely assume that it is. Just me. As a writer and as a columnist who holds the distinctly eccentric minority opinion that the arts and the environment are good things, I am one of those often blamed for the tyranny of political correctness.

And I apologize for foisting my elitist views on the rest of you. I know how easily you can be swayed by someone, still in his pyjamas, pounding away at a laptop. The media is a potent propaganda tool—especially after it has had a cup of coffee. I know how easily you can be dominated by the kind of liberal sensibility that, despite appearing on Page 3 of the *Globe Review* once a week, has actually been running everything in this country for the past 20 or 30 years.

As a minority of one, I certainly don't want to upset the vast and extremely sensitive majority with an opinion that might run counter to one that is not only universally held but, so we are told, rigidly enforced. Apparently, the dictates of political correctness rule the land. If you don't adhere to them slavishly in all matters of public discourse, you will be banished to beyond the pale. Or at least to Red Deer.

But my problem is that try as I might, I can't quite bring myself to believe that there is such a thing as political correctness any more. If ever there was. Heresy, I know. And I admit that I could possibly be wrong about this. But I was just wondering: Has there ever been a time when it was easier for any nut to say anything that crosses his (or her, to be perfectly fair) addled brain and to have a bigger, more attentive audience? But let's not spend too much time on Michael Coren. Let's talk politics. Has there ever been a time when anyone could more openly and more vehemently express a point of view and more easily find a more powerful, indignant, ready-to-be-rallied political constituency?

Let's see now. Executing criminals. Banning abortion. Dismantling the public broadcaster. Caning young offenders. Humiliating teachers. Abandoning the arts. Ignoring the environmental crisis. Demonizing homosexuals. Closing women's shelters. Shutting hospitals and firing nurses. Welcoming unregistered guns to the top drawer of every bedside table. We are told that the shackles of political correctness imposed by the cultural and political and media elite don't allow Canadians to speak openly about these subjects. We are muzzled. We are gagged. Which is odd—since, somehow, amid the tyranny of silence imposed on people by the enforcers of political correctness, Canadians keep electing popular, mainstream politicians whose primary political objectives seem to be all of the above.

I find it a little hard to believe, actually. It seems a bit of a stretch to think that for the past few decades—decades in which the politically correct, oh-so-sensitive, knee-jerk liberalism of Ronald Reagan and Margaret Thatcher and Brian Mulroney seemed to have had some influence on things—that in Tim Hortons and Country Styles and Coffee Times throughout the land, people sat over their double-doubles in terrified silence. I find it a little hard to believe that they have been afraid to express a point of view lest they have their knuckles rapped by the Birkenstock clad, granola-eating, bilingual PC police who were lurking behind the shelves of crullers, hammering together NDP policy and listening for errant tongues to slip off the straight and narrow of political correctness.

Is it really true that if, say, you are a highly educated, well-paid, federal civil servant within a hundred miles of the political and cultural elite that rules the land, controls the media, and, incidentally, keeps telling me how to write this column, and you so much as muttered under your breath that you are not really all that crazy about abstract expressionism, you'll end up selling matches in the Bytown Market? Or so we are told by those who are dedicating themselves so fearlessly during this election campaign to freeing us from our shackles.

But since, try as I might, I can't catch sight of these shackles—haven't seen them for years as a matter of fact—I can't help but wonder. And I do my wondering, I hasten to say, with all due respect. When people keep going on and on about political correctness—something which, so far as I can figure, does not actually exist—what are they really talking about? Is this some kind of code?

DISCUSSION QUESTIONS

1. Do either or both sides of the political correctness debate use their views to suppress debate on campus? Research this issue using sources like the CBCA index and cite specific instances.

2. Do a close analysis of the rhetoric used on the Society for Academic Freedom and Scholarship's Web site. Look particularly for metaphors which define the various writers' positions. Do the same for the articles in this chapter.

3. Use the Internet to find speech policies at various Canadian universities and colleges. Do an analysis of these policies.

 ## WEBLINKS

Society for Academic Freedom and Scholarship
www.safs.niagara.com/

Canadian Association of University Teachers
www.caut.ca/ (search: academic freedom)

American Communications Association Model Speech Code
www.uark.edu/depts/comminfo/www/campus.speech.html

Stalking the Wild Taboo
www.lrainc.com/swtaboo/index.html

Pinc (Politically Incorrect)
www.cycad.com/cgi-bin/pinc/apr2000/index.html

chapter four

Canadian Identity:
The Shifting Terrain

INTRODUCTION

Contemporary approaches to national identity have stressed, following Benedict Anderson's *Imagined Communities* (1983), that nations are "imagined political communities" Nations are produced, reproduced, and modified largely through discursive and symbolic means, including notions of common history, traditions, and shared systems of cultural practices and representations.

The question of what constitutes a Canadian national identity, or "Who are we?", has consumed more print and air-space than any other; it has been our national obsession, and current trends toward cultural globalization have only magnified our "crisis of identity." Canada has always been in the position of being neighbour to the most powerful nation in history—a power that is not only military and economic, but cultural as well. American popular culture *is* popular culture globally. Hollywood film and television, MacDonald's and the two "Colas" have become part of the culture of the world, threatening indigenous cultures in their dominance not only of the market but of our imaginations.

Rick Salutin frames his discussion of Canadian cultural identity in terms of the strength of our "national imaginary"—that cultural sense of self as part of a larger entity which has always been such a Canadian issue. Salutin views Canada as particularly at risk from the impact of American global corporate culture, since our sense of self is weaker than comparable selves in, for example, France or the USA.

Salutin argues that our particular sense of ourselves has never been as "mythical" as certain other national imaginaries—for example, we have fewer national symbols and beliefs than our neighbours to the south. However, we have concrete social institutions—art, health care, and the CBC, for example—which have served us better than myths precisely because they are concrete, real responses to the world. In the era of downsizing and the threatened destruction of our social institutions, we become particularly at risk since these social and economic changes profoundly affect our real dealings with the world. In the end, Salutin finds hope for Canadians in their traditionally ironic take on global culture, and finds tremendous creativity in our ingrained satirical stance which has the power to demythologize global, corporate culture.

Coming from a vastly different perspective, Bruce Wallace argues that Canada *in fact* lives on myths—myths of a kinder, gentler, more laid-back society—and that when all is said and done, these national myths make us complacent and uncompetitive in the larger world of corporate dealings. Wallace sees and celebrates a new aggressiveness in some Canadians who seek success on the global stage. Based on a more social-Darwinian model of cultural survival, Wallace praises a new Canada that is bolder and more assertive. Unquestioned in the article is whether or not the new corporate Canada would be a better place to live, and for whom it might be better. Unlike Salutin, who fears the ravages of the corporate state on the people, Wallace sees it as our road to survival.

Maria Tippett traces the evolution of Canadian identity through the growth and development of our arts. Like many cultural nationalists, she sees a strong connection between art—broadly defined as literature, visual art, music, film, and television—and our sense of our self as a diverse, but in the end identifiable, entity in the world. Her historical analysis traces the change from a largely English-Canadian artistic culture—which she calls the "faux nationalist project" because it was elitist and excluded Canada's non-English speaking artists—to a more inclusive multi-cultural form of artistic production which defines us for both ourselves and the world.

Lynn Coady locates the national imagery in our individual sense of belonging, which is fostered by our local/national pastimes like hockey—no matter how distant our relation to the game might be. As an intellectual and a woman, Coady is aware of how alienating "the game" is for women—it is a male game, but one which has far greater implications for local communities, regardless of gender. In a complex take on the game, Coady sees herself (and others) as both part and apart from the game—needing the belonging, but ironically detached from it for reasons of gender and intellectual aspiration. Here, perhaps, the issue of identity, local and national, is presented in its amusing, but oh-so-Canadian, fashion.

NATIONAL CULTURES IN THE AGE OF GLOBALIZATION: THE CASE OF CANADA

Rick Salutin *(Queen's Quarterly)*

Let me begin by explaining what I mean when I use the term "globalization"—and what I do not mean. I do not mean globalization in the sense of the communications revolution, the information highway, the Internet, and other breathless coinages. Every advance in communications technology over the past 200 years has been hailed as unprecedented,

Rick Salutin. National cultures in the age of globalization: The case of Canada. *Queen's Quarterly* 106(2), Summer, 1999. 206-215.

transformative, inaugurating a new version of human nature, extending democracy and so forth. During the French Revolution, the introduction of semaphore, for heaven's sake, was hailed in this way. It was going to make the nation state obsolete and lead to the integration of all humanity. Similar claims were made for the telegraph, film, radio, television—and of course the Internet.

The sense in which I do mean to use globalization refers to the global economic reach and power of corporate capital in our time. In its case, I would also like to enter a routine demur against the claim that it truly counts as globalization in some general and unique sense. It is certainly not the only form of globalization, or even the only form of economic globalization, which could be imagined or achieved. It is capitalist and corporate, it subjugates all human values and social possibilities to economic calculation and the profit advantage of a few huge players—and they are growing ever fewer. In the time it has taken you to read the first few paragraphs of this article, the number of major corporate actors has probably decreased due to mergers and acquisitions. This is concentration of power on a level that makes feudal accumulations of power look shabby and decentralized. It is not globalization in a general sense but in a very limited and particular sense. At most, it is one cramped version of globalization. In this light, the central contradiction of our time is not between global and local realities, but between corporate capital as a centre of power and all other possible sources of power.

Globalization in this sense is a terribly serious threat to the cohesion of societies and the welfare of individuals, one which seems to me comparable to the situation in Europe before the First World War. A savage, destructive global conflict is having massive deleterious effects, and so far we have only seen their beginnings. What little progress was made is being rolled back—in the Third World, in the cities of the First, in the immense and shameful gap between rich and poor everywhere. Globalization in this sense is a global social calamity for the majority, for structures and institutions—from nations to communities—and for the assumptions around which they have often organized their sense of self.

One of the most striking phenomena of our times is the increased importance of national cultures in this era of globalization. Given the great disruptions that globalization has occasioned in people's lives everywhere, it is predictable that they should turn to traditional sources of stability and identification. Whatever provides such a resource will be valued, clung to and, if necessary, resuscitated. We see this with the renewed attachment to religion in our time—from Islamic fundamentalism to the born-again Christians of the United States and Latin America. In his series of novels about the end of British rule in India, *The Raj Quartet*, Paul Scott has a character speculate that the rise of Hindu and Muslim militancy in India during the later years of British rule was due to the "comfort and support" religion provided in the face of British imperialism. "Hit a man in the face long enough," writes Scott, "and he turns to his racial memory and his tribal gods." In other words, modern imperial politics revived religion. In much the same way, you might say that modern global economics has revived national culture and ethnicity, along with religion. What I want to stress, however, is the intimate relationship between economic distress or catastrophe, and cultural response. I'm thinking here of the argument made by economist Karl Polanyi in his book *The Great Transformation*, published in 1943. Polanyi—a socialist but not a Marxist—wrote:

> Actually of course a social calamity is primarily a cultural not an economic phenomenon . . . the disintegration of the cultural environment of the victim is then the cause of the degradation. The economic process may, naturally, supply the vehicle of the destruction, and almost invariably economic inferiority will make the weaker yield, but the immediate cause of his undoing is not for

that reason economic; it lies in the lethal injury to the institutions in which his social existence is embodied . . . . Nothing obscures our social vision as effectively as the economistic prejudice . . . . Yet it is precisely this emphasis put on exploitation which tends to hide from our view the even greater issue of cultural degeneration.

He argued that when people feel great economic pressure, they naturally seek some confirmation that their lives make sense, and they look for this within their families and communities. If they can find such reassurance, they are able to withstand remarkable levels of economic deterioration and catastrophe. It is culture—that which makes sense of people's lives in relation to their community and the history of their community—to which they turn. On the other hand, argued Polanyi, if the sense of culture deteriorates, then even if the economic situation in some respects improves, the human results may well be disastrous. He argued, for instance, that this was the case for many Africans sold into slavery: ". . . their standard of life, in some artificial sense, may have been improved." But this was far outweighed by the cultural impoverishment the slaves suffered. A similar fate befell American native peoples moved onto reservations; they may have benefited "individually, according to our financial scale of reckoning. Yet the measure all but destroyed the race in its physical existence." In this light, it seems clear that culture—that which makes sense of our lives—matters to human existence more than purely economic "factors." Thus in an age of severe economic disruption, it is natural for people to turn to their cultures, including national culture, as a resource.

Our own Canadian culture is particularly threatened in the present age of globalization. The very nature of national culture in Canada (especially in English-speaking Canada) and the special role of institutions in that culture make it vulnerable. I refer both to institutions that are specifically cultural, like the Canadian Broadcasting Corporation, and institutions that are non-cultural, like the health care system. As well, some institutions are both cultural and non-cultural; the railway was originally a means of transportation which effectively created the national reality in the nineteenth century, but which also became a cultural icon described in works of non-fiction, like Pierre Berton's books, and works of art and music, like Gordon Lightfoot's "Railroad Trilogy." I make note of this because the kind of nationhood expressed in Canada has always been simplified; we're a sort of no-frills country, a kind of stripped-down, minimalist nation.

Most other countries have expressed their nationhood in more elaborate, sometimes even murky or mystical ways. You could say we lack the kind of glue which has characterized most national societies and held them together: glue such as a distinct national language, a long history, a deeply embedded culture or folklore, and a national mythology (the "American Dream," nineteenth-century England's "White Man's Burden," the French *mission civilisatrice*). Nations can survive severe political or economic dislocations when they possess that kind of glue. Harold Innis once pointed out that France puts on and takes off constitutions without the French ever wondering whether la France will cease to be; it is unthinkable. The French nation's language and culture guarantee its survival. Poland didn't exist on a map for 125 years, but its reality for the Polish people remained strong.

It is true that we Canadians (I should repeat here that I am speaking mainly of Canada outside Quebec) have a few symbols: a beaver, a cop on a horse, a game played on ice. But we lack a language that's uniquely our own, a long history, folklore or myths, even a cuisine, which should not be underestimated as a source of national sense of self. I'd say one thing we've counted on in the place of all these is a set of socially constructed institutions: the railroad, the CBC, our network of social programs, maybe the post office. These are real, not mythical, entities, but they serve a reassuring function, like myths and other glues. They not only deliver actual things like TV shows, pension checks, or mail—they give us the sense of a cohesive society.

And this situation accounts for the special role of artists in Canada, and the perpetual anxiety about Canadian culture. Many Canadian writers and artists, when they sit down to produce a work, feel responsible not just for expressing themselves but for proving the country exists. That's not a burden artists feel in France or the US. If we had more culture in the underlying sense, we might put less pressure on our novelists and filmmakers. I think this also accounts for Canadians' readiness to support the CBC even if they don't watch it. There is a witticism which states: Canadians are prepared to support the CBC so long as they don't have to watch it; there is a point here: an institution like the CBC is evidence that we have something to express, therefore that we exist in a collective, national way. Given the fairly mundane nature of the glue we rely on—institutions, individual artists—you can see why this has been a rough period for the Canadian sense of self. There has been a series of bloody assaults on those few national institutions, in the name of fiscal responsibility, privatization, and keeping up with the global economic trends. As for the arts, I'd rather not get into a debate on whether we'd be culturally deprived without our own versions of *Phantom of the Opera* and *Miss Saigon*, which have become typical of our theatre in the last ten years, but they certainly do not provide the kind of national sense that once came from Canadian plays. In addition, the last ten years have seen a series of political sneak attacks on our national sense of confidence. First came free trade: we were told we had to sign on or admit we were afraid to compete. Then Meech Lake: we had to swallow terms we found offensive or the country would disintegrate. The Charlottetown Accord carried the same threat. It's been a decade of nation abuse which I don't think any analogous national society can match.

This may sound like the beginning of a big whine, but actually I rather like our difficult, occasionally dire, way of being a country—including our emphasis on institutions as the basis of our national glue and sense of self. For one thing, it makes us unusual and possibly unique. For another, the trouble with basing your country on all that myth is that it's pretty mythical. I wouldn't want to believe, like Americans, that my country was "the greatest country in the history of the world," as President Clinton modestly says every chance he gets. It might make you feel good, but you'd pay the price of sounding stupid and being self-deluded. Personally I prefer things like a railroad or our social programs as the basis for a national sense of self—exactly because they're not mythical; they're concrete, they represent things we've done together, consciously, for and with each other.

To summarize, the relatively unique case of Canadian culture (not including, or in contrast to, Quebec and other cultures) makes it apt and particularly interesting as a case study for the postmodern, globalized world. But, at the same time, it follows that Canadian culture is particularly threatened by globalization: this is so because of the absence of traditional cultural "glues," and because in their place we have publicly supported—both financially and morally—institutions.

I'd like to be clear that I do not believe nations need to live forever, nor institutions. All of these come and go and justify themselves during their lifetimes, not by being eternal. At the same time, living in the aftershadow of free trade and NAFTA has given me new respect for what Canadians accomplished in the past by keeping this rather self-effacing little country going. I used to have much less respect for their achievement, but I can now see it was no mean feat. As to the current threats to our nationhood, I don't know what the outcome will be; I think that in this decade—when the Soviet Union disappeared and Nelson Mandela became president of South Africa—attempts at prediction are utterly stupid. But I can see certain reasons for optimism, or at least a certain wary hopefulness.

For one thing, the sad procession toward political, economic, and social demise can lead to cultural success. This is because the prospect of death concentrates the creative mind, in a way that leads to a deeper sense of the richness and meaning of life—individual or collective. I'm thinking here of the flowering of culture and the arts in Poland or in Ireland under severe conditions of political and/or economic disintegration.

In a cheerier vein, I would point to some of the rather surprising areas of current Canadian cultural success. I'm not referring to the altogether respectable Canadian showings lately in the respectable cultural realm of literature and the novel. I'm thinking instead of popular music and also of satire, especially television satire. In fact there's an impressive marshalling of the evidence for the vigour of a Canadian popular culture in Geoff Pevere and Greig Dymond's *Mondo Canuck*. What is this success really about? It seems to me it has to do with the prevalence of American popular culture on a global scale, in the era of globalization. It becomes the content everyone has to stand up to and define themselves against—as the French and others discovered during the last round of world trade negotiations. Well, to the extent that taking the measure of—and the piss out of—American popular culture has become a universal experience, we in Canada are way ahead of the rest of the world, and we always will be. Think of The Band, Neil Young, Leonard Cohen: these are cases of globally significant artists who were shaped by the encounter with American popular culture. Young and Cohen may have lived in the United States for decades, but they are, in my opinion, clearly Canadian in their sensibility. When Leonard Cohen, for instance, sings, "Democracy is coming . . . to the U.S.A.," this has an ironic detachment which I don't believe Americans are generally capable of with regard to their own mythologies. Americans tend to be too identified with those mythologies; when they critique them, they tend to express themselves with deep anger, as in the case of Bruce Springsteen. A satirical or ironic mode is largely beyond them; virtually the entire corpus of political and social satire in the American media in the past 25 years has been produced by Canadians. Finally, in an era which is apparently inevitably characterized as one of information and communications, Canadians may be especially well equipped. Throughout its history, this country has been about communications: from the far-flung connections of the fur trade, through the meshing role of the railroad, to the broadcast system and the odd attachment Canadians have to it—and then further, into the contributions Canadians have made to the theory of communications itself. This is a field more or less invented by Harold Innis, and developed subsequently by Innis's successor, Marshall McLuhan.

In everything I have ever written about or based in Canada, I've faced the problem of the ending: this is the challenge of how to be honest about how dire things are, yet not cause your audience or readers to despair. For, if that's your effect, then why write at all? So, for instance, I've ended a play about the failed Canadian revolution of 1837 with one character, about to be hanged, saying to another, "We lost." And the other replies, "No, we just haven't won yet." I even ended a play with the line, "Cheer up, there's no hope." I feel there is cause for cautious enthusiasm in our current national and cultural struggles. I'm thinking especially of the way in which there is room and even need for creativity in these efforts, in a way that may be unique in the current century. This has to do with the demise of all the hoary old shibboleths of the left, and what I'm convinced will be the imminent demise of those of the right. This vacuum of shibboleths and nostrums creates an opportunity and even a need for creativity.

My most recent novel takes place in the near future in Canada, and centres on an actor who in his youth has worked primarily in the theatre of improvisation and of collective creation, though later in his career he becomes a famous and successful film and television actor. But he looks around and sees the country in a mess, while all the old political scripts, those of the left and those of the right, are not usable any more. There is therefore no alternative in the political realm except to improvise—collectively. So he goes into politics himself, eventually becomes prime minister and . . . but let me end here.

WHAT MAKES A CANADIAN?

Bruce Wallace *(Maclean's)*

Come on people, is this the best we can do? Are Canadians really "spineless," which was one of the most popular responses when the *Maclean's*/CBC poll asked Canadians to choose one word to describe their compatriots? Tied at six percent of responses was "passive." But do spineless and passive really describe a country that likes to boast how its hockey players may be a little short on skills but long on heart and soul and guts? Is "laid-back"—another popular answer at four percent—the way we reacted when the call went out from our allies this year to fly bombing missions over Kosovo?

Sure, 12 percent came up with "friendly"—the most popular choice of those who could come up with an answer. But you have to wonder whether our self-image matches our accomplishments. Was one of the world's great trading nations built on lack of resolve? Were those Canadian soldiers hitting the blackened terrain of East Timor an example of "easy-going"? That 15 percent of respondents can't think of a single defining characteristic is astounding given the amount of breath our chattering classes have expended searching for the Canadian soul. ("A coalition of ideas based on an assumption of the public good," was one of author John Ralston Saul's eloquent stabs at it, though hardly in one word.) Uncovering Canadian identity has not been just an obsession. It is probably the defining characteristic of the place itself.

There is still, it seems, much to lament about our nation. Canadians may be certain we are a distinct society—or so say an overwhelming 90 percent of respondents to the *Maclean's*/CBC poll. "There are massive numbers showing that in spite of all the cynics who say Canada has lost its way, we still have a strong sense of identity," says Allan Gregg, president of The Strategic Counsel, which conducted the poll. But Gregg agrees that Canadians don't seem to know exactly what it is that makes us so different or unique. "We don't seem to feel the need to define it," he adds. "It is some vague sense that, well, we've got our flag. And it's cold here. We're Canadian, damn it. Our difference is us."

Scratch a Canadian about what makes us the way we are and you get a celebration of the obvious. The flag is the most important characteristic, according to 80 percent of respondents—and it is inarguably a great flag compared with all those other forgettable coloured stripes. Tied for first place is the pride we take in Canadian artists and scientists who have

Bruce Wallace. What makes a Canadian? *Maclean's* 112(51), December 20, 1999. 32.

become prominent internationally. (Imagine: a country branded by the Maple Leaf and Shania Twain's belly button!)

Smaller countries tend to show pride when their nationals rise to the top of the American-driven celebrity machine. But we are getting so good at it—start with Celine Dion and Sarah McLachlan and see how long the list grows—that it can be argued Canada now has a pretty fair star system of its own. Add to that the fame of such authors as Margaret Atwood and Michael Ondaatje, the Nobel achievement of economist Robert Mundell, the heroics of The Great One, Wayne Gretzky, among so many success stories, and Canadians are fairly bursting with national pride.

It is clear from the poll, however, that some self-delusion is at play. For example, 77 percent of respondents say it is a strong sense of our own history, rather than simply a desire not to be Americans, that defines us. This comes in a year when one of the top-selling books was Jack Granatstein's *Who Killed Canadian History?*, which mourns our poor grasp of the national story. Another two-thirds answer that our standard of living is as good as or even higher than the American level. (In purely economic terms) that is just plain wrong. The '90s, in fact, have seen our living standards fall further behind the Americans'. It is a lag that Prime Minister Jean Chretien ignores in favour of cheerier statistics, like the UN human development index, which has placed us first among nations for six straight years. As Thomas d'Aquino, president of the Business Council on National Issues, notes: "We have a government in Ottawa that fails to grasp the gravity of the situation facing the country."

Yet the American economic model, with all its aggressiveness and hairy-chested competition, remains anathema to large swaths of Canadian society. Which is fine if you want your country to be known in this new global economic jungle as a sort of 1960s-style hippie retreat, unrattled by the noise of an outside world in commotion. But what will others think of that? In a world that lives by images, nations can flounder unless they have a good one.

Listen to the warning from Ted Lyman, a senior vice-president at U.S.-based ICF Consulting, who was asked by a group of Ottawa high-tech business executives to study the region's prospects in the global economy. He reported back to them last month that the Ottawa high-tech sector lacks that "fire-in-the-belly, let's bet-the-ranch-on-a new-company" spirit that has made California's Silicon Valley such a success. Lyman said Ottawa's high-tech suburbs won't really take off until their entrepreneurs accept that failure is not a stain of shame to be hidden, but a badge of boldness.

Of course it no longer takes an outsider to point out our shortcomings. A growing number of Canadians argue the "American Way" is not a disease that might infect us, but inoculation against economic decline. In a speech titled "Storming the Status Quo" delivered in Toronto last month, d'Aquino decried the shortcomings of corporate Canada—"our lack of entrepreneurship and daring, our willingness to hide behind a weak currency, our hesitancy to reach into foreign markets, and our temptation to knuckle under to government bullying." D'Aquino's organization surveyed Canadian business leaders and found a "deep frustration at an underlying attitude of envy and entitlement" that runs through the Canadian culture. "There are still many Canadians who remain suspicious of the business community," he complained.

That frustration reflects a growing cultural divide. The traditional self-image of Canada as a kinder country, less individualistic, less obsessed with wealth, believing in government as a force for good, is no longer unchallenged. Attitudes are changing. The furies unleashed by the Free Trade Agreement with the United States, which tore at the country's fabric in the late 1980s, now barely register a blip on our emotional radar. Canadians may not think free trade has been all good but, like the monarchy, few seriously believe it is going away. In fact, more respondents think the Internet now has a greater impact on drawing us closer to Americans. Only 23 percent of those who think we are becoming more like Americans attribute it to free trade, while 34 percent finger the Internet. Most, however, cite the pervasiveness of American media (48 percent), followed by U.S. investment in our economy (35 percent).

Signs of a new cultural and political fault line show up in a question on whether Canadians would win or lose by having a common currency with the United States. Forty-four percent see some benefit in a common dollar; 42 percent think we'd lose out—a split. But the evidence of change is not all quantitative. It was once regarded as un-Canadian to grandly display personal wealth. Not anymore, as one look at the ostentatious "cottages" going up along the waterfronts of the Muskoka lakes north of Toronto can prove. And Ottawa's showy high-tech businessman Michael Cowpland at least does not offend everyone in town, as he once would have.

New language has also crept into our politics. For every old-style leader like Jean Chretien, who admits to taking an occasional swing at Washington because it plays so well at home, there is another like Ontario's twice-elected Premier Mike Harris, who sees benefits in making nice with the boys down south. At a recent Great Lakes Governors' Conference, Harris told his American audience: "We really see you as very, very strong allies, more so than many parts of Canada. What happens in Newfoundland and British Columbia economically," he added, "does not affect us as much as what happens in Michigan, Ohio, New York, Pennsylvania and Illinois." An economic truth, perhaps, but a once-unthinkable public utterance for an Ontario premier.

The current journalists' strike at the *Calgary Herald* is also, in part, a cultural battle, with management arguing that its left-leaning newsroom has been out of step with the go-get-'em city it covers. "The editorial pages were not well respected and, in the eyes of many in this city, seemed contrarian by nature and in constant opposition to the community the paper alleged to be serving," wrote editor-in-chief Peter Menzies in defence of *Herald* management. "This is a city that revels in hard work, imagination and excellence." Then there is the emergence of the *National Post*. Surely the fact there is a big audience for a paper so willing to sneer at traditional values is a sign the country is changing. To the surprise of many Canadians, the *Post* uncovered a good-sized market sympathetic to its rebelliousness against high taxes and meddlesome government, vigorously approving of its impatience with the enduring Canadian suspicion of the business community.

The old Canada is not dead, of course, and it would never be caught on the bus with a copy of the *Post* under its arm. That Canada still sees itself as the guardian of greater fairness, intolerant of frantic consumerism, a firm believer in life lived at a slower pace. It was also the old Canada speaking in the *Maclean's*/CBC poll finding that 54 percent believe it is the job of government to fight the forces making Canada more like the United States. That streak in our character has always seen government as the guarantor of Canadian distinctiveness. It also helped elect the federal Liberals, who are a reflection of that view of Canada: blissful, conservative, complacent. But keeping your independence and distinctness in an increasingly converging world may require more assertiveness than that. And in the end, some Canadians may find to their surprise it takes a dash of those so-called American values of daring and enterprise to save the country they love.

EXPRESSING IDENTITY

Maria Tippett *(Beaver)*

Colonial uncertainty dominated Canadian culture at the beginning of the twentieth century. But then came the Great War. Canada's pallid national identity flamed in the trenches of France, and Canadian artists, with growing self-awareness, began to behold the world in ways uniquely Canadian. By midcentury, the nationalist spirit in Canada was ablaze and the country's creators soared. As the century closed, new and different voices emerged, but ironically, just when Canadian culture seemed its most confident, the cultural environment, in a wired world, seemed most vulnerable.

It is a commonplace that, as we enter the third millennium, Canadian culture and Canadian identity are under threat. The reemergence of ethnic nationalism, the critical voice of deconstructionist theory and politically correct thinking, along with the worldwide recession, the revolution in communications technology, and the globalization of culture, are just a few of the things that make it virtually impossible for writers, artists, musicians, and others to speak with one voice. Yet it was no easier for cultural producers, promoters, and patrons during the last century. They had to work against the country's collective sense of negation and difference that thwarted—and continues to thwart—the production of a shared culture.

Southern Canadians have long thought of themselves as a northern people living in close proximity to the wilderness; yet most of them live in cities that are located within three hundred kilometres of the Canadian-American border. Many Canadians like to think of their country as a social democracy having state-supported social and cultural institutions, combined with an American standard of living. Yet the country's small tax base and vast geography, which requires an expensive infrastructure, makes this difficult to achieve. With medicare and gun-control laws in place, they believe that they have a superior lifestyle to the Americans. This does not prevent them from taking their holidays and consuming their popular culture across the border. The homegrown cultural products that the majority of Canadians do identify with, such as First Nations' artifacts and art objects, have little to do with their own experience. The symbols, on the other hand, which represent all Canadians—the country's vast geography, history, religious, ethnic, and linguistic diversity, the monarchy, and, in the last eighteen years, the Charter of Rights—have served to divide rather than unite its citizens.

For example, English-speaking Canadians take their sense of who they are from who they are not: they know that they are neither British nor American. French-speaking Canadians have a collective sense of who they are, yet they too like to point out that they are different from the French. Those not belonging to the English-speaking or French-speaking groups might have a clear idea of who they are, but their identity is often constructed from out-of-date or reinvented traditions that have no place in the dominant culture, let alone in the Old World or traditional societies from which they came.

However much Canadians have been—and continue to be—divided by geography, ethnicity, and language, there were moments during the last century when artists, writers, musicians, and others created works of art that reflected the mental climate of the majority. This happened twice in response to external events: the 1914–1918 War and the Great Depression of the 1930s. On a further occasion the patronage of the Canada Council, Expo '67, and the country's one-hundredth birthday gave Canada's cultural producers an unprecedented focus and a means of support.

Maria Tippett. Expressing identity. *Beaver* 80(1), February/March, 2000. 18–27.

It has long been recognized that the Great War was a crucial factor in forging Canadian national identity in a political sense. This is no less true in a cultural sense. Thanks to the efforts of Lords Beaverbrook and Rothermere, who set up the Canadian War Memorials Fund in 1916, writers and artists were hired to record on canvas and in print Canada's participation on the home and war fronts. What was painted, written, composed, and sung gave one sector of the country—the English-speaking community—a collective sense of identity for the first time.

Prior to the Great War, Canadians possessed a fragmented image of themselves. Writers drew inspiration from their immediate environment. Thus the traditional values of religion, the family, and the land, shared by residents living in the St. Lawrence River valley, were woven into the adventures of *Maria Chapdelaine* (Louis Hemon). The classic Canadian animal story emerged out of New Brunswick's *Tantramar Marsh* (Charles G.D. Roberts). The coastal rain forest of northern British Columbia provided the setting for tales of the immigrant logger (Martin Allerdale Grainger). Out of the imaginary town of Mariposa sprang satirical sketches mocking the political and social foibles of small-town Ontario (Stephen Leacock). The song the daughter of a Mohawk chief sang to her paddle shaped the romantic image of Canada's indigenous peoples (Pauline Johnson). And the story of an orphan girl named Anne would forever be associated with Canada's smallest and greenest province, Prince Edward Island (Lucy Maud Montgomery).

Most of what was written and painted before the Great War was, therefore, representative of a particular place or region. Yet it was also partly dependent on what musician and writer Leo Smith termed in the 1930s "foreign walking sticks." Books, essays, and poems were published outside the country. Artists, writers, and musicians took their styles and their standards, and even their artistic, musical, and dramatic training, abroad. The views and opinions of foreign cultural critics took precedence over what was said about Canadians' work at home. The private patron preferred to collect foreign paintings, listen to foreign composers, and attend plays written by British playwrights. It was the same for the country's cultural bureaucrats. Foreign works of art were favoured over local products in public galleries and concert halls across the country.

The Great War changed all of this. By 1916 artists and writers were forced to respond to something outside their local or regional experience. A.Y. Jackson painted shell-blasted trees along the frontline in Belgium and France. David Milne recorded hundreds of desolate graveyards in his spare, dry-brush watercolour style. F.H. Varley placed a gravedigger between a cart-load of decomposing corpses and a large open pit and called the painting *For What?* And the soldier-poet John McCrae gave Canada and the international community a site of memory and of mourning when he wrote the poem "In Flanders Fields."

After the hostilities ended, the image of the war-torn landscape of France and Flanders resonated through the canvases of A.Y. Jackson, F.H. Varley, and the other artists who formed the Group of Seven in 1920. The memory of the events surrounding the First World War gave writers such as Robert Stead and Charles Yale Harrison a motif for their novels. It also kept a group of soldier-entertainers called the Dumbells humming wartime tunes like "These Wild, Wild Women Are Making a Wild Man of Me" well into the 1920s.

The First World War not only gave Canadian writers, artists, and popular entertainers new subjects for their work. Exposure to Europe's landscape and Old World culture made them view Canada in a new light. Moreover the eagerness with which they responded to the challenge of interpreting Canada's role in the Great War did not go unnoticed. The success of the war artists' exhibition in London, New York, and across Canada demonstrated that

Canadian artists were to be taken seriously. The belief that culture had a role to play in the nation-building process unleashed a wave of public and private support for the arts. During the two decades following the Great War, an unprecedented number of plays, poems, novels, and paintings were produced; galleries, concert halls, and academies of music were built; and journals devoted to Canadian culture were founded.

Canadians have never been known to reach for their chequebooks when they hear the words "Canadian culture." But thanks to the wave of nationalism following the Great War, private patrons built concert and theatre halls from Vancouver to Halifax. They helped found academies and schools of music and fine art. They sponsored choirs, orchestras, and literary groups within their own companies. And they sat on the boards of virtually every cultural institution in the country.

Not to be outdone by the private sector, cultural bureaucrats like the director of the National Gallery of Canada, Eric Brown, saw to it that work by the Group of Seven and their contemporaries was not only bought for the national collection, but exhibited across the country and around the world. He encouraged American philanthropic organizations—the Rockefeller Foundation and the Carnegie Corporation—to sponsor national art lecture tours, to help found university departments of art and music, to support amateur drama groups, and, from 1933, to hand out funds through a body calling itself the Canadian Committee to public and private cultural institutions across the country. (More than twenty years before the founding of the Canada Council, culture was thus organized on a nationwide basis.)

Canada's British-born governors general were no less committed to the belief that the cultural community could uplift, educate, and unite the country's ethnically diverse population. Following the Great War, they brought amateur and professional artists, writers, musicians, and actors together through the Willingdon Arts Competitions for excellence in music, literature, painting, and sculpture (1928), the Dominion Drama Festival (1932), and the Governor General's Literary Awards (1936). Even an otherwise culturally uninterested Mackenzie King got into the act when his Liberal government licensed the country's first public broadcasting radio station in 1936. The Canadian Broadcasting Corporation sponsored Don Henshaw's, Rupert Caplan's, and Tommy Tweed's theatre productions from Toronto, Montreal, and Winnipeg respectively. It brought live performances of the Toronto Philharmonic Orchestra and the Montreal Symphony Orchestra into homes across the country. And it gave two artists from Montreal and Halifax—Anne Savage and Elizabeth Styring Nutt—an outlet for their critical commentary on Canadian painting and sculpture. Until television surpassed it in the 1960s, CBC radio was the strongest cultural force in the country.

Much of what was produced under the label of national culture during the interwar years came from Toronto. The Toronto-based Group of Seven claimed to represent all of Canada, though their most memorable subjects came from northern Ontario or, in A.Y. Jackson's case, from rural Quebec. (The Group's reluctance to accept anyone into their ambit who did not share their "nationalist project" disqualified the Montreal-based artists and writers who looked to the modernist French School for inspiration. It also ensured that the work of Emily Carr, Miller Brittain, and others outside of Toronto would be forever deemed as "regional.") In the print medium, Toronto's *Canadian Forum* purported to cover the nation while the *McGill Fortnightly Review* (1925–27) represented Montreal. And in music Toronto's Conservatory of Music set the standard for every serious musician across the country.

This centralist view of culture confined the cultural activity of "new Canadians" to the CPR's annual folk-art and handicraft festivals. Or to the community halls. (The Jewish

Workmen's Circle produced plays, Chinese dramatic societies staged *Bak Wah Kek* or skits, while the Ukrainians and Finns sang in *Prosvita* halls, labour temples, and *haali*.) The cultural traditions of Canada's indigenous peoples and the habitant were given even less space in the dominant culture. They were appropriated on the canvases of Emily Carr and James Wilson Morrice, in the musical scores of Ernest MacMillan, and in the poems of Duncan Campbell Scott.

Cultural domination by Toronto, and to a lesser extent by Montreal, left artists, writers, musicians, and dancers living in the regions with three choices. They could, firstly, conform to what might be called "the faux nationalist project" by moving to these cities. The artist Bertram Brooker and the writer Gabrielle Roy made good when they moved from Winnipeg to Toronto and Montreal respectively. The country's first art journal, *Maritime Art*, only received "national" status when its editorship relocated in Toronto where it was renamed *Canadian Art*.

Those living outside of Toronto could, secondly, remain in the regions and establish their reputations abroad. Gwen Pharis Ringwood did this by having her plays, *One Man's House* and *Still Stands the House*, premiered at the University of North Carolina. Martha Ostenso's novel *Wild Geese* was recognized in Toronto only after it won the *American Pictorial Review*'s prize for best novel of the year. And the Winnipeg- born composer Barbara Pentland found an appreciative audience for her avant-garde musical compositions in New York.

Cultural producers living on the periphery could finally find inspiration and fame by taking the road that led outside of the country. Claude Champagne composed his *Suite canadienne* while studying in Paris during the 1920s. A decade earlier Emily Carr discovered the forest as a motif for her art in a small wood above St. Ives harbour in Cornwall. Guy Lombardo made an international reputation for his dance band, the Royal Canadians, when he took them to Cleveland, Ohio, in 1923. And two dancers from British Columbia put their art on a professional basis by joining Diaghilev's famous Ballet Russe de Monte Carlo. Indeed, Denis Myers and Jean Hunt forsook more than their country. When the dance company toured Canada in the 1920s, they had become Alexandra Denisova and Kira Bounina.

However much the work of central Canada's faux nationalists was privileged over what came from the periphery, it could not speak for the whole country when the Depression hit the country in the early 1930s. As if in answer to Frederick Philip Grove's call a decade earlier for "socially significant" novels in which "crises and characters must be reflective of contemporary social conditions," writers representing all regions of the country—Irene Baird, Morley Callaghan, Gabrielle Roy, and Mary Quayle Innis—put pen to paper. So, too, did the country's artists and dramatists. Miller Brittain painted the unemployed longshoremen in Saint John. Leonard Hutchinson produced hard-edged woodcuts *Protest* and *Breadline*. And Carl Schaefer recorded the rusting agricultural machinery that he found lying in fallow fields in southern Ontario. In *Waste Heritage* Irene Baird dramatized the plight of the unemployed in British Columbia. And in *Relief* Millie Evans Bicknell told of the intolerable conditions facing the prairie farmers who had been forced to part with their implements and livestock.

It was not just unemployment that rallied the country's artists. The activities of the Communist Party of Canada, the labour unions, the Co-operative Commonwealth Federation (to become the NDP), the popular front against fascism, and the collapse of the Republicans in Spain set off a wave of activity. Dorothy Livesay and musician Jan Isnai Ismay wrote words and music for plays, songs, and mass chants. Earle Birney composed political poems. And a young worker from Montreal named Sidney Nicholls created the rousing mass recitation *Eviction*, which dramatized the shooting of an unemployed worker, Nick Zynchuck, by Montreal police in March 1933.

This nationwide response to the social and political turmoil of the 1930s was short-lived. The signing of the non-aggression pact between the Soviet Union and Germany and the outbreak of the Second World War made it clear that change was not going to be brought about by the poems and woodcuts that appeared in journals like *Masses* and *New Frontier*, or by the plays that were performed on the streets and in theatres across the country. Even so, what was produced at the height of the Depression showed that culture could best establish its claims if all of its forms—art, music, literature, and drama—emanating from all areas of the country were rallied behind one cause.

While patronage of the arts was haphazard and sporadic, amateur and professional cultural producers had more venues for their work than before the war. They had a place to study and teach, to perform, publish, and exhibit. Above all, they had larger audiences than had previously been the case. Prairie farmers and their wives drove hundreds of miles to attend the semifinal performances of the drama and music festivals. Ontarians crowded into the big tents set up by the Chautauqua Institute to hear Charles G.D. Roberts and Bliss Carman read their poems. And museums and galleries in Vancouver, Edmonton, Toronto, and Montreal had attendance records that today's gallery directors would envy.

When the Royal Commission on National Development in the Arts, Letters, and Sciences published its report in 1951 and the Canada Council was founded six years later, the nationalist culture was institutionalized. The commissioners, headed by Vincent Massey, favoured supporting high culture over low, the professional creator over the part-time amateur. They espoused an elitist moral vision of culture, which continued to ignore Canadians who did not belong to the English, and to a lesser extent to the French, linguistic groups. Above all they offered no antidote to the postwar infusion into Canada of American mass culture. They simply believed that Canadians would prefer to support homegrown high culture over foreign imports.

When the members of the Canada Council met in 1957 they carried out the spirit of the report. They favoured funding national over local or provincial cultural organizations; supporting English-Canadian over French-Canadian cultural institutions; established over unestablished groups and individuals; professional over amateur performers; and groups over individuals. Amateur producers thus found themselves closed out by the new emphasis on training, education, international exposure, and higher standards. And new Canadians continued to be left out in the cold. While the council was willing to fund folksong collecting in Quebec and native Indian carving projects in British Columbia, it was reluctant to support the development of the "national cultures" of new Canadians when the Canadian government had a policy of integration. It sometimes seemed that the emergence of a cultural bureaucracy in the form of the Canada Council limited rather than enhanced creativity, just as it would sometimes encourage an unhealthy competition for funding.

Despite its shortcomings, the existence of a government agency for the arts did improve the climate for many anglophone and francophone cultural producers. Cultural programs and institutions like the Art Bank, the National Library of Canada, and Telefilm Canada came into being. Private cultural organizations like the National Ballet of Canada and Les Grands Ballets Canadiens, along with theatres and publishing houses, were kept afloat by generous grants from the Canada Council. An attempt was even made to combat the influx of American periodicals, television, and radio programs. In 1964 the federal government made an effort to rework cultural law and policy by establishing a committee on broadcasting;

three years later it set up the Canadian Film Development Corporation; and in 1970 the Senate Committee on Mass Media tabled its report.

Public organizations like the National Film Board of Canada, founded in 1939, also got a shot in the arm. The introduction in the 1960s of lightweight equipment, the experimentations of the brilliant animator Norman McLaren and the emergence of the direct cinema movement, along with the appointment of a French-Canadian commissioner, Guy Roberge, revitalized the NFB. By the end of the 1960s it was a world-class film unit. Not to be outdone by the NFB, the emergence of CBC television made Canadians confront controversial political and social issues in such programs as "This Hour Has Seven Days.*"*

In 1967 Canada celebrated its one-hundredth birthday by hosting a world's fair, Expo '67, in Montreal. By this time the Canada Council's support of the "faux nationalist culture," which had emerged in the interwar period, was in full swing. Central Canadians from Robertson Davies, R. Murray Schafer, Glenn Gould, Maureen Forrester, Marie-Claire Blais, to Anne Hebert and Mordecai Richler had become household names. Canadian writers, Elizabeth Smart in *By Grand Central Station I Sat Down and Wept*, Hugh MacLennan in *Two Solitudes*, and Malcolm Lowery in *Under the Volcano*, had already produced international bestsellers. Farley Mowat made Canadians, and others, confront ecological issues in the novel *Never Cry Wolf*. And Central Canadian soothsayer, Marshall McLuhan, and literary theoretician, Northrop Frye, led the international debate on technology and literary criticism. Inuit and native artists found themselves favoured by government officials who had little time for the abstract canvases of les automatistes, the Painters Eleven, and the Regina Five. George Ryga's 1967 play, *The Ecstasy of Rita Joe*, spoke for First Nations' people. Margaret Laurence wove Cree legends and the Metis into her Manawaka novels. And in 1965, Hubert Aquin dealt with Quebec's separatists in *Prochain episode*. Popular culture was more representative of the country as a whole. Leonard Cohen, Anne Murray, Gordon Lightfoot, Ian and Sylvia Tyson, and Gilles Vigneault made people on both sides of the border sing "Suzanne," "Snowbird," "Early Morning Rain," "Four Strong Winds," and *"Mon Pays."*

Thanks to funding from the Canada Council and the wave of nationalism engendered by the new Canadian flag and by Expo '67, the professional cultural producer superseded the amateur. The star system had turned culture—as Marshall McLuhan predicted it would—into a business. But it was not just public money that accounted for the sheer quantity of cultural production. Canadians responded to gay rights by producing writers the stature of Jane Rule and David Watmough and playwrights the calibre of Michel Tremblay. The fallout from French and American feminism gave Canadian women, who had been marginalized in the grant-grubbing game, a fairer chance. Margaret Atwood represented them in her novels, faithful chronicles of their period.

By the 1990s Canadian culture was no longer being invented and constructed by a small elite in Central Canada. The worldwide resurgence of ethnic nationalism prompted those groups who had been excluded from the national cultural project to demand a place in it. Suddenly native playwrights, artists, writers, architects, and filmmakers like Tomson Highway, Robert Davidson, George Kenny, Douglas Cardinal, and Alanis Obomsawin were speaking for themselves. Writers of Italian and Chinese ethnicity were receiving the Governor General's Award for fiction. And women were directing public art galleries; one, Joyce Zemans, even presided over the Canada Council.

The emergence of deconstructionist theory, which seeks to expose underlying cultural assumption, and politically correct thinking also challenged the "faux nationalist culture." Emily Carr's paintings, the tunes that Ernest MacMillan had set to Quebec folksongs and native dirges, and the poems of William Henry Drummond and Duncan Campbell Scott were viewed through deconstructionist lenses. Similarly the Group of Seven was now referred to as the Ontario Group of Seven. Even Inuit carvings came under scrutiny as it became known that the educator and government employee, James Houston, had made pattern books for the Inuit carvers based on his knowledge of contemporary British sculpture—especially Henry Moore—and the demands of the nonnative purchasers.

The worldwide recession also had a part in undermining the national cultural project in Canada. It prompted the federal government to hand over some of its cultural territory to the provinces. (Decentralization, along with funding cuts to the CBC, the Canada Council, the NFB, and private organizations like the National Ballet of Canada, has weakened the institutions that have played a major role for half a century in defining the country.) The government's insistence that culture pay its own way has fostered block-buster, crowd-drawing exhibitions devoted to foreign artists. The need to fill seats in the concert halls has given preference to the compositions of the three B's and the big M, much to the detriment of Canada's composers.

The emergence of multinational conglomerates and the revolution in communications technology has posed a fourth and final challenge to the cultural nationalist project. Will CBC television be able to compete with a hundred channels? And will Canadians experience a crisis of identity when these new forms and technologies send them too many messages?

While all of these factors have weakened the dominant culture over the last twenty-five years, they have given rise to a more diversified and representative form of culture. It is our very diversity that has allowed Canadian authors like Michael Ondaatje to win the Booker Prize and Antonine Maillet to be the first non-French author to receive the Prix Goncourt. Moreover, Canadian singers and musicians are playing in opera houses and concert halls around the world. Canadian compositions and plays are performed at the Edinburgh and Salzburg Festivals. Canadian art is exhibited in every international art fair. The productions of Canadian filmmakers—Atom Egoyan, Patricia Rozema, and Denys Arcand—are seen on more screens outside than inside Canada. The jazz pianist Oscar Peterson and popular actors Michael J. Fox and Pamela Anderson are household names at home and abroad, while the stunning voice of the Quebec diva Celine Dion launched and sank one very big ship in the film *Titanic*.

If national identity arises out of the comparison and the competition of nations, perhaps Canada's best self-portrait has been painted by foreign observers. As Canada enters the new millennium, it is clear that there is a place for its cultural producers on the international level. The changing nature and meaning of cultural activity itself demands that we participate, because even though we can't change the past, we can certainly improve on the future.

HOCKEY NIGHT IN PORT HAWKESBURY

Lynn Coady *(This Magazine)*

My hometown's hockey team was called the Port Hawkesbury Pirates. Their colours were maroon and white and they had a fierce pirate's-head eyepatch emblazoned in the center of their jerseys. Their greatest rivals were the Antigonish Bulldogs. I remember one particular playoff where the entire town was mobilized against the mainland village of Antigonish. My

Lynn Coady. Hockey night in Port Hawkesbury. *This Magazine* 33(3), November/December, 1999. 26–27.

dad owned the Dairy Queen, and used its towering sign to denigrate everything about our neighbours on the other side of the causeway. Ho ho Shebo, he used to have up there, to the befuddlement of tourists looking for a deal on Brazier Burgers. Shebo was the name of the opposing team's coach. It was a chant the town liked to use whenever our team was ahead. Another day it was Port Hawkesbury Pirates versus the Antigonish Poodles. I thought that up. Dad was tickled, and thrilled me by enshrining it beneath the DQ logo for a whole two weeks.

I went to the big game with my dad. I was attired that evening in a Port Hawkesbury Pirates jacket zipped up over a Pirates jersey. Perched on my head was a Pirates cap. Clutched in my hand, a Go Pirates pennant. I loved everything about that night. Listening to Dad holler the most eloquent of personal insults at the nefarious Shebo, the guffaws of the surrounding adults. A woman swaddled head to toe in fox-fur cursing a blue streak like I had never heard. The hard benches. My brother's hand-me-down longjohns bunching underneath my clothes. The insane excitement all around me such as I had never experienced in that town before or after.

But I can't relate to you a single thing about the actual game. Because I didn't understand a goddamn thing that was going on. When the crowd screamed, I screamed. When the crowd booed, I booed. When the crowd threatened to disembowel the referee, I too became a mindless, homicidal maniac. I was having the time of my life. But when the actual game was going on, and the crowd sat in rapt awe, this is approximately what was going on in my head:

Guy skating, guy skating, guy skating. Another guy. Skate, skate, skate. Guy from other team. Skate, skate. Who has it now?

Oh. Fat guy. Skating, skating . . .

There you have, summed up, my eternally ambivalent relationship with the game of hockey and everything it represents. And it represents a lot, let's not kid ourselves. To grow up anywhere in small-town Canada is to grow up with the conviction that hockey is, if not the only thing that matters, one of the things that definitely matters most. In memories of my family, my town, my youth, hockey is always front and center. My dad coached, and my two older brothers played. Hockey-related pictures, trophies, plaques galore adorn my parents' home.

As a teenager, I was not permitted to be off in my room "sulking" when a Leafs game was on. It was a sacred time that I was expected to participate in, like when we said the rosary. Dad and the boys would eat chips with dip, drink pop, yell and bounce up and down in their seats. My mother would commandeer the couch and sneak in little naps between goals and intermission, when she would play Ron McLean to Dad's Don Cherry. A Toronto game is the only thing I have ever seen my father stay up past 11 for. I would sit at the very back of the living room with a selection of magazines on the table beside me.

You think I am not aware of what I sound like: Miss Priss, brimming with lofty notions and a hearty disdain for anything involving protective cups. "Really, faw-tha, another Leafs game? Can't you see I'm reading Joyce? If only we had an alternative cinema, I'd be so out of here." But it's not true. I was an adolescent, remember, and even more than screening the occasional Fassbinder film, what I really wanted was to fit in. Hockey wasn't merely my Dad's trip. It was everybody's. People spoke hockey, do you see? It was like a club, or a religion, and if you understood it, everybody else could understand you. You made sense to them. You fit.

Here are some terms and expressions I don't understand to this day.

Blue line.

Sudden death.

De-fense! De-fense! (I know what the word means, but why do people yell it over and over again?)

And what's with the octopi?

I have alternated my whole life from a fierce resentment of hockey to a wistful longing I can't quite put my finger on. The resentment is simple enough. It comes from having the overriding importance of hockey burned into me my entire life while at the same time understanding that someone like me (female) should never expect to have anything to do with such a vastly significant phenomenon. It comes from the fact that were I to admit this to any of my brothers they would assume I had not received enough oxygen to my brain as a baby.

So off I went into the world of books and English departments, where nary a taint of hockey fever could be felt—or so I thought. (Bill Gaston's newest novel is about a former pro-hockey player who becomes an English undergrad. The comedy writes itself.) Imagine my chagrin when I discovered that my own patron saint of Maritime Lit despised such stuffy havens for precisely the reason I sought them out. In *Hockey Dreams*, a veritable hymn to the gods of the rink, David Adams Richards tells of a variety of literary snotties who think it terribly impish to root for the Russians because "Wayne Gretzky's just so Canadian." Then there is the woman from Penguin Books who becomes awfully confused when Richards and a Czech writer strike up an animated conversation about the (Pittsburgh) Penguins. That would be me, I can't help but think. Desperately veering the conversation toward Kafka, praying no one discovered my pathetic ignorance about what really mattered—who made the big save, who got the most assists.

But what confounds me even more is how much I relate to this book. I understand, whether I want to or not. It is not so much the games Richards is remembering, but the way his friends floated in their oversized jerseys, the smell of wet wool, sub-zero Saturdays gathered around "Hockey Night in Canada." The feeling. Throughout the book, Richards struggles to explain the unexplainable, the mystery of hockey. There are those who understand and those who will never understand, he intimates. I know what he means, because I am both.

So that wistful longing makes sense, I suppose, when I look back on that Pirates versus Bulldogs game. I grew up with the understanding that hockey was all-important, hockey players were gods, and to be a hockey fan was to enter into some kind of enchanted circle that bestowed instant community and good fellowship upon you. That's what I was feeling that night. I was sitting on the Port Hawkesbury side of the rink, our rink, screaming for our team, on behalf of our town. I was 12 years old, sexually invisible, my days of artsy alienation far off in the inconceivable future. For a moment, I belonged. Because of hockey.

DISCUSSION QUESTIONS

1. What is the importance of art to the Canadian identity?

2. Is Canadian culture less mythical than US culture? Can you identify some Canadian myths? Are they in fact destructive to us?

3. Discuss the importance of hockey to our "national imaginary."

 WEBLINKS

Canadian Heritage
www.pch.gc.ca/

Association of Canadian Clubs
www.canadianclubs.ca/

Canadian Journal of Communications article on identity
www.wlu.ca/~wwwpress/jrls/cjc/BackIssues/16.1/goldman.html

Canadian Schoolnet project on identity
www.schoolnet.ca/grassroots/e/project.centre/toolkit/casestudies/case004.html

Council of Canadians
www.Canadians.org/

Citizine magazine
www.citizine.ca/

chapter five

Canadian TV:

Is Anybody Watching?

INTRODUCTION

The CBC and TVO (Television Ontario) are public television stations paid for largely by tax dollars, and, in the case of TVO, donations from residents of Ontario and from large corporations. The current Ontario government has considered selling TVO to private interests, much to the chagrin of many Ontarians. The Federal government is always fretting over the programming on CBC as well as its, by television standards, very modest budget. The issue here is, of course, whether government should be in the media business, and whether public broadcasters do a better job of producing Canadian programming than the private sector.

Patrick Watson, former chairman of the CBC, argues that the network has lost its way as a public service institution, in part because it has made unwise delivery and programming decisions, but also because it has been forced to compete with the private networks. Starved for revenue, the CBC has to rely increasingly upon advertising—advertising which interrupts and trivializes much of what is serious and entertaining in its programming. Advertising and foreign programming have caused the CBC schedule to become inflexible, making crea*tivi*ty in pursuit of ideas of national importance, or even topicality and innovation, far more difficult. Watson calls for a reinvented CBC—a network which will fulfil its important mandate for Canadian society.

Ian Austen does a close analysis of the problems of private broadcasting. He notes that a great deal of money is made by the private sector, but that often private broadcasters do not live up to their responsibility to produce Canadian programming. This is particularly disturbing because of the profits that the private sector has made from "signal substitution," or substituting Canadian commercials for American ones when stations broadcast American programs. Much of the money generated from this lucrative practice was supposed to be ploughed back into making Canadian programming; most of it appears to be merely profit for the owners themselves.

Noting that it is cheaper by far to show American programs than make homegrown ones, Austen argues that it would be better for Canadians if the private sector helped to develop Canadian talent rather than merely repackaging popular American sitcoms and dramas. The private sector seems to view Canadian content as mainly sports and news—hardly the intention of the CRTC regulations that govern Canadian content.

At the beginning of this chapter, Patrick Watson argues that the CBC has lost its distinctiveness and its audience. Taras Grescoe, on the other hand, argues that television in Quebec is alive and very well, if somewhat parochial. Popular television mini-series (*téléromans*) attract as many as two out of three French-speaking Quebecers per episode. Television, argues Grescoe, may be the cultural glue which holds Quebec together. Patrick Watson can only dream that the CBC could perform this important political and social goal. Famous and respected authors write for Quebec television, making it an important site for aesthetic experimentation and works of popular fiction that are widely admired and enjoyed.

A PROJECT FOR CANADA: NOW IS THE TIME TO CREATE A NEW SYSTEM OF PUBLIC BROADCASTING

Patrick Watson *(Maclean's)*

Here's a great millennium project for Canada. Let's build a public television system. We could use one. It could be an instrument to help restore the ancient and useful idea that there is such a thing as a Public Good, to recognize that Canadians have important things to say to each other and to do with each other. Television might be more usefully employed in that way than just to sell stuff to consumers.

Older readers will recall that for some years the CBC offered an authentically public television service. But then, under the presidency of Pierre Juneau from 1982 to 1989, commercial considerations began to loom larger. Whenever there was a financial shortfall, instead of trimming, say, the vast wasteful overheads at head office in Ottawa, the English and French networks were instructed to sell more advertising. As this was fairly early in the multichannel age, it would have been the right time for CBC-TV to develop a totally distinctive voice. Instead, it began to compete with and look more and more like its commercial competitors, trying to be something for everyone. And for nearly 20 years now, its preoccupation with ratings and advertising revenue has fatally skewed both content and style. It has largely lost its identity and almost totally lost its constituencies. Despite carrying more Canadian-made programming than ever, too many viewers confuse CBC-TV with those competitors.

Patrick Watson. A project for Canada: Now is the time to create a new system of public broadcasting. *Maclean's* 112(14), April 5, 1999. 58.

Over and over again I hear things like: "Say, did you catch that great documentary film last night?"

"What channel?"

"CBC, I think. Or, no, wait a minute. Was it Global? Oh, no! I know! It was History Television, or . . . well, I'm not sure. But it was really great."

It's partly the failure of the CBC to create a distinctive service, partly the success of the Canadian Radio-television and Telecommunications Commission, Telefilm Canada and the Canadian Television Fund in putting Canadian-made shows on commercial screens throughout the system. Audiences can see on History Television, Discovery Channel, Bravo!, Global, CTV, etc., publicly mandated programs that look like programs on the CBC.

CBC Radio, on the other hand, is still a public service for Citizens. The capital C here is not casual. In my vocabulary the word Citizen is a term of respect. To say that CBC Radio is a public radio service for Citizens means that it is designed to serve people who care about the country, who want to be involved, to know their fellow citizens, to know about the national life across its multifarious spectra, to have something cogent to say about where we go and how we get there. To that end they want song and story, information and comedy, nonsense and faith, conversation and performance, aspiration and fear, accountability and challenge, that speak to us out of our shared experience as a nation. A genuine public television service would deliver such material at places and times we can count on. Its only purpose would be service, its programming choices determined only by that thing called the Public Interest, and never by commercial or other partisan interests. CBC Radio, though cruelly starved for resources, still reliably delivers a public interest service that no other broadcaster duplicates. It has a constituency. CBC-TV no longer has one.

Politicians see that all across the Canadian television system there are Canadian-made programs much like what the CBC offers. They also see that when CBC-TV's budget is cut almost nobody, except people with vested interests, complains. And so they understand that closing down CBC-TV would not be much of an electoral liability, especially if part of the savings were redirected via the funding agencies, such as Telefilm Canada and the Canadian Television Fund, to increase the amount and quality of Canadian offerings on the commercial broadcasters and cable services.

Some of the specialty cable services are now doing excellent work of a kind that once made CBC-TV unique. Because their programming is distinctive and coherent, they can attract loyal audiences. But the specialty cable services are not public broadcasters: they are revenue-driven, depending on popularity and advertising. This leads even the best of them to carry some programming that has no intrinsic value but can be bought cheap to fill out the schedule.

I hasten to add that popularity is important. The early days of CBC-TV were often stuffy, self-indulgent, concerned only about the importance of its subject matter, indifferent to presentation and the special needs of television. Some programmers were insufferably arrogant and superior, a bit like some TV producers and editors today, except that they didn't care much whether people watched. If you watched, that proved you too were superior; if you did not watch, well, it wasn't the programmers' fault.

Such a posture was as irresponsible as the one that led to rigged talk shows—it has largely vanished. But so has the ethic based on serving the audience. Serve the audience has been replaced by get an audience. And while you cannot serve an audience if it's not there, you're not likely to provide much service if your only concern is numbers. The objective of much commercial television is to numb viewers into a state of mind that welcomes advertising intrusions instead of rejecting them.

This is a highly developed craft. CBC programmers are often as good at it as other North American broadcasters. But advertising revenue as the prime objective damages the kind of thoughtful and generous programming that the CBC still does from time to time. It is inimical to long-form documentary or drama of integrity because it forces structural breaks that have nothing to do with the requirements of the narrative or dramatic line.

It seems that most viewers accept such interruptions. They use television for escape, for narcotic, for reassurance that war has not started or pestilence broken out, or to prove in the workplace that they are up on the latest celebrity gossip.

But there is another kind of audience, people who feel there's a tacit contract with broadcasters that goes like this: "I, the viewer, will pay attention as long as you, the broadcaster, are enlarging my world and being truthful with your material." Such people are offended by violations of subject matter and of respect for their own judgment, and few are willing to waste the time that television advertising consumes.

Except for people in the public arena, or in the industry, I know very few serious-minded Citizens who use mainstream television much anymore, except for movies, the odd special, occasionally a newscast. The specialty services are different. Cable broadcasters like Bravo! and Discovery Channel appear to be winning loyal viewers. The numbers are small, but it is evident that there are people who want quality, and are willing to pay a subscription fee to get it.

An important Canadian component of that quality television is paid for by publicly mandated funds. But when it is distributed among many channels it doesn't appear to viewers as part of a public effort, something we did as a nation. Something that responds to the need we have to do, together, things in which we have a stake, to build instruments of consensus, of our collective life as a national community, instruments that belong to us, to which we can point with pride, and which respond to our declared national values.

The public discourse of the Canada I grew up in, which for six of those formative years was preoccupied with the 1939–1945 war, was richly strewn with the words "we" and "us" and "together." Together we could endure, survive, triumph. Such words have disappeared from the public discourse; our national leaders seem preoccupied with market values and fiscal probity, matters we used to think belonged in the world of taken-for-granted, but have now been elevated to the ranks of myth and shibboleth. And in those ranks they do not function as stimulants to national pride or unity, or to a sense of common concerns or objectives or pride.

The then-minister of the interior of France, Jean-Pierre Chevenement, said a couple of years ago, addressing the traditional French dislike of immigrants and prejudice in favour of old ethnic stock, that it would be better to define Citizenship as "sharing in a common project." Sharing in a common project! Five simple but electrifying words. And think how important having a common experience of our country must be if we are to recognize our common project when we see it.

That's what a public television service needs to be: a common project. It needs to reflect Canada's diversity of place and people, language and ethnicity, of land and space, of ambition and intent, in a way that allows us to use the words "we" and "us" meaningfully. This is not a matter of earnestness and furrowed brows. It has as much to do with a "This Hour Has 22 Minutes," a "Royal Canadian Air Farce," a Celine Dion, a "King of Kensington," as it does with documentaries and news.

It is also a matter of being inventively responsive to the changing winds of national life. Advertising prevents this even more than it prevents the reflection of diversity. CBC-TV claims, of course, that it is such a reflection. So why does it no longer have a loyal constituency? Simply because the reflection is so partial, so diluted, so narrowed by advertisers' requirements that there is little room for experiment, for real innovation, for risk. And one of the important forms that risk and innovation used to take—a readiness to respond rapidly to perceived need—vanished long ago.

It was common as late as the 1970s when the then-head of TV current affairs, Peter Herrndorf, inherited a tradition in which program heads made decisions and didn't nervously refer upstairs all the time. It was a time when, if the country was in a spasm, a programmer could say: "Look, we need to open up the network for a couple of hours this week to deal with this." In the October Crisis of 1970, CBC-TV stayed on the air all night. You didn't need to be on cable to be part of a nation on alert.

A few years later, when it looked as if there was a passionate group of articulate French- and English-Canadians who suddenly needed to talk to each other in public about the tensions among us all, current affairs producer Cameron Graham needed only about two weeks to mount two 90-minute specials, one in English, one in French, co-hosted in both languages by journalist Louis Martin and myself, in which several dozen participants, all bilingual, openly and courteously went at those national issues, first in French for Radio-Canada, then in English for CBC-TV, live to tape: because it was needed right then!

Not as part of the news magazine after "The National." Not as a laborious, several-months-of-preparation agony. But something that public broadcasters perceived to be appropriate and timely there and then. Because the next six months weren't already sold to advertisers, and because policy gave them some discretionary money for unexpected needs, the programmers actually controlled the schedule—for programming reasons! Graham and Herrndorf could get this project to air without six months of agonizing over policy.

On another occasion, the audience research people could say, "Last night's drama was a huge success, but a lot of people missed it because of a major sports event on another channel; we think you should open up a slot and repeat it right away." And that could be done.

In 1960–1961 I discovered Chris Bryant and Allan Scott, a couple of McGill undergraduate students who were doing stand-up sketch comedy in Montreal cabarets when they weren't working on their degrees in law and English. Although I was senior current affairs producer in the Ottawa region, and theoretically had no right to dabble in variety programming, within a week or two Scott and Bryant and I had not only designed "Nightcap," a late-night comedy/jazz/ interview show, but had got management to assign a modest budget and a time slot. It was only a few weeks between concept and launch. We and the audience had a lot of fun, and when it was over we went on to other things.

Please note: I am NOT suggesting that this was some Golden Age of public television. It was no such thing; there never was any such age. These were times that saw lots of disasters, lots of ill-considered initiatives, lots of management bungling and heavy-handedness. But there was a willingness to grope in public, to test, to invent under the scrutiny of audiences, to encourage young producers to go for a wild idea.

Now. What should this new public television system look like? Here are some principles and considerations that a government should declare when it asks a think-tank to design a new system and a model program schedule.

The service must be distinctive. In an age of specialty channels, it makes no sense for a broadcaster to try to be everything. So the new public television agency must be the Canada Channel: programs of quality—from nonsense to profundity, from fantasy to science, from goofiness to tragedy. Instead of cashing in on tried-and-true formulas, the public television broadcaster will take chances and break new ground. The primary criteria should include service, relevance and an ongoing invitation to know and take part in the life of the country. They should invite creative solutions to the challenges of content, distribution, finance, experimentation and risk-taking, and respect for both audiences and participants.

There must be room for the refined arts: the specialty arts channel Bravo! with its very small resources has done impressive, innovative work in raising Canadians' awareness of the performing arts, and there's more to be done. Yes, those arts generally reach only a relatively small group of people, but they are people who make a lot of decisions; they pay a lot of taxes, they teach in our schools and do community service, they head governments and corporations, they contribute a lot to the national life. And they get little back on their television screens.

And the high arts ripple out and refresh the popular arts: classical dance nourishes popular dance; experimental serious music finds its way into the pop stream and enriches it. No Bach, no "Whiter Shade of Pale." No classical string quartets, no "Eleanor Rigby". No Richard Strauss, no *Phantom of the Opera*.

Producers must be enjoined to make all programs as attractive as possible to a wide audience, consistent with the integrity and authenticity of the material. A public service using public resources has a political, moral and social obligation to be comprehensible and accessible to the widest possible audience.

Recognizing the large number of alternative attractions in the television spectrum, program schedulers must give audiences several opportunities to see new programs within the immediate period of their first release. This would entail a sophisticated and well-researched pattern of repeats that does not penalize the viewer who wants to see other programs on other channels within the Canadian system.

Next, is the issue of distribution. Based on a recommendation from a cable system designer, Sruki Switzer, the CBC engineering department was asked some years ago to consider putting the entire TV transmission service on satellites. Five or six transponders could serve the whole country and protect regional interests and time-zone needs by feeding local cable services. For the small percentage of homes out of reach of cable, it was argued, it would be cheaper to subsidize their purchase of direct satellite dishes than to maintain hundreds of terrestrial transmitters.

The reader will not be astounded to learn that CBC engineering, asked to evaluate a proposal that would have radically reduced its size and budget, did nothing. The underlying question is, does a public television system need a plant at all, studios, transmitters and so on? Or could it do what it has to do using existing facilities as carriers? That is, could the existing commercial broadcasters and cable services be instructed to open up regular time slots for programs from a public television agency that owns no hardware at all?

It is at least conceivable that the best Canadian instrument for the new century would be a public television agency that commissions all or most of its programs from independent producers, deploying public funds to make programs that existing services would be obliged to carry. When the existing CBC-TV disappears, Newsworld will lose its main source and will die as well. Our new public television agency could fund and set standards for a news service, probably as a separate, independent organization, supplying both the main service and, if viable, an all-news channel. The agency could, in effect, own or control a number of periods on commercial broadcast and cable services, regularly scheduled time slots that viewers could count on to be carrying the distinctive public service. Part of the compensation to those broadcasters would be a straight fee for service as a carrier and part the increased advertising revenue available to the rest of their schedule with a major competitor (the CBC) no longer in the advertising game. In any case, large publicly owned establishments of real estate and buildings and transmitters are no longer appropriate. Those facilities exist in a profitable private sector, which ought to be deployed, partly for pay and partly for public purpose, in the execution of a public television strategy.

I favour a combined approach: a distinctive "All Canada Channel" extended by a pattern of second windows amongst the other channels, something that has begun to happen already.

I think a national convention should be held to bring together the practitioners who are out there on the cutting edge of television, cultural development, entrepreneurship and social policy. Moses Znaimer of Toronto-based City TV has done more for innovative television than anyone else in Canada, so he should be empanelled. Evan Soloman, host of "Future World" on Newsworld, is far ahead of most of his colleagues in his thinking. Trina McQueen has made Discovery Channel sing, and long ago, as head of information programming at CBC, was brilliant at defining the role of a public broadcaster. The national convention should also canvass the recently adolescent coveys of genius who are designing Web sites and thinking the unthinkable.

This assembly or think-tank would not be a parliament, not a representative caucus: that's a recipe for paralysis. This must be a group of communications inventors. Put them together in a room. Give them a clear mandate in broad strategic terms. Their job is not to declare the purpose of the new public TV service—that's up to Parliament—but to devise the method and the machine. So give them a set of objectives about what the country needs and tell them they have six weeks to come up with a structure, a distribution system, a statement of guiding principles and a budgeted model program schedule.

It can be done. In 1984, a tiny task force, operating under the same kind of directives, designed a workable, low-cost second CBC channel to be known as CBC Weekend, only to have the CBC board lose its nerve and shelve the project.

It will need a name, this new agency. One is tempted to call it something like the Canadian Broadcasting Corporation—a name that once conveyed a grand dream and perhaps could do so once again.

CULTURE BETWEEN COMMERCIALS

Ian Austen *(Canadian Forum)*

Who's the real Izzy Asper? Is he the media mogul whose Global Television Network was effectively heralded as a force for Canadian culture in a late February press release from federal broadcast regulator Keith Spicer? "We are pleased that the licensee has exceeded the minimum expenditure of over $30 million a year on Canadian programming," the CRTC chairman noted while announcing a seven-year renewal of Global's licence.

Or is he the man whose broadcasting vision was portrayed on a cover of *Maclean's* that appeared just a few days before Spicer's announcement? "Izzy's dream," as the magazine called it, was depicted by a series of television sets showing Global's programming highlights. Four displayed top-rated, U.S. network imports; the fifth featured Izzy's face.

While the magazine illustrator didn't include Global's new Canadian series, "Traders," he was nevertheless much closer to the mark about Asper's record as a cultural force than

Ian Austen. Culture between commercials. *Canadian Forum* 75(849), May, 1996. 14-19.

Spicer's upbeat praise. Unfortunately, Asper—who wants to make Global the third national English TV network—has plenty of company. Despite years of effort and study, stacks of regulations and millions of government dollars, English Canada's commercial broadcasters remain largely distributors of the best Hollywood can offer. In short, we've been had, and amazingly, given the current focus on the CBC's sins, hardly anyone seems to be noticing.

Take, for example, most media coverage of the CBC, National Film Board and Telefilm Canada mandate review committee's report. Predictably, reporters were fixated on the panel's suggestion that a modest tax on things such as cable bills should pay the CBC's freight. Almost entirely ignored was the section on Telefilm, the semi-invisible federal agency that's the biggest investor in most entertainment programming on private TV, including the much-hyped "Traders." While the committee revealed lots of problems with CBC English TV, it was even harsher in its criticism of the private networks. "If the limited amount of Canadian programming (and particularly drama) on our television screens—and the disproportionate amount of time that Canadians devote to watching American programs—is not seen as a cultural crisis, it is only because English-speaking Canadians have grown too accustomed to this situation. It is not now, and never has been, a case of Canadian programs being provided and rejected by domestic audiences."

As the report suggests, the dismal state of private TV is hardly a recent development. Still, it's hard to imagine a more crucial time to start looking at private TV's invisible cultural crisis. As the CBC's resources continue to be squeezed, it becomes more important than ever to press the point that private broadcasters aren't doing us a favour by producing Canadian programming—it's the price of some very valuable considerations from the government. Over the coming months, opportunities to address the issue will surface, including eight CRTC commissioners' spots, among them the chairman's, becoming vacant; an internal review by the Heritage and Industry departments of the CRTC's role and operations; Asper's station licence applications to create his national network; and growing calls for regulatory change prompted by the so-called information highway, calls that have been dominated by industry demands for less regulation and lower Canadian content requirements.

If you only read private broadcasters' annual reports and their CRTC submissions rather than watching their programming or even glancing at the TV listings, you might think they actually are major forces for Canadian culture. It's rare that a private broadcaster doesn't appear before the CRTC without an introductory videotape that includes some aerial views of the Rockies, Canada geese in slow-motion flight and perhaps a quaint Innu woman for good measure. When private operators actually produce a Canadian show, their publicity departments do their best to ensure that everyone knows about it—Asper posed with the stars of "Traders" for publicity photos and even did a walk-on part in one episode.

But nothing turns private broadcasters into greater patriots than the emergence of anything they perceive as a threat to their profit margins—whether it's tax changes, increased regulation, the advent of cable in the '60s or, more recently, direct-to-home satellites. Any decline in their financial performance, they warn in usually apocalyptic terms, will doom Canadian production, if not the very fabric of Canada itself. New forms of electronic communications are emerging as the latest enemy. Last year's Canadian Association of Broadcasters' convention lamely attempted to lay claim to that territory with its theme "Private Broadcasting: Canada's Voice on the Innovation Highway."

On the whole, waving the Canadian flag while filling the airwaves with American shows has paid off handsomely. Asper alone is estimated to be personally worth $600 million, much of it generated by his company CanWest Global Communications Corp. In the first six months of its current fiscal year, CanWest's Global—which broadcasts in Ontario, but does not include the company's Saskatchewan and Atlantic Canada operations—saw its profits rise 36 percent to $66 million on revenue of $171 million. Most of that came from broadcasting popular U.S. sitcoms such as "Seinfeld" and "Friends."

Asper's performance is not an isolated example. Last year, Vancouver-based WIC, Western International Communications Ltd., owner of eight stations, a pay-TV network and half of the Family Channel, made $82.7 million. (The major English private network, CTV, has an extremely spotty financial record. However, its customers are for the most part its owners, including WIC, and their balance sheets are uniformly bright in large part because of the mostly American programming CTV provides.)

Despite all the extreme hype about a possible 500-channel universe and the current rush for more cable specialty channels, an over-the-air broadcast licence remains a remarkably valuable piece of paper. Though only Belgium has more of its population connected to cable than Canada, when Canadians turn on the tube they overwhelmingly select conventional, over-the-air stations. The audience gap with the cable channels is startling. Government-owned (at least for now) TVOntario is that province's smallest over-the-air network in terms of overall audience. Nevertheless, most of the time, more Ontarians are watching TVO than all the English specialty channels combined.

Licences aren't the only gifts given to private broadcasters. Few steps have been as influential in shaping private broadcasters' programming strategies and balance sheets as the CRTC's introduction of so-called signal substitution. Under the scheme, major cable companies must replace U.S. stations' signals with local Canadian channels' programming if both are airing identical shows. The identical programs are, of course, overwhelmingly American. Under signal substitution, Canadian stations grab 100 percent of the local audience for their commercials. Its unintended effect is less desirable. Signal substitution creates a powerful economic incentive for private broadcasters to flood key viewing hours with American imports that are sure to be popular with both audiences and advertisers. (The CBC also benefits from the rule when it airs U.S. shows, although the public network has vowed to eliminate its prime-time U.S. programming by this fall.)

Substitution has been a constant trade irritant with successive U.S. administrations. In theory, it should be worth the price of that aggravation. Private broadcasters were supposed to take a chunk of extra ad revenue the scheme generated and use it to develop Canadian programming. A CRTC background paper boasts that, thanks to signal substitution, "millions of dollars are returned to the Canadian broadcasting system." Perhaps to the system but not necessarily to Canadian programming, as former CBC president Tony Manera points out. "This is a case where a public policy has been created to favour the interests of private broadcasters without adding any real benefit for consumers," says Manera, now a consultant after quitting the CBC in 1995 over cuts to its funding. "If the private broadcaster wasn't running those American shows, the consumer would still have access to them. But they'd just have to watch American commercials instead of Canadian commercials. So, big deal."

"I think the private broadcasters owe some return to the Canadian system."

Most private broadcasters have the good sense to always honour the minimum CRTC Canadian content requirements. There are some exceptions, but generally private TV stations must make sure that 60 percent of their programming measured over an entire year is Canadian, including at least half the shows between 6 p.m. and midnight. Quantity isn't the problem; it's how the commercial operators reach the quota.

Asper's Global is a good example. The actual decision that renewed its licence reveals how the network became an overachiever: "The Commission notes . . . that Global's over-expenditures during the current licence term were made entirely on news programming and not on entertainment programming." Though Global and most private broadcasters have improved their performance, Canadian content on private stations remains overwhelmingly news and sports. Both attract ads and are relatively cheap to produce. But news shows that are heavily laden with U.S. network reports from abroad and Blue Jays baseball aren't really the stuff of national identity building. As well, neither sports nor news is what most viewers watch most of the time. Of the top 10 shows in the Toronto-Hamilton market early this year, none was a news program; one sports broadcast, CBC's "Hockey Night in Canada," made ninth place. Most were imported American entertainment series that appeared on Global and CTV.

TVO chairman and mandate review committee member Peter Herrndorf gives private broadcasters some points for trying—at least a little. "Private broadcasters have done significantly better in the last 10 years. They do a lot more drama than anyone might have thought possible in the early 1980s." Not enough though.

"Having said all of that, compared to Australia, compared to Britain, compared to the U.S., compared to France; the commercial broadcasters here do quite modest amounts of indigenous programming. They still are locked to a considerable degree into that economic logic that's prevailed in Canadian broadcasting from the 1930s on."

The statistics back that up. There isn't any overall tracking of private sector performance by the CRTC, but it accepts a CBC study that found only 8.2 percent of shows aired between 7 and 11 p.m. on Global in 1993 were Canadian drama or variety productions. The comparable figure for CTV is 7.9 percent, while the CBC reached almost 17 percent.

Indeed, the CBC research department's dismal findings may actually overstate the private networks' performance. Under the CRTC's and Telefilm's point systems for evaluating productions, some pretty strange things can qualify as Canadian content, especially co-productions. (The systems give up to 10 points for using Canadian talent such as actors, directors and cinematographers. A complex series of treaties, however, skews everything in the case of international co-productions.) CTV's "Canadian" offerings have included "A Family of Cops," starring Charles Bronson as Milwaukee's police chief. Programs filmed in Canada primarily designed for sale in the U.S. market that meet the bare minimum Canadian content levels are known in the trade as six-pointers. They've also become the greatest growth area in production, thanks in large part to the low value of the Canadian dollar. Turning parts of Toronto or Vancouver into Manhattan or Montana for a day certainly provides employment and revenue for independent producers, some actors and technicians. An occasional appearance by the odd Hollywood star is a nice diversion for passers-by, assuming they're not trapped in a film-related traffic jam. What most six-pointers do for Canadian culture, however, is at best unclear. Nevertheless, the push for more continues. The federal government's industry-dominated Information Highway Advisory Council, which reported last fall, was among the latest to join the cause. For cultural industries, it said, "[t]he objective must be a self-sustaining environment." Acknowledging that might not be completely possible, the report claims there's one way to reach most of the goal: "Government policies could do more to encourage the production of exportable content. As markets multiply and diversify, Canadian cultural products must stand out and appeal to consumers. They must strive to achieve maximum quality and marketability and not simply take up obligatory shelf space."

It's not hard to see from a pure business standpoint why private Canadian TV broadcasters have become essentially pipelines for U.S. shows. It costs about $700,000 to $1 million to produce a single hour of real Canadian entertainment programming—an eight- or more pointer. While there are a variety of funds and agencies to help finance the show, its chances for commercial success are dicey. Canadian programs receive only a fraction of the free publicity that falls on even the lamest U.S. shows. Three seasons passed before the CBC's "This Hour Has 22 Minutes" made two Canadian mass market magazine covers. "If it was an American show, it would have had 30 American covers by now and it would have had eight Canadian ones," says Herrndorf. By contrast, the formula for success with simulcasting U.S. shows is dead simple. You buy a big American hit for about $90,000 a one-hour episode. Selling commercials is easy. Many advertisers prefer to drop their money on a simulcast of a U.S.-made sure thing such as "America's Funniest Home Videos" rather than an unknown Canadian product. Those ads should pull in about $250,000, leaving a gross margin of $160,000. With numbers like that, why would you do anything else?

Despite the economic woes of the Ottawa Valley, the annual fall fair in Renfrew, Ontario, continues to prosper. Last year, mixed in with the tractor exhibits, Super Peeler pitchmen and back-bacon-on-a-bun booths, there were two outfits pushing direct-to-home satellite TV systems.

The continuing obsession of Canadian broadcast policy makers with distribution systems rather than programming has guaranteed a lot of attention for satellite TV over the past two and a half years. But despite all the hype and concern, satellite TV remains a tiny niche product used mostly by people in rural areas with either poor or non-existent cable service. In Renfrew's armoury, the fairground's biggest hall, the Women's Institute was dishing out apple pie and TV dealer Ben Sauvé had perched a pizza-sized RCA DTH satellite dish on top of a massive Hitachi set. On the screen was one of the 175 channels—none Canadian—beaming into Canada's so-called grey market from Los Angeles-based Hughes DirecTV. The system's clear picture and crisp, CD-like sound certainly attracted attention. After they admired the screen, however, visitors consistently complained to Sauvé about one major shortcoming: "Many people have been approaching us about it. But they're not interested right now because they want Canadian content. I'd say nine out of ten want Canadian content."

Many of those nine, it seems, define Canadian content as NHL hockey on the Toronto-based specialty channel TSN. But sports isn't the only draw. Just before the fair opened, Linda and Brett Hodgins had dropped about $2,400 for a conventional, three-metre dish for their home east of Renfrew. Instantly they went from receiving two English channels—Ottawa's CBC and CTV outlets—to over 130. The range is bewildering and includes RTP Portugal, BBC World Service News, internal U.S. networks and Canadian network news feeds. As her son watched Barney zapping down from God-knows-where Linda was already longing for some of the local shows on CJOH, the Ottawa CTV station controlled by the Eaton family.

It's one of the great myths of Canadian broadcasting—one that serves private stations well and one that caught the fancy of the Information Highway Advisory Council—that no one watches Canadian shows. "When Canadian programming is available, people will watch it. But it has to be available," says Manera. The CBC's peak viewing time analysis, like other studies, shows that the audience levels for Canadian content roughly match the amount available. In 1993, 25 percent of programming on all English stations between 7 and 11 p.m. was Canadian. It captured 24 percent of the audience.

Boosting the number of Canadian shows is a problem that has plagued Canadian television from the beginning. Thirty-one years ago, the Fowler Committee looked at private broadcasting and produced findings that were echoed this year by the mandate review committee: "Their program schedules are unbalanced; they do not provide sufficiently wide variety, and do little to further the development of the Canadian consciousness." The establishment of Canadian content quotas in 1970, the creation of the broadcast fund at Telefilm 13 years later, the establishment of the cable industry's Canadian Program Production Fund three years ago and a variety of tax measures were all hailed at their introductions as major steps to reversing the trend.

Most recently, an expanded range of cable specialty channels has been billed as Canadian broadcasting's salvation. Without exception, all the applicants for new channels have claimed that their services will be part of a new beginning for Canadian broadcasting. So far, there's not much evidence of that. "I am a skeptic about the specialty channels," says Herrndorf. "It's a nice thing to have. I happen to be a baseball fan, so I take full advantage of TSN. I like some of the things Bravo! does. But in many ways it's kind of a luxury. Given the economics of the specialty services, it is almost guaranteed that the level of complex original production they do will be minimal."

Sure enough, despite the specialty channels' bold promises to the CRTC, their production records have largely been disappointing. There are some exceptions, including YTV, Discovery and Bravo! to a certain extent. Most of the time, however, reruns and whatever's available at overseas program-buying shows are what specialty channels offer viewers. Reruns aren't necessarily a bad thing if they're Canadian programs. A second or third run is often what's needed to turn a profit. But reruns certainly don't add to the pool of Canadian programming. Programming that does get commissioned by specialty channels tends, on the whole, to be low end, what Herrndorf calls "pocket television." To a great extent, the whole specialty system has become a drain, drawing away ad dollars from over-the-air channels while making a minimal contribution to production.

The CRTC's answer to all this: a call for applications for even more specialty channel licences. Hearings begin this month, and the contenders, if anything, look less promising than the current bunch. They include The Horse Network: "All Horses, All The Time."

Despite the less-than-inspiring history of the Canadian content crusade, there are a couple of approaches that still haven't been seriously explored. Neither particularly costs government money, which should be good news for the deficit-obsessed federal Liberals. Both, however, demand strong political will from Heritage Minister Sheila Copps and Industry Minister John Manley.

Politicians generally aren't keen to take a hard stand with private broadcasters. Most broadcast licence holders have strong political ties. Asper, for example, is a former provincial Liberal leader. On top of that, the industry has been adept at creating phony crises whenever it appears its cozy relationship is in jeopardy. Don't be surprised, for example, if you soon hear private broadcasters talking about their need for higher profits and less regulation because of the corporate takeovers sweeping American broadcasting and telecommunications following the near total deregulation of that market in January.

The most important issue for Copps has to be the CRTC and its eight empty chairs. Her closed-door review of the commission indicates that the government isn't happy with the state of the CRTC. Where that's headed is something of a mystery. Manley has talked ominously about making the agency better fit the Liberal Party's values—whatever they may be—and mused about the limited need for regulation in the future. Copps, on the other hand, continues to defend both the need for a CRTC and the importance of broadcasting as a tool for Canadian cultural objectives.

The dismal record of private TV isn't entirely the commission's fault, although the CRTC is obviously part of the problem. Much of the problem lies with the commissioners. That doesn't mean they're dupes of private broadcasters or a gang of fools. For the most part, commissioners are well meaning and work hard for their generous pay. The CRTC's case-load is exploding but hasn't been matched by a corresponding increase in resources. Hearings are seemingly endless, and it's a rare week when at least one commissioner does-n't nod off during some droning presentation.

Offsetting the commissioners' good intentions is their traditional background. With rare exceptions, they tend to be former broadcast or communications managers, journalists or politically connected lawyers, engineers or academics. Certainly those skills can be use-ful. But others with equally large stakes in broadcasting and communications—artists, con-sumer advocates, film directors, novelists, actors, musicians—have been conspicuously absent. "I don't know if I'd go so far as to say the CRTC doesn't work very well, but it really needs balance," says Sandy Crawley, president of the broadcast performers' union ACTRA. "The commissioners don't really take our needs into consideration the same way that they do the money people, who can afford to have lawyers, bring them big briefs, take them out to lunch all the time and constantly lobby to get their people appointed to the commission." (Crawley has applied for an appointment but isn't optimistic about his chances.)

This pattern of past appointments has created commissions that try to squeeze the objectives of the broadcasting act, such as Canadian content, around the broadcast indus-try's corporate needs and desires. For most of the commissioners, the corporate world is where their ultimate sympathies lie. It won't be easy shifting that. One or two daring appointments, even in the chairman's job, aren't likely to be enough if recent U.S. experi-ence is any indication. Spicer's equivalent there, FCC chairman Reed Hundt, is a former anti-trust lawyer who came to the job just over two years ago with hopes of improving children's programming and maintaining telecommunications access for the poor. Since then he's spent much of his time arguing unsuccessfully with most of his other commissioners over such limited measures as requiring the world's biggest broadcasters to show three hours of educational kids' shows a week. Last fall *The New York Times* said Hundt is "looking more and more like the head of a dysfunctional family."

A balanced CRTC could be tougher on programming requirements. Other bodies inter-nationally certainly aren't afraid to push the issue. CanWest was the top bidder, in cash terms at least, for the right to operate a new fifth national network in Britain. But the U.K.'s Independent Television Commission went for a much lower bid after it found fault with CanWest's programming plans, especially its high level of reruns.

But to really effect change in Canada, Copps and whoever succeeds Spicer must take a hard public stand and push private broadcasters to do more real Canadian drama. They should require real programming plans and budgets and make it clear to private broadcast-ers that keeping a licence will require a dramatic change in attitude. Obviously, it won't be easy. Even small steps by the commission in the past have provoked major propaganda assaults from private broadcasting. But if they now have the courage, Asper's national net-work quest certainly provides an opening for such a brave move. Australia shows such a step can be effective. While Australia isn't next door to the U.S., its private networks have long been key sales targets of American program producers. The result was a domestic broadcasting system with programming that would be familiar to most Canadian viewers. Following government pressure, however, the three Australian networks—including one controlled by CanWest—all agreed to produce at least 100 hours of original, prime-time drama a year. In turn, they've been allowed to boost the amount of American programming they show in other programming areas and time slots. (The CRTC has a small measure along these lines, allowing a 150 percent time credit for some Canadian dramas.) "I've heard very few complaints from the Australian private sector about that," says Herrndorf. "They seem to have come to the conclusion that both for identity reasons, prestige reasons and ultimately for profit this was a good deal for them."

Will Copps take such a step? Historically, she's never been shy about speaking her mind, and the need for renewing the Canadian identity has never been greater. But the degree of the Cabinet's commitment to cultural issues is unclear. Much of the confidence instilled in Canadian cultural advocates by Copps's Cabinet appointment and the Cabinet's subsequent rejection of Borders Bookstores' plans for the Canadian market by Investment Canada faded in March when the budget further fuelled the CBC's funding crisis. Copps's main response, so far, has been only promises that some kind of completely new funding plan, completely undefined though apparently not the tax proposed by mandate review, will eventually appear. Manley also has considerable say in the CRTC's direction. Not surprisingly, however, as Industry Minister he tends to view broadcasting as a business rather than a cultural force.

Whether or not the government moves, a number of developments suggest that broadcasters should themselves start rethinking their view of Canadian content out of self-interest. While it's unlikely that we'll ever have 500 channels to choose from, it's not unreasonable to expect that 100 might be around by the end of the decade, thus diluting current broadcasters' market share. Similarly, there are growing threats from abroad that could upset the current system, threats that can't be solved by more special deals from the CRTC or government. Entertainment is the second biggest U.S. export after aircraft. Mired in the U.S. administration's support for Nashville-based Country Music Television's ludicrous argument that it has a guaranteed spot on Canadian cable was a message that Washington doesn't regard commercial broadcasting as a cultural industry exempt from trade action. More recently, the Clinton administration's hard-line attack on federal legislation blocking *Sports Illustrated*'s "Canadian" edition confirmed its attitude. Signal substitution may be Washington's next target.

Whatever happens in the future, the best long-term hope for Canadian private broadcasters is developing a distinct identity rather than just acting as American programming packagers. Their attempts so far have been exceptionally superficial. When John Cassaday left Campbell Soup early this decade to run CTV, he immediately began talking about developing a brand identity. There's not been much to show for it beyond a proliferation of on-screen network logos. By contrast, high-quality drama made for and by Canadians can allow Canada's private networks to stand out from the growing crowd. What's more; good, overtly Canadian shows have shown their export sales potential in the past—even if they don't have Charles Bronson. It's time for Izzy to substantially rethink his dream. Asper may not care about his role in Canada's cultural future, but his own financial future may depend on developing it.

TIVI NATION

Taras Grescoe *(Saturday Night)*

On a single winter evening four years ago, a world record was set in Quebec. It was a rather passive record, but a remarkable one nevertheless: on that night, between 7:30 P.M. and 8:00 P.M., two out of every three French-speaking Quebecers—4 098 000 of them—could be found in their living rooms, awash in the blue glow from their television screens, watching a character called Moman ironing a shirt still attached to the clothesline. It was an episode in the series "La petite vie," and it broke a world record for marketplace penetration, previously held by one of the hugely popular *telenovelas* of Brazil.

On yet another historic evening a few years before that, when the outbreak of the Gulf War interrupted a key episode of "Les filles de Caleb"—a *téléroman* that was then being followed by 3.7 million francophones—Radio-Canada brought in its star newscaster, Bernard Derome, to excuse the intrusion and promise that the show would resume after the briefest possible delay.

Apart, perhaps, from the fact that smoking is still permitted in laundromats, it's the first thing that strikes a newcomer to Quebec: people here watch a lot of television. Francophone Quebecers tune in an average of three hours and forty-eight minutes a day, compared with a Spartan two hours and fifty-four minutes for Albertans. What's more surprising, especially in a Canadian context, is that, on a week this March, for instance, the top thirty television shows in Quebec were all made in Quebec. In the rest of Canada, where the Nielsen charts are dominated by American shows like "E.R." and "Ally McBeal," an English-Canadian program that manages to attract a million viewers—in a market of twenty-three million—is considered a heartening triumph for Canadian content. A program rating that badly in French Canada—with only seven million potential viewers—could well get the axe.

None of this should come as a surprise: modern Quebec is defined by its *tivi* (the folksy French-Canadian diminutive, pronounced tee-vee, for what Parisians call the *télé*). And unlike other Canadians, the Québécois actually like their own television shows, which means their imaginations haven't been entirely colonized by Los Angeles and New York. If Europe's identity is literary (all discursive tradition), America's cinematic (Hollywood's self-righteous glamour), and English Canada's radiophonic (ethereal CBC static on the Trans-Canada), then Quebec is a televisual society, a *tivi* nation.

The basic francophone cable-channel package—available just about everywhere in the province except Montreal's largely anglophone West Island—provides viewers with two major public networks (Radio-Canada and the provincial government's educational channel Télé-Quebec); two private networks (TVA, recently made available on cable across Canada, and TQS, an aggressive upstart); and eleven specialized stations, including Canal Vie, a lifestyles channel aimed at the lucrative "women of a certain age" demographic. On a Monday night, I've watched an Italian gangster on Radio-Canada's trilingual crime drama "Omertà" kick a rival mobster out of a limousine with the words: "What the fuck are you waiting for? Get the fuck out!" as subtitles at the bottom of the screen helpfully translated, "*Dehors, hostie!*" I've gaped at the inexplicable "Dieu recoit" (God is Hosting) on TQS, a high-concept talk show in which God, played by a toga-wearing, Jack-Daniels-sipping actor, interviews Quebec celebrities while crew roving through the audience sport angel wings. I've even caught a few glimpses of a disturbingly retrograde xenophobia in Québécois

Taras Grescoe. *Tivi* Nation. *Saturday Night* 114(6), July/August, 1999. 68-75.

comedy. On this year's "Bye Bye," Radio-Canada's hugely popular New Year's Eve count-down show, host Daniel Lemire showed a picture of rosy-cheeked Micmac leader Ronald Jacques and snickered: "You only have to look at his nose to understand that the monsieur likes his firewater . . . ," to which the well-dressed studio audience responded with delight. Some English Canadians might have laughed at such a quip, too. If they were fans of "The Wayne and Shuster Show." And it was still 1972.

Even more surprising to an English Canadian, perhaps, is that in my few months of casual channel hopping I've seen more bare breasts in mainstream mini-series—and more pubic hair and writhing buttocks in such nightly dubbed porn shows as "Aphrodisia" and "Phantasmes"—than I've seen in a couple of decades of watching European art-house cinema. Québécois television is comically, exaggeratedly hot. In leading series like "Omertà" and "Caserne 24," you can usually count on a fairly explicit sexual encounter, of the nipple-and-buttocks variety, every couple of episodes.

It's especially striking for a society where, a generation ago, one of the highlights of the programming week was the service broadcast from Notre-Dame Basilica. In Quebec, it's a cliché of pop sociology to claim that Catholicism has been replaced by everything from dam-building and major-league hockey to New Age cults and separatist politics. Television, though, has a better-than-average claim to being a surrogate church: in the vast social vacuum left by the absence of such highly programmed rituals as weekly Mass, saint's day processions, and confession, *tivi* offers a gathering place that reinforces shared values through comforting, serialized morality tales.

Quebec's love affair with communications technology started early, and continued untrammelled into the television age. The nation's first radio licence was issued to Montreal's Canadian Marconi Co. in 1919, and XWA became one of the first stations in the world to offer regular, scheduled broadcasts. CBFT, Canada's first television station, went on the air in Montreal in 1952, and by 1960, nine out of ten Quebec households had plugged in a television set, compared with only eight of ten in English Canada.

According to former *La Presse* editor and UN ambassador Gérard Pelletier, French-speaking television instantly galvanized the people of Quebec. "The emergence of television in 1952—for me, that was our cultural revolution," he told journalist Pierre Godin in the early eighties. "It was an extraordinary magnet. The cinemas in Montreal emptied out completely. The theatre almost perished, at least to begin with. People stayed home! We couldn't even keep up meetings of associations—nobody came. It was a massive social phenomenon. While English Canadians were being lured away from homegrown programming by "The Jackie Gleason Show" and "Amos and Andy," Radio-Canada's domestic productions attracted huge audiences from the start. Transmitting only nine hours a day for much of the fifties, Radio-Canada mustered audiences of 1.5 million for "La soiree du Hockey," in which "the blessed Sainte-Flanelle"—the unbeatable Montreal Canadiens—turned the Stanley Cup parade into a regular civic event.

Quebec *tivi*'s most original creation, the *téléroman* (literally, the television novel), has no exact counterpart in world television. Generally centred on a single extended family, the *téléroman* is neither a soap opera nor a sitcom: unlike those never-ending sagas, "General Hospital" and "Melrose Place," the *téléroman* eventually comes to an end. Nor are they neatly resolved half-hour episodes, like "Leave It to Beaver" or "The Brady Bunch." Communications scholars say the closest equivalents in world television have been "Peyton Place," "Coronation Street," and the overwrought family sagas of the Brazilian *telenovelas*.

The prototypical *téléroman*, the one that introduced Canada to the archetypal modern Québécois family, was "La famille Plouffe", by the novelist Roger Lemelin. In the third season opener in 1955, Lemelin, dapper and devilish in a thin-lapelled suit and striped tie, a lighted cigarette between his fingers, tells us that Madame Plouffe—a roly-poly woman perpetually fussing about her children—and her husband have moved into the second-floor apartment of a classic Montreal triplex. Their daughter Cécile—the image of the strong-willed, if somewhat neurotic, urban wife—lives below with her bus-driver husband. Monsieur Plouffe, an ineffectual, overalled busybody perpetually playing with his tools, has set up a plumbing shop with his burly son Napoléon in the basement. The show is full of tiny dramas: the frugal Cécile wants to rent a room in her apartment ("sixty dollars a month and no dogs!"); Napoléon puts on a suit and proposes marriage to his girlfriend; and the family mounts an ingenious periscope-like pipe on the wall so that they can communicate with Cécile in the kitchen below. Ovide, the natty intellectual son, pulls out a deck of cards and announces that he's joined a bridge dub. An interkitchen shouting match develops after Cécile is called a tomboy by Napoléon, who finally drops a glass of water down the pipe to shut her up. Then everyone calms down, and the credits roll as the family shares a basket of grapes at the kitchen table.

And so it went, for a total of 194 episodes, little half-hour dramas in which nothing much happened—slowly. But for the people of Quebec, "La famille Plouffe" was a revelation: it was as if the glass-and-metal box in their living room was actually a picture window into the kitchen of the family next door. Anglophone families were also charmed by the Plouffes; an English-language version broadcast live on the CBC on Friday evenings until 1958, using the same actors, eventually built a loyal following in English Canada, where people delighted in the actors' big accents. "Many of the actors in 'The Plouffes' didn't speak English" points out Jean-Pierre Desaulniers, a professor of the anthropology of communications at the Université du Québec à Montréal, "including Amanda Alarie, the actress who played Madame Plouffe. They had to write her lines on the floor for her, and she'd read them without understanding a word. But she remembered the context because she'd performed the same material in French the day before."

Professor Desaulniers lives in a tastefully renovated home in a row of three-storey Montreal townhouses, any one of which could serve as the set for a modern revival of "La famille Plouffe." He sees a parallel between the recent history of Quebec and the fates of the Plouffe children. "Ovide is the intellectual," he says, using the corner of a Camel package to point to a cast photo. "He ends up being a top-ranking civil servant in Quebec City. Cécile's obsession is money. She eventually dies, but not before becoming rich. Napoléon, the young entrepreneur, is a plumber who starts his own company. And Guillaume, the hockey player, goes into public relations. The four pillars of the Quiet Revolution—political ideology, feminism, small business, and communications—are all present in the children of the Plouffes."

All this might sound like the over-analysis of pop academia (we are, after all, talking about a bunch of TV shows, the filler between ads for Vachon Snack Cakes and Volkswagens) if it weren't for the popularity and frequent high quality of Quebec's television. "When Lord Durham wrote in his famous report [in 1839] that we were a people without literature," Desaulniers says, "it was true! This was a society of peasants." Up until the 1940s, the history of fiction in Quebec was a rather barren one, punctuated by the occasional earnest historical novel celebrating "la race" and "le sang" But French Canadians had long had a reputation as impassioned storytellers—"*gens de parole*," people of the spoken word, as songwriter Gilles Vigneault put it—with a taste and talent for the tall tale. Such nineteenth-century oral traditions slid seamlessly into the electronic media of the twentieth century. It's not a huge leap, after all, from spending a night around the stove in the *cabane* listening to Grandfather's entertaining lies, and gathering around the *tivi* in a 5 1/2-room apartment to watch the follies of the family down the street.

From the start, Quebec's was a television not of the director, but of the *auteur*, and some of French Canada's most talented novelists and playwrights tried their hand at the *téléroman*. Victor-Levy Beaulieu is the author of fifty-four books, including an important biography of Victor Hugo. Described by *La Presse* columnist Pierre Foglia as "Quebec's greatest living author," Beaulieu writes stylistically sophisticated family epics, whose recurring characters recall the social portraiture of Balzac's "La Comedie humaine." Here's the plot of "L'heritage," his *téléroman*, which Radio-Canada ran for three seasons in the late eighties: in a small town north of Quebec City, a rural patriarch named Xavier Galarneau has an incestuous relationship with his daughter Miriam, who then flees to Montreal to have their child. Fifteen years later, Miriam returns to inherit the family farm from her dying father, who has cut her brother—his first son—out of the will. No moralizing, no easy answers, and definitely no "Days of Our Lives": a *téléroman* by Victor-Levy Beaulieu is to the standard soap opera what "Oedipus Rex" is to *Jurassic Park*.

Contacted at his home in Trois-Pistoles, Beaulieu isn't surprised to hear that many English Canadian intellectuals would consider television an inherently minor form. "It's a phenomenon that doesn't exist in English Canada—I can't imagine Margaret Atwood writing a series for television, for example. I think English Canadians subscribe more to the traditional myth of the author as a man or woman exclusively of books. It's the same in France: if you ask a French author to write a television drama, he's likely to say, 'Write *feuilletons* for the *télé*?'"—Beaulieu imitates the fluty tones of a Parisian bourgeois shocked at the mention of TV serials—"'Who do you take me for? *Voyons, donc!*' I'm more on the side of Jean-Paul Sartre, who said that the writer should occupy all available fields of discourse—including radio and television."

Beaulieu acknowledges that more pragmatic forces are at work as well. "There aren't many authors in Quebec who really make a living from their pens. It's such a tiny market." The author of even a moderately successful *téléroman*, on the other hand, can not only earn $5,000 for a half-hour episode, but also reach at least a million compatriots every week. "The *téléroman* contributed to making Quebec a kind of homogeneous whole," argues Beaulieu. "We now share the same spirit, the same speech, the same hopes, the same pains. For me, the *téléroman* has filled the same space that the works of Alexandre Dumas and Balzac did in the nineteenth century. In the final analysis, television has given us a grand period in our popular literature, like the literary *feuilletons* of the last century."

Beaulieu recalls a fellow named Galarneau from Montreal, who showed up at his door demanding to be introduced to the incestuous family in "L'heritage" with whom he shared the same last name. "I'd chosen the name because there was no Galarneau family in Trois-Pistoles," says Beaulieu. "He told me that the family in the *téléroman* resembled his, and insisted on meeting them. What's more, he was dressed in a cowboy hat and a leather jacket, exactly like the character Galarneau Junior! It took me three days to convince him that it was pure fiction."

Although some people in Quebec may occasionally have trouble sorting out fiction and reality, local programs should not be lumped in with such notorious low-culture icons as Jos. Louis snack cakes, Mitsou, and Mad Dog Vachon. Ambitious series such as "Omertà" and

"Paparazzi" have cost up to $900 000 an episode, and some are as self-conscious about form as any episode of "Twin Peaks" or "Ally McBeal." Nowhere is this *fin-de-siècle* spirit better captured than in "La petite vie," an often hilarious situation comedy—even its reruns consistently attracted two million viewers this year—that acts like a postmodern catalogue of a half-century of *téléroman* cliches.

The absurdly idyllic opening sequence, which shows the dysfunctional Paré family emerging from the orifices of their brick triplex, is played out to a tinkling piano line based on the theme for a trite seventies *téléroman*, "Rue des Pignons." As in "La famille Plouffe," most of the action takes place in the kitchen, a Day-Glo nightmare of polka-dot curtains and chrome furniture. The bearded patriarch of the clan, Popa, played by the show's creator, Claude Meunier, takes Monsieur Plouffe's love for his tools to an absurd limit, using an obsession with the latest in garbage-bag technology as a way to avoid all physical contact with his wife. (Fittingly, last year's launch party for Meunier's best-selling book about the world of "La petite vie" was held not in a bookstore, but in a Canadian Tire outlet.) The frustrated Moman, played by male actor Serge Theriault—perpetually clad in slippers and a housecoat—sublimates her stymied sex drive by whipping up dishes such as a lard turkey stuffed with Smarties. It's as if the white-trash family from "Married . . . with Children" had taken an immersion course in *joual* and sublet the Plouffes' townhouse in the east end of Montreal.

The Paré family is defiantly lower middle-class, xenophobic, and utterly indifferent to anything besides lottery tickets, recipes for *pâté chinois* (a kind of shepherd's pie with corn), and its tiny world of perpetual squabbles. Disgusted to learn that their prize in a sweepstakes is an all-expenses-paid voyage to Hong Kong, Moman and Popa trade it in for 100 trips to Plattsburgh, a New York state border town a forty-five-minute drive from Montreal. "La petite vie" is ultimately a celebration of self-satisfied parochialism, a send-up of all the pettiness, jealousy, and mean-spirited backbiting of a world of limited horizons—the "small life" of the show's title. Sure, Meunier is saying, Quebec can be *quétaine*, a little trite and kitschy. But then, who asked you anyway, you *maudit* bloke?

Richard Martineau, editor of the Montreal cultural weekly *Voir*, is the first person I've talked to who sounds a trifle exasperated with the local obsession with *tivi*. "Everybody talks about television. It's what keeps us together. We've replaced the church with the state, the myth of sovereignty, and the television."

In his late thirties, Martineau, dressed in loafers and a Chevignon bomber jacket, is often cast as the Generation X iconoclast to baby-boomer nationalist intellectuals like Jacques Godbout and Pierre Falardeau. He is notorious for his vitriolic columns, in which he has been known to lay into local group-think and upbraid his compatriots "for constantly suckling at the three nipples of Québécois popular culture: Celine [Dion], "La p'tite vie," and impersonation." Columns that have incited readers to send him parcels filled with human excrement, among other things.

Impatient as Martineau can sound with the limits of local pop culture, he's no elitist. Having grown up in the West Island neighbourhood of Verdun, where anglophone factory workers lived alongside working-class French, he remembers seeing his grandfather getting dressed up in a suit and tie to watch television, and politely replying *"Bonsoir, monsieur,"* when the newscaster addressed the camera. Martineau's 1993 book *Pour en finir avec les ennemis de la télévision* is an attack on intellectuals who use the medium as a scapegoat for all of society's ills. But he's notoriously impatient with nationalists who suggest that he should confine his interests to Quebec culture and television.

"Historical series like 'Les filles de Caleb' and 'Marguerite Volant' took us back to the time when everyone was white and spoke French, where there was the mother, the father, and the thirteen kids," he says. "The good old days. In reality, Quebec is exploding out-wards—there are people who speak different languages, lots of different ethnic groups. We want immigrants to change, to integrate, to become like us—as in, 'He may be Chinese, but he plays hockey like a Québécois.' When we watch television, we're reassured because it takes us back to the old face of Quebec, when it was more homogeneous, more closed. I think we're insecure about globalization in Quebec. People say that I'm too individualistic, too cosmopolitan, that I've lost my roots." Martineau shrugs. "But that's basically my generation. We don't know if we're European, we don't know if we're North American. We're split between French and English. I think this is so great! For a long time we saw this as a weakness, but I think it's Quebec's greatest strength. The future will belong to people who have various identities."

Television, like many aspects of Quebec society, is at a crucial point in its development, teetering between protectionist parochialism and a new generation's attraction to other cultures and outside influences. In the meantime, unfortunately, *la vie* in *la belle province* can continue to feel a little *petite*. Martineau and I part on rue Saint-Denis, but on my way back home, I'm waylaid by a camera crew for the cable network Canal Vie outside the Le Chateau clothing store at rue Rachel. The interviewer wants to know: *"Est-ce que t'aimes dire des cochonneries quand tu fais l'amour?"* In other words: do I like to talk dirty when I make love? I tell him *les cochonneries* are for *les cochons*—dirty talk is for dirty swine—which provokes a chuckle, and seems to provide a couple of seconds of sustenance for the local glass teat. Tonight, I realize as I walk away, I'll probably be seen on a couple of hundred thousand screens across Quebec, cast as the uptight Anglo in a series of man-in-the-street interviews.

Maybe I should feel flattered. After all, it means even my electrons can become part of the spectacle in Quebec. Like it or not, I've finally become absorbed by that comforting blue glow.

DISCUSSION QUESTIONS

1. Large corporations donate considerable funds to public television. Do you think that these businesses influence the content of programming on public television as a result?

2. Visit the Friends of Canadian Broadcasting Web site and do an analysis of their position on Canadian media.

3. Do an analysis of your own viewing habits. How much Canadian programming do you watch? Do you watch public or private Canadian stations?

4. Compare Watson's plan for a reinvented CBC to Grescoe's description of television in Quebec.

 **WEBLINKS**

TVO
www.tvo.org/TVOntario/TVOntario.html

TV Network Links
www.cgocable.net/cabletv/tvlinks.html

Friends of Canadian Broadcasting
friendscb.org/

CBC mandate
cbc.radio-canada.ca/htmen/1_2.htm

CBC Facts
cbc.radio-canada.ca/htmen/1_1.htm

Canadian Film: Not Coming to a Theatre Near You

INTRODUCTION

The discussion around the mission and value of Canadian movies has often been very rancorous. No other Canadian art form, with the possible exception of Canadian television, has been so hotly debated by critics, both academic and popular. Moreover, there has been a peculiar lack of connection between the critics and the audience in this debate. Many Canadian film critics are cultural nationalists who see Canadian cinema as a key component in the development and maintenance of a Canadian identity. However, Canadian audiences, outside of large urban centres, have traditionally had little access to Canadian movies, either because these movies never get shown in their local movie houses, or because they think, along with many other Canadians, that Canadian movies are inferior to the American product because they lack "action," powerful heroes, and flashy production values.

The first article in this chapter sets out the major issues in the economic and cultural aspects of Canadian moviemaking, noting that 97 percent of the films shown in Canada originate from outside Canada (most come from the U.S.), while only 3 percent are made in Canada. This article also adopts the model, derived from the *Massey Report* of 1951, that Canadian media and cultural production generally are essential to the maintenance of a Canadian identity.

The Pevere/Dymond article rejects the notion that Canadian directors should make "Hollywood-like" films when Hollywood does it so much better—and with so much more money. Citing the disastrous "tax shelter" years, they discuss the limited benefits that Canadian cinema gained by allowing investors to use movie-making as a form of income tax reduction.

Noreen Golfman lauds Federal Heritage Minister Sheila Copps for threatening to guarantee Canadian films exhibition in Canadian cinemas. She also argues that those who argue for bigger budget Canadian films have got it wrong. Why fund empty films like *Titanic* when we can distribute our tax money more widely to encourage new talent and regional filmmaking—as well as well-known Canadian filmmakers like Atom Egoyan? Big films are not necessarily good films. Arguing that Canadian films have always been made for adults, Golfman wants to take the chance that Canadians might grow to like Canadian cinema if only we can wean them off the Hollywood product.

Other Canadian critics have argued for alternative forms of cinema that express very Canadian views of the world—however that Canadian view is to be defined. An academic version of this important debate, sparked by an article entitled "The cinema we need," by Canadian avant-garde filmmaker Bruce Elder, can be found in Douglas Fetherling's *Documents in Canadian Film*. This passionate debate influenced the discussion of Canadian cinema, even among mainstream newspaper critics, for at least a decade after its publication.

CANADA AT THE MOVIES: MOVIES, CULTURE AND NATIONAL IDENTITY*

When filmgoers think of movies, they usually think of Hollywood. Canadians have for years enjoyed and supported American films, accepting the images, themes, and stories these films had to present. In 1922, one of Hollywood's pioneer producers, Lewis Selznick, was asked about the prospects of a feature film industry in Canada. He remarked: "If Canadian stories are worthwhile making into films, American companies will be sent into Canada to make them." In fact, between 1910 and the late 1950s, Hollywood companies made more than 500 feature films about Canada. That's about ten times the number of feature films that Canadians made about themselves. Ironically, most of Hollywood's "Canadian" films were shot on the backlots of Hollywood studios or in the California countryside. Their portrayal of Canadian life was stereotypical. In these films, Canada was basically about "moose and Mounties." There were no cities in Hollywood's Canada and little industry. Canada was a wild outback, sparsely populated by prospectors, lumberjacks, fur traders, and Indians. And, of course, there was always snow, snow, and more snow.

From the beginning, the Canadian film industry has lived in the shadow of Hollywood. By 1930 feature films were the most successful form of popular entertainment. At that time, virtually all of the movies shown in Canadian theatres were movies from someplace else—some from France and Britain, most from the United States.

Gradually, over the course of the last 60 years, Canada has developed its own film industry. However, even today less than five percent of the movies seen by Canadians, are made by Canadians. Why is this the case? Does it matter that Canadians mostly watch films from other countries, and especially from Hollywood? What steps have been taken to offset the influence that foreign films have on Canadian culture? To answer these questions we

---

*Centre for Canadian Studies, Mount Allison University/Canadian Heritage. "Canada at the movies: Movies, culture and national identity."

must explore the relationship between feature film (and other forms of popular culture) and the development of national identity. Also, we must understand something about the ways in which popular culture is made and marketed in modern societies.

MOVIES, CULTURE, AND NATIONAL IDENTITY

When we think of feature films (or television for that matter), we tend to think of them only as entertainment. Movies are something that we watch when we want to relax, to unwind, and to escape from the routines of daily life. But feature films and television do more than entertain. They provide us with ideas and images about the world around us. Social scientists who study the mass media—everything from newspapers and magazines, to feature films and television—have concluded that movies help form and transmit society's most important beliefs, attitudes, and values. Consequently, the culture of a society—its key ideas and practices—is in large part a product of the messages conveyed by the mass media. Movies (and the mass media in general) teach as they entertain and thus help to create the culture that makes us Canadian.

Since the 1920s, Canadians have been concerned about the flood of foreign mass media that washes over Canada's borders. And it is a flood. . . . Canadians spend an enormous amount of time reading foreign magazines and books, listening to foreign music, and watching foreign movies and television programing. These media forms transmit and often transfer culture. For example, the fashions worn, the music heard, the expressions used in films, if experienced often enough may be adopted by audiences for whom these behaviours are not the norm. Similarly, media presentations that readily depict different values or beliefs may alter the viewpoints and practices of those who consume them; they may even change their culture. Some commentators have suggested that Canadian culture—at least as portrayed in the media—is an "invisible culture." Certainly, one has to look rather hard to find it.

In 1951, one of the first government-sponsored inquiries into the many facets of culture and the mass media argued vehemently that the very survival of the nation was in jeopardy. The authors of the *Massey Report*, as it was called, believed that culture is the glue that holds society together. Culture gives us our sense of identity, both as individuals and as members of a group. Without a common culture, without at least a basic set of common beliefs and ways of doing things, there could be no orderly discussion, and people couldn't live together.

The report warned of an "American invasion by film, radio, and periodicals" that threatened to "stifle rather than stimulate our own creative efforts." In its review of the feature film industry, the *Massey Report* concluded that "Hollywood refashions us in its own image." According to the Report, without a common, "home-grown" culture, nurtured and supported by all elements of the mass media, Canadians would lose any strong sense of what it meant to be Canadian.

The Government Steps In

The *Massey Report* said that government needed to step in to encourage the growth of Canadian culture. Government should intervene not to restrict the inflow of foreign cultural goods (such as movies), but rather to increase the supply of Canadian cultural goods. This would give Canadians a choice: the opportunity to decide for themselves whether they were interested in a culture and a mass media with significant Canadian content.

Over time, Canadian governments have developed a variety of ways of supporting Canadian culture. In some cases, as (for example) the Canadian Broadcasting Corporation (CBC), Radio Canada or TV Ontario, governments own large institutions that are designed to provide significant amounts of Canadian culture. In other cases, Canadian governments have designed laws and regulations that require private companies, such as CTV, Global, or other private broadcasters to air a minimum amount of Canadian content. Finally, federal and provincial governments provide a whole variety of grants, loans, subsidies, and tax incentives to encourage the production of Canadian culture.

In each case the logic is the same. Without government support, the number of Canadian films, records and television shows would be much lower than it already is. As a result, Canadians would have little or no access to images and ideas that offer reflection and commentary on Canadian life.

The Business of Culture

If Canadian culture is so important to the health and survival of Canada as a nation, why isn't there more of it? Why is government support for Canadian cultural activities necessary? To answer that question, we need to understand two things. First, movies, magazines, newspapers and television are business ventures in which a lot of money is at stake. Second, the economic forces that affect the mass media do not favour the production of Canadian culture. Hollywood is one of the best examples of the business of making contemporary culture. Hollywood movies are expensive to produce. The average budget for a Hollywood film is currently just over $20 million. So-called "blockbusters" cost many times more (*True Lies*, for example, cost close to $100 million). Though Hollywood films are by far the most expensively produced films in the world, feature film-making everywhere is a relatively costly undertaking. The average budget for a Canadian feature film, by contrast, is roughly $3 million.

Given the high production costs, the major Hollywood studios (such as Paramount, Warner Bros., Twentieth-Century Fox, and Disney) spend an enormous amount of money and energy marketing their films. Hollywood "stars" are a very important part of this process; their lavish salaries reflect the fact that their names help draw people to a particular film. In an attempt to guarantee financial success, the Hollywood studios also operate on a worldwide basis. Their goal is simple: to ensure that their movies are seen by as many people as possible around the world. The large American marketplace provides a solid base for the Hollywood studios. They can recover most of their investment at home; sales in other countries typically represent extra profits. In pursuit of these profits, the Hollywood studios are very aggressive. In Canada, for example, the studios sign deals with the large theatre chains—Cineplex-Odeon and Famous Players—to ensure that their movies dominate theatres' screen-time. A similar arrangement exists with the major video distributors and retailers, such as Blockbuster. To get copies of the popular American films, theatre owners and video shops must agree to these deals.

As a result of Hollywood's control over the marketplace for films in Canada, most of the revenues from ticket sales and video rentals flow south of the border. The money that Canadians spend on feature films in Canada goes to the production of more films—in Hollywood. Given these business arrangements and the economic clout of Hollywood, Canadian films have a hard time competing successfully in the marketplace without some form of government assistance.

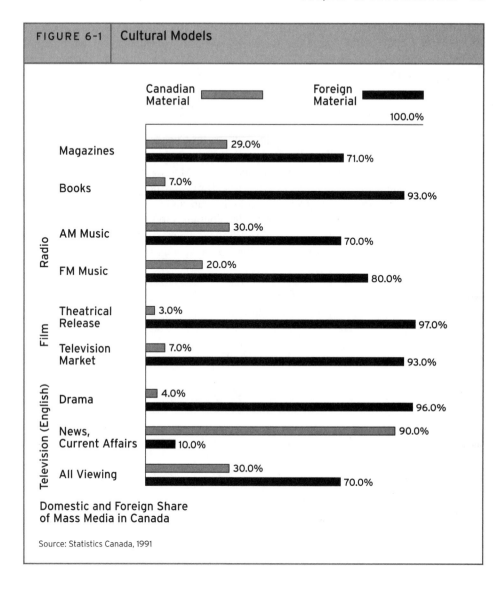

FIGURE 6-1 | **Cultural Models**

Canadian Material   Foreign Material

100.0%

Magazines
29.0%
71.0%

Books
7.0%
93.0%

Radio

AM Music
30.0%
70.0%

FM Music
20.0%
80.0%

Film

Theatrical Release
3.0%
97.0%

Television Market
7.0%
93.0%

Television (English)

Drama
4.0%
96.0%

News, Current Affairs
90.0%
10.0%

All Viewing
30.0%
70.0%

Domestic and Foreign Share of Mass Media in Canada

Source: Statistics Canada, 1991

A similar situation exists in the market for television programs. Programs produced in the United States, at enormous expense, are sold to Canadian broadcasters at a fraction of their cost. For example, a one hour episode of "Beverly Hills 90210" costs about $1 million. It is sold to Canadian broadcasters for about $50 000. Even if similar Canadian programs cost only $500 000 to produce, it is easy to see why Canadian broadcasters would generally prefer to buy American programs than make their own. . . .

Only about four percent of the dramatic programing on Canadian television is Canadian. This figure, however, is not a true measure of the popularity of Canadian drama among viewers (in fact, audience surveys show that Canadians watch Canadian drama in respectable numbers). Instead, it reflects the economics of television and the relatively high cost of producing

Canadian versus buying American programing. Therefore, the Canadian government regulates Canadian television to ensure that broadcasters spend more money on Canadian programing than they would otherwise. The government also provides loans and tax incentives that total close to $100 million a year to help defray the costs of producing Canadian drama.

New Initiatives for Survival

Early efforts to establish a feature film industry in Canada met with little success. Canadian-produced feature films, few and far between, could not compete successfully against films from the United States, Britain, and France. Moreover, Canadian theatre owners were quite content to exhibit foreign films. These films were cheap to rent and Canadian audiences soon developed a strong attachment to the stars and stories from elsewhere.

Ironically, a pattern emerged in the 1920s that continues to this day. Many Canadians who established successful careers in feature films (directors, screenwriters, and actors) moved south of the border and worked in Hollywood. Directors such as Ivan Reitman and

TABLE 6-1	Genie Award Winners
	Best Canadian Film
Year	Film
1980	The Changeling
1981	Les Bons Debarras
1982	Ticket to Heaven
1983	The Grey Fox
1984	The Terry Fox Story
1985	The Bay Boy
1986	My American Cousin
1987	The Decline of the American Empire
1988	Un Zoo, la Nuit
1989	Dead Ringers
1990	Jesus of Montreal
1991	Black Robe
1992	Naked Lunch
1993	Thirty-two Short Films About Glenn Gould
1994	Exotica
1995	Le Confessionnal
1996	Lilies-Les Feluettes
1997	The Sweet Hereafter
1998	The Red Violin
1999	Sunshine
2000	Maelström

Source: Association of Canadian Cinema and Television

Norman Jewison, and actors such as Martin Short, Jim Carrey, and John Candy are some of the more recent examples of a trend that started with the success of silent film star Mary Pickford. A cynic might conclude that there has always been a successful Canadian film industry, it just happens to be in Los Angeles.

The Canadian government has been involved in the film industry since the end of the First World War. In those early days, the government used films to promote immigration and investment in Canada. In 1939, the Canadian government established the National Film Board of Canada (NFB). During the Second World War, the NFB was primarily engaged in the production of propaganda films to support the war effort. But the NFB had also been given a special mandate. It was told to make films that would "interpret Canada to Canadians." Over the last 60 years, the NFB has done just that. Quickly, it became a world leader in the production of documentary, animation, and experimental films. It has been a pioneer in the development of new film techniques and equipment.

While the NFB's productions have won numerous international awards, including several Oscars, they have done little to solve the problem posed by the dominance of foreign films in Canada. NFB films have never been widely exhibited in movie theatres (with the exception of NFB's wartime propaganda films). Moreover, in its first two decades, the NFB stayed away from producing feature length films that might offer Canadians an alternative to Hollywood.

Not until the creation of the Canadian Film Development Corporation (CFDC) in 1968 did a Canadian feature film industry begin to emerge. The CFDC was given a budget of $10 million (about the cost of three Hollywood movies at the time) and a mandate to provide grants and loans to private Canadian feature film producers. In its first 10 years, the CFDC funded a number of critically acclaimed but commercially unsuccessful movies. *Goin' Down the Road*, a film about two young men from Newfoundland who move to Toronto in search of jobs and a better way of life, was one that many Canadians could relate to. *Mon Oncle Antoine*, a gritty and romantic film about the tensions between English- and French-Canadians in a small Quebec mining town, expressed a theme relevant to Quebeckers. Films such as these revealed a Canada seldom seen in Canadian theatres; to watch these movies is to learn something about the unique dimensions of Canadian life.

Since 1968, the CFDC, (which is now know as Telefilm Canada), has provided funds to more than 500 Canadian films. Telefilm's annual budget for feature films is in excess of $21 million. In 1993–4 Telefilm invested in the production of 26 movies, including Atom Egoyan's *Exotica*, the 1994 Genie Award winner for best film. Have you seen it? Probably not.

Unfortunately, most Canadians have seen only a handful of the Canadian movies produced during the last 25 years. As Claude Jutra, one of Canada's most noted directors, once said: "Not making the films you want to make is awful, but making them and not having them shown is worse." In the 1970s, Canadian movie theatres effectively discriminated against Canadian-made films by continuing to align themselves with the major Hollywood studios.

The Canadian government has attempted repeatedly to create some space for the exhibition of Canadian films, but each time its efforts have been thwarted by the combined economic clout of the Hollywood studios and Canadian theatre chains. Video stores have done little to improve the situation. Canadian films are not widely available or prominently displayed. They are treated, in many respects, like foreign films—of interest only to a very small and specialized audience.

Women and the Movies

One of the most important characteristics of the Canadian film industry is that it offers an alternative to the themes and styles that dominate Hollywood movies. To make this point, let's look at how women are depicted in Canadian as opposed to Hollywood movies. One of the most popular styles of moviemaking in Hollywood is the action-adventure movie. In films such as *Die Hard*, *Lethal Weapon* and *True Lies*, the heroes are strong and crafty men, who seem to know how to work every weapon and technical gadget that has ever been invented. The women in these films are typically depicted as meek and helpless. They need to be saved or protected; they are rarely capable of doing much to help themselves.

TABLE 6-2   A Sample of Recent Canadian Films about Women
Better Than Chocolate
Stardom
Emport Moi
Kissed
Lulu
Deux Seconde
Shadow-Maker: Gwendolyn MacEwen, Poet

Another recent trend in Hollywood movies is known as the sexual-thriller, films such as *Fatal Attraction*, *Basic Instinct*, or *Body of Evidence*. In each of these movies, single women are depicted as a threat to men and, in some cases, to the nuclear family. The lesson in these movies is that the "modern woman" can be dangerous, conniving, even psychotic. To say the least, the depiction of women in Hollywood's action-adventures or sexual-thrillers is not very flattering.

Canadian films provide us with a much more sensitive and reflective depiction of what it means to be a woman in the modern world. In 1974, the National Film Board established Studio D, a special unit devoted to the production of films about women by women. Over the next 15 years, Studio D produced an exceptional array of mostly short films and documentaries that focus on women's issues, including sexual abuse, stereotyping in the media, and employment equity. In 1984, Studio D produced a series of films on child abuse entitled *Feeling Yes Feeling No*. The series was widely praised by social agencies, schools, and parents and it became the largest selling item in the NFB's history.

Outside Studio D, a number of Canadian women have been given the opportunity to write and direct feature films. They have produced a stunningly rich array of films that reflect upon the lives and the histories of Canadian women. Cynthia Scott's *The Company of Strangers* chronicles the coming together of seven elderly women stranded in a typical Canadian landscape. Patricia Rozema's *I've Heard the Mermaids Singing* parodies the competition among women in the world of work. These movies and others like them portray women grappling with the real problems and challenges of living in the second half of the twentieth century.

Seeing Canada in the Movies

Unlike their Hollywood counterparts, few of the characters (male or female) in Canadian films display the qualities so characteristic of Hollywood's leading actors. Instead, Canadian films have focused more on relatively ordinary people trying to cope with the trials and tribulations of everyday life. Generally speaking, Canadian films are not as fast-paced as Hollywood movies, and for some people they are not as much "fun." But that is also their strength.

Canadian films tell the story of Canadians, their lives and their histories. In a land as vast as Canada, we need some way to understand and celebrate our rich diversity. Canadian films give us a sense of the various ethnicities and regions that make this country. Vancouverites can see something of life in a Newfoundland fishing village; a child living near the Rockies can witness the majestic St. Lawrence River as it flows by Quebec City; Nova Scotians can learn about life on the prairies; Torontonians can come to appreciate the history and ongoing struggles of Canada's Native peoples.

The government of Canada remains committed to providing financial support for the production of Canadian movies. They think it is money well spent. The Canadian film industry has become an important component of Canada's economy. In the long run, however, the biggest benefits are more cultural than economic in nature. Without Canadian movies, we would lose one of the most effective ways by which we can explore and make our own culture.

GO BOOM FALL DOWN: THE TAX-SHELTER FILM FOLLIES

Geoff Pevere and Greig Dymond *(Mondo Canuck: A Canadian Pop Culture Odyssey)*

In 1979, a record 66 feature films were made in Canada with the benefit of government support. *Sixty-six*. Bear in mind that a scant five years earlier, that number was three (!) and that in per capita terms this meant that Canada, a country with one-tenth the population of the U.S., had outstripped Hollywood's rate of production, if only for one year, by a staggering 50 percent. If these statistics tax one's credibility, they should, because you probably didn't see any of the films (most of them were never deemed of sufficient quality to be released), nor would your memory likely be jarred by the invocation of some of that stellar year's titles. Anybody remember *Meat the Cleaver*? *Crunch*? How about *Under the Cover Cops*? Oh, come on, certainly you've seen *Read On*? *Hog Wild*? Not even *Mondo Strip*? Really?

Nineteen seventy-nine was the peak year of a period in Canadian movie production variously characterized as the Tax Shelter Boom, the Capital Cost Allowance Era and, possibly most poignantly, the time of Hollywood North. Whatever you call it, it is a cautionary tale of distinctly Canadian dimensions. From that vaguely satanic 66 peak, the number would plummet significantly after two years (less than half that by 1983), once the industry and the government that supported it realized that the annual production of dozens of films that no one wanted to release, let alone watch, could hardly be pointed to as a source of cultural health or pride.

As much as one might be inclined to bury the period's memory in much the same manner as the period buried the movies it produced, the national folly that was Hollywood North

Geoff Pevere and Greig Dymond. Go boom fall down: The tax-shelter film follies. In *Mondo Canuck: A Canadian Pop Culture Odyssey*, pp. 214–217. Scarborough, Ont.: Prentice Hall Canada, 1996. (Reprinted with permission of Prentice Hall Canada Inc.)

cannot be forgotten, and for these reasons: first, because it reveals much about the inevitable schizophrenia that grips a country trying to produce commercial culture according to bureaucratic blueprints; second, because it stands as a particularly abject example of what tends to happen when Canadians attempt to be just like Americans, except without the history, money, population, promotional savvy or market base; and third, because it is a national farce of truly riveting dimensions. While it's fitting that the period almost inspired a movie of its own—called *Hollywood North*—it's even more fitting that the script was never actually produced.

To understand how it happened, one must recognize the historically dependent relationship Canadian movies have always had to forms of public support. Ever since the national movie marketplace was largely consumed by American interests early in the century, thus laying the groundwork for the development of Hollywood's most lucrative out-of-country market, the only way Canadians could indulge the enormously expensive practice of making moving images was by begging government for money to do it. Indeed, there may be no more important fact in the history of Canadian movie-making than this. It is what has made the greatest achievements in the national cinema possible—from Norman McLaren to Atom Egoyan, from animation to documentary, from Ivan Reitman to David Cronenberg, all that is noteworthy about Canadian movies was made possible through some form of government intervention in the industry. On the other hand, not only do governments (and government film policies) change like intemperate weather, they have proven notoriously reluctant to do anything that might upset the Washington-backed mega-industry to the south. If anything explains the frequent flights from reason taken by subsequent national film policies, it's this contradictory impulse to promote our own culture while not impeding that of the big guy to the south. Thus the fact that less than three percent of the national screen time in Canada is given over to Canadian movies. Thus the history of talented Canadian filmmakers who have had to move elsewhere to make movies. Thus Hollywood North.

The story of the tax-shelter boom really begins with the opening of the doors of the Canadian Film Development Corporation (CFDC, renamed Telefilm Canada) in 1967. The result of four decades of lobbying for some kind of government support to private-sector feature production, the founding of the CFDC is widely considered to represent the beginning of the feature industry in Canada. The problem was, the process of funding always took place in a supply-and-demand vacuum; that is, the CFDC could help get movies made, but it could—or would—do little to get them into more Canadian theatres. And every time someone suggested it ought to do so, through the introduction of policies that friends of Hollywood still like to demonize as "protectionism," the notion was usually beaten flatter than a seal pup on an ice floe.

By the early seventies, the government agency was, as ever, seeking ways to boost private-sector film investment and production without disturbing the status quo. That's when someone suggested tax shelters: the dubious practice of offering tax write-offs for investments in productions the government would designate as "certifiably Canadian." The shelter was called the Capital Cost Allowance, and its early results were sluggish. However, things tended to pick up as the government raised the ceiling on the shelter, finally offering a full 100 percent write-off for investors in movies meeting a bureaucratic checklist of Canadian ingredients. This is when things started to go boom.

Attracted by the low-risk investment shelter, a veritable stampede of investors started forklifting money into Canadian production: between 1974 and 1978, the number of certified Canadian productions assisted by the government rose from three to 37. The problem was, investments were (as they tend to be, Virginia) as often dictated by greed, opportunism and cynicism as they were a passionate commitment to the development of a distinct and vibrant Canadian film industry.

A host of producers from around the world flocked to Canada to cash in on the bonanza by making movies that were Canadian only in the checklist sense. As they were usually the result of doctors, lawyers, dentists and other upper-income professionals less concerned with art than a tax dodge, a number of commercially, not to mention culturally, hopeless productions were rushed into production which otherwise would rightly never have seen the light of script development. ("*Meat the Cleaver*? No prob: roll 'em!") Moreover, since the point-system process necessary to certify a production as Canadian was about as simple as astrophysics, a huge proportion of the budgets were sucked up by the various brokers, agents, lawyers and dealmakers who assembled packages for a living.

Sensitive to the enormous public expense of the tax-shelter production enterprise, while at the same time hamstrung when it came to doing anything about a commercial marketplace happily screening Hollywood movies for contented Canadian audiences, the CFDC started to invoke concepts like star systems, universal appeal and commercial competition as the justification for its if-you-can't-beat-'em-join-'em policies. The reasoning was as simple as it was mistaken: if we couldn't get our Distinctly Canadian movies into the marketplace, we'd make the kind of expensive, slick, culturally defoliated movies that would bring the marketplace to us. Of such logic was the yellow brick road to a vibrant national film industry theoretically paved.

To counter this rising cost of tax-shelter productions, producers, with the full endorsement of the CFDC, sought to make movies they thought would be surefire bets on the international marketplace. In many cases, this meant churning out movies that were paler-than-pale imitations of whatever genre—slasher films, science-fiction fantasy, disco— was hot at the moment. It meant a lot of Canadian-made movies pretending to take place in other, more universally appealing (read "American") places than Toronto or Vancouver, but it also meant making movies with stars who had international appeal. This was a tricky one, as no one making movies in Canada could really afford stars with international appeal (and especially not if lawyers and investment brokers had already made off with a major chunk of one's budget); much dimmer celestial entities would have to do.

To look down the cast lists for Hollywood North productions is to glimpse a roll call of the once-weres, might-have-beens and whatever-happened-tos of American movies and TV: James Coburn, Richard Burton, John Cassavetes, Lee Majors, Elliott Gould, Suzanne Somers, Robert Mitchum, Karen Black, Tatum O'Neal, Sally Kellerman, Bruce Dern—all worked in Hollywood North at least once, none in anything that turns up prominently on their résumés.

Tax-shelter productions also meant the virtual strangulation of the once-vibrant Quebec industry, as the language of universal appeal is English, not French. If many of the province's most gifted filmmakers, like Jean Pierre Lefebvre, Gilles Carle and Denys Arcand, simply went without work, others, like Claude Jutra, went to English Canada to make movies, with disastrous results. Needless to say, it was not a moment likely to fill the heart with national pride.

In retrospect, the tax-shelter system was not without its benefits. The fact is, the careers of David Cronenberg and Ivan Reitman were kick-started by the tax-shelter-production boom, and the sheer volume of movies made transformed Canada from a production backwater to a seasoned pro almost overnight. Some of the country's most successful export items, like 1979's *Meatballs* and 1981's *Porky's*, were tax-shelter productions, and people like Dan Aykroyd, Saul Rubinek, John Candy, Andrea Martin and Bill Murray all got their movie starts in Hollywood North productions. Moreover, the rare good tax-shelter movie did actually come along, like Bob Clark's *Black Christmas*, Daryl Duke's *The Silent Partner* and Louis Malle's *Atlantic City*. Not to mention all those great made-in-Canada George Kennedy movies.

By the early eighties, recognizing that it had helped make an international joke of the national film industry by facilitating the production of hundreds of lousy schlock movies, the government drastically reduced the tax shelter. The intention was to discourage what few investors hadn't already flocked elsewhere for fear of catching the stink of too many unreleased clinkers. People like Lee Majors, who even had a widely publicized fling with Canadian prima ballerina Karen Kain while filming some forgotten epic in Toronto, were returned to the televisual semi-obscurity from whence they came, and it was business as usual in over 90 percent of Canadian movie theatres, where American movies played to eager Canadian audiences who continued to live quite happily with the real thing, and without Canadian movies, Hollywood-slick or otherwise. Like a dream that fades with wakening, the false glitter of Hollywood North retreated to one of the darker corners of national memory.

WATCH WHAT YOU WISH FOR

Noreen Golfman *(Canadian Forum)*

Now is the winter of our Canadian content. Federal Heritage Minister Sheila Copps's recently calculated declarations about the need to guarantee exhibition of Canadian films in Canadian theatres immediately roused the queasy sensation that comes from having a long held wish finally granted. As countless Hollywood films have ceaselessly demonstrated, bearing the weight of a fantasy is far easier and more pleasurable than managing the matter of its materialization. What, after all, do you do with your wish when it is granted? Living up to its promise is so very hard to do. Even Canada's preeminent cinematic moralist, Atom Egoyan, disappointingly remarked that Copps's threats to overhaul the nation's film policy could lead to a backlash against enforced routing of the public's theatrical taste. This is the kind of cautious hey-now-wait-a-minute reaction we might be surprised to hear from someone like Egoyan, long an advocate of state-supported industry, but a reaction nonetheless that many Central Canadians probably share. Too bad. Copps should be encouraged to repeat her wish-list, if more forcefully. Moreover, heroic nationalist entrepreneur Robert Lantos of Alliance should speak for more than a few blocks on Yonge Street when he observes that the exhibition of Canadian films isn't really the problem, but that the marketing of his films is. Lantos, if you're listening, you need to get out more.

For the record, only about three *percent* of the films watched by Canadians are actually Canadian, a figure so pathetic you'd be inclined to make the whole matter a campaign issue for the Rhinoceros Party. Making sense of why this is so usually leads to the invocation of a holy trinity of problems Canadian movies, particularly in English Canada, are always already doomed by: limited distribution, small budgets and depressing themes. Ostensibly, too few Canadians watch low-budget films about suffering and death. The inverse proposition is that wider national exhibition, larger budgets and happier endings would draw larger Canadian audiences to Canadian theatres. In other words, if James Cameron had stayed in

Noreen Golfman. Watch what you wish for. *Canadian Forum* 76(868), April, 1998. 27-28.

Niagara Falls and badgered Telefilm into floating him a few gazillion dollars to make *Titanic*, we would have had more Canadians watching a Canadian movie than there are life rafts in the world. And anyone who tries to argue that *Titanic* is as sombre as *The Sweet Hereafter* does not understand the difference between an iceberg and an icy pond. *Titanic* is, in the final analysis, all American: a grandly spectacular melodrama morphed from an enormous tragedy, a sentimental hymn to hubris, as immodest in its ambitious nostalgia as *Gone with the Wind*. We are speaking here of tragedy for dummies.

Is this what we really want? More money for kitschier productions about grandly superficial themes? Surely the flag-happy Can-content-boosting federal minister doesn't intend to encourage big boys and model boats in overscaled bathtubs, just to ensure that we get the crowds queuing up to buy buckets of rancid popcorn in theatres near us. Perhaps we would all take a firmer position on the whole matter if Copps were clearer about what she does want, or thinks we need, and perhaps if she were resolute about her willingness to resist the arrogantly asinine declarations of Motion Picture Association of America bouncer Jack Valenti, a man clearly suffering from having grown up on an excess of Victor Mature movies. Indeed, we might then all be galvanized to take up a position that had some conviction, encouraged by more than thickly coated ambiguities about our national film policy. It is sometimes difficult to discern what Copps is trying to say when her caucus fellows cut the production studios at the National Film Board and choke the life out of the public broadcaster. But I've come here to encourage Copps, not to dissuade her.

First, it needs to be said that Canadian films do require wider distribution, and let's talk primarily about distribution in this country, before we start dreaming about European markets. *The Sweet Hereafter* might as well have joined the choirs eternal, because you can't watch this award-winning feature in most places in the country at any time. If Robert Lantos is happy that this Alliance film is being exhibited sufficiently, he should drop his spring vacation plans and take a national tour right now, courtesy of one of those Air Canada planes he rightly bullied into showing Canadian features. He ought to see directly for himself what is and what is not playing at the local Canadian Famous Players or Cineplex Canada or Empire theatrical venue, and then fire his management teams. The *Titanic* is sinking on almost every large screen in this country and probably will continue to do so long after all the Oscar tickets have been recycled into nacho cartons. If Copps means what she says, and if she means wider exhibition, she should say so loudly enough to burst Valenti's eardrums.

Second, bigger budgets for Canadian films would be pretty, but if we think size matters, we are never going to dismantle the master's marketing machines. The country's film industry needs support, not necessarily concentrated power in the hands of a few critically tested directors, courtesy of Telefilm or some ultimately elitist production fund. One implied consequence of Copps's announcement is that a sizeable film production fund would pass sizeable bucks into the hands of a mere few, thereby cutting down on the number of productions a year and resulting in blockbuster-budget spectacles. It is hard to see an Egoyan, a McDonald, or even a Cronenberg buying into that notion, especially at the expense of their own talent, let alone at the expense of developing film-makers or currently thriving regional centres of production. Nonetheless, an argument circulating in too many well-carpeted towers in this country is that production money is being unwisely deployed in the service of too many low budget—that is, unglamorous—efforts. Our firm view on this should be let's fund as many of the country's creative artists as we can, encourage diversity of genre and expression and inspire expatriate Canadians and other egomaniacs to launch, sink and soak the *Titanic* somewhere else.

Third, the matter of those depressing themes. Well, so what? Anyone can do melodrama or broad comedy or special effects for overfed audiences crawling from a six-hour-a-day television habit to a movie house. If Canadians aren't watching Canadian films, either they can't see them at their local theatres or they are utterly unfamiliar with and menaced by anything but Hollywood product. Canadian films have always been made for adults, so no wonder they are often as gloomy and enigmatic as a doomed yellow school bus. If we do not have enough adults in this country willing to watch Canadian features, then we should stop worrying about the whole business of audience altogether and promptly take charge. Copps is right. Just keep showing the stuff. And if Canadians won't eventually turn out to watch Canadian films, well, let's take away their voting rights, revoke their medical insurance and tax them for film production. I mean it. The whole tired matter needs some strategic enforcement, not just tax rebates for American co-productions. In view of free market ideology, a country full of near-empty theatres defiantly projecting Canadian films is about as irrational an idea as denying *Titanic* an Oscar. So let's do it.

DISCUSSION QUESTIONS

1. Should the Canadian government restrict the number of foreign films shown in Canadian movie houses by quotas or taxation?

2. Look at your own viewing habits. How often do you see Canadian films? How many of the films listed in the three articles have you seen, or had the opportunity to see?

3. How important is Canadian cultural production to the development and maintenance of a Canadian identity?

4. Two of the articles make assumptions about "Canadian character" and Canadian artistic traditions. Discuss the validity of these assumptions.

5. Can *Titanic* be considered a Canadian film?

 ## WEBLINKS

Telefilm Canada
www.telefilm.gc.ca/

Canadian Feature Film Policy
www.pch.gc.ca/culture/library/filmpol/econtent.htm

The National Film Board of Canada
www.onf.ca/E/index.html

The Film Studies Association of Canada
www.film.queensu.ca/FSAC/Home.html

Canada at the Movies
www.pch.gc.ca/csp-pec/english/about/movies/index.htm

chapter seven

Canadian Notes:
Singing a Different Tune

INTRODUCTION

From government to musicians, distributors, radio stations, and fans, everyone has something to say about Canadian popular music. One thing that is clear is that there is no industry that has been more affected by the new digital technologies than the music industry. Martin Melhuish has written an essay about the issues confronting the increasingly successful Canadian music business. His concerns range from the impact of download sites like Napster on intellectual property rights to the revolutionary changes in marketing and management that the new distribution systems will create. All of this is set against the background of the tremendous growth of the Canadian industry, from its international superstars to very popular homebased talent.

Chris Wood concentrates upon the impact of the "free" download sites on artists and the music business. He begins with the plusses for new bands who can distribute their music on the Web and help themselves to establish a fan base. Once well-known, however, the very same musicians can lose a small fortune to illegal downloads. He goes on to discuss the attempts of the recording companies to control Internet downloads through regulation, and also through developing their own delivery systems on the Net.

Samir Gandesha comes at the music industry from an entirely different perspective. A night at a punk concert in Vancouver in the 80s prompts him to think over the history of punk music and what it meant to its musicians and fans. Noting the vast difference between Canadian and British punk, Gandesha argues that British punk had a potentially revolutionary impact during its short lifespan. By turning culture back upon itself through its "shock" tactics, punk stood for a "ruthless criticism of all that exists." Unabashedly commercial, British punk mocked itself and the commercialization of the music industry with albums like the Sex Pistols' *Flogging a Dead Horse*. Ganesha finds Canadian punk, created in a far different culture, far less political and multicultural than the British version.

For further discussion of the place of rock and roll in North American Culture, see *We Gotta Get Out of This Place: Popular conservatism and postmodern culture,* by Lawrence Grossberg (New York: Routledge, 1992).

CANADIAN MUSIC BIZ OVERVIEW

Martin Melhuish *(Canadian Musician)*

When you look back at the past two decades of the Canadian music industry, you can't help being impressed with how far we've come and how much things have changed in that relatively short period of time. Some of the major transformations came from exterior forces, like the introduction of the CD in the '80s, and the BDS and SoundScan systems, which accurately track the airplay and sales of records, in the '90s, but for the most part, we have not done badly in taking care of our own business in this country.

The introduction of Canadian Content regulations for radio had an enormous impact on the industry here, as did the advent of video and the subsequent merger of sight and sound, pioneered in this country, in the late '70s, by an ambitious—for its time—program The New Music, which evolved to video networks like CHUM's MuchMusic, MusiquePlus, Bravo, MusiMax and MuchMoreMusic, and Shaw's CMT Canada.

The Foundation to Assist Canadian Talent On Record (FACTOR) was launched in 1982 with the voluntary support of broadcast sponsors. Since that time, FACTOR has distributed more than $25 million in loans and awards for projects which, over the years, have sold more than 18 million copies worldwide and generated more than $348 million in sales. Similar successes have been racked up by FACTOR's counterpart, MusicAction, in a Quebec market that has sustained its own star system, celebrated by the ADISQ Awards each year, and that traditionally sells more records per capita than most countries on the planet.

The world is now on a first name basis with our stars—Celine, Alanis, Shania, Bryan and Sarah—and, yes, for the most part they're women. (Heck, even a couple of our biggest guy-groups are Ladies—Barenaked or Our Lady Peace!) It's a trend that's carried over to the Canadian music business, where women now hold some of the most important positions in the industry. Prominent at the top of any powerbroker list in the Canadian music biz are Lisa Zbitnew of BMG Music Canada, the first woman to hold the post of president at a major label in Canada; Denise Donlon, the former VP/GM of MuchMusic and MuchMore Music and now president of Sony Music Canada; Laura Bartlett, the Canadian head of the Zomba Record Group (Britney Spears, Backstreet Boys); Daisy Falle, president of the Canadian Academy of Recording Arts & Sciences (CARAS); Heather Ostertag, executive director of FACTOR; and Sheila Hamilton, executive director of the Canadian Country Music Association (CCMA).

Martin Melhuish. The business. *Canadian Musician* 21(2), March/April, 1999. (20th Anniversary Issue), 67–80. (This piece is an updated version of "The business," originally published in *Canadian Musician*'s 20th Anniversary.)

There has been another major change in the industry over the last two decades. Once accused of being Torontocentric, the playing field in the Canadian music business has tilted somewhat in the direction of the West Coast where manager Bruce Allen (Bryan Adams, Anne Murray), manager/record exec Terry McBride (Sarah McLachlan, Barenaked Ladies) and manager/booking agency mogul, Sam Feldman (Joni Mitchell, Diana Krall) all call Vancouver home.

Oh, yeah, and remember that, "Disco is dead" pronouncement back in the early '80s? It's just plain old dance music now with a zillion different categories, but the rumours of its death had been greatly exaggerated. You need look no further than MuchMusic's "Electric Circus," the offspring of the '70s Citytv show "Boogie," to check the pulse. And isn't that Canada's own Deborah Cox consistently at the top of the international R&B charts?

So, the good news we bring is that the industry as a whole is still relatively healthy after all these years, though not without the frequent migraine headache.

Perhaps one prominent industry executive gave the most honest answer to the question of how things had changed in the Canadian music industry over the past two decades: "My hair's a lot grayer, I know that!" came the reply. And, if you're in the business of creating or selling music or protecting artists' intellectual property rights these days, chances are you've taken more than one longing glance at a bottle of Grecian Formula.

It's a pivotal moment in time for the music business, which is still trying to come to grips with the enormous impact that the digital age is having on the way that music is distributed and the ramifications of the new technologies and Web music providers like Napster and MP3 that have made it easy for the public to access, without payment, their favourite tunes. What was once known as bootlegging, these days, goes by the moniker of digital piracy and a recent conservative estimate by the Software Alliance of America suggests that it's costing the industry more than $4 billion a year and rising at an alarming rate.

CD Recordable technology has been available since 1988. In the early days, the recorder with associated hardware and software could set you back around $100 000. Today, you can pick up a recorder for $300. And, if you're not sure of how to download music from the Net, there are tutorials available to show you how to Rip [another way of saying Digital Audio Extraction] a track from a CD, transform it in an mp3 file and make a stereo-ready CD out of former mp3 files. You can also get legal advice, which generally concludes that there is nothing illegal about Ripping a track if it's for your own personal use.

"The concerns are that you've essentially got a vehicle that can produce almost CD quality downloads in a very high compression," says Brian Robertson, president of the Canadian Recording Industry Association (CRIA).

> I saw some figures the other day which indicate that the *Encyclopedia Britannica* can be downloaded in 30 minutes, so you can imagine an album would take just a few minutes. Then you have the development of hardware like the MPMan and the Diamond Rio, which are little hand-held players that are half the size of a Walkman, that can hold anywhere from 15 minutes to three hours of CD-quality music downloaded from a computer without paying. Of course, you've also got CD copying machines on the market, with which you put your pre-recorded CD in one side and your CD Recordable in the other and you've made yourself a nice little master-quality recording.
>
> At the moment, you've got tens of thousands of legitimate sound recordings, almost all the hits, up there, unauthorized that you can download for nothing. Obviously, this is cause for great concern for the record companies. There's a lot of independent product there legitimately, because they're using it for promotional purposes, but certainly the commercial stuff is absolutely, entirely vulnerable, and that's a huge problem.

Acknowledging that the industry continues to straggle behind new technologies instead of getting out in front and heading off potential problems, Robertson indicates that there is a new international initiative underway to try and stem the tide of anarchy in the music sector of Cyberspace. "It's known as SDMI—the Secure Digital Music Initiative—and it involves the five major record companies; IFPI, which is the international organization; America Online; AT&T; IBM; Microsoft; and hardware manufacturers, Matsushita, Sony and Toshiba," relates Robertson. "It's the first time that the service providers, record companies and hardware manufacturers have got together to speak with one voice. The aim is to establish a secure system for sound recordings on the Net. It's a watermark system, which will allow all the copyright information to be imbedded with a security device to prevent copying." (Updates at www.sdmi.org)

But even promising solutions need to be well-considered says Jim Griffin at OneHouse LLC, an entertainment technology consultancy firm, in an article he wrote for Album Rock Network. His warning is ominous: "All copy protection efforts are predicated on the eradication of the CD, and it might be even wiser to remember the old admonition that we should be careful what we wish for."

Griffin's comment calls to mind Nicholas Negroponte's keynote speech to a riveted industry crowd at The Record Music Industry Conference in 1993 in which he suggested, in part, that the days of record sales and video rentals are numbered. Negroponte, the founder/director of the M.I.T. Media Lab, contended that in a digital age, they are no longer in the record or broadcast business but rather they're in the bit radiation business and that will change everything:

> I'm not going to endear myself to too many [record] people in this room because packaged media is your primary delivery medium today but, I promise you, when you have this meeting 10 years from now, it will be, by far, your least significant and, in many cases, absolutely trivial. If I throw a lot of CDs in a shopping cart and push that shopping cart home, as it goes through my door, literally thousands of gigabytes per second have just entered my house, so it looks real efficient today. In the future, that will not be true, as the signal is distributed through fibre optics, and by other means. Packaged media's days are numbered.

If you carry Negroponte's logic to the next step, record companies are destined to become nothing more than administrators of intellectual property, which itself is facing a cataclysmic future.

"Changes in copyright over the next few years are going to be phenomenal," warned Negroponte. "If anybody tells you that being digital is not going to effect the copyright process, they're either lying or stupid, or both."

Brian Chater, president of the Canadian Independent Record Production Association (CIRPA), is neither a prevaricator nor anybody's fool when it comes to copyright matters. He's been on the frontlines of the battle for copyright protection and other matters of vital interest to the Canadian independent sector for longer than he's willing to recall, and the struggle continues:

> Not to sound depressing, but we've just moved and I was going through a lot of old files and Earl Rosen's [Chater's predecessor] stuff from 1982, that I could have written today, with a few minor changes. On the other hand, a lot of things have happened for the good. We have a lot more industry funding than we ever had before—the FACTOR/MusicAction money, which we lobbied for and got. We had an increase in CanCon (to 35 percent) and there were the intellectual property laws in 1998 and 1997 that we fought years for, which has done, and will do, the industry a lot of good. And, of course, there's the tape levy, which is another source of revenue and more money in the hands of the creators and their companies.

Acknowledging that the industry has made progress on neighbouring rights for performing artists and producers and a home taping levy over the past two decades, Robertson has been dismayed by the public's attitude to the latter:

> The only thing the public understands is their own self-interest; that they are going to have to pay more for blank recording media. I've done a whole bunch of phone-in shows and interviews and the level of selfishness is unbelievable. They don't care about ripping off the artists. They feel that they are entitled to this music and its abhorrent to them that they have to pay anything in terms of blank recording media. That fight was a 20 year-plus fight. The neighbouring rights battle started just before 1979 and has culminated with some degree of success now. The home taping fight started in the '80s.

Given the above, there may never be a better time to educate the public on intellectual property rights as they apply to home taping and access to music on the Internet. Writing in the Album Rock Network, Charly Prevost, that publication's former VP of Retail who is now an executive with Liquid Audio in New York, urged the industry to develop a strategy to educate music fans about copyright laws and suggested that perhaps one of the simplest and most direct ways to do it is to involve the artists. "No one has more at stake than the artistic community, and once solicited, this support will surely be forthcoming," contended Prevost.

Chater reckons that given the amount of money and resources CIRPA has had to work with over the years, they haven't done badly. "It's just that every time you turn around, you're fighting a lot of the same battles almost interminably and other ones, which are old battles in new clothes," Chater laments:

> You can see the new one coming up in the so-called Phase Three of copyright when you're talking about the users on the Internet. We want to make sure that we get exclusive rights of usage in all the stuff to do with Internet delivery and the whole electronic future. But, you think the broadcasters are bad, talk to Bill Gates and his friends: "You want us to pay? Here's a million dollars, now, piss off!"

This right of remuneration, Chater suggests, only works in a collective sense and is unlikely to work in the real world that we will be entering in 10 years time.

> There will be one-on-one availability, in other words, we're going to charge you 26 cents to use this, or 32 cents to use that, and it will be like a phone call almost; there's a billing per second involved. You can't do it yet, but it will come to that as sure as eggs are eggs. If you don't have exclusive rights, you are, as they say in the legal trade, "truly fucked!"

On the question of record companies ultimately becoming the administrator of rights, Brian Robertson and Brian Chater have a slightly differing view. Robertson feels that you'll never replace the retail experience:

> The Net is going to grab a piece of the market, but I don't think it will necessarily erode it. You go into a retail store and they have limited shelf space, so maybe they've got 1000 titles, but you've got 100 000 on the Net; you've got the whole catalogue there. You've got unlimited choice, sophisticated graphics, background stuff and you'll be able to sample the music. There will be a lot more opportunities to buy music than most people ever knew existed or that you could ever find in a store. But, I think it will enhance the business rather than erode it.

Chater tends to agree with Negroponte's comments but doesn't think it will impact for another decade. "You can see that with Internet shopping," comments Chater.

I saw in the paper today that Amazon.com increased their sales by some ridiculous figure, like 250 percent in the last quarter, and they're probably going to lose more money. There was another piece that I was reading in which the writer said that it was probably easier to go down to the local store and buy a book than to buy it on the Internet. We're going to have CDs and DVDs for the next 10 years before we see the turn over.

But, according to Robertson, there is a silver-lining to this cloud for canny musicians:

Certainly, the influence of digital has been remarkable in terms of the impact that it's had and continues to have. From an artist's perspective, the new developments in digital recording techniques are so far ahead of what they were in terms of what you can do with creating a first class master tape now. You can do it in your living room. Emerging artists are not anchored to a studio or anchored to those investments that they have to make to get into a studio. The ability to get to a master is better than it has ever been.

Since the late '60s, the radio and record industries have been at each others throats in this country where the words "radio" and "regulation" have almost become synonymous. The much-despised—by most broadcasters—30 percent Canadian content regulations were recently jacked up to 35 percent and now there's a Neighbouring Rights tariff to deal with. You'll get split opinions from broadcasters on the CanCon regs and across the board unanimity on new payments to artists and producers that they find neither right nor neighbourly.

One of Canada's top radio programmers, Doug Pringle, has seen both sides of the artist/radio equation. Back in the late '60s, Pringle was signed to Marc Bolan's record label in England as a recording artist and a songwriter. He eventually moved to Montreal, where he co-founded CHOM-FM as its first on-air announcer. He became a consultant to radio stations across the country in 1979 and now works as director of programming at RAWLCO Communications with whom he put stations like CISS-FM, Toronto, CKIS, Calgary. CJMJ, Ottawa and NCN – the New Country Network (now CMT Canada) on the air.

"The new 35 percent CanCon regulation is a good thing," says Pringle surprisingly.

I've always been for CanCon regs and I'm all for cultural regulation. You can argue forever about whether one should or shouldn't legislate taste or culture, but when you live next to America, it's necessary. I think a lot of the countries in the world are finding that, even across the Atlantic Ocean, you're still living next to America. If they can't take you over by force of arms, they'll conquer the world culturally and we, obviously, are, by far, the most vulnerable. The CanCon regs have been great for Canadian artists, but having said that, I don't think it has made any difference at all to the naturally world-class artist. They would have happened with or without CanCon, but there's a whole middle-ground of Canadian artists who are fabulous Canadian acts and CanCon has helped to ensure that they get the airplay that allows them to become the stars that they have become in Canada and, in many cases, nowhere else in the world. If that's the case, then you have to figure that there's something about the CanCon regs that have helped them.

To paraphrase one broadcaster's attitude to the Neighbouring Rights issue: "It's greedy." Broadcasters point to the fact that most research shows that by far the biggest factor in the sale of records is radio play which they feel has immense value and was not recognized in the debate on Neighbouring Rights.

The other side concedes that it will impact radio's bottom line but points out that that has been counteracted by the multiple ownership provisions that have now been granted broadcasters by the CRTC. It is not beyond imagination to believe that every single radio station in Canada will be owned by two different radio groups with the radio divisions of some proving to be tiny compared to their cable operations. Somewhere in the future, five or six companies will essentially own all the important radio stations in Canada.

"The biggest change in radio over the last two decades is in the actual execution," observes Pringle.

It was much less sophisticated and much less research-driven and, in many ways, more artistic-driven in the late '70s than it is today. We were living in a CRTC world of regulations which, in the case of FM radio, meant lots of foreground programming. For artists, that also meant there was lots of information and talk about them and their music, which was hugely beneficial to developing stars. One of the things we've lost with the demise of foreground programming is all the talk and all the backgrounding that makes the music we play on the radio three-dimensional. In terms of radio these days, it's tougher for an artist to get known than it was back then.

Of course, the advent of the video revolution of the early '80s picked up some of that slack and had people talking about the imminent demise of radio and its ability to impact on the careers of the artists whose records it was playing. But, video did not kill the radio star.

"What has been proven is that all video channels are essentially in the TV world and that's where they compete; they don't compete in the radio world," contends Pringle. "People think that because it's music then people make the choice to listen to it or watch it. In actual fact, people make a TV choice or a radio choice. If they make a TV choice, then the video channels are competing with "Seinfeld" in terms of people's viewing choice. Radio choices are made quite differently."

In many ways, radio and video have proven to be complimentary. Pringle agrees:

Video channels give a three-dimensional picture of an artist, which is hugely beneficial to new artists, although I think it hurts established artists, funny enough. One of the reasons why there aren't nearly as many superstars since the video age, is that I think video trivializes and overexposes artists, particularly artists that don't have quite enough talent to become superstars. If you want to be a one-hit wonder, then I think video is one of the best things that's ever happened to you. If you want to build a long career, then it's probably harder in the video age.

Over the past 20 years, television has become increasingly important, not only to individual artists, but also to the Canadian music industry as a whole. The CBC, which has a long history of providing invaluable exposure to developing artists in this country, first broadcast the Juno Awards in 1975. It was a modest affair during which singer/songwriter Ian Thomas quipped: "We owe this occasion to the CBC, and I'm sure they'd like to thank Alcan for the set." In 1979, Prime Minister Pierre Trudeau came to the show to help induct Hank Snow into the Canadian Music Hall Of Fame, and that was cause for considerable excitement. Today, the Junos celebrate in some of the biggest venues in Canada including Hamilton's Copps Coliseum and B.C. Place in Vancouver.

"The whole thing has grown so much," says Daisy Falle, president of the Canadian Academy Of Recording Arts & Sciences (CARAS), the organization that oversees the Juno Awards. "Back in those days, you were sitting around a table having dinner, and the awards followed. Now we've opened up the whole thing to the fans and the dinner is a gala reception beforehand, but even that's open to the public now.

The recognition factor and, of course, the talent base is huge now compared to what it was back in '79. We were scrambling to even get people to appear on the show. Now we're sitting around thinking, "How can we get a three-hour show out of the CBC?" The prime minister used to be a big thing. If he came, we used to say, "Oh, great! Now we've got a focal point." We relied heavily on the Hall Of Fame back in those early years to make a major impact. Now, we've outlawed politicians on the telecast. It's not their night. It's for the artists and it's getting more and more that way. I'm certainly pushing in that direction.

Brian Robertson, a former president of CARAS, figures that the Juno Awards helped an industry that was just beginning to mature in the '70s.

> In the early '70s, the music industry wasn't truly national. There were pockets of activity, but I don't think there was a true coast-to-coast industry. The Juno Awards helped this industry come together in all areas: artists, songwriters, record companies, retailers—everybody. It was quite a defining moment in our history when the Junos went to television. By the end of the '70s, we started to get it right a little bit and the audience grew. In 1979, I think the TV audience was 2.2 million. One of the things that has changed is the fragmentation of the ability to communicate because obviously back then, the CBC had a much larger market share than it has now and it was easier to get that kind of audience.

According to Falle, the Junos have reached critical mass as far as the number of categories, but every year the committee sits down and decides whether or not some of the categories should remain or be replaced. "We have 40 categories and only a two-hour show," explains Falle. "I don't see that we can go beyond that so we have to look at what we've got and see if each one is still relevant. We started out with a bunch of sales-based categories in country, classical and then jazz and now we cover so many different genres."

Television exposure has made a huge difference to the country music industry in Canada as well, given the past wide distribution of the CCMA Awards show, which was not only broadcast on CTV in Canada, but also on TNN: The Nashville Network across North America.

"The biggest change in country music is that it has become mainstream," states Sheila Hamilton, executive director of the Canadian Country Music Association (CCMA). "You could see that beginning to happen in the early '90s and, this past 10 years, it has really come into its own. The very first time that we really succeeded in holding Country Music Week as a business convention was in 1988 in Toronto."

> In a pro-active way, the best thing we did to help Canadian artists make the big jump to an international career—and certainly not the jump to the size of Shania Twain—was introducing ourselves to Nashville with our luncheons and showcases at the Country Radio Seminar (CRS). We did that from 1990 to 1995 and it legitimized us in the U.S. industry. It opened a lot of doors and proved to the people down there that there is a viable industry up here. Now we've got Shania and The Wilkinsons and so on. Would they have succeeded anyway? Certainly, because they're very good, but I think that the infrastructure was there to help them out. We helped managers and other people down there.
>
> Because of that networking and the contacts that we made, our awards show has been on TNN for the last few years, and was previously on CMT Europe. We recently managed to get on in the Pacific Rim in Australia and New Zealand.

And what of the musician's lot in an industry that has really adopted a do-it-yourself attitude over the last ten years? There's no doubt that the opportunities for learning abound. Music industry courses that cover every area of the business are on offer at institutions like the Trebas Institute, Fanshawe College and the Harris Institute For the Arts. There are a number of Canadian music industry directories available, so there's no excuse for not knowing where to go or who to call and over at the CCMA, they've even published a book, written by industry veteran Richard Flohil and titled *It's A Country Life*, which helps aspiring artists to avoid some of the major pitfalls that occur when the creative and business worlds collide.

There was an explosion of indie labels as the so-called alternative music scene flourished a number of years go, but few would have any meaningful or sustained success. "The problem is, you can make a very good buck vis-a-vis the Barenaked Ladies and others distributing your own stuff, but there comes a point where you can't go any further with it; you haven't got enough money," says Chater.

> The music business has become very much like the film business; you have to have a lot of bucks to play the game, and a lot of the time it won't work anyway. When I used to do this stuff, you could do a single and another single and, if they both worked, you'd do the album. Basically, your album was covered by the two singles, and you'd go and get reasonable advances from the U.S. and Europe. Now, if you don't invest three or four hundred grand on each project, nobody thinks you're serious. Do five of those and you've spent a couple of million dollars. You know what sort of house you can buy with that money?
>
> Generally, it has become a different ball game. I wrote a piece recently about getting serious structural funding in the industry. The reality with project funding is that you're always scrambling from A to B trying to pay the bills with the project money. What we want to see indies have access to is structural funding, so that you can operate a company rather than do projects.

On the major label front, the CRIA's Brian Robertson reveals that the investment in Canadian talent by the multi-nationals remains significant:

> They're now spending $40 million a year in Canadian Content production, which has escalated tremendously in the last ten years. They were always supportive and they always had tremendous relationships with independent labels through the distribution. Obviously, there's a recognition that there's a return on their investments, but it's a huge investment per year in Canadian music and Canadian artists and the resulting recordings.

Over at Toronto-based S.R.O. Management, the home of artists like Rush, The Tea Party, Matthew Good Band and Van Halen, among others, Pegi Cecconi laughs at the first reference point that comes to mind when asked her opinion on how the lot of the Canadian musician has changed, for the better or worse, over the past two decades. "That goes back to 1979, the year before Spirit Of Radio became a European hit for Rush. That's how I think. Rush is truly the soundtrack of my life.

> What has changed is that you could be a middle-class musician back then. You could work in clubs and make a living. You didn't have to have a big record deal; you were allowed to play covers. There were lots of venues because the drinking age was still pretty low at that point. Essentially, a musician could be a working musician and make a living without having to be a star. That's the main difference now. I don't think bands can make a living clubbing anymore. If they don't get their big deal, it's very hard to be a musician.
>
> There definitely has been a touring infrastructure built here in Canada. Evidence of that is Edgefest and what they did with Our Lady Peace. There is corporate money being put behind Canadian artists and that is putting bands on the road and allowing them to get paid.

And what has happened to the days when corporate sponsorship of rock 'n' roll in particular was considered uncool? "Well, the corporate thing happened in the early to mid-'80s, but it was unrespectable then," answers Cecconi.

> Now, it's virtually respectable. When you did deal with them, it was awful in those days, but then all of a sudden, Molson came up with The Blind Date and stuff that's really intriguing like, 'Wouldn't you like to go on a blind date?' It wasn't selling out so much because you didn't even know who the band was. When the corporate sponsors became creative and helpful in becoming part of the solution as opposed to a problem, it was a viable source of income and it has worked for a lot of groups.

Through good times and bad, new technologies and old, CIRPA's Brian Chater reckons there are some universal truths for aspiring artists always to remember:

> You go where the best deal is and where people are enthused about you. Someone has got to believe in the project, otherwise you're dead in the water. Talent will out most of the time, but I'd find the people who I felt most comfortable with, who seemed likely to spend some money on me, and roll the dice like everybody else.

FREE MUSIC

Chris Wood *(Maclean's)*

The crowd at Vancouver's venerable Commodore nightclub roars as the band on stage cracks out the opening chords of a rock anthem. Beneath its aural assault, "Leader of Men" is a song about self-doubt—an irony that eludes most in the audience. The four members of the group Nickelback don't mind. More important is the track's showing on the charts in the United States, where a potential breakout beckons for the B.C. band. But so does a discouraging new reality. Even as Nickelback's star is rising, so is a booming illicit trade in digital music files swapped over the Internet—featuring everyone from Celine Dion to the Backstreet Boys. For band guitarist Ryan Peake, growing fame is a two-edged sword: "The more you get known, the more people search for you on the Net. That's scary."

Scary or awesomely exciting, this is the new face of the record business. Music, digitally recorded for decades, is tailor-made for cyberspace. Once scrunched into a manageable-sized computer file using various compression techniques, anything from arias to zydeco can slide effortlessly across the Internet to consumers' ears, hard-drives, or a growing choice of portable digital music players. Stars—among them Canada's Sarah McLachlan and Alanis Morissette as well as Britain's David Bowie and America's Tom Petty—are using the Web to communicate with fans in novel ways. Up-and-comers like Nickelback and Newfoundlander Damhnait Doyle (whose second album was available free online for a limited time last month) use it to introduce themselves. The five giant corporations that control 80 percent of the global music industry—worth $60 billion annually—have taken notice. Edgar Bronfman Jr., who controls the world's biggest music company, Universal Music Group, told a business audience earlier this month: "Music and the Internet are truly a match made in heaven."

But the romance is bedevilled by the same characteristics that make music such a Net natural. In digital form, it can be duplicated in a few keystrokes. Since 1998, the popularity of the MP3 compression format (named after the standard-setting Motion Picture Experts Group)—and the wide availability of software to translate, or "rip," music from conventional compact discs into MP3 form—have fuelled an explosive illegal trade in pirated tracks. Between June, 1998, and June, 1999, traffic in music files over the Internet increased 20-fold, becoming "the single largest traffic component on the Web," according to Dermott O'Carroll, a vice-president of Toronto-based Rogers Cable Inc. "It's even bypassed porn."

Much of the credit for that dubious distinction goes to a young American. Shawn Fanning was 18 and at Boston's Northeastern University when he wrote a program called Napster last year. Available free from a Web site of the same name, it lets users troll the Internet for each

Chris Wood. Free music: Record companies face a huge challenge from the Internet, especially from digital pirates. *Maclean's* 113(12), March 20, 2000. 42–46.

other's collections of MP3s and download them. In one trial last week, Napster detected 6,890 collections around the Internet, with 804,802 music tracks available for download.

By far the largest concentration of such illicit archives is in North America—with many residing on large computers belonging to universities. Some are so massive they throttle other traffic. At the University of British Columbia, caches of MP3s are blamed for half a dozen disruptions in computer service this academic year, ranging from system crashes to e-mail that runs at a snail's pace. In addition to those who merely trade tunes for their own use, some entrepreneurial youths equipped with CD "burners"—the devices that copy files onto blank CDs—take orders for "custom CDs" of illegally downloaded music. The going price at one New Brunswick high school: $5, about a quarter of what a commercial CD costs when taxes are thrown in.

Dozens of commercial Internet sites offer other ways—most perfectly legal, others debatably so—to acquire music digitally. Streaming music, which plays directly over the Net through a computer's speakers, can include promotional releases from the likes of McLachlan or Bowie (consumers are not supposed to be able to save these on their own machines, but software is available to do so). Other songs are available by download to keep. Tunes by lesser-knowns are often free; those by established acts can cost from about 35 cents to $1.80 a track.

One Web music giant—San Diego-based MP3.com, whose shareholders include Canada's Morissette—has incurred almost as much wrath from the recording industry as Napster. It lets consumers choose from thousands of music tracks (mostly by unknowns) and have the songs burned into a CD, which is shipped to its buyer within 48 hours. Shoppers can also order regular CDs by established artists. So far, no problem. But according to the record industry, two other MP3.com services violate copyright law. One lets people who buy CDs listen immediately, rather than wait for the disc to arrive. Another lets them "upload" music from CDs they already own to MP3.com, where they can access the tracks later from any Internet connection. The Washington-based Recording Industry Association of America says the company illegally copied tens of thousands of popular CD titles onto its own computers, to avoid having to do so individually each time a consumer purchased or uploaded them. MP3.com insists it has done nothing wrong.

How badly all of this will harm musicians or the hugely profitable recording giants is a matter of intense debate. "I don't think there's any question artists are getting hurt," asserts Vancouver's Bruce Allen, who manages Bryan Adams and Martina McBride, among other stars. But, "Are we bleeding from the wrists and ankles?" says David Basskin, president of the Toronto-based Canadian Musical Reproduction Rights Agency, which represents Canadian music copyright holders: "I don't think so." Still, the stakes are escalating. Legal online music sales are running at $1 billion (U.S.) a year in the United States, says Bronfman, and will quadruple by 2004.

Those sales are mostly in conventional CDs. But the giants of the music business have not waited for the download bloodletting to become critical to respond. The RIAA has sued both MP3.com and Napster and launched a lobbying campaign to have universities and colleges block access to Napster on their networks. According to a Web site put up by students opposed to it, the RIAA's campaign has been successful at more than 130 campuses, including Ottawa's Carleton and the universities of Guelph and Western Ontario. Meanwhile, the Toronto-based Canadian Recording Industry Association sends up to 40 letters a week to the Internet service providers hosting illegal MP3 music sites, threatening legal action if the files are not removed from the Net. But the effect of such measures is questionable. The RIAA claims to have reduced the amount of illegal music on college sites by 10 percent, hardly a mortal blow to the digital pirates.

At the same time, the music majors have been working with consumer electronics manufacturers and software companies since 1998 to develop technical measures to foil illegal duplication. The first instalment of the Secure Digital Music Initiative was released last July. It applies only to digital music downloaded directly to computers or new-generation personal digital players like the Sony Music Clip or RCA Lyra. In essence a set of standards, SDMI requires record companies and electronics firms to use compression formats and hardware that limit users to making no more than four copies at a time of any protected track. "You can make convenience copies for yourself," says Larry Kenswil, president of Universal Music's eLabs. "You just can't copy at will for friends." A second phase of SDMI is supposed to make it harder to copy all new music tracks—including those on CDs—but work has just begun.

Still, all the major labels plan to begin delivering digital music directly to consumers during the course of this year. Some have already dipped their toes in the surf. GetMusic.com, a joint venture between Universal and Germany's BMG Entertainment offers music from both companies' catalogues for download. Warner Music Group (whose announced merger with Britain's EMI Group PLC is expected to create the world's biggest music company when complete) and Sony Music Entertainment sell music online through their jointly owned CDNow.com. Sony and EMI, meanwhile, are involved in a plan to install kiosks in U.S. music stores, where consumers will be able to download tracks directly into personal music players.

While the majors plot their cyber-debuts, individual artists, software makers and a handful of record labels are pioneering radical new ways to get music to fans. Cape Breton fiddler Natalie MacMaster recently performed two skirling medleys that were recorded and posted on the Web site of music retailer HMV, where e-buyers can download them for $2.99. Embedded codes ensure that only a credit-card holder with a Canadian address can download the music, and that it can no longer be downloaded once the offer expires.

The arrangement typifies the new role the Internet is playing in promoting performers. "It's become direct marketing right to your audience," says Nickelback manager Bryan Coleman. The Vancouver band's song "Leader of Men" has been downloaded tens of thousands of times, Coleman admits, without any return to the artists. But: "That's 30 000 or 40 000 kids that have heard at least one track off the album."

Until now, the Internet has been less successful at selling entire albums. Even David Bowie failed to move more than a few thousand copies of his CD *Hours*, when he initially made it available online from his own Web site (it was later released through conventional channels). One reason may be the long download time required for an entire CD over anything less than a high-speed connection.

But some visionaries believe the Internet's musical future lies closer to MacMaster's demonstration than Bowie's. Pollster Allan Gregg, who, with partners, sank $25 million last year into the creation of Canada's largest independent record company, Song Corp., predicts that in future the same downloadable music track may be sold at several different prices— with a lower tag entitling the buyer to fewer plays than a higher one. Software embedded in the music tracks will control how many times or for how long they can be played before reverting to digital dust. Universal's Bronfman foresees digital music streaming freely to wireless Internet receivers in automobiles where "you will be able to press a 'buy' button while listening to a song you like." Nearer the horizon are online subscription services, giving consumers access to vast libraries of music for varying monthly fees. "Pop music might be like basic cable, relatively cheap," suggests Universal's Kenswil. "But if you want the hottest hits of the day, it's going to cost more."

There may be other benefits for audiophiles. Kenswil predicts that future online fidelity will surpass CD quality. The lower cost of offering and selling digital files compared with plastic discs, moreover, holds promise for those with minority tastes such as bluegrass music, and fans of older artists dropped by their record labels. Competition from downloads (still less than one percent of all music sold) may even force down the cost of conventional CDs.

As e-music thrives, will bricks-and-mortar record stores perish? HMV Canada vice-president Andrew Pollock doesn't think so. "Retail," he insists, "still offers the experience of seeing the product and taking it home to hear it the very first time." And downloading, Pollock adds, will never become the social mainstay that store cruising is to mall-rats everywhere. But other industry players aren't so sure. "I find it difficult, in March, 2000, to think there won't be some physical exchange of goods," muses Deane Cameron, the president of EMI Music Canada. "I may have a different answer 10 years from now."

Much of the industry's optimism for legitimate online music sales depends on first defeating—or at least containing—the legions of Napster-inspired pirates. "If that doesn't get fixed," says Gregg, "all bets are off." And the fix is far from a foregone conclusion. Devices that limit what their owners can do with music stored on them "may work, they may not," suggests Eric Scheirer, a music researcher at the Massachusetts Institute of Technology's Media Lab. "They may not be acceptable to consumers." Experts already say there will be compatibility problems among the SDMI technologies used by different major labels: one player may not be able to handle them all. Then, too, the entire library of existing CDs, unprotected by SDMI, remains as vulnerable as ever.

Some critics applaud the potential shrivelling away of music giants they believe have too much control over artists. "The danger the Internet represents to the industry," says MIT's Scheirer, "is it gives artists new leverage to move away from labels and distribute their music in other ways." Up to a point, anyway. Vancouver's Allen, for one, agrees that e-music gives stars an extra card at contract time. "Established artists are going to say, 'You guys can have traditional distribution,'" he predicts, "'but we're going to withhold Internet distribution.'" But cross-town rival Terry McBride, who manages Sarah McLachlan, adds: "I laugh at the suggestion that MP3 was supposed to be a bonanza for young artists. You still have to promote, market and tour"—all activities that rely on record company expertise and bankrolls. If anything, argues Kenswil, "artists will need record companies more than ever, because they need to differentiate themselves on the Internet."

In the end, the marketplace will be the judge. And many in the music industry express the fervent—if unscientific—faith that most consumers will eventually agree to pay the piper when they call down the tune. "Once downloadable music is legally available, easy to use and not very expensive," says CRIA president Brian Robertson, "I think it's going to be quite attractive to those who are now stealing." Comparing the Napster phenomenon to the Seventies fad for dubbing to tape cassettes, HMV's Pollock notes: "When I was going to school, I taped albums. When I left, I stopped."

To the musicians of Nickelback, many of whose young fans are of prime Napstering age, the outcome is anything but academic. "I don't think people realize," says band member Peake, "that if they don't support the CDs and the bands they like, musicians won't be able to produce another album. They'll go broke." It is a riff other performers, managers and labels echo. But it has yet to catch on with legions of online music fans.

FLOWERS IN THE DUSTBIN, OR, REQUIEM FOR PUNK

Samir Gandesha *(Border/Lines Magazine)*

Sometime in the early 1980s I found myself at a gig by one of Vancouver's best, most infamous bands, DOA. The band's notoriety lay, amongst other things, in the homage it paid to Margaret Sinclair, former wife of Pierre Elliot Trudeau and consort to the Rolling Stones, by including her on an EP cover seated on the ground wearing a skirt, knees up to her chest, without any panties on. A parody of Rod Stewart's disco hit, "Do You Think I'm Sexy," the EP was entitled "Do You Wanna Fuck?" Before Joey Shithead and the rest of the band, including legendary bassist Wimpy Roy, formerly of the Subhumans, hit the stage of UBC's Sub Ballroom, I was accosted by a young punk who took exception to the t-shirt that I was wearing at the time. Pointing to the visage of Bob Marley on the front of it, he issued the following warning: "I'd be careful if I were you, Punks don't like Reggae." Disconcerted more by the punk's insouciant ignorance of music history than any evident danger in declaring divided musical loyalties, I continued on with the more serious business of getting another pint.

But the young punk's reaction to the appearance of a Reggae fan at the gig was not the exception but rather the rule in Canada. The notion that Punk and Reggae manifested divided loyalties owes to the manner in which Punk itself was so thoroughly commodified. To be sure, the band which started it all, the Sex Pistols, self-consciously made itself into the purest commodity, for instance, shamelessly issuing re-releases with titles like *Flogging a Dead Horse.* Nothing, however, was to top Malcolm McLaren's film, starring none other than that great outlaw Ronny Briggs, *The Great Rock 'n' Roll Swindle,* which offered a history of the Sex Pistols in the form of a sort of "twelve-step" program of instruction in generating "cash from chaos." Such self-commodification was also a parodic critique of the culture industry's ability to transform every oppositional, negative tendency in society into a profit. By the time of last year's "filthy lucre" tour, the joke had worn off. We already knew the punch line.

The experiences that Punk captured had to be "packaged" in order to be sold to kids in the US, Canada, Continental Europe, Japan, etc. It was necessarily detached from the particularity of those urban landscapes of abandoned factories as well as damp and decrepit council flats in which different classes and ethnic and racial communities jostled for position. Nonetheless, those milieus deeply penetrated the sensibility of the music. Owing to the specific nature of Canadian cities, there wasn't the same collision of cultures expressed in musical and subcultural forms. While the Canadian, particularly the once-thriving Vancouver Punk scene produced extraordinarily original bands such as DOA, the Subhumans, the Young Canadians, the Animal Slaves, the Modernettes, the Dirty Dishrags, the Viletones, Martha and the Muffins, and even a punk cowgirl—wearing cat's-eye glasses and invoking the ghost of Patsy Cline—named k.d. lang, it was not provoked in the same way by Black cultures that so decisively marked the British and, to a lesser extent, the New York scenes. What I want to suggest is that because of this encounter, contrary to its contemporary public image, Punk embodied a subterranean multiculturalism.

It was precisely because it was so thoroughly grounded in its own present that Punk's ethos was, to quote Neil Young, "It's better to burn out than to fade away." Which is to say, in its very attempt to glimpse the eternal in the moment, Punk signed its own death certificate. This is perhaps why, like Miles Davis's own judgment about Bebop, it is not possible to listen to Punk

Samir Gandesha. Flowers in the dustbin, or, requiem for punk. *Border/Lines Magazine* (45), 1997. 8-14.

anymore, at least not in the same way as we did in the late 1970s. Punk was stillborn as an aesthetic. In its declaration that "There's no future" Punk demanded that there be one. It could only reveal the world as a desiccated landscape by bathing it in the light of redemption.

But let us try to find the roots of Punk within the contradictions of the post-colonial city. Perhaps there is a structure of experience that Punk alighted upon that still might, twenty years later, have something to say to us. After all, if Punk is no longer around—ignoring what Iggy Pop calls the "middle-management music" of bands like Green Day and Social Distortion then certainly the social contradictions to which it bore witness undeniably are.

In contrast to the obsessive desire for the "safe," Punk sought out the dangerous, the risky, and the provocative which it found somewhere "beyond good and evil." Rather than establishing and maintaining rigid racial, sexual and other forms of identity, in its "ruthless criticism of all that exists," Punk actively broke down and reconstituted these identities in new and often imaginative constellations. In the process it sought to open itself up to the Other. For instance, in her adoption of the bondage and S/M gear so prevalent in the early punk scene, Poly Styrene, lead singer of X-Ray Spex, engaged in what the Situationists called *détournement,* the deployment of a specific object or sign for exactly the opposite of what it was originally intended—for example, Kung-Fu movies overdubbed with Maoist revolutionary dialogue. Poly Styrene's slogan was: "Oh Bondage Up Yours!" Such a strategy of detouring signs of authority and power would be crucial to Punk's policies.

The strange multiculturalism of Punk can be traced to the influence of Black culture which, itself, can be located in the crucible of the proto Punk scene in New York. This scene was heavily influenced, if not always in the musical forms themselves, by the style and sensibility of Black culture largely because it was music that expressed the essence of the "street hassle." The use of street style and language as a means of resisting the conformity and unthinking banality of American culture itself goes back to the Beat generation's adoption of the improvised idiom and riffs of Bebop culture. The Beats crucially cleared the way for the student and youth movements of the sixties by showing that the style and culture through which everyday life was lived was deeply political even when in the 1950s it was supposedly depoliticized.

It was not just traces of Black culture that appeared in the proto-Punk scene, but also that of other sub-cultures, particularly the sexual outlaw cultures of the Village and the Bowery as documented, for instance, in the photography of Nan Goldin. Patti Smith, Lou Reed, Iggy Pop (from Detroit), the Ramones, Stiv Bators and the Dead Boys, Richard Hell and especially the New York Dolls re-injected into American music the sexuality, indeed the polymorphous perversity, that had existed in Rock 'n' Roll ever since it had been damned as "devil's music." That was about the time Elvis's "pelvis" was censored during his famed appearance on The Ed Sullivan Show. The Dolls, by dressing in drag, were consciously identifying themselves with what was then—well before the likes of RuPaul, k.d. lang and Dennis Rodman—a particularly marginal subculture with the city.

Around the same time that Elvis was found on the bathroom floor of Graceland, fat, drugged and dead—consequently resurrected as the patron saint of middle America—New York bands were returning to the Black experience that had suffused the music of the young Elvis. The King had, so to speak, two bodies which can perhaps be read as allegories for two different "Americas": the brash, sexy body of his youth, which broke down the racial segregation of musical styles, and the bloated corpse found on the floor of Graceland.

Things, though, weren't quite so simple. While the New York scene drew upon the outlaw subcultures of that city, David Bowie, also deeply influenced by them, was at the time valorizing Hitler as the first "superstar" (which he, no doubt, was thanks to Leni Riefenstahl) and stating that what Britain needed was a dictatorship. As David has shown in his book *Beating Time,* Bowie even went so far as to stage a Nazi-style return to London from Berlin in a Mercedes limousine that, in the words of Widgery, "chillingly mixed rock star megalomania with Third Reich references." While he was later dissuaded from these coke-induced histrionics by some Berlin socialists, there was something particularly disturbing about the manner in which Bowie expressed a widely-held sentiment. As he was to put it later: "It was that hideous thing where as an artist you kind of feel there's something in the air ... You just sense a situation or an atmosphere and that can go into your writing." Around the same time, Eric Clapton, the musician perhaps most deeply steeped in the tradition of Mississippi Delta Blues, was publicly ruminating about the sexual endowments of black men and making statements in favour of Enoch Powell—the right wing Tory MP who delivered the infamous speech in 1968 predicting, in what was to become a self-fulfilling prophesy, that if immigration didn't stop, Britain would see "rivers of blood in the streets." Rod Stewart, whose own career would not have happened were it not for Smokey Robinson, Sam Cooke, Aretha Franklin and a host of black blues musicians, such as Big Bill Broonzy, himself declared that immigrants to Britain should just pack up and go "home." Never mind that Stewart himself was living in "tax exile" from Britain with a succession of blonde movie stars in L.A. Much to the derision of the fans of this ex-footballer, ex-gravedigger and erstwhile "working class hero."

The cities that gave rise to Punk as an aesthetic of collision and improvisation can be characterized as postcolonial inasmuch as these spaces were in the process of becoming transformed from what were once the industrial and political centres of Empire into places increasingly inhabited by colonial subjects: West Indian workers "invited" to work on British Rail and London Transport, workers from Pakistan and Bangladesh and refugees escaping racist dictatorships in Uganda and Malawi.

In the violence of its aural and visual assault, Punk simultaneously reflected and reflected upon the actual violence it saw around it in Britain, particularly that directed at those who were considered not to belong to the "nation." It was a gilt-edged polemic aimed at those who believed, to use the words of Paul Gilroy, "That there ain't no black in the Union Jack." Conscious of the manner in which Blacks and Asians, particularly Rastas in their obvious attempt to break with "Babylon," actively resisted the brutal conditions under which they were forced to live, Punk consciously sought a break, through its fashion, music and demeanor, with mainstream white society. The Clash called for a "White Riot" as an emulation of Black resistance to economic and social brutality. Punk, in other words, alienated itself from a society that dropped the hammer on those it considered aliens, a society that provided little hope for Black, Asian and white youth alike in an era of deindustrialization and diminishing expectations; as the Clash put it: "What we wear is dangerous gear/it'll get you picked up anywhere/though we get beat up we don't care/At least it livens up the air."

At the very moment when the symbols of Empire, in particular the Union Jack—in lethal combination with the jack boot—were becoming repoliticized, no doubt assisted by the comments of Bowie, Clapton and Stewart, in the year of the Royal Jubilee, Punk attacked these very symbols with a vengeance. In detouring the national anthem, the Sex Pistols made it into the anthem for a generation for which the "nation" either never had been or no longer was an option:

God save the queen and her fascist regime
it made you a moron a potential H bomb!
God save the queen she ain't no human being
there is no future in England's dreaming
Don't be told what you want and don't be told what you need
there's no future no future no future for you

This commentary spat out by Johnny Rotten, who was Irish and therefore felt particularly affronted by the unthinking conformism expressed in the Jubilee celebrations, was more than simply a dressing down of the monarchy. It was, rather, a critique of imperial history in its entirety; it presented a vision of history as a document not of civilization, but of barbarism. This was, of course, a history that was far from over: instead it was repeating itself on a daily basis in the stabbings, beatings and house-bombings of Blacks and Asians:

God save the Queen cos tourists are money
And our figurehead is not what she seems
Oh God save history, God save your mad parade
Oh Lord have mercy all crimes are paid

When there's no future how can there be sin
We're the flowers in your dustbin
We're the poison in your human machine
We're the future your future

The only progress one could discern in history was that leading, as Theodor Adorno put it, from the "sling shot to the Atom Bomb"—truly a "mad parade." The symbols of Empire were therefore transformed into signs of Anarchy; the glorious history of Pax Britannica into pure nihilism. While David Bowie and the National Front were invoking the name of Hitler, the Clash laid bare the fascism that was taking over the shop floors of whatever factories were still functioning in Britain and the US in the late 1970s:

Taking off his turban they said "Is this man a Jew?"
We're working for the Clampdown
They put up their posters saying we earn more than you
We're working of the clampdown
We'll teach our twisted speech
To the young believers
We'll train our blue-eyed men
To be young believers

What is crucial is the manner in which this song reveals fascism as the murder of cultural difference—"Taken to be melted down"—something that Punk confronted directly in its engagement with Black musical forms. For Hitler's "political theorist," Carl Schmitt, the essence of the political is the moment when the enemy comes into view. The gesture of stripping the Punjabi worker of his turban is precisely this instance: it is the moment when Punjabi and Jew come into view as identical victims of a calculated brutality. Meanwhile, in what is perhaps their most scathing attack, the Sex Pistols confronted the neo-Nazis' declaration of war on memory in their suggestion that the concentration camps such as Bergen-Belsen were holiday resorts:

Belsen was a gas, I heard the other day
In the open graves where the Jews all lay
Life is fun and I wish you were here
They wrote Jew postcards to those held dear
Oh dear

Sergeant majors on the march
Wash the bodies in the starch
See them all die one by one
Guess it's dead, guess it's glad
So bad!

So glad!
Be a man!
A real man!
Join our army!
Belsen was a gas!
Kill a man!
Kill someone!
Kill yourself!

In addressing the resurgence of the colonial inheritance in the midst of a social crisis, Punk asserted that "In 1977/I hope I go to Heaven/'cos I been too long on the dole/And I can't work at all." In 1977, the old music lost its ability to speak to the moment, to the social and cultural contradictions tearing the fabric of British society. In stripping rock 'n' roll down to its roots, Punk declared: "No Elvis, No Beatles, No Rolling Stones" in favour of the "roots" music of Prince Far I and Mickey Dread. This is what was precisely so dynamic about Punk: it brought Black and white musical forms into new constellations—each was influenced, provoked and, in some cases produced by the other. For instance, Dub-Reggae legend Lee "Scratch" Perry produced the Clash's "Complete Control," a song which addresses the "C-O-N-Control" wielded by a record company that initially promised "artistic freedom" to the band only to subordinate art to money. While deriding the violence of racist skinheads in "Crazy Baldhead," Bob Marley expressed solidarity with the Punks in "Punky Reggae Party," from the album *Bus to Babylon*. The Slits, driven by the primal drumming of Palmolive, articulated a unique style of Reggae that manifested an arresting form of "girl power."

In contrast to the often exploitive appropriation of Black musical forms in a way that was unthreatening to a white audience, many Punk bands covered Reggae tracks, not as a gesture of simple imitation, but rather in an effort to transform a certain idiom of resistance into their own. As Gilroy points out, the Clash's hugely popular rendition of Junior Murvin's "Police and Thieves" was often heard as a kind of soundtrack blaring from apartment windows during pitched street battles. Quite unlike Eric Clapton's popularization of "I Shot the Sheriff," the Irish band Stiff Little Fingers' blistering rendition of Marley's profoundly moving "Johnny Was" reinterpreted this document of random police violence in the streets of Kingston and Trenchtown, Jamaica, from a perspective rooted in the equally oppressive colonial realities of the "troubles" of Northern Ireland. To quote legendary music critic Lester Bangs "Somewhere in [punk's] assimilation of reggae is the closest thing to the lost chord, the missing link between black music and white noise, rock capable of making a bow to black forms without smearing on the blackface." In the process of bringing these forms together, Punk cleared the way for the Ska and Bluebeat revival of 1979–81 around the "Two-tone Label," with racially mixed bands like the Specials, the Beat and the Selector. But the culmination of the encounter between Black and white in Punk was the massive Rock Against Racism gig in Hyde Park in 1978.

The spirit of Punk lies anywhere but in the bands that try to produce Punk music today. These bands entirely miss the point that Punk attempted to grasp the eternal in the transitory rather than attempting to eternalize the transitory. Punk's legacy therefore lies, rather, in the hybridity of Bhangara, Ragga, Ambient, Jungle, Acid Jazz. It can be found in grrrl bands such as Hole, L7, and Riotgirrls, as well as in bands like BAD—featuring Mick Jones, former guitarist of the Clash and, for a time, Donn Letts, the Black filmmaker who did so much to document the early London scene, combining Chuck Berry riffs, dub, house and a hip-hop style sampling of the films of Nicholas Roeg. It lies in the work of Jah Wobble, formerly of P.I.L., who interprets the musical languages of the Middle East and Asia through dub-heavy bass but always with the unmistakable cockney accent of somebody who, had things turned out different, might have been a hooligan on the football terraces. It lies in the Punjabi-tones of Leicester's power-pop band Corner Shop, in the Ragga of Birmingham's Apache Indian and in the relentlessly hybrid styles of bands such as the Afro-Celt Soundsystem. It lies in the fusion of garage punk and hip-hop in the Beastie Boys and the deftly controlled anarchy of Chuck D, Flava Flav and Public Enemy. Closer to home, the interpenetration of styles Punk made possible can be found in the frenetic fiddling of Ashley MacIsaac—an invaluable counter-point to the mawkishness of Rita MacNeil and the Rankin family.

In shattering, if only momentarily, the opposition between high and low culture Punk threw down the gauntlet to the homogenizing logic of the culture industry in which every form of experience becomes magically transformed into an abstract quality of money. In the process, however, Punk was unable to escape destruction at the hands of the very commodification it protested against. Nonetheless, from the ruins of Punk's "creative destruction" new hybrid, provocative and truly "multicultural" styles were built. Such styles embody anything but the mendacious anything goes (and therefore nothing matters) ethos of postmodernism but rather a sort of restless modernism. In their desperate nomadic wanderings, such styles recognize that unless they "keep moving," in an effort to catch an ever elusive glimpse of Utopia, then the disciplining, dividing and classifying logic of capitalism—a logic with no soul, no vibe and no heart—will have had the last word.

DISCUSSION QUESTIONS

1. Discuss the issue of intellectual property. Do you download from Napster or other download sites?

2. How would you characterize the Canadian sound?

3. Access a few of the many fan sites for a Canadian rock band or a Canadian electronic fanzine. Do an analysis of what these fans/fanzines see as the Canadian sound.

4. Access one or two of the Canadian rock music distributors' Web sites (like Nettwerk). Analyze the strategy of address used to sell music to Canadian fans. Is there a difference between the Canadian approach and the approach taken by EMI Canada (a foreign distributor)?

5. Does rock and roll music have progressive, or even revolutionary, potential?

 # WEBLINKS

Canadian Association of Broadcasters
www.cab-acr.ca/index.html

Groove: Canadian Music at its Best
www.geocities.com/SunsetStrip/Stage/2199/music.htm

JAM: all Canadian music
www.canoe.ca/ACMI/home.html

Nettwerk
www.nettwerk.com/

Foundation to Assist Canadian Talent on Record
www.factor.ca/

Canadian Independent Record Production Association
www.cria.ca/

CBC Infoculture: on Napster
www.infoculture.cbc.ca/archives/newmedia/newmedia_02282000_napster.phtml

The Canadian Country Music Association
www.ccma.org/

chapter eight

Canadian Comedy—Funny, Eh?

INTRODUCTION

Nothing is more difficult to explain than humour. Many Canadian writers have tried to define a specifically Canadian form—with very mixed results. Given the multicultural nature of Canadian society and the vast differences in what people find humourous, this has always been a very tricky project. The writers in this chapter try to tell us what Canadian humour is by looking at comedians and television programs, but do these programs tickle the funny bones of all Canadians, or are they just the product of the elite few who get to bring their talents to television? Do ordinary Canadians spend most of their viewing time watching American sitcoms like "Seinfeld" and find them funnier than the harder-edged Canadian satires? Can we even say that the majority of Canadians share a sense of what is funny? And why have so many Canadian comics, like John Candy, Martin Short, Dan Ackroyd, Jim Carrey, and Mike Myers, to name just a few, been so successful in the U.S. if humour has national boundaries? These are just some of the questions that can be posed about humour and culture.

The chapter opens with an essay by Andrew Clark, who discusses an event held in New York to answer the question: why are Canadians so funny—particularly those who emigrate to the U.S.? Panelists speculated that Canadian comics get wonderful training in Canada because it is so far from Hollywood, and that when they go to the U.S. they often have years of experience in front of Canadian audiences. Another believes that Canadians are very familiar with American culture and can thus relate to American audiences; at the same time, they have a certain distance from the culture which allows them to satirize it with considerable glee.

Geoff Pevere is more interested in trying to define Canadian humour. Noting the amazing success of Canadian comedians in the U.S., he marvels that Canada has few stand-up comedians, and few successful sitcoms or talk shows. He argues that the true Canadian form may be the sketch comedy or short parody that concentrates on the process of humour rather than the punchline. He also notes our love of "stupid" comic characters like Ed Grimley and the MacKenzie Brothers. Like Clark, he points to the detachment of much Canadian humour and claims that it is so popular across North America because it is quintessentially postmodern in its ironic detachment.

The last two authors in the chapter discuss specific programs: "Made in Canada" and "Open Mike with Mike Bullard," two successful programs in genres which have not traditionally done well in Canada. Cheryl Binning argues that "Made in Canada" satirizes the Canadian television industry and those who abuse power. The show is gentler than "SCTV," and the show's producers argue that Canadians love to make fun of themselves—in fact, Canadian media celebrities like Moses Znaimer and Margot Kidder, among others, have appeared on the show to make fun of themselves.

Don Gillmor argues that Mike Bullard has succeeded where other Canadians have failed miserably: the late night talk show. Bullard began his comedy career in stand-up, riffing off audience members in a highly improvisational manner. In the beginning, Gillmor argues, Bullard struggled with the highly conventional talk show form—as an improv comedian, he was uncomfortable with the often scripted interviews which are conventional in the American genre. Occasionally this discomfort came to resemble a deconstruction of the genre like "The Larry Sanders Show." In the end, Gillmor argues, Bullard's success will depend on whether he can innovate within a genre that is clearly becoming tired.

See the various books by Linda Hutcheon, like *A Theory of Parody* (New York: Methuen, 1985) for further discussion of postmodernism and parody.

THE LAND OF LAUGHS

Andrew Clark *(Maclean's)*

Michael J. Fox begins with Wayne and Shuster, who appeared more times on "The Ed Sullivan Show" than any other act. The list continues: David Steinberg, Rich Little, Dan Aykroyd, Martin Short, John Candy, Dave Thomas, Leslie Nielsen (post-*Airplane!*), Mike Myers, Catherine O'Hara, Ivan Reitman, Lorne Michaels, Eugene Levy, Rick Moranis, Norm MacDonald, the Kids in the Hall, Jim Carrey. All Canadian, all top-notch comedians. Fox then poses the question: "What makes Canadians so funny? Would these people all have the same sense of humour if they were, uh, Latvian?" His quip gets the evening's first laugh from the audience of 1000 New Yorkers and Canadian expatriates, including journalists Robert MacNeil and Morley Safer. The mere thought that a country as reputedly mild and retiring as Canada might harbour a talent for the rebellious art of comedy sends the New York City crowd into hysterics.

Andrew Clark. The land of laughs: Americans find Canadian comedians hilarious. *Maclean's* 112(5), February 1, 1999. 66.

The gathering, assembled . . . in the Upper East Side's trendy 92nd Street Y, was hoping for insights as well as laughs. They had paid $18 a ticket to hear, along with Fox, "Saturday Night Live" creator Michaels, comedian and actor Short and "SCTV" icon Levy ruminate on the Canadian comedy phenomenon. Had the panel discussion—dubbed "Why Are Canadians So Funny?"—occurred in Vancouver, for instance, it would have sold out, but raised little surprise. After all, homegrown comedians have long been a source of national pride. But in the United States, comics such as Short and Fox are famous for being funny, not for being funny Canadians. So organizers were surprised when the evening, produced in conjunction with the Canadian Consulate, sold out in less than a week and attracted 30 newspaper reporters, seven television crews and a handful of radio journalists. "We've never seen anything like it," said one organizer.

Neither had the audience. "I don't think Americans give Canada a lot of thought," says Kendra Moyer, a 31-year-old arts administration student at Columbia University. "I'm surprised Canada produces so many big comedians. It doesn't seem like an in-your-face culture." It was this contradiction the audience wanted explained. To many Americans, Canada is a nice, cold, polite, rustic place, epitomized by Bob and Doug Mckenzie, the happy hosers created by "SCTV"'s Moranis and Thomas. Americans want life, liberty and the pursuit of happiness. Canadians seek peace, order and good government. How could such a culture produce a frenetic comedian like Jim Carrey, whose signature gag in *Ace Ventura: Pet Detective* was pretending to make his backside speak?

One factor, according to the four funnymen, is Canada's remoteness from the Hollywood machine. "You just assume nobody is paying any attention," says Fox. Canada is, thanks to the relative obscurity of its entertainment business, a place to experiment and hone your craft, explains Michaels. Canadian comics often have years of experience under their belts once they decide to cross the border. They arrive as unique commodities—seasoned newcomers.

Canadians leave because they feel they need the stamp of American approval in order to be taken seriously in Canada. Michaels worked at the CBC in the 1960s, producing and co-starring in "The Hart and Lorne Terrific Hour." "I told the then-head of light entertainment at the CBC that I wanted to stay but that I had offers from America," Michaels told *Maclean's* during an interview in his NBC office held after the panel discussion. "He told me, 'If you're that good, why are you here?'"

To Short, heading south is a matter of plain economics: "The money makes a drain to America. You have to come here." The Dumbells, a First World War serviceman's troupe, were the first Canadians to score in the United States. In 1919, their music-hall show "Biff Bing Bang" was a hit on Broadway. In the 1950s, Johnny Wayne and Frank Shuster succeeded both on the CBC and on CBS. The largest wave of Canadian comedians stormed the United States in the 1970s and 1980s. Michaels's "Saturday Night Live," the longest-running and most highly rated late-night comedy show, revolutionized the way North Americans watched television. It also made stars of Aykroyd and later Myers. "SCTV," a show born on Canada's Global Television and transferred to NBC, introduced American viewers to Candy, Short, O'Hara and a host of other Canuck comedians.

Curiously, British and Australian comedians do not experience the widespread acceptance of their Canadian counterparts. The panelists agree that Canada's exposure to American pop-culture and politics, first through the movies and radio, and later, television, gives its comedians an advantage. As Short points out, Americans watch television, Canadians watch American television. Adds Michaels: "I first realized the difference between Canada and America by watching American television. Canadian culture in the '50s and '60s had a markedly English accent. We were influenced by "Monty Python." In Canada, you got Canadian, English and American comedy." Canadians ingested American cultural icons, such as "Leave It to Beaver" (which SCTV later savaged), but felt removed from the American experience. This distance bred satire. The comedians most famous for lampooning Richard Nixon were Canadians Little and Aykroyd. "Saturday Night Live" brought political satire, which U.S. TV execs viewed as a ratings killer, to network television. "As a Canadian, I felt I had a God-given right to f— with American politics," says Michaels. "The network people just looked at the ratings, which were high, and said 'OK.'"

When Canadians did tune in to their own broadcasts, they were met with uniquely Canadian absurdities. Short, for instance, gave the New York crowd a brief lesson on the CFL: "It had eight teams, two of which were named Rough Riders. So, you could watch the news and hear: 'Rough Riders 28. [pause] Roughriders 7.'"

All four comedians feel an affection for Canada that is tinged with a sense of alienation. The Canadian love of rules and politeness, they observe, made comedy a socially risky venture. "I was considered strange," says Fox. "Then I came down here and was rewarded for doing the things I was ridiculed for at home. I thought, 'I do it here and they give me money.'" Michaels agrees, adding: "Canada is a country where celebrating is considered showing off. In Canada, it's called flag-waving. In America, it's called patriotism. If *It's a Wonderful Life* was made by a Canadian, it would be called *It's an All Right Life*."

The situation is changing. There is now room for comedians on Canadian television. The CBC boasts "The Royal Canadian Air Farce" and "This Hour Has 22 Minutes." "The Newsroom" director Ken Finkleman has established himself as a top-flight comedy series producer. The Comedy Network launched "Open Mike with Mike Bullard," the country's first successful late-night talk show. Still, the "drain" south continues, motivated, at least in part, by a desire to steal some of the spotlight that shines on the colossus next door. "I remember as a kid really taking it personally when an American announcer mispronounced 'Ottawa,'" adds Short. "He called it 'Oh-ta-wa.'" Such American gaffes will continue. Canada remains famous for hockey, snow and maple syrup. It can now add comedy to that list.

A JOKE IN THE TELLING: ON CANADIAN COMEDY AND THE MISSING PUNCHLINE

Geoff Pevere *(Teach Magazine)*

How perfect it would be to start things off with the ultimate Canadian joke. You know, some slyly perfect opener, a whole thesis conveniently packed into a single, geographically specific punchline. Two hosers walk into a bar maybe . . . Or should that be a tavern? A donut shop? Or should they ride a snowmobile?

Problem is, that joke seems not to exist, or at least not in the form that would do the job. While it's not difficult to think of jokes about Canadians—like the one about getting 25 Canadians out of a pool—or even jokes told by Canadians—that one, single, nation-defining gag just doesn't pop to mind.

And this relative state of jokelessness from a culture considered one of the funniest in the world; a country without which, it could be argued, there would be no Austin Powers,

Geoff Pevere. A joke in the telling: On Canadian comedy and the missing punchline. *Teach Magazine*, May/June, 1999. 42-44.

no Ace Ventura, no "Saturday Night Live," no "SCTV," no "Kids in the Hall." Or consider the key behind-the-scenes roles played by mirthmaking Canucks in some of the most popular sitcoms in recent network history: "M*A*S*H," "Seinfeld," "Mad About You," "Family Ties," "The Partridge Family," "Roseanne"—each boasted prominently-placed Dominion subjects in key creative roles, which only makes the question of why Canadians make such lousy sitcoms at home only more pressing and de-pressing.

A commanding, almost monolithic tradition of laughter, in other words, but hardly a joke to be found in the whole sprawling history of hoser-generated humour. Makes you think.

Maybe it shouldn't. After all, thinking—at least thinking in the theory-building, analytical sense—is the natural arch-enemy of humour, it tends to cripple forms of pleasure in general. Who really wants to know the anatomy of what makes you laugh? The experience is the thing itself.

When you embark on a project as challenging but inevitable as gleaning what's Canadian about Canadian comedy—because that's the kind of thing God apparently intended Canadians to do—some stabs at theorizing are ultimately inescapable, if only for the purpose of temporarily throwing a fence or two around an untamed herd. It may not hold them forever, but it makes them a lot easier to observe for the moment.

So let's start with a few fence-building propositions about Canadian comedy. It's Canada, and one thing we don't have to worry about is running out of wood. Our beavers might be good national symbols, but they're slow.

The relative lack of the punchline in Canuck comedy would seem as good a place as any to set first stakes for. When, for example, one places it in the context of the two other English-speaking traditions which press upon us, the pulling of the final punch would seem an almost perverse assertion of some kind of cultural sovereignty. Where British comedy loves the big, ugly and untidy visual gag, and American comedy boils down to a comic, a microphone and the squeezing off of rapid-fire rounds of jokes—they don't call it "killing" for nothing—Canadian comedy seems almost perversely disinterested in the pay-off.

Consider, in this light, the conspicuous absence of joke-tellers in Canadian comedy—no hoser Henny Youngmans spring to mind, no Canadian Hopes, Dangerfields or Berles. What begins to emerge is something completely different. Think of Leacock's sly evisceration of small-town delusions, Wayne and Shuster's elaborately goofy Shakespearean parodies, Rich Little's starstruck repertoire of showbiz impersonations, or even the closer-to-historical-home schticking of Carrey, Myers, "Kids in the Hall" or "This Hour Has 22 Minutes." Decades and hours of fullmetal mirth notwithstanding, there's barely a ripping yarn in the bunch.

What you do see—or hear or remember—are examples of comedy as process: elaborate parodic sketches ("SCTV," "Kids"), impersonations (Little, Carrey, Andre-Philipe Gagnon), semi-improvised ensemble sketch exercises (Second City, or just about any local comedy club with an improv component). A joke in the telling, in other words, rather than the telling of a joke. It's not where the chicken goes that makes the joke Canadian, but the fact that it's crossing the road. And, of course, that we care.

It would seem reasonable then to suggest that Canadian comedy is less about payoff than process, or at the very least in premise as much as punchline. To invoke some second-hand analogies, it's foreplay over orgasm, the game over the result, motion over destination. Why did the chicken cross the road? Who cares? How about how did the chicken cross the road?

In this dubious regard, there may be something significant in the fact that one of the recurrent motifs in Canadian comedy is how profoundly and bottomlessly stupid we can be. Indeed, is there any other national comedy tradition which is as brutally self-lacerating as ours: from

Johnny Wayne's gaseously offensive puns to Charlie Farquharson's artful meddling with the Queen's English, or from Ed Grimley and Bob Mackenzie to Wayne and Howie and *Dumb and Dumber* and "22 Minutes," stupidity runs through Canuck comedy as sure and impervious as the railway cuts through the Rockies. Indeed, when it comes to the missing-joke mystery in Canadian comedy, some clues might be offered by the fact that so much of our domestic mirth-making is perpetrated by people just too stupid to navigate their way through a joke.

All comedy is of course conceptual by nature. What we're suggesting, based on all this apparent fondness for goofs over gags, is just that Canadian comedy would seem to be more forthrightly so than most other kinds. Indeed, it's the idea behind the comedy which in many cases makes the comedy funny: Wayne and Shuster's "Shakespearean Baseball," Jim Carrey's impersonation of "post-apocalyptic Elvis," Mark McKinney's deranged "Headcrusher" character on Kids. If you laugh, you're as likely to laugh at the idea behind the gag as the gag itself. What makes "Wayne's World" funny? Wayne himself, or the idea that this cheerfully dim metalhead presides over "a world"? Is it Ed Grimley who cracks us up, or the sublimely ludicrous idea of Ed Grimley? As I'm sure you'll agree, these are the questions.

What we're talking about is another manifestation of that condition of chronic detachment which would seem to be the defining condition of so much English-Canadian cultural expression: the same capacity for sly observation which also makes Canadians such world-class journalists, media theorists, animators, landscape painters, statisticians and game show hosts. We like to watch, and we're damn good at it.

In terms of comedic inspiration, most of what we watch comes from somewhere else, delivered directly to our intellectual doorsteps (so to speak) by television, the medium which is to Canadian culture what eggs are to omelette. Essential.

Living in a large and sparsely-populated country with a relentless surplus of bad weather begins to explain why Canadians have become such formidable consumers and students of telecommunications technology: we love to talk on the phone and tumble through cyberspace, and we love to watch TV. But our love would seem to be conditional. We are, after all, descendants of stern and hard-working moralists, and we feel their stern spirits haunting the light flickering in our living rooms. We have turned watching into an activity, often a passionate one, as a way of justifying our epic slothfulness. McLuhan is one expression of this active passivity, the Mackenzie brothers another. Or Mike Myers.

Myers, who grew up in the geographic satellite dish of Southern Ontario—just like Aykroyd, Short and Carrey—is as good a model as any of the made-in-Canada comic. An avowed couch potato—and the first comedian to give the recroom its deserved pop-cultural status—Myers specializes in comedy which is process oriented, pop-obsessed and passionately-detached. Like countless other TV-nurtured Canucks, his worldview is hopelessly circumscribed by the media he consumed, and his way of marking sovereignty within that otherwise alienating experience involves interpretive regurgitation, i.e., reprocessing the life of observation into interpretations of things observed. The same thing Wayne and Shuster pioneered with their popcult pastiche parodies of the Fifties and Sixties. The same thing has been demonstrated by comedic byproducts from Little to Carrey—who even played a victim of televisual dementia in *The Cable Guy*—to "SCTV" and "Twitch City," which are both TV shows brilliantly and hopelessly about the world TV makes in its own warped image.

Parody, satire, impersonation—arguably the primary modes of Canadian comedic expression, all acts of critical interpretation made possible by a certain detachment, and best-served by the vehicle called sketch comedy. Sketch is about concept and process, and it might well be the ultimate expression of the Canadian comedic bent. Groups of people playing out ironic and critical riffs on the mediated world, something which allows the linking in time and tradition from Sullivan's Canadian pets through Lorne Michaels' Canuck-heavy "SNL", and from "SCTV" to "Kids." Indeed, even the current yin/yang of publicly-subsidized Canadian TV comedy—"The Royal Canadian Air Farce" and "22 Minutes"—are essentially pop-parodic sketch shows.

Common knowledge currently dictates that we are in the cultural grip of ironic postmodernism, a kind of collective, end-of-millennial been-there-done-thatness which manifests itself in increasingly disengaged, fractured and media-obsessed forms of media: nothing is new, everything is borrowed, and the direct expression of emotion is like, totally uncool. If so, then it would seem that the rest of the world has finally caught up to certain attitudes which Canadians, due to their unique position as the insects caught in the blinding high-beams of American culture, have been refining for years.

This explains why our comedy has proven one of the most successful Canadian export industries this side of stickhandlers and sweatshirts: comedy in general now wants what Canadians already have—an ironic take on a mediated world, the comedy or attitude or concept over the comedy of gag and punchline. Thankfully, however, there would seem to be more to it, for it's almost impossible to separate the overall shift in comedy toward ironic detachment from the forms of comedy which led that shift, many of which seemed to involve Canadians anyway. As far back as Rowan and Martin's "Laugh-In" and "The Smothers Brothers Comedy Hour," Canadians were playing prominently in the field of American network humour. And when it comes to the once-mighty "Saturday Night Live," the broadcasting equivalent to a terminal patient on life-support, the task of separating chicken from egg becomes downright challenging. Was it the innovations of that program, with its countercultural cynicism, sketch format and pop-fixation, which helped pave the way for the current Canuck domination of film and TV comedy, or was it the Canadians involved from the outset who were instrumental in making the shift possible? Either way, you're left with a commanding fact of cultural life at the lip of the millennium: whatever comedy has become, it has become somehow, strangely, more Canadian.

Needless to say, the very bankability of Canadian comedy has also meant that the rate of border-jumping among our comedically-inclined is higher than just about any other domestic industry this side of software. For all the funny people who have stayed behind, and who have concentrated their knack for critical irony on domestic affairs ("This Hour Has 22 Minutes" is a prime example), many more have packed up and fled southward, where salaries grow bigger and meetings with CBC executives are merely laughable poolside memories. But is this necessarily a bad thing? Certainly in the past, a huge element of one notion of Canadian nationalism has rested on the assumption that Canadian is what Canadians do in Canada. The assumption behind this was that Canadian culture was a thin and fragile and easily corrupted thing, and that American culture was the ravaging, rampaging monolith that flattens the distinction out of everything in its path. In this case, however, that argument might finally be demonstrated to have reached its limits. It's arguable that export forms of Canadian comedy have not just meshed with the American comedic mainstream, but have strongly influenced its direction, current and depth, for better or worse. That, quite the contrary to being diminished when introduced to the global entertainment mainstream, Canadian comedy has both maintained its particular proclivities and actually flourished when poured into a bigger tank. Now if only we could say the same thing about hockey.

As for that ultimate Canadian joke, the closest thing that comes to mind is a line quoted to me by someone else who forgot whom he heard it from in the first place: "If Canadians had a choice between going to heaven and going to a panel discussion on heaven, they'd pick the panel."

"MADE IN CANADA": AN INSIDE TAKE ON THE WORLD OF CANADIAN FILM AND TELEVISION

Cheryl Binning *(Take One)*

The big talk among Canadian TV-industry types today (right up there with the Canadian Television Fund guidelines and latest kerfuffle over runaway productions) is exactly who "Made in Canada"'s Alan Roy—that overly ambitious, conniving but charismatic CEO of Pyramid/Prodigy Productions—is modelled upon.

Over this past season, the sleazy showbiz exec (played by Peter Keleghan) has managed—with the help of his posse, Richard Strong (Rick Mercer), Victor Sela (Dan Lett) and Veronica Miller (Leah Pinsent)—to bring about the merger of two powerhouse entertainment companies. The head of rival Prodigy retired to "return to his first love, directing" and press leaks were avoided because, you see, all those privy to the secret information used code names like Jupiter and Pluto . . . oh, and Mickey and Minnie as well. Alan then handed out pink slips and watched stocks soar. However, crises continue to arise—a children's show host caught wife swapping just before merchandising deals are signed; former script writers launching law suits claiming the producers ripped off their ideas; going head-to-head at NATPE with Citytv boss Moses Znaimer to sell a format to U.S. broadcasters. But despite the obstacles, shows continue to be churned out at Pyramid/Prodigy: the turn-of-the-century family drama "Beaver Creek" (just think of an overly earnest CBC series) and the cash-cow action/adventure series "Sword of Damacles" (yes, one of those many rip-offs of "Xena: Warrior Princess," "Hercules" or "Sinbad").

Hmmm . . . it all sounds a bit too familiar. Perhaps it's no wonder that everyone in the Canadian TV industry has an opinion about who is being poked fun at each week in the Salter Street Films/Island Edge Entertainment spoof "Made in Canada." Well, guess no longer. About Alan Roy that is. "The truth is, he is everybody. He's the composite of every CEO story we have ever heard, all blended together," says "Made in Canada" executive producer Gerald Lunz, who created the show with Salter Street producer Michael Donovan and actor/story-editor Rick Mercer. "He has the sexual magnetism of a Robert Lantos, the good looks and intellect of Michael Donovan, the corporate structure of Michael McMillan's Alliance Atlantis and the production ideas of Kevin Sullivan."

The small, little world of Canadian television has the opportunity to have a laugh at its own expense each week as "Made in Canada" takes a peek inside a large publicly traded production company. All the daily dilemmas of TV production—those annoying actors who think they can direct; babysitting washed-up divas; outwitting rivals for the option on hot literary properties; schmoozing the press in the hopes of stopping a bad review; selling a family show to a German broadcaster who is really looking for edgy entertainment—are pushed just a bit too far and spoofed to the hilt. We can even see some of their own—CBC host Evan Solomon, actor Kiefer Sutherland, broadcast mogul Moses Znaimer—joining in on the fun and making cameo appearances as themselves.

Cheryl Binning. "Made in Canada": An inside take on the world of Canadian film and television. *Take One* (27), Spring, 2000. 15-19.

Richard: It's "Beaver Creek." There are not that many roles for women.

Siobhan: Well, do something about it.

Richard: I'd like to, but all the writers are men.

Siobhan: In this show all the women and children and aboriginal people are tired cliches.

Richard: Yeah, it's a family show.

Everyone is a fair target, even Lunz himself. "There's me in there, things I have done," he says. "In the Christmas show, I am the elf, the guy who makes the nuts and bolts and loves Christmas. You know those guys, the kind who say 'we have to get lights on this house.' Rick was making fun of me in those lines, and I had to sit there and take it. All my family and friends called after that episode aired and laughed at me."

But just how real is it all anyway? How close to the truth do these episodes sometimes get? "Well, you aren't going to get an answer from me," laughs Mercer, carefully sidestepping the question. "Although there are times when we are shooting we go 'Good God, we are going to get nailed on this one.'" "Writing about what we know is how we got into this," responds Lunz. "And the fact is, in our industry it's not hard to say there's a lot of egos, a lot of divas. We are dealing with a lot of creative people." Mark Farrell, who has written numerous episodes and served as costory-editor with Mercer adds, "When we keep it as real as we can the satire is really self evident because the things that happen are just silly. We don't have to invent crazy scenarios. We just have to find a way to turn these stories about production companies and how decisions are made into a half-hour format."

Alan: Comedy is the result of glandular problems. Yeah, it's true. Haven't you noticed the best comedy writers are always running to the bathroom.

Richard: That's where the cocaine is.

The "Made in Canada" story lines are based on the wealth of lore available in the TV business. "When you are sitting around in a green room with a bunch of actors, the funny things they talk about are the horror stories," says Lunz. "The craziest director, the most absurd production, these stories become legendary unto themselves. They are people's party pieces, and we started collecting these stories and working with the story line. There are touchstones of reality within the humour. People watch and say 'that's not me, someone said that's me.' No, maybe it's not you, but he has your hair, although he is sounding like Robert Lantos. I hope we see ourselves. When we do, I say, 'good, we're doing what we are suppose to.'"

Salter Street Films, itself, has provided much of the inspiration for the show, says Lunz. "When we first began creating the show six years ago, Michael's company was the biggest thing we knew about and the company was going through an initial public offering. As the machinations of a corporate change, there was a lot of good fodder there." So, in many ways, the Halifax-based production company is producing a show satirizing itself. In fact, the initial six episodes were shot on weekends at the Salter Street office after the staff had gone home. "As a story-editor," adds Mercer, "when the writers come to me about the episode they are going to write, I ask them to mine from their worst experiences, their worst director, the worst producer. You can't help but put your personal experiences into the show, but they are all composites."

While Mercer is best known for his sharp political criticisms on "This Hour Has 22 Minutes," he says "Made in Canada" is not meant to be a biting satire. There's no finger pointing. It's a spoof on the TV industry and its antics are not to be taken too seriously. "There's truisms, but no one is being hurt or slapped," adds Lunz. "We don't have any axe to grind.

We aren't getting back at anyone. That's not funny." The basis of the humour in "Made in Canada," says Lunz, is that unique Canadian ability to laugh at ourselves, mock our successes and chuckle over our failures. With the tremendous growth in the Canadian TV industry over the past few years, it was about time to poke some fun, look at our rapidly expanding TV industry through a cynical, yet humorous lens, point out the essential silliness of it all and knock our egos down a few pegs. Put ourselves back in our rightful lowly place.

"Canadians are good at this," says Lunz. "Most of our conversations with our friends are similar, self-deprecating and cynical but really funny about it. It's a Canadian trait. We don't take ourselves or others too seriously. We have a great laugh at ourselves and move on. Viewers say, 'Hey look they are making fun of us,' but it's okay because they are making fun of themselves too." And the industry is playing along with the joke. Like Moses Znaimer poking fun at his reputation for being totally out of the loop and hiding in an ivory tower at the Citytv building on Toronto's trendy Queen Street West (he doesn't realize that Citytv already has a very popular "Intimate and Interactive" franchise) and alluding to having killed people in the 1980s.

"They play with their reputations and see the humour in it," says Mercer, pointing to the script he wrote with Moses Znaimer as the guest character. Then there's Margot Kidder taking on the role of a washed-up American actress who is brought in as a guest star on "Beaver Creek" and totally disrupts the set with her tantrums, hallucinations, ravings and eventual breakdown. "Now that's self-deprecating humour and not taking yourself too seriously," says Lunz. "We asked her to play a diva, with all sorts of problems. Margot is a Canadian. She got the humour in a second. She thought it was a gas."

A long list of who's who in the Canadian entertainment world have agreed to play themselves on the series or take on some far-from-flattering roles: "Road to Avonlea"'s Sarah Polley as the leader of the Spirentology Cult who's out to make some cash, spoofing the strong relationship between Scientology and the entertainment industry; Kiefer Sutherland as himself, trying to break in to TV producing; Maury Chaykin as an oversexed, wife-swapping children's entertainer; "Trader"'s Bruce Gray as the penny-pincher at the helm of rival Prodigy Productions; Ann Medina as a journalist who does a scathing undercover report on Alan Roy; and Peter Gzowski, Gino Empry and Evan Soloman—all starring as themselves.

But while the TV-production business provides the backdrop for the show, the bottom line is that industry insiders are a small percentage of the viewing population. While one level of the humour is aimed at those on the inside, all the jokes have to hit the funny bone of the general viewer. "Ultimately it's funny that wins," says Lunz. "It's the funny that got 887 000 people to tune in on a Monday night. Most of my audience doesn't know who Kevin Sullivan and Michael Donovan are, but if I draw these big, wealthy, ambitious people— everyone can relate. It's their boss."

"Sure insider jokes are planted in the episodes," continues Lunz, "but not at the cost of the plot nor at the cost of the one basic concept we hold to and that's the Dilbert reality. What happens inside Pyramid/Prodigy could happen inside a manufacturing company, or Canadian Tire. It's people working together in a publicly traded corporation at the mid-management and upper-management level. That's the corporate stuff that happens anywhere."

Farrell also says that the industry satire is second to the ultimate goal of creating a sitcom that is entertaining to its audience. "Yes, we are writing a show about the TV industry, but it wouldn't be wise to aim it just at the industry. I don't want the show to become one big inside joke, like night two at the Geminis. We are trying to get a lot of people to watch."

And take away all the trappings of production sets and scripts and at its heart "Made in Canada" is a satire on corporate climbing, office politics and the sad but true reality that the dumb guy who dotes on the boss rises to the top while the ones with the real brains are still down on the ground shining the bosses' shoes. No one trusts anyone else, each is out for themselves and will stab in the back a co-worker they joined forces with just the day before. Alan, the paranoid boss, hires a detective who pretends to hire his staff away, just to prove their loyalty. And since the world of TV production has become so corporate, the entertainment aspect melds well with the spoof on office politics. "The TV business has the same bureaucratic structure as other offices," says Farrell. "It's very much about the idiots in every office, the people in charge who don't know what the hell they are doing, the underlings who do all the work and the overlords who get all the credit. It's an age-old bureaucratic story we are telling. We are making fun of people who abuse power."

> Alan: Here's the problem [with the show]. The problem is no one is in jeopardy or peril.
>
> Richard: Jeopardy and peril cost money.

Ironically, when executive producers Michael Donovan, George Lunz and Mercer first discussed doing a new series together, the backdrop did not include a film and TV production company at all. "We wanted to do a show about an individual's Machiavellian rise to the top. A person who would not care who he hurts on the way up, who is entirely focused on moving up the ladder one rung at a time," explains Mercer. They brain stormed about setting this overly ambitious character in a number of situations—Parliament Hill, an advertising agency, even a MuchMusic-type setting was considered. "That would have been fun to write, but I would be making it up," says Mercer. "I haven't worked in that environment so I would have to guess what's going on. The most important rule of satire is to satirize what you know, and we knew this industry," explains Mercer. "We felt we had a voice of authority. I know that sounds egomaniacal but all it means is if you know it well enough you can satirize it."

With 19 half-hours and two seasons wrapped, and fresh fodder for new episodes never far away, the producers are hammering out ideas for a third season. And with "Who Wants To Be a Millionaire" the latest craze, Lunz thinks Pyramid/Prodigy should jump on the game-show bandwagon as well. Oh, and he also thinks it would be too much fun to get Jim Perry, the host of "Definition," on the show.

CAN WE TALK?

Don Gillmor *(Saturday Night)*

In the comically small green room of Yuk Yuk's Superclub in midtown Toronto, Mike Bullard chain-smokes Export "A" Lights and tells me about other talk show hosts: Johnny's reign; Dave versus Jay; Conan's slow, agonizing triumph. "Letterman was like me. He was an emcee in the clubs, he didn't really have an act," Bullard says. It is twenty minutes before the opening show for his cross-country stand-up tour to promote "Open Mike with Mike Bullard," the late-night talk show that has put him in the national spotlight. He is forty years old, an awkward age for a comic, though a good age for a talk-show host.

Don Gillmor. Can we talk? *Saturday Night* 113(7), September, 1998. 38-44.

The room is full and expectant and Bullard comes out to big applause, looking down at the front rows on display under the harsh stage lights. A bald man calls out that he and Bullard have the same barber.

"Apparently I got out of the chair a little sooner," Bullard says, and the sparring begins. He spritzes with the audience, creating a dialogue. Among peers, he is considered the best spritzer in the business; his impromptu abilities are what got him the television show. His openings are standard Vegas exordiums: What's your name? What do you do? Anyone here from out of town? But like an opening move in chess, the dull, undeviated beginning leads to a more sophisticated attack.

On the surface, Bullard's act has the rhythms of stand-up comedy, but it takes more from theatre. He doesn't have a prepared act; the routine is created extemporaneously using information the audience offers. In the course of the evening, he creates a large, dysfunctional family, using the crude elements available in the first four rows. Tonight is like a guerrilla version of a Eugene O'Neill play; strangers in the audience are linked, their foibles drawn out and exaggerated.

Bullard's blue-collar bulk, blunt features, and crooked smile all lend his work appeal. When he laughs, his shoulders heave as if they were being operated by someone backstage. If he were slicker, some of the jabs would be less palatable. Occasionally, there is a hint of Don Rickles's thuggishness, but Rickles's verbal assaults are driven largely by volume. Bullard is witty and his barbs work toward a larger point.

He is getting slightly agitated as the show goes on and there is now a hint of forcefulness behind the lines. With an American woman, he debates cultural superiority. "You didn't invent the telephone. We did. It was invented in Brantford. Not Boston. Brantford. You know how I know?" He moves forward menacingly, bends down, his face red, like a cop who knows the man he is interrogating is guilty. "Do you know how I know?" He steps back and relaxes slightly. "Because when we called you guys the next day, no-one answered. Thank you everyone. Good night." Bullard leaves the stage and the crowd erupts.

After the show, he works the room, greeting friends, fans, media, and industry people. You killed, people tell him. Destroyed. Bullard goes into the tiny green room and sprawls across a small armchair and physically deflates, though he is jittery and high from the show. A year ago, he was working at Bell Canada, where he had worked for nineteen years. Now he is the next great hope for a late-night Canadian talk show, a format that comes with an unfortunate history in this country. In a gesture of faith and publicity, CTV recently bought the Masonic Temple, a historic building on Toronto's Yonge Street, for $2.4 million, and announced that it would be the new site of "Open Mike" in its second season. The network is investing heavily in Bullard's ability to talk.

The set has exhausted him, but he is still talking. Doing it professionally, he says, is easier than his former job. The club has emptied, and the waiters are scurrying in the buoyant vacuum. Bullard lies back in his chair, on the cusp of celebrity, and recalls his previous existence as a Bell corporate investigator.

"We're trailing these two heroin addicts who've been stealing equipment out of Bell trucks," he says. "We're looking at two-hundred-grand worth of stuff. A lot of stuff. We know they're doing it, but we have to catch them in the act. So we plant a truck full of equipment at the Mount Pleasant cemetery and sit in our car and wait. Sure enough, an hour later they show up, break the window with a hammer, start filling up green garbage bags with phone sets. There's people walking by, it's broad day-light. We go over and say we're Bell corporate investigations, you're under arrest. I just assumed they'd stand there. They take off. I go after this guy, his name is Russ something. I'm puffing, he's getting away. So I yell, "We know where you live, Russ." Great. So now he's not going to go home. The cops finally pick up Russ and sweat him and he tells them the other guy lives in a rooming house in Parkdale. We go over there at two a.m. with the police. Someone pulls the fire alarm, which is what the residents do to warn everyone the cops are coming. There's five cops with a battering ram. They break down the door but the guy's right behind it and the door falls on top of him and I start laughing. One of the cops tells me you're not really supposed to laugh at these things. The heroin addict is living with another guy, a fence. A bad guy. A known bad guy. This is maybe the worst rooming house in Parkdale. The fence's teeth are all pointed, they're like a dog's. Really pointy and weird. And yellow. Terrible teeth. The guy says to me, "You know who I am? Do you know who you're dealing with?" I say "No." He says, "I'm the mayor of Parkdale." I say, "Well, you'd think they'd have a better dental plan."

The late-night talk show, as defined by Johnny Carson and exemplified by David Letterman and Jay Leno, is an American creation. It has a peculiarly American energy, driven by false enthusiasm and a cultural preoccupation with celebrity. "Open Mike" is the second real attempt to produce a Canadian counterpart. The forebears that are invoked, usually as cautionary tales, are Peter Gzowski's "90 Minutes Live" and "Friday Night! With Ralph Benmergui," though "Friday Night!" was weekly and essentially a variety show. Gzowski's brief foray into television (1976–78) is a wound that still hasn't entirely healed. In their book *Mondo Canuck*, authors Geoff Pevere and Greig Dymond write, "the program sure felt like bargain-basement Carson, which is to say a 'Tonight Show' rip-off too poor to bag the big guests." There was a cultural catch-22; not only were we imitating our neighbours, we were doing it badly. This combination was potent enough to haunt "Friday Night!" when it debuted almost twenty years later, despite the vast difference in format.

Bullard's first television appearance was on the Benmergui show in a semi-regular bit called "Two Minutes of Hate," a short comic rant that brought him to the attention of Ed Robinson, currently vice-president of programming at The Comedy Network. At the time, Robinson was with the CBC and involved with Benmergui's show. "After 'Friday Night,'" Robinson says, "Mike did an episode of 'Comics' for us at CBC." The segment included a mock talk show with Bullard playing the host and Knowlton Nash as the guest. "It was great," Robinson adds. "From that point on, whenever Mike and I encountered one another, he would always say to me, 'Are you ready for me to do my talk show yet?'"

When Robinson went to The Comedy Network, Bullard and Allen Magee, an old friend who is now co-producing the show, came to pitch him a talk-show idea. It was an ambitious, expensive proposal that was winnowed down to accommodate a realistic cable budget (about $20 000 a show). "Open Mike" debuted last November, and was shot live in Studio 99 in Wayne Gretzky's Restaurant in the heart of Toronto's tourist district. Its viewership on The Comedy Network was roughly 50 000 a night, excellent for a specialty channel, and it became its flagship show. "Open Mike" earned an impressive sheaf of media praise for Bullard. The talk-show format has eluded us in the way the sitcom had until "The Newsroom," and the pattern of acclaim, which suggests deliverance from years of mediocrity, was similar.

The format of "Open Mike" broadly follows the American model of Leno, Letterman, et al. There are filmed comic bits with people on the street, a prepared monologue, and regular desk bits. But the current crop of American hosts have stolen their structure as well.

Much of it was created by Steve Allen, the first host of "The Tonight Show," which debuted in 1954. He took a camera outside the studio and did comic bits with passers-by. Long before Letterman, Allen did novelty stunts, facing off against a woman wrestler, or jumping into a vat of Jell-O. He had a segment called The Question Man, which presaged Johnny Carson's Carnac the Magnificent routine. Allen's show was intensely eclectic: he interviewed poet Carl Sandburg for ninety minutes; Lenny Bruce and the Three Stooges appeared on the same night. To demonstrate the state of driving drunk, Allen once drank six double vodkas during the course of the show. He realized the potential of the new medium for impromptu comedy, for a fresh approach.

Over the years, comedy replaced talk. No one was going to chat with a poet for three minutes, let alone for ninety. The format became dominated by celebrities, who came on to advertise a new film, or a TV series, or their breasts. The host set up the pitch, kept it short, light, and funny, and then cut to commercial.

The first season of "Open Mike" was tailored to Bullard's strengths, which, like Steve Allen's, were partly improvisational. Each show opened with Bullard talking to members of the audience, doing a short version of his club act. Dealing with guests was a trickier prospect. "Mike had never been an interviewer before," Robinson recalls. He had to learn the technical language, the cue to commercial, the intros and extros. In the early shows, Bullard interrupted some guests with insistent witticisms, while on other occasions authors rambled unchecked as they plugged their books. His interview with British comedian Eddie Izzard resembled two lead guitarists who couldn't agree on a song. Other interviews—Denis Leary, Tracey Ullman—took flight and had an unforced comic energy. His interview style eventually emulated his club rapport with audiences, an edginess that is mitigated by vulnerability or flattery.

Following the lesson of the Benmergui disaster, the network deliberately didn't hype the show, hoping to develop it quietly in the shade of cable. "We were allowed to make mistakes," Robinson says, "to change things as we went, to find out what worked."

It wasn't just Bullard who had to learn how a talk show worked. "Everyone," says Robinson, "the audience, the guests, had to learn how it worked." The audience had to realize that it was part of a show rather than simply watching a show. Associate producer Laura Mac Donald, who books guests for "Open Mike," says that not all guests understood that they were giving a performance. "It's very different from giving an interview," she says. "They have to have stories, good stories." They need more energy; they are entertainment as well as information. They also need to be there. "It was difficult to book guests at first," Mac Donald says. "We were begging people to come on the show." Some went AWOL, among them actor David Cubitt ("Traders") on the second night, who never received his publicist's message that he was supposed to appear on the show.

Early on, Bullard incorporated the learning curve into the show, addressing the audience directly: "What the hell's the matter with you people, can't you act?" Later in the season, he said, "I must commend you folks, you're really starting to laugh in all the right places." When actor Patrick McKenna ("Traders") wandered briefly, Bullard interrupted and said, "What I did there was cue you." It looked, on occasion, like "The Larry Sanders Show," a deconstruction of the genre.

The remote bits were often brilliant, taking a simple premise (Bullard going door to door, offering people $300 for their vacuum cleaners), and adding his deadpan improvisational skills. The vignettes sometimes had the look of short foreign films. And the tight, lively contributions of Orin Isaacs and the Open Mike Band ably filled the odd niche that talk-show bands occupy, which requires them to be musically spontaneous and to act as foil to the host.

In the early shows, Bullard's opening dialogue with the crowd was truncated and couldn't develop the depth of the club act, though it still contained shining moments. On one show he addressed a pinched-looking woman who said her name was Rhonda.

> Rhonda, you seem bitter.
> No. I'm not.
> What do you do, Rhonda?
> I'm a pharmacist.
> Maybe you're not bitter, Rhonda. Maybe you're experimenting.

At his best, Bullard's comments evoked an instant, disturbed snapshot of a person. In some of the exchanges, the camera stayed on the faces of the skewered audience member a few beats longer than necessary. In the club, his victims are largely abstractions. Most of the audience can only see the backs of their heads, and the halting responses are lost in the club din. But on television, we are faced with their full-frontal images: tongue-tied, unmiked, glistening in the TV glare, speckled and lumpy, their eyes like those of laboratory animals searching for escape. The element of danger that fuels a club performance doesn't always translate well to television, where it can become merely awkward.

In the pantheon of American talk-show hosts (Carson, Paar, Allen), and among the dead (Merv Griffin, Chevy Chase, Arsenio Hall), and the undead (Tom Snyder), few have ventured out into the audience. Most hosts lack the necessary skills and the crowd can be unpredictable. Some are now making tentative forays. Letterman, whose skills as a stand-up were largely improvisational, does it with some success. Leno is stiffer and keeps it to a minimum. The risk (a moment of discomfort or embarrassment on a medium that stresses comfort) outweighs the reward (fresh, unscripted humour).

Bullard's forays are more successful, though he has been accused, in *The Globe and Mail*, of being mean. In the early shows, those who sat in the front rows did so reluctantly, and their timidity lent Bullard a bullying tone. But as the viewership increased, people rushed to the front row, looking for recognition and a few unkind words. The supposed meanness has less to do with his material than with the demeanour of his targets.

Last January, CTV, which is the majority owner of The Comedy Network, gave "Open Mike" a three-week trial in a late-night slot. The show maintained the existing audience (about 120 000 viewers) for the late movie, so CTV committed to the program. This season, The Comedy Network will continue to air "Open Mike" at 10 p.m., before CTV shows it at 12:30 a.m. But eventually, the specialty channel may find itself in the position of the Montreal Royals baseball team, which nurtured Jackie Robinson, allowing him to develop quietly, only to lose him to Brooklyn, to the big leagues.

CTV could find itself in the same position if Bullard follows that well-established pattern and heads south. He has a season of good tape to shop around Los Angeles, but he is a rabid nationalist and says he wants to stay put. Perhaps as a reminder of California hubris, Bullard had Alan Thicke on as a guest in the first season. Thicke had a successful talk show on CTV in the early eighties that ran for three years. "It could have gone longer than that," he told Bullard. "But I went to the States to do the show that was intended to take the country by storm ['Thicke of the Night'], but we took it by drizzle and got cancelled in a year."

Bullard just stared at him impassively, blinking rapidly, the way people do when they've just received bad news they've been expecting.

In his club act, Bullard isn't confessional, there are no neurotic rants about relationships, parents, sex, or childhood. The rich vein of material from working at Bell remains untapped. Instead, he gets the audience members to reveal their frailties, while keeping his own hidden. In our interviews, he deflected personal questions and brought along a foil, his friend and producer Allen Magee. For the last decade, he has usually worked seven days a week, often long hours. His longest conversations have been with audiences. His personal life is a rumour, his marriage now reconciled after a period of transition. A talk show, he has said, is all he's ever wanted.

"I'm a fan of the genre," Allen Magee says. "As is Mike." They are in a pub near their offices, talking about talk shows, pulling them apart and examining them like doctors checking for signs of disease. Bullard talks compulsively and easily to whoever is near: waiters, fans, clerks, asking them questions, drawing them out. He is a talk show.

"You watch 'The Tonight Show,'" says Magee, "or you watch Letterman, they format those shows to the second. To the second. What does that tell you about the show? It tells you they're not really expecting anything to happen. They're predicting that they're going to be done with Harrison Ford in five and a half minutes, which is a great example of someone who's going to be done in five and a half minutes because he's got nothing to say. We've left our show open so that if something starts to flow, we can go with it."

"We don't script it," Bullard says. "On Letterman and Leno the guests come in at eleven in the morning and get pre-interviewed on the set by someone playing Leno or Letterman. When he says this, you say that . . . . Americans we've had on—I won't say who—they came and said, 'Here's what you're going to ask me. I have my [cue] card, here's yours.' One was very apologetic, told me he thought it was funny the way the interviews went, but he didn't want to take the chance."

"We're prepared to keep the show very flexible," says Magee, "We'll let someone go on twelve, thirteen minutes." The show is closer in spirit to Steve Allen's original concept, both in its spontaneity and in the eclecticism of its guests, though part of that is due to the limited size of the national talent pool.

Musically, the country has great depth. "We could put on three bands every week and it's not a problem," Bullard says. "And they're easy to get. One band drove twenty-four hours from Halifax to be on the show." And there is a surfeit of talented comics, an underexploited resource that tends to flow south to work in television. Film and television stars present more of a problem. Once you get past the cast of "Traders" (four of whom have been on "Open Mike"), the ranks thin. In his stand-up routine, the "Open Mike" writer Greg Eckler quips, "You're watching the Gemini Awards and some actor you've never seen before is on the screen. And he's getting a Lifetime Achievement Award."

But the pool is sufficiently larger than a few years ago, large enough, the producers are hoping, to address the daunting math: three guests a night, five nights a week, forty weeks. "If another show came along, we'd both be gone," Bullard says. "You'd get into a talent fight. There's no way you can have that kind of thing in this country. It'd be over in ten minutes. We'd like to be in the position to create celebrities."

An occasional feature of "Open Mike" is The Canadian Way vs. The American Way, a comic bit that divides an issue along cultural lines. Choosing a talk-show host who is a comic is the American Way (Carson, Leno, Letterman, Bill Maher). The Canadian Way has been to choose a journalist (Gzowski, Pamela Wallin). Canada is still linked more concretely by radio, by the CBC, than by television. "This Morning" and "As It Happens" are where we hear the nation. Bullard is hoping that "Open Mike" can evolve into a forum where we see the nation.

"I think we can become what the Carson show was," Magee says. "In the end, it all comes down to whether or not the host can pull it off."

With CTV's $2.4-million expectations riding on their shoulders, both Bullard and Magee have decided that the key to success in hosting is creating the impression of familiarity. "I'm positive that's what it is," Bullard says. "Someone you think you know." It is ironic that those hosts we think we know—Gzowski, Carson, Letterman, Leno—tend to be private, in part because so much of their lives are lived in public. We don't know them. As long as we don't know Bullard, he can maintain the illusion that we do.

While the host is key, the format itself shows signs of weariness after forty-four years. "The Tonight Show" has the look of a reliable, bland franchise. The staleness of the form is also signalled by the potency of "The Larry Sanders Show," a parody of a talk show that, in reruns, is one of the lead-ins to "Open Mike" on The Comedy Network. The celebrities who appear on "Sanders" offer neurotic self-parodies that are fresher and more honest than their appearances on real talk shows. In one episode, Robin Williams, who is on Larry's show to promote a new film, delivers his customary antic monologue. When they cut to commercial, Larry whines about how Williams is appearing on competing talk shows as well. As they cut back from commercial, their television smiles beginning to form, Williams turns to Sanders, "It's a business," he says. "Get used to it. Blow me."

It is a business, and in the U.S. at least, an increasingly desperate one. To flourish, the show must have the kind of freshness that Magee and Bullard emphasize, but to reach a wider audience, it may need to become more like its American counterparts. In February, Dave Foley ("Kids in the Hall," "NewsRadio") was a guest, promoting his movie *The Wrong Guy*, a comedy he had co-written, co-produced, and starred in.

"It's much funnier than *The Sweet Hereafter*," he told Mike. "Oh sure, I laughed when the kids died. . .," he said, offering a glimpse of the dark comedy of his early career. The audience let out a tentative groan. "Oh, like I'm serious. . . ."

"Dave," Bullard said, "This might be a good time to remind you that you're mainstream now."

"And so are you," replied Foley.

DISCUSSION QUESTIONS

1. Is there a specifically Canadian form of humour? By watching the Canadian Comedy Network, analyze any differences you find between Canadian and American programs.

2. Discuss the methods that might be used to define Canadian humour. What individuals or groups are the butts of Canadian jokes?

3. What is the function of humour in Canadian society? Is it primarily a weapon, or the glue that helps hold our society together?

WEBLINKS

"Open Mike with Mike Bullard"
www.open-mike.com/

The Comedy Network
www.thecomedynetwork.ca/comedy.html

"This Hour Has 22 Minutes"
www.salter.com/22minutes/22hour.htm

"The Royal Canadian Air Farce"
www.tv.cbc.ca/airfarce/

"SCTV"
www.secondcity.com/SCTV/index1.html

CBC Comedy
www.tv.cbc.ca/html/comedy.html

chapter nine

The Writing's on the Wall:
Youth Culture in Canada

INTRODUCTION

Samir Gandesha sees the Harris' government attempt to rid the streets of Toronto of some 200 windshield-washing squeegee kids as part of an international attempt to rid the middle class of its "millennial anxieties." By appropriating the language of feminism, in the form of the "rhetoric of safety," the Harris government exerted an authoritarian scapegoating posture over youths whose real social circumstances the government does not wish to address. Those who adopt this cleaning-up-the-streets approach, called the "communitarian" or "fixing broken windows" strategy, believe that by cleaning up graffiti, broken windows—or squeegee kids—neighbourhoods will return to their former crimeless, peaceful condition (however mythical that utopian condition might have been).

Gandesha sees this over-concern with safety as one of a series of what Lawrence Grossberg, in *We Gotta Get Out of This Place: Popular Conservatism and Postmodern Culture* (New York: Routledge, 1992), calls "affective epidemics," such as the moral panics mobilized by governments around "the deficit," "the war on drugs," or "welfare mothers." Bereft of either the will to help or compassion toward impoverished youth, increasingly authoritarian governments, he argues, invent these panics to steer the public's attention away from real social issues like youth poverty and joblessness. The true panic caused by squeegee kids, he argues, is that by making themselves visible, they make it impossible for the wealthy to turn up the stereo and accelerate through "an increasingly impoverished, bombed-out urban core."

Jake Reichert is interested in graffiti as a form of youth art which incorporates hip-hop culture or other forms of rock, depending on the city in which it is found. From simple tagging, or naming, to elaborate murals, graffiti has been both destroyed and adopted by the dominant culture. Most cities, Winnipeg included, have declared war on graffiti, erasing it wherever possible—and refusing any consideration of it as a form of artistic expression; on the other hand, corporate culture has frequently co-opted graffiti as a logo or sales device to market clothing or other consumer goods to youth. In either case, the original liberating, artistic function of graffiti is destroyed.

Douglas Rushkoff makes a similar argument for raves. He argues that the original rave culture gave Canadian youth a movement that many believed would change the world. Comparing it to the early potential of the Internet, he argues that it was a truly democratic form—joyful, international, and utopian—but like graffiti, it became subject to police and parental pressures. In the end it became commercialized, controlled, and lacking in the very spontaneity and existence outside of commercial culture that participants sought above all else. Rushkoff's rather sad meditation on raves does raise a key issue in youth culture: can a seemingly apolitical form like the rave truly have the potential to change Canadian society, or is this merely a youthful utopia which in the end is only about sex, drugs, and rock and roll?

The last article in this chapter raises some key arguments about youth and the Internet. Sarah Elton wonders whether youthful computer hackers are really political terrorists (cyber-guerrillas) or merely hyper-capitalist, free market vandals. Noting that the Internet was invented by the U.S. government, and is increasingly devoted to consumer capitalism, Elton questions the medium itself as a tool for political liberation—especially given that many of the hacker arguments seem to centre on freedom for pornography and other questionable forms of liberation.

WHO'S AFRAID OF SQUEEGEE KIDS?

Samir Gandesha *(Canadian Dimension)*

The government of Ontario is presently in the process of introducing legislation aimed at eradicating "aggressive panhandling." In actual fact, such legislation targets the so-called "squeegee kids," who have been an increasing presence on the streets of large urban centres in the province, particularly Toronto, since the Tories came to power and inaugurated their slash and burn neo-liberal agenda.

In light of the economic and political crisis that has recently enveloped the world, what could possibly be so compelling about the question as to whether 200-or-so youths roughly between the ages of 15 and 25 decked out in mohawks, leather jackets and body piercings, should be permitted to continue plying their trade.

Was this not a trivial issue?

Yes. And no.

It is trivial in the sense that the level of rhetoric marshalled against the squeegee kids in the name of an almost pathological obsession with public order and a sense of personal security has been inversely proportionate to the degree to which they actually pose a threat to

Samir Gandesha. Who's afraid of squeegee kids? *Canadian Dimension* 34(1), February, 2000. 19-22.

public order. Like good Canadians everywhere, the squeegee kids are, perhaps to a fault, almost always polite. Indeed, herein lies their importance: the panic they have engendered can be read as a symptom of our millennial anxieties.

Toronto is far from unique in proposing legislation that would abrogate basic constitutional guarantees of freedom of expression and association, ostensibly in the name of protecting and maintaining public order. Similar measures have been undertaken in Rudolph Giuliani's New York City and Tony Blair's Britain, to name but two celebrated examples.

As has been much discussed, in New York, the mayor, a former DA whose main claim to fame is having brought organized crime to heel, has embarked on an extremely draconian project of cleaning up the mean streets of the city, specifically the sex trade of Manhattan's 42nd Street. In Britain, as a continuation of the Tories' "law and order" agenda, the New Labour government has arguably subsumed virtually every aspect of public policy under the rubric of public safety. The difference between the old Tories and the new Labour lies in the fact that while the Tories straightforwardly scapegoated blacks and youth, New Labour articulates its agenda in terms of an ambiguous concept of "community values."

A Discourse of Fear

This is a point to which I will return: with the disintegration of social solidarity as a result of the rampant individualism of the 1980s and 1990s, the only way to revive a sense of community is through a discourse of fear; the only thing that we have in common is a panoply of shared insecurities.

In the specific case of the proposal to get squeegee kids off the street, the argument is that it is legitimate to compromise the individual's freedom in the interest of "safety."

As a spokesperson for the Ontario Attorney General's Office announced: It is a priority of the government and the ministry to allow Ontarians, particularly women, to feel safe and not be harassed on city streets. Or, as Jim Brown, Tory MPP and member of the Crime Central Commission, put it: "People want to get rid of them—there are people like my wife who feel very intimidated by them when they come downtown."

Significantly, the Ontario Government, not otherwise known for its pro-feminist stance, is deftly able to appropriate the language of feminism, particularly its rhetoric of safety, in an attempt to enact an authoritarian crackdown on squeegee kids, and the homeless more generally.

The ease with which the Tories are able to do so is due, in part, to the fact that certain forms of feminism already possess a similar logic. The elective affinity between feminism and the "law and order" agenda reached its apotheosis in the celebrated Butler decision— a decision on which U.S. feminist legal scholar Catherine McKinnon had a direct impact resulting in an extremely narrow definition of obscenity. This led to a consequent crackdown not on the billion-dollar, mainstream porn industry, but on gay and lesbian bookstores, books and magazines.

This is especially true of academia where feminists of a certain (but by no means every) stripe and other advocates of identity politics have called for zero-tolerance in unacceptable speech and behaviour. Arguably, this does little to address the underlying social causes that give rise to such forms of speech and behaviour. It simply represses them in a manner not unlike the prohibition on discussing problems of race in the former East Germany. The result of the foregoing was made eminently clear in the Rostock fire-bombings. What the politics of political correctness and authoritarianism have in common is an anti-libertarian emphasis on social adjustment; they simply differ on the content of the moral norms to which the individuals must adjust themselves.

Fixing Broken Windows

The policy of eradicating even the most insignificant form of disorderly (or non-conformist behaviour) is both the cause and the consequence of the heightened perception of fear on the part of the public. Lying directly behind the proposals discussed by Toronto City Council and similar measures in New York and Britain is the "communitarian" approach to policing first set forth in an article entitled "The Police and Neighbourhood Safety," published in *Atlantic Monthly* by James Wilson and Gary Kelling in 1982. In that article, the authors state the case for community policing not just as a way of increasing contact between police and the community, but also to create a climate of security and law and order. This approach, which later came to be known as "fixing broken windows" (which is incidentally also the title of Kelling's most recent book co-authored with Catherine Cole), holds that by eliminating what are considered to be the signs of urban decay, such as, well, broken windows, graffiti, dilapidation, etc., one eliminates the climate in which more serious crimes like mugging, breaking and entering, drug-dealing, etc. usually take place. By fixing broken windows, the neighbourhood demonstrates that it will not tolerate disorderly behaviour, and therefore, crime.

What the authors assume is that there is no possibility that a neighbourhood community could be strengthened rather than imperilled by graffiti or a mural if it takes the form of a collective project dedicated to public art, an assumption belied by the examples of many communities in the San Francisco Bay area and other inner cities throughout North America.

Theirs is a specifically "communitarian" approach because it is premised on the notion that the good of the particular community must take precedence over the right of disorderly, belligerent, non-conforming, but otherwise law-abiding individuals. The problem with this approach to crime is that, while we might want to hold that the interests of the community may legitimately take precedence over self-destructive individualism and mindless consumerism, it is vital that there be put into play what Habermas calls a "discourse ethic"; that there exist democratic channels through which the interests of all members of the community affected by a given regulation can be articulated and heard. Without it, communitarianism takes a sharp turn in the direction of authoritarianism.

This is precisely the problem with "fixing broken windows": it makes no allowance for such procedures to determine precisely what community interests might look like. Rather, by default, they come to be articulated by those with the most power—homeowners and small-business people for example—at the expense of sex-trade workers, the homeless and, of course, squeegee kids, in particular.

The reason why the notion of safety is vague is because it relies on public perceptions, perceptions that may or may not square with reality. Despite declining levels of violent crime in North America, public perceptions of danger have not correspondingly decreased. To the contrary, they are palpably on the rise. Where, then, does this rhetoric of safety come from? The heightened fear of violent crime is part of the larger sense that life is becoming increasingly precarious at the millennium's end.

Consider the manner in which the public sphere is flooded with reports of impending ecological catastrophes, "global warming," Mad Cow disease, genetically modified foods, the threat of viruses—computer and otherwise—tainted blood, etc. It is as if in the wake of the Cold War, we have gone from the threat of one big catastrophe, i.e. the annihilation many times over of life on the planet, to that of many small catastrophes that nonetheless add up to something big.

The Preoccupation with Safety

One example that crystalizes this experience of fear in everyday life is a television advertisement for a recreational vehicle aimed at young, upwardly mobile professionals. The commercial parodies a B-Movie plot line in its portrayal of a young couple's "Escape from the City." At every step of the way, against a grim backdrop of poverty and urban decay, this hapless couple is terrorized by menacing bicycle couriers and speeding 18-wheelers in their attempt to escape to the calmer and more secure precincts of the suburbs during rush hour. While the menacing bicycle couriers clearly represent the anomie, if not nihilism, of Generation X, the speeding truck signifies the ever-present threat of organized labour's demands for wage increases and portends every investment banker's worst nightmare: "runaway inflation."

The generalized context of urban decay suggests none-too subtly the increasingly multicultural and therefore violent and threatening nature of the city.

Clearly, while the automobile was the privileged signifier of social mobility in North American culture in the decades following the Second World War, the sport-utility vehicle, with its tank-like exterior, is now the privileged metaphor of security. "Freedom" has been supplanted by "safety" in the North American imagination.

The preoccupation with "safety" has its roots firmly in the late 1970s, when the welfare state showed the first signs of the crisis that is currently reaching its apotheosis throughout the so-called advanced industrialized world. With the crisis of the global economy that was brought on, as Robert Brenner has recently argued in the pages of the *New Left Review* not by a lack of competition, but, rather, because of a surfeit of it resulting in the familiar problems of over-production and over-capacity, the welfare state entered into a period of accelerated decline. In an economic period characterised by both stagnation and inflation, it became increasingly difficult for states to maintain a steadfast commitment to levels of social spending that had been in place in the years following the Second World War.

In successfully pushing for fewer restrictions to its mobility across national borders, capital was able to gain the upper hand.

One of the justifications for lowering of trade barriers was that it would rationalize production inasmuch as only the most efficient firms would survive the jungle logic of the market. Indeed, it wouldn't be too far from the truth to argue that fear came to play a central role in the prevailing economic wisdom. For such wisdom—monetarism—was geared towards creating a so-called "favourable climate" for capital investment, hence the term "supply-side economics." Such a theory involves not only lowering the rate of corporate and personal taxation in addition to reducing the overall level of regulation, it also necessitates an increasing commodification of the services provided by the state. In Canada, for instance, social spending dropped from 8.1 percent of gross domestic product in 1984 to 7.1 percent in 1989–90.

Escape from the City

The reasoning behind such a rollback of the "safety-net" is that, in addition to reducing the tax burden, such measures would create an ever larger "reserve army of the unemployed," thereby driving down the cost of labour and consequently its power. At the same time, it disciplines labour to ever higher rates of productivity, as workers become increasingly fearful and anxious about losing their jobs and quickly sinking into abject poverty. It does not take much, of course, for such anxiety to be transformed into a hatred of the migrant, the stranger, the other—precisely the kind of anxiety seized upon and exploited by the likes of Pat Buchanan in the U.S. and the Reform Party in Canada.

The processes of globalization have led to the formation of what German sociologist Ulrich Beck has called the emergence of a "Risk society." In such a society, Beck argues, individuals must understand themselves as centres of action, meaning that they are forced to assume greater responsibility for their own fates. Beck underestimates, however, the degree to which this responsibility is more and more difficult to assume, owing to the volatility and uncertainty of the global economy.

This is well-exemplified by "Escape from the City." For what the advertisement maps out is the middle class's attempt to escape not just from the city but also from the networks of solidarity that had comprised the post-war social contract. To put it differently, the middle class is exercising its right to choose by "opting out"; by withdrawing from public institutions, by paying less income tax, sending their children to private schools and their parents to private American hospitals. As a consequence, citizenship is stripped of its meaning.

Creeping Authoritarianism

The combination of this heightened perception of fear and a profound lack of confidence in politics and political solutions to social problems has led to a creeping authoritarianism. Apart from the Lewinsky scandal that has so obviously turned the American political system into a farce, Western democracies as a whole are suffering from unprecedented levels of cynicism on the part of their citizens. For one of the effects of so-called "globalization" has been a profound diminution of the power of the nation state, both from above by supra-national institutions, like multinational corporations, and from below by sub-national forces such as regionalism, nationalism and ethno-particularism.

In the absence of political solutions to the problems of unemployment, poverty, urban decay, etc., there is an increasing tendency on the part of neo-conservatives, following Daniel Bell's celebrated formulations, to suggest that the causes are "moral" in nature, i.e. due to increases in immigration, "multiculturalism," a proliferation of single mothers, a lack of discipline, decline in the work ethic, etc. Waiting in the wings, of course, is the strong father, the leader, who is able to lay down the moral law—a touchstone of absolute certainty amidst a world swept up in the turbulence of the global economy.

In the specific case of the squeegee kids, little mention is made, for instance, of the fact that for youths between the ages of 15 and 24, the unemployment rate in 1997 was 16.7 percent, nearly double that of the 25-to-44 cohort. Neither is a correlation drawn between steadily decreasing levels of participation in the economy within the same group between 1993 and 1997, from 63.5 percent to 61.2 percent, and the rise in ranks of the squeegee kids. Rather, the argument is that the causes of this phenomenon lie in a specifically moral crisis, necessitating a redoubled emphasis on regulation and social adjustment.

The rancor against the squeegee kids results from the fact that their approach to "job creation"—a kind of punk, do-it-yourself Keynesianism—aggressively calls into question the expected distance between vehicle and pedestrian. In the process, they challenge those who believe it is possible to escape the realities of increasing levels of poverty, homelessness and suffering by simply rolling up their windows, turning up the stereo and accelerating through an increasingly impoverished, bombed-out urban core.

It is testimony to the fact that the moral panic over safety is one of the direct, immediate and ultimately inescapable effects of the elimination of the safety-net over the past two decades. Far from manifesting it, therefore, the communitarian ethos underlying the "fixing broken windows" is testimony not so much to the presence as to the absence of community.

A WILDERNESS OF WALLS

Jake Reichert *(Canadian Dimension)*

Past and Future of Graffiti Writing in Winnipeg

Property owners panic and are quick to alert the police whenever they see kids tagging, as if they expect their homes or businesses to be sacked. This excitability, together with the enthusiasm over the Pan Am Games, has led to a concerted effort to paint over, sandblast, or cover with murals any wall whose appearance seems to have escaped the control of its owner. It is unfortunate that graffiti should be dismissed as mere vandalism on par with tire slashing and window breaking, because for many young people, who often exhibit considerable talent, graffiti constitutes an aesthetic discipline.

Graffiti has existed in one form or another as long as writing. The earliest known cave paintings dating from 20 000 years ago sometimes seem to have more in common with modern graffiti than with writing. Confining a person's avenues of graphic and decorative expressions to books, canvases and printed pages—instead of spreading them out on communal surfaces—is a relatively recent practice and is part of our culture's obsession with private property. On the other hand, merely writing one's name for others to see (tagging) is a somewhat limited pleasure, and it is unlikely such a thing could become a subculture on its own. Graffiti plays an important function on what we call "the street," and as such, various commercial and ideological interests have adopted it, and hold it up to show their rootedness in urban culture.

Early Waves

By far, the bulk of Winnipeg's graffiti is of the tagging variety, which first caught on in New York and Philadelphia around 1970. A 1971 article in *The New York Times* suggests that a teenage courier, who wrote "Taki 183" everywhere he went, was the individual who kickstarted the phenomenon. Taki was his nickname; 183 the street he lived on. Almost immediately, a host of competitors arose, asserting themselves on subway lines, and within a few years, the famous, colourful spraycan "pieces" became an essential element of the battle.

A second wave began in the early eighties, according to noted graffiti writer and author William Upski Wimsatt. This period saw graffiti exported to other large American cities like

Jake Reichert. A wilderness of walls: Past and future of graffiti writing in Winnipeg. *Canadian Dimension* 33(6), December, 1999. 20-26.

Chicago, L.A. and San Francisco, borne along on the rising popularity of hip hop music. When Henry Chalfant's documentary film, *Style Wars*, came out in 1985, graffiti, break-dancing and rap music were all seen as elements of hip hop culture, and it was in this context that they spread. As Chicago graffiti writer Demon tells Upski in the latter's book, *Bomb the Suburbs*, "In Chicago, our whole concept of hip hop comes straight out of *Style Wars*. We swallowed it as a whole package: breaking, rapping, DJing and graffiti together. We never split them apart."

The earliest writers, however, did not experience the hip hop connection. The founding members of the legendary NYC graffiti crew TC5 (begun in 1973 and still going) were into "rock and roll and funk guitars," according to a recent article in *Blaze* magazine, while the subsequent generation (1978 and on) were into hip hop. Similarly, Seen, of the seminal NYC crew United Artists, used to listen to the rock group Kansas on his boom box while painting subway cars. The connection, while real for many people, becomes cloudier the longer you look at it. Chicago graffiti writer Orko goes so far as to reverse the order portrayed in *Style Wars*, which has graffiti as one of the four elements of hip hop culture, and claims that "Graffiti is the center of hip hop. That's why the best MCs were all graffiti writers: KRS-One, Rakim."

Actually, Upski's description of hip hop as "the music with little culture and no politics of its own" would seem an apt description of graffiti. Writers' letters have been made to carry the weight of all kinds of ideological and cultural notions. Graffiti is a vivid and tangible urban artifact, signaling, at the very least, the writer's disrespect for the institution of private property and his/her willingness to take risks. As such, it is easy to see how other cultural movements, underground or otherwise, might emulate it, or use it for their own purposes. The news media, as an extreme case, can be quite cavalier in associating images of graffiti with all manner of social ills.

Graffiti writers, whether they realize it or not, collude with this state of affairs. This is apparent in the attitude of some writers toward painting for the public. There is a trend, especially in California, toward full-scale productions featuring elaborate scenes and characters, which are easier to appreciate. The cartoon-like characters that one often sees alongside a tag are, in part, a response to public expectations. Some writers, such as those featured in the underground U.S. video, Malicious Mischief, feel that this is a departure from true graffiti, in which "letters"—the tag-name alone—is what it's all about.

That tagging graffiti, in its purest form, is essentially meaningless until appropriated by other interests may seem an odd claim, especially considering, as Winnipeg writer Fair points out, that most graffiti writers write not so much for the public as for one another. Far from kowtowing to any ideology, the writer's mission seems to be to find an honourable place in the cadre of writers, by writing the tag-name as often, in as many places, and as skillfully as possible.

In the broader cultural context, this makes perfect sense. Tag-names—these basic units of fictional street identity—are so empty of intrinsic meaning that they seem to beg to be brought into some larger ideological home. Early forms of rap music, for example, often sought to inject "intellect" into ghetto life—to initiate a ghetto renaissance, so to speak—and graffiti may have been embraced as a part of hip hop culture at this point. Increasingly, graffiti is used by commercial interests, like the music, clothing and sporting-goods industries, to help make youth culture tangible and thereby carve out a market niche for themselves. "Graffiti is rebellious and individualistic," they imply. "Just like you will be if you wear our clothes, watch our movie, buy our CDs—for this is what youth culture is."

Graffiti: Third Wave

Graffiti evolved throughout the eighties, Upski says, until "with the aid of magazines and videos, writers from different cities mingled; the nationwide graffiti scene took form." Coping with increasingly hostile municipal authorities, writers began to look toward freight trains and the idea of a national and international audience as an outlet. Movies glamorizing gang life, such as Colors (1988), hired graffiti writers to create an alien urban landscape, further popularizing and recontextualizing graffiti. This universalization of graffiti in the late eighties and early nineties constitutes graffiti's third wave and accounts for its spread to hundreds of smaller cities in North America, including Winnipeg.

As graffiti "becomes universalized," says Upski, "its unity weakens and it splinters off, like rap, into smaller subcategories which have less and less to do with each other." The local scene bears this out. Winnipeg's first writers were not hip hoppers, either. According to the writer known as King Ada, there was very little graffiti here prior to the formation, at Glenlawn Collegiate in 1988, of a crew called Swarm. Members of Swarm patterned their street personas on a story from an X-Men- or Spiderman-type comic book, and they listened to rock or heavy metal music, rather than hip-hop or rap.

Other varieties of graffiti have been grafted to the basic stalk. Many writers insist on the hip-hop mythology, for example. On the other hand, on mentioning Concave of the Elf Skate Crew, you might be told that skateboarder graffiti is different; yet Concave's tags are stylish and he is a capable piecer. Gang members, too, incorporate tagging graffiti into their experience in a number of ways. A few writers consider it a wholly independent activity. The fractiousness of Winnipeg's graffiti scene reflects the various cultural influences that have staked a claim to it. Even when—or perhaps especially when—writers assert graffiti's independence, it serves as an exemplary trailblazer of urban youth culture. Consequently, graffiti owes to these interests both its popularity and its tendency to branch apart.

One branch seems to be centred on the more affluent neighbourhoods of Winnipeg's south side, in crews descended from the TNC crew of '92 and '93. These crews, particularly TMB and ASP, boast some of the most experienced writers in the city and some of the best skateboarders. They are wary of later writers, who they feel are "destructive" and bad for the scene.

Street Gangs and Graffiti Crews

In '94 and '95, graffiti began to spread rapidly across the city. Fair, as a former high-school student in the North End, is very open and knowledgeable about this phase. He appears to have been a founding member of the large and historically important crew, Ever Phat Dusters (EPD), whose members spawned numerous other crews over the past several years (SAB, AK3, the DBS and DNA crews, TC, PBA and Showlords). Fair related an interesting story of his early attempts to mix with and learn from some of the writers who are now with TMB (The Mad Bombers). He found them closed to outsiders, almost snobbish. Zer, acting as TMB spokesperson, counters that they are simply a tight crew: "Not just anyone can get into TMB." Nevertheless, the rift between this branch and the middle-class writers from the north side of the city (the EPD descendants) endures.

Another branch, which seems to have arisen from within the EPD line, involves what in the U.S. are called "tagbangers": gang members who do tagging graffiti. Winnipeg has between 1000 and 2000 known gang members (and many more associates or wannabes), whereas there are probably less than 100 consistent graffiti writers. The presence of an incredibly aggressive graffiti scene in the North End suggests that in the future many of the experienced writers will come from that area. Crews such as EWD, RW, ORM, BIO and DOA, seem to range freely throughout the territory of the Indian Posse street gang. Several people have informed me that Casper and the rest of the EWD and ORM crews are certainly gang members, though the graffiti they do is almost exclusively non-gang. In other words, their graffiti doesn't mark turf, and does not, for the most part, serve to "represent" for their gang.

It is a mistake to suggest that graffiti crews will, as time moves on, come to be synonymous with street gangs. The two pursuits are basically unrelated, if not mutually exclusive. At most, frictions between writers are likely to become more cautious as the tagbanger scene develops. There appear to be numerous shades along the spectrum: writers that are "down with" particular street gangs—Shorty B., for example—and hard-core gang members who do non-gang graffiti. In addition to many of the Indian Posse taggers, Task, of the 9-Os, and Enzo, of Deuce of Central, would also seem to fit the latter description.

Tagging graffiti is quite distinct from territorial gang graffiti. Its goal is to demonstrate to others that the writer is "king"—in terms of style, skill and/or quantity. It is a title that goes beyond any particular geographic region. The presence of other writers is usually tolerated and, when frictions develop, a battle is sometimes used to prove who's got the skills. Fair described such a challenge between himself and a TMB member. The fact that he had only five cans of paint weighed against him, he said, as did the fact that the TMB writer called in a more experienced replacement. The piece by Mesk, of the ASP crew, was in that case judged superior.

What often appears to be an intractable rivalry between crews can sometimes be resolved quite simply. Amer (SAB) related that an intense war with DVS in the summer of 1997 died off rather abruptly when the two of them became aware that they already knew one another. Even the most intense personal rivalries are qualitatively different from gang rivalries. When Cose (TMB) challenged Arse (SAB), in the summer of 1998, to settle their feud (and for 50 cans of paint), the battle never materialized. TMB members claimed Arse showed up without paint, while SAB members claimed they waited for hours and finally gave up. The matter finally spilled over into violence at the Osborne Street Festival, when Arse was assaulted by Cose, at which Zeaba and others came to his defense. Apparently, all writers are "toys," who deserve to be written or painted over until they can prove otherwise. (Upski's first rule for graffiti writers is: "You suck until further notice.") Cose had been referring to SAB members as toys for some time before Arse eventually—and quite deliberately—went over a piece by Cose. And the war was on. Again, this is not gang behaviour in the usual sense: it is not about money or drugs or territory, but about who is best, aesthetically.

Winnipeg's graffiti scene, as disunified as it is, is still evolving. The city has bought into the idea of an anti-graffiti imperative, and prime, downtown walls are being abandoned in the face of the anti-graffiti assault, in which graffiti is removed on an almost-daily basis. As a result, some writers have become more aggressive in their methods: members of the Merit crew (Tank, of TMB, along with Semp and Test) have, among others, been climbing onto rooftops two or three stories above street level, where their work is less quickly buffed. Other writers (Mesk, Payz, Cose and Newton, for example) have experimented with scribing their tags into glass using sandpaper, now that bus shelters have proven to be quickly and effectively cleanable—perhaps signalling a trend for the future. Seeing the phenomenon of graffiti only in terms of cleanliness or vandalism, the public becomes unsympathetic, and civic politicians more keen, on anti-graffiti initiatives. It gives them another line in the budget to spend on businesses, bolstered by the cant of civic pride.

At the same time many writers have taken advantage of the carrot dangled by Steve Wilson's Graffiti Gallery. With their talents otherwise unrecognized and misunderstood, many of the best are eager to make the transition to the "gallery scene." Mr. Wilson provides the canvas and a percentage of any sales. Thus lured into the limelight, the glamour of the "street" disappears. The young kid with a chip on his shoulder no longer has any aesthetic role models beyond the impersonal corporate advertising that dominates public space.

Ultimately, it seems likely that the efforts of the anti-graffiti task force will have an effect. The central business district now appears to the graffiti writer as a wilderness of blank walls that swallow whatever he has to offer. And while the interest in graffiti continues to expand in some segments of the population, only time will tell if the greater effort and risk involved—and the centrifugal "tug" of other cultural forces—will eventually sap its popularity and send it into a decline. Few people would suggest that graffiti could ever be completely annihilated. The only questions are what form it will take, and what the activity will represent for the graffiti writers of the future.

RAVE AGAINST THE MACHINE

Douglas Rushkoff *(This Magazine)*

Rave culture once promised something truly extraordinary—a radical social community, capable of transforming the world around it. Today there's a party going on every night and promoters rake in the profits, but the spirit is gone. Is this the counterculture we were building?

It was all thump and bleep. Simple analog computer sounds that, amplified to discotheque volume, somehow suggested a new future for the human race. A thousand kids, wearing no style in particular, dancing sexily, rhythmically, or even just spasmodically, committed themselves to pushing through until dawn and beyond. Maybe it was the drugs. Or maybe they were on to something.

My first exposure to rave culture, back in 1988, was perhaps the most significant dose of pure possibility I had experienced since my psychedelic initiation 10 years earlier. Too young to have any direct contact with whatever the 1960s may have heralded, I was convinced we had stumbled upon something truly novel: a social scene capable of transforming the greater world around it.

In a room or field with no agenda other than a 120-beat-per-minute pulse, a few thousand intimates could liberate themselves from conventional closed-mindedness for long enough to touch something else. While we had many names for this "other"—from the strange attractor, to God herself—it all boiled down to experiencing ourselves and one another in a new way: as a collective, in motion and evolving. Blindly but boldly, we would go where no man or woman had gone before—or so we thought.

Rave was meant to be as democratic as the Internet itself: there was no boss, anyone could participate and the more contributions from around the world the better. The object of a rave dance was to bring a large group together—at least temporarily—into a single, joy-

Douglas Rushkoff. Rave against the machine. *This Magazine* 33(3), November/December, 1999. 37–39.

ful, coordinated being. How much closer to the utopian dreams of the Internet can a cultural movement get?

See, the beauty of the ecstatic experience, whether you're using Ecstasy (MDMA) or not, is the freedom it offers from values systems. Everything is delightfully up for grabs. This is what distinguished the nineties Ecstasy kids from the sixties acid generation. The hippies picked up signs and fought the war, their parents and the system. The "man" was real, and he needed to be brought down. By the 1990s, these enemies could no longer be held as real. It seemed as if the establishment's faulty foundations would crumble under their own weight. Just turn up the bass a little to speed up the process.

All we had to do was dance, and the rest would take care of itself. As we told ourselves with our music, everybody's free to feel good. We believed in the power of love, and cheered as we watched everything from the Berlin Wall to apartheid topple in its wake.

I understand why we strove for rave to not be about anything in particular. If it got too grounded in one or another brand of politics or religion, the scene would lose its healing levity. But the problem with having no agenda is that you're open to the agendas of others. The scene can be co-opted.

The Criminal Justice Act in the U.K. and over-zealous police forces in the U.S. brought about the first wave of change. Although we had a sense that it would diminish a certain something, we took our parties indoors to commercial venues. Who cares, I remember thinking, as long we have the music and the people? A few extra bucks to the police let us keep the right chemicals in the mix, and a few more to the club owners kept the power on through morning.

But everything had changed. When we were off the map, we could keep our bearings. Traveling three hours to a rave and having to spend the night in an open field forces an intentionality all its own. The trip requires a commitment, and the event itself is a tribute to our resourcefulness.

Today, you can find something called a rave almost every night of the week at a club within walking distance. Some of these parties are taking place in the very same rooms where your parents went every Friday night after a long week of work to let off steam—with booze and boogie instead of tryptamines and Tricky. By current estimates, a million hits of E are consumed every weekend in the U.K. So why is club culture so devoid of everything that rave appeared to herald?

For one, the ecstatic experience doesn't work if it happens every week. Sure E itself has effect. But when it's taken in weekly doses, the empathic qualities quickly give way to simple stimulation, provoking the same sorts of hooliganism that everyone else succumbs to on a weekend binge.

Rave deteriorated because we allowed the movement to become part of business as usual: a weekend release, no different from the pub crawls of any other worker who, given a break to blow off some steam, can go back to work on Monday morning without complaining. We failed to figure out exactly which part of the rave experience was most important to bring indoors. And that, even more than the beats or the chemicals, was the economic principle behind rave.

Rave parties had been part of what could only be considered a gift economy. Collectives would form spontaneously, gathering enough money to rent a sound system and print up some flyers. If there were extra cash from a successful event, the money would go to pay for a few meals for the organizers and the rest toward the next party.

While the cops and government officials hated the idea of kids doing drugs and making noise in abandoned spaces and remote fields, business hated it even more. The young people who should be buying alcohol, Top-40 records and paying for admittance to the disco, were instead participating in an alternative economy—dropping psychedelics, exchanging remix tapes and driving to the country.

When rave became a club event, it merged this gift economy with the business of night-clubbing—and this is where it all went bad. We all know the story by now. Clubs make money selling drinks, but kids at a rave ingest E, not booze. The solution? Sell bottled water to the dehydrated trippers. To insure this lucrative business, club owners began confiscating any water the kids brought themselves, and shutting off the water in the bathroom. Some would argue that the first vastly publicized deaths due to "ecstasy overdoses," may have been cases of simple dehydration. The kids were killed as much by the water-sellers as by the drugs.

The rise of the commercial rave effectively destroyed the very real but unstated ethic of the gift economy. Rave promoters, initially forced to raise their prices to pay for venues, learned that a few more dollars added to the price of a ticket could yield tremendous profit. Promoters who were used to breaking even found themselves tens of thousands of pounds or dollars richer by morning. This drew new legions of would-be promoters into the ring, whose glossy flyers would compete with one another for attention at the record shop.

What had been a spontaneous expression of community turned into good old-fashioned free-market competition. With five or more separate clubs competing for the same audiences on the same nights of the week, distrust and ill-will between rave posses ruled. DJs who used to be anonymous became headliners who performed on stage under spotlights. The number of gigawatts of bass became an advertising pitch. Promoters worked hard to prove through their graphics and slogans that they were the exclusive purveyors of the "original" integrity that defined the great raves of 1988. But no matter how good the sound, the lights, the DJ, or the drugs, the commercial parties were missing the ingredient that used to hold it all together.

By reducing its participants to mere consumers, rave lost its claim to the sacred. As economic and business forces became the driving force of the culture, the imperative to have profound experiences was replaced by a financial imperative to sell more tickets to more people in less time. We no longer took weeks to prepare both practically and mentally for the ritual. It was reduced to mere entertainment—appropriately listed alongside concerts and movies in the weekend newspaper.

But what made rave so revolutionary was its economics. The reason we felt so removed from the workaday reality is that we had disconnected ourselves from the cycle of consumption and production that degrades and dehumanizes so much of the rest of our daily experience. Just as Wired magazine reduced the community-inspiring Internet to a shopping mall called the World Wide Web, commercial interests reduced the rave movement to an "Electronica" category in the record shop.

It was not its existence outside the law that made rave so special, but its separation from corporate culture and the market economy. We were striving toward a celebration of the sacred. Instinctually, we realized that our vision would be compromised by business and politics. Business used the power of government's enforcers to drag our parties indoors, and while we managed to hold on to our stashes, we didn't hold on to much else. In the end, we simply didn't know enough about what we doing to fight for the part that mattered.

COWBOYS IN CYBERSPACE

Sarah Elton *(This Magazine)*

In late October 1998, Bronc Buster, an American computer hacker, broke into the Web page belonging to the Chinese Society for Human Rights—a page featuring China's official line on human rights—and made his statement. "I simply [cannot] believe the total bullshit propaganda on this Web site," he scrawled. "China's people have no rights at all, never mind human rights. They censor, murder, torture, maim, and do everything we [thought] left the earth with the middle ages."

Then, in December of the same year, he and a group of hackers disabled a number of firewalls that prevent Chinese citizens from accessing censored information. Their moves were bold. On the international digital stage, they sent a public message to the Chinese government. Buster made newspaper headlines and was quoted in the media. Since the hack, Buster says, the Chinese government has been poking around, asking journalists he spoke to for information about him. He has also received death threats. Post-hack, Buster was transformed into a political dissident, an activist. Featured in the North American press and monitored by the Chinese, the Internet cowboy was promoted to Internet revolutionary.

Hacking is becoming an increasingly popular pastime, with numbers of reported hacks multiplying rapidly. Here in Canada, government networks are the target of hundreds of attacks a day, according to David McMahon, a computer engineer at EWA, a firm that does contract computer security for the Canadian government. Some of these hacks come from "script kiddies"—pubescent boys in their parents' basements who tend to rely on downloaded software—while other attacks are the work of "hacktivists," people such as Bronc Buster, who have a clear political message. Hackers are such a busy bunch that governments and the private sector have stepped up computer protection, creating a new infrastructure to deal with the problem. The United States, a world leader in what is dubbed "information protection," has thrown heaps of money at the problem, even forming a special division to police the hacks. It's the Cops and Robbers of the 21st century, and the attention from the authorities has reinforced the folklore around hackers, mythologizing them into online heroes.

It is no surprise really that hackers such as Buster, fervent believers in open access, have been embraced as cyberguerrillas. After all, the Internet—that creation of the American military now adored by the corporate world and the masses alike—is a bastion of free speech, a giant public space where the individual rocks the world. Online, you can fulfill your own private dreams: create your own e-zine, post do-it-yourself porn on your own pay-per-view site or just buy stuff at the click of a button. On the Internet, the individual triumphs, which is why the place has come to embody America's last frontier. It's today's Wild West, where down-home, American, pioneer values of freedom for every individual flourish once again. Hackers, most of all, live this individual freedom on the Internet. They're the ones with the technological know-how to navigate the Net's open spaces and—for the politically minded—to make their views heard there. Where else can a lone guy (and they are usually guys) take on a government or a multinational corporation with success? Indeed, a popular challenge among hackers is to throw themselves up against a corporation: take the Hotmail hack of last summer that ridiculed Microsoft's security flaws.

Sarah Elton. Cowboys in cyberspace. *This Magazine* 33(4), January/February, 2000. 20-23.

And so, hacktivists such as Bronc Buster and Zyklon—another American hacker with a message for the Chinese government—seem like anticorporate, rights-for-the-citizens types. Yet, while such moves appear to have the ring of solidarity with the people, it is hard to identify exactly what power their fight-the-power rhetoric resists. Hacktivists have already come under criticism over the question of how their actions amount to sustained political activity. The problem may run even deeper. When you probe their politics, there's really only one thing that emerges as sacred: a fervent belief in their own rights as free agents in a liberal democracy.

The hacker world can be divided up into three different camps. There are the "white hat" hackers, who sell their technological savoir-faire to the state, the military, the corporate sector—and protect computer systems from "black hat" hackers, who hack maliciously. (Black hat hackers sometimes wreak havoc on computer users with damaging viruses, such as the Melissa worm that tore into e-mail systems last year, but often they just break into places they aren't supposed to go.) Then there are hacktivists, hackers with a social conscience, who use their hacking skills to agitate for change. Like Bronc Buster, they choose a cause and go to work.

Myles Long, an earnest hacker-turned-Internet politico, is one who falls on the more idealistic side of that spectrum. Long has been hanging out on the Internet since 1993. At 21, he's a veteran hacker and a passionate hacktivist who says he uses his skills to back his convictions. "I've seen a lot of worldwide political upheaval. I've seen the Berlin Wall fall. I've seen the students in Tiananmen Square standing in the way of tanks, fighting for what they believed was right," he says. "I don't want my children to have to worry about these things. I want the world to be a better place."

It wasn't the idea of social change that got Long interested in the computer underground. He got hooked when he read an article about hackers and got together with his friends to write a History Fair project about the rivalry between two hacker groups. Soon after, he was teaching himself hacking skills in his spare time and hanging with members of the Cult of the Dead Cow (the oldest hacker group in the computer underground, it dabbles with network administration software). Then he had an epiphany about what his skills could accomplish. "We can change the world. Our parents did it by marching, protesting, rallying. We're doing the same thing through computers," he says.

He won't disclose details of his hacks for security reasons, but he sees hacktivists simply following in the footsteps of the student movements of the 1960s. They just happen to work in a different medium, calling attention to issues through Web site graffiti, server attacks and other hacks. Long doesn't pretend to be a radical. He admits he'll probably end up like most of us, married, with a home and a car and 2.5 kids. But that doesn't take away from his passion for keeping government restrictions off the Net. "Information should be free. It does not belong to any one person," says Long. "The people of China or Iraq should have the same rights to read or not read, view or not view whatever they choose [like] the citizens of the U.S. or Canada."

It's hard to argue with Long's anticensorship argument—or with the fact that high-profile hacks do create some public awareness around issues. The trouble is, for many hacktivists, the politics begins and ends here, with the free movement of all information and (at least theoretical) access to communication for all. The roots of this political vision are found in the Wild West ideology of the Internet, articulated by self-declared techno-sages such as Alvin Toffler. In the early 1990s, a handful of cybervisionaries working in southern California and fancying themselves Internet experts, began to write about the Internet. They attempted to establish a formal ideology for the new space, mimicking the great writers of the past who laid out the blueprints for the liberal democracy (in the model of Plato's Republic).

Their titles borrowed from the language of revolution. Cyber-science fiction writer Bruce Sterling wrote "The Manifesto for January 3, 2000," a document outlining the route society should take to create its "technocultural" Nirvana in the new millennium. John Perry Barlow, former Grateful Dead lyricist and present-day writer and commentator on the Internet, penned "A Declaration of the Independence of Cyber-space." (Perry Barlow, now a Republican, co-founded the Electronic Frontier Foundation and is a fellow at Harvard Law School's Berkman Centre for Law and Society.) "Governments of the Industrial World," he declared. "On behalf of the future, I ask you of the past to leave us alone. You are not welcome among us." Only a handful of years since these words were written, the current state of the Internet reflects their vision.

That's despite the fact that, until the early 1990s, the Internet was the government's domain, a military operation tool designed to improve command and control. In the 1980s, it flourished as a scientific project, with scientists across the United States hooking up to the government-funded network. But late in the 1980s, Vint Cerf, one of the men credited with creating the Internet, had an epiphany at an industry trade show. When he saw the number of companies that had created Internet-related products for the government project, he realized that the private sector had a role to play. The Internet could be a public good, a space for many people to use, if the corporate sector joined the game. "I remember just thinking, people are spending a lot of money on this. It must have commercial value," he says today. Within a year, the cyber-world had opened its doors to the free market. And the free market came willingly, creating Internet Service Providers, mergermania and corporate services to facilitate Internet use. It was around this time that Perry Barlow, Toffler, and the rest of the California crowd wrote their tomes. Today, as the Internet increasingly becomes a vehicle of e-commerce, their ideas have almost become prophetic.

On top of wanting government out of Internet regulation—a key demand in Perry Barlow's declaration—today's hackers also subscribe to the Gnostic view that information will free you. Like the original Gnostics, who in the first centuries AD, integrated Jewish, Iranian, Babylonian, Egyptian and Greek culture, and believed that a combination of self-knowledge and knowledge of God would release the inner human soul from the bonds of the physical world, today's Gnostics think knowledge will set the individual free. As articulated by academic Eric Dery, they believe that what we know will liberate us. And computers are the vehicle to this enlightenment, the ultimate instrument to aid in the elevation of the consciousness. Here, autonomy of the individual is supreme in order to reach this information salvation. Tied up with these beliefs is a repulsion for institutional authority. And inexorably connected to the reverence for freedom of information, is the hypercapitalist free market. Capitalism is fundamental to the distribution of the liberating information. To free your soul you've got to first free your market. "Commerce is the ocean that information swims in," writes R.U. Sirius, co-founder of one of the first Internet magazines, *Mondo 2000*.

Bronc Buster and company are, metaphorically speaking, the sons of those Gnostic gurus. Computer hackers are, after all, a largely North American phenomenon. Thanks to a telecommunications system that doesn't require you to pay for every call you make, hackers on this continent have had the time online to develop their skills—unlike their European counterparts, who must pay for each call they make, pricing hacking out of the average person's league. By participating in the Internet community, North America's hackers inherently espouse the views of Sterling, Perry Barlow and friends (called the California Ideology because the new Internet thinkers were from the freewheeling West coast), embodying the popular movement of the slightly more intellectual California group.

Perhaps not surprisingly, no matter how strong their beliefs or how much hacktivists resemble cyberguerrillas fighting for a world free from information oppression, hacktivists lack the eloquence and romance of real-life revolutionaries. It is hard to imagine any hacker being canonized like Che Guevara or Zapatista Comandante Macros. That's in part because protests on the Internet seem to be as much a show of power and skill as a political state-ment. For one thing, consider the nature of hacks today. Web site defacements all too often feature immature messages—and even pornographic images or sexually explicit writings with loud misogynist undertones. The Web page belonging to the Canadian hacker group hack-canada, in addition to housing an updated catalogue of recent hacks of Canadian sites, features a disturbing image of a voluptuous bikini-clad woman locked in a cage that bears the label "e-slut." It's hard to crown such yahoos kings of politics.

Even well-meaning, earnest hacktivists such as Long, who really wants to change the world for his kids, aren't doing much for the cause. After all, governments with restrictive information policies, such as China and Iraq, are easy targets. And they are targets shared by the American establishment. Unofficially teaming up with your government isn't the most revolutionary action. It's like agreeing with your parents or working with the high-school administration. There's nothing terribly risky about it.

But hacktivism's lack of revolutionary lustre is also a reflection of a more fundamental problem: the close connection between the Internet and the establishment. The Internet, pri-marily in the hands of the U.S. and catering to the corporate interests of a few relatively large players, just isn't that revolutionary. The medium as we know it today thrives on a basic lib-ertarian notion of freedom of the individual, and the hackers who love this space subscribe to its worldview. They are complicit with the politics of the Internet. And this fundamental ideology of the Net links black hats to white hats to hacktivists. When it comes down to it, there is little difference in their thinking. Whether online pranksters or cyberguerrillas fighting for the right of the Chinese to log on to American porn, their belief in the doctrine of the Internet exists beyond their actions.

"I don't think hackers are motivated by conventional politics," says Oxblood Ruffin, the so-called foreign minister of the notorious hacker group, the Cult of the Dead Cow. "Generally speaking, they are libertarian-style, [pro-] freedom of the individual, individual rights," he says. "They'd hate to hear the words 'conservative' and 'hacker' together in the same sentence, but it's true."

In hacker culture, one manifestation of this libertarian politics is their antistructure ide-ology, their resistance to anything that reminds them of a bureaucracy. The Cult of the Dead Cow that Ruffin describes as an unusual hacker organization because of the group's use of humour, (their homegrown network administration program is called Back Orifice, its logo a giant cow anus) mocks such structure. (When asked to confirm that he remains "foreign minister" of the cDc, Ruffin chuckles. The formal title was created not out of respect for institutions or a desire to recreate them, but purely for kicks.)

It's an ironic turn of events, that the children of the Internet have turned out to be right-wingers, against government intervention. Today, the Internet is ruled by the invisible hand of the market, the Net's government-funded roots long forgotten. It is impossible to escape the corporation online. Even vanity pages—where average people showcase their life for no reason beyond solipsism—are more often than not flanked by corporate ads. By espousing the rhetoric of antiregulation and freedom of information, the new hacktivists—even if they see themselves as political radicals—are in reality working to keep all the power structures in place. They remain silent about the flaws in the structures through which they themselves move so easily. With all of their talk about individual rights, they are supporting the unfettered flow of commerce on the Internet, seduced by the idea that information can only be dispersed freely by the free market.

So when it comes down to it, Bronc Buster is not fighting for human rights in China. Whether he knows it or not, he's fighting for the expansion of corporate America's fervent belief in the right of every person to choose freely. He's fighting for good ol' Uncle Sam. And rather than bringing social justice to the world, his fight will probably only improve people's rights as consumers. And the status quo will live on, carried into the future on the broad shoulders of these radical, pro-establishment revolutionaries.

DISCUSSION QUESTIONS

1. Does rave culture constitute a potentially progressive political arena for Canadian youth?
2. Discuss the representation of squeegee kids, rave culture, hackers, or graffiti in the Canadian press in terms of Grossberg's notion of "affective epidemics."
3. Is graffiti an art form? What does it communicate?
4. Are there progressive political uses for the Internet, or is the medium inherently conservative?

WEBLINKS

Vancouver Rave Scene
www.loungex.com

Rave Flyers
Rave.victoria.bc.ca/

Nocturnal Magazine
www.nocturnalmagazine.net/

Edmonton Raves
www.geocities.com/happe_place/

graffiti
www.visualorgasm.com/

Art Crimes: Best graffiti sites
www.graffiti.org/index/best.html

Anti-graffiti links
www.dougweb.com/grlinks.html

Shaw Magazine
www.fazeteen.com/pshaw

Media Bias: Slants on the News

INTRODUCTION

This chapter has a dual focus: media bias and content analysis. Media bias is one of the oldest debates in the history of the media, and "objectivity" the Holy Grail of many media commentators. This chapter consists of some very different views of the Holy Grail.

Clive Thompson discusses the apparently "leaked" or stolen media agenda of the conservative Fraser Institute. Thompson is concerned with the power of lobby groups over the media, and in this case, their agenda for controlling the content of the news. Noting the amount of money that the Fraser Institute can spend, as opposed to the relative poverty of leftist organizations like the Council of Canadians, Thompson is concerned about both the Institute's agenda and its ability to garner media attention. Despite what he terms the "technicolour weirdness" of the Institute's economic arguments, Thompson is worried about its growing influence over the press and the biased reporting that springs from this.

Sky Gilbert, artist, writer, and gay activist, found himself short of money. When a friend suggested that he write some pieces for the *National Post*, he was attracted by the money but concerned about writing for a paper whose politics he found repugnant. After an initial good experience with them, he was later told that if he wished to continue to write for *The Post*, he would have to get "onside" with them. Worried about what "onside" might actually mean, and also worried about becoming a token gay author whose work could be co-opted by a clearly anti-gay editorial policy, Gilbert concludes that *The Post* is nothing more than a mouthpiece for Reform Party (Canadian Alliance) policies—and, worse yet, they attempt to hide their extreme social conservatism behind the apparently "fair" inclusion of occasional leftwing columns.

Content analysis is one of the most common methods of analysis used in the social sciences to quantify data about the media. Those who find it useful claim that it is an objective, empirical method for tabulating the number of occurrences of a particular word, group of words, or concept. Those who are critical of the method claim that it is biased because of subjective elements that are impossible to eliminate from the categories created to quantify the samples taken. These critics also claim that content analysis is unable to get at the context of the particular use of the words, ideas, or images under study or their interpretation and significance for the reader/viewer.

In "Manufacturing Media Bias," Doug Saunders argues that content analysis is not a good tool for media analysis. Citing the issue of context, and how words and pictures must be interpreted to get at their meaning, Saunders also argues that many companies, or lobby groups, commission studies done in this manner because they expect the analysis to confirm a predetermined conclusion and support an already established position.

James Winter's article on "Media think" is a critical essay on the "dumbing down" of the media. Winter criticizes what he sees as the vacuousness of much newspaper reporting and the depoliticization of citizenship, which he argues is produced by the inaccurate "tabloid style" of news reporting. Referring to Project Censored Canada's analysis of what was not covered in the news (a sort of non-content analysis), Winter discusses the political and economic significance of the top 10 under-reported stories in Canada. He proposes that for one dollar a month in membership dues from its five million members, the Action Canada Network could produce a "progressive national daily newspaper."

See Edward S. Herman and Noam Chomsky, *Manufacturing Consent: The Political Economy of the Mass Media* (Toronto: Random House Canada, 1988) for a detailed discussion of the workings of the media.

FRASER ATTACKS!

Clive Thompson *(This Magazine)*

Michael Walker figures the document was stolen from right under his nose.

It was last November and Walker, director of the Fraser Institute, was holed up in a hotel. It was time for the annual weekend conference of the right-wing think-tank, when the staff traditionally gathers to chart plans for the future. This time, Walker had brought along a special mind bomb: a confidential 28-page brief in which he outlined an aggressive expansion plan.

To this day, Walker doesn't know how it got out—whether it was someone on the inside, a hotel staff person or someone else entirely. But at some point on the weekend, a copy went missing. "Someone," says Walker, "must have purloined it."

A few weeks later, Linda Goyette, a left-leaning columnist for *The Edmonton Journal*, got an anonymous, unmarked brown envelope in the mail. She opened it and found a copy of the stolen document inside. Sensing a great story, she began reading the plan—with a

Clive Thompson. Fraser attacks! A leaked document reveals the right-wing Fraser Institute's five-year plan for media domination. *This Magazine* 30(6), May/June, 1997. 18–21.

mixed sense of amusement and alarm. It called for a doubling of the institute's massive $2.5-million budget. A good chunk of that money would be spent on media outreach for the institute's particular brand of free-market ideas, including privatizing health care, lambasting judges who make anti-market decisions and more. "It was such an ambitious project, I couldn't tell if the thing was real," she says.

So she called Walker to find out. When Walker heard she was calling with a leaked copy, he went to the phone in a flash and went ballistic. "How the hell did that document get out?" he barked at Goyette. The plan was indeed his, he confirmed. But, he said, "it wasn't meant for public consumption."

If Walker is touchy about the document, it's with good reason. The institute's five-year plan is a compelling look into how deeply the group understands the modern art of media wrangling. In that field, appearances are everything: pressure groups frantically pour as much cash as possible into manipulating the press, while pretending it's the last thing they'd ever do. The trick is to stay prominent and above all retain your *savoir faire*—never get caught trying. And if you do, backpedal like mad.

The Fraser Institute's reputation has always rested on its phenomenal ability to attract media attention. It's all the more remarkable when you consider its less-than-illustrious origins. The institute was launched in 1974, after a MacMillan Bloedel executive collected seed funding for Walker and a few like-minded friends. But in the "just society" seventies, the institute's hard-core libertarian stances—blaming unions for unemployment in an early book, for example—were mocked, and journalists and politicians alike dismissed them as a group of economic cranks.

Times changed—and how. Today, the institute commands a massive media audience, with 2053 mentions in worldwide media in 1995 alone. It's a particular favourite of *The Globe and Mail*, which has used the Fraser Institute as a source more than 200 times in the past two years; in comparison, the left-wing Council of Canadians received just over 50 mentions. *Globe* editor William Thorsell even hired one of the Fraser's senior policy analysts, Owen Lippert, for a four-month stint writing editorials. Meanwhile, at Conrad Black's new *Ottawa Citizen*, two members of the new editorial board—William Watson and John Robson—are longtime Fraser associates.

And its success isn't just in mainstream media. A large part of the institute's profile comes from its rigourous targeting of alternative news sources—particularly the ones the Canadian left has generally neglected, such as talk radio. According to the five-year plan, Fraser Folios (shortened versions of their major papers) have been faxed out to 450 talk-radio stations, forming the sonic backdrop of thousands of workplaces. In the plan, Walker also writes of its past success in "acquiring" 105 hours of coverage on CPAC, the parliamentary television network.

This has all happened in spite of the almost technicolour weirdness of the institute's economic arguments. In 1987, for example, Walker argued that "in some cases . . . poverty is simply a reflection of the fact that the sufferers were dealt an unlucky intellectual or physical allocation from the roulette wheel of genetic inheritance." At other times, the Fraser Institute has made it clear that it regards democracy as a serious hassle for those who revere the free market. Its National Tax Limitation Committee, for example, exists to study how "the self-destructive economic forces unleashed by democratic political choice might be restrained."

But the institute's media job has been so successful that some of its ideas are no longer associated with the Fraser thinkers—they're just, well, ideas. Tax Freedom Day, a concept they invented in 1977, is now so commonplace that many people don't know it came from the institute. Last year, several newspapers didn't even attribute it when they wrote stories on the day, which commemorates the moment when, theoretically, Canadians have made enough money to pay their taxes (June 25 last year). When you get that level of the "mind-share"—a fave buzzword among media buyers—you no longer need to put forward an argument; hell, you're setting the language of debate. In that sense, the Fraser Institute is an essential part of how neoconservatism became the operating system for politics in the 1990s.

As I read through their five-year plan, I had to keep reminding myself of the Fraser's long-term success. Otherwise I'd have been tempted to dismiss the whole thing as insanely ambitious. "A central focus of our program during the next five years," Walker writes, "will be the expansion of our penetration into the national media."

No kidding. One plank in this platform is to drastically increase the profile of the "Fraser Forum," its monthly newsletter. Currently the vehicle for articles such as "Why the Flat Tax is a Good Idea," Walker calls for the "Forum" to become a mass-circulation, general-interest magazine. He wants to see it increase from its current 1333 subscribers to 20 000 by syndicating columnists such as P.J. O'Rourke, adding book reviews, "comments on popular culture" and—in a nod to the achingly dry prose of the economist-written "Forum"—including "more humour in the articles to attract and retain regular readers."

Similarly, Walker calls for the institute to inject more material directly into the daily media, particularly in the area of privatizing health care. The Fraser, he argues, should create "a regular column for Canadian newspapers on health-care issues," which it would syndicate to downsized, over-worked editors. In addition, the institute should organize lists of "patients who have been waiting longer than the Medically Desirable Time for surgery," and release the names of those willing to talk to the press.

Even more nakedly, Walker recommends the institute "develop a database of journalists who respond to our material and catalogue the extent to which particular journalists cover our releases." Another is "to receive more coverage in *The Economist, The Wall Street Journal* and *Business Week*"—which isn't as crazy as it sounds, given that *The Economist* recently profiled the institute's "freedom index" (its method of ranking various countries' levels of privatization and deregulation). Yet another plan calls for the institute to place "relatively less emphasis" on its book publishing, in exchange for more focus on its shorter "critical issues" newsletters. It's a significant media move: promoting books takes more energy and demands more intellectual rigour from both writers and journalists.

Walker even plans to take on Canadian information at one of its most important sources: Statistics Canada. He argues that the institute should "convince Statistics Canada to publish our Measurement of Poverty as the poverty line. . . ." Currently, Statistics Canada publishes "low-income cutoff" lines, which measure poverty as a percentage of the average income in a region. The institute's poverty lines, in contrast, are roughly one-half as high. Whereas Statscan figures $15 479 represents poverty for a single adult living in a midsized city, the institute argues it ought to be only $7480.

The institute doesn't plan to stop at Statscan, either. Walker calls for it to "target" the studies produced by the liberal Vanier Institute for the Family—or, as the plan puts it, "the Vanier Institute for (well, against, actually) the Family."

Among the other goals, one last that is worthy of note is Walker's desire to take the institute's "freedom index" and make it "the most reliable and utilized index of economic freedom in the world." To do so, it will enlist "the help of no less than 25 multinational companies."

The total price tag for this plan, according to an appendix, is an additional $2.704-million—more than doubling its 1995 budget of $2.536-million.

Walker is convinced the institute will achieve it. "We've always exceeded the targets that we've set," he tells me. "I fully expect that we'll accomplish what's in that document."

Fraser critics, too, are betting it'll happen. As Duncan Cameron, president of the Canadian Centre for Policy Alternatives says, "They have a big budget, which helps a lot." It also has a board of trustees that, to put it mildly, represents a kick-ass posse of the Canadian corporate world. As of 1995, there were representatives from monoliths such as Nesbitt Burns, Bata Ltd., the Bank of Nova Scotia, CIBC and Imasco Ltd., with Barbara Amiel thrown in for good measure. A 1983 analysis of the institute's trustees showed that, even back then, they collectively accounted for $248-billion in corporate assets. Given those ties, it's not hard for the institute to raise one-third of its donations from corporate supporters, as it did in 1995 (another one-half came from foundations, while one-sixth came from individuals). Against this sort of financial juggernaut, left-wing groups such as the Council of Canadians are mere pikers. David Robinson, co-ordinator of research and communications for the COC, says his jaw dropped when he saw the institute's budget for expansion in the leaked five-year plan. "I drooled," he jokes.

Michael Walker wasn't terribly thrilled when I called him to discuss the five-year plan. Why, he asked me, would he be interested in discussing the institute's plans with, er, its "opponents"?

His reticence was revealing, because it points at the double-tongued nature of media-suasion tactics. To wit: a media-manipulation strategy works best when nobody knows you have one, particularly if it's an unusually aggressive plan. Journalists do not like to be taken for easily manipulated fools, an anxiety that, when you think about it, speaks volumes of their vulnerability. Journalistic desire operates under an almost romantic logic: the press most often chase after those who don't claim to want attention. After all, if a lobby group is too obviously jockeying for coverage, no self-respecting journalist can take its material, whack it on page one and call it a scoop. In this sort of minefield, groups such as the Fraser Institute have to walk a careful tightrope between appearance and reality.

So once the cat was out of the bag, the institute moved swiftly into damage-control mode. The second best way to hide a media plan is to make it fully public and hope nobody will pay attention if it isn't "hidden"—sort of like the Purloined Letter. So Walker immediately posted the plan on the institute's Web site (www. fraserinstitute.ca). That, as he told me, was intended to remove the "stigma" of it being an internal document. As the institute's director of communications, David Hanely, wrote to the *Journal* in a letter of response, the plan could be found "in all its clarity" at the online site.

Well, partial clarity, anyway. One potentially embarrassing detail got edited out in the process. Possibly worried that it would look too conspiratorial, they removed plans to target the Vanier Institute—one place in the document where the plan's invocation to information warfare becomes the most naked, and, consequently, where the mainstream media go bonkers if they catch you at work. Witness last February's nine-day wonder over the Non-Smokers' Rights Association. It began when *The Globe* leaked an NSRA internal document that included plans to "mock and embarrass" a Liberal MP, a tobacco industry representative and *The Globe* itself. Splashed across the front page, *The Globe* story was followed up by a column by Report on Business columnist Terence Corcoran denouncing the NSRA's plans. "I've had to spend most of my days since just defending the organization," NSRA head Garfield Mahood told me.

Walker, too, understands the battle-like nature of these realms. "He's been quoted as saying the media is lazy and he's going to take advantage of it," says the CCPA's Duncan Cameron. With the proliferation of think-tanks today, pushing information has become as competitive a job as producing cheapo Third World-manufactured running shoes. Walker regularly talks about outpacing his "competitors" in the world of policy analysis, and refers to the institute's book and studies as "products." "As everybody now knows," he writes in the plan, "we have outpaced not only each and every one of our competitors, but the sum total of their efforts in this area."

After reading over Walker's five-year plan a few times, the thing that sticks most in my mind is one of his more poignant phrases. It's a point where he refers to the media as "secondhand dealers in ideas." It's a wonderful phrase—both derisive and respectful, acknowledging both the power of the press and the grungy, free-market style of modern "dealing" in ideas. Walker has nailed perfectly the role of the modern press: creators of few ideas on their own, and shoddy purveyors of the ideas of others. In that context, it's not surprising that a group like the Fraser is focusing its energy not so much on developing brilliant new ideas to challenge conventional thought, but simply honing the rules of engagement.

ADVENTURES AT THE *NATIONAL POST*

Sky Gilbert *(Canadian Forum)*

My adventures at the *National Post* began on a bright sunny day last November, a week before World AIDS Day. I wasn't feeling either ambitious or inspired. But I was feeling poor. I got a call from my journalist friend Frank: "Have you heard that the *National Post* is paying fifty cents a word?" Hmmm. *Fifty cents a word.* Music to my poor writer's ears.

"Oh, but I could never write for the *National Post,"* I told Frank. "Have *you* ever done it?"

"No," he said.

"I could never do it," I said.

"Sure you could," said the always pragmatic Frank. "Couldn't you put your principles aside for fifty cents a word? I certainly would, if I had an idea for an article."

"Hmmm," I said.

Frank set me to thinking. The *Post* had been out for more than three weeks but I had vowed not to read it. I felt the same way about the *Post* as I did about the *Toronto Sun.*

I never actually *buy* the *Sun.* I'll admit that I have *read* the *Sun,* though. Actually, I'm interested in two things about the paper. Sensational tabloid journalism holds a strange fascination for me, and so do Sunshine Boys. So when I'm eating at Mr. Sub and somebody leaves a copy on the counter I usually grab it guiltily and check out the gossip and the hunk of the week. But I refuse to *buy* it. After all, I am a person of principle.

Well to me the *Post* seemed a lot like the *Sun,* but published for people who are richer, better dressed and with more education. And I always found Conrad Black and Barbara Amiel nauseating and smug. I certainly didn't think they would want an aging, lefty, homosexual drag queen writing for their new prestigious "national" paper.

But on that fateful day, I decided to pick up a copy of the *Post.* Sure enough, I found the editorial particularly offensive. The gist of "Outing AIDS Myths" was that we have become complacent about AIDS. "This is still a very scary disease," the editorial warned us,

Sky Gilbert. Adventures at the *National Post. Canadian Forum* 78(879), July, 1999. 9-13.

recommending "abstinence" for young people and "mandatory reporting of HIV status to partners." It was wearying to hear yet again the politics of fear used to frighten people into antisexual celibacy. My position has always been that information, not fear, is the most effective prophylaxis for sexually transmitted disease.

Suddenly, I had an idea. After all, World AIDS Day was coming up—why not offer the *Post* an editorial comment written by a bona fide gay activist? How could they refuse? No matter what the actual politics of the *Post* they would certainly want to *look* liberal (witness Linda McQuaig's occasional column). I looked at my bankbook and noticed that the recent royalties for my first novel were one dollar per *book*. It would be nice to vent my spleen about AIDS politics for fifty cents per *word*.

My first experience writing for the *Post* was a good one. I received a fat cheque and the editor (Natasha Hassan) didn't change *a word* of what I'd written (I could handle her fiddling with the commas). The *Post* seemed fine with publishing an editorial comment that directly countered the sentiments of an official editorial one week earlier. I began to think that maybe they weren't so bad at all. Maybe I was just jealous of Conrad Black because he was so rich and powerful, and his wife was beautiful and smart to boot.

The genesis of my second experience with the *Post* was a front-page story in *The Globe and Mail* reporting that Olympic medal-winning swimmer Mark Tewksbury was gay. This story irritated me and I wanted to respond to it in the *Post*.

After all, Tewksbury was "out" in the gay press long before this official "coming out" in the straight press. It occurred to me that I could write about the "gentleman's agreement" that allows mainstream newspapers to ignore information from gay magazines and present old gay news as a scoop. So I thought that perhaps the *National Post* might be interested in an article that would make them appear savvy enough to criticize the mainstream press. And I thought I could make some valuable political points about how straight newspapers ignore gay issues.

Now my experience with my second editor at the *Post* (Peter Scowen) was not as benign as the first. After reading the first draft of my piece, he called me and told me that it was a bit too "personal" for him. This surprised me; I had tried my best to clear the piece of all vestiges of my trademark chatty style and give it the unmistakable homogenized sound of mass newspaperspeak. I asked him what he meant by "personal" and he said, "Well, when you talk about homophobia, it's—well it's something we hear about all the time, you know?" Ah. So my piece was too "personal" because it dealt with homophobia. That made sense in a homophobic sort of way. Again, I was very poor and needed the *National Post* dollars for my words, so I deleted the offending remarks—only to find my piece butchered and rearranged in the *Post* the next day, all completely without my permission.

But I got over it. The money seemed to assuage whatever writerly integrity I was dragging around, and besides (I assured myself) *some* of my ideas were still evident in the published article.

But I wasn't prepared for Cam Cole's take on Mark Tewksbury two days later. Cole is a sportswriter for the *Post*. In the inaugural edition of the *Post* on October 27, Editor-in-Chief Kenneth Whyte had introduced Cam Cole as "easily the best sports columnist in Canada today." Well, I beg to differ. You judge for yourself when reading Cole's remarks about Buddies in Bad Times, Toronto's premier gay and lesbian theatre:

> You certainly look at the venue he [Tewksbury] chose for his coming out ceremony—Buddies in Bad Times Theatre—where playbills on the front window advertise the feelgood story of the

season "A Dyke City Christmas" and despair for the human race . . . Mark, Mark, Mark what the hell are you doing in this place?

The blatant homophobia of Cole's remarks made me very angry. But what made me especially angry was that I felt partially responsible for them! Cam Cole must have read my article of two days before, and I couldn't help thinking that it might have emboldened him to write his. After all, the *Post* wasn't likely to be accused of homophobia after just printing an article by known gay activist Sky Gilbert, an article that all but criticized the mainstream media for being homophobic (and would have, if the editor had let me).

Suddenly the tables were turned. I had taken advantage of the *Post*'s urge to appear open-minded to persuade them to publish my editorial comment on World AIDS Day. Now they were using the same balancing act against me, or so it seemed. They were countering my gay-positive article with blatantly antigay material.

Heroically, I vowed never to write for the *Post* again, but my vow didn't last long. My greed (and a pile of debts) got the best of me. So one desperate day I e-mailed the books editor, Noah Richler, and told him I was available to review books. I semi-hoped he wouldn't reply. Noah indicated that he had (you guessed it) a *gay* prose anthology (*Contra/diction*) that needed reviewing. I agreed to review it, and casually mentioned that I understood the fee to be fifty cents a word.

I was certainly not ready for his angry e-mailed reply. Mr. Richler stated that he had *never* paid writers fifty cents a word. He wondered, in fact, *who* I imagined myself to be that I was so sure my writing worth that much. He complained about writers who were only in it for the money. He said, sarcastically, "I assume you read the *Post* every day." He also said that the *National Post* was only interested in writers who were "onside" with the newspaper.

I was upset by the vicious e-mail, but thinking of my empty pockets I decided—apologize, tell him you're "onside," and write the book review! Which I did.

With this final compromise, I really felt like I had sealed my pact with the devil. But I couldn't get Noah Richler's words out of my mind. Particularly one word: *onside.* What did "onside" with the *National Post* mean? I e-mailed Noah Richler and asked him. I received no reply.

You see, I had always suspected that there was an agenda at the *National Post*; Noah's e-mail confirmed my suspicions. And then I thought I might be able to deal with my guilt about my financial pact with the devilish *Post*. Hey, if I could find enough evidence to expose the *Post*'s hidden agenda—whatever it was—then maybe I'd have to stop writing for them! I decided to do some research and discover the exact nature of being "onside" at the *National Post.*

I started my research with the inaugural edition and the philosophy of Editor-in-Chief Kenneth Whyte. In this introduction to the new paper he states that "an intelligent daily should also be entertaining" and that Conrad Black hopes this newspaper will "enhance prospects for a genuine national community in Canada."

Whyte also points out that the *Post* will not be like other newspapers that are "presuming to speak for the whole country." The reference to the Torontocentric *Globe and Mail* is pretty obvious. But what I find amazing about Whyte's little introduction to the *Post* is that he is strangely silent about the political agenda of the newspaper. Is the paper's much vaunted "nationalism" actually the *Post*'s only mandate?

I've got nothing against a newspaper or magazine clearly stating its political mandate in its inaugural edition. I *do* have something against a publication that is deliberately vague about its philosophy and then proves to have a very specific political agenda. I mean, are we to believe that the mandate of the *Post* is merely to provide a newspaper that is more "entertaining" than *The Globe and Mail?*

I probed further, poring through back copies. What I found, on closer examination, was a very clear and consistent political bias. Of course, *The Globe and Mail* and the *Toronto Star* and the *Calgary Herald* and other newspapers are biased too. The word "newspaper" itself is a misnomer. I believe that *there is no such thing* as "the news," and that in our inane world of instant sensational journalism *all* news is "gossip." We can't really blame Conrad Black for founding a newspaper and pretending he's providing the news, any more than we can blame the person who invented the "newspaper" for not calling it the "gossip-paper" instead (although we *can* wish that they had each been a bit more honest).

What I found in the *Post*, however, on the editorial page and the front page, were articles with a very extreme agenda. Again and again, the headlines and editorial pages of the *National Post* present ideas that are so "out there" on the radical right that I sometimes thought I'd mistakenly bought the *Toronto Sun* (or perhaps William F. Buckley's *National Review!*). And unlike the *Sun* papers, the *Post* positions itself as a "thinking person's paper." Remember the ubiquitous billboards and TV ads that advertised the *Post* before the first issue? The word *PRE* accompanied a picture of a candle, in contrast to the word *POST*, which featured a searchlight. A searchlight, we presume, shining its penetrating beam on our muddled brains.

I think that the *Sun*'s Sunshine Girls (and its open working man's pro-police bias) give it, at the very least, a kind of refreshing honesty. At least we know what the *Sun* is up to. The *National Post*, on the other hand, is (as I will set out to show) a Trojan Horse for the Reform Party—wearing the trendy costume of a hip "entertainment" newspaper. The *National Post* is part of Preston Manning's makeover. Its "Avenue" section and "Toronto" pages, its occasional columnists from the far left (like me), are intended to pull the wool over our eyes. Just like Preston Manning's new glasses or haircut. Just like Manning's pointed assertions that there are no racists in the Reform Party.

From the start, the headlines in the *Post* focused on Alberta, the cradle of Reform. In the first days of the newspaper (late October 1998), while *The Globe* was preoccupied with Jean Chrétien's gaffes and the election in Quebec, the *National Post* was preoccupied with whether or not Ralph Klein and Joe Clark would join their Tories up with Reform and unite the two Canadian right-wing parties. The editorial on the second day stated that Joe Clark could not refuse the "united right." And the fifth day's edition contained a letter from Preston Manning himself about the same topic. A weekend visit with the Preston Mannings "at home" was soon to follow (that sure was glamorous!).

Sure, the *Post* occasionally published views opposed to the Reform position. But that further proves my point. What clarifies a paper's mandate is not the various opinions they publish about "the news" but *what they choose as news*. There's no more subtle way for the media to manipulate us than to claim that they're just reporting the news from different angles. But who defines *what is news* (i.e. Who defines the issues)? To *The Globe* that week, it was Quebec. To the *Post* that week, it was Alberta. Each paper's regional focus indicated its respective bias—not that it was a "national" newspaper.

But that didn't stop the *Post* from using Alberta news to try to look "national." In fact, early editions carried the "national" obsession (with Alberta) to a ludicrous extreme. One of my favourite early front-page *Post* headlines is, "Banff mayor encounters bull elk in backyard." Yeah, wow. That is news. (I had a unfortunate encounter with a female elk in heat during the one and only week I was in Banff. Regrettably the *Post* wasn't around yet, so they missed the scoop!)

But there's less obvious and more convincing proof of my Trojan Horse theory. Not only does the *Post* blatantly attempt to make the Reform Party news; there is also a quiet but concentrated effort to re-argue basic Reform Party positions and make them more palatable to "liberals." For instance, the *Post* has—on its editorial pages and in front-page headline articles—consistently tried to defend Reform platforms on immigration and multiculturalism as "non-racist." They have also made sure to consistently inform us about the latest liberal "hysteria" around poverty and social and cultural change.

Take, for example an article on March 30, "Immigration: Canada's Taboo," which attempts to reposition attacks on immigration as nonracist. John Robson suggests that, after all, "immigration is about culture, not race." And to support his case he supplies a statistic. "72 percent of Canadians wanted immigrants to adapt to our way of life, not preserve their own." But, he sighs, "The Canadian establishment is committed to the notion that culture means race." Robson plays semantics, in hopes that his opposition to certain "cultures" won't be considered racist. Just to back Robson's thesis, an editorial comment on March 17, has a label for multiculturalism—"the next big anti-democratic idea."

Now let's turn to the *Post*'s reporting of so-called liberal hysteria over poverty and other social and cultural issues. An editorial comment about the power of the mass media (on November 2) assures us that "fears of monopoly or excessive media concentration are paranoid fantasies" (well thank God we can put those groundless fears to rest!). And an article by Tamar Lewin on December 16 suggests that "the myth that schools shortchange girls is dangerously wrong," and talks of "affirmative action for boys." Lewin criticizes a 1992 study by the American Association of University Women, which talks of "inequality between men and women."

In another editorial comment James Bowman is weary of "Hollywood's obsession with sexual liberation." And an early editorial on October 29 informs us that "Toronto does not have a homeless state of emergency." A front-page story on December 12 warns that as "Canada redefines poverty" the "millions of poor will rise." So in other words, we should ignore those scary, hyperbolic statistics. These articles (and many others) are devoted to exposing the hysteria behind "liberal" causes such as feminism, sexual liberation and poverty.

The *Post* routinely makes fun of left-wing political correctness in its editorials and commentaries, with a snide, insider tone. One typical editorial comment, by Ian Hunter, regrets taking the "Boys" out of "Boy Scouts of Canada" (which would make the new moniker "Scouts of Canada"). He deplores the fact that it has become "politically correct" to let girls into the Boy Scouts. He touts the mandate of Britain's newly formed Baden-Powell Scouts (named after the founder of the scouting movement, Robert Baden-Powell), where "the scout must have a connection to a major formal religion" to be a member. (What, in heaven's name, is a major *formal* religion?) Then, anticipating more hysterical liberal political correctness over this edict, he jokes, "What will the human rights commission say!" (I hate to prick Ian Hunter's balloon, but many historians now believe that his idol Lord Baden-Powell was a repressed homosexual pedophile, who channelled his suppressed feelings into the creation of the Boy Scouts!)

If you think I'm harping on the *Post*'s obsession with feminism and sexual politics, you're correct. It's my view that social conservatism is the heart of the public policy of the new right in Canada and the United States. The new right intends to fight and win its first and major battles over abortion, feminism, divorce and homosexuality; the rest will come easily. And if you're looking for social conservatism you'll find it saturates the editorial pages of the *Post*.

I was astounded to find an attack on Jane Doe in the fifth issue of the *Post*. Jane Doe is the pseudonym for the person who sued the police for neglecting to inform the women in her Toronto community of a serial rapist. Christie Blatchford condemned her for being "in the limelight without paying the price" (i.e. for using a pseudonym) and defended the police who were "hamstrung by a myriad of rules."

Susan Marinuk is another woman writing for the *Post* who, in countless editorial comments, condemns feminism through her attacks on birth control and abortion. On December 18, she says birth control teaches children that "sex had no consequences." John Collins confirms this worldview in another editorial comment on December 17 when he writes, "For the sake of the children . . . we've got to go back to the fifties." Collins's is one of many articles urging us to remember that divorce is not harmless.

The *Post*'s front pages are always the first to inform us about sagging Canadian support for health care. In fact, there seems to be no end to excessive government spending (usually related to Native issues and other social causes). The *Post*'s radical right ideas amount to a series of campaigns—a campaign against antipoverty spending, a campaign against feminism, and a campaign for a new united right-wing Canadian party, for instance. The *Post* has led editorial campaigns to free Augusto Pinochet, to stop the prosecution of split-run magazines, and to end the criticism of nuclear power.

By attacking the foundations, by seeking to expose so-called liberal hysteria, and by developing loosely veiled arguments for racism, the *Post* is clearly and systematically attempting to pave the way for the Reform Party and the "United Alternative." What's so dangerous, though, is that the *Post* is not honest about its agenda, and attempts to veil it by placing these ideas beside interviews with New York City hairdressers ("he'll do Celine Dion but not Rita MacNeil!"), interviews with Kate Moss or Naomi Campbell, and features by Sky Gilbert or Linda McQuaig. By peppering its campaigns with interviews on transgendered people or putting a chat with "Canada's top chef Claude Bouillet" in it's glossy entertainment section, the *Post* may fool some readers into believing that these reactionary campaigns are acceptable, maybe even new, and possibly trendy.

In fact, dressing up Reform Party platforms to make them more acceptable to the general public is a key Reform strategy. At a recent town hall meeting for Ontario members of the Reform Party, Preston Manning said, "There is a way to say things that is positive or negative." If Reformers think Quebec has too much power, Manning said, they should talk about "equality of the provinces." If they don't like the country's official bilingualism, they should talk about leaving language policy up to the provinces. If only Conrad Black could be as forthcoming about his tactics as Manning himself.

So just one last message to Noah Richler—don't bother to answer my e-mailed question asking what being "onside" at the *National Post* means. I think I've pretty well figured it all out for myself. Being "onside" at the Post means fitting Preston Manning with new eyeglasses and styling his hair in a more contemporary "do."

MANUFACTURING MEDIA BIAS

Doug Saunders *(The Globe and Mail)*

Content analysis has become a popular way of determining where Canada's newspapers and broadcasters stand on the issues of the day. But is the exercise worth even the paper it's written on?

It is well known that there is a left-leaning, anti-business, big-government bias in the reporting of *The Globe and Mail*, the CBC national news and *Maclean's* magazine, a bias that tends to favour politically correct welfare-state solutions and to downplay market realities.

Don't agree? Then try this one: Canada's national media have a right-wing, corporate-agenda bias that tends to favour solutions that benefit the wealthy and powerful elite, a bias that often excludes the voices of the marginalized and ordinary working people.

Take your pick. Each of these theories has a strong following in the Canadian imagination. And they're not just opinions any more: In recent years, each has had a burgeoning industry built around it, an industry that uses scientific-looking methods and rigorous analysis to prove that the nation's reporters and editors are putting an ideological spin on the news.

Content analysis, as this strange science is known, has been pulled from the dusty backrooms of academia to become a fixture in Canadian public life. By counting and categorizing the headlines, quotes, sound-bites, sources, images and opinions sent to Canadians over a period of weeks or months, analysts can "prove" that the public is being ill-served, misled, brainwashed or (occasionally) served well by their reportorial servants.

Federal departments and big corporations use content analysis as evidence that the media aren't repeating the messages they'd like sent. Organizations ranging from the right-leaning Fraser Institute to the left-nationalist Council of Canadians use it to turn out regular bulletins on the lack of "balance" in print and on screen.

The results of all this indexing and counting often have the look and feel of impartial, scientific data—even though different analysts have been known to study the same material using the same methods and come to opposing conclusions.

For instance, in his recent book *Democracy's Oxygen: How Corporations Control the News*, University of Windsor professor James Winter uses a careful reading of Canada's media to show that reporting overwhelmingly favours the voices of corporate owners and managers—that is, the news is "a management product."

On the other hand, the Fraser Institute's National Media Archive has published an equally rigorous study that "proved" that the national media tend to favour labour voices and are largely critical of management.

Amidst the vast and stormy sea of words and pictures that make up the daily media, it's not surprising that analysts are able to fish out whatever they need to confirm their personal theories.

Even ardent advocates of content analysis admit this. University of Calgary professor Barry Cooper's 1993 book, *Sins of Omission: Shaping the News at CBC TV*, uses voluminous content analysis to confirm his theory that the CBC's coverage has been biased in favour of Marxist regimes and against the U.S. government. Yet he is not surprised that other studies have come to the opposite conclusion.

Doug Saunders. Manufacturing media bias. *The Globe and Mail*, March 22, 1997, D2. (Reprinted with permission from *The Globe and Mail*.)

Mr. Cooper, an unabashedly conservative scholar who co-authors The West column on this page [of *The Globe and Mail*] and helped set up the Fraser Institute's Media Archive, draws his inspiration and methods from many of the same sources (including U.S. culture critic Neil Postman) as his left-leaning counterparts such as Mr. Winter. He finds it quite natural that they have used the same tools to find a right-wing bias in the media. "It all depends on what you're looking for," he says.

But, as veteran journalist George Bain recently discovered, people don't always get what they want.

One day last year, Mr. Bain answered a phone call from a Toronto consulting firm at his home in Mahone Bay, Nova Scotia. The woman at the other end, Kadi Kaljuste, of OEB International, wanted to know if he could be contracted to analyze some newspaper clippings on behalf of a corporate client. He soon learned that the client was Chapters Inc., the bookstore chain. In a letter to Mr. Bain, Chapters CEO Larry Stevenson explained that he believed *The Globe and Mail*'s coverage had been biased against the chain's large stores.

Mr. Bain knew why they had chosen him. The author of a media column in *Maclean's*, a former King's College journalism professor and the long-time author of *The Globe*'s national-affairs column, he obviously knew the media well. But more significantly, his 1992 book *Gotcha!* is a detailed work of content analysis in which he contends the Canadian media, especially *The Globe*, is unduly critical of powerful people and institutions.

"I think that's why they turned to me, because they thought this was a guy who was going to give them a very severely critical analysis of the media in general and *The Globe and Mail* in this case in particular," Mr. Bain says. However, he adds, "I was quite content with my own feeling that I wasn't going to be swayed by what Mr. Stevenson wanted, that I was going to write whatever was going to be the case."

What he ended up writing in a five-page letter to Mr. Stevenson, after spending several weeks studying the clippings, was that *The Globe*'s coverage had been balanced and he could find no bias against Chapters. A few days later he received a letter from Ms. Kaljuste, informing him that her firm was no longer interested in his analysis. He was later paid a small honorarium for his work.

"They wanted an analysis done that would show that *The Globe and Mail* was biased against them," says Mr. Bain. "I didn't find that, and it came to an end over that."

Ms. Kaljuste offers a different version of events. She says Mr. Bain was never expected to conduct a full analysis, and that his five-page letter had been a "sort of stream-of-consciousness ramble."

This is not the only time recently that a content analysis hasn't produced the desired or expected results. Last year University of Regina journalism professor Jim McKenzie was commissioned by the Council of Canadians after Conrad Black's company, Hollinger Inc., bought the *Regina Leader-Post*. His assignment was to see what effect the takeover had on the editorial content.

Mr. McKenzie's detailed report was unlikely to have pleased the council, which has campaigned against Mr. Black's stranglehold on Canada's newspapers. "By and large, the editorial stance of the *Leader-Post* has not changed since Hollinger took over," he wrote. He concluded that the paper was "mediocre" both before and after Mr. Black's jarring incursion. (To the council's credit, the report was released.)

In February, a leaked document from the Toronto-based Non-Smokers Rights Association revealed that the organization was trying to commission a content analysis from a Carleton University professor in the hope that it would make *The Globe and Mail* appear to have developed a pro-tobacco bias under editor-in-chief William Thorsell. "It would help, in my view, if a story got out about just how bad *The Globe* has been since Bill Thorsell took over from former editor Norman Webster," said a memo from the office of executive director Garfield Mahood. "I believe such a comparison, if credible, could go some distance in undermining *The Globe*'s credibility on tobacco policy."

After the memo was leaked, the association abandoned the idea, but has filed a notice of libel against *The Globe* for publishing a story about the leaked memo.

Things might have been worse if they had gone ahead with it. After all, the professor they had hoped to hire, Alan Frizzell of Carleton University, is a man who has become deeply skeptical about the value of content analysis (he also says he wouldn't have taken the job).

Mr. Frizzell feels that most content analysis is little more than a foil for someone's foregone ideological conclusion. "You can use content analysis to justify Jim Winter's conclusions, you can use it to justify the Fraser Institute's conclusions," he says. "That tells you a great deal about the value of content analysis."

Content analysis got its biggest boost in the early 1980s with the publication of *Manufacturing Consent* by Noam Chomsky and Edward Herman, an enormously popular work that took a detailed, critical look at the international news reporting in the pages of *The New York Times*. Its authors concluded that the *Times* had repeatedly distorted the news and buried important facts in order to support the foreign-policy goals of the U.S. government. The authors took this analysis a step further, arguing that the inevitable role of the media in a capitalist society is to support the state in its goal of protecting big business.

More than 15 years later, *Manufacturing Consent* reads like a good study of *The New York Times* as it appeared under editor-in-chief A.M. Rosenthal, who made no secret of his desire to use his paper to support America in its overseas ambitions. However, the book's conclusions seem wildly overstated and simplistic when applied to the *Times* today, or to virtually any other major media organization.

Nevertheless, *Manufacturing Consent* became the most popular model for content analysis: First, make a broad assertion about the organizational culture of a media organization; then find ideologically disagreeable items in its reporting; finally, conclude that the latter must be proof of the former.

With little variation, this is the approach taken by left-wing works such as James Winter's *Democracy's Oxygen* (which baldly concludes that "far from being independent-minded professionals, most journalists are employees who do the job the boss wants in return for a pay cheque") and conservative studies such as Barry Cooper's *Sins of Omission*, which finds in the media a cultural conditioning that avoids moral certainties in favour of entertainment. Like all works of content analysis, neither book examines the actual cultures within media organizations, whose workings are usually extremely difficult to reduce to mechanical slogans.

At its root, content analysis is built on a daunting task: To reduce words and images, infinitely slippery commodities, to simple numbers and "trends." This is far more likely to raise questions than to answer them. If a thing is shown or mentioned, or a person quoted, does that mean the reporter is in favour or against? Does a photograph of an angry striker count as favourable or negative labour coverage? Do many quotes from Conrad Black mean that he is getting an unfair amount of press or that he is being allowed to hang himself with his own words? Does an increase in stories about the military mean a paper is biased for or against the military?

Proponents of content analysis describe it as a "useful tool" to test theories about the media. And while it has certainly produced some fascinating work, it is unwise to call something a research tool that so often obscures reality.

By erasing the notion that the news is reported by fellow citizens who bring to it their distinct and individual voices, by insisting that the media must be a monolithic machine that produces "trends" and "balance"—in short, by taking the actual reporting out of reporting—content analysis is far more likely to demolish the contours of reality than to sharpen them. And that does not describe a very good tool.

MEDIA THINK: THE ROLE OF THE MEDIA IN SUPPORTING THE ESTABLISHMENT

James Winter *(Canadian Dimension)*

Darn, we hate this stuff but what can we do? The public has a right to know.

Two points seem to have gone unmentioned amidst the occasional regrets and media hand wringing over their voluminous and sensational coverage of the Paul Bernardo and O.J. Simpson murder trials.

The first point is the important role the news media play by filling their pages and the airwaves with endless lurid and sleazy details. Coverage of violence such as this inevitably feeds the pro-gun, pro-cop, police state mentality. Reform Party leader Preston Manning has exploited the Bernardo coverage by proposing a national referendum on restoring the death penalty. Ontario Premier Mike Harris has eliminated photo radar vans on the highways and vowed to replace them with more police officers on the street.

As University of Toronto criminologist Richard Ericson has pointed out, today's news media provide audiences with the same kind of entertainment formerly offered up by public hangings, the guillotine, stocks and pillories. In so-doing, they are a crucial link in the system of social control. Journalists point to examples of extreme deviance (Bernardo), promote possible solutions (should we bring back the death penalty?) and reinforce the system of social control. The media do not merely report on social control, they are part and parcel of such efforts.

The second point was made by the late, great Canadian communications scholar Dallas Smythe, who observed that the media are adept at the magician's trick of misdirection, or distracting audiences away from important matters and directing them towards the trivial and unimportant. More recently, American academic Noam Chomsky made the same point in the National Film Board documentary made about him, entitled *Manufacturing Consent*.

Chomsky said of sports, it offers people something to pay attention that's of no importance. That keeps them from worrying about things that matter to their lives. There is an analogy of course between spectator sports violence, as parodied in the James Caan film, *Rollerball*, and the revolting details on which these murder trials have dwelled.

Yes, there is a chance that another Paul Bernardo type will abduct our daughters, especially given all of this wanton publicity for his pathology and his methods. But realistically, the odds of it happening are somewhere between that of winning the Lotto 649, and being struck by lightning. So what is it that really matters to our lives that we could have been hearing and reading about all of these past months, but we haven't been?

James Winter. Media think: The role of the media in supporting the establishment. *Canadian Dimension* 29(6), December 1995/January 1996, 1996. 48-50.

Finding answers to this sort of question is the goal of Project Censored Canada (PCC), which looks at stories that are under-reported or ignored altogether by mainstream news media. PCC has just completed its second year of operation. It was modelled on Project Censored in the U.S., which was founded in 1976 by Carl Jensen, a communication professor at Sonoma State University in California. *Regina Leader-Post* reporter Bill Doskoch and other members of the Canadian Association of Journalists initiated PCC, along with professor Robert Hackett of Simon Fraser University, in the spring of 1993.

For 1994, about 150 stories were nominated from the mainstream and alternative media, as well as newsletters and so forth. All stories were researched and evaluated at Simon Fraser and the University of Windsor, with the result that about 20 were sent to a national panel of journalists and public figures in the spring of 1995. These judges came up with the following rank-ordered list of the top ten under-reported stories.

1. $300-million cleanup of toxic hazards at AECL's old nuclear facilities.

2. Provincial Trade Agreement may have dealt away their powers.

3. Third World battles GATT over plant patenting which risks jobs.

4. Corporate and white-collar crimes overlooked, obsession with violent offenses.

5. Cigarette manufacturers' complicity in smuggling.

6. Reducing interest rates provides an alternative for debt reduction.

7. The Canadian Wildlife Federation hides its hunting connections from donors.

8. World Bank development forced resettlement of 200 million people.

9. Fish farming could risk environmental disaster without more stringent controls.

10. Governments quick to lessen damage to NAFTA caused by Chiapas rebellion.

The Law of the Jungle

Economic interests may be seen to underlie virtually every single omitted or under-reported story, with the possible exception of number seven on the Canadian Wildlife Federation. We seem to be seeing evidence for the systematic exclusion of material which presents free market economics and private enterprise in a negative light: as the law of the jungle.

When it comes to the news media, an analysis of corporate ownership and influence, the process of newsroom socialization, the assertion that the news is largely a management product, all of these would lead us to expect that the news media would either discourage or preclude entirely, those views which challenge or oppose corporate ownership values.

With this in mind, a look back at the top ten stories from last year provided additional support. Indeed, it appears as if all ten of the under-reported stories in 1993 revolved around similar economic interests. They were as follows:

1. Oil prospects in Somalia.

2. Tories forgive wealthy millions in taxes.

3. Canada's cozy trade and aid relationship with Indonesia.

4. Business grabs the environmental agenda.

5. NAFTA: a new economic constitution for North America.

6. Corporate, media ties to political power.

7. The BC government giveaway to forestry industry continues.

8. Canadian mismanagement and the cod fisheries collapse.

9. Canada's peacekeeping image: arms exports outpace peacekeeping spending.

10. The environmental and economic costs of military pollution.

These stories also have been evaluated as important and newsworthy, yet have been under-reported or overlooked entirely by the mainstream press. In all then, in 19 out of 20 cases these top censored stories had as their central focus views which challenge or oppose corporate ownership values: specifically in relation to the economic underpinnings of the capitalist system, the law of the jungle.

Media Think

By leaving out altogether some stories such as these, and taking a predictable slant on many of the stories which they do include, the mainstream news media in Canadian society predominantly may be seen as promoting a narrow ideological consensus on the world around us. Perhaps we could think of this as Media Think, a form of group think on a vast scale which permeates the lives of elites, news workers, and much of society at large. It stems from a socialization process that begins at birth. It has its beginnings in a process of enculturation, a value system that stretches through history, across generations and races, classes and gender. The nature and presentation of Media Think is honed, both deliberately as well as unintentionally, in the corporate and editorial boardrooms and newsrooms of the nation's media. It is the process by which the mainstream, corporate media have come to function, wittingly and unwittingly, as the delivery system for neo-conservative dogma.

Some writers have referred to this as a naturalized, common sense perspective. It's the means by which the media create particular pictures of the world in our heads, all the while omitting and thereby preventing the formation of alternative, competing pictures. This is the misdirection of magicians. This whole process is so natural, so much taken for granted, that we are generally unaware that it is even taking place.

The product of Media Think is a conventional wisdom which is presented as a view of the world that is eminently reasonable, evidently the result of a long process of rational and objective evaluation by policy makers whose overriding concern is the public interest. Anything and everything else is the unthinkable. In recent years, this conventional wisdom has included, in part, an emphasis on the glory and inevitability of globalization, free trade, and competitiveness, with the resultant downsizing or layoffs and transfer of jobs to still more leaner and meaner economies elsewhere. Recently we've seen the manufacture of deficit hysteria as an excuse for slashing and burning the social safety net (the federal budget, Ralph "Albertosaurus" Klein, "Iron" Mike Harris, etc.). But in addition to being used to target social programs, as Linda McQuaig points out in her book *Shooting the Hippo: Death by Deficit and Other Canadian Myths*, deficit hysteria also is part of a broader, pro-free market strategy for reducing the role of government in society, promoting privatization, increasing unemployment, and driving down wages. All of these goals are synonymous with the neo-conservative, corporate political agenda. They have had ramifications in every area of society, ranging from the environment, to health, education, unemployment, welfare or workfare, economic disparity, poverty, and so forth.

Young neo-con extraordinaire Andrew Coyne of *The Globe and Mail* is a case in point, when it comes to Media Think, the conventional wisdom, and avoiding the unthinkable. Following the release last spring and success of Linda McQuaig's book, Coyne wrote a column in which he belittled the author and the book, in the time-honoured journalistic tradition of ad hominem attacks. He wrote, for example that Ms. McQuaig's incoherent arguments put her in league with Noam Chomsky, in the intellectual tradition of conspiracy theory. Not bad company to keep, in some quarters. Following yet another great journalistic tradition, Coyne misrepresented McQuaig's thesis, and then proceeded to tear down his own distorted concoction. But in the process he made some revealing observations in defence of the vast consensus that now exists on certain economic questions, concluding that, some things are not worth debating. Barely three weeks later the Royal Bank implicitly admitted Ms. McQuaig was right, by attacking the high interest rate policies of former Bank of Canada Governor John Crow as being responsible for the severe 1990 recession. *The Globe and Mail* saw fit to put this on its front page.

Dumbing Down

With their mind-numbing control over the mass media, or what Dallas Smythe liked to call the Consciousness Industries in our society, the ruling elite has succeeded in spreading its narrow doctrine far and wide. As we saw in Alberta and more recently in the Ontario election, a significant portion of the public bought into the ludicrous neo-con view that welfare recipients or cheaters are somehow to blame for our current fiscal mess. Ralph Klein responded by giving people on welfare one-way bus tickets to Vancouver; Mike Harris has cut Ontario welfare benefits by 21 per cent.

Working in conjunction with other ideological institutions in society, such as the education and political systems, the news media have successfully propagated the neo-conservative agenda. For our part, we have been transfixed by O.J., and Bernardo, and the sports circuses, in addition to tending to the kids and putting food on the table. When we do glance up to take in the world around us, we are inundated with corporate Media Think.

The result is the further depoliticization of the populace, the dumbing down of political thought. Our ability to converse intelligently is increasingly proscribed, to the point where we are left with the banal exploits of the previous night's game or murder trial. It's high time for some diversity. It's time to dummy up, instead. We need to get alternative views out there, where they can be seen and discussed and numbered amongst the options facing us. We can't simply be restricted to the narrow, dogmatic and self-serving ideas of the corporate elite. We need to begin serious discussion of the things that matter to our lives. It's time for us to take back the thoughts and the talk which reflect our position as communal, interdependent and compassionate human beings.

We can only do this if we have our own local and national news media. Not just monthlies, but weeklies and eventually dailies, television and radio stations as well. Impossible? Here's one suggestion. The Action Canada Network claims to be an umbrella organization for five million members, through its affiliated organizations such as the CLC, the OFL, the Council of Canadians, the teachers' federations, and so forth. If we could arrange for a monthly dues checkoff of just one dollar from each of those people, we would have $60 million dollars annually to put towards a progressive, national daily newspaper.

DISCUSSION QUESTIONS

1. Take a sample of the news from Canadian television or from a Canadian newspaper and discuss whether or not there has been a "dumbing down" of the news.

2. Go to the Newswatch Canada Web site and discuss the implications of the top 10 under-reported news stories.

3. Do a close reading of a news story and attempt to detect bias in the reporting. If a photograph accompanies the story, discuss the role that it plays in creating a point of view.

4. Discuss the qualities that define "objectivity" in news reporting. Visit the CBC or other television or newspaper Web sites where the standards and practices of journalism are discussed.

5. Conduct a content analysis of one week's worth of a Canadian newspaper. Do an analysis of any bias that exists in the categories that you have set up.

 **WEBLINKS**

CBC
www.cbc.ca

Fraser Institute
www.fraserinstitute.ca

Canadian Association of Journalists
marlo.eagle.ca/caj/

Canadian Commentary
www3.sympatico.ca/dylan.reid/

FAIR (Fairness & Accuracy In Reporting)
www.fair.org/

Flipside: the Canadian Alternative Media Homepage
www.mnsi.net/~flipside/

Institute for Alternative Journalism (U.S.)
www.alternet.org/an/

Newswatch Canada (formerly Project Censored Canada)
edwina.cprost.sfu.ca/newswatch/index.html

Content Analysis of the *Regina Leader-Post*: Comparing the paper under Armadale and Hollinger ownership
www.media-awareness.ca/eng/issues/mediaown/part2.htm

chapter eleven

Media Ownership:
He Who Pays the Piper

INTRODUCTION

In this era of the merger of huge telecommunications (and other) companies, media scholars and journalists are concerned that a small number of individuals or corporations will control most of the newspapers and media outlets in Canada, including the Internet. The assumption here is that the consequences of media ownership are different than for ownership of other kinds of businesses because the media help to "manufacture consent" or create public opinion. Those concerned with this issue fear the development of "Big Brother-like" figures that have a monopoly over all of the information that gets into Canadian homes.

John Miller proposes "citizen journalism" to replace the crippled newspapers in many small Canadian communities. Miller and a few friends who live in Port Hope, Ontario, were distressed with the quality of *The Evening Guide*, their daily newspaper, which had been bought by Conrad Black's Hollinger group. Arguing that the new corporate publisher has destroyed the paper's integrity and its roots in the local community, Miller maintains that local newspapers must arise from the community itself, and not from profit driven corporations that are more concerned with shareholders than readers.

Bruce Livesey believes that Canada needs labour newspapers that will concern themselves with issues of importance to the working class. He sets out the history and the difficulties of such ventures, including the vexed issue of advertising. Advertisers, and big business, he argues, destroyed early Canadian labour newspapers by monopolizing advertising revenues and underselling the labour papers. The result is that current Canadian media do not represent labour issues fairly (or at all) because they see labour as the enemy of big business and are actively disinterested in working class issues.

Turning to the new media, Vincent Mosco argues that there have been two views of the Internet: one a utopian, democratic view which sees the Internet as empowering individuals, and the other which he calls the Internet of "selling goods." His view is that the commercial interests have won out and that the mega-corporations already control much of the access, content, and uses of the net. He argues that there will be no publicly funded, free Internet access in the era of "neoliberalism."

Dwayne Winseck asks, "should those who control the medium control the message?" His answer to this question is no. He argues that the conservative nature of many large corporations like BCE is counterproductive for new media like the Internet, and that they destroy the "evolutionary path characterized by uncertainty, risk and omnidirectional information flows." Nor does corporate ownership increase Canadian content, judging from the behaviour of current conglomerates.

GET MAD! RECLAIM YOUR NEWSPAPERS!

John Miller (The Globe and Mail)

One morning a year ago, something strange and revolutionary got thwacked down on every doorstep in a small town just east of Toronto—a 12-page protest newspaper, fat with local ads, that proclaimed "Port Hope deserves a better newspaper." Some of the ads even had special messages of support for independent, local journalism.

A strongly worded editorial criticized Conrad Black for emasculating the prize-winning local daily, which had served the community well for 120 years. Under his ownership, it quickly became an embarrassment, a paper stripped of any means of keeping track of local issues and full of typographical clunkers like "Diana, the Princess of Whales." It was run by a publisher who'd been plucked out of an ad department at one of Mr. Black's newspapers in British Columbia and told to get as much profit as he could out of the poor *Evening Guide*. (As a success in Hollingerland, he's since been given a larger paper to ruin.)

What happened in Port Hope is a case study in the dangers of concentration of newspaper ownership, for nowhere has it been more ruinous than in the small communities across Canada that form the bulk of Hollinger's 59-paper empire. Having been used primarily to provide cash flow for Mr. Black to purchase bigger properties elsewhere, they are now being cast aside, and offered for sale to the highest bidder. The only fortunate thing is that Mr. Black hasn't owned them long enough to completely destroy their franchises.

But what happened in Port Hope also provides a model of hope. Some communities wish to reclaim their newspapers from the press barons and restore them to public service. And it is by encouraging this, not by opening the door to foreign owners, that Heritage Minister Sheila Copps will serve Canadians best as she leads us in an overdue public debate about who should be allowed to own our newspapers.

John Miller. Get mad! Reclaim your newspapers! *The Globe and Mail*. Friday, May 5, 2000, A13. (Reprinted by permission of *The Globe and Mail*.)

We revolutionaries of Port Hope didn't set out to publish a newspaper. We were just a group of friends—including a train engineer, a gardener, a nuclear plant worker, author Farley Mowat, a bed and breakfast owner, a retired politics professor and a journalism professor—who began meeting in a local bar to lament the loss of good journalism. One night we each tossed $100 into a hat and decided to do something about it. We found we had just enough to produce a paper and deliver it to 7000 homes. Our first editorial was a challenge to Hollinger/Southam to improve the *Evening Guide*, and it said: "In a move that we believe is unprecedented in Canada, we are asking the community to speak up for its newspaper."

Gordon Fisher, a Southam vice-president, set the tone for the company's response when he dismissed us as "a bunch of disgruntled left-wing agitators." His publisher accused us of going to great lengths to destroy the paper. He promised to clean up the typos and form a community editorial board (as we suggested he do). But that was it. Our facetious offer to buy the *Evening Guide* for $1 (all it was worth, we figured) was answered with corporate bluster about its importance to Hollinger shareholders and the future of the free press.

The people of Port Hope spoke louder. Two hundred e-mails and letters urged us to keep trying to improve the *Guide*, but also to keep publishing ourselves. One person wrote: "This has been the first time in years that I have read every word of my local newspaper!" Two businessmen offered us free offices on main street. Forty advertisers signed contracts to keep us going. *The Crier* was born.

Promising to provide our community with a "strong, independent, local and intelligent press," we went to bat for people being harmed by bureaucracy, questioned local council decisions, and campaigned successfully for a health study to examine the long-term effects of low-level radiation on town residents—all stories that the *Evening Guide* was no longer equipped to cover.

We just celebrated our first anniversary, and were recently honoured with two Ontario Community Newspaper Association awards for commentary, but we are still largely a volunteer paper that gets put together over coffee once a month in a restaurant called Doo-Doo's. We are not a substitute for the crippled daily paper that Conrad Black will leave in his wake, nor can we be serious bidders for it. But we can be an enabler, helping the community articulate what kind of journalism it expects any new owner to provide.

In my book, *Yesterday's News: Why Canada's Daily Newspapers Are Failing Us*, I predicted that concentration of ownership would lead us to this perilous state of stripped franchises, homogenized journalism, and possible state intervention.

But I also laid out a blueprint for what can take its place, something I call "citizen journalism." That's the kind of journalism we are trying to practise in *The Crier*, a journalism that is not detached or cynical but that has a stake in the betterment of its community, a journalism in it for the long run (and not with Conrad Black's short corporate attention span, geared to the needs of shareholders, not readers), a journalism that doesn't preach but instead conducts a kind of "town hall meeting in progress" with its citizens.

Journalism that wrings profits from its communities and gives little back in return cannot prosper for long. The *Evening Guide*s of this country cannot generate the kind of wealth that keeps lenders and shareholders happy any more. So there will be no more Conrad Blacks. As he said when he bailed out of Massey Ferguson years ago, it's time for him to transfer his flag to "a more seaworthy vessel."

But a new model might be found in small regional alliances of independent community newspapers, which can satisfy the public's almost insatiable appetite for news that directly involves them and their neighbours. Such alliances cannot be forged by chains. They must grow from the communities themselves, much like the Wilson family did in Port Hope. They had the audacious vision to establish a daily newspaper in a town that never had more than 3500 subscribers, and kept it going, against all odds, for nearly 100 years.

Many people remember old Ralph Wilson, the last of his line and an engineer, tending to his daily chores of publishing the news and making sure the old clock on the top of town hall was running precisely every day. How we need that caring stewardship over our local affairs again.

A LABOUR NEWSPAPER: PIPE DREAM OR POSSIBILITY?

Bruce Livesey *(Canadian Dimension)*

Does Canada's labour movement want its very own independent newspaper? During an Action Canada Network assembly held in Toronto, this topic was placed under a microscope during a special forum.

In a cavernous hall located in the bowels of Toronto's city hall building, a couple of hundred delegates listened to four keynote speakers—one of whom was myself—opine on whether a labour newspaper was really feasible. Overall, people were enormously positive to the idea, the one voice of pessimism coming from Jean-Claude Parrot, executive vice-president of the Canadian Labour Congress. He said the CLC had looked at this issue and concluded that the expense and resources were simply too overwhelming.

Parrot's bucket of cold water was a reminder of how labour's bureaucracy is either feet-on-the-ground realistic, or simply trying to dissuade people from a project that union leaders don't feel comfortable backing. In 1996, compelled by the prodding of Darrell Tingley, then-president of the Canadian Union of Postal Workers (CUPW), the CLC set up an ad-hoc committee to review the possibilities of establishing an independent newspaper. But despite some half-hearted discussions, the CLC has shown no sign of taking any further action.

It's long been apparent there's little support at the CLC's executive board for starting up a labour-friendly weekly, a conclusion strengthened by a letter I received in January from Mary Rowles, executive assistant to CLC President Bob White. Rowles suggested the money for such an endeavour was too rich and doubted a large-enough audience existed to sustain a newspaper. "If the general public is like union members and they get their news from TV, maybe we're looking at the wrong media," she added. Rowles may also be chary of admitting that in the fractious, faction-riddled and thin-skinned labour movement, many union leaders would never support an independent newspaper that would actually cover their very own unions.

Rowles wrote me in response to a discussion paper I'd cobbled together and mailed out earlier this year to a number of trade union leaders, activists and people on the Left. The paper contained the results of a survey I conducted with four unions, asking workers whether they wanted a labour newspaper. With the assistance of CUPW researcher Chris Lawson, I've been pursuing a long-held dream of founding an independent labour newspaper, especially in light of how stories and issues about working people are rarely addressed by the mainstream media.

Bruce Livesey. A labour newspaper: Pipe dream or possibility? *Canadian Dimension*, 33(4/5), Fall, 1999. 35-38.

As a journalist, I've written about the labour movement for about 15 years, primarily for *Our Times* magazine. For a couple of years in the mid-nineties, I was even a columnist and writer for *Labour Times*, a monthly paper published by Canada Law Book. *Labour Times* was around for about five years before the company killed it off and turned it into something more banal and pro-management called *Workplace News*. Yet *Labour Times* proved that an independent labour publication could cover the labour movement, garner an audience and not lose money (admittedly, it never turned a profit, either). And stories that were not "anti-union" *per se*, but were not obsequious towards labour's leadership and the NDP, could appear in print.

After *Labour Times* died, I thought it would be a worthwhile endeavor to see if there was support for an independent, self-sustaining labour publication that appeared more frequently than *Our Times*, and was more controversial and militant. In so doing, the question has emerged: why doesn't Canada have its own independent labour newspaper?

Why Not?

The reasons are numerous. One is because labour's leadership has not seen the need for such a publication, generally being wary of any media, fearing its potential independence.

Yet Canada once did have a very vibrant working-class, labour and socialist press. In fact, nearly 250 labour journals were established between 1867 and 1948, with 70 publishing by the end of the 'forties, having a combined circulation of more than 300 000; publications like *Labour Record*, *Labour Advocate* and *Canadian Labour Reformer*. It's even said that Toronto once had 13 dailies, some of which were working-class newspapers.

But according to Noam Chomsky and Edward S. Herman, authors of the 1988 book *Manufacturing Consent*, the reason such newspapers aren't around today is because of advertising. The working class press that once flourished in many Western countries in the 1800s and early part of this century was often enormously effective in reinforcing class-consciousness, unifying workers based on an alternative value system, and promoting social change. Not surprisingly, this radical press was considered a major threat to the ruling business elites. Attempts to suppress labour newspapers using taxes and libel laws failed. What did succeed was using the marketplace to drive the working class press out of existence.

True, the capital costs of starting up and maintaining daily newspapers have risen persistently over the decades. In the early days of the daily press, launching a newspaper and breaking even required surprisingly little capital. But as the media became more concentrated, and the economies of scale much larger, the money needed for establishing a daily newspaper began to run into the hundreds of millions of dollars.

The Rise of Advertising

However, advertising was most responsible for killing off the working class press. Prior to newspapers displaying ads, what a newspaper made at the newsstand had to cover the costs of publishing it. But with the emergence of advertising, newspapers that attracted ads could lower the price of their product at the newsstand. In effect, advertising is a direct subsidy from the business sector to those newspapers that reflect their ideological and class outlook—in other words, right-wing and pro-business. Those newspapers unable to attract advertising were then put at an enormous and ultimately fatal disadvantage. Indeed, right-wing newspapers were able to drop the price at the newsstands to such a low level that it effectively drove the higher-priced labour newspapers out of the market. Moreover, labour readers tended to be of modest means, so they weren't of much interest to advertisers anyway.

Not much has changed since then. Working class and radical newspapers or broadcasters are always going to be at a serious disadvantage because it's unlikely they would attract enough advertising, and therefore the revenue, to truly compete with the right-wing media.

The newsstand price issue should not be poopooed: in recent years, Conrad Black and Rupert Murdoch fought a pitched battle in the U.K. over marketshare, between their rival dailies *The Times* and *The Daily Telegraph*, by lowering the price of the newspapers. This method worked, with the circulation of both newspapers rising considerably.

But what about the so-called free alternative weeklies that have popped up in most major cities in recent times and are solely sustained by advertising, while containing generally left/liberal content? In Toronto, these include *Now* and *Eye* (where I work as a staff reporter), *The Mirror* in Montreal, and *The Georgia Straight* in Vancouver, among others. These weeklies rarely cover the labour movement, however, and if so, not always in a positive light. They're bereft of more serious ideological content, with discussions about socialism, class struggle and political philosophy never appearing. Furthermore, these newspapers garner advertising primarily because they have a strong entertainment/popular-culture component, with their news holes usually being a minor part of the overall content.

If So, Who Would Read It?

Ultimately, is there an audience for a left-leaning labour publication? After all, an alternative press does exist with periodicals like *This Magazine, Canadian Dimension, Our Times, Canadian Forum*, and *New Maritimes* publishing year after year. The labour movement itself has a bevy of newspapers, magazine and newsletters. The CLC, for instance, publishes *OUTFront*, a periodical distributed to 50 000 people. Yet the alternative press has a combined circulation and reach that's miniscule if compared to that of the corporate media.

So does the precarious existence of the alternative press infer that workers aren't interested in its content, no matter how intelligent or perceptive they may be? After all, if the statistics are correct, two-thirds of union members get most of their news from TV. That may mean they are not big readers. And about one-quarter of any union's members are probably functionally illiterate. Meanwhile, most workers don't see themselves as unionists first, but as parents, sports fans, chess players and sport fishermen. And then there is the problem of media overload. With so much printed and broadcast matter currently available, why would workers want to devote time to one more?

Still, I believe the reason alternative periodicals have small circulations is because they cannot hire the writers, the foreign correspondents, the art designers and photographers that the corporate media can. The right-wing press can afford to launch marketing and circulation campaigns replete with TV ads, and then publish on glossy stock with colour photographs. Which is exactly what *Time, Newsweek, Maclean's, The Globe and Mail, The National Post, Vanity Fair* and *Chatelaine* do.

I believe an audience for a labour newspaper exists. I say this because of two surveys I have. One I conducted myself last year to see if there was the political and financial wherewithal to sustain a labour publication and, if so, what it should contain.

My survey was completed by 266 members of the Canadian Auto Workers (CAW), the Canadian Union of Postal Workers (CUPW), the Canadian Union of Public Employees

(CUPE) and the Ontario Public Service Employees' Union (OPSEU), who work in a wide range of industries and occupations.

They were asked whether Canada's labour movement needs its very own independent publication, and told to respond on a scale from one to ten, with one being not at all, five being indifferent and ten needing a publication a great deal. The reply? 8.77. In other words, the vast majority of respondents felt there was a need for such a publication. Moreover, 88.1 percent felt the mainstream media was anti-labour, with only 10 percent thinking it was neutral. When asked if the news analysis in the mainstream media fulfils their needs adequately, some or none, the responses were 3.4 percent adequately, 68.2 percent some, and 28.3 percent none at all.

The survey also asked them how much they would be willing to pay for a subscription for a publication that contained all that they wanted. Most said under $50, but were more likely to pay more if they were spending their union's money.

I also asked them how much money they would donate or invest to help see a publication started up. The response was again most under $50, although 45 percent were willing to invest more than $50 of their union's cash.

At the same time, I managed to get hold of a Vector Poll conducted for the CLC in March, 1997. It examined the potential market for a labour paper. The Vector Polling Group does polling, social marketing and media training for unions, and is funded by the CLC, the United Steelworkers of America and CUPE. This particular poll found that nine percent of adults across the country would be "certain" to buy a national labour newspaper if they could afford it. This would translate into a national audience of 1.8 million readers. Another 32 percent of the population claim they would "likely" read a labour paper (another 6.4 million readers).

The poll said that while advocates of a national labour paper will be encouraged by these findings, market researchers know that surveys on buying intentions are notoriously unreliable as predictors of consumer behaviour. Only those who say "certain" to buy would be the primary target readers if such a paper were ever launched. Moreover, these are readers and not necessarily buyers. And, of course, price dictates audience size—the lower the individual cost, the more likely people will purchase it.

What are we to make of the results from my survey and the Vector poll? There's no question that the 266 trade unionists I polled are the sort of readers a labour publication would be targeted at: they are mostly trade union activists and have a certain level of labour and class-consciousness. Not surprisingly, they recognize the need for an independent labour publication, and see the mainstream media as inherently anti-labour. They also prefer the publication to be a newspaper, rather than a magazine, and its content be accessible through the Internet. They also would prefer it appear at least monthly, more preferably bi-weekly or weekly.

The Bottom Line

But are they willing to pay for it? Again, it's evident that cost is an issue: the more expensive a subscription, the less likely people are going to buy it. This is a quite an understandable reaction.

The Vector poll shows that there is a large number of people willing to at least read and possibly subscribe to a labour newspaper. A larger number would be sometime readers. At the very least, the Vector poll suggests a big enough audience base exists in Canada to sustain a publication.

Yet the age-old problem remains: how to finance and sustain a newspaper?

For starters, my survey suggests that people are not willing to spend enough on a sub-scription to keep a weekly afloat, or at least without having a lot of advertising dollars to cover most of its costs. Some believe that advertising revenue could be found. I am more skeptical. Corporations and governments hate unions, or tolerate them grudgingly, and rarely donate to the NDP, and never donate to parties more radical than the NDP. So it's unlikely they will fund a newspaper that actively works against their class interests—a newspaper aimed at strengthening unions, calling for more militancy among workers, and discussing a politic more left-wing than the NDP. This isn't to suggest that advertising could not be garnered—say from small businesses, labour law firms, unions and NGOs. But probably not enough to keep a daily, or even a weekly afloat.

The only compelling reason why workers would financially assist a publication above and beyond what they're asked for by other newspapers is if they actually own and demo-cratically control it. One model I envision calls for capital to be raised by selling shares to individuals, starting at $50. Unions and locals would be asked to buy either more than one share, or buy a share for more than $50. No one could individually own enough shares to give them a controlling interest, or even more of a say in how the newspaper is actually operated.

These shares would give its holder certain rights. Such as access to the newspaper's pages to voice their own opinions. As well, they can elect the publisher and editor, along with a board of directors. This model would call for some form of democratic forum—perhaps designed along the lines of the CAW's Canada Council—where every six months or so shareholders can come together and express their views on the newspaper's progress, its con-tent and political direction. In order to raise capital on an on-going basis, shareholders could be asked to renew their share every year or so.

This model, if successful, would preclude the necessity of depending on advertising and subscriptions as the only source of funds (although it would seek advertising where it could be found). It would also be truly socialist, where working people get to democratically own their own media. While this model sounds somewhat Utopian, and may be too unwieldy to work, it also has enormous potential to galvanize working people around ideas, information and politics.

One other model was posited by CUPW's Chris Lawson, who sat on the CLC's ad hoc committee that reviewed the possibilities of starting up a labour newspaper. His idea called for a weekly that would operate at arm's length from labour with a board appointed by unions but enjoying editorial independence.

How would it be sustained? This model would have the newspaper distributed free of charge to union members' households. Unions keep lists of where their members reside. Using those lists, the paper would have a guaranteed audience. Given the fact that many union households are an appealing demographic for advertisers—earning a fair amount of disposable income—it's presumed companies would be attracted to advertising in such a newspaper. Thus the publication would be entirely advertising-financed.

Starting up a labour newspaper would be no easy endeavour, requiring enormous com-mitment from trade unionists to see it realized and then sustained. However, with virtually the entire media we consume owned by right-wing corporate or state interests, the neces-sity for such an alternative media is greater today than ever before.

MEDIA CONCENTRATION IN A DOT COM WORLD

Vincent Mosco *(Canadian Dimension)*

Two visions have dominated most thinking about the Internet. On the one hand, there is the Internet that promotes democracy by expanding communication, citizen participation and popular involvement in social movements and the political process worldwide. It is the Internet that breaks down traditional barriers between authors and readers, producers and viewers, the powerful and the rest of us. Moreover, it is the Internet that removes all traces of class, race, ethnic, gender, or sexual identity, enabling us to enter cyberspace and not only go wherever we want, meet whomever we want, but also, and almost magically, be whomever we choose. It is the Internet of the rebels in Chiapas beaming their provocations from laptops in their village hideouts.

The second sees the Internet and cyberspace as a giant shopping mall, one large electronic office, or a television set on speed. This is the vision of cyberspace that makes corporate executives and not a few government policy makers salivate at the prospect of using the net to produce and market more of everything. It is the Internet of selling goods, information, services and audiences to global markets that transcend time, distance and culture.

Since the start of the new millennium, a series of mergers have reconfigured the Internet to make it much more likely that the second vision will triumph. Mind you, events at the close of the last millennium did not exactly augur well for democratic communication. At that time a handful of mainly U.S.-based global conglomerates dominated the worldwide production and distribution of information and entertainment. The web of connections linking just eight companies—Microsoft, Disney/ABC, Time Warner/Turner, GE/NBC, AT&T-TCI, CBS/Viacom, the News Corp, and Bertelsmann—shaped almost every major sector of cyberspace. They dominate the new electronic services arena, which includes cable television, TV and film production, Internet technology and content, telephone and wireless telecommunications, home video and games, sports teams and stadia, satellites, newspapers, magazines, books, television broadcasting, music and recording, and theme parks.

Canada had its own version of monopoly as every sector of our communication and cultural industries came under the control of a dominant firm. Conrad Black's Hollinger corporation in newspapers, Rogers in cable and magazines, Chapters in book distribution and marketing, and Bell Canada Enterprises in telecommunications, are the major examples. The U.S. plays a growing role in these companies, with AT&T holding a major stake in Rogers, and Barnes and Noble, the giant U.S. bookseller, in Chapters.

The new millennium did not skip a beat. On January 10 the largest Internet company, America Online, bought Time Warner, the largest owner of intellectual property in the world. The deal gives AOL access to an entertainment and information empire that includes CNN, Home Box Office, Warner music and films, *Time* magazine, and a network of 13 million cable television subscribers. Time Warner gets access to what is by far the largest Internet connection company in the world with 22 million paying subscribers.

Less than a month later, Canada's Rogers became the dominant force in Canadian cable television across the country by spending close to $6 billion to purchase Quebec's Le Groupe Videotron. The deal puts Rogers cable into 3.7 million Canadian households, making it the national leader. It also gives the communication giant 260,000 high-speed Internet

Vincent Mosco. Media concentration in a dot com world. *Canadian Dimension* 34(3), May/June, 2000. 16-17.

customers, placing it third among high-speed providers in all of North America after AOL-Time Warner and AT&T. With characteristic forthrightness, Rogers said that it will join Videotron's strength in Quebec with its own cable operations, largely based in Ontario and British Columbia, as well as fully integrate services such as Rogers' AT&T wireless to kill off the competition by offering bundles of services including cable, Internet, wireless, business services, publishing, radio, home security and home telephony.

About two weeks later, Bell Canada Enterprises, having stuffed itself with cash from the sale of Nortel and other assets, opened its wallet and offered to spend $2.3 billion to buy Canada's largest private broadcaster CTV. BCE controls Bell Canada telephone, Sympatico, the largest internet service provider in Canada, as well as wireless telephone, direct broadcast satellites, and investments in telecommunications and new technology enterprises across Canada. CTV owns television stations nationwide, a national television network, national headline news and sports networks, and has pending the purchase of speciality channels The Sports Network and the Discovery Channel.

Finally, in a sell-off that will likely deepen media concentration in Canada, the Thomson Corporation, owner of *The Globe and Mail,* put all of its remaining newspapers on the block in order to devote more attention to its online information businesses. Up for sale are five Canadian newspapers, and Conrad Black's Hollinger, which now controls 61 dailies across the country—over half the English-language dailies—is eyeing them. It especially would like the *Winnipeg Free Press*, which would give the company either a monopoly or a significant position in every major English-language newspaper market in the country, and more room to promote its right-wing agenda.

These deals signal an acceleration in the already substantial pace of concentration in the communication business. Each grows out of specific concerns. AOL-Time Warner brings together the largest provider of access to the Internet with the largest owner of content. BCE-CTV is similar, but the content is more focused on broadcast media. Rogers-Videotron is mainly a move into a new market—the King of Anglo cable buys subscribers in Quebec. Finally, the Thomson move places the bets of one large company squarely on the Dot Com world and opens the door for the largest holder of newspapers in this country's history to grow even fatter. But beyond the specific implications of the deal, there are consequences, and not very good ones, for the promise of democratic communication.

The growth of the online world led some to expect that media concentration would slow, particularly in the short term, because cyberspace added too much real estate for even large media companies to buy up rapidly. In fact, they have done so with remarkable ease, managing to put together global firms that bring together control over conduits (access to media) and content (entertainment and information).

Alongside concentration, we can observe the rapid commercialization of that real estate, as companies design new ways to market access (expensive monthly fees for high-speed, video-quality connections), to sell products and services through e-commerce, and to sell, as they say, eyeballs to advertisers through sophisticated and privacy-invading means of measuring viewership. Companies like AOL-Time Warner will use their new power to brand the desktop with portals for their companies, easing access to their own material, and with advertising for companies sufficiently flush to rent space on the big firm's real estate.

These developments are in line with the history of modern mass media. When the telegraph came along it was hailed as an instrument of democracy. Within a decade, the Western Union Company had established its monopoly power and relegated the telegraph to commercial use. Practically the same can be said for telephone, radio and television. Nations were nevertheless able to preserve some measure of public control, some alternative to commercial content, some limit on monopoly pricing of access and services. They established public systems like the CBC or regulated both conduits and contents, at the very least keeping companies from controlling both. These measures came after long public struggles and we enjoy their admittedly eroding benefits today. These include universal access to telephone, public radio and television, and measures to ensure even a minimal level of Canadian content.

Even the United States, the beacon of free enterprise, was made to regulate telecommunications and broadcasting, reserve non-commercial channels for radio and television, and establish content rules for commercial television that, however weak, provided some measure of diversity and fairness on the airways. Three decades ago, public pressure made ITT withdraw an offer to purchase the ABC television network because, even in the business-friendly Nixon era, there was widespread fear of big business control over a TV news network. Today the ITT case sounds sadly quaint, a period piece from a bygone era. Where is the concern for how CTV might cover the next strike at Bell Canada or the next complaint about bad service and pricing ripoffs?

Cyberspace can still be a site for democracy. But, as in the past, the technology does not guarantee it. Sadly, in the cold climate of neoliberalism, the relentless pressure of global business, which supports a near-religious enthusiasm for the wonders of the Web, has led governments to strip away policies that once provided for some democratic access to old media. Furthermore, governments refuse to entertain anything but the slightest interest in extending public-interest policies to new media.

Canada has become widely recognized as a pioneer in libertarian media regulation with the CRTC the first among regulatory authorities explicitly ruling our regulations of the Internet. Barring substantial public intervention of the sort that gave the prairies low-cost telephone service and all of us the CBC, don't expect a public lane on the Information Highway or policies that promote public uses. Cyberspace knows but one god and its name is business.

TAKE COVER, HERE COMES MEDIASAURUS

Dwayne Winseck *(The Globe and Mail)*

As BCE moves to consolidate its control of CTV and *The Globe and Mail* against a backdrop of a slew of similar transactions that have dramatically transformed the Canadian mediascape over the last year, a fundamental question stands out: Should those who control the medium control the message?

The off-the-shelf answer is usually yes and, moreover, that this is necessary and desirable in an age of media convergence. Convergence, so the arguments go, has created a need to fill "new media" channels with content and robbed governments of any compelling reason to impede ownership consolidation. Information abundance is the reality of our times and no single outlet can exert an inordinate influence over citizens' access to information. Proponents also claim that the new national champions will ensure that citizens have access to a steady flow of CanCon, going so far as to suggest that these information gladiators will even ensure Canada's very survival in the "global information age."

Dwayne Winsek. Take cover, here comes Mediasaurus. *The Globe and Mail*, February 27, 2000, A17. (Reprinted by permission of *The Globe and Mail*.)

Yet, what evidence is there, for instance, to support the claim that there is a lack of content to fill the new media? In fact, the idea that we are living in an age of missing information is a myth. We have an unparalleled abundance of information from numerous sources. The more pressing concern for corporations appears to be owning specific kinds of content that will generate revenue sufficient to finance acquisition binges and high rates of profitability—TV programs, subscriber-based services, video on demand, and other forms of "old media" content.

This would not have surprised the early guru of cyberspace, Marshall McLuhan, who observed that old media typically become the content of the new media. However, unlike McLuhan (who saw this as an inherent feature of media technologies), ownership consolidation is a stronger factor explaining the absorption of old media by the new.

Ownership consolidation is transforming cyberspace into the image of old print and broadcasting cultures, making them appendages to familiar patterns of ownership, commercialism and existing forms and sources of content. In the process, new technologies are being diverted from an evolutionary path characterized by uncertainty, risk and omnidirectional information flows. Thus, ownership is a broad and powerful influence that shapes the entire media environment and people's experience of that environment.

Of course, BCE's acquisition spree does not remake the Internet in its own image. But, couple it with AOL's merger with Time Warner, AT&T's acquisition of nearly half of the cable systems in the United States, the division of Canada into regions of exclusive monopolies by Rogers, Videotron/Quebec and Shaw, the reinforcement of this family compact by these companies' joint control over high speed Internet access over cable (the @Home service) and its allied Internet portal, Excite—and the trajectory of media evolution is clear.

Even if there is a need for vast new sources of content, why should such content be owned by those who provide the networks? The constant claim that bigger companies with deeper pockets will result in more CanCon is not supported by historical evidence.

Open media systems encourage those who control the pipes to earn their profit by attracting as many users and content providers as possible, rather than by offering privileged access to their own services. Allowing those who own the medium to control the message leads to closed media systems where in-house content is favoured. This happens either in a heavy handed manner, such as by refusing access to networks altogether (the history of the cable industry and specialty channels), or more subtly by designing user menus, search engines, portals and so on, in ways that give priority access to some sources of content and not others.

These latter practices are already being extended into cyberspace as, for instance, the cable companies refuse to implement CRTC requirements to open their networks to unaffiliated Internet service providers (ISPs), and as their @Home service restricts downloads of video content from unaffiliated sources, limits the amount of information subscribers can transmit, and biases the distribution of content in a myriad of other ways.

In short, networks are powerful entities that both include and exclude. Those who control them influence the access of content providers to users and users' access to content.

These problems also apply to BCE's proposed amalgamation with CTV and *The Globe and Mail*. While BCE defends these actions as a means of obtaining content to fill its distribution channels, BCE does not have to own *The Globe* or CTV to distribute them. Moreover, Bell could produce its own content, something that would nominally increase the availability of Canadian content.

BCE's moves are also problematic in light of the fact that it has no experience in journalism, news or entertainment while aiming to take over two of Canada's leading players in these fields. BCE's very history and organizational culture pose significant threats to quality journalism and media freedom. Bell has had a rigid and bureaucratic approach to management. It has resisted the formation of labour unions, strictly supervised its labour force through intensive surveillance and offered little autonomy to those in its employ. Bell operators are monitored electronically and subject to 65 different surveillance measures to assess their work and interaction with customers.

This deeply entrenched approach to management and labour at BCE is anathema to the values of autonomy, freedom and unevenly structured work that are the hallmarks of the entertainment industries and quality journalism. The threat of BCE to quality journalism is unlikely to be expressed directly. Instead, it will more likely be filtered through the screens of corporate culture and what isn't said.

We must also look further afield at some of the implications of corporate consolidation and convergence in the communications field. A key consideration should be that the enormous cost of media ownership transactions typically results in the diversion of resources from the production of content to financing debts.

This was especially apparent in the U.S. during the late 1980s and 1990s. Ownership changes at the major networks led to the closure of foreign bureaus, news staffs cut by one-third to one-half, and there was an overall decline in the amount of news programming, especially international news, at each of the networks. The reduction of international news was especially disturbing in light of the so-called "trends of globalization." Similar patterns have affected CTV, with ownership changes quickly followed by pared down news budgets and cuts to its journalistic workforce in recent years.

Additionally, BCE's pledges to plow money into new programs at CTV need to be assessed in light of promises made by the company to the CRTC in the 1990s. At that time, BCE and the telephone companies across Canada promised huge investments in a national information highway to be available to 80 percent of all homes if the government and the CRTC rewrote the legislative and policy framework to permit media convergence.

Between 1994 and 1996, the Liberal government and the CRTC removed all restrictions on the telephone companies' ability to get into broadcasting, the Internet and print-based media. Canadians, however, are still waiting for their information highway, as the sorry state of high speed Internet access offered by the telephone companies and their declining rates of investment in the network infrastructure attest.

The key lessons to be drawn from this recent history are that BCE's promises cannot be trusted and that, just as the government and CRTC shifted in the mid 1990s from preventing to promoting convergence, so too can they now step in and stop the idea that convergence is merely code for the consolidation of corporate control of cyberspace.

DISCUSSION QUESTIONS

1. Does the presence of the *National Post* (free) on campuses threaten student newspapers? Should universities or colleges allow the *Post* free access to campuses?

2. Do a close analysis of one week's worth of the editorial page of your hometown newspaper, or *The Globe and Mail*. What is the political position of the editorial writers? Who owns the paper?

3. How do Canadian newspapers handle labour issues? Analyze the language used to represent labour and trade unions.

4. Winseck argues that the Internet now appears to be dominated by consumerism and that its democratic, anarchic potential is rapidly being eroded. Is he correct?

5. Do an analysis of the "free" newspapers available to you. How does their content differ from mainstream publications? Do these papers provide a useful alternative to traditional publications?

WEBLINKS

Media Ownership
www.screen.com/mnet/eng/issues/MEDIAOWN/Mediaown.htm

Canadian Association of Journalists
Marlo.eagle.ca/caj/

Canadian Newspaper Association
www.can-acj.ca

Who Owns What
www.screen.com/mnet/eng/issues/MEDIAOWN/owns.htm

Flipside-The Canadian Alternative Media Homepage
www.mnsi.net/~flipside/

chapter twelve

Gender: Speaking of Girls

INTRODUCTION

The four articles in this chapter discuss female stereotypes in accounts of "violent girls," sport, teen magazines, and the narrow range of female representations among models and actors. These articles share some common assumptions: all four presume that mainstream media have an immense power over women because they offer traditional, if questionable, pleasures to them—despite the changing roles of women in society—and three of the authors wonder if the way in which women are represented can be changed, and if women might find these changes pleasurable or beneficial.

Nicole Nolan argues that recent media reporting on the "girl crime wave" plays upon very old stereotypes which depict women as either "angel[s] in the house" or as the victims of their own "irrational and vice-ridden natures." Noting that the media tend to exaggerate stories about waves of female violence, she stresses that many of these stories have an anti-feminist bias that connects feminist principles to the development of a new breed of violent girls. She argues that a more reasoned approach to female violence might connect it to issues of sexual abuse, poverty, class, and race rather than popular, ideologically anti-feminist discourses.

Rachel Giese is interested in women's sport and the depiction of female athletes in the media. She argues that while women are increasingly involved in a wide variety of sports, the athletes still struggle not only with far lower rates of pay and funding than their male counterparts, but also with "homophobic and sexist notions that they are either too fluffy or too butch." The emphasis in magazine articles or television depictions of female athletes is on their "femininity" and good looks rather than their abilities. Giese argues that the homophobic aura around women's sport discourages many women from pursuing careers as athletes or coaches.

Marnina Gonick discusses her attempt to help "empower" some female high school students by creating a magazine that would address issues that both interested the students and were pleasurable to read. When it becomes clear to Gonick that her own feminist principles are becoming a barrier between herself and the students, she undertakes an analysis of the pleasures that mainstream media offer to teens—and what pleasures these teens seek out for themselves in their reading. Gonick ponders the satisfactions offered to women by mass-produced fiction, and goes on to ask what role "cultural texts," like those found in teen magazines, play in constructing desires for women in ways which might ultimately be seen as hurtful to them.

For a more detailed discussion of the representation of women in the media, see *Representing Women: Myths of Femininity in the Popular Media* by Myra Macdonald (New York: Edward Arnold, 1995).

GIRL CRAZY

Nicole Nolan (*This Magazine*)

Seventeen years ago, when I was in the sixth grade at Courcelette Elementary School in Toronto's east end, I left school because a girl threatened to beat me up. I don't recall being particularly surprised by the incident, just afraid of what a beating by the incongruously named Brenda Love might feel like. Nor do I recall anyone paying much attention, even when Brenda planted a well-aimed punch to my back in the school hallway. In the end, I solved the problem myself. When my family moved a few blocks west and the chance came to switch schools, I gladly abandoned Courcelette. Later, I was threatened by girls, heard of girls threatening other girls and beating them up. My best friend Kathy even pummelled another girl in the head with the heel of her stiletto. Once, I even got in a fight myself.

It was with my somewhat violent and (I suspect) very average childhood in mind that I watched the recent spate of panicked hand-wringing over the rise of girl violence. The question of whether violence of this kind is on the increase has been swimming vaguely around in the Canadian psyche (or, at least, the media) since the mid-1990s when Karla Homolka's crimes were revealed. It would surface in the odd weekend newspaper feature or mid-day call-in show—intriguing, but hardly a hot topic.

But when Reena Virk was murdered, allegedly by teenaged girls, last November in Victoria, British Columbia, violence by young women was catapulted straight into the country's frontal lobes, as everyone from *Maclean's* magazine to CBC Newsworld's "Benmergui Live" discussed the question.

In light of such a brutal and horrifying crime—followed closely by the murder of a 58-year-old youth worker in Saskatchewan, allegedly by two 15-year-old girls—the answers seemed starkly obvious. Soon, experts and authors were appearing on TV and radio talk

Nicole Nolan. Girl crazy. *This Magazine* 31(5), March/April, 1998. 31-35. (With research assistance from Jill Toombs.)

shows trumpeting—with the solemn self-importance that always accompanies adult laments about the various wickednesses of youth—the shocking fact that, according to the Canadian Centre for Justice Statistics, crime by young girls has increased 200 percent since 1986.

Girls, *The Globe and Mail* advised, were "the fastest-growing group of violent offenders in the country." Even staid *Maclean's* remarked, in a cover story headlined BAD GIRLS, that Canadians were now asking themselves "some painful, seemingly unanswerable questions," the most important of which were "Why is violence among young girls sharply on the rise? And what, if anything, can be done to halt the trend?"

By the time Toronto police announced the January arrest of five 15-year-old girls at a Toronto high school on charges of extortion, the rhetoric had taken on a tone so lurid, it wouldn't have been out of place on a poster for last summer's teen slasher flick. What we were dealing with, concluded *Globe and Mail* reporter Isabel Vincent, was "a cross-Canada crime wave of escalating violence by teenaged girls."

It would all be terribly disturbing if the reports were accurate. But they weren't.

A less appalling, (but easily accessible) piece of information that didn't find its way onto the front pages was that serious violent crimes such as the Virk murder are not increasing. According to statistics compiled by the Canadian Centre for Justice Statistics and the University of Toronto, in 1991–92, there were 53 girls (defined as between 12 and 17 years old) charged with the most serious level of assault (including attempted murder) and 7 girls charged with manslaughter or murder. In 1996, the last year for which crime stats are available, the number actually dropped—to 39 and 2, respectively.

Nor did many journalists mention that the "200-percent increase" was mainly due to a jump in charges for minor assault—pushes, shoves or slaps that didn't cause serious injury—with a lesser increase in the second level of assault charges. These second-level charges are more serious (threats and assaults with a weapon), but again, are usually applied only when there isn't serious injury.

Nor did journalists note that many respected criminologists and youth specialists are convinced that there is no increase in crime by girls at all.

It's easy to dismiss the "girl crime wave" as just another instance of media sensationalization—a case of journalists overlooking inconvenient information in an attempt to find a hook on which to hang an incomprehensible act of violence. But hysteria of this sort should be taken seriously. In the aftermath of the Virk murder, commentators and journalists have not only sensationalized girl violence, they've made some sweeping generalizations about all young women. Following long-standing misogynist traditions, they've made the assumption that the behaviour of a few reveals the brutality of all girls and that increased freedom for women—brought about specifically by feminism—is responsible for the supposed rise in young women's violence.

This is not to say that it's wrong to talk about women as perpetrators of violence. Women's violence is notoriously under-researched. Nor is to say that some of the discussions around the Reena Virk murder haven't been sane and informative. But we can't talk about it without understanding how the spectre of the violent/aggressive female has historically been used to justify control of—and even violence against—women. This omission has led to the repetition of some pretty scary ideas in the past couple of months, ideas that function as justifications for increasing social controls on women and girls.

If you believed the media coverage, you'd assume that there is no debate about the rise of girl violence but, in fact, it is a hotly debated and ideology-laden subject. If there are youth workers and criminologists who say violent crime by girls is on the rise, there are just as many who disagree. In a recent paper for the *Canadian Journal of Criminology*, U of T's Anthony Doob, one of Canada's most prominent criminologists, and his student, Jane Sprott, condemned media assertions of increasing and worsening girl violence. In fact, says Doob, "There is no evidence whatsoever of increases in the most serious kind of violence."

As for the increases in more minor assaults, Doob and Sprott believe it is more likely to reflect changes in adults' attitudes toward violence, than youth behaviour. In recent years, he says, Canadian society has become less tolerant of youth violence. This is evidenced in policy changes such as Ontario's "zero-tolerance" approach, requiring that police be called in to deal with student fights that would previously have been the purview of parents or teachers. "Such policies can be expected to result in increased numbers of minor cases of violence— these are the cases that are likely to have been ignored in the past," wrote Doob and Sprott.

Kim Pate, executive director of the Canadian Association of Elizabeth Fry Societies, worked with delinquent girls 10 years ago. When she talked to young women who had been picked up for shoplifting, it wasn't uncommon to hear stories about fights and assaults. But none of those girls were ever charged. Now, she says, they probably would be. "We're seeing an increased focus on behaviour that used to be ignored or rationalized away in other ways. Girls fighting, taunting and teasing is not a new phenomenon. What's new is to have it result in charges of assault."

In fact, talking about increases in girl violence for anything more than the past several years is a pointless exercise. Fred Matthews, a community psychologist with Central Toronto Youth Services, has been doing research on girls' violence for 10 years. He says that his organization is getting more calls to deal with violent and aggressive girls, but it's difficult to tell if actual violence has increased because the subject was rarely studied until the mid-eighties. When Matthews asked students to answer questions about violence in school he found "that we've had this problem for a while."

So if its supposed increase is so debatable, what makes girl violence such an urgent subject right now? It's not the incidents themselves that are selling newspapers, it's the significance that's being attached to them. These incidents are being cast not simply as a story about crime or about girls but about women's characters generally.

The most articulate and visible proponent of this argument is Patricia Pearson. Pearson's book, *When She was Bad* (subtitled *Violent Women and The Myth of Innocence*) hit the bookstores last fall. Her thesis is that women are as capable of violence as men, and she self-consciously casts herself as the truth-teller against what she claims are long-standing Western ideas of femininity.

According to Pearson, "our most cherished notions" of women are that they are gentle "saintly stoics who never succumbed to fury, frustration or greed." The murder of Reena Virk seemed tailor-made for Pearson's thesis, and, not surprisingly, she has been busy propounding her views in newspapers and on TV talk shows. The Virk murder, Pearson wrote in *The Globe and Mail*, "has shattered our illusions about the gentler sex." She counselled readers to imagine satchel-carrying schoolgirls "beating one another to death."

But the angelic image of woman—which Pearson feels so strongly must be eradicated— is an ideology limited to a very specific place, time and class, namely the middle-class Victorians (and, to a lesser extent, 1950s America). There is no doubt that this conception of womanhood has influenced us, but it is only part of the story. In fact, what runs consistently through Western culture is not so much a view of women as the "gentler sex" but an insistence on their irrationality, weakness of intellect and moral turpitude. Men were assumed capable of applying reason and logic. Women, on the other hand, were believed to live closer to nature. As a result, they could be more emotionally nurturing than men, but were also thought to be dangerously vulnerable to impulse and selfishness. It is this notion that has been Western culture's central intellectual justification for women's social and political inferiority.

Far from being ignored, the violent, aggressive woman was regularly trotted out as the culture's best advertisement for ensuring that women were subject to rigorous social control. In the West's most spectacular example, the 16th- and 17th-century witch trials, a belief in women's greater capacity for corruption and vice prompted European authorities to execute more than 100 000 women. Women, according to the *Maleus Malificarum*, a popular tract of the period authored by two Dominican priests, were creatures "who always deceive" and who found "an easy and secret matter of vindicating themselves by witchcraft." Moreover, women were more vulnerable to the devil because, as everyone knew, they were "more carnal" than men— "insatiable" in fact.

On a more mundane level, violence against women was frequently justified by their irrational and vice-ridden natures. One popular European proverb lumped women in with animals and inanimate objects as things better moved by force than reason—"A woman, a horse, a walnut tree, the more they are beaten, the better they be."

These ideas easily co-existed with their apparent opposites. In 1866, at the height of the Victorian cult of the "angel in the house," the editors of *Cornhill* magazine, a London journal, could still make the following assertion about women: "It is notorious that a bad man . . . is not so vile as a bad woman. If we take a man and a woman guilty of a similar offence in the eye of the law, we shall invariably find that there is more hope of influencing the former than the latter."

Like a cart on a well-worn track, the recent commentary on girls has jolted right back into these misogynist ruts. After a 17-year-old girl assaulted another girl in Kitchener, Ontario, *The Globe and Mail* ran a front-page headline informing its readers TEEN'S TORTURE AGAIN REVEALS GIRLS' BRUTALITY (a generalization that surely would never be tolerated if it referred to a racial minority or any other group). And despite the fact that they make up less than a quarter of violent youth crime charges, girls are often described as "worse" than boys.

Other than the obvious manipulation of statistics, one of the most remarkable features of the "girl crime" hysteria has been the alacrity with which commentators have pointed the blame for increased violence on women's increasing freedoms. Feminism has long been a familiar character in the pantheon of culprits wheeled out to explain youth violence—generally tied in to neglect of children by working mothers or the breakdown of the nuclear family—but this time feminism has taken on a whole new character. Instead of being blamed for indirectly victimizing youth, it has been cast in the more active role of actually urging them on to greater acts of evil. Having freed girls from the repressive ways of the past, feminism, the theory goes, has also freed their aggressive natures.

"We shouldn't be surprised by what's happening," Detective Brian Keown of the Metro Toronto Police remarked to news reporters. "What we're looking at is ladies coming of age in the 1990s and girls are taking on a much more aggressive and violent role." Why are girls acting out? Patricia Pearson asked and answered, "Probably because girls are thinking: it's okay now, if you're female, to be demonstrably angry. It's okay to express yourself forcefully." In the *Edmonton Journal*, psychiatrist Mitchel Parsons attributed the increase in violence to the fact that girls of today "have stopped repressing their anger or disciplining their emotions."

The rhetoric was so intense, it was no wonder that Charles Cook of Toronto was whipped up into such a frenzy that he wrote a letter to *The Globe and Mail* remarking with bitter irony on the havoc feminism had wrought. "The bra burners of the sixties must be very proud. The number of girls who begin intercourse before the age of 16 is increasing rapidly . . . while incidents of extreme violence by women multiply daily. What was that story about putting a canary in the same cage with a sparrow to teach it to sing? At the end of the month, the canary was chirping."

Feminism is part of the cultural atmosphere, and teenage girls, like the rest of us, absorb its influence. That it causes confusion when it collides with other ideas about gender roles is understandable. But to believe that increased freedom causes girls' violence is to believe— much like the misogynists of the European tradition—that women have volatile natures that can only be held in check by restrictive social controls.

The theory that feminism will lead to more violence is nothing new. It's been a fiercely debated subject in criminology circles since the 1970s. But despite repeated attempts, criminologists have been unsuccessful in finding a link between feminism and violent crime by women. There is plenty of evidence, however, to indicate just the opposite.

Even those who believe girls' violence is on the rise have rejected the connection between feminism and girls' violence. After intensively researching the lives and families of six violent white girls in British Columbia for her book *Sex, Power and the Violent School Girl*, University of Victoria professor Sibylle Artz concluded that women were given even less value than usual in violent girls' homes, that violent girls tended to be more rigid than other girls in applying conservative gender mores (they frequently referred to other girls as "sluts" and "whores" and expressed the belief that girls who violated sexual mores deserved a beating), and that the low value they placed on women was reflected in the ambivalence of their friendships with other girls.

"It seems peculiar," wrote the American criminologist Meda Chesney-Lind in a 1992 book on delinquent girls titled *Girls, Delinquency and Juvenile Justice*, "that so many academics would be willing to consider a hypothesis that assumed improving girls' and women's economic conditions would lead to an increase in female crime when almost all the existing criminological literature stresses the role played by discrimination and poverty . . . in the creation of crime."

It's a short jump from the thesis that girls have been made more violent by being given more freedom to concluding that the key to stopping this "dangerous trend" is to restrict them once again. The rhetoric of panicked urgency surrounding this supposedly "sharply rising" girl violence favours quick solutions over progressive ones—the punitive over the therapeutic.

"Many prosecutors and social scientists," advised *Maclean's*, "caution against easier treatment for girls than boys." In the same article, Halifax Crown attorney Catherine Cogswell remarked that the system should not deal "with girls with kid gloves."

As I sat shivering in the girls' washroom stall for an hour after school each day in the final, agonizing weeks at Courcelette, waiting for Brenda Love to give up her vigil—my most acute feeling was frank physical terror. My second feeling, only slightly less acute, was an intense frustration. Having taken in my own generous share of the touchy-feely *I'm Okay, You're Okay* psycho-jargon of the seventies, I was sure that if I could just talk to Brenda, if we could just communicate, we could work the whole thing out. We had, after all, once been friends.

Maybe Brenda was set on her mission to beat me up, maybe no amount of talking would have healed our breach. At any rate, it's useless to speculate, since we never got a chance. Having dismissed our problem as just kids stuff (and perhaps also "just girls cat-fighting"), the adults didn't take either of us seriously enough to interfere.

The question of whether girls should be held responsible for what they do is not the issue. Of course they should. If adults had taken Brenda and me seriously enough to help us work out our differences, it would have helped both of us. The problem is when taking responsibility becomes equated solely with punishment, when reform equals authoritarian control.

This issue needs attention—but the right kind. Those who have spent a lot of time thinking about severely violent girls tend to believe that exploring the girls' own experience—including factors such as sexual abuse, poverty, race and class—is a more useful long-term solution than reforming the Young Offenders Act or giving girls stiffer punishments.

Fred Matthews puts it quite simply: "These young people are accountable for their behaviour. We are accountable to provide what they need, so we can help them out."

SHE GOT GAME

Rachel Giese (*This Magazine*)

The Nike Air Swoopes basketball shoe, which hit the market in 1995, comes in black with a white stripe and a red logo for winter, white with a black stripe and red logo for spring. ("Black is a symbol of toughness to me," the shoe's namesake, former Texas Tech all-American guard Sheryl Swoopes, told *The New York Times*.) The sneaker is designed specially to support Swoopes's narrow size 10 1/2 feet and weak ankles and has a basketball encircled by an "S" at the top of the tongue. When the wearer goes up for a slam dunk, another big "S" on the sole is visible to the mortals left earthbound on the hardwood. Swoopes, there it is.

But what's really newsworthy about the Air Swoopes is that it's the first sneaker to be named in honour of a woman. And what a woman. Swoopes is one of the greatest female college basketball players of all time—she once scored 47 points in a National Collegiate Athletic Association final. These days, she plays forward for the Houston Comets of the year-old, professional Women's National Basketball Association (WNBA). She appeared on the cover of the premiere spring 1997 issue of *Sports Illustrated Women Sport*—a basketball in one hand, the other resting on her pregnant belly (the birth of her son last June forced the 27-year-old to sit out most of the WNBA's first season).

But it's really the shoe that counts. In the money-crazed, corporate world of sports, it's the endorsements that prove an athlete has really arrived. In fact, the future of female athletes depends as much on how well they can sell themselves as it does on how well they play. And aggressive, media-savvy women like Swoopes—along with a handful of others, such as Mia Hamm, the humble star of the U.S. Olympic soccer team, and Hayley Wickenheiser, the golden girl of women's hockey and a member of Canada's 1998 Olympic team—are rising to the challenge.

Although it doesn't yet even approach male sports in terms of status, opportunity and cash, women's athletics are thriving—developing its own heroes, culture and fan base. The past five years have seen the development of two professional women's basketball leagues, tremendous viewership of women's events in the 1996 Atlanta and 1998 Nagano Olympic Games, and a subsequent surge of media interest. In fact, there are a half-dozen new magazines devoted to women's sports and fitness alone.

Rachel Giese. She got game. *This Magazine* 32(1), July/August, 1998. 10-12.

But underneath the new opportunities and hype, the playing field is far from even. Sports programs for women on an amateur and collegiate level remain vastly underfunded compared with men's. And outside of the Olympics, women's sports are barely covered by the media. Female athletes continue to struggle against homophobic and sexist notions that they are either too fluffy or too butch. In order to be viable, women's sports have to be as aggressive, exciting and, well, masculine as men's sports; but in order to be accepted, women have to prove that playing sports doesn't compromise their femininity. It's the woman's classic double-bind: act like a man, but don't ever forget that you're a girl.

Despite long-held fears that sports cause every affliction from shriveled ovaries to rampant lesbianism, there have been prominent female athletes since the turn of the century, renowned not only for their talents, but also for their ground-breaking endeavours. In the 1920s and 1930s, American Mildred "Babe" Didrickson was an international star, a three-time Olympic medal winner in track-and-field, an accomplished golfer and cofounder of the Ladies Professional Golf Association (LPGA). Another American, Althea Gibson, broke the racial barrier in women's tennis in the 1950s, winning multiple Wimbledon and U.S. Open championships—despite being barred from most whites-only clubs and tournaments.

But it was the 1970s feminist movement and its modern attitudes about women and their bodies that really boosted women's and girls' involvement in sports. In Canada, Abby Hoffman—who'd been infamously booted off a boys' hockey team in the late 1950s when it was discovered she was a girl—rose to prominence again in the 1960s and 1970s as a track athlete. The 1972 passage of Title IX in the U.S., a federal law legislating equality in funding, opportunities and resources for female athletic programs, gave girls a leg up in that country. And the legitimacy of female athletics was sealed by Billie Jean King when she wiped the sexist smirk off self-proclaimed "male chauvinist" Bobbie Riggs's face and solidly trounced him in their famous tennis match in 1973.

Throughout the 1980s, women's involvement in physical fitness and sports continued to rise. The aerobics craze popularized a new ideal for women's bodies—strong, toned and fit. Olympic heroines such as track star and heptathlete Jackie Joyner-Kersee and gymnast Mary Lou Retton became celebrities, garnering major endorsements. And more recently, rower Silken Laumann became a global hero for her grit and tenacity when she won a bronze medal in the 1992 Olympics only two months after she almost destroyed her leg in an accident.

But despite these achievements, women have had very few opportunities to enjoy the usual spoils of athletic success. Until recently, the Olympics and collegiate sports were the pinnacle of achievement. Outside the fields of golf, tennis and figure skating, few women were actually able to make a career out of sports. No one figured that women could be taken seriously as professional athletes—let alone draw an audience.

Atlanta and Nagano put those myths to rest. Some of the Games' greatest buzz centred on women's tremendous showing in rowing, soccer, softball and hockey. Not only did these athletes show they could play, they demonstrated that women's sports provide as much drama, personality and flair as men's.

The boys with the big bucks were paying attention. Both the WNBA and its poorer, less promoted rival, the American Basketball League (ABL), debuted within the last two years with much fanfare. And rumours are flying that professional soccer and hockey leagues are on the way. Corporations have also become interested in female athletes as a way to reach a growing market of active women. At its peril, Nike ignored women during the fitness boom of the 1980s—leaving Reebok to scoop up the lucrative market. Today, Nike has become a huge sponsor of *Sports Illustrated For Kids'* special "Girls and Sports Extra" supplement—which appears about six times a year—and has launched an ad campaign, titled, "If You Let Me Play," which points out that, among other benefits, involvement in sports bolsters girls' self-esteem and makes them less likely to contract breast cancer. But this ain't just about boosting girl power. A media kit for "Girls and Sports Extra" pointed out that "supporting girls in sports yields tremendous marketing benefits for advertisers [because] the women's sports market is currently a $10-billion market and growing."

As spokespeople for their sport and its products, these new female jocks are undeniably appealing. They are an untapped source of entertainment for an almost insatiable sports audience, as well as a surefire draw for female viewers.

Physically, these Amazonian athletes are a far cry from the most familiar athletic women's bodies: the muscley, munchkin forms of prepubescent figure skaters such as Nagano gold medalist Tara Lipinsky. Canadian hockey dynamo Hayley Wickenheiser (5'9" and 170 pounds) and beach volleyball star Gabrielle Reece (6'3" and 172 pounds) provide a liberating challenge to the asparagus stalk female body ideal. Even pregnancy is proving to no longer be a hindrance to an athletic career. Last year, golfer Laura Baugh continued on the LPGA tour until she was almost nine months' pregnant. In 1995, U.S. ultramarathoner Sue Olsen gave birth only 30 hours after she finished a 24-hour-long race.

Which isn't to say that concerns about being too masculine don't still dog female athletes. The people who cover women's sports are obsessed with the issue. While personal profiles and sentimental human interest stories have always been a part of sports reporting, you aren't likely to see Michael Jordan on the cover of *Sports Illustrated* cradling his kids in his arms, discussing how fatherhood changed his game, the way coverage of Swoopes and her new motherhood eclipsed discussions of her athletic prowess. Nor do we—as Megan K. Williams and Elizabeth Etue point out in their 1996 book, *On The Edge: Women Making Hockey History*—hear Eric Lindros being described primarily in terms of his looks. When Quebec goalie Manon Rheaume became the first woman to play professional hockey on a men's team in 1992, journalists harped endlessly about her delicate prettiness. In a *Toronto Star* column, Rosie DiManno described Rheaume as "a comely nubile with hazel eyes, a glowing complexion, and a decidedly feminine grace. There is no hint of testosterone in her nature."

Some of this new breed of female athlete even play into the glamour trap. At least three prominent athletes—Gabrielle Reece, French track gold medalist Marie-Jose Perce and the WNBA's Lisa Leslie—moonlight as fashion models. That these women can still be beautiful and strong eases all those penis-shrinking fears, the same way that the endless contextualizing of female athletes as daughters, girlfriends, mothers and wives demonstrates that they would never be so foolish or selfish as to put their career first. During the Nagano Olympics, the CBC ran a human interest profile on the Canadian women's curling team, focusing on their husbands and children. The whole gushing story seemed designed to allay concerns that these mannish-looking women were not "that way."

In fact, if you believe all of the stories, very few female jocks are that way. Lesbian athletes are deeply closeted—and have good reason to be. A 1994 U.S. survey found that 53 percent of women's college athletes, coaches and administrators were concerned that their involvement in sports would lead others to assume they were gay. And 49 percent of female athletes and 51 percent of female coaches said they felt homophobia was a hindrance to attracting and retaining women in athletic careers. Tennis great and out lesbian Martina

Navratilova, with 50-odd Grand Slam titles, earned far less in endorsements than her less successful heterosexual rivals such as Steffi Graf.

In golf, one of the most female-friendly sports, CBS golf commentator Ben Wright stuck both feet and a couple of limbs in his mouth back in 1995 when he told a reporter that lesbians on the LPGA tour hurt corporate sponsorship and that women were hampered in their golf swings by their "boobs." Wright, who recently apologized for his remarks, was suspended by CBS in 1996.

When Canada's Shannon Miller made history as the only full-time, female head coach of a national women's hockey team at the Nagano Games, she was under fire right from the beginning for her coaching choices. But when her critics set their sights on her sexual orientation, the attacks became downright ugly—including a *Frank* magazine expose titled "Bettys On Blades," which accused Miller of sleeping with her players and playing a game of lesbo-favourites with her rookies.

On the flip side of these negative attitudes about female athletes being too masculine, there's the expectation that women's "feminine" approach will clean up the professional sports industry. Since most women's sports are still played on an amateur level and the pro sports are still in their infancy, the thinking goes, they provide the perfect antidote to the increasingly bloated and bratty—but high-paying—world of men's sports. Women's athletics—with its numerous stories of defeating the odds, playing for no money and training in near obscurity—conjures up all kinds of romantic ideas of playing for the sheer love of the game. But increasingly, female athletes are less interested in purity and more interested in making a decent living. So the big question remains: can women's sports stand on its own and create its own culture and ethic, or will it be overwhelmed by the style and attitude of men's competition? In hockey, there are concerns that if the women's game does go pro, it'll have to go more macho—incorporating tougher play and body-checking. Female basketball players are in their own peculiar bind. The ABL has a reputation for better players, friendlier management and a longer season (October through February), but has a much lower profile, smaller game attendances and fewer endorsement possibilities. The WNBA has all of the loot and marketing savvy of the NBA behind it, but the players get a shorter season (June through August) to accommodate the men's games.

Female athletes are themselves divided on the direction of women's sports. Some see themselves as part of a greater movement that will affect opportunities for all women, others just want to play their sport, politics be damned. Many female hockey players were less than thrilled over the hype that ensued when Manon Rheaume joined a professional, men's hockey team in 1992. There were concerns that Rheaume's move diverted attention and support away from women's hockey and demonstrated that women's professional aspirations could be met by playing with men.

In an even less traditional sport, boxer Christy Martin has earned herself few allies for her grandstanding and me-first attitude. A member of Don King's stable who has fought on a Mike Tyson undercard and earned upwards of $75 000 for a fight, Martin is a thug of a fighter. She trains only with men, smears other female boxers with dykebaiting comments, and plays up her femininity by fighting decked out in pink trunks, boots and tank top, her long hair loose.

When it comes to being tough and ambitious, some women are already on par with male athletes. In hockey, Hayley Wickenheiser has been known to throw down her gloves and start slugging. As for trash talk, the WNBA is as guilty of it as the men's league. And in terms of sheer ambition and moneymaking opportunities, women are jumping right in—shilling for everything from shoes to shampoo. WNBA hoopster Lisa Leslie has called the ubiquitous basketball player/rapper/movie star Shaquille O'Neal her "entrepreneurial role model."

But even if they wanted to, it's still unclear how much power women have to change sports institutions. How do you undo the "Dream Teams," the commercialism, the need to win and the money-grubbing agents that characterize men's sports? And, secondly, why should it be up to female athletes to do so?

In fact, it's both demeaning and infantilizing to assign women's sports the chore of cleaning up the industry. Why, just as women are coming into their own as athletes, should they be held back from earning even a fraction of the cash and a small part of the fame of their male counterparts? It's not that women's athletic competition should turn into a blood sport, or that it's wrong to value cleaner, fairer, more principled play. But rather, women shouldn't be relegated to the ladies' auxiliary of men's sports—making less money and getting less attention, but proud in the knowledge that their play is uncorrupt.

As female athletes take over the courts, the rinks and the playing fields, they should play because they're talented, ambitious and exciting to watch. They should be able to be as gracious as Mia Hamm or as cocky and attitudinous as tennis star Venus Williams. Women should play and be watched because they've worked hard and earned our attention.

TEEN MAGAZINES AND FEMINIST PEDAGOGY

Marnina Gonick (*Canadian Dimension*)

With her face down close to the page, her finger marking her place, Tam, a grade six student at a Toronto public school, is reading from *'Teen* magazine to a group of four of her friends.

They are participating in a program initiated by a school concerned about student "apathy," especially among young girls. As part of my graduate work, I volunteered to work with the students to develop a program that would involve them in the school community. The key to the program's success was premised on the students' participation in identifying their own needs, designing and implementing a plan of action and being largely in control of the final product. "Empowerment," "having a voice" and developing a sense of "can do" were all catch phrases that went around the room as the planning committee consisting of the school principal, teachers, school board staff and community members gathered to address "the problem."

Tam and the girls she is reading to are all of Asian backgrounds: Vietnamese, Chinese and Cambodian. They live in a largely working-class, immigrant area of the city, and many of them have recently arrived in Canada. The project we have been working on together is to design a magazine about issues that are important to girls. My goal was to offer the girls an alternative to the concerns of beauty, fashion and "how to get and keep a man" so widely subscribed to by teen magazines on the market. In offering something different, my thinking went, subjectivities beyond the passive femininity prescribed by teen magazines and in so many other spheres of their lives might be considered and taken up.

However, it became clear that my own agenda of producing a magazine that would be both feminist and critical in outlook clashed with the interests of the girls at our very first meeting.

I had come prepared with some copies of *NEW MOON*, a non-commercial feminist magazine with many articles written by girls the same age, thinking that this was close to what

Marnina Gonick. Teen magazines and feminist pedagogy. *Canadian Dimension* 30(5), September/October, 1996. 27–29.

could be produced by the group. What I had not anticipated was the girls' complete and immediate dismissal and uninterest in even looking at *NEW MOON*, never mind considering using it as a model of what could be produced by our group. Instead they spoke of models, make-up, movie stars and fashion found in the teen magazines they read.

Here is my dilemma: If I am to adhere to the premises laid out by the planning committee that the program must be student-initiated and controlled, then my own feminist, critical project is in danger of being subsumed by the girls' desire to reproduce media forms that reinforce power relationships, stereotypes and the objectification of women. And yet, the mere reproduction of these media forms, assuming we could even come close to achieving the "look" of a teen magazine, would surely be counter to the goal of empowerment that was the impetus for the program in the first place.

This clashing of agendas raises a series of dilemmas in attempting to introduce a feminist project into schools. How far do I go in insisting on my own agenda if not only are the girls not interested in mine but if mine suppresses theirs? How am I to be sure that what I think I have to offer them in terms of a feminist perspective is ethically and politically right for them?

In an effort to salvage my critical feminist project, I decided to take a closer look at the teen magazines the girls read. If I was going to be able to begin to answer these questions I needed to know more about what attracted these girls as readers. What are the desires and investments that are activated through the girls' readings? I also needed to understand what the rejection of the feminist teen magazines was about.

Reading 'Teen and *Sassy*

At the next group meeting I came prepared with a stack of different teen magazines. Two seemed to attract particular attention. 'Teen, a magazine they were all familiar with, was praised for its fashion, its models and its stories. *Sassy* (a self-proclaimed feminist teen magazine they had not seen before) was criticized for its "old-fashioned" clothes, its little-girl hair styles and its lack of any stories at all.

It was their fascination with one of the stories in 'Teen that provided my first clue as to the contrasting allure of 'Teen, with *Sassy*'s complete failure to engage them. The girls returned to this story—"I Had Sex With Him, Now I'm Sorry"—over and over throughout our discussions. Their reading and rereading of this story opened up a glimpse for me of what might lie beyond the girls' stated likes and dislikes to another level of how as readers they structure, understand and derive pleasure from their readings.

I Had Sex With Him, Now I'm Sorry

Subtitled "Melinda's Story," this is a tale told in the first-person narrative about the romancing of a girl by her older but still teen-aged boyfriend, his persuasive tactics to have her agree to have sex with him, her reluctant concession and his eventual abandonment of her.

In the reading and rereading of the story, the narrative form, the photograph, as well as the story's content, performed important functions in successfully catching up its readers. This is some of the discussion after the second reading of the story:

> Trinh: (reading) When I was thirteen, I met this really cute guy at the mall. His name was Trevor. He had the most gorgeous green eyes . . .

> Mai: (leaning over to look at the photography) Is this a true story? He's cute.

. . . the story continues . . .

Marnina: So, what do you guys think of the story?

Trinh: He's using her—it's a good story, I like it.

Marnina: What do you think about what happened?

LeLy: She shouldn't have sex with him.

Sang: (laughing) Gee, you're smart.

Trinh: (pointing to the picture of Trevor) He's cute, eh?

Mai: Yeah, he's cute.

Marnina: So, the story then. You think she made a mistake about having sex with Trevor? What do you think she should have done?

Mai: Say no.

Sang: She say (sic) no. No way. I'm going to kill you if you do.

Mai: If you love me, then don't pressure me to have sex.

Trinh: Yeah, I know. That's what she should have done.

Tam: She could have said no. I don't want to do it. I don't want to have sex until I'm married— something like that.

Melinda's story resonates with what the girls understand and know about the world of heterosexual teenage sex. It underscores the pleasures of romance and the yearning to be found desirable by men at the very same time that it warns of the dangers to them of being the object of male sexual desires. The girls demonstrate this very contradiction as lived when at one moment they comment on their attraction to Trevor while the next they castigate Melinda for falling prey to his seduction.

It is the combination of providing a piece of a familiar world along with the promise of a world the girls aspire to become a part of: the world of romance, glamour, sexuality and fantasy that so successfully engages them as readers. 'Teen makes use of the girls' desire at the same time as it participates in constructing it.

Lesbians, Russians, English Canadians

What of Sassy's failure to engage the girls as readers? It is as important to understand this failure as it is to understand 'Teen's success if the goal of unsettling the bounds of the old structures and discourses is to be realized. It was during a discussion about the covers of 'Teen and Sassy that this became clear to me. Previously the girls had claimed to be able to tell from the cover if the magazine would be good or not. 'Teen's cover shows a conventionally attractive caucasian couple: A young woman and man embracing. Framing the photograph are headings of the articles contained inside. Sassy's cover shows a photograph of two young women cheek to cheek with arms around each other. Down one side is also a list of articles to be found inside. This exchange took place on the second day of discussions.

Tam: (pointing to *'Teen* cover) These people are English-Canadian people, (and then to *Sassy*) and these people are maybe another language.

LeLy: Russian.

Marnina: You think these two are Russian, eh?

Trinh: (pointing to *Sassy*) If they do that, right? People might say, "oh, they're gay."

Tam: No, lesbian.

LeLy: (comparing covers) Maybe this and this is a different story. (pointing to *'Teen*) This is a boy and girl story—We're more interested in this one than two girls' story.

Mai: Yeah, I think so too.

Marnina: Why?

Tam: Because teenagers love boys. Teenagers doesn't (sic) like girls because they don't want to be lesbians.

Here, the girls seem to be suggesting that there is some distance between what they might want for themselves and what *Sassy* seems to be offering. The models, although caucasian like *'Teen*'s models, are "some other language—maybe Russian." The girls' reading of the picture of the two women embracing as the possibility they might be lesbians suggests that a discourse of queerness is being offered and rejected by the girls. This is stressed in the second segment when LeLy rightly points out that the two magazines have different stories to tell. For in being "a boy and girl story" *'Teen* relies on the hegemonic discourses of heterosexuality. *Sassy* does not. What LeLy calls "two girls' story" and interpreted as a discourse of lesbianism, seems to me to be a rather androcentric discourse of sexuality. The discourse of sexuality *Sassy* offers is decidedly unglamorous and not the least bit romantic. The one story even mentioning sex is about sexually transmitted diseases. It sets out to educate the reader, using medical discourses, and just cannot compete with Melinda's confessional tale of romantic love and betrayal.

In its attempt to present an androgynous alternative, Sassy failed to recognize the deep investments girls have in the media produced images of femininity, heterosexuality, glamour and beauty.

Lessons for a Feminist Pedagogy

What are the lessons here for feminists who want to introduce feminist projects into the classroom? Clearly the task of generating new story lines that have the power to disrupt and displace the old is extraordinarily complex. It is obviously insufficient to assume that all that is required is to produce more stories or that any new story will do. Introducing young girls to alternative views and images through the "simple realism" of much anti-sexist literature fails because it assumes a rationalist reader who will change as a result of receiving the correct information "about how things really are." Instead, feminist pedagogy needs to be concerned with the social construction of female desire and with the way in which cultural texts differently position women in relation to such desire. The role cultural texts might play in constructing such desire differently is crucial for feminists interested in undoing the bounds of old stories and making way for the new.

DISCUSSION QUESTIONS

1. Discuss the depiction of violent women in the media. Do these depictions differ from those of violent men?

2. Identify some of the female stereotypes in Canadian dramatic television or teen magazines. Are they different from their American counterparts?

3. Are there positions of resistance and empowerment available to women in mainstream media? If so, what are they and how do they work?

4. Have a look at the depictions of female athletes in the popular media. How are they different from the depictions of males?

 ## WEBLINKS

Daniel Chandler's Media and Communication Studies Site: Gender Links
www.aber.ac.uk/~dgc/gender03.html

Assorted Gender & Race in Media Links
www.uiowa.edu/~commstud/resources/GenderMedia/assorted.html

LesBiGay & Queer Resources
www.igc.apc.org/lbg/lbg.resources.html#MED

Canadian Advertising Foundation (CAF) Gender Portrayal Guidelines
cii2.cochran.com/mnet/eng/indus/advert/gender.htm

Sports femmes
www.sportsfemmes.com/

Canadian Association for the Advancement of Women and Sport and Physical Activity [CAAWS]
www.caaws.ca/

chapter thirteen

Race: Stereotypes and Appropriations

INTRODUCTION

Given the optimism of many public discussions about racism, it would seem that racial stereotypes should be a thing of the past—especially in a country like Canada, which thinks of itself as very tolerant. Sadly, this is not the case, as the authors in this chapter argue.

"White peril" by Taras Grescoe is a controversial experiment using satire and irony to make a point about negative stereotypes. Grescoe, in what was intended as a humorous, but pointed, dig at racist reporting, trots out all of the anti-Irish/Scottish/Caucasian stereotypes he can find. He combines them with statistics on crime and scenarios borrowed from other racist writing and television shows to make a strong point about how easy it is to promote negative views about any ethic group. To his dismay, some readers did not appreciate the irony and wrote scathing letters to the magazine which published the article.

Terry Glavin, who finds Grescoe's article extremely humorous, briefly discusses the fallout it created. He argues that racial tensions in Vancouver, where the article was published, run high and Grescoe had hoped that those who held negative "media-induced" ideas about Asian and Indo-Canadian immigrants might see the foolishness of their position when they saw themselves represented in a negative light. Both Glavin and Grescoe argue that there are not enough efforts in the Canadian news media to discuss issues of race and gender.

Robert Fulford recounts a very strange story about a white man who spent most of his life passing himself off as an Indian. It was not until after his death that his real identity was discovered. Fulford argues that so many people fell for Archie Belaney's game because Belaney had cleverly mastered all of the stereotypes that Canadians use to represent aboriginal people—in effect, those Belaney fooled became victims of their own racist stereotypes. One of the great dangers of racial stereotypes for Fulford is the negative effect that racist popular culture has on native people's own self-images. Growing up surrounded by images of "noble savages" and the idea that Indian culture is a thing of the past not only alienates native people from non-native people, but from their own culture as well.

Do Disney animated films contain negative racial, gender and class stereotypes? Gail Roberston, among others like James Winter and Henry Giroux, argues that they do. Concerned about foreign entertainment teaching Canadian children to discriminate against others and accept dated gender stereotypes, she argues that parents should watch films with their children and discuss controversial subjects with them. In the end she maintains that the media, and popular culture in general, are, for better or worse, powerful educators.

WHITE PERIL

Taras Grescoe (*The Georgia Straight*)

As he walks past the small, carefully tended gardens of Strathcona, Vancouver's oldest residential neighbourhood, Mr. Sang Lee can recall a time when he didn't have to knock used condoms out of the rosebushes or flick syringes into the gutter with the tip of his umbrella. During the past year, the president of the Strathcona Property Owners and Tenants Association—one of Canada's oldest neighbourhood-rights groups—has watched drug-related crime hit the streets in earnest, an overflow from the incessant dealing at the nearby intersection of Hastings and Main. "The very selling of drugs seems to be very active over the last year. Some people who are not residents of this area are trying to bring drugs and prostitution to this neighbourhood."

Who are these arrivals, the dealers, pimps, and burglars poisoning life for the residents of Strathcona? Mr. Sang Lee doesn't have to think twice. "Most people involved in local criminal activities are Caucasians."

Its one of the tragedies of Vancouver's urban geography that the city's oldest residential neighbourhood, peopled by the founders of the city—farmers from China's Guangdong province, whose families have prospered in the New World—is bordered by one of Canada's hotbeds of white crime. On any given day, Mr. Sang Lee can watch Irish and Scottish-Canadian dealers on Hastings Street peddling heroin outside the bars and welfare hotels. When their clients run out of cash for their habits (and statistics show that drug addiction in Canada is an overwhelmingly white problem), they break into the respectable homes of Strathcona—then sell what they've stolen to pawnshops on Hastings. Not coincidentally, many of these shops are owned by other Caucasians.

The problem may be concentrated in the streets around Vancouver's Chinatown, but it is by no means limited to Strathcona. In British Columbia, the tabloid headlines that record the province's most savage crimes are a litany of Caucasian Canadians. Stephen Stark: a 17-year-old Caucasian male who kicks an older man to death outside a convenience store—

Taras Grescoe. White peril. *The Georgia Straight*, June 1–23, 1995l. 11, 13, 15.

striking with such force that he leaves the imprint of his running shoe on his victim's face. Jason Gamache: an adolescent of European descent who strangles a six-year-old child, then crushes her corpse. David Schlender: a Caucasian killer-for-hire who is convicted of shooting Surrey resident Manut Nareg in the face and confesses to killing a 19-year-old woman in her apartment.

When Mr. Sang Lee came to Vancouver in 1967, he—like many other settlers—was looking for a safe and prosperous place to raise his children. But it's becoming clear that in this paradise on the Pacific, all is not as advertised. The tourist brochures and magazine articles that have attracted settlers from Hong Kong, India, and Singapore may dwell on the city's scenery, but they inevitably fail to mention that it is also home to a burgeoning Caucasian underclass. What's at work is a disturbing social trend: while 41 252 immigrants from around the world came to B.C. in 1994—by far the nation's wealthiest immigrants— almost as many, 38 649, came from other Canadian provinces. Many of these "immigrants" were poor and most of them were white. Alongside peaceful residential neighbourhoods, the city's swollen welfare rolls and overflowing skid-row bars are breeding a Caucasian criminal class with no scruples about the race of their victims.

It's long been a truism among criminologists that, in Canadian prisons, white faces tend to outnumber those of visible minorities. Statistics released by the Correctional Service of Canada show that Caucasian Canadians are regularly overrepresented in federal pens. In British Columbia's penitentiaries, where 2114 prisoners are incarcerated, 1573—or 74 percent—are Caucasian. People of Asian descent, who account for 11 percent of B.C.'s population, account for only 4 percent of the province's federal prisoners. Nationwide, the figures are even more telling: although only one in a hundred prisoners is Asian, fully eight percent are white. These unsettling statistics are finally forcing observers and experts to ask some tough questions. Why do so many whites turn to crime, and in numbers out of all proportion to their representation in the population at large? Is it merely a cultural failing—a lack of morality in a group for whom family values and tradition are falling by the wayside—or, more ominously, is it something genetic, an innate propensity toward crime?

Can anything be done about these monsters in our midst?

These days it's a question many new Canadians are asking themselves on an all-too-regular basis. Almost any morning of the week, the pages of *Sing Tao* and *Ming Pao*, two of Vancouver's leading dailies, tell of Caucasians involved in yet more crimes: such as the European-Canadian principal of a residential school who systematically abused his young Native charges, or the notorious international all-white motorcycle gang described by the RCMP as a sophisticated organized crime ring with its local chapter headquartered in East Vancouver, or the Caucasian transient incarcerated on a weapons charge who is considered the prime suspect in the kidnap and murder of eight-year-old Mindy Tran in Kelowna last summer.

The headlines only tell part of the story, however. It's the relentless day-to-day crimes that are at once the most unnerving and the most seldom reported. Mr. Sang Lee tells of a Union Street flophouse whose white tenants toss their hypodermic needles into the yards of neighbouring home owners, then vandalize their mailboxes and door locks if they complain.

But Mr. Sang Lee doesn't blame all whites for the crimes of a few. Before moving to Strathcona in 1989, he spent 25 years selling vegetables from his farm in Richmond to Chinatown merchants, and his work brought him into contact with many decent, law-abiding Caucasians. "I find that those Caucasians who are living in this neighbourhood are very good and nice neighbours, and they aren't involved in these kind of criminal activities." Mr. Sang Lee believes that it is transients from other provinces and cities who are breaking the law. "These people are the troublemakers. They are the real ones who are involved in the criminal activities."

Keeping track of these troublemakers is part of Const. Joseph Chu's job. As a beat cop at the police department's Chinatown crime-prevention office, Chu has been posted in the midst of a maelstrom of white crime, the few square blocks of Chinatown that border both the propriety of Strathcona's Chinese-owned homes and the squalor of Caucasian-dominated Main and Hastings. With his spiked black hair and the leather jacket and wraparound shades he wears on stakeouts, Chu looks more like the Terminator than a beat cop. But an imposing image is a prerequisite when you're dealing with white criminals, especially in this area of small grocery stores and restaurants. Burly white shoplifters count on merchants being too intimidated to chase after them, and street-smart Caucasian thieves spend their days seeking out cars with out-of-town plates, often driven by tourists and timid new Canadians hesitant to approach the police. Tactfully, Chu says crime is not necessarily a question of race, but he acknowledges that most of these incessant petty crimes are driven by drug addiction. What's more, he's noticed that it's usually not the Chinese who are stealing, scoring, and shooting up.

"We don't have a lot of drug-dependent Asian people down here. It's a cultural difference: I just don't often see Asians using needle drugs." His partner agrees: "We find people, white people, who do thefts in Chinatown, high-quality items. They don't steal for themselves. Whoever their supplier is they steal what he wants, and they know that they can trade it for some drugs." Chu explains why Caucasians so often end up on the streets, ripping off the merchants on his beat.

> With Asian families, people tend to take care of one another; a lot of my Caucasian friends, by the time they were 18 they were out of the house. With Chinese families, you often don't move out of the house until you're out of university and married. It keeps people off the street, for one thing. Caucasian kids often say to themselves: "I'm 18 now; I have to go out and make it out there." Well, times are tough now, and when you've got no life skills or job skills and no education, how do you make it out there? For those kinds of people, society becomes their family.

Someone with a privileged outlook on the sordid criminal milieu of the Caucasian community is Salim Jiwa, crime reporter for Vancouver's *Province* newspaper. Since the mid-'80s, his efforts to untangle the complex world of white crime have been recorded in banner headlines—providing a morning shock to the law-abiding citizens of Vancouver over their coffee and corn flakes. In the cafeteria of the Pacific Press Building, he puffs on a cigarette between glances at his watch, always aware of his evening deadline.

> In my time as a reporter with this paper, 11 years, I look back and ask myself how many stories have I done. Perhaps an average of 300 stories a year, including many, many headline stories on crime—because our paper does tend to concentrate heavily on crime—and I can only remember a handful of events, of major stories, that involved ethnics. The rest of the crimes—man kills wife, murder-suicides—the vast majority of these are done by white people.

For Jiwa, it's not simply the numbers—more than anything, he finds the kinds of crimes that European-Canadians commit disturbing. "Drug dealing is massively white, no question about it. Bank robberies—my God, how many of these robbers are brown or Chinese? The vast majority of them are white. Homicides: the vast majority are committed by these people. And these are random, senseless homicides; they are not tied to the killer by family. There's no connection apart from the thrill. Thrill crimes, which involve sexually tormenting someone and killing them, believe me, those are western, white crimes." He says that in the country where he grew up, Tanzania, figures of authority such as scout masters and priests could be trusted. But given the stories of abuse that seem to surface almost weekly in Canada, he says he would be "very afraid" to send his child on a three-day field trip with a Caucasian scoutmaster.

What's the explanation for this apparent savagery? Jiwa admits it's a question that's kept him awake at night.

> I've always looked at this situation and said to myself that some of the crimes that I have seen committed by so-called white folks tend to be vicious beyond proportion and unmotivated and crazy— there are no patterns. . . . I've thought about it many times. Is it drugs? Is it the drug culture of the '60s? Is it spiritual bankruptcy? . . . Something has gone wrong in western white society. There's no doubt in my mind about that.

Where did the white community go wrong? Ironically, it's often the Caucasians themselves who offer the deepest insights into why so many of their number become thieves, killers, burglars, and rapists. Elliott Leyton is that rarest of phenomena, a European-Canadian anthropologist who studies the culture of his own people. In *Hunting Humans: The Rise of the Multiple Murderer*, an examination of serial killers worldwide, he notes that the serious crime most often associated with Caucasians is mass murder. Contacted at his home in Newfoundland—a province where 90 percent of male, and 100 percent of female, convicts are white—Leyton makes no excuses for the criminal behaviour of his people.

> Oh, absolutely, serial killers are mostly white—well, that's about as broad as you'd want to be with a sample that small, even in North America, but they're overwhelmingly just that: Caucasians. In my book, I allude to this interesting phenomenon, that there are relatively few black and Asian serial killers, and none in Canada.

Leyton's academic training allows him to look at his own people with a rare objectivity. "You see, white people come from brutal and insensitive cultures that are accustomed to imperialistic rampaging across the planet, and their personality structure has been forged by this kind of racist and sexist behaviour backed by violence in expanding their empires for economic and political purposes. So it's not surprising that they commit these kind of crimes. There may even be a genetic carryover." He singles out the Scots and Irish, the notorious Celtic minority of Caucasians historically associated with some of the worst crimes in Canada. "These people seem to have a genetic inability to handle alcohol; they drink vast amounts of it all the time in their cultural rituals. It wouldn't be surprising that you'd see them overrepresented in prisons."

In fact, the propensity of the Celtic Caucasians—the Scottish, Irish, Welsh, and Bretons—toward crime has been considered axiomatic by criminologists almost since the founding of their discipline. Most of the research concentrates on Scottish and Irish offenders, who from the start were overrepresented in penal statistics. Cesare Lombroso, one of the founders of modern criminology, noted in 1911 that: "In our civilized world, to note the proof of the influence of race upon crime is both easier and more certain. We know that a large number of the thieves of London are of Irish parentage."

Since Lombroso made this key observation, other criminologists have struggled to discover why the Scottish and Irish—collectively referred to as Celts or Kelts—and their descendants have been such enthusiastic tenants of the world's prisons, Borstals, and lockups. Irish militancy and hatred of authority are well-documented, not surprising in a group that comes from a country whose cultural traditions include kneecapping and Guinness abuse.

More disturbingly, research is beginning to emerge that shows many Caucasians, but especially Celtic Caucasians, might actually be predisposed to crime. Leyton has alluded to the tragic Celtic love affair with drink—and the well-established link between alcoholism and criminality. An article in the *American Journal of Studies on Alcohol* suggests this is much more than a mere stereotype: "In statistics of admissions for alcoholic disorders to various hospitals in this country, the Irish have consistently had rates two to three times as high as any other ethnic group."

But the most damning evidence comes from Earnest Hooton's *Crime and the Man*, one of the most ambitious studies of North American criminals ever undertaken. He singles out what he calls the Keltic types—the Scottish, Irish, Welsh, and Bretons—recognizable by their "deeply wavy hair, ruddy skins, thin nasal lips, absence of jaw protrusion, and multiple loss of teeth." Where French Canadians are inclined to armed robbery (according to a 1987 study by University of Ottawa criminologist Thomas Gabor), the Scottish and Irish tend to be predisposed to just about every offence in the book:

> Criminologically, the Keltic type is notable in its conformity to popular impression. It ranks first in assault just as in red hair, first in sex offenses, first in offenses against the liquor laws, second in first degree murder, and third in burglary and larceny. . . . On the whole, this type specializes in crimes against persons, if it can be said to specialize. It bats a generally high average.

Hooton, like most criminologists, stops short of calling for mandatory sterilization of these most consistently vicious of Caucasian criminals.

Who are these people, the members of this underclass that shares our streets and fills our prisons? Historians point out that Vancouver's Caucasian community is notoriously hard to pin down. They were already on hand when Sikh and Chinese city fathers were settling Vancouver; the 1901 census shows the Irish and Scottish as being the city's two largest ethnic groups. The Irish show up on prison rolls as early as 1879—they were consistently booked for selling liquor to Natives, and the first person hanged in the province was an Irishman. One thing is certain: the ancestors of these first Caucasians have multiplied since their arrival. Today, the common Scottish prefixes "Mc" and "Mac" fill 55 pages of the local white pages, from McAbney to MacWillie.

Many of them are concentrated in an area called Shaughnessy, located between Arbutus and Oak. Recently the site of heated controversy over its ostentatious monster homes, Shaughnessy makes no attempt to hide its Celtic-Caucasian ethnic background. Even the street names—Angus, Devonshire, McRae—conjure up exotic images. Police sources say the Caucasian community is notoriously tight-lipped: when a crime is committed, Irish and Scottish Canadians tend to close ranks rather than cooperate with police. When Mindy Tran's suspected killer was still at large, I attempted to penetrate this close-knit community by visiting South Granville, a bustling street swarming with white shoppers.

Outside Edward Chapman Ladies Shop—a bazaar where flocks of British women can be found fingering the tartan fabrics they favour at their social gatherings—a Scottish-Canadian woman in her 70s eyes me suspiciously before she agrees to go on the record. She's a handsome Scot, though her face is crisscrossed by a tracery of burst veins, the sad result of a lifetime of gin abuse. She says she has a nephew in Kelowna who has been in some trouble with the law; he was out drinking with his rugby friends and hit a cop. When I ask her if he might have some connection to the Tran case, her face becomes an expressionless mask. Muttering a Gaelic expletive, she turns and hobbles away without giving her name.

Two blocks to the south, the owner of a butcher shop is happy enough to show off his haggises and blood sausages, but when I ask him what the word on the street is about the Tran case, he shows me the door. It's the same story up and down Granville—from the women whispering over their teapots at the Normandy Restaurant to the panhandler singing "Danny Boy" for spare change outside the liquor store. Stonefaced silence. These people are obviously scared. Part of it is suspicion; many Caucasians don't make the distinction between journalists and cops. For them, both are symbols of authority to be avoided. But I can't help wondering if fear of recrimination is an equally important factor.

Outside the Bank of Nova Scotia at 12th and Granville, three redheaded boys in brightly coloured mackinaws are loitering by the door to the automatic teller, they only reluctantly step aside to allow an elderly gentleman in a turban to walk by. As he walks out, stuffing his deposit slip into his wallet, the tallest boy extends his leg and the Sikh gentleman stumbles. In an admirable display of self-control, he pauses, eyes the boys up and down with measured contempt, and walks on.

Here on the sunny side of Granville Street, in Vancouver's Celtic ghetto, violence walks with everyone—even children. For most European Canadians, brutality, drunkenness, and fear are part of the tissue of day-to-day life. For the first time, experts are coming to a conclusion that should give our leaders and policy-makers pause. Random, predatory crimes—from rape to serial murder—are on the rise, and they're tearing our cities apart. In fact, we are the ones who allow them to happen, but only because we still allow a group with a proven predilection toward crime to roam our streets.

(Thanks to the people who contributed to this story, and a nod to those who refused and their very good reasons for refusing. Special thanks to George Hui, of the Strathcona Community Centre, for his invaluable interpreting services.)

WHITE PERIL: WHEN IT COMES TO STEREOTYPES, WE'RE ALL SUCH HICKS

Terry Glavin (*Canadian Forum*)

We have all heard the story about Orson Welles' 1938 radio drama, the one that gave real-life news treatment to a story about an invasion from outer space, and how North Americans were set off in a panic.

It happened during a time when mysterious forces were shaking society's foundations. The industrial world was convulsing, and there were rumours of war. The radio was a new and magical thing, and we sat and we listened and we believed. We were all such hicks back then.

The June 16 cover story of Vancouver's *Georgia Straight* magazine bore the scary head-line: "White Peril: Is Vancouver Safe From the Caucasians In Its Midst?"

Written by 28-year-old freelancer Taras Grescoe, the story applied investigative-feature treatment to a proposition: Almost all the outrages covered by Vancouver's crime-obsessed news media could be traced directly to British Columbia's white community.

In 1995, mysterious forces are shaking Vancouver's foundations. Thousands of people are settling here from Asia. The real estate industry is booming like nowhere else in North America, but for some reason, unemployment and poverty are chronic. Scary headlines

Terry Glavin. White peril: When it comes to stereotypes, we're all such hicks. *Canadian Forum* 74(842), September, 1995. 12–13.

about Asian youth gangs are commonplace. When people with Punjabi names were recently arrested in a gruesome murder case, reporters went into the city's Punjabi market to ask passers-by what they knew about the killings.

The *Georgia Straight* story opens with a Mr. Sang Lee, reflecting sadly on his Strathcona neighbourhood, a formerly pleasant, working-class section of Vancouver's 19th-century Chinatown district. The decaying sidewalks are littered with syringes and condoms. The streets have become scenes of muggings and stabbings and murders. The right question is put to the elderly Sang Lee, and he states the obvious: "Most people involved in local criminal activities are Caucasians."

Grescoe's feature makes the point that Asians are underrepresented in the country's prisons, but white people, particularly those of Celtic origin, are alarmingly overrepresented. His investigation reveals that in 1994, while 41 252 immigrants came to the province from offshore countries with law-abiding traditions, almost as many new arrivals came from head-clubbing regions of Eastern Canada with exotic names like "Newfoundland" and "Quebec."

Criminologists confirmed in on-the-record interviews that serial murder, beyond dispute, is a white-crime phenomenon. Social scientists revealed "disturbing research" to demonstrate how white people of Celtic origin are predisposed to drunkenness, bedlam and murder. It has reached the point that 55 pages of the Vancouver phone book are now taken up with names that begin with "Mc" or "Mac," from McAbney to MacWillie.

People with European-sounding names were arrested in a gruesome murder case, so Grescoe went down to the close-knit and notoriously tight-lipped white enclave of Shaugnessy to stand on a mansion-lined street and ask passers-by what they knew about the killings.

It was hilarious.

At the *Georgia Straight* offices on West Pender Street, the telephone wouldn't stop ringing and the letters arrived with the ink still wet. The mayhem lasted for days. Charles Campbell, the magazine's 35-year-old editor, says the reaction has been quite unlike anything he has seen in his ten years with the magazine. A store and a coffeeshop called in to say they would never carry the magazine again. An anonymous middle-of-the-night caller warned Grescoe to watch his back or he would be killed.

Georgia Straight is a mass-market, free distribution magazine. It does not confine itself to any particular social, political, intellectual or economic niche market. Its readership surveys show that almost 300 000 people put their feet up with the magazine in their laps each week.

To be fair, Campbell reckons that a careful assessment suggests that most people probably enjoyed "White Peril." But at least one in four people just didn't get it. They actually thought it was serious. They were indignant and offended and shocked.

White Canadians took umbrage: "My neighbour had a bicycle stolen, and I can tell you it wasn't a white guy." Asian Canadians were disgusted: "Being an Asian-Canadian—I was repulsed by the article."

The anger came from the left: "His statements were inflammatory. His claims were supported by incomplete evidence and selective portrayal of the facts . . . It is the usual blind, hate-supporting material that uses race as the excuse for our society's ills."

The anger came from the middle: "To find this kind of polemic receiving front-page coverage in your magazine is, to me, deeply disturbing."

And the anger came, in spades, from the right: "The majority of crime here is Asian and Oriental crime. They now own the majority of businesses here in town, with money from crime. . . . You guys are fighting a losing battle over this stuff. Your NDP government, your politically-correct bullshit is a thing of the past. The Chinese hate us."

Campbell shakes his head about it all. He says he realized it was possible that some people might be taken aback by the cover's "White Peril" headline, and by the cover illustration of a white man's profile with a colour-coded map of the regions inside his exposed brain: Criminal Predilection, Spiritual Bankruptcy, Thievery, Laziness, Senseless Savagery. So, in advance of its delivery to the stands, Campbell warned the magazine's distribution manager to clue in the drivers in case a nervous storekeeper wondered what it was about.

Still it would appear that thousands of people who read the entire feature, which was accompanied by a sidebar detailing the stupidity of racist stereotyping, along with a note of thanks to the "experts" who played along with the joke—still didn't get it.

"Humour is a funny thing," Campbell said.

Some readers who did get the point were sincerely concerned that Grescoe went too far in the way he employed anti-racist satire at the expense of the Scottish and Irish. Similarly, some readers who didn't get the point were bursting their very blood vessels over Grescoe's Celtic references.

Campbell, of Scots-Irish ancestry, observed that the magazine's staff is dominated by Scots and Irish descendants. Grescoe's mother is Irish, and since the hateful, 19th-century pseudo-scientific "research" he relied upon for "White Peril" is relatively silent about his father's Ukrainian ancestors, it was Grescoe's mother's people whose legs got pulled the hardest. Although he made use of claptrap that has made the rounds about other European nationalities, Grescoe dredged up every preposterous Irish stereotype he could find in the literature. In a follow-up editorial, Campbell advised the magazine's readers it was okay to calm down, because "White Peril" was a work of semi-fictional satire, and Campbell apologized if Grescoe's attempt to put the shoe on the other foot had pinched any white person's toes.

But ethnicity, politics and class provided no warning signs about what an individual's response to "White Peril" would be.

I come from an Irish immigrant family that claims to have the same contempt for bigotry, soft-heartedness for felony and love for true water that right-thinking people expect of one another the world over. My dignity wasn't offended a bit. But one caller to *Georgia Straight*, who called himself Mick and who claimed to reside in the neighbourhood Grescoe described as Vancouver's Celtic Ghetto, said: "I'm Irish. I've got a lengthy criminal record. I drink a lot. I live in this neighbourhood. I don't see anything satirical about it."

Grescoe said that quite often the demarcation line was easy to see: these people know what satire is; these people don't know what satire is. But it was fascinating to watch the pattern of lines that seemed to form up, only to disappear into the underbrush, and the unlikely bedfellows the various encampments allowed.

He said his intent was simply to take the kind of thickheaded rubbish that has been an underlying feature of the Vancouver media's conventional treatment of race, turn it all around and point it at itself. The hope was that white people who might harbour a range of media-induced ideas about Asian immigrants, Indo-Canadians or other minorities might be more able to recognize the daftness of their notions if they spent a few minutes admiring themselves in "White Peril"'s funhouse mirror.

"The challenge these days is finding a forum, to explore these things. Race issues, gender issues—these things are not really explored in the news media," Grescoe said. "People still don't really question what they read or see. You can base a story on objective fact, manipulate fact, and use selective facts to attack just about any ethnic group, or say the most outrageous things about anyone, and people will believe it."

In 1938, they came from outer space, and it was a war of the worlds. It had to be true; they interviewed experts and everything. It was on the radio.

We were all such hicks back then.

LET'S BURY THE NOBLE SAVAGE

Robert Fulford (*Rotunda*)

One night in the 1930s a young salesman from Macmillan Publishing was escorting one of the company's star authors, Grey Owl, across the lobby of the King Edward Hotel in Toronto. They were on their way to a banquet in Grey Owl's honour, and the great man was wearing his standard uniform, an elegant fringed-buckskin jacket. His hair, as usual, was pulled back in tight braids, revealing a noble brow and the stern look of a visionary with a profound belief in his mission.

As they walked past the open door of the beer parlour, several drunks spotted them. "Hey, Chief!" one of them shouted, "Where's your squaw?" Furious, Grey Owl wheeled around, his right hand reaching for the knife at his belt—also a standard part of his public-performance kit. The young man from Macmillan stepped nervously in front of Grey Owl, smiled placatingly at the drunks, and hurried his charge towards the elevator. "You should-n't let fools like that bother you," he said. "I suppose you're right," Grey Owl replied. "But you see how it is. In this country I'll never be anything but a *god-damned Indian*!"

Thirty years later the young man, John Gray, by then the president of Macmillan, told me the story with a mixture of amusement and wonderment. What he recalled most vividly was Grey Owl's angry racial pride, and how genuine it seemed. John didn't doubt for a second that Grey Owl was an eloquent, sensitive, thoughtful Indian, the most famous Indian alive. But, in fact, Grey Owl was a fraud, which is what makes the encounter with the drunks so rich in irony. The drunks were racists of the usual sort, but they were directing their racism, unknowingly, at another white man. It was as if John Gray and the drunks were the unwitting actors in a play about the mistreatment of Indians, with a non-native voluntarily playing the role of the Indian.

For me, that incident has always summarized perfectly the way whites deal symbolically with natives. The scene had all the necessary elements—anger, bigotry, nobility, and the presence of a man with a powerful image. It had everything but a native.

As a supremely talented fraud, Grey Owl deserves the place of prominence that he is given in *Fluffs and Feathers: An Exhibit on the Symbols of Indianness*, organized by the Woodland Cultural Centre, which will be displayed in several museums and public galleries across Canada, including the Royal Ontario Museum (ROM) from 7 November 1992 to 28 February 1993. Shortly after Grey Owl's death in 1938, the whole world learned what a few dozen people, not including his publishers, had known for years, that Grey Owl was an Englishman, Archie Belaney. Belaney had radically rewritten the script of his life and turned himself (with the help of a little makeup) into a Canadian Ojibway. He wrote popular books about native life, like *Pilgrims of the Wild* and *The Men of the Last Frontier*. He appeared in government-sponsored films and went on lecture tours, preaching respect for nature. When he went home to England to lecture and to sell books, he was cloaked in the magic aura of Indianness that he had acquired in Canada. The young princesses, Elizabeth

Robert Fulford. Let's bury the noble savage. *Rotunda* 25(2), 1992. 30-35.

and Margaret Rose, were his fans, so he went to Buckingham Palace for a command performance. When he was leaving—in a flagrant but quickly forgiven breach of protocol—he clapped King George VI on the shoulder and said, "Goodbye, brother, I'll be seeing you." He had the born con man's ability to pull off an outrageous gesture.

Belaney's value to our understanding of cultural history lies in his vibrant relationship with white audiences. Having spent his English boyhood dreaming of Indians, he was able to play into white people's extravagant fantasies of native life. Intuitively, he understood the sort of Indian who would appeal to whites, and he invented his character to fit the requirements. He created a woodland nobleman who was solemn, dignified, and taciturn. He dressed as whites expected Indians to dress, and uttered the sort of Thoreau-like wisdom, seasoned with mysticism, that whites liked to hear. "I have been asked where I got the power to talk to people," he said in a 1937 speech to the Empire Club in Toronto. His explanation was modest, rather like that of a TV evangelist who gives Jesus all the credit for his own eloquence. "It is not me at all. I have behind me that immense north country. I have the power of it standing behind me, greater than you or I. I am only the screen for the picture I wish to show. I am the mouthpiece."

His career illustrated the truth that those who present themselves as untutored, uncomplicated, and "natural"—from the poet who claims to know nothing of poetry to the politician who eschews book-learning and insists that he is just an ordinary guy—usually turn out to be purveyors of clichés and stereotypes. This is not to suggest that stereotypes are innately harmful, or fraudulent. Most human wisdom begins with the creation of categories (a nicer word for stereotypes). We spend our lives mentally organizing the objects and people around us into categories. Modern botany, for example, began in the eighteenth century with Carolus Linnaeus carefully sorting plants into genera, classes, and orders. Humans are pattern-making animals. None of us would get through the day without frequent reference to our internal systems of classification.

But we distort this healthy and necessary process when we rely not on experience or careful study but on manufactured fantasies, those hallucinations of mass culture that have a nasty habit of displacing intelligence. "Indianness," in its many forms is one such fantasy. It transforms natives into cardboard cut-outs. It screens the actual human beings, and limits the imagination and perception of whites.

It can be more devastating, however, to natives, who grow up with mass culture in the same way other North Americans do, automatically absorbing its imagery. Deborah Doxtator, the curator of *Fluffs and Feathers*, recalls that, "for the longest time I didn't know what to say when someone asked if I was 'really Indian.'" What, after all, is a real Indian? From movies, books, cartoons, and school film strips she had learned that "real Indians" were mysterious romantic figures, yet with some flaws—"such as ruthlessness, a lack of self-control, and technological backwardness." People were conditioned to believe that "real Indianness," as she says, "had something to do with not talking very much, never smiling, wearing fringed clothing, being mystical, being poor, and riding horses."

Living beneath this barrage of images, natives can easily grow up alienated, not only from the larger society but also from the people, including fellow natives, who are close to them. Developing a sense of identity, never an easy matter, becomes even more difficult when your ethnic connections are defined, almost always wrongly or inadequately, by the larger culture—and when the larger culture is composed mainly of those outside your own group. Blacks, Jews, and any other minorities have known this problem in various forms, but it comes to natives with something else attached, something both baffling and ominous—an implication that whatever is genuinely native is part of the past.

For as long as anyone can remember, the larger culture of North America has discussed native culture in the past tense. Native culture is assumed to be something that once was, is no longer, and therefore can best be commemorated in museum displays depicting past ways of life. This assumption can be held maliciously (by those who wish to see natives disappear or be assimilated), but it can also be held by those whose motives are generous; as Doxtator point outs, anthropologists and ethnographers usually take it for granted that they are dealing with the end of a civilization, no matter how much they may respect it.

The great ethnographer, Marius Barbeau, who collected and described native art and artifacts (including some of the ROM's), wrote in 1923: "It is clear that the Indian with his inability to preserve his own culture . . . is bound to disappear as a race." When Barbeau set those words down, that belief had already been part of popular culture for close to a century. It was given a terse summary in the title of James Fenimore Cooper's 1826 best-seller, *The Last of the Mohicans*. Cooper understood the sentimental pleasure to be found in reading about people who may be extremely admirable but are on the point of leaving the planet forever and therefore cannot possibly threaten anyone. That nostalgic theme was picked up by many other novelists, then by filmmakers, then by TV producers. There are now few living humans who have not absorbed it through one means of communication or another. Those who know that their race rules the world can enjoy mourning those races that are slipping into oblivion—and can even admire themselves for mourning.

All this is the subtext to *Fluffs and Feathers*. In a sense, the exhibition expresses one part of the native agenda for museums, an attempt to reorganize the way our great public institutions deal with aboriginals. For many years natives have argued that museums use native cultures carelessly, even to the point of exhibiting the bones of their ancestors. "My Grandfather is not an Artifact" was the theme of a recent conference in Hull on archaeology and native issues.

Tom V. Hill, director of the museum of the Woodland Cultural Centre, was a co-chair of a task force, "Turning the Page: Forging New Partnerships Between Museums and First Peoples," sponsored by the Assembly of First Nations and the Canadian Museums Association. The task force came about after the intense controversy over *The Spirit Sings*, the 1988 exhibition of native art and artifacts put together by the Glenbow Museum for the Calgary Olympics. Three points in the task-force report emerged as central to the native agenda for public institutions: repatriation of some objects to institutions run by natives; improved access to collections of native artifacts by natives; and greater involvement by native people in the use of native materials.

The exhibition and task force are part of a long-range effort to persuade the greater North American public to reconsider its view of native life as something purely historic. As Trudy Nicks of the ROM's Department of Ethnology and the other co-chair of the task force says, "It brings across the idea that native people aren't just figures in history; they're living people, right here, and if we see them only through these stereotypes, we're missing a lot."

Our tendency to place native culture exclusively in the past arises from an idea that is at least four hundred years old—the idea of prehistoric native purity. Europeans have understood, at least since the Renaissance, that their own society and the societies they created in the Americas and elsewhere, are constantly changing. The changes may be good or bad, and may or may not be the result of contact with other cultures; but they do not make European civilizations any less European. Yet we imagine that aboriginal cultures, in North America or anywhere else, are not only affected by contact with Europeans but are ruined by it. A glance at a few catalogues will show that some of the most admirable products of aboriginal cultures (Haida carving, Micmac beadwork, Inuit sculpture) followed contact with Europeans. Yet we persist in the idea of purity, an idea that is necessarily pessimistic about the future of native life. If natives also accept and believe, as given, the traditional views of the media and the museums, then they are finished before they start.

Doxtator has ingeniously constructed a native analysis of a white culture's use of native life in *Fluffs and Feathers*, thereby creating a neat reversal of the traditional ethnographic process. Her goal is to subvert those traditional views displaying the copious absurdities of "Indianness" as contrived by North American mass culture. Materials exhibited run from posters for Buffalo Bill's Wild West shows in the 1880s, advertising "two hundred Indians of various tribes" enacting an attack on a train of white settlers, to Pontiac hood ornaments, wooden cigar-store Indians, and contemporary airport souvenirs executed in vaguely native designs. Doxtator also presents a fairly lengthy look at Hollywood Indians, and notes how often natives are depicted by non-natives. Elvis Presley, Mary Pickford, and Yul Brynner all played natives; Rock Hudson starred in *Taza, Son of Cochise*, and Jeff Chandler played Cochise himself in *Broken Arrow*, the 1950 film in which Hollywood inaugurated a new spirit of kindliness towards natives but did not carry tolerance to the extent of actually giving them starring roles.

"Rarely," Doxtator wrote in the book accompanying *Fluffs and Feathers*, "have Indians been treated by Canadian society as equals." The symbolism of popular culture has helped to create the atmosphere that makes racism possible. There is a large tragedy in this subject, the tragedy of blindness, incomprehension, and exclusion—and in *Fluffs and Feathers* the tragedy never quite disappears. But people who visit the exhibition, non-natives and natives, will also see the comedy in this bizarre assemblage of comic books and beer labels, biscuit tins and city crests. Doxtator has played satirically with her material, often emphasizing what is funniest about it. It's her way, an ancient and honourable way, of leading us gently towards the truth.

SNOW WHITEY? STEREOTYPING IN THE MAGICAL KINGDOM

Gail Robertson (*Canadian Dimension*)

When you wish upon a star,

Makes no difference who you are...

Through the lyrics of this song, sung by the lovable Jiminy Crickett, Walt Disney and his successors have welcomed viewers into a world of enchantment and fantasy. Yet, who you are makes a world of difference, even in the Magic Kingdom.

So great is the stereotyping in children's animated films that you would think we were living in the United States in the 1940s.

Although it tends to be relatively ignored, this unofficial education system aimed at children is possibly more influential than the school system everyone has been talking about.

Gail Robertson. Snow Whitey? Stereotyping in the Magical Kingdom. *Canadian Dimension* 32(5), September/October, 1998. 42-44.

Television, movies, videos, toys, and video games are enveloping our youth and influencing their impressionable young minds.

Pennsylvania State University professor Henri Giroux focused his attention on Disney films after watching them with his three sons. "This isn't just entertainment," he says. "It's teaching our children. Popular culture is a powerful educational force, regardless of where you are politically. And there are things going on in popular culture that aren't very friendly to kids," he said in an interview.

This is what communications guru Marshall McLuhan had in mind when he wrote almost 50 years ago, about "an unofficial program of public instruction" in the media, which he said "has mainly neutralized the much smaller program of official education with its much smaller budget and much less well-paid brain-power." These words are even more apt now than they were when McLuhan wrote them in *The Mechanical Bride*, in 1950.

Today, children spend far more time every week with the media than they do in school. And if we're worried about the quality of classroom education, it's decades ahead of the unofficial variety.

Adults would do well to look closely at children's films—a world filled with racism, sexism, ageism and heterosexism. A world with sharply defined classes, where the working class is shown as stupid and incompetent. A world that encourages a sense of powerlessness.

And for Canadians, the programming often stems from the United States. So we're not just adopting their "free market" approach to our social programs, but we're also inundated by their media and products, as a result of integrated global marketing.

For example, Disney owns the Capital Cities/ABC radio and television network, along with film and record companies, book publishing, newspapers, home video, theme parks, magazines, hundreds of Disney retail stores, as well as hockey and baseball teams and insurance companies. In their book on global media, U.S. academics Edward Herman and Robert McChesney say "Disney's stated goal is to expand its non-U.S. share of revenues from 23 percent in 1995 to 50 percent by 2000." Disney is no longer going it alone, preferring to gobble up as many joint ventures as possible, including deals with McDonalds for exclusive toy distribution with its kids' Happy Meals, and Pixar (computer animation specialists responsible for the 1995 hit *Toy Story*).

But beyond the mergers, acquisitions and profits, what's the scoop on Disney films?

In children's animation, females, minorities and workers have few redeeming qualities, says professor Giroux, who lectures and writes extensively in the area of children's education and culture.

"Popular audiences tend to reject any link between ideology and the prolific entertainment world of Disney. And yet Disney's pretense to innocence appears to some critics as little more than a promotional mask that covers over its aggressive marketing techniques and influence in educating children to the virtues of becoming active consumers," Giroux wrote in the 1997 book *Kinderculture*.

At first blush, movies like *Hercules, Pocahontas, The Lion King* and *Beauty and the Beast* are hugely entertaining. They captivate—even enthrall—with songs, slick animation and story telling. Creatively, they are works of art. Additionally, anything by Disney is viewed as ideal and above suspicion. Criticizing Disney is like questioning motherhood. But check out these scenes the next time your little ones sit down to a Disney video:

- In *The Little Mermaid* women are either evil or without a life of their own. Ariel not only trades her voice for legs to pursue the handsome Prince Eric, but she gives up her whole undersea world to be with him. Ursula the sea witch tells Ariel that taking away her voice is not so bad because men don't like women who talk too much.

- In *Beauty and the Beast* you see the very svelte Belle dancing around the countryside, looking down upon townsfolk like the baker and tailor as she yearns "for more than this provincial life." In the end, like Ariel, her aspirations are limited to marrying the bad-tempered and at times violent, prince.

- In *Aladdin*, Arabic culture is portrayed in the opening song as a faraway place where camels roam and "Where they cut off your ear if they don't like your face/ It's barbaric, but hey, it's home." And throughout the movie the bad guys have beards, bulbous noses and bodies, evil eyes and heavy accents. Yet the hero Aladdin has a small nose, no beard or turban and no accent. He sounds and looks very American.

- The shapely Pocahontas, with her Asian features, is a strong female role model, but the plot takes huge liberties with Native American culture and history.

- *The Lion King* is rife with race and sex-role stereotyping. Mufasa, the proud lion ruler, and his son Simba are key characters while mom is relegated to a supporting role. The fair-haired Mufasa is good while his evil brother Scar is the dark-skinned, female-abusing lion "Queen" (with the lisping voice of Jeremy Irons). Scar prefers the company of his blackguard hyena "henchmen," with voices by Whoopi Goldberg and Cheech Marin.

Even the music shapes views. In *Aladdin* we have the street urchin singing about showing the world to the naive princess Jasmine. And in *The Lion King*, Elton John sings about the Circle of Life as a "wheel of fortune" with winners and losers.

The entertainment factor is almost enough to make us overlook the films' serious shortcomings, says Dr. James Winter, professor of communications at the University of Windsor, who teaches media literacy. "Take a film like *The Lion King*, which wasn't a fairy tale. Disney invented it from scratch, and it earned them more than $1 billion. Here, they had an opportunity to create what they wanted."

What they produced is a story that, on the surface, is about a lion cub that prevails in the face of adversity. But the real story of the Lion King is the marginalization of females such as Nala and Serabi, the vilification of gays personified by Scar, the ghettoization of Blacks and Hispanics, represented by the dreaded hyenas, and the glorification of hierarchy and paternalism symbolized by Mufasa and Simba. "It's a film whose imbedded messages can only be described as despicable," says Winter, who taught a workshop on media, including children's programming, to a Workers of Colour course at the CAW's Family Education Centre in Port Elgin, Ontario, in April.

In addition to the stereotyping, the films promote American ideals. "It's not just trade agreements that undermine our cultural sovereignty," Winter says. "Our children are repeatedly exposed to American values such as individualism, the glorification of the private at the expense of the public, and so forth."

Movies and children have become as inseparable as the profits they engender. For Disney, kids' flicks bring in hundreds of millions of dollars annually. With 1997 sales of nearly $24 billion, Disney is the closest challenger to Time Warner for the status as the world's largest media firm.

As with television, the marketing and selling of products is far-reaching, from spin-off toys, books and videos to sequels, clothes and jewelry. Such overt commercialism has a great impact on how young minds view the world, says Giroux.

As far back as *Dumbo* in 1940, blacks were portrayed in two ways: as jive-talking, hip crows, and as-dumb-but happy workers singing about how "we throw our pay away." For the past 60 years, women have either needed to be rescued (from Faline in *Bambi*, to princess Jasmine in *Aladdin*) or play horrific villains such as the wicked stepmother in *Snow White* (1938) to Cruella De Vil in *101 Dalmations*, or Ursula the sea witch in *The Little Mermaid*, which revisited theatres in fall, 1997, and was re-released on video tape this past spring.

For the most part, females are marginalized or non-existent, as the boys take over the screen, in everything from the Muppet movies to *Robin Hood* and *Peter Pan*. Even Miss Piggy is played by a man. Where female characters have the lead, as with Thumbelina, Ariel and Belle, their roles are traditional. Belle stands up to Gaston, but aspires only to wed the beast-turned-prince. In this respect, Pocahontas and Esmeralda from *The Hunchback of Notre Dame* are partial exceptions.

Disney titles like *James and the Giant Peach* get good reviews until you watch them closely and see the underlying messages. Meanwhile, children watch them dozens of times, helping even the subtle messages to become ingrained.

After a few weeks watching children's movies with a critical eye, I was discouraged to find so few that avoid racism and/or sexism. As for any positive gay or lesbian characters, forget it!

Parents must reclaim their children from the clutches of filmmakers like Disney—no matter how much we need a babysitter. Giroux says parents shouldn't blindly accept or ignore these films. Parents need to understand how much of their children's views of the world and their own lives get shaped by animation, he says. It's a powerful tool to teach children right or wrong. Often characters who are not white and middle class are shown as deviant, inferior and ignorant, he says. Parents must watch the movies with their children and address issues of racism, sexism and working-class bias, says Giroux.

"This isn't just about entertainment, it's about education. We have to take pop culture seriously and put it into our curriculums," he says. "Students have to learn to read the culture. We're not just dealing with friendly Walt."

Winter says "parents should minimize children's exposure. When the kids do watch, parents should watch with them and point out the problems, to innoculate the kids against the stereotyped and harmful messages."

But while it's important for parents to act, most of the responsibility should be collective, Winter says. "We must insist that regulations and laws protect citizens, especially the little ones. Our elected representatives should act on our behalf."

The world can be a wonderfully magical and imaginary place in movies. It can also be a violent, angry place, and one that is filled with negative stereotypes.

DISCUSSION QUESTIONS

1. What was your response to the Grescoe article? Is irony a useful way to communicate ideas about race?

2. Collect some advertisements which use ethnicity to sell products. Analyze their approach to race.

3. Look for depictions of race in Canadian television programs, or on the news. Are the depictions stereotypical or innovative?

4. Watch a Disney cartoon like *The Little Mermaid*. Do you agree with Robertson, or do you find it has redeeming values?

WEBLINKS

Daniel Chandler's Media and Communication Studies Site: Ethnicity Links
www.aber.ac.uk/~dgc/gender02.html

Canadian Media Awareness Network: Portrayal of Diversity Links
www.screen.com/mnet/eng/issues/minrep/default.html

Gender and Race in Media
www.uiowa.edu/~commstud/resources/GenderMedia/

Eye on the Media
www.erols.com/eombr/index.html

Media and Race Index
ctl.augie.edu/dept/COTH/coth380/race/home.htm

chapter fourteen

Political Minorities:

"The Invisible Man (sic)"

INTRODUCTION

This chapter deals with some Canadian political minorities: Native Canadians, gays and lesbians, and women in general. Although large in number and increasingly vocal, few of these groups have any significant political power—indeed, all are marginalized by negative stereotypes and discriminatory practices.

Nicole Nolan argues that the world's most powerful women are those who become popular culture icons—women like Princess Diana, Oprah, or Kathy Lee Gifford. Traditionally, western cultures have associated qualities like rationality and disinterestedness with masculinity, and emotion, irrationality, and self-abnegation with women. Given these stereotypes, is it any wonder, she asks, that women do not fare well politically? Noting that statistically the number of women in politics is only marginally ahead of 1955 levels, she maintains that democracy must change to acknowledge women's concerns and give women a role in the public sphere.

Sky Gilbert argues against the blanding out of the gay image in mainstream culture. He positions himself as a visibly gay man who embraces the values and politics of queer culture, and fears that blending or becoming part of the sexual "continuum" might in fact be a setback for gays. He expresses considerable discomfort with the idea that sexuality is merely a style that one can try on or discard at will. Despite the seeming acceptance of gays in the media, Gilbert notes that violent homophobia is still alive and well.

The last article in this chapter deals with another politically active minority group: Native Canadians. The argument in "Indians are not red" concerns the lack of interest in the media about native issues in general—except, of course, when there is a violent confrontation between native activists and the police. These violent conflicts make good television. Stereotyped as "noble environmentalists, angry warriors, or pitiful victims," natives don't make the news unless they commit violent acts. Maurice Switzer argues in this article that reporters generally know little about native culture, and, as a result, their stories are full of "misinformation, sweeping generalizations and galling stereotypes."

GIRLPOWER: FROM PRINCESS DI TO OPRAH WINFREY

Nicole Nolan (*This Magazine*)

From Princess Di to Oprah Winfrey, the mavens of pop culture pack a powerful punch on the international political stage. But if we can give women our respect, our tears, our trust and our bucks then why don't we elect them?

A few months before her death, Princess Diana—trailing her usual retinue of photographers, journalists and television cameras—visited a land mine field in Angola. Just as she intended, the cameras dutifully recording her casual denim ensemble couldn't help but pan over the legless and armless stumps of Angolan children who had been injured by land mines. Proponents of the land mine ban were gleeful: "Only someone like Princess Diana," burbled Minister of Foreign Affairs Lloyd Axworthy, "could give this worldwide attention."

That the Princess was playing political hardball was obvious to the flailing British Conservatives, who haplessly accused the royal "loose cannon" of influencing the coming elections in favour of Labour. They might have known better. The Princess, deploying a foolproof underground explosive of her own, responded to the charges with sweet, feminine bewilderment. "I'm only trying to highlight a problem that's going on all over the world. That's all," she fluttered to the cameras. Labour? "I don't know what you're talking about."

It was a lie, of course. As the Princess herself certainly knew, she had enormous political clout. Expertly manipulating a public and media fascination with her looks, her love life and her motherhood, the "pop culture Princess" carved out a considerable moral authority in the public sphere. Where she led, the voting public followed. As a result, her word and her advocacy had influence equal to that of a Bill Clinton or a Boris Yeltsin. The Exxon *Valdez* of commentary released after her death took Diana at her doe-eyed word, ignoring her political power in favour of predictable paeans to her naive, "instinctual" devotion to good works. What has gone entirely unnoticed is that Diana is the most extreme example of a bizarre cultural phenomenon in which women in the so-called democratic West exercise far more political power as pop culture icons than as elected representatives.

Popular culture is the only realm that can compete with democracy for the prominence and public authority it confers on its chosen ones. And it has conferred that power on women to a far greater degree than democracy has ever done. Women continue to achieve only small numbers in democratic assemblies. Even fewer have become presidents and prime ministers. Meanwhile, popular culture has produced women like Princess Diana, Oprah Winfrey and Kathie Lee Gifford—female public figures who, for all their pop culture kitsch, are exercising astounding levels of influence in the political sphere. Their suc-

Nicole Nolan. Girlpower: From Princess Di to Oprah Winfrey. *This Magazine* 31(3), November/December, 1997. 11-13.

cess is an indictment of democracy's failure to create an environment in which women can gain access to power, and a telling sign of how little has changed in our cultural assumptions since women first gained the vote.

In a report released to little fanfare or public attention last February, the Interparliamentary Union (IPU), a Geneva-based organization of 135 parliaments, noted a disturbing trend: despite what the union called "the global tide of democracy," the number of female legislators worldwide had fallen to 1970s levels. The study, which surveyed 179 parliaments, found that women hold only 11.7 percent of all seats, barely ahead of 1975 numbers and only marginally ahead of the 7.5 percent of female legislators in 1955. The levels had fallen from a high of 14.6 percent in 1988.

"Women," the IPU noted after its World Conference on Women in 1995, "remain sidelined at all levels of decision-making, especially in politics." What is at stake, the IPU has argued, is not just the rights of women but the legitimacy of democracy itself. For how can any nation call itself a democracy when it consistently marginalizes more than half its population? The most damning figures in the IPU report showed that the countries who most often congratulate themselves as democratic leaders had poor representations of women. The U.S. ranked 41st among 135 countries (right after Senegal). The United Kingdom and France ranked even lower, with only 9.5 and 6.4 percent representation of women respectively. Canada fared somewhat better, coming in 17th in the world with a Parliament that is 20.6 percent female—but that's behind countries such as Vietnam and Eritrea, to mention a few.

The need for female leadership has been shown by innumerable studies and polls that document clear differences in the political values of men and women. Some recent examples include a poll taken during the 1996 B.C. election, which revealed female voters put more emphasis on health issues and job skills and less emphasis on the deficit than men. Studies by Pauline Horn in New Zealand and Jeya Wilson in Canada have showed that female legislators are more likely to be feminist and more likely than men to raise women's concerns in the legislature.

With her fluffy blond coif, brownie recipes and pastel sweater outfits, Kathie Lee Gifford, co-host of "Regis and Kathie Lee," probably wasn't the first person that American unionists would have named as a major political force for the left. But after the New York-based National Labor Committee revealed that Wal-Mart's "Kathie Lee" brand clothes were being sewn by exploited Third World workers, Kathie Lee became just that, throwing her weight behind a campaign to end sweatshop labour. And where Kathie Lee led, a scarily large portion of the voting public followed.

"I really have to give a lot of the credit to Kathie Lee," NLC director Charles Kernagan admits somewhat sheepishly when asked to explain the secret of the campaign's success.

Interestingly, the female pop culture icons whose political activism has been most effective lobby on behalf of issues that are decidedly to the left of the political spectrum. The "Oprah's Angels" campaign, for instance, has everyone from sorority sisters to Alabama housewives doing their bit to attack the class barriers in American education by collecting pennies to send poor kids to college. Princess Diana's pet issues—landmines, AIDS, child poverty, disabilities—read like an NDP policy paper.

Clearly, the public (particularly the female public) are ready to hear arguments for social accountability and collective values. Moreover, they're willing to follow female leadership. So why are we willing to give women our attention, our trust, our respect and our dollars, but not our votes?

People like Heritage Minister Sheila Copps (who, incidentally, objects to what she calls "another article on woe betide women in power") characterize it as a structural problem that will disappear as our culture becomes less sexist. "Parliament will change as society changes," she says.

Of course, there are myriad structural reasons to account for women's invisibility in politics: from their greater family duties to their relative poverty. But it doesn't explain why women have been shut out so completely. Why, in other words, is Margaret Thatcher the only notable female head of a leading democratic nation to emerge in the entire history of G7 nations? Maybe democracy is part of the problem rather than the prize at the end of the struggle.

From its beginnings in 17th century Europe, Western democracy has been founded on a division between public and private—between areas that the government can legitimately regulate and those that are off limits. "Liberalism," writes the British feminist scholar Anne Phillips, "sprung from the imperative to protect citizens from those who rule. . . . The pressure for greater democracy in the public sphere went hand in hand with a pressure to restrict the spheres in which democracy was relevant." Government was a contract between property-owning individuals who consented to governmental power in certain areas of life because it was necessary, but eschewed the role of government in other areas—particularly in their homes and the management of their property. The public world of politics is therefore idealized as the realm of what is abstract, general or disinterested. The private is situated as the realm of self-interest—an area from which politicians are supposed to divest themselves as much as possible in order to rule in the public interest.

The definitions of public and private concerns have shifted over time. Socialism and feminism have pushed the boundaries, insisting that formerly private areas such as child welfare and the workplace come under government regulation. But current democracies maintain their public-private distinction in documents like the Charter of Rights. Pierre Trudeau's famous statement that the state has no place in the bedrooms of the nation is testimony to the fact that Western liberal democracies still operate according to public-private distinctions.

The distinction was (and is) also one of gender. Women occupied the world of the household while men were charged with the task of venturing forth into the public domain. The qualities of disinterestedness and rationality associated with the public sphere are also culturally "masculine" qualities. Meanwhile, women are identified with the qualities of the private world: sensuality, emotion, irrationality, caring and self-abnegation. To be political then, is, quite literally, to be un-female according to the definitions of femininity set out by Western culture and supported by the structures of liberal democracy.

It's worth noting that the democratic countries where women have fared the best are the Nordic states where the public sphere has a much wider definition. Still, even when women do reach positions of power, their ability to secure the public trust is hampered by our apparent inability to accept and trust women as democratic representatives. During her years as leader of the NDP, Audrey McLaughlin struggled to be taken seriously. She recalls that when she brought up the issue at a parliamentary panel meeting of women from all parties, "all the women immediately agreed and knew what I was talking about. It really is the theme that runs through the way a woman and a woman leader is dealt with. We're just not seen as serious or as intellectually good as a man. We just don't take women as seriously. It's as simple as that."

Patricia Schroeder was a U.S. congresswoman for 24 years before stepping down prior to the 1996 election. In 1988, Schroeder's political profile was so high that many were encouraging her to run for president. She declined. Now Schroeder says the problem facing women with their sights set on the White House is that "a woman just doesn't look presidential. We have all these images from history of what a president should be like and none of them is a woman."

Attacks on Sheila Copps have demonstrated how even the most basic, physical characteristics of femininity are construed as evidence of political ineptitude. "People have said I'm shrill. I'm not shrill. I happen to have a female's voice," she says.

Popular culture has given women a space to express their concerns within the context of culturally acceptable feminine roles because pop culture is not founded on the ideal of a rational disinterest separate from the private sphere. In fact, it's exactly the opposite. Springing from the "irrational" world of art and stories, pop culture embraces the personal both as a source of entertainment and as the defining factor in our ability to understand and change the world. All the trappings of femininity that have been such obvious liabilities for women in public office are sources of strength for pop culture icons like Diana. The public fascination with female looks and clothes—the same fascination that has been so successful in undermining female politicians—was what allowed Diana to publicize the causes in which she believed. And family is such an anguished issue for female politicians that the recent Liberal election handbook for women warned "Invisible children can be 'spun' into neglected children. Visible children can generate an undue amount of concern about exploitation." Diana's motherhood, on the other hand, was the foundation of her authority, the basis upon which she was credited with a special knowledge of and commitment to children.

Kathie Lee Gifford and Oprah Winfrey are similarly identified with the private emotional world. Barely a month passes that Kathie Lee and her adorable children are not adorning the cover of some women's magazine. And despite the fact that Oprah has displayed some obviously anti-domestic tendencies by remaining childless and refusing to marry her long-time partner Steadman Brown, she has made a considerable fortune by exploring the world of family and marriage relationships.

This is not to say women with political ambitions should concentrate on running talk shows, marrying well and looking good in a Versace mini-dress. Pop culture is only capable of promoting women within the restricted confines of their traditional roles. Women like Diana and Oprah are really just postmodern versions of the Greek *hetaerae*, winning their points through influence rather than manoeuvering the levers of power themselves. And Oprah notwithstanding, pop culture is notoriously biased in favour of the white, the wealthy and the beautiful. What it does show, however, is that creating a truly democratic system isn't just a matter of changing cultural stereotypes of femininity so that women can "fit in" to democracy. Democracy has to change to fit women.

EVERYBODY IN LEATHER

Sky Gilbert (*This Magazine*)

American lesbian comic Lea Delaria used to tell a great joke: "I was in this store in Provincetown run by these two dykes. They put up a sign that said: Lesbian Discount 20 Percent. I mean, what difference would it make to call yourself a lesbian for five minutes, just to get a 20 percent discount?"

Sky Gilbert. Everybody in leather. *This Magazine* 33(4), January/February, 2000. 12-14.

I always laughed at the joke. And it has particular relevance to the queer community right now. After all, it's hard to tell just who might lay claims, or refuse to lay claims, to that label these days. Everyone seems to be reacting against labels or calling for an expansion of their meaning, or calling for their destruction altogether.

It started with Gay Pride Day. Lesbians felt excluded by that name, so it became Gay and Lesbian Pride Day. Soon, bisexuals and the transgendered spoke up. Then the term "queer" became popular for its comfy inclusivity. And if we called ourselves queers—the way blacks called themselves niggers—we could defang the word and, at the same time, make it a proud label.

Queer is often today's chosen inclusive moniker. But for some, it's not inclusive enough. Nowadays, it's the queer-positive, straight academics who are complaining. In a new book, *Straight With A Twist*, edited by Calvin Thomas and published by University of Illinois Press, sympathetic straights try to figure a way to refigure queer politics to include them.

Thomas's essay is heavy with postmodern lingo, but huddling behind the verbiage is a little heterosexual male desperately wishing to be a card-carrying member of the gay community. I've met lots of men like Calvin Thomas; sometimes they're the only straight men I'm interested in courting as friends. Their dicks point toward women, but they hate masculinity, heterosexism and white male privilege, and wish to be included in our queer family.

Others are against labels altogether—Canadian author Bert Archer, American theorist Daniel Harris, and (according to *The Globe and Mail*) lots of girls at Queen's University in Kingston, Ontario.

Bert Archer started out as a gay man. But in *The End Of Gay* he posits that the label "gay" is no longer relevant—since he and a lot of his friends are experimenting with members of the opposite sex. He says: "The most basic thing about sexual attraction, other than its very existence, is that it changes. On the most basic level, when we are young, we are most attracted to young people and when we get older, we are mostly attracted to older people. . . . There are obvious exceptions, which do not disprove the standard."

Since sexual desire—according to Bert—is fluid, the need for labels such as "gay" and "straight" have become superfluous.

The idea is trendy these days. Remember *The Globe and Mail*'s interview with a gaggle of university-age, bisexual, Kingston girls? According to Stephanie Nolen's article about the group, which appeared in the Saturday *Globe* last year, girls just want to have sexual fun, and identity politics have become a cumbersome burden: "It's like eating Indian food without joining an antiracism group. . . . It's about young women sleeping with other women without feeling any need to take on questions of sexual identity, and without worrying about the L-word—not because they reject it—but because they're not interested in any label at all. This is not about feminist response to patriarchal society; it's about girls on a Saturday night."

When the idea is expressed with such cheery, apolitical naivete, how can one disagree? Why, indeed, should carefree university girls be forced to carry such egregious labels? Again, like our straight professor, Calvin Thomas, their genitals are doing one thing, and their brains, well, their brains are going every which way, it seems—but certainly not there, toward a queer identity.

Then there is Daniel Harris, who agrees with Bert and the Kingston girls. Harris's book, called *The Rise And Fall Of Gay Culture*, posits that "gay" is over. Unlike Bert, he doesn't so much theorize about sexuality as plot what he sees as the inevitable demise of gay culture. Drag and leather were once potent expressions of the gay identity. But drag is now "totally devoid of erotic content," and sadomasochistic (S/M) sex is now "a safe, if somewhat unconventional, form of therapy, an acceptable method of self-discovery sanctioned even by the human potential movement."

Harris would see Ally and Ling's notorious kiss on "Ally McBeal" as a perfect example of this mainstreaming of gay culture. He constantly reminds us—much as the religious bigots do—that our queer images are all over the TV screen and mainstream movies. The result is that the rebellious displays of our political might—our hysterical queens and dykes on bikes—have become sad wax figurines, ideologically impotent, from a rapidly vanishing era.

Well, I have a number of problems with this position. Analysts like Harris, when they call drag and leather passe, have forgotten sex. Drag and leather aren't recent flashy inventions of gay culture. They are visual manifestations of the power play that is fundamental to sex. Sex is not about genitals. What's really erotic (and universally human) is power. Who's on top? Who's in charge? Straight culture traditionally gets its sexual kicks from insisting that men wield power over women. Recent queer theory suggests instead that power is a game, not an absolute—that it's sexy for both genders to dress up and/or wield power. Drag and leather, which have become symbols of queer culture, are the visual signals of the possibilities for that power play.

Besides, Harris has got his facts wrong. Leather isn't "safe." Sure, there's a new S/M restaurant in New York City where the waitresses are dominatrixes, and customers can eat dinner and get spanked. But this is sexual dilettantism. Fleeting S/M images in rock videos and heterosexual girls having an experimental kiss on "Ally McBeal" are just cultural tourism. But when was the last time your local priest advised solving your marital problems with a trip to Dora The Dominatrix? The fag leather bars and dyke house parties are as raucous as ever. And the cops seem keener than ever to bust them. And if drag is so passe, then why are the young kids still dressing up—and taking it into such radical areas? Maybe the boys don't do Barbara Streisand the way they used to. Instead they do Madonna, Ani DiFranco and Alanis Morissette. They enjoy dressing up as bisexual or lesbian icons, because these gals are now getting the mainstream glam treatment.

As for Bert's argument that desire is fluid, and the Kingston girls who want to do dyke sex without the labels and Calvin Thomas, the straight academic who identifies as gay? There's a problem with relying on personal, anecdotal evidence to shape sexual theory. For instance, my own experience is different from Bert Archer's. I've spent my whole life being attracted to men of a very particular age and look—no fluidity in sight. But you won't find me suggesting that people's sexual desires are unchangeable. No, I can only generalize that human sexuality is wonderful, inexplicable and varied.

But I swear that if I hear one more person talk about the "continuum" of human sexuality, I'm going to throw up. Yes, okay, there is a continuum and we're all on it. And sure, everybody probably has a little bit of attraction to just about every body type on earth. But the existence of a sexual continuum does not strip sexuality of its politics—any more than a colour bar strips race of its politics. I mean, it's one thing to say that few people are really black or white, since so many people exist somewhere in the middle. But that's not much solace to the very dark black person, who—in North American society anyway—has a much harder time of it than someone who is pale caramel.

The interesting thing about gays and lesbians is that (unlike most blacks) a sizable number can "pass" for being a member of the dominant culture. And, of course, the queers who can pass for straight, do. Like Bert and those Kingston girls, who are still in a better position to get a good job, or affordable housing, or the respect of friends and family, much more than a visible queer. But for those who cross the gender lines—the transgendered, say—life is difficult. Matthew Shepard couldn't help it that he looked and acted girly. It's no accident that many effeminate fags still become hairdressers, tellers, florists or waiters, and that lots of butch dykes are gym teachers and marines. They need a safe place, where their frightening visibility is tolerated.

I hope some day (by the year 2050, perhaps?) we will live in a world without labels. But I guarantee the name-calling won't stop in my lifetime. And yes, I've got nothing against straight academics like Calvin Thomas who, acutely aware of the privilege they accrue as heterosexuals, want to fool around with sex and power. But until a leather dyke and effeminate queen are delivering the nightly news, labels ought to be ubiquitous. And queers should claim them, embrace them, and revel in the differences they signal. The pretense that labels have disappeared plays right into the hands of the homophobes. Their hate flourishes in secret. After all, the gains of gay liberation are pretty recent. In eliminating our own visibility when it's just starting to be accepted, we actually cede that ground.

On a recent show of "Pamela Wallin Live," Bert Archer said my opposition to *The End Of Gay* was typical of "the older generation." True, I'm 46 years old. But oldie Gary Indiana (ex-Beatnik, writer) is a big supporter of Daniel Harris, and aging Bruce LaBruce is a big supporter of the antigay stance. Attitudes about labeling don't fall along age lines. It all has to do with power and privilege. Bruce LaBruce is a pornographer, and Gary Indiana is a writer who has never made an issue of his sexuality. Bruce is "out" in one of the few professions (besides hairdressing) where it doesn't matter, and Gary has always been somewhat closeted.

I wish to be taken seriously as a writer. But because I'm openly gay, promiscuous and effeminate many personal and professional doors are closed to me. Heck, even when I order a burger at McDonald's, people turn and stare. They can't help it—when I talk, I wave my hands around like a girl.

Lea Delaria is right. Those house-wives still aren't lining up in those Provincetown stores for the "Lesbian Discount 20 Percent." That says something. Until women are willing to lie about their genital preferences to get a bargain, or until faggot boys are no longer left for dead tied to Wyoming fence posts—call me crazy—but I'll have a weird affection for labels.

INDIANS ARE NOT RED. THEY'RE INVISIBLE

Maurice Switzer (*Media*)

The stories of a people who were thriving on this land long before the Egyptians built their pyramids—and who have survived five centuries of uninterrupted genocide—would make for some fascinating journalism. But mass media news coverage is inextricably linked to political agendas, and governments don't want to deal with native issues, so there have been far more headlines in this country about Helms-Burton legislation than there have been about, say, the report of the Royal Commission on Aboriginal Peoples.

[In November 1996] the royal commission tabled its six-volume, 3500-page report, optimistic that a government prepared to invest $58 million to investigate the underlying causes of soaring rates of aboriginal poverty, suicide and unemployment must be serious about trying to reverse those trends.

Maurice Switzer. Indians are not red. They're invisible: *Media*, 4(1), 1997. 21-22.

Royal commission co-chairman Georges Erasmus was particularly testy in a year-end interview with veteran *Globe and Mail* reporter Rudy Platiel, accusing commentators and critics of never having actually read the commission's report, and of basing their opinions on inadequate news coverage.

"It's a partial discussion, never a complete discussion," said the former Assembly of First Nations grand chief. "I haven't read a complete story on it yet, but even when the stories are written, you don't get a full story on finances."

So concerned were commissioners about apparent media indifference to their efforts that in January they distributed to community newspapers a series of 11 camera-ready articles dealing with various aspects of the watershed report, an extraordinary display of media spoon-feeding.

Ironically, media attention helped trigger the establishment of the royal commission by a Mulroney government embarrassed about headlines from the 1990 confrontation between 4000 Canadian soldiers and Kanehsatake Mohawks unwilling to let Quebeckers play golf on the graves of their ancestors. But it was the elements of conflict in the so-called Oka crisis that appealed to journalists, not the underlying historical issues of aboriginal autonomy and land rights. Mainstream media coverage focused on flashpoints like blockades, confrontations, and the death of a single police officer. Native story-tellers like filmmaker Alanis Obomsawin took the longer-term aboriginal perspective; Obomsawin titled her feature-length documentary about the 78-day stand-off *Kanehsatake: 270 Years of Resistance*.

The Royal Commission on Aboriginal Peoples reminded Canadians that their government had dispatched a larger armed force to Oka to besiege 63 people—including 22 women and children—than had ever been sent as a peacekeeping mission to such war-torn global trouble spots as Cyprus, Bosnia, or Somalia. But their report also underscored the potential damage caused by out-of-context journalism.

"In all the television, radio, and newspaper coverage, one image was repeated again and again: that of the 'warriors'—bandanna-masked, khaki-clad, gun-toting Indians. The image bore a remarkable resemblance to the war-bonneted warrior—the dominant film and media image of aboriginal men in the last century," the report concluded.

"Media images that focus predominantly on conflict and confrontation make communication more difficult and reconciliation more elusive."

Lynda Powless, editor of *Turtle Island News*, an award-winning weekly on the Six Nations Reserve near Brantford, Ont., had founded the Native Journalists Association when she testified before the commission in May of 1993.

"Non-native reporters showed us through their spotty and dismal understanding of the issues that led to and provoked Oka and subsequent coverage, that they are not as well-versed in native issues as they pretend to be."

But the most damning indictment the royal commission would hear about mainstream coverage of the aboriginal beat did not relate to the stereotypical and sensational reporting of Oka, nor did it originate from within the native community. In a November, 1993 appearance before the commission in Ottawa, Canadian Association of Journalists then-president Charles Bury minced no words about his assessment of the coverage of native issues in this country:

> The country's large newspapers, TV and radio news shows often contain misinformation, sweeping generalizations and galling stereotypes about natives and native affairs. Their stories are usually presented by journalists with little background knowledge or understanding of aboriginals and their communities. The large media outlets include shamefully few aboriginals either on their staff

or among their freelance journalists. As well, very few so-called mainstream media consider aboriginal affairs to be a subject worthy of regular attention . . . The result is that most Canadians have little real knowledge of the country's native peoples or of the issues that affect them.

In their final report, commissioners concluded that access to mainstream media by aboriginals was critical to Canadians achieving wider understanding of native identities and aspirations:

Aboriginal people are not well represented by or in the media. Many Canadians know aboriginal people only as noble environmentalists, angry warriors, or pitiful victims. A full picture of their humanity is simply not available in the media. Mainstream media do not reflect aboriginal realities very well. Nor do they offer much space to aboriginal people to tell their own stories—as broadcasters, journalists, commentators, poets or story-tellers.

Commissioners recommended that private and public media outlets provide for a greater aboriginal presence in their offerings by developing and implementing employment equity plans and, specifically, that the CBC purchase and broadcast programming from independent aboriginal producers. They also urged federal government support for aboriginal media training, and funding for aboriginal-controlled media ventures.

Six summers have passed since Kanehsatake, and there has been little indication that Canada's print and broadcast journalists feel any obligation to provide substantial coverage of native affairs. The eruption of media attention aboriginals received surrounding Oka began to dissipate almost as soon as the barbed wire and barricades came down, and native issues resumed their familiar position at the bottom of both the House of Commons order paper and newsroom assignment rosters.

The Globe and Mail has been the lone exception, setting the news-gathering agenda for the nation's media in aboriginal issues as well as most other areas. But long-time native affairs specialist Rudy Platiel took early retirement in March, and wasn't sure if Canada's "national newspaper" intended to replace him.

"I was never really assigned the aboriginal beat to start with," Platiel says. "I just started doing stories on native issues, and the desk just kept passing assignments over to me. But I doubt that the *Globe* will maintain a distinct beat."

Some large dailies—like the *Ottawa Citizen*—can boast native issues reporters, but they operate nominally, lumping in the beat other Parliament Hill duties in much the same way as they would assume coverage of an emerging trade dispute over softwood lumber. In fact, only a handful of the thousand daily and weekly newspapers in this country provide any local enterprise copy on aboriginal issues. I can only name two Ontario dailies regularly carrying native affairs columns—the *Peterborough Examiner* and *Belleville Intelligencer*—and I am the source for both of them.

Among broadcasters, CBC Radio and Television staffs have traditionally set the standard for native-issues journalism, but their coverage is gradually being eroded to an event-driven basis.

Native issues were a bottom-rung newsroom priority before the media industry's restructuring turmoil of recent years, so dwindling budgets can't be blamed for inadequate coverage.

Nothing better illustrates the shoddy reporting of aboriginal issues by Canada's media than poll results that indicate that 40 percent of the general public think that natives enjoy a standard of living as good as or better than theirs. This at a time when 30 percent of aboriginals subsist without the luxuries of indoor plumbing.

Not all native Canadians live in hovels, nor do they loiter around the gates of 24 Sussex Drive, waiting for daily handouts from the Great White Father.

It is up to this country's journalists to find out who aboriginal people are, and what they have been doing for the past 20 000 years or so. Until they do, the issues affecting 800 000 members of Canada's First Nations should dominate *Media* magazine's annual list of under-reported stories.

The onus is on journalists to make native Canadians a visible minority.

DISCUSSION QUESTIONS

1. Discuss the ways in which feminist and gay activists depend on telecommunications to further their goals.

2. Research the newspaper or television coverage of the Oka "crisis." How did the visual images and the text combine to create a "picture" of the events?

3. Discuss the recommendations (recounted in the Switzer article) made by the Royal Commission on Aboriginal People on ways to increase the participation of native people in the media. How successful have these recommendations been?

4. Locate an Internet site created by a native, gay or feminist group and discuss the ways in which they represent themselves. Do these images differ from what appears in mainstream newspapers and on television?

 WEBLINKS

WeblinksAnti-Racist Action home page
www.web.apc.org/~ara/

Windspeaker
www.ammsa.com/WINDHOME.html

Assembly of First Nations: Weblinks
www.afn.ca/links.htm

FAIR (Fairness & Accuracy In Reporting) Stereotypes and Bias Link
www.fair.org/system-bias.html

Sky Gilbert's Website
Home.istar.ca/~anita/

National Action Committee on the Status of Women
www.nac-cca.ca/

chapter fifteen

Into the Heart of Africa: Museum Pieces

INTRODUCTION

"Hypocrisy with style" and "never having to say you really mean it" are two witticisms that have been used to describe irony. Journalists and literary critics have traditionally been rather suspicious of ironists. On the one hand, the use of irony has been seen as a political act of resistance or even subversion as, for example, in Jonathan Swift's famous "A Modest Proposal," which made devastating use of it against the British Empire for its treatment of the Irish by suggesting that the British might finally eat Irish children. On the other hand, irony has been seen as indicative of a "cool" and "detached" stance that indicates a lack of engagement on the part of the ironist, and even a way of indirectly supporting some unworthy cause because speakers get to say one thing and mean another—and who is to say what is really meant?

Although this debate took place some time ago, it still casts its shadow over museums and art galleries who deal with controversial subjects—or do not deal with them, fearful of mounting an exhibition which might create a controversy as painful as the ROM debacle.

Into the Heart of Africa was an exhibit mounted by the Royal Ontario Museum to show some artifacts that had been donated to the museum by white Canadian missionaries, soldiers and their families. These artifacts included a very violent depiction of a white soldier killing an African and other disturbing materials. The museum claims that the show was intended as an anti-racist exposé on how the missionaries felt about people whom they considered "primitive"; however, some people in the African-Canadian community felt very differently about the exhibit and accused the museum of racism. A large part of the dispute centred on the appropriateness of the use of irony to expose the racist attitudes of an earlier era.

Both authors in this chapter note that irony is a very dangerous tool to use in this context, since it can easily be misunderstood or missed altogether. Robert Fulford gives a very complete version of how the dispute developed between the museum and the community, and how painful and ugly it became. He also argues that the exhibit played into several important and highly political debates that were raging at that time, particularly "Eurocentricity" and "cultural appropriation."

Brenda Austin-Smith is interested in irony as a device. Noting that it has a long and distinguished career as a "vehicle for cultural and political criticism," she worries that irony has lost its bite in a consumer society and that the exhibit in fact supported racism by placing whites at the centre of the visual part of the show. She also, and more importantly, notes that people who have suffered the brutalities of racism can hardly be expected to preserve the detached and disinterested stance of the ironist in their response to the exhibits.

For a more complex discussion of the Royal Ontario Museum and irony see Linda Hutcheon, *Irony's Edge: The Theory and Politics of Irony* (New York: Routledge, 1994).

INTO THE HEART OF THE MATTER

Robert Fulford (*Rotunda*)

They could never for a moment have imagined what many of us think about them today, less than a century after their time of sacrifice and high adventure, the time when they went forth proudly to do what they believed was God's own work. Many of us regard the missionaries sent to Africa from Canada—including those depicted by *Into the Heart of Africa*, the most controversial exhibition in the history of the Royal Ontario Museum—as arrogant and narrow-minded imperialists. On that point, at least, most of the people publicly involved in the argument at the ROM seemed to agree. What they violently disagreed about was whether the exhibition demonstrated this view, as its defenders said it did, or instead expressed a form of racism by focusing on white Canadian missionaries and soldiers rather than Africans.

In all the public discussion—newspaper articles beyond number, endless argument on radio and TV—there was hardly more than an occasional flicker of lingering respect for the missionaries who inadvertently planted the seed of this fierce debate by collecting many of the objects in the show. Clearly, old-time Christian missionaries are now almost beyond the range of human sympathy. That fact in itself demonstrates the shifting ethical imperatives of liberal society, and perhaps leads us towards some understanding of the astounding events at the ROM last year. Racism is no longer just one among many social issues; it is an issue that towers over others. Racial discrimination is not a sin like others; murder aside, it is *the* sin. The needs, hopes, and pressures of a multicultural democracy have altered the status of racial discrimination, moving it steadily upwards on our list of public concerns. The proof is in our attitude to South Africa: judging by our public debates, we believe that oppression based on race is immeasurably worse than oppression based on any of the other

Robert Fulford. Into the heart of the matter. *Rotunda* 24(1), 1991. 19-28.

reasons currently claimed as justifications by despotic governments of all colours around the world. As the New York writer Dorothy Rabinowitz said recently in the *Wall Street Journal*, "The issue of discrimination has now become the prism through which all other matters are judged." Nowhere more than at the ROM in 1990, where principles of scholarship and academic freedom were suddenly called into question.

As an accusation, racism can turn the heroes of one era into the villains of another. The missionaries, no matter how much they claimed to love Africans, were clearly bigoted, by any definition we now use: they believed it was their duty to bring the benefits of Christianity and the West to Africa, whether Africans wanted them or not, and they believed that their own form of civilization was the only one worthy of the name. Those ideas, self-evidently truthful and beautiful to a Canadian clergyman late in the nineteenth century, are self-evidently false and ugly to many Christians (as well as many other people) late in the twentieth.

How could we explain this to a man such as the Reverend A.W. Banfield of Toronto, who was in Nigeria from 1901 to 1930 and took photos that became part of *Into the Heart of Africa*? Missionaries like Banfield saw themselves as exceptionally courageous and daring, and they were confident that they acted out of Christian generosity. Narrow-minded? What, in their view, could be less narrow-minded than the desire to take the gospels, literacy, medicine, and many other benefits all the way to Africa? Banfield himself learned the Nupe language, wrote an English-Nupe dictionary and a Nupe grammar, translated the Bible into Nupe, built the first printing press in Nigeria, and published a book of Nupe proverbs. He promoted local crafts and industry, against the wishes of the British government, and introduced a higher-yield cotton seed. A life, he would probably insist, of admirable accomplishment.

But consider how he regarded the people he claimed to be saving. The catalogue for *Into the Heart of Africa* quotes his caption for a picture in his book, *Life Among the Nupe Tribe in West Africa*, published in Canada in 1905: "I had a hard job taking this photograph as the woman had to be held while I set up my camera. Just as soon as she was released . . . she ran away again. Poor creature, she thought I was going to kill her with that horrid looking thing, the camera. One cannot blame her." No, but one can blame Banfield for his moral blindness: he believed he was acting decently when he ordered that terrified African be held in place so that he could photograph her, and he was so blissfully ignorant of what this said about him that he passed on a chatty account of it to his Canadian readers. He may well have held the standard missionary view that he and others would eventually elevate Africans to the level of Canadians, but on that occasion—and, we have to assume, many others—he treated an individual African as he would have treated an animal. A man of some imagination, did he for a moment imagine what a female member of his own congregation in Toronto would have felt on being held against her will while a Nupe pointed an unfamiliar machine in her direction? Probably not: that wasn't the sort of thing missionaries thought about, in the early days.

His words, of course, were set down for people who shared his assumptions; if we judge him harshly now, it's because our assumptions differ so radically from his. He wrote a text in the belief that it carried only one meaning, but we may now read into it a meaning based on our knowledge and feelings—we inscribe our own understanding on top of his intentions. On very different levels, this is exactly what happened at the ROM in 1990: both the exhibition itself, and the controversy it produced, were based on divergent readings of texts.

"Reading collections as cultural texts" is a phrase that appears in the catalogue of *Into the Heart of Africa*. The exhibit was a way of examining—"reading"—the ROM's modest African collection to determine what it could tell us. Being scattered and extremely incomplete, made up of haphazard donations from soldiers, missionaries, and their heirs, the collection was unlikely to say anything fresh about the magnificent and richly documented artistic accomplishments of African civilizations. But might it instead say something historically valuable about the people who collected this work and the context in which they acquired it? Might we not learn something about modern Canada by considering the attitudes towards Africa of these missionaries and soldiers, many of them leading Canadians of their day? And might this material also tell us something about museums and how their collections are formed?

Nothing like this would have occurred to the people who donated the objects. They saw them as souvenirs of an exotic world, and no more. But because we think differently of Africans (whatever our race), because some of us bear a measure of guilt for our imperialist past, and because we know something about the tragedies of the colonial and post-colonial periods, we have a much more complex understanding of both African objects and the white Canadians who collected them. *Into the Heart of Africa* was an imaginative and ambitious attempt to expand that understanding.

But if the exhibition was a reading of the material according to certain historical assumptions, the negative response to it was a reading of *the exhibition* according to a different set of assumptions. And the space between these two readings was so huge that it appalled everyone who caught a glimpse of it. That space, apparently, was just as great as the space between A.W. Banfield's intentions in 1905 and our reading of him in 1991.

For one thing, a number of viewers considered *Into the Heart of Africa* racist. The missionaries' belief in their own superiority was one of the subjects of the exhibition, but for some visitors the exhibition actually seemed to embody that belief: it was accused of a crime it depicted. It was as if a museum, after mounting an exhibition concerned with ecological disaster, found itself accused of advocating the destruction of the environment. This was a museologist's worst nightmare come horribly true.

Long before the opening on 16 November 1989, the ROM understood that this exhibition might attract criticism from the black community in Toronto. Accordingly, the ROM hired a publicist from the black community, discussed the title of the show and its advertising with black leaders, and then—in June, with the opening of the exhibition still four and a half months in the future—invited black community leaders to hear the exhibition explained at a reception. In July, advertising and promotional material was tested on two focus groups, each made up of eight prominent blacks. In the course of all this, the ROM changed the title (originally it was *Into the Heart of Darkness*, a phrase many find offensive) and junked $25 000 worth of promotional leaflets because they used words about Africa (such as "mysterious" and "unknown") that some blacks considered objectionable. Most of those involved, including the blacks, thought this process was constructive, and as it went on the ROM was also building a program of lectures, films, and concerts around the exhibition. There was so much optimism and good feeling in the air that the ROM moved the closing back a week, to 6 August 1990, so that it could be seen by many of the thousands of black Americans and Canadians who come to Toronto for the Caribana parade and celebration.

There was little or nothing in the press reports of the opening to suggest that a political issue was in the air, and in fact picketing didn't start until the exhibition had been open for about four months. In private, though, there were signs of trouble. One was a report from an official at the Toronto Board of Education suggesting that racism in the exhibition's point of view might make it unsuitable for school visits. That opinion reached Harold Wright, who is staff adviser to the Afro-Canadian Club at Oakwood Collegiate, perhaps the most ethnically mixed of all the Toronto high schools. Late in November Wright visited the ROM by himself and decided that the exhibition was in a sense racist but should nevertheless be seen by the club.

Around the same time, I also visited *Into the Heart of Africa*, and saw nothing racist in it. It was Wright who indirectly alerted me to this issue and made me start thinking about its meaning. As Wright and his club were preparing for their visit to the ROM in December, they invited non-black Oakwood students to join them. One of the two who did was my youngest daughter, who later told me something of her fellow students' feelings. Before they entered the exhibition, Wright told them that while it contained much of value, the show itself demonstrated systemic racism. Wright, in other words, was suggesting that the students look at it anthropologically, as evidence of contemporary Canadian society, just as the exhibition looked anthropologically at the missionaries as evidence of Canada in their time. Didn't that (he was asked later) run the danger of influencing the students before they saw it for themselves? "I would have abdicated my responsibility if I hadn't warned them," Mr. Wright said. "I think they might have felt I was betraying them by leading them into that."

Even so, they were startled—the blown-up drawing of a Zulu being stabbed by a British officer, near the beginning of the show, was an unpleasant shock to them, though Wright had specifically mentioned it. The slide show, in which a voice, purporting to be that of a Canadian missionary, condescendingly explained some photos of Africans to fellow Christians back home, was particularly disturbing. "The kids found it insulting," Wright says. "Sure, it said that this was how people talked then, but it was like shouting out an insult and then saying, 'That's what I would say if I wanted to insult.'" There was no equivalent African presence to offset that view. The visual (and to some extent musical) culture of Africa was represented, but there was no explicit verbal statement of African views. A white man, Wright was conscious that this was a show from a white point of view, mainly about whites—though it started out with African culture.

"Two girls came up to me with tears in their eyes," he recalls, "and said, 'Why do they have to do this?'" Wright could not understand, and so was in no position to explain, the value there was in showing African culture through European eyes. "Africa was shown as a place where Europeans did things," as he said later. Some members of the club appeared not to care about the exhibition one way or another, but the most serious members (in Wright's view) were upset. A few months later, two or three of them were among the picketers.

Opinions like those held at Oakwood (where black students wrote a letter of protest to the ROM) remained relatively private until Saturday, 10 March 1990. That was the day about 25 people appeared on the steps of the Museum representing an umbrella organization that no one at the ROM (and few elsewhere) had heard of before—the Coalition for the Truth About Africa (CFTA). They handed out a leaflet criticizing the exhibition, in words much more restrained than those that would be used later. The leaflet said the show should be called "Into the Heart of the Interpretation of White Missionaries And Soldiers About Africa." It went on to say that the exhibition slighted Africa's contribution to world culture, ignored the real crimes of imperialism, and insulted Africans with words such as "savage"— though those words were in quotation marks and attributed to the missionaries.

Some blacks, it became clear, brought to a major exhibition about Africa certain expectations that this one couldn't begin to fulfill and didn't even claim to encompass. At an early demonstration a young woman seized a bullhorn and said: "All my life I've been looking for my roots. I come here looking for them—and you've shown me nothing." One of the people in the crowd she impressed was Tom Kierans, the director of the C.D. Howe Institute.

Kierans had become chairman of the ROM in the summer of 1989, and the upcoming African show had been the first item drawn to his attention. He thought well of the show, but he also understood that concerns as serious as those the young woman was expressing had to be addressed. During the next four months or so, he and his fellow trustees tried, unsuccessfully, to do just that.

After that first demonstration, and a somewhat smaller one the following Saturday, the Ontario government's Race Relations Directorate met with ROM representatives to discuss the problem. They passed on some of the concerns of the CFTA, and the ROM representatives agreed to consider their views. Privately, the people at the ROM decided they could comfortably make five or six changes in the show and held them in reserve as items for negotiation. As it turned out, negotiations never reached that point. Over the next four months both the ROM and the protesters found these contacts frustrating. The CFTA came to believe that the Museum was not interested in its complaints; the Museum, on the other hand, found that the CFTA's demands were shifting. Sometimes CFTA representatives declared that they wouldn't even appear at a meeting unless the exhibition was closed down first.

Meanwhile, the criticism grew louder and the demonstrations violent. On 14 April, demonstrators entered the ROM and blocked the entrance to the exhibits; police were called to move them outside. On 21 April they entered again, and were ejected by police again. This time the front doors had to be closed to the public. On 5 May, demonstrators went into the Museum yet again and this time fought with police. On 11 May the Ontario Supreme Court granted the ROM's request for an injunction ordering the demonstrators to stay at least 50 feet from the Museum.

After a few weeks the rhetoric intensified. A CFTA statement of 7 May, for instance, spoke of the ROM aiming "the bullets of psychic murder right at the heart of Africa." Arguments about how properly to approach the material were now replaced by a blunt statement: "This exhibit promotes racism and race hatred." Signs denounced the "Racist Ontario Museum."

From the beginning, supporters of the exhibition held the view that much of this criticism was perverse and self-promoting. A few radicals, this argument went, had seized on the ROM as a way to promote themselves and their causes—for instance, they incorporated in the ROM demonstrations protests over Toronto police treatment of blacks. Certainly this view was nourished by the fact that some demonstrators admitted they hadn't even seen the show. And what, after all, was the CFTA? It was new and unknown, and at least 15 of the groups it claimed to represent had the same address, an office provided by the University of Toronto for the African and Caribbean Student Association. At one point the CFTA claimed to speak for 40 different groups, but its demonstrations usually drew fewer than 40 individuals. A well-established organization, the Black Business and Professional Association, issued a statement noting that "the CFTA has no grounds to claim that it speaks for the entire community, and to demand that the view it holds is the only one that should be heard."

Even so, the Black Business and Professional Association said, "Most others in the black community are critical to some degree of the exhibition," and commended the CFTA for bringing these concerns to public attention. And as the controversy ground on it became evident that serious argument over the exhibition reached far beyond the black community. Paul Lovejoy, professor of African history at York University, wrote a letter to *The Globe and Mail* questioning the central idea of *Into the Heart of Africa*: "An exhibit on Africa should educate the Canadian population about Africa itself, not the missionary experience there. The failure to provide a clear focus on Africa exposes the ROM to charges of racism." Michele Landsberg of the *Toronto Star* called it "an insensitive white-point-of-view exhibit. . . ." Peter Desbarats, dean of the University of Western Ontario School of Journalism, wrote (also in *The Globe*) that he found the focus on Canadians a mistake: "If I had been a Canadian of African rather than European origin, I would have been appalled. As it was, I found it embarrassing."

Several negative articles and letters focused on what many saw as the irony in the show: this exhibition, they wrote, requires a fairly sophisticated understanding of irony, so that when a curator quotes a missionary using the word "savage," the public is supposed to understand that the curator understands that this was a bigoted statement; but, these commentators said, not everyone can deal with irony in this way. And this in turn—as Brenda Austin-Smith wrote in *Canadian Dimension*, the Winnipeg socialist magazine—placed another burden on blacks who felt offended by the show: "Either black viewers submit to a white culture's model of ironic art, or they listen to art critics tell them that they just aren't culturally literate enough to know irony when they see it."

At the same time, a good many commentators not only approved of the exhibition and its contents but also applauded the presentation. Christopher Hume in the *Toronto Star*, for instance, argued that it "dealt openly and honestly" with the cultural arrogance of the missionaries and that the decision to cancel its appearance elsewhere set "a potentially disastrous precedent." He suggested that the protesters were "a tiny but vocal minority within a minority." In *The Globe and Mail*, Michael Valpy, a political columnist, wrote two pieces defending the exhibition as an accurate portrait of certain significant attitudes within a Canada that no longer exists. Like many who wrote about *Into the Heart of Africa*, he used it as a way of describing the Museum's role. "Museums exist," he said, "to help us understand our cultural selves. The message from the exhibit can be the same to black and white kids: this is how racist attitudes in Canada were given shape. A useful teaching tool." A history professor at Wilfrid Laurier University in Waterloo, Terry Copp, decided that the exhibition depicted both the missionaries and the Africans even-handedly. "Anyone with an open mind," he claimed in a letter to *The Globe*, "is able to understand that the curator is attempting to promote respect for African culture without expressing contempt for those who saw it through nineteenth-century eyes."

After the show closed, the board of trustees received a request from a ROM security guard, Tony Hanik: could he give them his views of the controversy? He was invited to do so, and his carefully worked-out presentation impressed the trustees. "I saw it at least three times a week," Hanik said, "and it took me ten months to figure out what they were doing and why it didn't work." In his view it was a specialist show, comprehensible to a select few but open to misinterpretation by anyone else. He cited a point made in a ROM report on another exhibition in 1985: nearly every study of museum-goers shows that they usually take away no appreciable increase in their knowledge of the subject of an exhibition. Quite often, they read few or none of the captions. What they take away instead is an impression.

Hanik argued that *Into the Heart of Africa* asked visitors to pay attention to the texts and seriously examine not just the artifacts or the makers of them but the perceptions of the people who collected them—and then to judge those perceptions false. But what if the visitors acquired only a visual impression? They would go away, Hanik claimed, with a powerful image of white racial superiority. "Walk through the exhibit and pretend you can't read. You will find image after image of superiority: the mounted swordsman over the spear carrier; the military leader over his troops, the missionary over the convert. . . ." Wherever whites and blacks were pictured together, whites were superior. It was, Hanik suggested, "a bombardment of superiority." The liberal view of the texts was simply overwhelmed by the much more powerful imagery.

But if Hanik and others thought that *Into the Heart of Africa* inadvertently showed missionaries as superior, certain admirers of missionaries vehemently disagreed. They were far fewer in number than those who expressed sympathy only with the Africans, but they were just as convinced that the exhibition was misguided and bigoted. A letter in the *Toronto Star* from the Rev. A.W. Banfield's son, a retired Brock University professor, claimed that his father was unfairly denigrated. A paper prepared by a Canadian mission organization, SIM, said that the ROM stereotyped the missionaries, failed to understand their goals or their accomplishments, and ignored the many ways they respected and helped preserve African culture. They also said that relatives of SIM missionaries, "having generously contributed artifacts in good faith . . . now feel betrayed and abused."

One of the most eloquent of the many letters that arrived at the ROM during the exhibition came from an African who defended both the missionaries and the exhibition. Maria Chela Chikueka, an Umbundu from Angola who lives in Toronto, wrote about her gratitude to Canadian missionaries (including some in the exhibition) for their warmth, their love, their teaching, and their courage. She recalled that in the struggle against the harsh Portuguese colonial regime, "In our anguish the missionaries sided with us. They went to jail for us; they tasted our tears and we tasted theirs in our sorrows; and they rejoiced with us in our happy times." On the subject of culture, Chikueka made a point that, as much as anything else, the entire story of the exhibition demonstrates the ambiguous nature of cross-cultural relationships. The Portuguese, she said, thought everything African, from food to sculpture, was "savage," and would happily have obliterated all of it; but "the missionaries protected our culture." She saw *Into the Heart of Africa* as "an act of peace-making, for it brings a better understanding between people of different cultures."

That must have been among the goals of Jeanne Cannizzo, who was both the chief creator of the show and, in the end, its main victim. An anthropologist who has done field work in Sierra Leone and taught at the University of Western Ontario, she was working as a research associate at the ROM when she began to see that the African material in the vaults told a story. She proposed an exhibition that reflected current thinking in both museology and anthropology—a question-raising exhibition rather than an inert collection of objects. As Margo Welch, head of exhibitions, said recently: "The idea evolved into something that was more and more exciting. It was clear that it was going to involve the attitudes of people in Canada in the late nineteenth and early twentieth centuries. It was extremely original. No other museum was producing an exhibition that showed how material came into the museum's collection."

As for the missionaries and their attitudes, Welch thought all along that the story was so clear at this point in history that visitors could come to only one conclusion. In Welch's view, Cannizzo did not use or misuse irony—her quotation marks, for instance, were just that, not signals of derision. The idea was to tell the story clearly. In Welch's view, "Visitors will have a much more meaningful experience if they come to their own conclusion rather than if the Museum forces it down their throats." But that leaves open the question of what happens when some then come—as in this case—to conclusions that the curator could not have imagined, or pick up entirely false ideas of what the exhibition says.

Communicating is one of the major interests of Jeanne Cannizzo, yet somehow in this case communication broke down—tragically, for Canizzo. Her private life was invaded and her career, for the moment, brought to a halt. Enemies of her exhibition not only slandered her in public but wrote racist graffiti on the exterior of her house and then, in September, invaded her anthropology class at Scarborough College in the University of Toronto. They harassed her, shouted her down, and made it impossible for her to teach; on her doctor's advice she took sick leave. It was an occasion of great shame for the University of Toronto, the first time in memory that a professor had been effectively banned from a classroom for political reasons.

For Cannizzo it was the climax of a long season of trouble—as Tom Kierans put it, she was shellshocked almost from the time the demonstrations began. "And," as Kierans added, he expects "the Museum to support her career for a long time into the future, to help make it up to her." It will be hard, however, to compensate for either the personal hurt she endured or the professional setback over the cancellation of her show. Her colleagues at the ROM defended—and continue to defend—her scholarship; they kept the exhibition open as long as scheduled. But under the pressure of bad publicity and the threat of picketing, the four other museums that had booked it—in Ottawa, Vancouver, Los Angeles, and Albuquerque—announced one by one that they had altered their plans. Tom Kierans wrote from the ROM to Peter Herrndorf, chairman of the Canadian Museum of Civilization in Ottawa, to say that the decision to cancel was an act of censorship and the director of the CMC should resign. *Into the Heart of Africa* was to have been on the road until the summer of 1992; but when it closed in Toronto last August, it closed forever.

Those who knew Cannizzo's record were astonished to see her at the centre of this controversy. Not only did they agree that any charge of racism against her was preposterous; they also knew that on the subject of museums and their messages, she is exceptionally thoughtful and well informed. In 1982, for the CBC Radio program "Ideas," she wrote a three-hour series, "Old Images/New Metaphors: The Museum in the Modern World," in which she spoke eloquently of the democratization of the museum as a necessary process. That series also contained some of the seeds that produced *Into the Heart of Africa*. Cannizzo was interviewing Linda Nochlin, an American professor of art history.

> Cannizzo: "Is there . . . something that we can be taught in a museum, something other than how to articulate our admiration for this wonderful art?"
>
> Nochlin: "What about a show that, say, in some way centres on ideology and reveals the ideological biases of whole groups of works of art, and shows people how to read these as you would read the ideological messages of advertising or propaganda?"

Later in the series Cannizzo expressed her own view of what happens when visitors encounter the drama of a museum exhibit: "The Museum as a theatre doesn't present just one play, it presents as many plays as there are visitors. Because I think that the visitors are the playwrights and the directors and the audience as well."

This central idea, of all museum-goers freely and imaginatively recreating each exhibit in their own minds, reflects not only a hopeful view of the public but also a thoughtful appraisal of what happens as the human mind absorbs information. It ran into trouble at the ROM when it encountered a quite contrary expectation: that an exhibition at a public institution should have a clear, simple message.

More important, *Into the Heart of Africa* faced some of the most dangerous controversies of this period. It was often accused of being "Eurocentric," a word seldom heard a decade ago but now frequently used to condemn any person, book, or thought that seems to show only Western influences; because of the idea embodied in that word, curricula in many major universities are being re-assessed and the very notion of an established core of literary and philosophical classics is under severe attack. At the same time, an idea that for the moment lacks a name—call it "ethnic possession"—has been gathering strength. Increasingly, racial groups are laying claim not only to objects produced by their ancestors (and now in museums) but also to the culture and history surrounding those objects. Blacks demonstrating outside the ROM attacked the Cannizzo exhibition for not telling the African history that they, the blacks, believed to be true; they clearly assumed that for reasons of race they automatically understood more about Africa than someone who had merely studied it. That idea might have been condemned as racist no more than a generation ago; today it may still be fundamentally racist but it can't easily be dismissed.

The troubles surrounding *Into the Heart of Africa* also demonstrated our society's unspoken but deeply felt attitude to museums. Images of contemporary blacks being killed by whites or blacks are available in hundreds of movies. Why, then, is it upsetting when the stabbing of a nineteenth-century Zulu appears in an old drawing in a museum? Because museums are places of special honour and reverence, like cathedrals and unlike movie houses. In some dim but important way we expect museums to be decorous rather than challenging. We have looked for decades at medieval armour without once wondering who wore it or in what cause. Teaching us to do otherwise will not be easy.

We also expect museums to maintain a higher standard of public morality and sensitivity than other institutions. In San Francisco last summer the mayor wrote to the trustees of the San Francisco Fine Arts Museums, insisting that they either get a new sponsor for their 1991 exhibition of Dutch seventeenth-century paintings or cancel the show. The sponsor was Royal Dutch Petroleum, parent company of South African Shell and a target of anti-apartheid groups; for that reason, the people organizing Nelson Mandela's tour of California had decided to boycott San Francisco. In the end, though the trustees decided to drop Royal Dutch Petroleum, Mandela visited Oakland instead. To the director of the museums, Harry Parker, the lesson was clear: "We must realize that as institutions we are in politics and public affairs."

Museums must also deal with the fact that our sense of authority is not easily changed. Cannizzo, in defence of her show, wrote: "The display and discussion of attitudes from the past should not be confused with the endorsement of such attitudes. . . ." That's clearly true of a book or magazine article, but the point is not as easily applied to a museum. A museum with ROM's stature possesses a special authority, and wraps that authority around everything it shows. When it exhibits a Greek vase or a Haida mask, we assume that the object is presented for admiration. In the case of *Into the Heart of Africa*, it's now clear, some visitors automatically assumed that the admiration they were encouraged to show for the African objects also extended to the ideas of the missionaries, or perhaps even the actions of the Englishman killing the Zulu.

When the events of 1990 were over, the ROM was subtly changed. For one thing, it was now—paradoxically—working towards better relations with the black community. Blacks were more interested in serving on committees at the ROM, and the ROM more interested in recruiting them (though as late as April 1991, this process had still not produced a consensus on *Into the Heart of Africa*). There was something more pervasive, a sense that the ROM was a public actor in a way that it hadn't been in recent years, a performer in the drama of public affairs—and, painful thought it might be, that was a better condition than obscurity. Many of us used to say that the ROM was the central cultural institution of Toronto, a fact demonstrated by its generative role in the young lives of artists ranging from Harold

Town to Margaret Atwood, but that in the 1980s it had grown less important. Perhaps 1990 brought it back to the centre.

Still, there were lingering regrets. Tom Kierans summarized them best: "What we experienced was a missed opportunity to bond with an important part of the community. I don't think the ROM did anything wrong, but it was missed nevertheless. It is still very painful, because we are not above the community, we are of it." A point made by *Into the Heart of Africa* with exceptional force.

INTO THE HEART OF IRONY

Brenda Austin-Smith (*Canadian Dimension*)

It's becoming increasingly difficult to maintain cultural currency without a well-developed sense of the ironic. So much of late twentieth-century culture is infused with irony that a whole issue of the trend-spotting magazine *Spy* has been devoted to it, which is a sure sign that a figure of speech has well and truly arrived. Irony is the rhetorical necessity of the age, the critical accessory no one should leave home without. It has also replaced patriotism as the last refuge of scoundrels, for it means never having to say you really meant it.

Irony is, as you may recall, the literary and rhetorical figure that commonly depends upon an intended disjunction or gap, between what is said or depicted and what is "really" meant. To miss that gap, to associate the surface of what is presented to you in the ironic artifact with the deep structure or intended meaning of the artifact, is to misread it. Such a misreading may result not only in confused or inappropriate responses to cultural productions that employ irony, but also in embarrassment and humiliation when your failure to negotiate that intentional gap is exposed.

Irony has a rich history as a vehicle for cultural and political criticism, with artists in various media using it as a sly, often witty means of attacking dominant cultural beliefs and practices. The attraction of irony for oppositional cultural production is precisely its duplex nature: it can pass, in the right light, for the real thing, but eventually reveals a hidden structure which renders it radically incompatible with the dominant cultural, political or social discourse that it at first resembles. Or so one expects. Many problems attend the use of irony as a discourse or gesture of resistance or opposition, but two strike me as immediately apparent. One is the question of co-optation; another is the matter of intended audience.

In a world of happy face t-shirts it's clear that irony is everywhere, and that it functions in many ways, not all of them critical or progressive. In fact, its sheer ubiquity renders the status of irony as a critical mode highly unstable. Often, irony is not so much a mark of political or cultural difference as it is a sign of being fashionably cool, or on the cutting edge of not caring. That very temperateness indicates distance from, or even diffidence towards, the subject, attitude ("Have a nice day"), or practice being "ironized." In such a cultural climate, how is one to distinguish between the "truly" oppositional and the merely arch? This is a vexed question both for the artist who uses irony to oppose mainstream culture, and for the perceiver of cultural artifacts or performances. Has it finally become impossible to resist, let alone talk back, to the dominant discourse of capitalism through ironic art because that avenue of dissent has now become a commodity in its own right? Am I nostalgic to think it wasn't always this way?

Brenda Austin-Smith. Into the heart of irony. *Canadian Dimension* 24(7), October, 1990. 51-2.

The danger of being mistaken for, or co-opted by, what you are criticizing has always been one of the risks of using irony, but it's even more likely to happen in a hyper-con-sumerist culture in which people want to buy one of your ceramic wall safes (comments on the fragile illusion of private property), insure it heavily, and install it in their foyers. Irony as product undermines irony as process. But what's a cultural worker to do, especially in a time of cuts to government support for the arts? I certainly have no answer but watching irony lose its ability to create a snafu in the mainstream, seeing its potential for subversive sting domesticated and used to support the very structures it was trying to destabilize, is painful to me. It also makes me think about the recent controversy over the Royal Ontario Museum's (ROM) exhibit, *Into the Heart of Africa*, and the ironic audience.

I will not talk about its content; I am interested here in the response to the exhibit, and how irony supposedly functions in that response. The debate is over the nature of an exhibit of artifacts "collected" and brought back to Canada from Central Africa by soldiers and mis-sionaries in the 19th century. According to the ROM, the exhibit is offered as an historical record of the missionary perception of the African continent and its peoples, a perception distorted by racism, imperialism, and Christian notions of "civilization." To many members of Toronto's black community, the exhibit perpetuates these very perceptions by not point-ing out to visitors that they are, indeed, distortions. A recent write up in *FUSE* mentions that in the view of many visitors to the show, "the organizers of the exhibit relied too much on the ability of viewers (regardless of age, culture or ancestry) to read between the lines of irony, presupposing an audience that is both knowledgeable about and possesses a sense of empathy with Africa's peoples."

Perhaps the organizers of the show relied too much on an assumption of its audience's emotional and political detachment from the pain of the distortions being re-presented in the exhibit itself. Irony requires a degree of coolness, a measure of distance on the part of the perceiver in order to succeed. That distance comes easily to those whose history has not been one of brutal oppression. It is difficult to remain detached from depictions of racism "in his-tory" when racism itself is not history. It's still here. Asking black audiences to put aside their lived experience in order to participate as ironic perceivers of themselves seems to pit the ROM's expressed intention of using irony as a way of questioning historical perceptions of blacks, against blacks themselves.

For whom, then, is the show intended? If the intended audience is white and middle-class, then perhaps it will be a success, for that audience has access to the luxury of detach-ment. But if the intended audience is conceived of in broader terms, then the possibility that ironic distance is indeed another luxury, available to those who enjoy a certain amount of race and class privilege in this society, was not considered. In this way irony really does turn on itself, becoming not a method of unravelling the assumptions of an oppressive culture from the inside, but a recuperation of them, a reinforcement of the line between those-who-get-the-joke and those-who-are-the-joke.

Two more distressing ironies proceed from this. The first is the increased security at the ROM as a result of weekly demonstrations against the exhibit. Talk about recontextualization. It's really hard to see the oppositional effectiveness of an ironic cultural exhibit when the police are called in to protect it from the people it was apparently expressing some solidarity with.

The second has to do with comments and discussions about the black community's sup-posed inability to "read" the exhibit properly. I've heard the show compared to Jonathan Swift's *A Modest Proposal*. I'm not at all certain how appropriate the comparison is. Swift *was* Irish, and time after time in that masterpiece it's possible to see through his ironic pose and hear him rail passionately in a charged, authentic voice against the injustices suffered by the Irish under English rule. There is enough of a gap between Swift the eiron and Swift the social critic to allow a reader into the work without humiliating her. I see this as a potential problem with the ROM exhibit. Both sides may misunderstand and misread each other but the protesting community seems to have been put in an impossible situation by the ROM's defenders. Either black viewers submit to a white culture's model of ironic art, or they listen to art critics tell them that they just aren't culturally literate enough to know irony when they see it. The attitude of the (ironized?) missionaries inside the ROM replicates itself in these responses. Humiliation, in some form, seems the inevitable outcome. This is not what oppositional practice could be.

DISCUSSION QUESTIONS

1. Define irony and discuss its use in the media.
2. Visit the Web sites on cultural appropriation listed below and do an analysis of what First Nations authors have to say about it.
3. What view do the Web sites of the Royal Ontario Museum, or other museums, take of culture? Is their viewpoint "Eurocentric?"
4. Take a look at the African Canadian websites listed below. How do they present the African Canadian experience?

 ## WEBLINKS

Royal Ontario Museum homepage
www.rom.on.ca/

Cultural Appropriation
www.tbe.edu/lib/resource/bibs/bib1.html

Cultural Appropriation and Aboriginal Literature
www.ammsa.com/WindspeakerClassroom/CLASS3appropriation.html

Many Rivers to Cross, The African Canadian Experience
citd.scar.utoronto.ca/88p/Exhibits/Many_Rivers/index.htm

African Canadian On-line
www.yorku.ca/research/aconline

chapter sixteen

The Valour and the Horror:
The War on Documentary

INTRODUCTION

The Valour and the Horror, a three-part documentary about some of Canada's more disastrous moments in World War II, was broadcast on the CBC in early 1992. It immediately set off one of the most heated and ugly debates in the history of Canadian television—debates that were carried out in the media, the Canadian Senate, and finally in the courtroom. Brian and Terence McKenna, the makers of *The Valour and the Horror*, take the position that Canadian troops were often terribly unprepared for war, that blanket bombing raids on German cities was both barbaric and unproductive, and that the Canadian government was careless with the lives of its men and indeed, long after the war, still have not recognized their suffering. By and large, they argue that average Canadian soldiers and airmen were courageous but badly treated, and that the fault for the high casualty rate in World War II—both military and civilian—rests with the Canadian government and its subservience to the British establishment who ran the war.

Canadian veterans took violent exception to this, arguing that the McKenna's documentary was full of lies, errors, and misrepresentations. Woven into this was an examination of the role of the CBC in Canadian society and the standards it sets for objectivity and accuracy in documentary. The veterans argue that the CBC has an obligation to ensure that publicly funded television programs meet with high standards of fairness and honesty. The veterans found the use of actors and "re-created" scenes, as well as errors of interpretation, particularly problematic in *The Valour and the Horror*. They were also very upset that the CBC planned to make *The Valour and the Horror* available to Canadian schools.

This chapter comprises the report of the then CBC Ombudsman, William Morgan, on *The Valour and the Horror*, and a brief to the Senate Sub-Committee on Veteran's Affairs by Brian McKenna. The Ombudsman's report, while upholding the CBC's mandate to investigate any and all aspects of Canadian society, finds that *The Valour and the Horror* is "flawed" because the directors tried to insert the historical evidence into frameworks that in the end might have distorted the historical "facts." Morgan concludes that the program does not live up to the CBC's journalistic policies and standards.

In his brief, Brian McKenna wonders about the fact that the public hearing on his program is taking place in the Senate rather than at the CRTC, where such issues are usually discussed. Claiming "political correctness" around anything that deals with World War II and the mythologies that have been created around it, McKenna argues the validity of his research for *The Valour and the Horror* and the media's right to examine even the most painful of historical issues. Going beyond debates over the accuracy of specific points, McKenna points out that this debate is far larger than *The Valour and the Horror* alone, as it also concerns freedom of the press and who gets to interpret history in a democratic society.

There are two important Web sites on the program—one maintained by Galafilm, which includes the producers' detailed response to the CBC Ombudsman Report, and another by some Canadian veterans who take issue with *The Valour and the Horror*.

REPORT OF THE CBC OMBUDSMAN

William Morgan

Gérard Veilleux
President
Canadian Broadcasting Corporation
Ottawa
6 November 1992

Dear Mr. President:
I initially wrote to you on September 26, 1992, in response to your request that, in light of all the material we had discussed, I should prepare a final written summary of the full review I have conducted for you on the program series *The Valour and the Horror*. Since then we have received further representations and material from the producers and program makers of the series. I have reviewed what has been made available and, where appropriate, have made adjustments. Virtually all of what follows is already known to you, of course, and you have seen the material from the producers. So this letter now represents the final summary report which you requested.

Background

On January 12, 19, and 26, 1992, *The Valour and the Horror*, a three-part series, was broadcast on the CBC English Television Network.

William Morgan. Report of the CBC Ombudsman: *The Valour and the Horror*. 1993.

There was a strong reaction to the broadcasts, with a substantial volume of calls, letters and other more detailed communications coming in to the CBC, many of them expressing anger or complaining about perceived errors or distortions in the programs as broadcast. Other letters and calls expressed satisfaction with the programs and praise for the producers.

A second airing of the series had been planned to take place on CBC Newsworld beginning Saturday, 28 March 1992, and, in an effort to respond to complaints and concerns which had been expressed, in particular, about the second episode of the series, "Death by Moonlight: Bomber Command," CBC program managers arranged for the second airing of that episode to be followed immediately by a discussion program involving the writer-director of the series and Bomber Command veterans who had expressed objections to that episode after it was first shown.

Controversy about the series continued, however, and the President of the CBC, as is his right under the mandate of CBC's Ombudsman, asked the Ombudsman to conduct a full review of the series for him and suggested that the process include consultation with qualified historians.

Procedures

In carrying out this review the Ombudsman took the following steps:

- Tapes of all three programs, as originally broadcast, were screened a number of times.
- The latest available transcripts of the programs were obtained from the producers and reviewed in detail.
- All correspondence received by CBC on the program series was sought and was read with care and interest. (This correspondence included a number of substantial briefs whose contents have been, in various ways, thought-provoking and helpful.)
- Initially, three historians who were approached agreed to provide detailed commentary on programs in the series. David Bercuson, Professor of History and Dean of Graduate Studies at the University of Calgary, and Sydney Wise, until recently Dean of Graduate Studies and Research at Carleton University, agreed, as requested, to comment on all three programs. Denis Richards, a British author and historian who had written a short history of the RAF in World War II and had met and interviewed Sir Arthur Harris, Commander-in-Chief of Bomber Command from 1942 to 1945, was asked and agreed to comment on the Bomber Command episode only.

Subsequently, two further Canadian historians, whose names were provided by the writer-narrator of the series as historians he and his colleagues would choose to have the Ombudsman speak with, were consulted. They were Steven Harris, an historian with the Directorate of History at the Department of National Defence and co-author of the directly relevant volume of the history of the RCAF, who stressed that he was speaking strictly as an individual, and Carl Vincent, Government Archivist and author of *No Reason Why—The Canadian Hong Kong Tragedy—An Examination.*

Also considered carefully were the comments of other historians, including those who had written more or less supportive letters at the request of the program makers or the producers of the series.

- Because the time and space constraints of television tend to militate against inclusion of all evidentiary material, the production company was presented by the Ombudsman with a number of written questions and requests for the documentation to support and justify various portrayals, assertions and statements of fact in the programs.

- Upon receipt of responses which the production company had been able to supply, and taking fully into account the comments of all the historians consulted, the Ombudsman proceeded with the final detailed examination upon which the findings in this summary report are based.

Roles and Relationships

The auspices under which this series was contracted for and produced are complicated. Principals of Galafilm Inc., the independent production company involved, have stressed, quite correctly, that the series was co-produced with them by CBC and NFB and with the participation of Telefilm Canada.

This review of the series does not, however, concern itself with those or any other administrative or contractual arrangements among co-producers. It concentrates, as the work of CBC's Ombudsman normally does, on the content of the programs as broadcast.

It should also be noted from the outset that the role of The National Film Board is not considered or dealt with at all in this report.

The CBC's Ombudsman is mandated to deal with CBC programming. The NFB is a separate entity with its own structures and standards and, unlike the CBC, does not hold broadcasting licences.

This review has been conducted entirely within the framework of CBC's own particular policies, standards and traditions. What follows should be read in that light only and not as a reflection of any kind on The National Film Board of Canada.

Nor is freedom of expression an issue in this review. The key creative people involved in the series are familiar with CBC journalism policies and aware that anyone producing a program for the Corporation, whether independently or as a member of staff, accepts the constraint of abiding by those policies.

As to the CBC's own responsibilities and traditions, the very first thing that must be said is that the CBC has not merely a right, but an actual responsibility to broadcast programs in the category to which this series generally belongs. Whatever faults may be observed in this particular piece of work, they should in no way be seen as a justification, or even an argument, for an organization like the CBC to draw back, either through fear of causing upset or of political consequences, from the production and presentation of programs which raise difficult and uncomfortable questions, or which force us to look again, for legitimate reasons, at issues on which our views may be settled.

In this particular case, the veterans, despite the unrepayable debt of gratitude that most citizens feel they are owed, do not own an exclusive right to analysis of the events in which they personally participated. Indeed, almost all of those veterans, conscious that they fought, and that many of their friends and comrades died, in defence of our democratic way of life and our personal freedoms, including freedom of expression, would themselves instinctively reject any such idea.

Still, with freedom goes a certain responsibility. Those who make such programs have a duty to ensure that, in questioning conventional views and interpretations, they do not let themselves slip into using their own privileged access to the airwaves to become advocates.

No matter how appealing any new or unfamiliar theory or interpretation may be, or how persuasive the exponents themselves may find it, their presentation should still give reasonable attention to all significant evidence which does not support their theory and should allow us to hear any theory tested against other relevant views, including strongly divergent ones.

This does not mean that there is a policy requirement for delicacy. Sensitivity towards the feelings of people directly concerned in a program's subject matter is largely a matter of courtesy, and perhaps of maturity. It is not a requirement of responsible journalism.

Accuracy, however, is such a requirement, and not always an easy one to fulfill. Accuracy is not achieved simply by making sure that the facts actually chosen for presentation are right. To be accurate means ensuring that all of the relevant facts are present. Accuracy involves a determination to get at the truth and to share it with the audience, even when the result may not perfectly accord with the writer's or producer's preconceived notion. If truly controversial issues are involved, a range of relevant opinion as well as facts should be offered. Even those engaged in analysis and interpretation must try to be fair.

Broadcast journalism—or broadcast history—is a particularly difficult and vulnerable enterprise. In the academic world, the historian who presents or publishes work has often done all of the key research personally or has delegated it to graduate students whom he or she has personally trained. In broadcasting, a whole team of researchers from different backgrounds and disciplines may be involved, and they most often do not themselves write the final version of the script. Indeed, by the time that final version is completed several other hands and influences may have been involved. The task of accurately capturing and encapsulating the results of detailed research, often with the researcher not personally present for consultation, under the inevitable pressure for brevity which broadcasting exerts, trying to match a handful of words precisely to the visuals in a few seconds of stock footage, is an extremely demanding and difficult one. Even capable, experienced people doing their honest best to get it right can make slips and errors and the program managers who accept the finished product, doing so on trust, just as a producer does from a writer, or a writer from a researcher and that researcher's contacts, are in a similarly vulnerable position.

CBC Policies and Standards

In order to help program makers and managers to avoid the dangers inherent in these processes, CBC has developed official written policies, approved by the Corporation's Board of Directors, and has made them available in book form to those who work in and with the CBC on journalism or related programs. It may be worthwhile to set down here, from the Corporation's book of journalism policies, the principles upon which those policies are based and some key paragraphs from those policy statements which appear most relevant to this review.

The Corporation's information programming is expected to reflect certain essential principles of journalism:

> Accuracy: the information conforms with reality and is not in any way misleading or false. This demands not only careful and thorough research but a disciplined use of language and production techniques, including visuals.

> Integrity: the information is truthful, not distorted to justify a conclusion. Broadcasters do not take advantage of their position of control in any way to present a personal bias.

> Fairness: the information reports or reflects equitably the relevant facts and significant points of view; it deals fairly and ethically with persons, institutions, issues and events.

Under the terms of CBC's journalism policy, especially when the subject matter is rarely visited and the views or interpretations to be presented are evidently controversial, real and substantial efforts to ensure fairness and balance are required.

> Programs dealing with an issue of substantial controversy on a one-time basis should give adequate recognition to the range of opinion on the subject. Fairness must be the guiding principle in presentation, so that the audience is enabled to make a judgement on the matter in question based on the facts.

Another area where particular care is required, especially in light of the highly complex assembly of elements that is involved in a series such as this one, is in the proper editing and juxtaposition of these elements.

> The editing process must result in a true reflection of what was originally seen and heard and any terms agreed upon during the preparation of the program.

> Editing, the abbreviation of recorded visual, sound or written material, is an essential technique and one of the most demanding in journalism because of the time limitations imposed by radio and television production and the need to be concise and clear. It would be impractical to expect the whole of reality in an edited program. *What in fact results from selection and editing is a compression of reality, a slice of reality—which must nonetheless reflect the essential truth without distortion.* [Emphasis in original]

Under the heading "Mixture of Actuality and Dramatization," the policy states:

> Journalistic programs must not as a general principle mix actuality (visual and audio of actual events and of real people) with a dramatized portrayal of people or events.

> The audience must be able to judge the nature of the information received. The mixture of forms renders such a judgement difficult because it may lend the appearance of reality to hypothesis.

> Should a situation arise in which such a mixture of forms is the only adequate method to convey the necessary information, the dramatized portion must be well identified.

General Remarks and Findings

While I do find serious fault with the programs in this series, I want to stress, as I tried to do earlier, that programming which raises legitimate questions about our history, just as about events and circumstances in contemporary society, is an important part of CBC's mandate to inform.

I believe those who made these programs understood this and were trying to carry out their responsibilities to the best of their ability and I find no reason to conclude that they deliberately set out to distort the facts or to mislead their audience.

Nor do I consider, as some people appear to do, that the programs in the series are entirely without merit. One cannot help but admire the courage and humanity of the many Canadians whom members of the audience were able to encounter through these programs, people who clearly saw an unmistakable evil and were ready to risk everything to defeat it and to preserve freedoms we today take for granted.

Even some of those who were not there in person left letters and diaries from which much can be learned. Just a couple of sentences of Martin Favreau, for example, remind us of a proud tradition of voluntary military service among the oldest and most cultivated French Canadian families.

The most powerful and touching parts of the programs—and often the most sound journalistically—are those involving the three pairs of veterans who personally appeared in the films, recalling their own experiences. Their dignity and evident decency were enough to make any Canadian proud to be their compatriot and one might readily apply to any of the six a comment which one of the historians consulted made about the two who appeared in the first episode of the series:

> I must record my heartfelt admiration for the two veterans of Hong Kong who appeared in this episode. They were quintessentially Canadian, wholly believable, and some of the sequences in which they appeared were inexpressibly moving.

No program which enables us to meet people like these and to understand something of what they went through can possibly be all bad.

Regrettably, it must also be said that, in some respects, these programs are flawed. Each of the programs seems designed to fit its subject matter within a framework, of which the program makers themselves were apparently convinced, of incompetent, brutal or obsessive and villainous leadership, protected by secrecy or a conspiracy of silence now broken at last by those who made the programs and who are letting the audience hear the "full" or the "real" story for the first time.

The problem is that the case against the leadership is for the most part not proven. The secrecy was either understandable in the context of the time or not evident to others than the program makers. And much of what the narrator claims to be revealing has been known for some time.

In the Bomber Command program and in the Normandy program, attempts to persuade the audience of the villainy of one particular commanding officer, who had been singled out by the program makers, went beyond the available supporting evidence in criticism of the officer in question.

Arthur Harris remains a controversial figure. But even the historian among those consulted who has the least favourable opinion of Harris says that it is wrong to present him as being uncaring about the aircrew in his command.

Similarly, one of the historians consulted observed that the Normandy program seemed to be "stacking the deck" against Lt.-Gen. Guy Simonds. Even Col. Carlo D'Este, an American historian who wrote, at the producers' request, to comment on the Normandy episode, disagreed with the portrayal of Simonds, saying that he was exceptional among senior Canadian commanders.

In these ways, as in others, apparently through efforts to fit the material into a rather arbitrary framework, combined with the pressures of such substantial and complex production activity, the programs fail to meet policy requirements, including, in some cases, the essential test of accuracy.

Reputable, professional historians have pointed out a number of instances where, because important context is not provided to the audience, the information actually presented, or its implication, becomes seriously misleading.

Thus, RAF/RCAF area bombing of targets in Germany, the central issue of the program in which it is discussed, is presented as if precision bombing without calamitous losses of aircraft and men was available as a viable alternative in 1942 and 1943 and as if area attacks were simply preferred by the Commander-in-Chief of Bomber Command because he was obsessed with destroying German cities and killing German civilians. Without exception, however, the historians consulted on this program agree that precision bombing of German targets by Bomber Command was still only becoming increasingly feasible in the Fall of 1944.

Similarly, there are instances in the selection and editing of material from the writings or non-broadcast interviews of people who are represented in the programs by actors where important context and balance were lost.

So, though the actor portraying Roger Cyr is heard in the Hong Kong program talking about the possibility that their government knowingly sent the two Canadian battalions as lambs to the slaughter, we do not hear that, elsewhere in the non-broadcast interview with him, Mr. Cyr says the government decision was based on "the availability of the intelligence and the information of the day."

Similarly, when the same program presents, through an actor, the words of Nursing Sister Kay Christie recalling her concern at hearing rifle instruction sessions on the ship transporting the Canadians to Hong Kong, the audience does not hear the next words from her non-broadcast interview:

> But they weren't sent over to fight, they were going over for garrison duty, just to strengthen the British.

Historians may not all agree on the "garrison" argument. It is, however, seen by a number of them as important context, but omitted here.

The audience can also be misled, however inadvertently, by a shift of context, as in the Normandy program where, several times, words from a book by Donald Pearce of the North Nova Scotia Regiment, delivered by an actor, are inserted into discussion of events taking place in Normandy during the summer of 1944, although Donald Pearce did not even arrive in Normandy until later in the year.

There are also errors or confusions of fact, of which a few examples may be illustrative. Kurt Meyer's 12th SS Division are described as eventually being pushed off Verrières Ridge, while all indications, including those from the program makers, are that they were on Bourguébus Ridge and that the producers were trying to simplify to avoid confusing the audience.

General Simonds is described as having "never answered his critics," though he in fact wrote a detailed analysis of Operation Spring. The audience is told that "half of the regiment (The Queen's Own Rifles) lay wounded or dead" on the beach on D-Day, while historians report the Queen's Own to have sustained 143 dead, wounded or captured on D-Day. Tragic, but not half of the regiment. In the Bomber Command program the narrator states that the 545 aircrew killed in the Nuremberg Raid of March 30, 1944, was greater than the number who died during the entire Battle of Britain. The actual figure for the Battle of Britain was 1485 aircrew killed. In the same program we are told that Arthur Harris, though ordered to have Bomber Command assist with "Overlord," the Allied invasion of Europe, "would have none of it." This is simply not true. While Bomber Command continued to target Germany it did participate actively in support of "Overlord" and Harris was thanked for that support by General Eisenhower.

The programs contain various interpretations and assertions which the producers were unable adequately to support with documentary evidence and which were questioned or challenged by the historians consulted, including those recommended by the program makers themselves.

Even the Hong Kong film, though the veterans are so impressive and the story of the fall of Hong Kong and its aftermath is generally told well, is marred by several significant unsubstantiated assertions or implications. The notion that the Canadian Government know-ingly sent 2000 of its young men to the slaughter is featured prominently, both near the begin-ning and the end of the program. Elsewhere, the narration suggests that the decision to send the two battalions was made as a result of the Canadian Government's "accepting the Mother Country's assurance that the men would not be in harm's way." Later in the program it seems clearly implied that Canadians were sent to die there because the British did not want to risk any more of their own. The program also suggests that what happened to the two battalions sent to Hong Kong was for a long time suppressed by the Canadian government.

However, the historians who commented on this program challenged these assertions. Even Carl Vincent, who wrote the book on the Canadian Hong Kong tragedy, and who was recommended for consultation by the writer-narrator of the series, while he finds the pro-gram reasonably accurate in content and very accurate in theme, had reservations about use of the word "knowingly" and is clearly not convinced that the evidence supports the asser-tions that the British were willing to sacrifice Canadians rather than risk their own, or that the British provided assurances that the Canadians would not be in harm's way. On the final point, that of suppression, Carl Vincent, while he clearly feels that the Duff Commission report was a "whitewash," says there is no evidence even of deliberate isolation of documents concerning Hong Kong and that treatment by the Canadian government of information on this particular matter was no different from the normal handling of documents in wartime and subsequently by Canada or its allies. Vincent also reports that when he was researching and writing *No Reason Why*, none of the material that he needed was particularly difficult to obtain. In fact, he says, with justifiable pride, that he did not have to resort to oral his-tory because "it was all there in the documents."

Similar assertions or implications in other episodes, including depiction of the Dams Raid in the Bomber Command program as if it was planned from the beginning partly as a publicity stunt needed by Bomber Command to improve its image, and in the Normandy program, where Montgomery's decision to attack Caen was presented as being for public relations purposes, are disputed by the historians who were consulted on those programs.

The last and, in many respects, the most significant area of difficulty with these programs lies in the use of drama techniques. CBC's journalism policy makes it clear that use of drama in journalism programming is discouraged as a general principle because the mixture of forms may make it difficult for the audience to judge the nature of the information presented and because dramatic techniques may "lend the appearance of reality to hypothesis."

Even if one takes the position that, because a number of the people the producers con-sidered it necessary for the audience to hear from are dead, the use of drama segments to pre-sent their words may be justified, one cannot avoid the fact that the use of drama in these programs had the effect of helping to create other serious problems and distortions.

If a decision is made to use drama in an information program, the drama segments should be properly identified. That was not done.

Nor, though statements at the beginning of each program seemed to provide an assur-ance of exact quotation from writings and interviews, were the words put in the mouths of the various people who were represented by actors in every case their own actual words or even a precise reflection, with appropriate context, of what they had actually written or had said on tape when interviewed.

So, at least one quotation delivered by the actor representing Arthur Harris consists of words we have no record that he ever said or wrote. Another quotation, appearing to offer

Harris's view of "colonials," seriously distorts the burden of what he actually wrote and the view of him which the audience might draw from it. And, through an important omission, and a shift of context, Harris is shown seeming to say, immediately after pictures of the devastation at Hamburg, that bombing was a comparatively humane method, that there is no proof that women and children died at Hamburg in disproportionate numbers and even seeming to lie about this latter point. Examination of the text of his book shows that important context for his statement about bombing was omitted and that the actual casualty figures he was discussing were for all of Germany, not Hamburg.

Harris is no longer around to speak for himself. Chosen to represent him was an actor who apparently neither looked nor sounded like Harris did, an actor who, in recent years, until his untimely death, had specialized in playing villains, indeed may well have been associated in the minds of members of the audience with any of the many villainous characters he had portrayed, an actor who delivered a number of his lines with a look of cruel menace and, occasionally, even with a curled lip. The dangers in the use of drama in information programs are particularly evident here.

From these examples, and from all of the other material I have discussed with you, I believe it is clear why I find that the series as it stands is flawed and fails to measure up to CBC's demanding policies and standards.

Yours truly,
William Morgan
Ombudsman

BRIEF TO THE SENATE SUB-COMMITTEE ON VETERANS' AFFAIRS

Brian McKenna

Mr. Chairman, honourable Senators:

First I want to thank you for giving me the opportunity to appear before this Sub-committee of the Senate of Canada to discuss the television series *The Valour and the Horror*.

At the outset, I want to go strongly on the record as opposing the whole principle of these hearings. In its wisdom the Parliament of Canada has vested the power over radio and television to the CRTC. They are the regulators of broadcasters, and it is to them broadcasters must answer. For one of the houses of parliament to launch this sort of inquiry into the so-called "authenticity" of a television series is a dangerous precedent.

Of course this exercise is also designed to shelter a politically correct view of history and put a chill in the creative air. The veterans' organizations and this committee are sending out a terrible warning to anyone contemplating such a project again.

But having made that point, I want to observe that I understand that these hearings are much more than a public debate over six hours of television. They are about history and who gets to tell it, they are about truth and who gets to interpret it, but most of all, I think, they are about pain, and who gets to speak about it.

Brian McKenna. Brief to the Senate Sub-committee on Veterans' Affairs.

Filming in the Senate recently brought home to me how deep a shadow the story of Canada at war casts over the Red Chamber. Those huge canvasses from the Canadian war art collection remind you, every day you're sitting, about the valour of our soldiers and the melancholy nature of war itself.

The canvasses depicting scenes at the front and soldiers taking a respite from battle are personal statements about war from the artists. Some cast a nostalgic glow, others are as austere in their depiction of the battlefield as a searing poem. But each one, like the television series *The Valour and the Horror*, represents an evocation of war.

Every member of this committee, and anyone following this debate would have their own favorites among these paintings. Some they would hate with a real passion. In the same manner, many veterans can eulogize the Hong Kong episode of *The Valour and the Horror*, but reject the episodes on Bomber Command and Normandy.

The war art collection, like the television series *The Valour and the Horror*, was financed largely with money from the people of Canada.

During the Second World War, and in the five decades since, the Canadian Broadcasting Corporation has been given public money to tell the story of Canada at war. During the war, CBC and other reporters were sworn into the army to do battle with typewriters and microphones as deftly as others fought with Sten guns. Their dispatches must be treated as the work of honourable men writing, as Charles Lynch said, propaganda for a cause.

The National Film Board produced probably a thousand short and long documentaries to shore up morale on the home front with uplifting films by Canadian men and women, French and English, overseas, doing their best in a multitude of small and large ways to defeat the forces of Hitler's Third German Reich. The dark side of any war was of course not reflected in these films, or in radio broadcasts, or newspaper and magazine accounts.

When I was growing up there were lots of American movies and books on the war, but the only Canadian images I retain from my youth were from television. I remember being glued to the set as the old black and white CBC ran the black and white NFB thirteen-part series called *Canada at War*.

That series was produced under the watchful eye of six historians from the Canadian Department of Defence. The imprimatur on the bottom of every film was C.P. Stacey, the official army historian from 1945 to 1959. Again, these were official stories, prepared by honourable men and women reflecting the politics and perception of the times. Nowhere in the series is there the battle of Verrières Ridge, the second blackest day, after Dieppe, for the Canadian Army in the Second World War. There is no discussion of the 1500 dead and wounded we suffered as a country, and why it happened. It's not even mentioned in passing.

Similarly, the short account of Bomber Command, in the *Canada at War* series, focuses on these brave airmen and the extraordinary job they did, flying night after night over Hitler's Germany. There was no mention of just how savage the casualty rate was at the peak of the bombing offensive in the winter of 1943–1944 when German night fighters were killing two out of every three crews before they could finish thirty missions. When the films do describe Bomber Command targets, they cite the factories of the Ruhr valley, and precision targets undertaken, such as the Penneemunde raid, giving the impression this was the way Bomber Command was principally used in the Second World War.

There was no discussion of a policy that resulted in the Royal Canadian Air Force being used as an instrument by the Allied high command to deliberately destroy every German city with a population over 50 000. Appearing before your committee, historian Steve Harris, who is at this moment finishing the official air force history, confirmed the main thrust of our film, that Bomber Command spent most of the war leveling the residential sections of German cities.

But in the 1950s, even though the debate about bombing German's civilian population was aflame in Britain, there was no debate here in Canada.

It was too early for Canada to confront this difficult moral dilemma and discuss whether in war anything goes.

In the 1960s and 1970s more films along the same lines were produced and broadcast by the CBC. Often written and filmed by either veterans or those very close to them, the films reflected a nostalgic view of the battlefields.

In the last decade or so, the story of Canada in the two World Wars, quite frankly, looked in danger of being forgotten by the National Film Board, and especially by the Canadian Broadcasting Corporation. Why would the new generation of journalists and filmmakers, except for the writing of stock stories on Rememberance Day, be interested in a series of events fifty years old, that seemed to have no bearing on their lives. Over and over again, as I began my quest to raise the financing for these films on war, I was asked why I was going back to look at an old dusty story, five decades old.

Every day now, I ask myself the same question.

Some of the Senators have questioned my motives, so I will take this opportunity to explain how *The Valour and the Horror* came to be made.

On a grey November morning in 1987, I stood with my children in front of the Westmount cenotaph. It was Remembrance Day. We were all decked out in scarlet poppies, watching old soldiers in blue berets and clinking medals, remembering and praying.

After the ceremony the three children examined the granite roll of honour inscribed on the cenotaph. Robin, my eleven-year-old daughter, ran her fingers over the name Adrian Harold McKenna. "Is he related to us, Daddy?" Daddy said he was ashamed to say he didn't know, but would find out. The search began in local archives at Westmount Library and at the city hall. I was astonished that they had no records explaining the names on the monument. The quest came to Ottawa and the National Personnel Records Office of the Department of National Defence. There, amongst hundreds of thousands of carefully kept files of every Canadian who has served his country in war, was the dossier on Adrian Harold McKenna.

Adrian was my grandfather's kid brother. He graduated, as I did, from Montreal's Loyola College at the age of 21.

The last entry in his medical file reads: "Killed in Action: bullet through the right lung. January 16, 1916." He bled to death in no-man's-land.

Adrian Harold McKenna was one of 60 661 Canadians killed in the First World War. Canada suffered more casualties per capita than any of her allies.

To bring the story to a new generation we proposed to the CBC a production that came to be known as *The Killing Ground*, a two-hour film documenting the First World War. Despite its often controversial nature it was acclaimed by veterans, critics and the military as a fair and moving assessment. After its broadcast, near Rememberance Day, 1988, we investigated the possibility of doing similar films on the next war.

In the space of 30 years this country had lost many of the best and brightest of two successive generations. As one veteran wrote us:

> To be hit like that two times in a row can traumatize a small nation. Understandably, one of the ways a people can continue to live with a double whammy of that magnitude is to dignify, revere, ritualize, and ennoble it in memory and imagination, till it becomes not just a function of public

attitude but something of a landmark, of indeed, almost religious significance: like twin peaks, so to speak, for us to set our course in life to.

We made a deliberate decision to base the films on the accounts, not of generals or historians, but on the stories told by ordinary Canadian men and women who saw combat, and to cover the story as if it were happening now.

As modern journalists experienced in covering war and revolution, we applied our experience and training to a Canadian war five decades old.

We consider that war still alive. We believe that there is no statute of limitations on the crimes perpetrated by Nazi Germany. That is why I went to the Auschwitz death camp and spent a year tracking Nazi collaborators hiding in Canada. My brother feels the same revulsion for those crimes. That is why he investigated the Josef Mengele story in Germany and Latin America.

But we also take it as self-evident that most Canadians know that Hitler started the Second World War and that he was the leader of a criminal regime. As a result we believe that it is unnecessary to list all these crimes every time a film is produced about Germany and the Second World War.

From the vast amount of positive and negative comment received about the series it is clear that just about every Canadian who watched the series had those basic reference points. Even children are constantly reminded in feature films such as the Indiana Jones trilogy (*Raiders of the Lost Ark*, etc.) that the Nazis in black uniforms and black hats are the bad guys.

Without the military constraints that handcuffed the generation of journalists who came before, we approached the field to tell a dimension of the story of Canada at war that has never been told in the mass media.

In one area in particular there is a dangerous void: the story of Canadians of French background who volunteered to risk their lives for their country—by the tens of thousands. Because French Canada fought conscription during the war, a myth arose that French Canadians were not a significant force in combat. In Bomber Command, in the fields of Normandy, in the hills of Hong Kong, the French Canadian volunteers gave their all, but in giving, won almost no recognition from more nationalist Quebecers and scant from much of English Canada. So believing that if the country understood how we died together in battle we might begin to find a way to better live together in peace, we introduced the country to men like Joseph Favreau, Armand Bourbonniere, Joseph Le Bouthelier, and of course a war hero known to many, former Chief of the Defence Staff Jacques Dextraze.

After six months of initial research, three stories began to take shape.

Despite a number of good books on the topic, few Canadians knew about the 2000 soldiers dispatched to Hong Kong in 1941, to a battle where those who survived came to envy those who perished. From the west, steadfast Bob Manchester volunteered to relive his war, and from eastern Canada, the remarkable sergeant, Bob Clayton, agreed to a mission which proved very painful indeed.

Bomber Command was the subject of the second film, the theme suggested by historian Desmond Morton: "Canadians who had joined the RCAF to escape their father's memories of trench warfare found themselves in no less bloody and hopeless a struggle in which their own survival became improbable and their most likely victims were women and children." The 10 000 airmen killed in the campaign represents the highest toll for Canada of any campaign ever. This was worse than Passchendaele, worse than the Somme, in the First World War, and worse than Italy, Normandy or the savage battle for the Scheldt in World War II.

Yet while the catastrophe at Dieppe has spawned a cottage industry of books scrutinising every detail of the political and military blunders, there was not a single serious volume doing the same for Bomber Command.

Doug Harvey's honest and entertaining memoir, *Bombs, Boys and Brussel Sprouts*, led us to choose him as one of the main guides through the Bomber Command story. After interviewing dozens more, we chose as his crew mate the Canadian hero from the Dams raid, Ken Brown. He won the Conspicuous Gallantry Medal for his courage on that most famous of missions.

In Normandy, we were struck by the scale of the battle and Canada's immense role relative to her population—and the stark fact that her troops suffered casualties as grievously as their fathers had in Passchendaele and Vimy Ridge less than 30 years before. When we came across the story of the slaughter of the Black Watch at Verrières Ridge, it was clear that this was a story that should be investigated and given a fresh telling. As the main storytellers, we chose two military heroes, both officers during the battle and men whose good judgement and skill had led them to the top of their profession after the war, General Vernon Radley Walters and General Jacques Dextraze.

To bring the stories home, even more powerfully, we decided to take the letters and stories of the men and women who fought and bring them to life employing the skills of professional actors. The central reason for this technique was to communicate to the new generations of viewers that inside the old men with blue tams and clinking medals are the young men who went to war.

When we filmed the air force sequence involving the story of Bomber Command navigator Jim Moffatt and his crew, we invited Moffatt as the only survivor to come to the old air base where we filmed so that the smallest detail would be correct. When Moffatt was introduced to the actors depicting his crew, he immediately whispered in my ear that the actors were all too young. So I had each actor tell Moffatt his age. In every case, the actor was the same age or slightly older than Moffatt's dead mates. When Moffatt realized how he too had forgotten how young they all were when they went off to war, the old tailgunner had tears in his eyes. And so did the young actors.

To portray the air crew relaxing in the mess, we recruited the militia units of the Royal Hamilton Light Infantry, and the Argyle and Sutherland Highlanders. We wanted those participating to know what the toast "to absent friends" meant. For the hundreds who participated in the making of these films, this was far more than just another job. So many told me how proud they were to be telling the story of their country.

These films have actors, but are not docudramas. They did not employ a standard dramatic technique of blending various real characters together to make a single powerful figure. The words spoken by all the actors in the films are based on scrupulous research. A good illustration is the story of John Payne. Captured and executed by the Japanese when he tried to escape, Payne left behind a series of luminous and evocative letters. To bring his words to the screen we recruited a splendid young actor. Payne's story was carefully woven into the tapestry of the Hong Kong story. When the film was screened for the Hong Kong veterans and their families, there wasn't a dry eye in the house.

That night Bob Clayton's wife, Jesse, said the return to Hong Kong and Japan for the filming had awakened the old demons and that the nightmares he suffered for years after the war came back again. In a sense, however, Bob Clayton has been trying to work out his pain by speaking it.

The trauma is so deep and the pain so profound that most veterans surviving combat never speak about it. Some have told us that their experience is so radically at odds with the glorious story told to the folks back home that they wouldn't know where to start.

After the Vietnam war, doctors finally woke up to the indelible effect of horror on combatants, and gave it a name: post traumatic syndrome. Of the men exposed to fighting in Vietnam, three out of four suffered from the aftermath of horror. It is calculated that roughly the same proportion suffered trauma in the Second World War, but the nightmare was given no name, and the guys were expected just to jump back into normal life.

If our television series, unsparing in its approach to the full horror of war that those men endured, triggered a resurgence of the horror in some veterans, then we understand their anger, and regret any pain we may have unintentionally caused.

We scoured the shire reading all the histories we could get our hands on. We did our homework, spending thousands of hours in archives in Canada, England, the United States, Germany, and Japan. In every case we walked the battlefields with the men who fought. We interviewed by letter and in person hundreds of veterans. We acquired thousands of feet of war footage and hundreds of photographs, all central to the telling of a story on film.

There has been little reason for most veterans to keep up with new material declassified every year, evidence periodically published by the major international historians in the field. So some of the information we broadcast came as shock.

"When you air a program about WWII," wrote veteran Donald Pearce, "that deviates from the mighty stereotype—that is, that quite sanely cuts back on the romantic aspect of the story rather than picturing the desired succession of noble deeds and heroic actions— obviously you're going to stir up a hornets' nest of wrath and vengeance in some viewers."

We also discovered that Hell has no fury like an historian scorned. From the beginning I was critical of many military historians for failing to draw the obvious conclusions from archival material they have long had access to. Buried in Canada's various splendid archives are sheaves of documents embarrassing the political military establishment.

Because so much of Canada's war history is entrusted to historians hired directly by the Department of National Defence or by historians dependent on the good will of the Defence Department as well as organizations such as the Canadian Legion their criticisms and conclusions are often muted.

As the series went to air, I repeatedly quoted *Globe and Mail* writer David Martin, who wrote on Remembrance Day 1991 that his father died twice, once at the hand of the enemy and the second time at the hands of Canada's historians.

Generally, most historians don't like history on television, unless of course they've written the program themselves. But most historians who have the slightest inkling of the power and need for popularizing history, support the television series. They approach it as they would a book—some parts you like, some parts you don't, but it is only one of hundreds of television programs dealing with the Second World War. The reaction from these leading historians has been gratifying:

Pierre Berton urged that:

Every schoolchild be given the chance to see this documentary so that they may realize the horror, the misery, the cynicism—yes, the incompetence, too—that accompanies every war.

Carl Vincent, Canada's leading expert on the battle of Hong Kong, called our film about that tragedy, "an immensely moving presentation" and he has strongly defended it on several occasions.

Max Hastings, of Great Britain, the world's leading expert on Bomber Command, wrote:

> I think the general tenor of your film reflects a fair picture of the bomber offensive and pays full tribute to the courage and sacrifice of the air crew who carried it out.

Colonel Carlo D'Este of the United States, the world's leading expert on the battle for Normandy, said of our film:

> *In Desperate Battle* attempts to come to grips with, and to tell the story of, the Canadian army in Normandy, warts and all . . . I do feel the film was a sincere attempt to present the viewer what obviously has become, in the eyes of some critics, some unpalatable truths.

Military historian Brian Villa, of the University of Ottawa, who you refused to hear in this forum, wrote the following appraisal of our three programs:

> This series, superbly directed, nicely paced and full of dramatic moments, shows how instructive good documentaries can be and I have no doubt that the public is much better informed by this one series than it has been by a half dozen programs in the last decade . . . Honesty is often controversial but I applaud CBC for the courage shown in this searing series.

Instead of these opinions, you've chosen to dwell on the complaints of a parade of minor historians, many of them with personal axes to grind against the filmmakers.

Take Colonel John English, for example, with whom I had a bitter and personal argument when he tried to disrupt our filming in Normandy. To top it off, just as his new book on the battle was coming out and he could have used the publicity, the scenes we filmed with him ended up on the cutting room floor. So he put his uniform on and came before this committee and called me names.

Another historian who attacked me in quite unreasonable terms was Terry Copp of the University of Waterloo, the co-author of a series of self-published coffee table books on Normandy and other battles along the Maple Leaf Route. He testified that we had a dispute as to whether he would be employed as a researcher on this series, a dispute about which he is obviously still bitter.

Copp and his co-author, Robert Vogel, who also attacked me here, have written remarkably uncritical accounts of the activities of the Canadian army in Europe. Terry Copp has even suppressed some of the very stories we told in our films.

It was in the footnotes of a Copp manuscript that I discovered the story of how General Rod Keller had been repeatedly upbraided by General Crerar for his excessive drinking. It was in those footnotes that I also discovered the story of how Brigadier Dan Cunningham refused Keller's demand to commit his Highland regiment to an obviously suicidal attack during the battle for Verrières Ridge—a refusal which cost him his job.

When I congratulated Terry Copp for unearthing these stories, there was a long, uncomfortable silence on the other end of the telephone. Then he said he was not going to use the story. He said he didn't want to embarrass anyone. I thought this was at best a curious attitude for an historian, and at worst intellectually dishonest.

This is the kind of kid glove treatment that has been given to Canadian military history by the sort of historians who have been so hysterical in attacking these films.

Now I am going to tell you a shocking story, a profoundly damning indictment of the manner in which Canada's military history has been written. It involves the Directorate of History at the Department of National Defence and the man who was for many years Canada's leading military historian, a man I have long admired, the late C.P. Stacey. As you know, Colonel Stacey was the official army historian from 1945 to 1959, and subsequently the founding director of the tri-service Directorate of History, until his retirement to the University of Toronto.

First a little background. Our Normandy film, *In Desperate Battle*, recounts the story of a 26-year-old major named Phillip Griffin, a British Columbia native, who was a student at McGill University and joined Montreal's renowned Black Watch regiment. During the battle for Verrières Ridge, Major Griffin found himself in command of the regiment, after the commanding officer and the next-in-command had been killed by machine gun fire. The film tells the story of how a combination of bad generalship and bad luck resulted in Griffin being forced to lead his battalion into a suicidal advance up Verrières Ridge, a battle that one surviving officer compared to the charge of the Light Brigade.

Griffin died heroically on Verrières Ridge, but his gallantry was not recognized with a medal. In fact, after his death, the generals chose to blame him for the failure of the attack. For many years his family fought to discover the truth about what really happened on that Ridge, and pressured the army to grant some posthumous recognition.

In 1972, Phillip Griffin's brother, H.H. Griffin, himself a veteran of the Normandy battle, wrote to C.P. Stacey at the University of Toronto. Stacey had publicly suggested that many of the classified Second World War records should be declassified. H.H. Griffin asked for Stacey's help in discovering the true circumstances surrounding his brother's death.

On February 9, 1972, Stacey wrote back to Griffin, expressing "interest and sympathy," but in fact he was being less than forthcoming. On that same day Stacey wrote an astonishing letter to historian Sydney Wise, a former Bomber Command pilot who had taken over Stacey's job at the Department of National Defence Directorate of History. The Stacey letter appears under the logo of the University of Toronto's Department of History.

The letter to Mr. Wise reads:

Dear Syd,

The attached letter to Mr. H.H. Griffin is largely self-explanatory. See The Victory Campaign, [pages]191–192. It is a sad case. Mr. G[riffin] has been discussing it with [army historian] Murray Hunter.

After the war we made a detailed study of Operation Spring, of which this grim affair was part (25 July 1944). The study led to bitterness between General Charles Foulkes and Simonds (in 1944 respectively GOC [General Officer Commanding] 2nd Can Div and GOC 2nd Can Corps) and they agreed between them that the draft report should be destroyed. All the copies were destroyed, except by some strange mischance, one. It may still be somewhere in your office. In the event of a visit from Mr. Griffin, it would be well to make sure that he doesn't see this particular piece of paper. All the best . . .

Yours sincerely,

Charles (C.P. Stacey)

Nine days later, as a result of Stacey's letter to Wise, the Directorate of History took the following action. The remnants of the destroyed report and another confidential analysis of Operation Spring were pulled from the accessible files, with the notation from Mr. Wise's deputy:

Not to be released to non-DND researchers without the approval of the Director, DHIST. 18 February 1972.

Make no mistake about the impact of what you've just heard. This is Charles P. Stacey, the most acclaimed Canadian military historian of his generation, the author of the official account of every major campaign, including the deeply controversial Dieppe, Hong Kong and the battle for Normandy. This document reveals that he is not only aware of a cover-up of a military catastrophe, but he is party to it.

Realize what's going on here. A military tragedy takes place, an official report is written. The generals don't like it and so the report is ordered destroyed. Twenty-six years later, the historians of the Department of National Defence are still conspiring to hide the truth.

H.H. Griffin, a lawyer, a veteran and a recipient of the Military Cross, is being deceived by Canada's pre-eminent military historians as he doggedly tries to uncover the real circumstances surrounding the death of his brother and most of the Black Watch battalion over a quarter of a century earlier.

What does this document tell you about the systematic suppression of damning evidence by the Department of National Defence, its Directorate of History and some of Canada's military historians? How many more documents are there like this one?

We said that our documentary was an examination of the largely untold story of the disasters that befell the Canadian army in Normandy. We stand by that statement as we stand by all of our stories

There is much still classified about the Second World War in Canadian archives, including the early drafts of C.P. Stacey's official history, which were censored by the generals. Fifty years after the war, it's time for a full release of all those documents.

All of us who researched, wrote, directed, produced and assisted in innumerable ways in the broadcast of *The Valour and the Horror* are proud of how we told the story, unburied the past, shook up the powerful, and showed historians that journalists have not only a right to question the official version of history, but a duty.

DISCUSSION QUESTIONS

1. Discuss the techniques used by documentary filmmakers to argue an authoritative case. Consider the creation of "the truth" in your discussion.

2. Discuss the effect of the use of "re-creations" in *The Valour and the Horror*.

3. Go to the CBC Web site and access their Media Accountability policy. Discuss one episode of *The Valour and the Horror* in the context of this policy.

4. Speculate about the possible results of "libel chill" on the Canadian media.

 WEBLINKS

The Valour and the Horror Galafilm site
www.valourandhorror.com/

Alternative views of *The Valour and the Horror*: the Bomber Harris Trust Site
blvl.igs.net/~jlynch/index.htm

Letters from veterans about *The Valour and the Horror*
www.blvl.igs.net/~jlynch/bharis16.htm

CBC Media Policy
cbc.radio-canada.ca/htmen/7_2.htm.

chapter seventeen

Cultural Policy: A Taxing Issue

INTRODUCTION

As you read this chapter, note that Europeans refer to the process of one culture taking over the culture of another through the media as "Canadianization."

This chapter, which concerns itself with the preservation of culture, consists of three articles with very different, but passionately expressed, views on how to preserve a distinctive Canadian culture. New economic realities make control over the content of what Canadians see and hear and read very problematic, particularly in light of the North American Free Trade Agreement (NAFTA) and the negotiations around the Multilateral Agreement on Investment (MAI).

Victor Rabinovitch examines the fragility of the Canadian "cultural ecosystem," pointing out all of the problems of a cultural sector that must deal with underfunding, a vastly multicultural population, and serious competition from an aggressive and wealthy cultural industry in the United States. Rabinovitch favours government funding ("the patron state") of cultural activity, pointing out how much our arts and media have developed since World War II because of public funding. He argues that our cultural expression depends on six qualities: freedom of expression; promoting Canadian choices in the arts and broadcasting; audience access to these choices; a wide range of funding tools from direct funding to tax credits; promoting funding partnerships between government and the private sector; and preserving our natural and human heritages.

Hal Jackman disagrees with Rabinovitch. He argues that government subsidies to the arts and broadcasting have been counterproductive. He maintains that government money goes to the same old projects year after year, with little innovation or impetus for private citizens to support the arts. He goes on to argue that only "bad" Canadian movies seek government funding, and that culture must arise spontaneously from the people—not from a government view of what qualifies as culture. He does note that our arts appear to be thriving, and, unlike Clarke and Barlow, he credits the low Canadian dollar and NAFTA.

Clarke and Barlow take the "doomsday" approach to the effect of the new trade agreements upon the cultural sector. Industry by industry, they note the disasters that lie in wait for Canadian culture if the Americans dominate the MAI agreement. Perhaps the most galling of the pitfalls that they point out is a scenario wherein a foreign company could come to Canada, make a film or publish a book, hire no Canadians, take all of their profits home, but still be eligible for money from the Canadian government in the form of industrial incentives. For Clarke and Barlow, MAI spells the end of Canadian cultural industries.

METHOD AND SUCCESS IN CANADA'S CULTURAL POLICIES

Victor Rabinovitch (*Queen's Quarterly*)

We begin with the market. Perhaps it seems strange to start an account of Canada's cultural policies by referring to something so mundane as the marketplace. We routinely separate "culture" and the "arts" from the everyday pursuit of jobs, trade, and commerce. Yet public policies on the creation and distribution of cultural products have always been concerned with market pressures. The reasons are as Canadian as the Rideau Canal. Cultural and artistic issues of creation, voice, and authenticity must yield equal time to questions of market size, access to distribution, and financing of risk. And these practical matters inevitably focus on the dominance of the largest player, almost always American.

Popular culture and mass communications are inseparable. As the modern radio era came into being, American broadcasters quickly established their presence across the continent, with several stations in Canada linked into US networks and with Canadian listeners in border areas able to tune into American programs directly. The federal government took notice of this new medium and, in 1928, established the legendary Royal Commission on Radio Broadcasting chaired by Sir John Aird, who was also president of the Canadian Bank of Commerce. Aird's report pointed to the related problems of size and market penetration that bedeviled the expansion of a Canadian radio presence. His proposed solution to this challenge was the creation of a publicly owned radio system, with the mandate to carry Canadian programming to its listeners. Aird's recommendations were summed up with the memorable words, "it is the state or the United States."

In response to Aird, the Conservative government of R. B. Bennett in 1932 established the Canadian Radio Broadcasting Commission (CRBC) to operate a national public radio network and to administer a licensing system for competing private radio companies (radio spectrum being a publicly owned resource). These decisions set public policy onto a distinctive Canadian course by creating a publicly owned cultural entity similar to British Broadcasting while also licensing a competing privately owned system, similar to the Americans. Four years later, the Liberal government of Mackenzie King created the

Victor Rabinovitch. Method and success in Canada's cultural policies. *Queen's Quarterly* 106(2), Summer, 1999. 216-231.

Canadian Broadcasting Corporation to succeed the CRBC, with strengthened financial and administrative independence. This model flourished during and after the Second World War; it only moved in to new directions for national cultural expression some 30 years later, with the establishment of the Canadian Radio and Television Commission (CRTC) and the subsequent expansion of broadcast programming and systematic rules for Canadian content on licensed stations. (The CRTC mandate grew again in 1976 with the added responsibility of telecommunications regulation, thereby anticipating the current trend to "convergence" in communications.)

Fear of being swamped in an American market has been a consistent note in the chorus of studies and policy directives which have shaped cultural policy since Aird's report. It was a major theme in the 1951 Royal Commission on National Development in the Arts, Letters and Sciences, chaired by Vincent Massey. It was the dominant chord in the still influential 1982 Report of the Federal Cultural Policy Review Committee, led by Louis Applebaum and Jacques Hebert. It has been amplified in numerous parliamentary and departmental studies, such as the Mandate Review Committee which concluded in 1996 that

> . . .the bottom line is that the vast majority of all the entertainment on Canadian television and theatre screens is American and this is unlikely to change. Many Americans are worried about what television and radio offer to them and to their children. At least their programming does not originate in a foreign country.[1]

Some have denied that Canadian cultural expression is threatened by the American colossus (or by the lesser but significant French and British cultural powers). But this argument is without factual foundation. The challenge of promoting "Canadian voices" and gaining access to them in "Canadian spaces" remains as central today as it ever was. If anything, the growing multicultural diversity of Canadian society has added to the complex challenge of cultural expression. The gratifying international success of small numbers of Canadian stars—notably some writers, popular singers, and film people—does not solve the continuing problems of most creators who seek to be produced, distributed, exhibited, and rewarded here at home. In fact, the concentration of cultural production and distribution into megalith operations, such as Bertelsmann, Barnes & Noble, News Corp., and Time Warner, will make the challenge even more difficult for small cultural markets such as Canada's.

Is this just a whine about the obvious? Everyone knows that Canada has a modest-sized population, divided into two principal linguistic groups, scattered over 5000 kilometres of linear distance, in a few urban centres, mainly within easy reach of American centres. But this demographic and economic reality is no longer accepted as a sufficient reason to protect business undertakings from the disciplines of international competition and global product mandates. Is there any reason for arts and culture to be treated differently under the current economic orthodoxy? Subject to certain limits and disciplines, my answer is yes, culture is very different. It is exceptional.

Culture is at the heart of what makes a community unique. Through language, customs, values, and lifestyles, it is possible for communities to differentiate themselves, express their identities and create a sense of uniqueness and belonging that is central to human comfort and security. This is not to say that the cultural practices of any community or nation should never be criticized. Cultural challenge and exchange is an endless process whether in biblical times or in our digital era, but for a challenge or a transfer to take place, a community must have a cultural identity to begin with.

Nor can we wish away the ritualized dance between English-speaking and French-speaking communities within Canada. Anyone who ignores the centrality of cultural identity to national survival misses an essential dimension of our national angst. Recall the words of René Lévesque in 1968 as he forged the creation of a Quebec nationalist party, based in part on a self-conscious appeal to a cultural legacy.

> We are the heirs of that fantastic adventure which first made America almost entirely French, and of that collective stubbornness which enabled part of it to remain alive in Quebec. . . . This is how we distinguish ourselves from other people, particularly other North Americans, with whom we have most other things in common. . . . This means that we must be able, in this place, to earn our living and lead our careers in the French language. It also means that we must build a society which is true to our own self-image but which is as progressive, as effective, and as "civilized" as all the others. . . . We must give ourselves enough reasons to be confident in ourselves and proud of ourselves.[2]

Thirty years after Lévesque's political and cultural manifesto, similar ideas are still being expressed, but often by English-Canadian political leaders in their quest for pan-Canadian national unity. At a UNESCO Intergovernmental Conference held in Stockholm in 1998, the comments by Canada's Minister of Heritage, Sheila Copps, warmly praised the intrinsic worth of cultural diversity.

> Culture is the soul of a people and the very essence of nationhood. It reflects our history, our values, our dreams and our view of the world. And it holds a cherished place in the hearts and lives of every individual and every country. . . . Therefore, it is vitally important to find new ways of protecting our respective national identities so that we can continue to hear our country's history spoken in the language of our people.[3]

As ever, the problem remains for us to discover how to live together, with two languages and two cultures in one country.

In response to the unique importance of cultural expression and the pervasive presence of American culture, a Canadian model of "cultural affirmation" has emerged. This model evolved over time and is the outcome of a pragmatic combination of state involvement and private expression, public financing and individual activity. It has superficial similarities to the "National Policy" phase in Canadian development, which guided economic policy for more than half a century after Confederation, but it is very different in key aspects such as timing, objectives, domestic context, and international outlook. Overall, it has a degree of coherence that is remarkable, particularly as it is not the product of a single vision or the creation of a single sponsoring authority.

The federal government has acted within the cultural sector to achieve two basic goals: the development of indigenous content and access to such content. The concept of cultural content includes categories of information and creativity such as the reporting of news and analysis, the performing and the visual arts, and the production of popular works in music, film, publishing, multimedia, and communications. This cultural model has given rise to measures that have shaped the entire continuum of arts and heritage activity: creation, production, distribution, promotion, consumption, and conservation. It has six main elements, which are:

1. Upholding freedom of expression: respect for cultural choice and expression is both necessary and desirable in a democratic and diverse society.

2. Promoting the creation of Canadian choices: a variety of measures to encourage Canadian artists, writers, performers, and producers have the overall effect of increasing cultural freedom by ensuring the availability of Canadian content.

3. Expanding access to Canadian products: it is essential wherever technically possible to provide for the presence of Canadian cultural contents on the distribution "shelf space" because access is the controlling factor that determines audience reach.

4. Using a wide range of policy tools: the mix of policy and program instruments, such as direct funding, regulation, or tax concessions, varies depending on the type of cultural undertaking, its particular challenges, and the climate of public opinion.

5. Forging partnerships: all facets of the culture continuum can benefit from joint activity between not-for-profit, voluntary, and commercial sectors, as well as between the different levels of government institutions.

6. Preserving natural and human heritage: the personality of a community and its members is shaped by the memories, stories, landscapes, and artifacts that are saved as part of a shared inheritance.

This affirmative model is a particularly Canadian blend of the private and the public, but it is not the product of a full-blown, methodical policy agenda. It has evolved from specific solutions to particular problems at a moment in time. In broadcasting, for example, the CRBC was created in 1932 in response to pressures from the rapidly growing American radio system. There was an urgent need to occupy a portion of the radio spectrum with a Canadian entity, and a parallel need to allocate other parts of the Canadian airwaves in an orderly manner. Pressures increased again in the 1960s with the expansion of US border television stations and the commercial installation of cable distribution systems. In response, the CRTC was set up as the independent regulatory body with a mandate of promoting more coherence in broadcasting, applying clear Canadian ownership rules and obtaining greater amounts of Canadian content in return for the valuable licences granted to private broadcasters.

Policy changes during the past 30 years in broadcasting have moved in parallel with developments in commercial technology. Measures such as the creation of Canadian content rules for music on radio, the application of content policies to television, evaluating what is "Canadian" to qualify for funding and broadcasting credits, the licensing of new genres of programming, the creation of competing Canadian-owned networks, the licensing of specialty television channels carried on the cable distribution system—all flow from the original concepts of John Aird, expanded by later generations of public and private broadcasters as well as by the visionary administrators of the regulatory system. The annual Juno Awards for recorded music honour one of these public administrators, Pierre Juneau, who was the chairman of the CRTC when it adopted the Canadian content rules for radio music programs in 1970. How Canadian! In what other democratic country has the popular music sector associated its highest awards with a national regulator?

In contrast with broadcasting, Canada's accomplishments in film policy are more mixed in their outcomes. The National Film Board was created in 1939 as a wartime film unit to make and distribute education and documentary material. Once the war ended, the strong leadership of its renowned director, John Grierson, and the reputations of its creative and technical staff helped persuade the government to legislate a broader mandate to "interpret

Canada to Canadians and to other nations." The NFB succeeded in doing this, and in doing much more, namely the creation of a nucleus of filmmakers with the expertise to branch out beyond the documentary, animation, and education genres.

The NFB, however, was not able to transform its technical and non-commercial strengths into large-scale feature film production. In 1967, frustration over the continuing absence of a national cinema led to the establishment of the Canadian Film Development Corporation (CFDC) whose primary goal was to boost feature film production through administrative and financial initiatives. If the weakness of a Canadian presence in cinematic exhibition was bad, the failure to produce significant film materials for Canadian television broadcasting was even worse. An eloquent warning issued by the CRTC in early 1983 described the problem succinctly.

> With the exception of the Canadian Broadcasting Corporation, Canadian English-language broadcasters offer audiences virtually no Canadian entertainment in peak viewing periods and next to no Canadian drama—light or serious—at any time in their schedules.[4]

The transformation of the CFDC into Telefilm Canada in the mid-1980s, with a wider mandate and larger budget (partly funded through a new tax on cable TV services) was the federal response. Like the original decision to create the NFB, this initiative was a specific solution to a particular problem: the expansion of American border stations and the improved reception of imported US signals carried by Canadian cable systems. The Telefilm solution, especially its Broadcast Fund set up to assist domestic TV production, has been robust and long-lasting, with immense benefits to both English and French filmmakers in Canada.

Similar stories can be told about the establishment of programs for book publishing, recorded music, promotion of museums, maintenance of professional training schools for theatre and dance, adoption of tax breaks for newspapers and magazines, and many other federal initiatives. Canada's cultural affirmation model has been implemented through many programs, agencies, and regulations. Detailed designs of interventions for specific sectors have depended on the difficulties being experienced and on the preferences of leading ministers. Often, an initiative has taken place only because a problem has gained public attention or captured the personal interest of a cabinet minister.

No single pan-Canadian approach exists for cultural initiatives, funding, or regulation. Federal programs are often paralleled by provincial and municipal initiatives, usually financial but sometimes with a regulatory dimension (particularly in Quebec). Some overlaps also occur between different agencies and regions. This absence of a single "Canadian Cultural Policy" has been criticized for being confusing or imprecise, but the lack of neatness reflects the complexity of the multiple activities grouped under the catch-all title of "arts and culture." Variety in regulatory, promotional, and financial approaches has been a source of strength providing flexibility to manoeuvre. Television, live theatre, film, multimedia, magazines, books, musical performance, and recording: these types of performance and communications media are highly specialized, requiring tailored program and policy interventions. They can also be interrelated, with productions and expertise in one form transferred to another. To create a one-size-fits-all policy, with a single governing body, would have been unwise for many reasons, whether creative, administrative, or political.

Several high-profile private funding initiatives have received much publicity recently, with the implied message that private philanthropy can displace public money for cultural funding. This would be an important change to the Canadian cultural model if it were true; it is not, however. The endowment of the annual Giller Prize for English-language authors, the creation of the Harold Town Prize for Visual Arts, and the controversy-plagued contribution to the National Arts Centre by the Ottawa Senators hockey star, Alexei Yashin, are three notable examples. These follow many years of financial support for arts and culture by the Bronfmans, the Molsons, the Chalmers, the Kahanoffs, the Gelbers, and many others. An important responsibility of the Canada Council is to administer awards created through various endowments. Overall, there is no doubt that private contributions can be immensely important, particularly for one-time capital needs such as the recent campaigns for the Stratford Festival Theatre and the Halifax Neptune Theatre. But this must be kept in perspective.

Favourable publicity for donors should not obscure the fact that governments in Canada are by far the largest source of funding for all forms of arts and culture. In publishing, for example, while the Giller Prize is worth $25 000 and is the richest Canadian book award, the annual contribution of the federal government to authors and book publishers exceeds $30 million each year. Every sector of arts and culture reflects this financial reality. The importance of the "patron state" remains undiminished despite budget cuts during recent years. We should celebrate what is positive in this. State patronage is administered openly, subject to public finance rules and expert juried selection of recipients. Although government administrators are targeted for lobbying by individuals or companies that seek grants and favours, they operate in a manner that is far more transparent than private patrons, even though these sponsors and donors are also state-assisted through tax concessions.

Can we measure the results achieved through the Canadian cultural model? By any standard, the results are very positive, particularly in some sectors. Yet there are areas where Canadian productions remain strangers in their own land. Let's review some key statistics, while remembering that statistics do not explain all the factors that go into creating the strong core of arts, culture, and heritage activities now present in Canada.

- In television broadcasting, the operation of Canadian-owned networks and specialty channels on cable or satellite (which must carry a specified portion of domestic programs as a condition of their CRTC licenses) ensured that a total of 39 percent of the total programming available in 1996 was Canadian in origin. Audiences for Canadian programs also represented an average of 39 percent of viewing time, although higher for French-speaking viewers than for English-speaking.

- In book publishing, Canadian authors accounted for 46 percent of sales by Canadian publishers in 1996. Looked at in another way this means that Canadian books are mostly produced and distributed by Canadian-owned publishers who account for about half of domestic book sales and who produce between 80 and 90 percent of all new Canadian-authored books.

- In recorded music, despite the major presence of the six multinational companies that dominate worldwide sales, Canadian "independents" continue to play an important role and release about 80 percent of Canadian-content recordings. Access to domestic radio audiences is achieved by the CRTC rules that require 35 percent of English-language radio music and 65 percent of French-language music to be Canadian.

- In film and television production, more than 400 titles were certified in 1995 by the Canadian Audio-Visual Certification Office as achieving the Canadian content requirements specified for tax and program purposes. This sector produced only three certified titles in 1975.

- Magazine publishers produced some 1500 Canadian periodicals in 1996, with a readership share of about 50 percent of the domestic market. This contrasts dramatically with the situation before federal magazine rules came into force (in 1965) when there were barely a handful of national circulation periodicals.

- Not-for-profit performing arts companies (a total of 493 in 1994) and heritage institutions such as museums, galleries, and libraries (a total of 2390 in 1995) are well-established and provide the back-bone for the hundreds of annual theatre, music, and folklore festivals that are a hallmark of Canada's regional cultural landscape.[5]

Numbers are only part of the picture. Cultural expression is important for public policy because it enables individuals to share their visions, tell their stories, and contribute to social cohesion, community identity, and shared values. This is more than just entertaining a local audience. Think of the importance of a book like *Fugitive Pieces*, by Anne Michaels, for its loving portrayal of a refugee's experience in Toronto and its poetic rendering of the horrors of genocide. Or the poignant memories in Roch Carrier's stories, particularly his children's classic, *The Hockey Sweater*. Or the warmth and humour of the French-language film, *Les Boys*, whose box-office receipts outdrew the opening weeks of *Titanic* in Quebec. Or the bitter-sweet heroics and brilliant staging of *Billy Bishop Goes to War* (which is now being revived to renewed theatrical success). Statistics cannot assess the significance of these cultural products, whether to us as Canadians or as reflective individuals.

The current state of culture is like the proverbial wine bottle that appears a quarter full to one person but three-quarters empty to another. Although 50 percent of magazine sales are for Canadian titles (overwhelmingly through subscriptions and mail delivery), who can be pleased that over 80 percent of newsstand space goes to foreign titles? Or that 86 percent of prime-time English-language drama on Canadian television is foreign, mainly American, and 60 percent of all English-language programming available in Canada is non-Canadian? Or that 84 percent of retail sales of sound recordings (including 69 percent of French retail sales) feature foreign content? The picture drawn by one eminent commentator, Jeffrey Simpson, seems conclusive.

> The notion of a level playing field in culture is almost completely bogus. . . . The fight for Canadian cultural space in a continent (and even a world) dominated by U.S. cultural influences has never been easy. . . . After all, the U.S. eagle already has just about all it could want in Canada.[6]

The aberrant situation in feature film exhibition, where less than five percent of screen time goes to Canadian products, deserves special comment. Our instinctive reaction is to blame ourselves with the false explanation that we don't know how to make good films. Canadians can sing, write, act, create broadcasting networks, and make so many television programs . . . but somehow the American-owned theatre chains are unable to promote and show Canadian feature films in Canada. Feature film policy is uniquely underdeveloped when compared to other cultural sectors such as book publishing, magazines, recorded music, and broadcasting. There are no cinema sector rules to require majority Canadian ownership and control, or to mandate access by Canadian products to theatre screens. Film distribution remains largely under foreign control. When efforts have been made by the federal government (and by Quebec) to increase some aspect of Canadian participation, even modest proposals have been stopped by a brilliant combination of threats, promises, and celebrity lobbying by the American film industry and some Canadian allies.[7]

The exhibition of English-Canadian feature films in theatres in this country is rare, with only a slightly better record for French-Canadian films. There is no Canadian equivalent to the screen-access rules that apply in France and other countries. The recent sale of the Cineplex chain to the Sony-Loew's theatre group without long-term undertakings to ensure the showing of Canadian films, or Canadian decision-making on program selections, will likely mean that screen time for domestic films will not expand at this important chain. Similar access problems are also now evident in the video rental market which is a key part of the commercial film world. The dominance of American distribution and retail operations, and the absence of any obligations to identify, display, or promote Canadian products, means that Canadian films are literally classified as "foreign" in stores such as Blockbuster Video (owned by Viacom which also owns Famous Players Theatres).

The apparent impossibility of creating a niche for Canadian cinema in the domestic exhibition market demonstrates the need to use a wide range of intervention instruments to assure a presence of "Canadian voices in Canadian spaces." The interventions must include a choice of financial methods (such as tax credits, allowable deductions, direct grants, matching contributions) and regulatory instruments (such as content requirements, ownership rules, promotional undertakings, program packaging). The interventions must occur over the full range of the cultural continuum, including creation, production, distribution, promotion, consumption, and preservation. If cultural policy instruments are limited to financial subsidies, as some economists have proposed, and if there is no legal mandate to ensure that some "shelf space" is reserved for indigenous creators, Canadian cultural policy will eventually fail. The logic of the market—the size, financial depth, distributional power and pervasive presence of the dominant foreign groups—will sweep aside the smaller players. Financial subsidies alone will mean that Canadian voices are marginalized into minor regional whispers on the American soundstage.

We have seen how over the past 70 years a unique cultural ecosystem has blossomed on the Canadian landscape. At its heart are multiple policy measures that promote artistic and cultural expression, production, and distribution. Public policies, programs, and institutions have become increasingly complex in response to the demands and sophistication of Canada's linguistic and cultural communities. This ecosystem is now producing a rich harvest of works that are reflective of Canadian experience, setting, and tastes. Some of these works also appeal to broader audiences beyond our borders, but the main consumers of Canadian culture are located in the "home" market.

On balance, the Canadian cultural ecosystem remains breathtakingly fragile because the essential context of this country has not changed. Factors such as audience size, regionalism, linguistic divisions, under-financing, inadequate distribution, and the ubiquitous American presence continue to challenge potentially self-sustaining Canadian cultural undertakings. New developments in diverse fields such as information technology and international trade law are now introducing even more difficult challenges for both Canadian and global cultural diversity. It remains to be seen how the successful Canadian policy model, and the resulting cultural system, might be adapted and applied within the logic of an emerging global information society.

Notes

1   *Mandate Review Committee—CBC, NFB, Telefilm, Making Our Voices Heard: Canadian Broadcasting and Film for the 21st Century* (Ottawa: Supply and Services Canada, 1996), p. 22. Emphasis in original.

2   R. Lévesque, *Option Quebec* (Montreal: Les Editions de l'Homme, 1968), pp. 20–5. Translated by the author.

3   S. Copps, "Speaking Notes for Canadian Delegation Plenary Intervention at UNESCO Conference on Cultural Policies for Development," Stockholm, 31 March 1998 (Hull: Canadian Heritage, 1998).

4   *Canadian Radio-television and Telecommunications Commission, Policy Statement*, 31 January 1983 (Hull: CRTC, 1983).

5   *Canada's Culture, Heritage and Identity: A Statistical Perspective* (Ottawa: Statistics Canada 87–211, 1997). See also *Canada Year Book 1999* (Ottawa: Statistics Canada, 1998), pp. 257–95.

6   Jeffrey Simpson, "Un-American Activities," *The Globe and Mail*, 23 December 1998.

7   The attempt in 1987 by Minister of Communications Flora MacDonald to sponsor a Film Products Importation Act is one example. This legislation would have established access for Canadian-owned film distributors to bid on foreign film distribution rights for the domestic market. This limited goal was strongly opposed by the American industry; the legislation was dropped at the time of congressional approval of the Canada-US Free Trade Agreement.

BIGGEST THREAT TO CANADIAN CULTURE: OTTAWA'S BILLIONS

Hal Jackman *(Canadian Speeches: Issues of the Day)*

Madam Chairman, it is indeed an honour to be invited to be a speaker at one of your meetings celebrating the millennium, although I must say I was very nervous when you suggested that I should talk about culture, particularly that rather elusive entity, Canadian Culture.

I looked up three dictionaries to that find a definition for culture—one Canadian, one American and one English. The dictionaries, of course, all gave many definitions, but it was interesting to see which definition each dictionary listed first.

The first definition in the English dictionary said that culture was "a refined understanding of the arts and other human intellectual achievement."

The American Webster Dictionary called culture "a set of shared attitudes, values, goals and practices that characterize a company or a corporation, or traits of a racial or religious group." Note the difference.

The Canadian dictionary stated as its first definition "the cultivation of plants, the rearing of bees, silkworms, etc.," or "a quantity of bacteria grown for study."

I am being, of course, somewhat facetious here as all the dictionaries gave alternative definitions and came around to approximately the same position.

But of the definitions cited I personally prefer the first definition in the Oxford English Dictionary, "a refined understanding of the arts and other intellectual achievement," which implies a knowledge and understanding of the arts acquired through intellectual and aesthetic training. Culture so defined transcends national boundaries. It represents the highest quality of the human spirit. It rejects a narrow "jingoistic" definition. Appreciation of fine

Hal Jackman. Biggest threat to Canadian culture: Ottawa's billions. *Canadian Speeches: Issues of the Day*, 13(6), January/February, 2000. 3-9. (Speech to The Canadian Club of Toronto, Millennium Series, November 22, 1999.)

art, music and literature is a personal attribute attained through study, rather than a national characteristic. Encouragement of art and cultural expression of all kinds, not just Canadian, is a legitimate avenue for government support as the greater appreciation of art and culture enriches our lives.

I suspect, however, for the purposes of your Canadian Club Millennium series, we are attempting to define the word culture in the American Webster Dictionary sense as being "a set of shared attitudes and values which might characterize us as a nation." This is a much broader definition and could include social attitudes, consumer preferences, the sports we enjoy, attitudes towards government, etc., all of which might define us, but are hardly examples of artistic expression. In this sense the word "culture" is synonymous with "identity" and is far broader than simply appreciation of the arts.

The problem in Canada, particularly when it comes to government policy, is that we tend to confuse the two definitions. Policies that encourage an exploration and appreciation of arts and the humanities should and do receive government support in most civilized societies. Government policies on the other hand that deal with "identity" are much more of a problem. Much of Canada believes that the state should have no role in promoting a specific identity. The problem is compounded by the fact that there seems to be no consensus in this country as to what our identity truly is.

Can we define Canadianness with a country spread out over thousands of miles with differences which in the past 100 years have grown greater rather than lessened? The twin forces of globalization on one hand and the growth of regionalism are much stronger now than they were 100 years ago. Does this make the search for our Canadian identity or culture even more elusive?

Governor General Adrienne Clarkson articulated sentiments in her installation speech that many Canadians might support. Perhaps she was less successful two weeks later when she read the Speech From The Throne, though she might be excused as she had a different speechwriter on that occasion.

That the government is concerned about the lack of a Canadian identity goes without saying, as witnessed by the myriad of programs and dollars that are lavished on our so-called cultural industries in an attempt to define "identity" with questionable relevance to artistic merit. Developing cultural policy is not an easy task, particularly in the absence of any consensus as to what culture it is we are trying to protect.

And yet, in spite of this cultural ambiguity, artistic expression in Canada seems to be in pretty good shape.

At the moment our so-called "cultural industries" are enjoying remarkable growth. Canada is becoming a cultural powerhouse. Canada's artists and cultural entrepreneurs have made Canada one of the top exporting nations against countries two or three times its size. Books by Canadian authors in terms of both titles and sales have trebled in the past decade and foreign-rights sales are booming. In the 1960s only 5 percent of books sold in Canadian bookstores were by Canadian authors. Now the figure is over 30 percent.

Much of this growth is fuelled by the 1988 Free Trade Agreement and the cheaper Canadian dollar. Canadian film and TV production, according to a recent Price Waterhouse survey, now totals $3 billion, double the figure seven years ago. Between them, Alanis Morissette, Shania Twain and Celine Dion have sold 155 million albums, of which 95 percent are sold outside of Canada. Private TV networks are voluntarily increasing Canadian content, a development that would have been unheard of only a few years ago.

Yet in spite of all this, many Canadians suggest that much of this may be simply a symptom of further Americanization of our society.

One of the chief problems with our quest to find our identity is that we keep making comparisons to the United States. In fact, we are in danger of developing a mega-sized inferiority complex which seems to tell us that if only the United States were not here we could develop on our own and that the huge U.S. engine south of the border is somehow destroying our separate and distinct culture. We label American culture as self-assertive, expansive, vigorous and robust. In spite of the tremendous growth in Canadian film, theatre, music, and books we still continue to say that our culture is fragile and undernourished. Our federal arts bureaucrats, concerned with their own budgets and those dependent on government handouts, encourage this perception.

Since Americans are characterized as being brash or harsh, we take refuge in calling ourselves "a kinder and gentler people," an assertion that may have little ground for legitimacy. In other words, our obsession with the United States means that discussion of culture in this country which should be a celebration of the remarkable achievements Canadians have made in the "arts," tends to be a hand-wringing wake where we wallow in our own supposed cultural deficiencies and ask for more government funding.

This has led to a huge cultural establishment at the federal level which supports organizations like the CBC and the National Film Board, and the Museum of Civilization which gobble up the lion's share of the Department of Heritage budget. The question of what it is we are trying to protect, however, never seems to be answered.

A Canadian magazine may get a different tax treatment from an American magazine. What is the difference between an American and a Canadian magazine? Answer: the Canadian magazine gets a different tax treatment. Does this mean that it is only the extent of government support that defines its Canadianness?

What is a Canadian book? I just finished reading a biography of the late John Marshall, former chief justice of the United States during the early 19th century. A friend of mine asked me why did I not read a comparable book about our Canadian judicial system? The book I read was certainly published by an American publisher, but when I read the fly-leaf the author was a professor at the University of Toronto who wrote the book in Canada. Is this book Canadian? A biography of Laurier published by the Oxford University Press—written by an Oxford professor who did his graduate work in Canada—is this a Canadian book? Probably not by our government definition.

Some years ago I was walking to my home and my way was blocked by a film crew who were shooting a movie. I asked someone who appeared to be in charge whether this was a Canadian movie. The person I questioned turned out to be the Executive Producer who said, "hell, no, this is definitely not a Canadian movie." I asked him "why not?" It was my understanding there were a lot of grants given to Canadian productions. He said, "if this were a Canadian movie the distributors would not touch us." Admittedly this was some years ago, but it was obvious that Canadian government funding was the last resort of bad movies. Good movies, or at least commercially successful movies, could and did receive money from the private sector.

Canada as a movie capital at the moment is booming. Twenty-five percent of Hollywood's movies are now made outside of the United States, most of them in Canada. Are these Canadian movies? According to our cultural bureaucrats most of them are not. By definition Canadianness of a film can only be defined, like publishing or magazines, by reason that they receive government subsidies. If you do not get a Canadian government grant you are not a Canadian movie and presumably are not contributing to our cultural fabric. Yet until you see the credits at the end of the film it is often very difficult, if not impossible, to determine the film's nationality.

The biggest threat to Canadian culture, in my opinion, is the faulty logic coming from Ottawa which defines our identity in terms of government support. The CBC, which soaks up over a billion dollars of our taxpayers' money, presumes to give Canadians a common sense of identity even though its television audience is only a small fraction of what it once was a few years ago. Any discussions of the CBC, including the present press surrounding the hiring of the new president, makes it very clear that the CBC itself has no clear idea as to what its mandate should be. Yet this lack of purpose does not prevent the CBC from asking for more money. CBC supporters will say the very existence of the CBC is a reflection of our identity. What it may or may not broadcast therefore becomes secondary. In other words, according to Ottawa and our cultural mandarins, Canadian identity is defined by government policy and largesse. In the absence of any clear ability to define who we are, perhaps they may be right. Government handouts have certainly become part of our culture.

Although we do not have an authoritarian regime in this country, cultural policy still remains subject to political pressure and the dictates of what might be called the politically correct. The CBC a few years ago came up with a documentary entitled *The Valour and The Horror* which, according to some, denigrated the service of the Canadian armed forces during the Second World War. The issue here was not an artistic question but their interpretation of history which was vigorously criticized by veterans groups. The CBC apologized.

There is a lesson to be drawn here. Surely an artist may write or publish or produce anything he or she wishes, but should they do so if it is produced and funded by governments? Contrast this with the tremendous number of anti-Vietnam War feature-length films that have come from Hollywood. These movies, I am sure, were to some Americans as equally offensive as *The Valour and the Horror*. Yet there was no public outcry. Why? The difference was that they were not funded by governments. In a country that believes in free expression no one really has the right to complain. But if it is the government or the CBC that funds one point of view to the exclusion of other viewpoints you can see the problem.

The Canada Council, which again prides itself as an agent for allowing the "avant garde" to express itself, came out with a program to celebrate the millennium. What were these avant garde themes the Canada Council wished to promote? Well, there was giving our native peoples a voice which had so long been denied them; expressions of celebrating our multiracial, multicultural diversity; recognizing the place of women in our history and our society; and recognizing the duality of French and English languages across Canada.

Now these sentiments, however laudable, are hardly "avant garde." "Avant garde" is meant to shock and to raise questions and challenge established tastes and values. The Canada Council here is simply reconfirming what our government feels is politically correct.

Similarly, government funding, as practised by the Canada Council, simply because it is one Council, inevitably leads to a uniformity of cultural choices which everyone must agree is detrimental to the creative process. It is far better to have a multiplicity of funding sources. Patron "A" may be eccentric in his choice of art but his or her eccentricities are cancelled out by the eccentricities of hundreds of other patrons. It is only from this variety of tastes that true art or culture can emerge. There are still many in the federal government who feel that private sector funding is somehow corrupting and that government should be the exclusive funder of the arts. The truth of the matter is that private sector donors are far less subject to political pressures than governments.

What, therefore, is the answer? I have said earlier that our preoccupation with our identity, particularly our insecurity relative to the United States, is self-defeating, perhaps even soul destroying. It prevents a healthy, robust culture from ever developing at all. I believe that we should not try to define ourselves; we should simply let it happen. We are very different people living in this country. The fact that we are different does not make any of us less Canadian. It is not the government or the CBC that gives us our identity. The government should be a reflection of what we are, not someone who tells us who we should be.

What then do we have in common? For 200 years now the northern half of this continent has decided to live separately from our neighbour to the south. Why did we do it? Our history tells us why, which leads me to ask, why in the interests of political correctness have we stopped teaching our history in Canadian schools? But that is another story. Our history would show that Canada is not the product of a revolution against authority as was the United States, but is the product of the counter-revolution. We are the product, not of a proclamation of a set of principles or a way of life, but are the product of a pragmatic, evolutionary process which perhaps resists ringing declarations such as an "American" or a "Canadian" way of life. Perhaps because of the evolutionary nature of our development, our culture or identity is therefore incapable of being defined. Nor should it be defined. For in spite of our differences we have created a nation on the north half of this continent, sprung from ancient traditions, nourished and enriched by the countless millions who came to these shores to join their destiny with ours.

We do not need the government to tell us who we are or what we should be. Culture and artistic expression, however you define it, must come from within; it cannot be imposed.

Government funding of the arts should be limited to art in its truest sense. I again quote the Oxford Dictionary, "a refined understanding of the arts and other human intellectual achievement." We do this through the support of our schools, universities and other cultural institutions.

I said earlier that we have been told that we are a kinder and more generous people, particularly when compared with the United States. That statement only rings true if we talk about government programs. If we measure the words "kind" and "generous" in terms of volunteerism or charitable giving, the facts show otherwise. Volunteerism as measured by the number of volunteers relative to population is three times greater in the United States than in Canada. Charitable giving, according to the House of Commons Finance Committee, is also three times as great in the U.S. relative to personal incomes.

Why then do we seem to be less generous? It is not because on a personal level we care less, but simply because in Canada our government leaders have told us they would do more and therefore as individuals we need to do less. We therefore have a system of medicare, hospital and unemployment insurance, government grants to arts, culture and public broadcasting which are much greater here than in the United States. Whether these should be carried out by the government or whether the private sector should play an increased role can be a matter of debate. However, there is no question that there is a correlation between government support and lack of private sector support.

Whatever one feels about government involvement in the arts or society in general, it is clear that if government programs do not expand then private philanthropy must fill the gap. Therefore it must follow that the purpose of both public and private policy as we approach the millennium should be to take the necessary steps to ensure that government policies should be designed to encourage greater private support.

For the past two years I have had the honour of being chairman of the Ontario Arts Council, which distributes funds to artists and not-for-profit arts organizations. We have undertaken many changes, some of which are controversial, in the arts community. The most important change however is to change the focus from government arts bureaucrats giving out money to not-for-profit arts organizations on a basis of what is generally called "peer group assessment," a flawed process heavily influenced by the Arts Council officers themselves, which has frequently been criticized as elitist and which tends to perpetuate the same grants to the same organizations year after year and more often than not, prevents newer and more experimental organizations from gaining access to the system.

We have changed all this to emphasize policies which reward arts organizations that help themselves by gaining a wider degree of public acceptance and private sector support. The centerpiece of our program is the Ontario Government's Arts Endowment Fund which is making millions of dollars in taxpayers' money available to those organizations which match government funds from private fundraising. After one full year of operation this program has achieved remarkable results—$25 million in new endowments have been set up. To put this amount in perspective, this program has already put almost twice as much into the hands of arts organizations than the annual grants that the OAC makes under its regular assessment process. These expenditures of taxpayer funds are not driven by government telling us what we should do; they are driven by the charitable giving, individual generosity of countless Ontarians. This is a tremendous shift in public policy, away from the elitist Canada Council model, and has perhaps not been adequately covered by the press nor understood by the public.

In effect governments are saying not that you deserve less money from government, but that your future destiny must lie within yourself. If you give generously the government will effectively match your gift. Thus Canadians have been given the opportunity to prove that they are as kind and generous as we keep saying we are.

We have a great tradition in our country. Reliance on government is not one of our traditions; it is simply an act of dependence. Our traditions embrace freedom, self-reliance but also a commitment as individuals to help those organizations which enrich our lives.

Volunteerism and philanthropy are not just characteristics of Canada; they are Canada. Canadians are clearly willing and eager to take control of their daily lives. Canadians are ready for what might be called "a new citizenship for a new millennium." And for a great many Canadians it will mean that we will finally be getting our country back.

THE WAR ON CULTURAL RIGHTS: WHAT THE FTA AND NAFTA DIDN'T TAKE AWAY, THE MAI WILL

Tony Clarke and Maude Barlow (from *MAI: The Multilateral Agreement on Investment and the Threat to Canadian Sovereignty*)

The Multilateral Agreement on Investment (MAI) will establish a revolutionary new set of global rules for investors giving transnational corporations the unrestricted "right" and

Tony Clarke and Maude Barlow. The war on cultural rights: What the FTA and NAFTA didn't take away, the MAI will. *Canadian Forum* 76(865), December, 1997. 20–24. (Excerpted from *MAI: The Multilateral Agreement on Investment and the Threat to Canadian Sovereignty*, published by Stoddart.)

"freedom" to buy, sell and move operations whenever and wherever they want around the world. The agreement would require Canada to treat foreign investors as if they were Canadian citizens. Last month, Minister of Trade Sergio Marchi and chief MAI negotiator Bill Dymond assured the Parliamentary Sub-Committee on International Trade, Trade Disputes and Investment that Canada will stand firm with France to request cultural exemptions. However, most critics feel it is unlikely that the United States will agree to even these cultural exclusions. The MAI is currently on a fast-track for negotiations among the member countries of the Organization for Economic Co-operation and Development (OECD), with an April deadline for signing the agreement.

The MAI represents a lethal attack on what remains of all three forms of cultural protection in Canada: subsidies, Canadian content quotas, and, most particularly, investment rules. The Business and Industry Advisory Group to the OECD, which includes Canadian representatives, has advised the OECD to oppose any "cultural carve-out" for the MAI. No cultural sector or practice, not even national treasures, would be included in the general "sovereignty" exceptions to investor protection in the proposed draft of the MAI.

On close examination, it becomes clear that the U.S. entertainment industry has carefully and systematically used trade and investment agreements to take apart Canada's cultural regime, piece by piece. An OECD working group anticipates that the MAI would supersede the provisions of earlier trade agreements, including NAFTA's cultural exemption and the weak protections of the GATT.

Canadian government officials insist they are seeking a general exemption in the MAI for culture, a move the U.S. strongly opposes. Having successfully kept culture out of the WTO (World Trade Organization), the U.S. is hardly likely to put it back into the MAI.

The U.S. insists that if Canada wants to protect its culture, it must seek an individual country-specific reservation. This would allow the Canadian government to save face on this politically sensitive issue and sell the deal to the Canadian public, without even slightly jeopardizing the U.S. position. For country-specific reservations would simply set Canada's cultural policies up as a moving "hit list" which could be picked off one at a time under the non-negotiable "standstill" and "roll-back" clauses.

The standstill clause means that no new policies or protections could replace those that have been negotiated away, abandoned as part of cost-cutting measures, or lost in decisions like the WTO ruling on magazines. As well, any new technology developed for the hardware that delivers culture would not be subject to Canadian content rules on software. The MAI's roll-back provision, however, would place even current policy at risk; it would be used to enforce conformity to open investment rules over any area where culture and investment meet. Over time, roll-back would eliminate any reservations for culture that Canada might acquire temporarily.

Further, the principles of national treatment and most favoured nation would apply to the granting of investment incentives, subsidies, and grants, which could not be restricted on the basis of country of ownership. This goes beyond NAFTA, which explicitly excluded subsidies from national treatment provisions. Andrew Jackson of the Canadian Labour Congress explains, "This provision would mean that cultural subsidies. . . . could not be allocated exclusively to Canadian artists, publications, production companies, etc."

Because the MAI would also extend the national treatment and most favoured nation clauses to the privatization of public enterprises, any federal or provincial cultural institution that has been run as a non-profit by government and is now slated for privatization would have to be tendered to the corporations of every country that is a signatory to the treaty. The government in question could not even give Canadian companies the advantage of prior notice, nor could it make special arrangements with Canadian workers or communities to buy the cultural institution or to distribute shares to the general public.

In privatization-crazy Canada, it would be almost impossible to maintain production or content control over institutions that have formed the core of Canadian culture. For instance, if the MAI is in place when the Harris government moves to privatize TVOntario—as it has promised to do—it will not be possible to require that production or content control of TVO stay in Ontario or even Canadian hands.

Magazines

The Canadian magazine industry is fighting for its life in the wake of the WTO ruling. As it is, 80 percent of magazines bought on Canadian newsstands are now foreign, and seven out of ten Canadian magazine titles don't show up on Canadian newsstands at all. The removal of borders for magazine trade would dramatically favour the American industry, which ships $700 million worth of magazines into Canada every year, compared with the only $10 million in exports of Canadian magazines to the U.S.

The giant U.S. media companies like Time Warner are now poised to flood the Canadian market with versions of their mass-market magazines, such as *Time*, *Sports Illustrated* and *People*. George Gross, executive vice-president of the Magazine Publishers of America, says the American industry is "waiting to see when they'll be free to get into heightened Canadian activities." The "Canadian" version of these—the split-runs that are now legal in Canada—will bleed advertising dollars from domestic magazines, threatening their survival in the small Canadian market.

Gordon Ritchie, a former deputy minister of industry who helped negotiate the FTA, said, "Having probed the weak spot in the wall and been able to get through, the Americans are going to step up the assault. There's no question that they're on a crusade here. This is the thin edge of the wedge." Canadian ambassador to the U.S. Raymond Chrétien noted with surprise "how widely perceived, distributed, noticed this decision is" in the U.S.

The only remaining protections for Canadian magazines in the wake of the WTO ruling are very costly direct government subsidies to the industry and a tax measure that allows businesses to deduct the cost of advertising in domestic—but not foreign—periodicals. If disputed under the GATT, the former would likely be allowed, and the latter struck down. However, the MAI's national treatment provisions would prohibit the use of both of these measures unless American magazines were given the same rights and access to the same subsidies. Canadian trade expert Peter Clark explains, "Anything that treats Canadian magazines differently from foreign magazines is going to run into national treatment problems."

Broadcasting and Film

In a recent report by the U.S. trade representative, the Canadian Broadcasting Act was identified as a barrier to U.S. exports and targeted for elimination. The WTO has scheduled negotiations for the global deregulation of broadcasting for January 1, 2000. Areas for discussion include the definition of broadcasting, ownership and control of broadcast licensees, and "access and reciprocity to domestic and foreign markets." The Canadian government is working with the pro-privatization U.S. government and industry to come up with a "common North American position" to take to the WTO. This process, combined with the MAI, would doom Canada's domestic industry.

All of the policies and practices that protect Canadian broadcasting and films would likely be illegal under the MAI. Canadian content rules would violate MAI national treatment and most favoured nation rules. The MAI clause on performance requirements would mean that a foreign film or broadcasting company would not have to locate in Canada or hire Canadian artists in order to operate here and receive the going subsidies and tax breaks. And these companies would be free to take 100 percent of their profits out of Canada. Parliamentary subsidies to the CBC, the Canada Council, and the National Film Board could be challenged.

The government could no longer require radio stations to play Canadian music, television to air Canadian programs, or film companies to produce Canadian material to qualify for grants and tax breaks. In fact, all tax breaks would have to be granted equally to the entertainment corporations of all the OECD countries (and eventually to the 182 countries of the WTO as well), or cancelled. The CBC could not be treated differently than ABC, CNN, CBS, NBC, and their counterparts in the other OECD countries. The MAI would also prohibit simulcasting, the process in which Canadian viewers watching a U.S. show on a U.S. channel receive a cable signal that switches the show to the Canadian channel with the broadcast rights, so that viewers see Canadian instead of American commercials. Bill C-58, the income tax law that makes it advantageous for Canadian companies to advertise on Canadian stations, could also be challenged under the MAI.

The Canadian government could no longer restrict foreign film companies from granting Canadian distribution rights for their independently made movies to the Dutch entertainment giant, Polygram; as a result, Canadian distributors could quickly be shut out of this lucrative business. The business community is ready. Several telecommunications giants testified before the Senate committee hearings on the future of broadcasting and film in Canada (the hearings that produced Wired to Win) and found Senate members to be a receptive audience. The corporations' recommendations foretell the future for Canadian broadcasting and film under the MAI:

IBM Canada recommended a three-phase transition period that would, within a period of roughly 10 years, see the complete phasing out of all regulations in the area of licensing, foreign ownership, Canadian content, and mandatory contributions to Canadian production. The final phase would see the lifting of all rules: unconditional exemptions, 100 percent foreign ownership, no content rules, and no mandatory expenditure on Canadian production.

Publishing

Canada's fragile book publishing industry could be greatly affected by the MAI. The Book Publishing Industry Development Program would have to be open to foreign publishers or cancelled, as would the $3 million the federal government allocates annually to Canadian publishers for book distribution and marketing. Investment controls whereby foreign firms may not establish new undertakings in the book trade, nor acquire a majority of any Canadian company, would violate national treatment and most favoured nation provisions. Nor could Canada continue to require that an indirect acquisition by foreign firm of a Canadian publishing subsidiary of another foreign firm be "of net benefit" to Canada.

Under the MAI, a U.S. book publishing giant could buy up a major Canadian publisher and refuse to produce any creative works by Canadians, but still qualify for industrial incentives offered by the Canadian government. Book distribution would be open to continental competition, as would bookstores. There would be no stopping the entry into Canada of the several giant American book chains that have closed down independent stores all over the U.S. There would be no way to force foreign publishing, distribution, and book companies operating in Canada to employ Canadians, in either the arts or business end of the industry.

The audience for all books would now be North American; under the economics of scale of a continental industry, Canadian writers would have to appeal to an American audience in order to be published. The book you are reading now might not find a publisher in a post-MAI jurisdiction that allowed no policy to promote books written for and about Canada.

Copyright

Canada's new Copyright Act provides a series of what the Canadian Conference of the Arts calls "economic and moral rights" to the creators and owners of intellectual property. Among other things, the Act provides compensation to Canadian musicians and producers for radio airplay, and maintains a fund from a tax on sales of blank cassette tapes to compensate Canadian performers and producers for the home copying that deprives them of royalties.

The U.S. has placed Canada on a "watch list" for possible trade violations arising from the Copyright Act. The watch list is the first step to launching a full-scale trade dispute. Charlene Barshefsky says her government is "very, very concerned" about it. "This is a violation of national treatment, among other violations, and we are looking at the possibility of bringing a case on that matter."

The Canadian government claims it has a defence for copyright under NAFTA and the GATT, though the language they are relying on is ambiguous at best. But the government would not have a leg to stand on after ratification of the MAI; under the national treatment and most favoured nation rules, and the ban on performance requirements, the artists and producers of American and other OECD countries would have to be given equal access to any compensation funds or Canada would be in clear violation of its treaty obligations. The MAI would kill Canadian copyright before it ever had a chance to work.

Newspapers

Canada's magazine industry was not the only sector to be negatively affected by the recent WTO ruling. Canadian newspapers also lost the right to preferential postal rates. Now, the only remaining support for Canada's newspapers is a provision of the Income Tax Act that restricts foreign ownership by allowing businesses to deduct 100 percent of their advertising costs only if they advertise in Canadian publications. Because this practice puts foreign publications at a distinct disadvantage in attracting advertising revenues, it would clearly be illegal under the MAI.

A senior federal official admitted in May 1997 that the MAI would lead to the elimination of all foreign ownership restrictions, including those that protect newspapers. The assistant deputy minister of heritage, Michael Binder, told *The Globe and Mail* that the government would "absolutely have to revise" the four-year-old Telecommunications Act, which contains restrictions limiting foreign ownership in the telecommunications sector. Similarly, ratifying the MAI would mean opening the door to foreign media corporations. Canada would find itself out of the Conrad Black frying pan and into the Rupert Murdoch fire.

The threat to Canadian culture by the proposed MAI, with its twenty-year lock-in, cannot be overstated. If Canada endorses this treaty, a vibrant domestic industry, with its Canadian perspective on the arts, news, and history, may be lost, perhaps forever.

DISCUSSION QUESTIONS

1. Does government funding of the arts and the broadcasting industry stifle innovation? In what direction would you like to see Canadian film, television and the other arts develop?

2. Outline and discuss Canadian content regulations and their effectiveness in promoting Canadian artists.

3. Will the protectionist model for cultural survival work in the era of the new technologies? How might Canadians use new technologies to ensure the survival of their cultural industries?

4. The Jackman essay is considerably different in its approach to the funding of Canadian culture than that of either Rabinovitch or Clark and Barlow. Which model will benefit Canadian culture more?

5. Is Jackman correct in stating one of the main problems in the *Valour and the Horror* issue was the expenditure of tax dollars on something that some Canadians found offensive? Would such productions be funded by private funding sources?

WEBLINKS

Council of Canadians
www.canadians.org/index.html

Multilateral Agreement on Investment Sites and Links
www.dfait-maeci.gc.ca/english/trade/need2-e.htm

pascal.math.yorku.ca/sfp/mai/index.html

www.foe.org/ga/mai.html

avoca.vicnet.net.au/~unmployd/MAI.htm

Canadian Cultural Statistics
www.pch.gc.ca/culture/library/statscan/stats_e.htm

chapter eighteen

Stern Radio: Taming the Shock Jock

INTRODUCTION

The Howard Stern Radio Show hit the air in Toronto and Montreal in the fall of 1997 and immediately generated controversy. While the audience share of the two stations broadcasting the program soared, the Canadian Broadcast Standards Council was inundated with complaints about the program's perceived profanity, sexism, racism, and poor taste. The CBSC, established by Canadian broadcasters as a self-regulating body, produced its decision in mid-November.

The decision, an edited version of which is included here, contextualized the issues involved in the Stern case by summarizing the significant differences between U.S. and Canadian approaches to regulation and freedom of expression in broadcast media. The document categorized the types of complaints received, summarized the responses of the radio stations to those complaints including their defence of their right to air the program, and outlined the regulatory basis of the Council's decision.

Briefly, the CBSC found that the program regularly violated the broadcasters' code of ethics with respect to four of the six identified categories of complaint: anti-French comments, abusive comments against identifiable groups (i.e., racial, ethnic, gay/lesbian), sexist comments, and suitability for children. Complaints about the program's political commentary and whether it was in "bad taste" were judged to be beyond the mandate of the CBSC.

To comply with the CBSC, the two radio stations were required to broadcast the results of the decision during prime time and to notify the CBSC and all individuals who had sent letters of complaint that this had been done. In their response to the CBSC, both radio stations indicated a commitment to "monitor" the program to ensure that it complied with Canadian broadcast standards.

The CBSC decision provoked a strong response amongst those who perceive media regulation as a threat to freedom of expression. Andrew Coyne's column in the *Ottawa Citizen* ("Broadcast Standards Council, not Stern, is really offensive") provides a stinging critique of the CBSC decision and media regulation in general. Ronald Cohen, National Chair of CBSC, responds to Coyne's argument and provides a defence of the Stern decision and media regulation in general in "Why we need broadcast standards."

A more recent decision of the Broadcasting Standards Council in August of 2000 condemns Stern for comments about developmentally disabled persons as "tasteless, rude, insulting, offensive and unpalatable to responsible and socially mature adults." The decision, which can be found at a Web site at the end of the chapter, advises that in future the radio station in question will be more careful to edit out material which does not conform to the voluntary Broadcasting Standards Code.

DECISIONS RE *THE HOWARD STERN SHOW*

Canadian Broadcast Standards Council

Canadian Broadcast Standards Council/Quebec Regional Council
CHOM-FM re *Howard Stern Show* (CBSC Decision 97/98-0001+)
Decided October 17, 1997.

and

Canadian Broadcast Standards Council/Ontario Regional Council
CILQ-FM re *Howard Stern Show* (CBSC Decision 97/98-0015+)
Decided October 18, 1997.

The Facts

The Howard Stern Show is produced at WXRK-FM in New York City each non-holiday weekday morning. It begins at approximately 6:00 a.m. and, in principle, finishes at 10:00 a.m., although the ending time of the show is not fixed; in the time period dealt with in this decision, the show generally ran 60–90 minutes beyond the 10:00 a.m. projected ending.

On Tuesday, September 2, 1997, the show was syndicated in Canada for the first time. Two Canadian stations, CHOM-FM in Montreal and CILQ-FM in Toronto, began to broadcast the show on that date. During the course of that initial episode, the host made many comments about which listeners to the stations immediately objected. The initial complaints received by the CBSC were followed by complaints signed by over 1000 individuals to date in relation to the episode of September 2 and other specific dates in the first two weeks, as well as *The Howard Stern Show* generally for the period. The substance of those episodes which required CBSC review will be described below. There were also letters of support for the show received directly and indirectly by the CBSC.

Canadian Broadcast Standards Council. *Decisions re The Howard Stern Show*. Ottawa: Canadian Broadcast Standards Council.

Canadian and American Approaches to Broadcast Speech

Before delving into the specific issues raised by the initial episodes, it seems appropriate to deal with certain themes which will be common to the CBSC's treatment of all issues raised by *The Howard Stern Show*.

The CBSC considers it appropriate to draw certain distinctions between Canadian and American approaches to the free speech issue which might result in the non-acceptability of a broadcast in one country and the acceptability of the same program in the other. In broadest terms, the texts of the First Amendment in the American Bill of Rights and the first and second sections of the Canadian Charter of Rights and Freedoms are materially different. The American approach is far more sweeping. It provides that:

> Congress shall make no law respecting an establishment of religion, or prohibiting the free exercise thereof; or abridging the freedom of speech, or of the press; or the right of the people peaceably to assemble, and to petition the Government for a redress of grievances.

In Canada, freedom of expression is nowhere declared to be as absolute. In the Canadian Charter of Rights and Freedoms, Section 2(b), which declares the existence of the fundamental freedoms "of thought, belief, opinion and expression, including freedom of the press and other media of communication," is expressly declared to be subject to the limitation imposed in Section 1, which declares:

> The Canadian Charter of Rights and Freedoms guarantees the rights and freedoms set out in it subject only to such reasonable limits prescribed by law as can be demonstrably justified in a free and democratic society.

Thereafter, neither the American Communications Act of 1934 nor the recent Telecommunications Act of 1996 contain any provisions which purport to restrict freedom of speech whereas the Canadian Broadcasting Act and the regulations created under it do. The logic of those restrictions begins with the principle enunciated in Section 3(1)(b) of the Canadian law, which states that "the Canadian broadcasting system, operating primarily in the English and French languages and comprising public, private and community elements, makes use of radio frequencies that are public property . . ." It follows that the CRTC, as the body administering the Act, the Regulations and the licences granted under those instruments, could be expected to impose standards which would have the effect of restricting access to those licences by imposing both positive and negative proscriptions. One of the most fundamental positive requirements is that "the programming originated by broadcasting undertakings should be of high standard." There are also negative restraints, one of which, Section 3 of the Radio Regulations, 1986, clearly restricts untrammelled freedom of expression, and is relevant to the matter at hand. It provides that:

A licensee shall not broadcast

(a) anything in contravention of the law;

(b) any abusive comment that, when taken in context, tends or is likely to expose an individual or a group or class of individuals to hatred or contempt on the basis of race, national or ethnic origin, colour, religion, sex, sexual orientation, age or mental or physical disability;

(c) any obscene or profane language;

(d) any false or misleading news;

Furthermore, all Canadian broadcast licencees know perfectly well that there are public rules in Canada to which broadcasters must adhere as well as others to which private broadcasters have chosen to adhere. In this latter category fall the Canadian Association of Broadcasters Codes, of which there is no equivalent in the United States. These are, however, viewed by Parliament and the CRTC as a necessary and integral component to our broadcasting system.

The CBSC has frequently observed that freedom of expression is the basic rule which it applies in the rendering of its decisions but it believes that this principle is not absolute. It is and must be subject to those values which, in a free and democratic society, entitle all members of society, on the one hand, to speak freely while, on the other hand, remaining free from the abrogation of those other values in which they and other Canadians believe. Free speech without responsibility is not liberty; it is licence. The freedom to swing one's arm ends where it makes contact with one's neighbour's nose. The length of that arc is what the CBSC must determine from case to case.

It must also be recognized that the scope of freedom of expression will be greater in a private or even limited public environment than it will be on the airwaves. As noted above, the airwaves are public property. They are also a scarce resource and available only to those who will exercise their broadcast entitlement by the rules. Access to a broadcast licence is a privilege, not a right.

The Issues

The Regional Council members listened to the tapes or reviewed the transcripts of the following September programs (September 2–5, Monday, September 1, having been Labour Day, and September 8–12) and reviewed all of the correspondence relating to complaints for which Ruling Requests had been received by their respective meeting dates, as well as a significant sampling of support letters and other complaints for which there had been insufficient time to generate Ruling Requests as of the time of the meetings.

The various programs of the first two weeks of *The Howard Stern Show* give rise to numerous issues which return with regularity. With respect to many of these, as will be noted below, the Councils consider that the broadcasters have breached one or more of the Codes. With respect to certain others, the Councils do not consider that there has been any breach. Their reasons are discussed under each heading.

1. **Bad Taste**

   Many of the complaints received regarding *The Howard Stern Show* related to questions of taste. Stern was accused of being offensive, vulgar, adolescent, rude, unsuitable, outrageous, sick, tasteless and so on. . . . The Quebec and Ontario Regional Councils are, however, agreed that, under the present Codes, matters of taste must be left to be regulated by the marketplace. Such choices remain those of the listener. This is the time when the on/off switch is the listener's coping mechanism.

2. **Anti-French Comments**

   The CBSC's Quebec and Ontario Regional Council considered the complaints relating to the French and French-Canadians under the Code of Ethics of the Canadian Association of Broadcasters (CAB). Clause 2 of that Code reads as follows:

CAB Code of Ethics, Clause 2:

- Recognizing that every person has a right to full and equal recognition and to enjoy certain fundamental rights and freedoms, broadcasters shall endeavour to ensure, to the best of their ability, that their programming contains no abusive or discriminatory material or comment which is based on matters of race, national or ethnic origin, colour, religion, age, sex, marital status or physical or mental handicap."

- The CBSC has no hesitation in finding that, in this case, the expressions "pecker-heads," "pussy-assed jack-offs," "scumbags," "pussies," "Frig the French" and "Screw the French" are clearly . . . abusive. . . .

The Comedic Defence

- In the present case, Stern indicated on September 2 that "This is another silly comedy show".

- In their responses to the complainants, the broadcasters had also defended Stern's statements on the grounds that they were not intended to be taken seriously.

- There are in this country limitations on what a broadcaster is free to air and the use of abusively discriminatory language such as he used on September 2 clearly surpasses the permissible. Even had his comments been understood as comedic by some elements of his audience, they would be excessive by Canadian standards.

- The suggestion has been made that the abusive comments may have been made worse by reason of the make-up of the station's [largely Franco-phone] audience. The Regional Councils disagree. Every Canadian, regardless of nationality, is diminished by abusively discriminatory remarks which are aimed at any identifiable group. ... It is clear that representatives of English and other linguistic groups have been as offended by the comments directed at one group of Canadians as the Francophone members of that group have been. That has also been as true of Canadians outside Quebec as Canadians inside Quebec.

- Consequently, the Quebec and Ontario Regional Councils find that CHOM-FM and CILQ-FM are in violation of Clause 2 of the CAB Code of Ethics with respect to the September 2 broadcast.

3. Political Commentary Relating to Quebec, France and Canada

The Regional Councils note the importance of differentiating between insults aimed at identifiable groups and comments related to the political or historical environment in Canada and in France. The breach they find is limited to the comments mentioned in the foregoing section. Those comments relating to the state of radio in Canada, the use of English in Quebec, the value of French culture, Canada as an appendage of the United States, the role of the vanquished French in Vichy France, the issues relating to separatism, and so on, are the host's opinions and . . . they are his to espouse.

It is the view of the Regional Councils that these political and historical comments fall squarely within the bounds which freedom of expression is meant to protect.

4. Abusive Comments Directed at other Identifiable Groups

Stern's remarks relating to French-Canadians were, in fact, only an example of his casual attitude toward abusive commentary directed at identifiable groups by virtue of their race, gender or sexual orientation. There is a regular flow of racial, homophobic or gender-related offensive comments, some of which are brief digs, and others of which extend to longer discussions. In the period reviewed by the Regional Councils, he has targeted Japanese, gays, Poles, Sikhs, blacks and Arabs among others.

[The comments above regarding abusive and discriminatory comments relating to the French and French-Canadians] apply equally to these comments made regarding other identifiable groups. The point, in the CBSC's view, is that such comments are in violation of Clause 2 of the Code of Ethics and that they will be ongoing, day after day, episode after episode.

5. Sexist Comments

One of the most continually recurring categories of Stern comments reflects his on-air commentaries regarding women. . . . Those comments which exceed bad taste and violate Sex-Role Portrayal Code provisions fall into the area of words and expressions used, degrading remarks regarding individual callers, and comments reflecting on the intellectual and emotional equality of women generally.

In addition to terms such as "pieces of ass," "horny cow," "dumb broads," "dykes" (referring to women with even moderately feminist views), and "sluts," which sprinkle the dialogue on the Stern Show, he frequently deals with female guests on the basis of their physical attributes and sexual practices rather than, or occasionally in addition to, the skills or talents which are the reason for their common recognition. In the case of callers, he regularly avoids the subject with respect to which they have called in order to seek details of their bust size and weight as well as their sexual practices, despite the fact that this information is utterly irrelevant to the subject of interest.

The Decision Regarding the Sexist Comments

The Quebec and Ontario Regional Councils considered Stern's sexist comments under Clauses 2 and 15 of the CAB Code of Ethics as well as several of the provisions of the CAB Sex Role Portrayal Code. The texts of the relevant Code clauses follow (except for Clause 2, which has been cited above). Clause 15 (Sex-Role Stereotyping) of the CAB Code of Ethics reads as follows:

> Recognizing that stereotyping images can and do cause negative influences, it shall be the responsibility of broadcasters to exhibit, to the best of their ability, a conscious sensitivity to the problems related to sex-role stereotyping, by refraining from exploitation and by the reflection of the intellectual and emotional equality of both sexes in programming.

The original CAB Code of Ethics was followed by a more detailed Code which expanded on the principles contained in Clause 15 of the earlier Code. The CAB Sex Role Portrayal Code provides, among other things, the following rules.

> Negative or inequitable portrayal and representation of women or men can be expressed explicitly in programs and commercial messages, as well as implicitly through images, dialogue and character portrayal. Canadian broadcasters recognize the cumulative effect of negative and inequitable sex-role portrayal, and seek to address this issue effectively and responsibly with this Code . . .

In its definitions, the Code provides that:

> Negative or Inequitable Sex-Role Portrayal refers to language, attitudes or representations which tend to associate particular roles, modes of behaviour, characteristics, attributes or products to people on the basis of gender, without taking them into consideration as individuals.

Clauses 2(c) and (4) of the Code specifically prohibit the type of exploitation which is endemic to the Stern Show:

(2) Diversity:

(c) Television and radio programming shall respect the principles of intellectual and emotional equality of both sexes and the dignity of all individuals. Television and radio programming should portray women and men as equal beneficiaries of the positive attributes of family or single-person life. Women and men should perform in a range of occupations and function as intellectual and emotional equals in all types of thematic circumstances.

(4) Exploitation:

Television and radio programming shall refrain from the exploitation of women, men and children. Negative or degrading comments on the role and nature of women, men or children in society shall be avoided.

The unrelenting use of terms such as "pieces of ass," "dumb broads," "fat cow," "dykes" (to refer to women because they may have even moderately feminist views), and "sluts" and the like are exploitative and unacceptable.

It appears to the CBSC that every Stern episode reviewed by the Regional Councils has revealed sexist comments which fall afoul of one or more of the foregoing provisions.

6. Suitability of Subject Matter for Children

While the type of comments dealt with above which breach the Codes would do so at any time of the day, the CBSC is, with respect to other matters, greatly concerned by the time of day at which the Stern Show is broadcast. It was at least a persistent theme in many of the letters of complaint was the inappropriateness of the content of *The Howard Stern Show* for the time of day in which the program is broadcast, between 6 a.m. and approximately 10 a.m. on weekdays.

The Decision Regarding the Suitability of Subject Matter for Children

Children represent an important value to Canadian society. This is reflected in Section 3(c)(iii) of the Broadcasting Act, which states that the Canadian broadcasting system should "serve the needs and interests, and reflect the circumstances and aspirations, of Canadian men, women and children . . ." Out of concern for children, Canada's private broadcasters, supported entirely in this regard by the CRTC, in 1993 adopted the Voluntary Code regarding Violence in Television Programming, which contains strong proscriptions regarding television programming containing violence intended for adult audiences.

In the introductory language of the Violence Code, it was declared,

Canadian private broadcasters are publicly endorsing the following principles:

1.2   By their adherence to this Voluntary Code of practice,

1.2.1 that programming containing gratuitous violence not be telecast,

1.2.2 that young children not be exposed to programming which is unsuitable for them,

1.2.3 that viewers be informed about the content of programming they choose to watch.

1.3   By the adoption of this Voluntary Code Canadian private broadcasters shall ensure these standards are met in the production, the acquisition, the scheduling, the promotion and the telecast of their programming.

It is worth adding that the issue of content suitability for children has also been addressed more recently by Canadian television services in the development and application of a program classification system. Even though the CRTC only required broadcasters to develop a classification system for violence in programming, the broadcasters voluntarily added sex, nudity, language and mature themes to their comprehensive rating system, as their extensive field research had shown that these content elements were also of concern to parents.

It is a small irony that the host of *The Howard Stern Show* states that, in his own view, his "show is not appropriate for an 11-year old. I'm a parent and, as a responsible parent, I wouldn't let my kid listen to the show." In any event, it is the Canadian broadcast standards which apply to this program and the stations which broadcast it and, in the view of the Quebec and Ontario Regional Councils, descriptive opinion and comment such as that . . . regarding the sex life of Stern and his wife, details of which were broadcast during hours when children could be expected to be listening to radio is certainly not proper material for Canadian children. The Regional Councils also have no hesitation in concluding that Stern's language is not at all suitable at an hour when children could be expected to be listening to radio. Moreover, the issue of unsuitable language and the graphic discussion of sexual situations occurs with consistency, day in and day out on *The Howard Stern Show*.

While the CBSC has always advocated the importance of the vigilance of parents in determining what their children should watch and see, the Canadian solution has always been more pro-active than that. There is a belief among Canada's private broadcasters and on the part of the regulator that there ought to be rules in common, applied by the broadcasters themselves, to ensure that the entire responsibility for what is viewed or listened to in Canadian homes is not left solely to parents.

The globalization of the late twentieth century village does not mean the abdication of the maintenance of order within its Canadian borders. The existence of other standards in other parts of the global village cannot weaken the need to apply home-grown standards within the Canadian bailiwick. The bar should not be lowered in Canada just because it is set at a lesser height elsewhere in the village.

In addition, therefore, to the other concerns expressed by the CBSC, it is its view that the time period in which *The Howard Stern Show* plays is entirely inappropriate and that the unsuitable language and graphic discussion of sexual situations which the CBSC found in the two weeks of episodes it reviewed will be repeated on a daily basis in future episodes, thus rendering the broadcasters carrying it in constant ongoing violation of the Code of Ethics.

Content of Broadcaster Announcement of the Decision

Each of the stations is required to announce this decision forthwith, in the following terms, during prime time and, within the next thirty days, to provide confirmation of the airing of the statement to the CBSC and to each of the complainants who filed a Ruling Request.

In the case of CHOM-FM [and CILQ-FM]:

The Canadian Broadcast Standards Council has found that CHOM-FM [and CILQ-FM] has breached provisions of the industry's Code of Ethics and Sex-Role Portrayal Code. The Council found that each episode of *The Howard Stern Show* during the weeks of

September 1 and September 8, 1997 contained abusive or discriminatory comments directed at French-Canadians and other identifiable groups, made sexist remarks or observations, or contained unsuitable language or descriptions of sexual activity during a broadcast period when children could be expected to be listening to radio.

BROADCAST STANDARDS COUNCIL, NOT STERN, IS REALLY OFFENSIVE

Andrew Coyne (*Ottawa Citizen*)

As it was reported in press accounts, Howard Stern, the foul-mouthed New York disc jockey whose syndicated morning radio show recently debuted on stations in Montreal and Toronto, has been ruled unfit for Canadian airplay by something called the Canadian Broadcast Standards Council. The council is invariably described as an "industry watchdog," the broadcasters' attempt to police themselves in matters of ethics, sexual stereotypes and the portrayal of violence.

This contemptible bunk is the kind of mincing fiction usually reserved for children and citizens of totalitarian states. The CBSC is a fraud, a front for the regulatory ambitions of the only body whose opinions really count in Canadian broadcasting, the Canadian Radio-television and Telecommunications Commission. The facade of self-regulation is quite useful to the CRTC: It can indulge its censorious urges behind a discreet veil of concern for civil liberties. Self-censorship has ever been the censor's preferred technique: the long arm of the law remains at rest, leaving the busy work of expurgation to the short, chubby fingers of servility.

The council might legally be a creature of the Canadian Association of Broadcasters, but its inspiration is pure CRTC, its every method, principle and responsibility tailored to the regulator's specifications. The council's Web page fairly bursts with pride at the approving notices the CRTC has bestowed upon it over the years: The CAB's proposed guidelines on sex-role stereotypes, for example, were received as "excellent statement of principle," while the council itself was blessed with the regulator's "whole-hearted support" in 1991.

Nor can there be any doubt as to the ultimate source of the council's authority. Broadcasters may in theory be free to ignore its rulings, but would leave themselves exposed to the CRTC's wrath at licence renewal time. Council chairman Ron Cohen left no doubt that he expected the two stations implicated in the Stern ruling would "find a way to conform," noting that "the decision reflects the kinds of standards which one would expect the CRTC to uphold in anything they would decide."

This puts the stations in a bad way. There's no doubt that Stern has struck a chord with Canadian listeners: Both stations' morning audience numbers have shot up since the show, broadcast live in more than 40 American cities, began its Canadian run. As the council found fault with virtually every line of the shows it examined, and there is precisely zero prospect of Stern toning down his material to suit its sniffy tastes, the only way the stations could "conform" with the ruling would be to take him off the air which, given the tenuous state of their finances, might well result in both stations going under.

What we have is a clear case of suppression of speech, made all the worse by the enthusiastic participation of the industry in its own confinement. Had the CRTC, as an agent of

Andrew Coyne. Broadcast Standards Council, not Stern, is really offensive. *Ottawa Citizen*, November 13, 1997. (Reprinted with permission from Southam News.)

the state, presumed to order Stern off the air, a great outcry might have been expected, perhaps an appeal to the courts for the protection of the Charter of Rights, with its guarantees of "freedom of thought, belief, opinion and expression." But so long as the issue can be portrayed as an internal industry matter, to do with "voluntary" codes of conduct and the like, the CRTC can carry on undisturbed, censoring at one remove.

What is most alarming in all this is the reasoning the council offered for its decision. There is no disputing that much of what Stern says is disgusting, puerile, even hurtful. But that does not make it any less speech, or any less deserving of protection as such. The council draws a distinction between "political commentary," as the kind of speech "which freedom of expression is meant to protect," and "abusive comments directed at identifiable groups," such as French-Canadians, whom Stern, with characteristic subtlety, referred to as "peckerheads."

The distinction between "political commentary" and mere "abusive comments" suggests that speech qualifies for protection only on the basis of its usefulness to society. But that puts the onus on the speaker to prove that his speech is useful, not, as it should be, on the state to prove the speech is actually harmful. If anyone wishes to suggest that Stern's speech is harmful—that it would lead to attacks on French-Canadians, say—there are already laws against incitement to violence. It is not enough merely to show that his comments are offensive or unedifying.

The rights of a free people precede the powers of the state. We do not have such rights as the state sees fit to give us. The state has such powers as we see fit to give it.

WHY WE NEED BROADCAST STANDARDS

Ronald I. Cohen (*Ottawa Citizen*)

Andrew Coyne is nothing if not consistent ("Broadcast Standards Council, not Stern, is really offensive," Ottawa Citizen, November 13, 1997). It was only three years and a week before that article that his piece on the Canadian Broadcast Standards Council (CBSC) and the "Power Rangers" appeared in *The Globe and Mail* under the title "The day the Power Rangers met the Mighty Morphin CRTC."

In 1994 he called the Council "a front, the standards it enforces designed and dictated by the evil empire itself, the Canadian Radio-television and Telecommunications Commission." This time, his tune hasn't changed, but the Council has now been elevated to "a fraud, a front for the regulatory ambitions of the only body whose opinions really count in Canadian broadcasting, the Canadian Radio-television and Telecommunications Commission."

Rubbish. Self-regulation was proposed by the broadcasters to the Commission, not the other way round. The concept, which had been mulled over by the private broadcasters as early as 1986, was cohesively packaged by the Canadian Association of Broadcasters (CAB) in 1988 and advanced to the Commission, which finally approved the principle of a self-regulatory broadcast standards council in 1990.

The Council began dealing with complaints in 1991 and handed down its first rulings against broadcasters in June 1993. Since I became National Chair in July 1993, the CBSC has rendered 70 decisions, of which 52 have favoured the broadcasters against whom the Canadian audience's complaints were made and 18 were negative.

Ronald I. Cohen. Why we need broadcast standards. Ottawa: Canadian Broadcast Standards Council, 1997. (This is the uncensored version of Mr. Cohen's response—published in the *Ottawa Citizen* of November 13, 1997, A2—to Andrew Coyne's editorial criticizing the CBSC decisions.)

Coyne slips out into public view on this issue when it is convenient to do so. Not a whisper for the other 16 negative decisions as they were released or posted on the CBSC Web site. Nor a whimper for the 52 occasions when the Council decided that the broadcasters were not in breach of the Codes it administers.

The Council administers four Codes: the Code of Ethics, the Sex-Role Portrayal Code, the Violence Code, and the Radio and Television News Directors Association (RTNDA) Code of (Journalistic) Ethics. Both the Sex-Role Portrayal and Violence Codes have been approved by the Commission, it is true, but both were created by the broadcasters themselves. Moreover, the Code of Ethics, under which the Stern decision was rendered, has never been approved by the CRTC. This has been, may I add, a sore point to the Commission over much of the time I have served as CBSC National Chair.

As to the Code of (Journalistic) Ethics, it was created in 1970 by the RTNDA and, as the sole result of a joint CBSC-RTNDA initiative, began to be administered by the CBSC in the fall of 1993. We informed the CRTC of that initiative after the deal was done.

It is not immediately apparent why Coyne should single out broadcasters as being disentitled to have their own standards and to have these rigorously administered by their own self-regulatory body, in pretty much the same way as any other group of professionals in this country. The Canadian Medical Association has its own Code of Ethics, the Law Societies theirs. So, too, the Architects and so on. The last time I checked, but please don't tell Mr. Coyne, even Canadian newspapers face Press Councils in nine of the provinces.

It may be that Andrew Coyne does not like the CBSC decision in the Howard Stern case. He certainly did not like that in the "Power Rangers." It may even be that he supports unfettered, untrammeled freedom of speech. No limits. No holds barred. Or perhaps only barred by him, on the basis of his standards, if there are any which he would apply to broadcast publishing. It's a funny thing but I expect that neither Coyne nor his editor would permit the Stern excesses in their newspapers.

Which identifiable group would they label "p***erh**ds," "sc****gs" or "p***y-a**ed j****ffs" [originally "peckerheads," "scumbags" or "pussy-assed jackoffs"] in their columns? Which letters to the editor would they deem publishable (or not publishable) on the basis of the bust size of their authors? Which humorous Southam columnist would be allowed to say, as Stern did, "Oh, I just wanna take that piece of a** [originally "ass"] body, put tape over her mouth, and do things to her. . . . And have her lay by my pool in a bikini and have her come out and service me. [Stern's words excised by *The Citizen*: And I'm laying by my pool, in comes that nude with just a pair of heels. And then like, I reach in, I yank out her vocal chords and then she just orally satisfies me by the pool. Oh, she's totally a mute Kim. And she's totally nude. . . . And then I break her legs and position them in the back of her head so that she's sitting, and they're permanently fixed like that. We let them knit and mend.]" Cute, isn't it? Good for the newspapers? I doubt it. Good for the broadcasters? Definitely not.

In any event, that's how the CBSC sees it. And that is how Canada's private broadcasters have chosen to deal with their responsibilities to the public for the programming which they air.

The private broadcasters actually prefer a system in which they set their own standards in the form of codes and in which they submit the measure of these, on a level playing field basis, to their own arbitrator to judge. The broadcast stations and networks are all, at the end of the day, made up of men and women who often play roles of significance, whether public or less visible, in their own communities. That's where they go home each night and, unlike Howard Stern, who says that he would not let his 11-year-old daughter listen to his show but doesn't care whether yours does, the broadcasters do care.

As to the notion of free speech, broadcasters believe that there are and ought to be limitations, just as newspapers do. Newspaper editors determine what is and is not suitable to publish just as station managers and broadcast executives do. They just do it in private and don't tell the public what they have chosen not to run. No one accuses them of stomping on free speech. Nor the various Press Councils when they land on a writer with a thud.

Perhaps their negative determinations are not picked up by the media. Nor are most of our negative decisions. This one was. It doesn't change the issue, which is that free speech is not the only Canadian value. It is an important value, to be sure, but one to be balanced against other important Canadian values. In Canada, we respect freedom of speech but we don't worship it.

This was a fine country when the "Mighty Morphin Power Rangers" was on Canadian television. Its disappearance from those airwaves did not destroy the fabric of this nation. To some, it may seem hard to imagine that Canada functioned before September 2, when Howard Stern arrived in Montreal and Toronto, but it did.

Despite the fact that the CBSC has rendered 18 negative decisions in four and a half years, despite the fact that broadcasters have no doubt smarted from time to time as a result of one or another of those, despite the fact that broadcasters have certainly made choices about what they will or will not air because of the CBSC's interpretation of those standards, life has gone on in Canada. Perhaps even imperceptibly better for those standards. And, despite the Stern decision, it still will.

DISCUSSION QUESTIONS

1. In light of the decisions, evaluate the major points made by the radio stations in defence of the program.

2. Is there a role for media regulation in Canada—either by the government or self-regulation by the industry—or should the market alone determine what is broadcast?

3. Discuss the broader social implications of the differences between the Canadian Charter of Rights and Freedoms and the First Amendment in the American Bill of Rights.

4. Discuss the stereotypes of women and minorities used on the Stern show. What effect do you think these stereotypes have on those who listen to the program?

5. Do you find Stern's humour progressive or parodic?

 ## WEBLINKS

Canadian Broadcast Standards Council
www.cbsc.ca

Complete texts of the Stern decisions and supporting documents
www.cbsc.ca/english/decision/decision.htm

CRTC
www.crtc.gc.ca/

August 2000 Broadcast Standards Decision
www.cbsc.ca/english/decision/000831b.htm

chapter nineteen

Media Violence: Remote Controls and Twitch Instincts

INTRODUCTION

The debate about violence on television is almost as old as the medium itself, and there is virtually no agreement among researchers about how it affects children. Beginning with Newton Minow, former Chairman of the U.S. Federal Communications Commission, who defined television as a "vast wasteland," many different governments, both Canadian and American, have sought to regulate content on television. It is clear that both governments and conservative groups are convinced that television is far too violent and has a bad effect upon young children.

Joe Chidley notes some of the complexities of television viewing habits: that parents who think that children are harmed by violent television get this information from television itself—the vicious circle of media hyper-reality. Chidley is also concerned about the stereotypes prevalent on television and the commercial "imperatives" offered by programs which market toys based upon television series.

Thelma McCormack offers the most complex analysis of children's viewing habits. McCormack sees attempts to reduce violence on television as just censorship in another guise. Noting that studies of children and television have been done only in "experimental laboratory situations," she underlines the fact that no study of children and television can be considered conclusive. McCormack also notes that most studies set out to study violence, not non-violence. She asks if this were not the case, would studies find that television shows "had more non-violence than violence, more acts of kindness, cooperation and care" than the "alarmists" would allow?

Clive Thompson finds himself puzzled about another form of popular entertainment that appears on television screens—video games. A long-time aficionado of violent video games himself, Thompson starts from the position that video games have little to do with teen violence. On a research trip to interview "killology" expert Lt.-Colonel David Grossman, however, he finds that he himself is a good marksman, even though he has never fired a gun before. He concludes that his video game "murder simulator" practice has indeed given him some skill with a gun. Given that this is true for teens as well, does it make them violent, or are other social factors more important than video games in youth violence?

TOXIC TV: IS TV VIOLENCE CONTRIBUTING TO AGGRESSION IN KIDS?

Joe Chidley (*Maclean's*)

Nick Workman's favorite program is "The X-Men," a cartoon featuring mutant superheroes with names like Gambit, Rogue and Wolverine—the latter a misanthropic man-beast whose razor-sharp claws have a hair trigger. "I like the action," says Nick. "I like it when they use their powers." He also likes "The Simpsons"—especially Homer, father to the animated show's dysfunctional family, "because he always says, 'D'oh!'" Now, at age 7, Nick feels he's ready to move on to more mature fare: "The X-Files," the graphic sci-fi show that explores paranormal activity. Trouble is, Mom won't let him watch it. "She thinks I'll get nightmares," Nick says. In fact, Mom—aka Deborah Irvine, a 40-year-old speech-writer who works from her home in Maple Bay, B.C., an hour's drive north of Victoria—is worried about more than nightmares. Nick, she says, is well below his grade level in reading, and she suspects that his love affair with TV may be responsible. Of three sons, Nick is the only one "that we have to be very firm with and turn off the television," Irvine says. "It creates huge arguments. He'll grab onto my feet when I'm leaving the room and beg for the TV to stay on."

The scene has been part of North American family life since the television explosion of the 1950s—the child crying to stay up and watch, the parents getting angry, defensive or defeatist. But in the 1990s, the tenor of the TV debate has taken on a dark new tone. Increasingly, Canadian parents and educators are worried about the effects of the tube on kids. Much of their concern—fuelled by a recent spate of gruesome, lethal crimes committed by mere children—revolves around TV violence. And on that front, the September release of the so-called V-chip, a device that allows parents to screen out violent programming, promises to provide a new weapon in parents' battle for the minds of their children. If parents actually use it, the V-chip will permit unprecedented control of the household's most-used appliance.

But the problems of television go far beyond the powers of any quick techno-fix. They involve not only what kids are watching but also the fact that they are watching at all. Even in the 100-channel universe, where TV will offer something for everybody, parents will have to confront a question that transcends violence: what is television really doing to kids? Is it doing them harm? To put it bluntly, is TV toxic?

Joe Chidley. Toxic TV: Is TV violence contributing to aggression in kids? *Maclean's* 109(25), June 17, 1996, 36–41.

In its nearly 60-year history, television has been blamed for a host of societal ills, and not always fairly. "If the television craze continues with the present levels of programs," Boston University president Daniel Marsh declared in *Maclean's* in 1951, "we are destined to have a nation of morons." Arguably, that has not happened—yet. There is a lot of fine programming on North American television. But the issue of TV's effects is not only about what is on, but also about the interaction of the medium and its viewers—how they watch it, and what they take away from it. By the time most Canadian children reach high school, they each will spend between 10 000 and 15 000 hours watching TV—more time than is spent going to school, playing sports or talking to parents. No wonder that communications guru Marshall McLuhan called television "the first curriculum" for modern youth.

But what do they learn? Violence is one part of the picture, but increasingly sociologists and media critics are concerned about other, more subtle effects. Through the cathode tube, children learn about sexual stereotypes, about the "appropriate" roles for men and women in society. And they are told over and over again what they should buy: American communications guru Neil Postman estimates that the average kid has seen about half a million TV commercials by age 18. Perhaps most important, television is the primary source of information for children—as it is for adults—providing not only a refuge from, but a window on, the real world. And it is a very narrow view, indeed.

On a chilly night in April, 1995, a 13-year-old boy helped beat retired Montreal priest Frank Toope, 75, and wife Jocelyne, 70, to death with a baseball bat and a beer bottle; sentencing the boy to three years in detention and two years' probation last March, Judge Lucie Rondeau remarked that he showed no signs of remorse. Last April, a six-year-old boy crept into a home in Richmond, Calif., and beat one-month-old Ignacio Bermudez Jr. almost to the point of death; prosecutor Harold Jewett later said that the boy had told friends he assaulted the baby because members of the Bermudez family had "looked at him wrong." In Toronto last month, a 13-year-old accused an 11-year-old boy of raping her.

There is an ongoing and contentious debate over whether youth crime is really on the rise. But whatever the reality, the perception persists: what, parents and educators ask, is happening to kids? In the search for answers, many point to TV as, if not the culprit, then at least an accomplice. "Television violence is eroding, scrambling up, the value systems of children—oh, absolutely," declares Rose Anne Dyson, chairwoman of Canadians Concerned About Violence in Entertainment (C-CAVE).

Violence has long been an element of the TV landscape—and of kids' programs, from "The Three Stooges" to the "Bugs Bunny" cartoons that baby boomers were raised on. And of all the effects of television, the link between depicted violence and heightened aggression is the most thoroughly researched. Some dispute the statistics—there is real contention about what defines a violent act—but the numbers are still alarming: by the age of 12, according to one study, a typical Canadian will have witnessed as many as 12 000 violent deaths on television.

Many psychologists say that TV violence can lead to heightened aggression in the short term. Other research suggests that children who watch a lot of violence can become desensitized to real-world violence, and less empathetic to the pain and suffering of others. And then there is the so-called mean-world syndrome, in which children exposed to television violence develop a view of the world as more dangerous or sinister than it actually is. Tellingly, the same effect has been reported in adults, particularly among the elderly.

Doug Hallstead, a Grade 2 teacher at Stevenson-Britannia School in Winnipeg, sees those effects every day in the schoolyard. "I haven't seen Red Rover or tag on the playground for years," says Hallstead. "The standard now is 'play-fighting,' often with kung fu moves.

But there is a real lowering of empathy—their standard line is, 'I was just joking when I kicked him.'" More disturbing for Hallstead is what happens in the classroom. "If we're talking about the Second World War and we mention something violent, there are always a few boys who will go, 'Yeah, right on,'" he says. "There are kids in my class who take delight in something a previous generation of students would have responded to with shock."

But the TV-violence connection is complicated. Wendy Josephson, a psychologist at the University of Winnipeg who compiled a survey of TV violence research for Canadian Heritage, says that male children are more likely to be affected by TV violence than girls, and that children who have been abused are more sensitive to televised aggression—and tend to watch more of it. Still, a few experts doubt that televised violence has any real-world effect. Jonathan Freedman, a psychology professor at the University of Toronto, claims that while heightening aggression through exposure to violent imagery is possible in a laboratory setting, the violence studies do not reflect the way kids actually watch TV—in their own living-rooms, with outside distractions.

And the links between television and individual acts of violence are problematic, at best. In October, 1993, a five-year-old boy set fire to his family's mobile home in Moraine, Ohio, killing his two-year-old sister, Jessica Matthews. The girl's mother said the boy lit the fire after watching "Beavis and Butt-head," a notorious cartoon about two ne'er-do-well adolescents with a taste for pyrotechnics. The case was widely reported in the United States, and in response MTV, the music-video cable channel, moved the cartoon to a late-night time slot. What got less media attention, however, was the fact that the mobile home in which Jessica Matthews died did not even have cable.

> You will see a procession of game shows, violence, audience-participation shows, formula comedies about totally unbelievable families, blood and thunder, mayhem, violence, sadism, murder, western bad men, western good men, private eyes, gangsters, more violence and cartoons. And, endlessly, commercials—many screaming, cajoling and offending. And most of all, boredom.

—U.S. Federal Communications Commission chairman Newton Minow, May, 1961

Thirty-five years after a stunning indictment of television that came to be known as the "wasteland speech," Newton Minow—now chairman of the Carnegie Foundation, a philanthropic organization that helped fund, among other projects, "Sesame Street"—says little has changed. "I think in many ways, sadly, it has deteriorated," he told *Maclean's*. "We have a much wider choice, with the advent of cable and public television. But I think that the level of stuff thrown at kids, especially, has gone down."

Why? Minow and other U.S. critics point to the increasing commercialization of children's television during the 1980s, when the FCC deregulated the field—and when broadcasters threw out their voluntary code on advertising to children. Canadian broadcasters, in contrast, adopted a strict code on children's advertising—limiting, for instance, the number and air time of commercials. But thanks to the vagaries of the TV market, four-fifths of programs watched by English-speaking Canadian kids are American-made.

There are exceptions to the rule—the success of the youth-oriented YTV in Canada and of Nickelodeon in the United States—but for a variety of reasons, broadcasters cannot demand top advertising dollars for children's shows. From a research standpoint, kids are notoriously hard to keep track of, and advertisers cannot tell whether they are watching a show or just sitting in the room. The result is that ad rates for kids' programs are about one-fifth those for adult shows. As one industry executive puts it: "Broadcasters can make more money running infomercials."

When they do get made, Canadian children's TV productions—like "Fred Penner's Place" (CBC) and "The Big Comfy Couch" (YTV)—raise few concerns about violence or suitability for kids. "Children's television produced here is absolutely stellar," says Kealy Wilkinson, national director of the Alliance for Children and Television. The problem, Wilkinson says, is that there is simply not enough quality Canadian programming for children on the air.

The realities of children's TV in Canada are highlighted by the case of the "Mighty Morphin Power Rangers." The U.S.-produced show, which is exported around the world, follows the exploits of a group of squeaky-clean teens who transform into karate-kicking superheroes to battle evil forces from outer space. In 1994, the Canadian Broadcast Standards Council ruled that the show, which ran in Canada on YTV and CanWest Global, violated the broadcasters' code on violence. YTV pulled "Power Rangers" and, after running an edited version briefly, Global followed suit in July, 1995. But the show is still broadcast in Canada—thanks to Fox Network stations in the United States. On top of that, "Power Rangers" has given birth to such knockoffs as VR "Troopers" and "Masked Rider," both of which air on Canadian TV.

Some critics point to a link between violent entertainment for children and commercial imperatives. "There are so many other cultural commodities that go along with television programs," says C-CAVE's Dyson, "that the half-hour shows become commercials in themselves." There is practically no American-made children's program—from "The X-Men" to "Barney & Friends"—that does not have related merchandise. The all-time winner is "Power Rangers," whose figurines and accessories are now a billion-dollar business.

When Lukasz Zalewski was a kid—he is 15 now—the "Teenage Mutant Ninja Turtles" were all the rage. "Power Rangers" "is newer, because the Ninja Turtles were all guys, but the Rangers have girls," says Zalewski, a high-school student in Pickering, Ont. "Every show tries to trigger certain groups—they show things and they know that the little kids are going to bother parents to buy it for them." TV, he says, manipulates little kids. "But I guess teenagers, too," Zalewski adds, "because if you're watching MuchMusic, they have all these stereo systems on—all this cool stuff teenagers want."

Amid the feel-good news shows, the cartoons, "Sesame Street" and "Barney" on other channels, MuchMusic offers something different: an interview with the lead singer from the rock group Marilyn Manson. An androgynous figure dressed all in black, he opines that "there's no real difference between artists and killers," and describes how the group's latest album, *Smells Like Children*, is "about abuse of all sorts." What is remarkable is not the interview—run-of-the-mill anti-establishment rock stuff—but its airtime: 9 o'clock, Saturday morning.

Every generation of adults has viewed youth culture and its medium of choice—radio dramas in the 1940s, horror comic books in the 1950s, rock music in the 1960s—with suspicion. And although parents often say their concern is violence, their worries about television go much deeper. "Simply to go on what is relatively simplistic cause and effect about violence is to miss the bigger point," says Alan Mirabelli, executive director of the Vanier Institute of the Family in Ottawa. "Violence has been a way of articulating a disease with the medium. But we've never gone beyond it."

Too often, television offers little more than stereotypes, especially of women, like the curvaceous babes of "Baywatch." In a recent study, E. Graham McKinley, a lecturer at Rider University in Lawrenceville, N.J., looked at the ways 40 girls, from sixth grade to college age, talked about the hit high-school soap "Beverly Hills 90210." The show revolves around six beautiful teens living in a beautiful neighborhood. The show does occasionally look at socially relevant issues—drug abuse, AIDS, physical disability. But McKinley found that no matter what the ostensible issue, the women in the study talked about a limited range of topics: "Hairstyles, makeup, eyebrows, clothing and boyfriends," says McKinley. "The show established a community of viewers, who shared expertise on how women look." From a feminist perspective, she adds, the results are disturbing: "Do we want our young women to take a deep, abiding pleasure in the idea that you are what you wear?"

Adolescents, in particular, are highly imitative—a casual look at the baggy jeans and backwards caps worn in malls across the country is evidence enough of that. "Adolescents are the most prone to visual images," says Marshall Korenblum, a psychiatrist at the Hincks Centre for Children's Mental Health in Toronto. And teens learn to pattern their behaviour after stereotypes they see on television, often with disturbing results: a 1986 University of California study found that teen suicides tend to rise after TV news stories about suicide.

The trend in many commercials, meanwhile, is to stereotype parent-child relations: parents are clods, kids are cool. One ad for Apple Jacks, for instance, has a father wondering to his preteen daughter and her friends why they like the cereal when it doesn't even taste like apples. The response: "Da-ad!"—as if he just committed some sin to all things hip by asking an honest question.

It is worth pointing out that adult perceptions of youth are also shaped by what they see on TV. Some shows, like CanWest Global's "Ready or Not," CBC's "Straight Up" and WIC Communications' "Madison," attempt to transcend stereotypes of youth culture—and they do it well. But television, Korenblum argues, still tends to portray adolescents either as victims or as "leather-jacketed amoral thugs"—feeding an "us-versus-them" mentality among adults, and raising public hysteria about juvenile crime even while many researchers say youth violence is actually declining. One example: a promo for an NBC Nightly News special report last week made a clear pitch to adult fears with the lines, "Younger and younger criminals are terrorizing our cities. How can we stop them? How should they pay?"

In at least one respect, Elizabeth Bonnell of Halifax is an unusual 11-year-old: she watches only half an hour of television a day. She says she "sort of" likes TV. "But sometimes I don't like it," says Elizabeth, whose mother is a preschool teacher. "Like, sometimes I get bored watching it." She seems to make the most of her time: at school she takes cello lessons, sings in the choir, swims and plays basketball. After school, she takes jazz and tap dance lessons. And then, Elizabeth says, "I walk the dog."

Everyone who watches television knows the feeling—lying on the couch, bleary-eyed and bored, flipping vacantly through channels that offer nothing particularly worth watching. It is the most familiar TV effect and yet it may also be the most pernicious. According to Statistics Canada, the average Canadian spends 22.7 hours in front of the tube every week. Teens and children 2 to 11 actually spend less time watching television than the national average. And viewing hours for those ages have decreased—from 20.3 and 22 hours, for teens and children respectively, in 1986 to 17.1 and 17.7 hours in 1994, the last year for which statistics are available. Part of the reason for that decline, however, is that the numbers do not take into account time spent playing video games.

What worries many parents is the fact that kids watching television could be doing something else—like cutting the grass, playing with friends, reading, anything. On the other hand, parents who contemplate turning off their TVs altogether risk cutting off their kids from the cultural reference points of their generation: every kid at school knows the "Power Rangers" by name. And TV does have an undeniable role as a refuge. "For many households," says

Mirabelli, "there is so much stress that it's really come down to a question of television or Valium." In an era of broken families, many kids find a sense of belonging in the virtual families depicted on television. Some even claim to find enlightenment: in a 1994 American survey of kids aged 11 to 16, more than a quarter said daytime talk shows—the likes of "Jerry Springer," "Geraldo" and "Oprah"—do the best job covering people their age. The fact is, says Mirabelli, "somebody who spends that much time watching TV will begin to develop a perception of the world which is not real."

According to Wilkinson, 80 percent of parents say they monitor what their children watch on television. But in the age of latchkey children and two working parents, taking control of how long children watch is not always easy. The V-chip will help. And many parents and educators are already coming up with creative ways to address the problem. In Winnipeg, Grade 2 teacher Hallstead is waging what he calls "emotional nuclear warfare" against television. At the beginning of every school year, he invites parents to two evening sessions to discuss how they can help their children perform well in school. His main message: turn off the television and start reading to your child. He also offers parents placards to put on their fridge or on top of their TV sets. One asks, "Who do you love? Who do you spend time with?"—over an illustration of a set of scales balancing a TV set with a blank space for a picture of their child.

Some parents, meanwhile, are turning to a more traditional method: bribery. Bonnie Lovelace, a provincial civil servant from Edmonton, and her husband, David Hudson, a business development consultant, began to worry about their two kids' TV viewing about a year ago. "More and more, we found that whenever they had time to spare, they turned on the television," says Lovelace. So they made an offer to Michael, 15, and Leigh, 10: if the kids could watch a maximum of three hours a week for a year, beginning on April 1, 1995, then the parents would pay them $200 each. Lovelace says that Leigh stopped watching TV altogether and collected her $200 last March. But Michael "fell off the wagon," his mother adds, although he did cut back on his TV viewing—and earned himself a consolation prize of $100. Now, the kids are back watching television, but not as often, and not in the same way. Says Lovelace: "Now when they watch TV—and I don't know if this is a big step forward—they are conscious of what they are doing."

Deborah Irvine finally gave up—on television, that is. "We're going to cancel cable for the summer," she decided. "And where we live, if you don't have cable, you virtually don't have anything." How did she break the news to her son Nick—lover of "The X-Men" and "The Simpsons"? "I told him the TV's going on summer vacation, just like he is," Irvine recalls. "What I have to do is wean Nick off television from being his best friend."

TV AND THE CHILD SAVERS: BAD HABITS AND THE BOOB TUBE

Thelma McCormack (*Canadian Forum*)

The child savers are on the job again and this time the villain is television. Chief among them is Keith Spicer, Chairperson of the CRTC, who has put pressure on the private broadcasters to tighten their violence code "or else." Meanwhile a new group of public and private broadcasters, Action Group on Violence on Television, has recently issued a press

Thelma McCormack. TV and the child savers: Bad habits and the boob tube. *Canadian Forum* 72(824), November, 1993. 20-22.

release proclaiming its own good intentions. "Programs which contain gratuitous violence," it said, "will not be shown on television." In addition, an all-party Commons committee has recommended new amendments to the Criminal Code concerning violence shown on television and in videos. The composition of the committee may change with the next Parliament, but not the intention.

In reality there is less violence on television now than in the past, according to George Gerbner of the University of Pennsylvania's Annenberg School of Communication, who has monitored TV violence for more than a decade. But there is less tolerance of it, and more displacement. Parents who would like to hold the schools more accountable and schools that would like to blame parents for low educational performances can both agree that television is the common enemy.

The new censorship of Spicer et al is different from the older forms where community groups, often religious, put pressure on the schools directly to remove certain books from the curriculum and the school library. According to David Booth, writing about Canadian schools in *Censorship Goes to School*, these local groups are still active and have the same concerns about language, sex and social values on television. Whether it is a handful of individuals or an organized church group, they are blunt, ethnocentric, driven by a moral-Biblical vision that precludes any special consideration for works of art. They are successful to the degree that textbook publishers are unwilling to jeopardize their profits or future business by offending them.

The new censorship, on the other hand, is top-down, secular in spirit, and initiated by regulators and legislators who appeal to some abstract notion of "the public good." Instead of the thundering rhetoric of Bible-belt fundamentalism, there is an appeal to rationality. In theory they base their policies on scientific evidence of harm but, in practice, choose the evidence selectively. Better educated and more sophisticated than the older grassroots censors, they listen to the voice of cultural elites who have their own vested interests in protecting us from a dependency on trash culture. Although the two groups start from different perspectives, they end with the same demands for prior restraint and preemptive censorship. And it is this demand for censorship that brings them into conflict with the children's rights movement.

Children's Rights

Do children have cultural rights? Although Canada was a signatory to the 1991 United Nations Convention on the Rights of the Child, it is doubtful Canadians read it as anything more than helping Third World countries reduce infant mortality and illiteracy. Now they are beginning to have second thoughts. Immunization programs in South East Asia are one thing; children divorcing their biological parents is another. The recent highly publicized cases in the U.S. are just a beginning; the next 25 years may see many more bitter struggles over the rights of children, including those related to censorship issues.

Ironically, the pressure to eliminate violence from the screen comes at a time when the academic community has changed its direction. *Big World, Small Screen*, a recent report by a blue-ribbon panel of American psychologists, documents a shift in concern from violence to family values, from the study of behaviour to attitudes, from media effects to the sanctioning function of the media.

The authors have not retracted their earlier views that images of media violence cause violent behaviour, or desensitization, but admit candidly that these correlations are primarily in experimental laboratory situations and that the jury is still out on any long-term behavioural effects. More importantly, they have dropped the notion that the criterion for judging research is cumulative evidence. For example, a recent CRTC report, *Scientific Knowledge About Television Violence*, begins by saying, "No single study ever proved a hypothesis conclusively. It is the weight of evidence that accumulated from various sources that persuades us of the validity of a supposition." *Big World, Small Screen* dismisses that kind of feeble apology; more studies do not mean better studies, nor do they make the results more valid. In that sense the new agenda is both a reproach and a big step in a different direction.

While the new agenda represents an improvement, the catch lies with what the panel calls "a healthy family life." Parents who themselves grew up on Saturday morning cartoons and have never worried about them for their children are less open-minded when it comes to depictions of dysfunctional families or the polymorphous perverse guests who turn up on Geraldo, Oprah, Sally, Shirley, Maury and Phil. There is a latent anxiety among parents about television and the family. Instead, then, of a discussion of the rights of children to movies, television, comic books, and other forms of popular culture, we have parental guilt, moral panic and demands for the CRTC to use its muscle or for Parliament to criminalize more people within the cultural sector.

Blaming television for brainwashing our children is not a new phenomenon nor is it peculiar to us. Parents in all modern work-centred societies sense that their authority is challenged by a medium dedicated to pleasure. In the former U.S.S.R., for example, where children's television was everything Canadian parents and educators could wish for—non-commercial, interactive, written and produced by the best writers and actors, no competition from adult programs on other channels—Soviet parents were still dissatisfied. Too much sex and violence, they said. There could hardly have been less, but, Freud notwithstanding, the myth created by modernity is that prepubescent children are asexual. It is a myth dear to the hearts of parents whose heads may tell them otherwise, but it fits our belief that Lewis Carroll's *Through the Looking-Glass and What Alice Found There* is just a charming story of primal innocence.

Parents may deceive themselves about the phallic symbolism of Carroll's books for children or of *Red Riding Hood*, not to mention *Lassie* and *Black Beauty*, but they are realistic enough to know that their own efforts to screen what their children see on TV are ultimately defeated by a neighbour whose set is on all the time and whose kids watch everything. There comes a time in a desperate parent's life when it seems easier to turn control over to the state as surrogate parent, as if the state did not have its own, hegemonic interests in framing our consciousness.

The only groups to resist state regulation are the industries, and not on grounds of principle. Here, as elsewhere, the corporate mind regards self-regulation as the lesser of two evils.

The LaMarsh Commission and the Politics of Violence

According to the report of the 1975 LaMarsh Commission in Ontario, *Reflections on Violence*, violence can result from all sorts of indirect stimuli. When, for example, children see too much luxury on the screen, their expectations are raised and since these are not likely to be realized, disappointment can lead to frustration and eventually violence. In short, the LaMarsh report indicated unintentionally that what the state fears most about violence is not the expressive violence of a street brawl or the instrumental violence of the police, but civil disorder, a crisis in its own legitimacy.

This report, like so many others, raises a question of class bias and the stereotype we have of the poor as more brutal, more impulsive, more violence-prone than the middle classes. Hence, we censor pulp magazines and exempt works of literature accessible to the more literate, a view that was strongly defended by one member of the LaMarsh Royal Commission when confronted with the gratuitous violence in Shakespeare.

At the other extreme is the apolitical, the personal-pathological model represented by Frederic Wertham's *Seduction of the Innocent* in the fifties and, more recently, by the British publication *The Plug-In Drug* by Marie Winn. For these authors, popular culture is the opiate of children, conjuring up an image of young children hypnotically drawn to a medium that does irreversible harm. Before they have had time to grow up, they are victims of their parents' ignorance and irresponsibility. In *Unplugging the Plug-In Drug*, Winn shows how "to help your children kick the TV habit" by what amounts to making your home into a detox centre. Your child remains, not really cured, but, as they say in addiction circles, in a lifetime state of "recovery."

What is it about these metaphors of sexual or substance abuse that appeal to us? Whenever I have suggested to students that they study non-violence, or examine communities or groups with low rates of violence, the idea is received with polite indifference. Serial killers and child molesters, psychotics and suicides are more interesting.

But this predisposition introduces bias. If investigators coded programs differently, they would discover that television has more non-violence than violence, more acts of kindness, cooperation and care, more examples of friendship and bonding than is apparent from the statistics on TV murder cited by alarmists. This was, in part, the upbeat message of a recent British publication by Marie Messenger Davies, *Television Is Good for Your Kid*, but hers was a voice in the wilderness.

Children's Culture

In the typical research design, scenes of violence are isolated from the overall story and, similarly, television is examined apart from the larger realm of children's culture which includes school, games, sports, secret passwords, songs, music, rhymes, books, jokes, stories, comic books, slang, codes and private languages, board games, Disney films and a whole underground of fart-jokes, scatological stories and verses—the folklore of childhood described by the Opies in *The Lore and Language of School Children*. Television is only a small part of this larger world, a world that is varied, rich in diversity and often clandestine. The result is that our studies tell us little about violence or the culture of childhood.

What Do We Know about Children and Television?

Social psychologists emphasize the way in which children interpret television scripts in terms of their own experience and needs; developmental psychologists emphasize the way children interpret in terms of their own cognitive development. Both groups insist that children and adults differ in what they see and hear.

We know that children like television and watch a great deal of it, but less than parents estimate, and more on weekends than during the week. We know that viewing tapers off as children become adolescents; that larger families have the set on for more hours than small ones, but attention to it is intermittent; that the younger children are, the shorter their span of attention; that older children are more attentive but do less watching.

By the time children are five, they understand that television is make-believe. The people are real, they tell us, but the guns are not. Older children are impressed by realistic drama which they recognize as fiction but also, as they say, it could be real. By the time they are seven, children prefer adult programs to those packaged for them. It is as if the more fervently we construct childhood as a total institution, the more determined children are to know what mysteries lie on the other side.

Pre-school children like cartoon programs, where most of the violence is located; their older brothers and sisters who no longer watch cartoons like adult violence, but they rank comedy higher. Preschool children understand very little about the story or the action taking place on the screen; older ones, grade two for example, understand sequence but not causal relations. Both age groups recall little of the story and what they do recall is very different from an adult description of the plot. Boys and girls differ in their cognitive development, but in trying to make sense of what is on the screen they look to cues. And cues are what alert children to excised scenes which they themselves fill in. Ellen Wartella, an American expert who has surveyed the research, concludes that children are not passively absorbing what adults regard as the message, and their level of cognitive development determines what children see and how they understand it.

Finally, what children find frightening on television is not adult one-on-one violence, but any kind of abuse, threat or neglect of children. I learned this the hard way when I rented a video of *True Grit* for my granddaughter. She was nine at the time, and *True Grit* seemed to me a wonderful story for a little girl. But the film starts with the little girl visiting her father's grave, and that is as far as we got.

What We Don't Know

What criteria, then, should we use? Many critics question the assumptions in studies that show children learning anti-social behaviour from television role models. Others suggest that the problem is not in the findings but in their interpretation. Sooner or later all children are exposed to stimuli that are frustrating and raise levels of anger and aggression. The measure of mental health is knowing how to handle anti-social impulses and how to resolve conflict. Overprotecting children undermines their social and psychological development.

Television, because it is an indirect form of communication, and because it cannot reward or punish children as parents and teachers can, is a poor and inefficient medium of socialization.

At the same time television is great source of pleasure. Psychologists who study emotion, such as Percy Tannenbaum at the University of California, have long insisted that the media are primarily entertainment, and that the mental set and mood all of us, adults and children alike, bring to entertainment are different from those we might bring to other situations. Whether it is "Laugh-In" or *Macbeth*, we are engaged through a willing suspension of disbelief. Thus Tannenbaum and other psychologists who work in aesthetics turn to different theories and explanations. Tears and laughter, they say, bring great relief to children as well as to adults, when they seek escapism, fantasy or magic. Bruno Bettelheim, the child psychiatrist and educator, saw this as a normal part of personality growth and, in *The Uses of Enchantment*, urged parents not to censor the cruelty and mutilations in Grimm's fairy tales. He had great respect for the subconscious logic of these stories and feared the greater damage done by either depriving children of them or presenting the stories only in expurgated versions.

With all of these questions about the data, doubts about the concepts, and contradictions in the findings, any rush to censor through regulation ought to be challenged.

Television is part of the culture of childhood, replacing, supplementing and retelling the traditional stories and myths children have read or heard in our cultural history. It is like a counterculture, disturbing to adults who are looking for trust, and it is not easily comprehended by those who read it literally. What is needed now rather than more regulation of television, "in the interests of children", is a new understanding of how children create, process and interpret television within the larger context of their historical culture, and the acceptance of a more robust children's aesthetic. But that is the one thing the bureaucratic mind cannot grasp and the conservative mind cannot tolerate.

GOOD CLEAN FUN?

Clive Thompson (*Shift Magazine*)

The sun beats down like a hammer on the Mississippi firing range as Lt.-Col. Dave Grossman crouches on the ground. The heat is furious and he's beginning to sweat a bit, his army crew cut glistening as he punches in the combination to open his safety box. Inside are two guns. Grossman pulls out a .22-caliber pistol.

This, he tells me, is the same model that fourteen-year-old Michael Carneal stole from his neighbor's house in Paducah, Kentucky, on December 1, 1997. Carneal took the gun to a high-school prayer meeting and opened fire on the group. "He fired eight shots and got eight hits on eight different kids. He killed three and paralyzed one for life," Grossman notes grimly in his slight Arkansas accent. It was an astonishing piece of marksmanship—a hit ratio that many highly trained police officers can't achieve. Last year, for example, four experienced New York City cops shot at unarmed Amadou Diallo, firing forty-one bullets from barely fifteen feet away; fewer than half hit their mark.

But perhaps more startling about Carneal is another salient fact: He'd never shot a handgun before. "So how did he get such incredible aim?" Grossman asks. "Where did he get that killing ability?"

His answer: videogames. In a controversial book out this fall, *Stop Teaching Our Kids to Kill*, the forty-three-year-old Grossman details how Carneal had trained for hours and hours on point-and-shoot games. The teenager had practiced killing literally thousands of people virtually; he'd learned to aim for the head in order to dispatch each victim with just one shot.

Videogames have long been blamed for provoking violence, but rarely by someone of Grossman's background and expertise. A military man and Pulitzer-nominated authority on the psychology of killing, Grossman shot to prominence after the Columbine school massacre. In countless media appearances, he has argued that modern videogames are eerily similar to the training tools that military and law enforcement agencies use to teach soldiers and officers to kill. Kids learn these skills, he writes in his book, "much the same way as the astronauts on Apollo 11 learned how to fly to the moon without ever leaving the ground." The proof, he argues, is in the profusion of mass high-school shootings in recent years, where kids with limited experience in using guns have displayed excellent aim and tactical maneuvers, not to mention a view of murder as fun.

Clive Thompson. Good Clean Fun? *Shift Magazine* 7(7), December, 1999. 46-52. (Clive Thompson is technology columnist for *Newsday* in New York. He can be reached at clive@bway.net.)

I am here to test Grossman's theory. I have never even held a gun, let alone fired one. But for two decades, I've been avidly playing videogames, including the wickedly violent arcade shooters that Grossman considers the most military-like "murder simulators." I'm particularly good at these—I can usually finish Area 51 or Time Crisis for only about three bucks in quarters. If Grossman is right, I should be as deadly as Michael Carneal.

I look down the range at my target, a human-shaped silhouette. It's twenty feet away, roughly the same distance from which Carneal shot his victims. In the blazing heat sweat drips slowly down the small of my back. I raise the barrel of the gun.

The videogame debate has been going on for years, but Grossman has arguably brought it to a new level. He is a peculiar combination of ultra-pundit (known for his crisp sound bites on violence) and career soldier. Unlike other critics, who typically hail from the media-literacy or family-values camps, he has direct experience in the domain of killing. During his twenty-three-year stint in the army (from which he retired in 1998), he participated in the Panama invasion. He has taught the psychology of killing ("killology") at the West Point military academy and the University of Arkansas. Today, as founder and director of the Killology Research Group in Arkansas, he works full time training police officers—and remains an enthusiastic ambassador of military culture. He says "roger" and "check" instead of "OK," and calls everyone "brother."

Grossman's epiphany about videogames came through a circuitous route. Research for his psychology PhD eventually became the source of his 1995 book *On Killing*, which examines a little-known aspect of war: that soldiers, even highly trained ones, are profoundly resistant to shooting people.

As Grossman points out, surveys of World War II veterans show that eighty percent of riflemen never once fired a gun during active combat, even when enemy bullets were flying around them. During the American Civil War, according to data collected after battles, many soldiers only pretended to fire their weapons, loading them again and again without actually discharging a shot. On some level, it seems, they simply couldn't bear the prospect of shooting other human beings. Had they done so, casualties would have obviously been much higher.

Faced with armies full of reluctant gunners, the U.S. military began devising new techniques to definitively train men to shoot—and shoot to kill. The answer lay in classic "operant conditioning" methods made famous by American psychologist B.F. Skinner in the fifties. In a series of experiments, Skinner trained rats to push on a bar, after which they were rewarded with food. Positive or negative reinforcement, he argued, could make any form of activity virtually automatic, overriding conscious objections.

For the military, this meant setting up realistic shooting simulations. Soldiers were put into mock combat situations, filled with noise and riot; they were taught to fire at pop-up silhouettes until it became a twitch instinct. The conditioning worked well. By the Korean War, Grossman found, such training brought the firing ratio up to fifty-five percent. In Vietnam, the number skyrocketed to ninety-five percent.

In the eighties, the armed forces began using an even more powerful and cheaper training tool: video- and computer-graphics-based simulations. Many were modeled directly on videogames. One popular military sim was a barely-modified version of the early Nintendo game Duck Hunt.

Which is when Grossman began to look away from the battlefields and into the arcades. If the army was using game-like sims to train its killers, were the arcades doing the same thing, inadvertently, to youth?

An incendiary chapter in his 1995 book blames Hollywood violence and the rise of super-realistic videogames for the seismic increase of "serious assault" cases in the U.S.— which had nearly doubled between 1977 and 1993, from 240 to 440 incidents per 100 000 people. In Grossman's analysis, different forms of entertainment provide different elements of violence training. Hollywood and TV desensitize youth to the consequences of violence, a proposition generally backed by study after study. More controversial is the role he assigns to videogames as teachers of gun-handling skills. It is a theory supported by scant scientific evidence; Grossman bases his claims entirely on military research and his personal experience. In his own pistol-training classes at West Point, he says, some recruits displayed an uncanny facility with weapons. "Out of every class of about twenty kids, you'll often get one or two that are extraordinary shots but who'd never fired a gun before. And almost without fail, if you ask them, 'Where did you get to be such a good pistol shot?' they'll look you in the eye and say, 'Duck Hunt.' Or 'Time Crisis.' The skills transfer over immediately."

Still, for all their explosiveness, Grossman's ideas would probably languish in obscurity if not for the Michael Carneals of the world.

High-school shootings in the U.S. have been going on for years. In fact, the 1992 to 1993 academic year was the worst in sheer numbers, with nearly fifty deaths. But they were almost all one-on-one incidents, either revenge- or gang-related. In 1997, however, the peculiarly large-scale shootings began, during which the killers fired indiscriminately at groups of people they barely knew. Consider a partial list: In October 1997, Luke Woodham shot up his high school in Pearl, Mississippi, killing two and injuring seven. A few months later, Carneal went on his prayer-group rampage. In March 1998, two kids opened fire on a school in Jonesboro, Arkansas, killing five and injuring ten. Not long after, a student in Springfield, Oregon, cut loose in a crowded cafeteria, murdering two and injuring eighteen. And then came the most violent one of all—the April 1999 shootings at Columbine, which left a stunning thirteen dead and twenty injured.

Grossman figured his prophecy was coming true. It had also hit home. In a brutal coincidence, he actually lives in Jonesboro, across town from where its school shootings occurred; he was even summoned to the middle school to help counsel traumatized teachers. The ensuing weeks and months saw Grossman appear regularly in the media, from "60 Minutes" to *The New York Times*. An expert strategist, he decided the time was ripe to strike. This summer, he and co-author Gloria DeGaetano (a media literacy consultant) quickly completed work on *Stop Teaching Our Kids to Kill*, which slams violent games, movies and TV, and demands that they be legally restricted to adults only. Grossman has also trained lawyers nationwide in how to launch class-action suits against videogame companies on behalf of families whose children are killed in school shootings, as well as consulting on draft laws for videogames. The ripple effects are already here: this spring, the parents of three of Michael Carneal's victims sued, among others, several videogame companies that they felt had incited the rampage.

Now, as the media prepare for still more shootings, Grossman has arguably become the most prominent player in the videogame debate. "This whole industry is going down, and going down hard," he says with conviction.

But a question remains: Is he right?

I take a deep breath and start firing like mad, squeezing the trigger again and again until my finger aches, blasting round after round. Things are looking good: My aim is steady, my heart rate low. As I fire, bodies drop on impact—chunks of flesh flying off in all directions.

It's the day before my meeting with Grossman, and I've decided to go for a warm-up at a local arcade in Pearl, the Mississippi town I've come to to speak with him. I'm holding a plastic pistol in front of Midway's House of the Dead, blowing away endless platoons of zombies. A few days before, over the phone, Grossman spoke about the sheer physicality of guns like this one—arguing that they make games like House of the Dead preternaturally similar to a Fire Arms Training Simulator, which police officers use to hone their twitch-shooting instincts. Warming up on this stuff, he'd figured, would get me "really fired up" for the main event.

Indeed, from the time I first suggested this experiment, Grossman has displayed an almost perverse enthusiasm for it. He urged me to fly down from New York the following weekend to join him in Pearl, where he was due to guest-lecture at a police sharpshooter conference (taking place just a few miles from the high school that had its own shooting in 1997).

When we meet for lunch, he pulls out ads he has collected for various videogame companies, gleefully poking fun at them. One, for Quake, features a photo of a human foot with a toe tag; the caption says "he practiced on a pc." Another, an ad for a force-feedback joystick, reads "psychiatrists say it is important to feel something when you kill." He slaps his thigh. "These things are mass-murder simulators—and in their own ads, they're saying so!"

I'm not so sure. I've been a long-time defender of videogames, on TV panels and in radio debates. Games need defending, I've always felt, simply because they're the chief pastime of the young, unathletic geek, a cohort with whom I feel a personal sympathy. For these kids, gaming is a crucial refuge in a teenage world that glorifies physical power and beauty. Videogame critics frequently come from outside this geek demographic—as does Grossman—and thus inevitably err in their analysis of it. They ignore, for example, the social aspect of games—the robust culture of camaraderie and information-swapping that surrounds them. Or they focus on a few gory games that comprise a small portion of the market, such as Quake. During the Columbine coverage, clueless journalists cited Doom as if it were actually a current game, when nobody I know had played it for about four years.

Perhaps most problematically, critics assume that players are hopeless dupes of the videogame experience—that they are unable to critically assess what they play and are doomed only to be "influenced" by it. These critics rarely look at games as pieces of a living, breathing culture. In fact, you could argue that the tongue-in-cheek irony so prevalent in shooting games and their cartoonishly over-the-top gore are more of a comment on violence than a true enactment of it. Indeed, as gaming critic J.C. Herz once noted, the gun-toting protagonists of videogames are inevitably policemen, marines or soldiers—not mercenaries or lawless killers. What sort of social comment is that? As I sit here blowing away zombies in House of the Dead, my primary reaction is, as always, to giggle. Part of the fun is simply the deep surreality of the action.

To his credit, Grossman gives these arguments their due. Sure, games are useful socially, which is why he doesn't have any problem with non-violent ones. He also sees the irony of the gorier titles. But he doesn't think young children do. "They accept it on a different level," he says.

I was skeptical of Grossman's theory, but something happened at the Pearl arcade that gave me pause. I'm halfway through a round of L.A. Machinegunners when I notice a young man in fatigues watching me. I introduce myself, and discover that he's Sgt. Scott Sargent, a U.S. military reservist out recruiting. A recruiter in an arcade? I ask him if he wants to join me for a game.

Soon, Sargent and I are merrily annihilating virtual terrorists on the streets of L.A., using throbbing, simulated machine guns. Watching him, I see that Grossman's theory seems to apply in reverse. Sargent has had extensive training on real-life weaponry, but he's never played Machinegunners until now. Nonetheless, he's astonishingly good. And Machinegunners is one of the most difficult shooters to play—my wife becomes nauseated just watching the vertiginous, rapidly shifting angles. Despite my long experience playing this game, Sargent is better than I am, racking up more kills and sustaining fewer injuries.

As the round ends, I ask him how the game compares to real life. He pauses for a second, fingering the machine-gun controls that have a simulated recoil when you fire. I've always assumed the game recoil is a pale shadow of a real one. Apparently, this is not so. "It's actually very similar to the kick of an M-16," Sargent says. "I've trained with those things for years. It feels almost exactly the same."

The next day, training is over. I'm at the range, holding one of Grossman's pistols.

Several National Rifle Association officials and five police officers, here for a sharp-shooting competition, stand in a semicircle behind me, eyeing me worriedly. I can hardly blame them: The prospect of a neophyte blasting away is clearly unsettling. It's obvious that I don't even know how to correctly hold the thing; one officer has to gently suggest a two-handed approach. He stands next to me to make sure I keep the gun pointed down-range and to tell me when to fire. Grossman looks on with excitement. "Imagine it's House of the Dead," he calls out.

After everyone is safely a few paces back, the officer gives the nod. He leans over and touches a lever on my pistol. "The safety is down," he announces. "It's ready to fire."

For a second, I feel an odd sensation of danger, as if I'm only now realizing how deadly this thing really is. It's like driving along the edge of a cliff and suddenly visualizing yourself veering off into space. I have a brief, unbidden thought that at any moment I could swivel around and shoot three or four of the cops in the gut. I banish the notion immediately, then grip the gun more firmly and focus.

Guns are a peculiarly modernist combination of form and function, which is part of their allure. They have no extraneous elements: Just point and shoot. I squint down the range at the silhouette target. I squeeze the trigger.

Bang.

A hole appears in the upper left shoulder of the target. Whoa: I've hit it squarely, though I aimed too high. I fire again, and again. I'm nervous, far more than I expected, and trembling like a leaf. Perhaps it's because five cops are staring at me. Perhaps it's because I'm trying to fire as quickly as possible, to emulate the speed of Carneal and the other teen killers, who had little time to line up their shots.

Yet for all my panic, it's quickly become apparent that I'm actually doing quite well. After only a few shots, I have learned to correct my high aim. Within thirty seconds I've fired off every round and reloaded. Grossman urges me to try some head shots. This is harder, but again, after an initial error, I can see the holes popping in the head of the silhouette and the sun peeking through.

By now it's clear that whatever else about his theories I might question, Grossman's right about one thing: The .22-caliber pistol is remarkably similar in feel to an arcade gun—the kick is miniscule and it's only slightly heavier. In fact, arcade guns have a heavy cord dangling from them, so after hours of playing, you feel an added weight. You tend to develop muscles that can clearly hold a .22 quite steady.

We decide to take things up a notch. "Now," Grossman says, "I want you to try something with a bit more kick to it." He hands me a much bigger gun—his .45-caliber Springfield pistol, the weapon carried by the FBI. A .22 is a potentially lethal gun, as

Michael Carneal proved, but ultimately it's pretty lightweight stuff. A .45, however, can really mess someone up.

Including me. The first shot shocks me with the power of its kick, and the bullet flies harmlessly over the top of the target. I swallow deeply. My hands are shaking badly. Far more than the .22, this gun is very, very real, and nothing like an arcade toy. The way it kicks around, it's like it has a mind of its own.

Still, what happens next is revealing. Despite my nervousness, I automatically compensate for my panic. Even as my hands tremble, even as I sweat under the gaze of the cops, even as my mind races, my aim instantly improves. Some subconscious part of my brain takes over, and by the second shot I'm again hitting perfectly in the chest area. Shot after shot rips through the target, and I realize in a flash that this is what training is supposed to do—allow you to perform well even under great stress, or when your mind is occupied with other details. Some form of Skinner's operant conditioning, it seems, is in effect.

Then the hammer clicks on the empty chamber. The last shot has been fired. I hand the gun back to Grossman, and he races off to examine my targets.

According to Grossman, the accuracy of neophyte soldiers in training is relatively low. After one week of pistol training, fifty percent of recruits can hit the man-shaped silhouette "with some regularity," and one-quarter can concentrate their shots in the central chest area. Only five percent can place their shots in a small, silver-dollar-sized area. I've checked these stats with other police trainers; they agree the estimates are sound.

As for me? Grossman brings my targets. The shots are all in the center-chest area, the "9" and "10" scoring rings. It's unsettling, yet riveting to look at these close up. The bullet holes are clustered in what seems to be a shockingly tight radius. If this were a real person, hell, I'd have blown their torso to shreds with the first few shots alone.

Grossman seems thrilled. "I would say it was head-and-shoulders above the average first-time shooter." I'm not on par with the best he's seen, he says, but I'm shooting as well as a trainee would at the end of a week of training—a week. He gestures to the target. "That would be an A. You're scholarship material. You were rocking and rolling!"

Now comes the inevitable question. Grossman grins at me. "To shoot like you did with that .45 is truly extraordinary. And you've never fired a gun before. Where did you learn to do that?"

On the flight back from Mississippi, my shooting targets crammed into a garment bag, I replay the experience in my head—what it means, what it doesn't. I'm still relatively unsettled by my aptitude with deadly force, and impressed by how well Grossman's theory has played out. But I'm also disappointed. On some level, I realize, I didn't want to prove him even partially right. Too frequently, critics assume all gamers are sociopathic freaks. I hardly wanted to push that stereotype further.

But even if Grossman's idea about gun training is correct, it still can't explain what's going on in American high schools—specifically, the motivations of the killers. Hand-eye co-ordination is one thing; seething rage is quite another. Sure, kids may be able to go on mass rampages, but why would they want to?

Investigators studying the Columbine shooting admitted this fall that they were still baffled by what motivated Dylan Klebold and Eric Harris. "I've been working on this nonstop daily since April 20th and I can't tell you why it happened," lead investigator Kate Battan told *Salon* magazine. The killers' hatred, it seems, was freefloating in the traditional manner of persecuted teens. Jocks, gays, other nerds, popular kids, minorities, racists—everyone was up for grabs. None of this would shock anyone who went through an even mildly bad adolescence—they know that high school is, socially and psychologically, a shark tank, pitting clique against clique. In that context, it's hard to finger House of the Dead as a singular cause of teen angst. On the contrary, teensploitation TV fare like *Manchester Prep* or *Popular*—with their phalanxes of glossy, milk-fed socialites and ugly, brainy losers—is probably more likely to blur your sense of reality. And though largely devoid of physical violence, shows like that are quite capable of training you in the art of teen psychological warfare, a battle in which no gun license is necessary.

Guns themselves, of course, are another obvious issue in recent shootings—and another wrinkle that makes Grossman's theory seem overly pat. Videogame guns don't kill people; real ones do. Yet Grossman, a soldier who wholeheartedly supports the NRA, isn't out there fighting for enhanced gun-control laws. Rather, he thinks current laws are adequate. He also claims kids' access to guns hasn't increased, so guns can't solely be responsible for the rise in shootings. "I grew up with a twelve-gauge shotgun in my bedroom," he notes.

Perhaps most damaging to Grossman's case, however, are academic videogame researchers, some of whom say he has no science to back up his theories. A recent survey by media think-tank Mediascope found that only sixteen studies exist that probe the relationship between videogames and aggression, and their results are mixed. Even if every study agreed that games are homicidal in their impact, sixteen studies is a scientifically insignificant number, say the scientists. It doesn't yet prove anything.

Jeanne Funk, author of several videogame studies and a respected psychologist from the University of Toledo, sighs when I mention Grossman's name. She admires *On Killing*, but thinks his videogame theories have no serious scientific foundation. "He says things have been proven when they haven't," she says. "The fact is, we're just beginning to examine this issue. We don't know. The data are so thin." In pushing his ideas, Grossman relies instead on the thousands of studies that successfully link violent TV shows with aggression, and on the military's experience using simulators. But neither, Funk argues, are easily applicable to gaming. Videogames could have benevolent effects; on the other hand, that could be far, far worse than Grossman's worst nightmares. "But we have nothing to go on right now," she insists.

This, ultimately, is the most frustrating part of the issue. Surrounded by all the firing guns, panicked parents and the media frenzy, simple answers are more seductive than further debate. But every time I'm tempted to dismiss Grossman, I open my closet and pull out those silhouette targets. I check out the cluster of holes in the chest. I remember the jolt of the .45.

DISCUSSION QUESTIONS

1. Which is preferable: top-down or bottom-up control over television violence?
2. Visit the Canadian Broadcast Standards Council on the Web and analyze its policy on children and violence.
3. What role, if any, should children play in decisions regarding the content and type of programming or video games aimed at them?
4. Do video games condition players to commit violent acts? Does violence become a conditioned reflex in habitual players?

 **WEBLINKS**

Canadian Broadcast Standards Council
www.cbsc.ca/english/canada.htm

Hincks Conference on violent television
www.screen.com/mnet/eng/issues/violence/resource/reclaim.htm

House of Commons Standing Committee Report on Communication and Culture
www.screen.com/mnet/eng/issues/violence/resource/reports/fraydoc.htm

Media Issues: Media Violence
www.screen.com/mnet/eng/issues/VIOLENCE/default.htm

Killology Research Group
www.killology.com

mediascope
www.reseau-medias.ca/eng/med/home/resource/ntvs.htm

chapter twenty

Censorship: Hate in the Media

INTRODUCTION

How should we deal with the vexed issues of freedom of speech and of the press, censorship, and the publication of material that is clearly racist and filled with hateful slurs on ethnic minorities? This has been a very troubling and complex issue for the Canadian media and anti-racist groups like the B'nai Brith.

This chapter begins with an essay by Alan Borovoy of the Canadian Civil Liberties Association, who sets out some of the troubling complexities of this issue. He notes that the many Canadian human rights statutes contain statements directed against material "likely to expose people to hatred or contempt on the grounds of race, creed, gender and sexual orientation." He asks how such statements can be used to punish real hate mongers while allowing freedom of speech in other areas. One of his examples is particularly difficult: should libraries, for example, have books on the shelves that might create a "hostile environment" for some patrons? How far should we go to protect ourselves from hatred; will we reach a point where nothing remotely controversial can be said at all?

Paula Brook recounts the story of Doug Collins, a holocaust-denying writer for Vancouver's *North Shore News*. Collins' case was particularly ugly, but also significant since it revolved around Holocaust denial and freedom of the press. Numerous press associations supported Collins' right to speak his mind; many (but not all) deplored his ideas. This essay is a well-told tale of how complex and divisive an issue this was, and is, even within the Jewish community itself.

While the Internet has been available for more than a quarter of a century, its use, until very recently, has been largely confined to members of the military or academic communities. However, since the massive success of the personal computer in the home market, public interest in and access to the Internet and the World Wide Web has exploded. As with the introduction of all new communications technology, the popularization of the Net has generated debate around its potentially problematic content and public accessibility to that content. A short piece by the B'Nai Brith discusses hate on the Internet and proposes ways to control and eventually eliminate these hate sites.

The chapter concludes with an edited piece by Jeffrey Shallit, a professor of computer science and a founding member of Electronic Frontier Canada, a group dedicated to fighting censorship of the Internet (see gopher://insight.mcmaster.ca:70/0R0-19485-/org/efc/doc/ten-fallacies.27apr94 for the complete article). He summarizes and rebuts ten frequent arguments used to justify censoring the Net.

WHEN HUMAN RIGHTS GO TOO FAR

Alan Borovoy (*The Globe and Mail*)

Having campaigned vigorously many years ago for the creation of Canada's first human rights commission, I have been disquieted by the recent erosion of respect in human-rights circles for the importance of free speech. There would be little problem if the issue were simply speech connected to discriminatory acts. It has long been unlawful—and properly so—for businesses to advertise, "No blacks allowed." But human-rights commissions have also been moving against expressions of opinion.

Certain human-rights statutes now target statements "likely to expose" people to "hatred or contempt" on grounds such as race, creed, gender, and sexual orientation. Recently, the Canadian and B.C. human-rights commissions took action under those provisions over opinions expressed by Holocaust denier Ernst Zundel and Vancouver journalist Doug Collins. These two men understandably attract little sympathy. But a wise concern for human rights must address not only current cases but also longer-term implications. In short, who else could be targeted under these statutes?

The issue is not the desirability of suppressing hate propaganda, but rather the virtual impossibility of formulating a law so precise that it will net the vituperations of a Zundel without catching a lot of legitimate speech as well.

Consider this situation: One group in this country once called another group "a selfish, devilish operation desperately attempting to gain control over all peoples of the Earth." This statement was made not by anti-Semites about Jews but by Jehovah's Witnesses about the Roman Catholic Church. It expressed the Witnesses' belief that the Church was involved in the very real persecution they suffered under the mid-20th century Quebec government of the repressive Maurice Duplessis. Despite his best efforts to prosecute the Jehovah's Witnesses for this kind of material, Mr. Duplessis was unsuccessful. Happily, there was no law then against such speech. For vulnerable groups like the Witnesses, the right to censure their perceived oppressors has always been crucial.

Alan Borovoy. When human rights go too far. *The Globe and Mail*, June 1, 2000, A 15.

Today, however, the Jehovah's Witnesses could well be nailed for any repeat performance. Thus, the crunch question is: in order to stop a non-entity like Ernst Zundel, to what extent is it worth the risk of muzzling tomorrow's Jehovah's Witnesses?

It might have been acceptable if these laws against hate speech had simply banned incitements of violence. But "hatred" and "contempt" are such vague terms. Remember, free speech is sometimes most important when it expresses strong disapproval. But where does strong disapproval end and "contempt" or even "hatred" begin?

In targeting statements "likely to expose" people to "hatred or contempt," these human rights laws do not require an intention to promote hatred or contempt and there are no defences for truth or reasonable belief in the truth. Suppose, then, a complaint were filed regarding some of the serious scholarship in which it is contended that in certain places occupied by the Nazis, their Holocaust-related activities were enthusiastically supported by the indigenous populations. Couldn't such scholarship be seen as "likely to expose" the people of those places to "hatred or contempt"? Could these human rights laws, therefore, make it an offence to tell the truth about the Holocaust?

Currently the Saskatchewan Human Rights Commission is in proceedings against the *Saskatoon Star-Phoenix* and a self-styled Christian fundamentalist who had placed an ad in that newspaper. The ad showed a diagonal line drawn through the image of two men holding hands. To be sure, a repugnant ad. Nor was it redeemed by the inclusion of biblical citations. If the newspaper had rejected it, I would have applauded. Illegality is another story.

The Saskatchewan commission argued that barring the ad would interfere minimally with the fundamentalist's freedom of religious expression. According to the commission, he was still free to read his bible, donate money, talk to his fellow believers, and distribute bibles. But, in order to have their views even considered, activists must often employ attention-getting measures. To confine proselytizers to polite discussion is to replace freedom of communication with freedom of soliloquy.

Although the Ontario Human Rights Code has no such anti-hate provision, the Ontario commission has nevertheless been following suit. This commission is now acting against a printer who had refused to print the stationery of a gay and lesbian organization. As a "born-again Christian," the printer insisted that he conscientiously objected to this job. While I share the commission's disdain for this printer's views about homosexuality, I believe that his position should be defended. We should insist that he serve gay people but not gay causes.

In the mid-1990s, a former administration of the Ontario commission proceeded against certain convenience stores for selling allegedly pornographic magazines including *Penthouse* and *Playboy*. The complaint was that the stores had created a "hostile environment" for women and had thereby discriminated against them. According to this logic, book stores and even libraries would violate the Human Rights Code by disseminating *The Satanic Verses* by Salman Rushdie. In view of the many Islamic reactions to Rushdie's "blasphemy," couldn't his book be seen as creating a "hostile environment" for Muslims? If this complaint had succeeded, the Human Rights Code could have become an authority for pervasive censorship.

Thus, tomorrow's Jehovah's Witnesses might well blame the human-rights community for enabling a reincarnated Premier Duplessis to persecute them more easily. I don't believe Canada's human rights activists would wish to create such a legacy. Nor do I believe that such a risk is necessary in order to contain the influence of our society's hate-mongers.

FREEDOM'S JUST ANOTHER WORD . . . FOR SAYING 6-MILLION DIDN'T DIE.

Paula Brook (*Saturday Night*)

"Give me a break." Peter Speck is pacing briskly between a window and couch in his office at the *North Shore News*, self-described "Voice of North and West Vancouver since 1969." The paper that Speck launched and still runs is jettisoned three times a week onto 60 000 driveways and doorsteps stacked up the steep side of Burrard Inlet, and he's made a healthy profit almost from the start. Enough to see the fifty-eight-year-old publisher ensconced, a good part of each week, at his country retreat on North Pender Island, and enough to have caught the fancy of Southam, which bought up most of the shares in 1990 for more than $13-million, though they promised to keep their hands off the editorial and Speck was thankful for that. It's still very much his Voice, for better or worse. Right now, you could say it's for worse.

I'm sitting on the edge of the other couch, watching him pace, watching the bow tie vibrate every time he says give me a break. (We're at three, and counting.) "I've published Doug Collins for fifteen years," Speck says. "He has written 1500 columns for us, and he's a fine man, a fine journalist, he's a pro, he's the recipient of a military medal, he served with distinction in the Second World War, he was captured by the Germans and he escaped ten times. Ten times!" Speck spins on his heels. I'm working hard to get all this down in my notepad seeing as he forbade me to use my tape recorder. He says he doesn't trust tape recorders, by which he means he doesn't trust me.

Not that I blame him. At the time of this interview we are midway through a five-week-long human-rights hearing into a complaint against the newspaper and its seventy-six-year-old star columnist, and it's been hell for Speck, and I've certainly done my bit to stoke the flames. I'm a columnist myself, with a weekly spot on the *Vancouver Sun's* op-ed page, and have been pretty hard on Collins and Speck over the last weeks. That's my job: to be hard on people I think deserve it, to trade in emotion, to wield facts as much as use them. I guess you could say Collins and I are alike, is what I offer Speck by way of conciliation—though I wasn't yet born when Collins earned his medal, and have no quarrel with multiculturalism or homosexuality or the accepted history of the Holocaust, and have never been hauled in front of a human-rights tribunal for speaking my mind. "No, not yet," says Speck, burning me with his eyes.

Of course there's also the fact that I'm what Collins would call a "racial comrade" of the complainants in this hearing, the Canadian Jewish Congress (CJC). Collins uses phrases like that in his column all the time. I know. I have read almost every word he's written for the last two and a half years, starting with a column published on the eve of the 1995 International Conference on AIDS which brought thousands of "sodomites" to Vancouver whom Collins could clearly have lived without, considering "they brought their troubles on themselves through filth piled on filth." My husband and I had moved our family over the Lion's Gate Bridge that very week. I had picked the paper up off my doorstep and, on reading Collins, was immediately seized with fear that we'd chosen the wrong suburb.

For a few weeks after that we tried to stop circulation to our house, but calls and letters to the editor had no effect. I suppose we might have intercepted the carrier, or tried what Peter Newman did when he lived up here a few years ago: send the paper back by courier,

Paula Brook. Freedom's just another word . . . for saying 6-million didn't die. *Saturday Night* 112(9), November, 1997. 58-71.

COD. But we didn't think of that, and so it kept coming and perversely I kept opening it to page seven to see how mad Collins would make me this time. I soon learned his code: you've got your sodomites, your leather-clad lesbians, your multiculits, and your racial comrades. I have never in my life felt more like a racial comrade, which might explain why I jumped in with both feet when the human-rights tribunal got going last spring, setting a media attendance record and ranting regularly in the *Sun* about what I saw. It was just too rich.

The business of the tribunal was a March 9, 1994, column entitled "Hollywood Propaganda" in which Collins had written what his editor Timothy Renshaw later described to the tribunal as a movie review of *Schindler's List*, except that Collins hadn't seen the movie and he'd called it "Swindler's List." Renshaw, incidentally, doubles as restaurant critic at the *News*, and confessed to the tribunal that he wouldn't review a restaurant he hadn't eaten at. But Collins can pretty well do as he pleases in his semi-weekly spot because he is considered a pro: since moving from England in 1952 he's worked at the *Calgary Herald*, the *Vancouver Province*, the *Vancouver Sun*, CBC-TV public affairs, and a number of community newspapers, mostly in three-year stints; he is also considered very good for business—controversial, recognizable, his bulldog face perfect for giant mugs on the sides of buses with captions such as "Hard Lines," to quote a recent campaign.

The column in question is full of hard lines, the gist being that Spielberg's movie would sweep the upcoming Academy Awards—but not for the usual reasons. It would win thanks to "the Jewish influence" in Hollywood and the "Jewish-owned media" across North America, and because "what happened to the Jews during the Second World War is not only the longest lasting but also the most effective propaganda exercise ever." The goal of that exercise, he writes, is to bilk "billions of dollars" out of innocent Germans to compensate Israel and Holocaust survivors—"of whom there seem to be an endless number." The 6-million figure is "nonsense," according to Collins, who has said the same thing and more in other columns. He has written, for example: "I do not believe in the gas chamber stuff." He has frequently suggested that the death toll may be as low as a few hundred thousand.

Those are "reasonably held statements of material fact," according to Speck. He said so in a special "Freedom of Speech" fund-raising supplement published by the *News* in August. Renshaw agrees. Referring to the column in question, Renshaw told *The Globe and Mail*: "I think he makes some valid points. I wouldn't have approved the column if I thought it was over the top." Which has left more than a few readers to puzzle out the implication: are Speck and Renshaw publishing Collins in the interest of free speech—or because they agree with him? And would they go to the wall defending my constitutional rights to express views they consider unreasonably held? The Canadian Jewish Congress's Pacific region directors didn't waste time puzzling. They simply named both the columnist and his publisher in their complaint under Section 2 of the provincial Human Rights Act—a piece of law amended by the NDP government in 1993 to prohibit publication of material "that is likely to expose a person or a group or class of persons to hatred or contempt because of the race, colour, ancestry, place of origin, religion, marital status, family status, physical or mental disability, sex, sexual orientation. . ." you get the picture. And if you've read much of Collins you know he's targeted most of those groups at one time or another, with Speck's tacit approval.

Speck doesn't buy this assessment at all. His newspaper, like all good newspapers, is a marketplace of ideas where offended readers are welcome to offend back, in the letters column, he says. Alternatively, they're welcome to turn the page on Collins—no-one is forced to read him. And when they do turn the page they'll find a good variety of community-service features written for and by people of every size, shape, and colour: "We print all view-points. We run lots of multicult features. We have multicult contributors. I have Iranian friends. I have Jewish friends," he tells me, still pacing. "We've been tarred with the brush of racism. It's very painful." But couldn't you have avoided the pain, I ask him, by editing some of the more offensive material out of Collins? "Do you want me to publish pap? Give me a break." There goes the bow tie. "The winds of political correctness are blowing, and it's a dangerous thing because there's a self-censorship going on in the mainstream press. A sort of Damocles' sword hanging over our heads. *The Sun* and the *Province* won't print [Collins] because he's too dangerous."

A David-and-Goliath theme runs through this story, but with a twist: both sides see themselves as David. David is the little publisher who, along with his bulldog columnist, is preyed upon by state censors and powerful special-interest groups—i.e., the Jews. But David is also the Jew, the Sikh, the gay or lesbian reader who is wounded by the columnist's pointed words, and by his publisher's refusal to soften them or apologize for them despite the newspaper's claim to be their voice. While it's true offended readers can turn the page, some of them are wondering—why should I? And why shouldn't I fear repercussions when my impressionable neighbour doesn't turn the page? And yes, I can write to the editor—but there is no guarantee I'll be printed, and there's always the risk Collins will strike back. Master of ad hominem argument, Collins never seems to forget an insult or a name, and his editor does not stop him from fiercely attacking critics in his column. One West Van reader, Jack Chivo, got the full treatment after he wrote a letter challenging Collins's gas-chamber observations. "Chivo is a Jew from Romania and a Doug-hater," Collins noted, going on to wrap up the debate: "Hatred is a bad adviser, Chivo. And you would get more sleep if you went back to Romania." One thing is for sure: no reader will ever have his mug plastered on the side of a bus.

So who's bullying whom? Tough call, at least for those of us observing at close range. *The Georgia Straight*'s annual "Best of Vancouver" issue noted the "Best excruciating dilemma for local journalists: Support Doug Collins or censorship?" Even the defence lawyers seemed to lose resolve at times, as witness this exchange between a journalist and one of Collins's lawyers during a break in the hearings. Asked by the reporter whether his intent was to try to show that the government framed this piece of legislation specifically to muzzle Collins, the lawyer answered: "No. I'm not trying to get to that, because, ha ha, that might justify the goddam legislation. Just kidding. Don't print that!"

Yet, from a safe distance (such as Toronto), it seemed rather easy to find the real David and root for him. Peter Worthington, writing in *The Toronto Sun*, had no problem: "The CJC is wrong to let its dislike (dare one call it 'hatred'?) of Collins and what it thinks he stands for, lead it into supporting anti-democratic legislation—over a movie review!" PEN Canada chimed in, being "convinced that government repression of speech, however hateful and disgusting the speech may be (and Holocaust denial, a species of thinly disguised racism, fits that description) is unacceptable in a free and democratic society." Ditto from the Writers' Union of Canada, who wrote directly to Premier Glen Clark to push for repeal of this "censorship" law. Former premier Bill Vander Zalm sent a cheque to the *North Shore News*'s "Free Speech Defence Fund" as did the former mayor of Victoria, Peter Pollen, and hundreds of other citizens, from Europe and the Orient and just down my street—all of which was duly noted in the *News*.

The more mail and money that rolled in, the harder it was for the other David to be heard. Starting last March, the paper's defence fund was loudly monitored in each issue, with a banner on page one, a contributions-to-date thermometer above the masthead, tributes to Collins from readers, and indignant editorials by Renshaw and senior editor Noel Wright. "On the North Shore, democratic principles matter," went the May 14 editorial, a few days after the hearings started. "News readers don't take kindly to having their thinking being done for them by someone else. They don't take kindly to having the government tell them what views are right and what views are wrong. They have said so to the tune of $70 000 thus far." By the hearing's close six weeks later, the fund was up to $101 000—half of what Speck would need to cover legal bills. And his paper would need a lot more, he told his readers, if the ruling went against them and they were compelled to appeal it to the Supreme Court of Canada. "This newspaper won't rest until the NDP's bad bills are dead and buried."

This was no marketplace of ideas. It was war. And it quickly evolved into a war of ideas more than of words, which was inevitable considering that almost everyone involved—with the exception of Speck, Renshaw, Collins, and his most ardent fans—agreed that the actual words contained in that column were indefensible. Even David Sutherland, chief counsel for both the columnist and the newspaper, backed away from defending what Collins had said about the Jews, electing to focus instead on his constitutional right to say it. Indeed, the old Voltaire saw—"I disapprove of what you say, but I will defend to the death your right to say it"—proved to be the rallying theme of the defence side, eloquently supported by the B.C. Civil Liberties Association and by the B.C. Press Council, which represents all major daily and community newspapers in the province. Both organizations were granted "intervener" status in the hearings, allowing their lawyers to submit arguments on behalf of the defence. On the complainant's side, there were four interveners: the Attorney General of B.C. and the B.C. Human Rights Commission, both of whom came to defend the human-rights legislation; and the B.C. Human Rights Coalition and Chinese Benevolent Association of Vancouver, who were there to fight racism. Chairing the tribunal was a diminutive, brown-skinned feminist law professor from the University of British Columbia named Nitya Iyer. Collins must have used all the restraint he could muster not to use code on her.

Most days there were eight to ten lawyers in the room, a few reporters, half a dozen-odd observers, and a couple of security men. Security was beefed up when Collins was called to the stand—the hearing moved premises that day, from a meeting room adjacent to the B.C. Police Commission offices in downtown Vancouver to a nearby hotel ballroom. A crowd was anticipated and it materialized, consisting largely of Collins fans—eighty or so mostly grey-haired white people, a few bearing signs and handouts warning of democracy's imminent demise. They were not disappointed with the show. "This whole exercise is a farce," Collins half-shouted at one point, looking straight at his audience. "They could hang me up by the heels, and they wouldn't get an apology." His fans cheered, then Collins turned back to his cross-examiner, CJC lawyer Gregory Walsh, Q.C., and grinned thinly. Walsh was unmoved. After all, it was not his job to get Collins to apologize. Everyone in this town knows you could hang him by his heels, and shoot off a few toes, and still come up empty (Allan Fotheringham says Collins is the toughest man he's ever met). Walsh's job was to persuade the tribunal to grant a cease-and-desist order to protect readers from similar anti-Semitic columns in the future. To achieve this end, he and his co-counsel Gerry Cuttler had to prove that grievous harm had been done by this one.

On this particular day, Walsh was working on a line of questioning designed to catch Collins in his own trap—to get him to agree that words can cause harm, that harmful speech bears a price, and that even he has relied on the courts in the past to remedy harm done to himself by those who would falsely malign him. And Collins came through for Walsh, admitting that innocent Germans are harmed when Jewish filmmakers malign them, that he is harmed when someone maligns him, that he has no qualms taking legal action against such parties (as he has done to *The Vancouver Sun* and *Reader's Digest*), and that by doing so he contributes to a chill on freedom of the press—a chill he evidently deems necessary and even good when it is an individual, such as himself, who is defamed.

When a group of people is defamed—well, that's a whole different story. There's no effective legal remedy for that, except here, in a human-rights hearing, where many people suddenly get squeamish about the possibility that the law will impinge on their freedom. Walsh and Cuttler spent a good deal of their time trying to show the hypocrisy of this, suggesting that fundamental freedoms are already limited by our courts and are only slightly more limited by human-rights legislation like British Columbia's—which is almost identical to human-rights codes used by most of the provinces and by the federal government, and by many of the 146 countries around the world that have ratified the United Nations Convention on the Elimination of All Forms of Racial Discrimination. Significantly, the United States is not a signatory of this convention, nor any other that threatens to erode First Amendment rights, and those who defend hate laws often remark that their critics might be happier living there.

Canada is not only a signatory but an author of the granddaddy convention against hate: the Universal Declaration of Human Rights—the UN's postwar answer to what the organization regarded as the greatest violation of human rights in recorded history: the Holocaust. The spirit of the declaration was described by then UN secretary general Dag Hammarsskjold: "There is not now and never has been any such thing as unlimited liberty. Each man's freedom is limited by that of his neighbours."

"All the rights guaranteed by our charter reflect one common value, and that is the dignity and worth of the individual," argued Walsh in his closing submission. "In this case, Mr. Collins and the *North Shore News* say they are entitled to expose people to hatred and contempt because of their race or religion. They say they are entitled to do that regardless of the harm it causes. They say that in the name of free speech, the fundamental values in our free and democratic society permit them to pursue a commercial enterprise, for profit, without being responsible or accountable."

There are legal precedents in Canada for limiting speech rights in the interest of protecting individuals from discrimination that would interfere with their equality rights. The most notable was the 1990 Supreme Court of Canada case, Taylor versus the federal Human Rights Commission. An anti-Semitic telephone message service called Canadian Liberty Net, operated by Western Guard party leader John Ross Taylor, was ordered by the Human Rights Commission to cease and desist. Taylor defied the order, went to jail, and eventually beat a path to the country's top court to put the ruling to a constitutional challenge. The majority ruled that the original cease-and-desist order was a justified infringement of Taylor's speech rights, given the harm caused to the community by Liberty Net. Quoting the UN Covenant on Civil and Political Rights, Chief Justice Dickson wrote: "The opinions that Mr. Taylor seeks to disseminate through the telephone system clearly constitutes the advocacy of religious hatred which Canada has an obligation under Article 20(2) of the Covenant to prohibit."

The Taylor judgment was quoted probably a hundred times in the Collins case, by the CJC and their interveners. They believed Collins was doing much the same damage as Taylor was, and they were looking for a similar remedy—not to gag Collins entirely; just to ban future columns on this subject. It hurt Jews, they argued. Especially Holocaust survivors who didn't need to hear the *Voice of North and West Vancouver since 1969* deny their memories and their pain.

But it also hurt Jews to be vilified as censors, to be called "thought police" and even "Gestapo" for their role in taking an opinion writer to court for bad opinions—a first for Canada and a terrifying precedent in the mind of anyone who considers press freedom sacred. Many Jews wanted no part of it. Even the *Western Jewish Bulletin* (whose owner is American) joined the free-speech brigade, infuriating the CJC and alienating many readers: "Our refusal, through our editorials, to condemn Mr. Collins's right to express his views caused some readers to ask, 'Are you Jews first, or are you journalists?'" ran an editorial in the September 26 issue. "The answer is both. . . . to distort the case to comfort ourselves would be unforgivable as journalists—and as Jews."

"This hurts us in so many ways," Robert Waisman told me one day during a lunch break at the hearings. Waisman, who survived Buchenwald as a child but lost his parents and four brothers, was part of a small delegation to the tribunal from the Vancouver Holocaust Centre Society, and I had watched him squirm in his seat all morning. Sitting directly behind him in the public gallery were three Collins supporters who had been whispering derisively about Jews. "We're damned if we speak out, and we're damned if we don't. We don't want to give him the publicity, yet in the thirties someone got up and started in the same way and we ignored it because, we said, he's a madman. So we can't just sit back and say, well, look, he's just a nut."

Rabbi Imre Balla is not so sure. "I see that Doug Collins is in the papers, he's on television—isn't this exactly what he wants?" The rabbi of Har-El, the North Shore's only Jewish congregation, had invited me into the trailer that served as an office and chapel for more than a year while his synagogue was under construction. (It opened in time for Rosh Hashanah.) The imposing structure, its southern wall made of stone imported from Israel, stands just downhill from West Vancouver's British Properties—one of Canada's wealthiest neighbourhoods (where Jews were not welcome to live until the early fifties). The new synagogue is the first real home to the North Shore congregation that has been renting church and school space for more than two decades. And it's geographically correct: Har means mountain; El stands for God. Connecting the main building to the Hebrew school is an artfully landscaped bridge over a creek, symbolic of the bond with nature and neighbours. "This is part of our mandate, to build a bridge to other communities," says Balla. "And to cross the bridge, through education."

We share a laugh, at the bridge's expense. We're talking about the Lion's Gate now. Jews who live on this side of it are a somewhat different breed from those who live "over town." We're a smaller and quieter minority up here, on the *har*, which fits the overall demographics of these burbs. The North Shore has been largely insulated from the rapid changes that immigration brought in the seventies and eighties to Vancouver and its south and east bedroom communities. As recently as 1991, more than eighty percent of North Shore residents spoke English as their first language, compared to fifty-seven percent in Vancouver. The quaint, upscale shopping enclaves of Ambleside in West Van and Edgemont in North Van are likened to Vancouver's Kerrisdale back in its Jolly English heyday of the sixties. Only in the last few years have wealthier immigrants started moving across the bridge in any numbers— at their peril, some say. I've heard older residents bemoan the unpleasantness of strolling the Ambleside sea-wall these days: you hardly see any "Canadians" there. North Shore Jews, for the most part, just mind their own business.

This might explain why no-one from Har-El attended the Collins hearing. If there were boosters among the congregants, they made no attempt to organize or voice support. Many, however, have stopped circulation of the *North Shore News* to their homes. "Time is too short," is Rabbi Balla's outlook. "There are only twenty-four hours in a day and I want to use them to focus on something positive in my community." He had the same response a year and a half ago when, on a Friday night, swastikas were spray-painted across a half-built wall of the new synagogue. By Saturday morning there was no sign of vandalism: members of the neighboring Unitarian Church had formed a midnight posse and painted over the deface-ment, turning an ugly incident into a "positive story," in Balla's books.

"What good will come of this hearing? What good would a boycott do? Do you think it would stop Doug Collins? Do you think it will stop his followers? It can end up like a cru-sade," argues Balla. "It can go underground, and it can be even more dangerous because peo-ple will say, 'the Jews are silencing us.' If they do go underground, you never know where they will surface. Don't you think that in another part of the world, in another part of the city, somebody will take over? There will be others; there will always be others."

Balla, forty-nine, came to Har-El from Hungary in 1982—the second son of Holocaust survivors who lost their firstborn infant in Budapest's disease-ridden Jewish ghetto. Before the war, Budapest was the heart of Hungary's very old Jewish community of 800 000. About 600 000 perished in the war. "Maybe it was 599 000. Maybe it was 601 000," notes the rabbi, who heard his calling as a boy, growing up in a city haunted by empty synagogues. "I wanted to carry on the lives of those who were murdered. And what if it was only 550 000? What difference does it make, questioning the numbers? The danger in this revisionism—the real test—is yet to come, when the survivors are all gone. Is everything going to be nego-tiable then? This is why we need to focus on education, why we need to support the work the Holocaust Centre is doing."

This is Balla's answer to a rhetorical point made by Peter Worthington in a July 1 col-umn. "For some reason," the *Toronto Sun* columnist wrote, "the numbers in the Holocaust experience are important to Jews." Perhaps you have to be Jewish to know just how impor-tant, and how maddening it is to be made to feel defensive, even guilty, for relying on schol-arship to understand history. "No-one who has studied the subject seriously on the basis of the most recent evidence and scholarly work believes that the number is less than 5.2-mil-lion and most of us now think that the number is close to or over six million," says Leonidas Hill, a professor emeritus of history at the University of British Columbia who specializes in twentieth-century Germany and has published two large volumes on the subject, in German. In a written submission to the tribunal, he argues: "No serious scholar doubts that very large numbers of Jews were murdered in gas chambers with gas. There is much pho-tographic and written wartime documentation about how Jews were killed, including reports written by perpetrators as well as by Jews who escaped from camps or survived them. Massive documentation was combined with extensive testimony at the post-war trials, first the International Military Tribunal in Nuremberg, then many other trials in a number of countries, including eastern Europe." But such facts, says Hill, make no headway against deniers who maintain the myth of a Jewish plot—"in this case supposedly to sustain Israel and to slander German history and bleed the German people through reparations."

If scholarship and reasoned debate make no impact on revisionists, what does? "When they come out from under a rock, you beat them. And when they come out again, you beat them again!" offered an otherwise mild-mannered friend of mine. We were at a dinner party where the chatter was, typically, all about Collins. Like most middle-aged Jews I know, my friend broke his teeth on Holocaust history, his parents lost relatives, his friends lost parents, and memories of all those losses are sacred. And like many Jews of the snake-beating variety, he fears that the numbers game played by people like Collins is designed to cleanse the sullied reputation of National Socialism and usher it into the North American mainstream. As far as he's concerned, these people belong underground, on the lunatic fringe. They don't belong in a newspaper with a large mainstream readership and the clout to influence opinion.

To which the Holocaust denier replies: that's his opinion, and he ought to be free to print it. Free speech is the touchstone of revisionism—you can pick up the theme in Collins and trace it back through the legal trials of dozens of others. Recall Victoria lawyer Doug Christie's freedom-fighting words in defence of Jim Keegstra, Malcolm Ross, John Ross Taylor, and Ernst Zundel—all of whom Collins has invoked as examples of free speech in action. "Freedom of Speech" was emblazoned across the hard hat worn into court by Zundel, Toronto author of *The Hitler We Loved and Why* and distributor of *Did Six Million Really Die?* Christie called Collins as an expert witness in Zundel's defence, most of which revolved around Christie's contention that "the Zionists" were wielding their power to curtail freedom of speech with the result that the public was prevented from challenging the "propaganda" about the 6-million.

Collins still refers to the Zundel victory—the Supreme Court having ruled, on a four-three vote, that the archaic False News law did indeed pose an overly broad violation of speech rights. It was at Zundel's trial that Collins met Fred Leuchter, an American gas-chamber "expert" who reported that there could not have been homicidal gassings at Auschwitz, Birkenau, or Majdanek. Leuchter was discredited on the stand, admitting he was not an engineer as he'd claimed, and was later arrested in and deported from England. He is now under order by the U.S. government to stop making racist statements or risk facing prosecution for practising engineering without a licence, but Collins continues to believe Leuchter was right—hence his stand on the gas-chamber "myth." Among Collins's other favoured sources are: David Irving, an English academic condemned by the British House of Commons as a "Hitler apologist" and currently banned from entering Canada, Australia, New Zealand, Germany, Italy, and South Africa; Robert Faurisson, a former literature professor from the University of Lyons who wrote that the gassings were a "gigantic politico-financial swindle whose beneficiaries are the state of Israel and international Zionism"; the late Paul Rassinier, author of *Debunking the Genocide Myth*; and Arthur Butz, who wrote *The Hoax of the Twentieth Century*—a book Collins describes as a seminal influence.

Like Irving, Faurisson, Rassinier, and Butz, Collins has had his work published by the California-based Institute for Historical Review, whose bi-monthly journal is banned in Canada (though Collins has informed his *North Shore News* readers how to send away for it). In fact, his *News* column has been reprinted verbatim in that journal, about which Speck says he knows nothing. Speck also shrugs at the mention of the *Council on Public Affairs Digest*, a newsletter published out of Salmon Arm, B.C., which has reprinted a number of Collins's columns lifted straight out of the *News*—mugshot, headline, and all. The same digest runs ads for a video called "Doug Christie in the Holy Land," produced by Zundel's Samisdat Publishers, in which "you can walk with Doug as he tours holy shrines in Jerusalem and other places in Palestine. . ." as well as for a tape by "the courageous American execution expert" Fred Leuchter which includes footage from his research trip to Auschwitz and Majdanek.

By cloaking themselves in a veneer of academic respectability, revisionists gain access to a mainstream audience, writes Deborah Lipstadt, chair of Modern Jewish and Holocaust Studies at Emory University and author of the 1993 book *Denying the Holocaust*. But strip away the veneer and at their core they are no different from neo-fascists, she writes. "They hate the same things—Jews, racial minorities, and democracy—and have the same objectives, the destruction of truth and memory. But the deniers have adopted the demeanor of the rationalist and increasingly avoided the easily identifiable one of the extremist. They attempt to project the appearance of being committed to the very values that they in truth adamantly oppose: reason, critical rules of evidence, and historical distinction. It is this that makes Holocaust denial such a threat. The average person who is uninformed will find it difficult to discern their true objectives."

Lionel Kenner is not the average person—not by a long shot. Peter Speck calls him "a nutcase." I've joined Kenner for coffee on the deck of the Lonsdale Quay Public Market, and I'm a little embarrassed because he's been badgering our waitress about all the noise she's making moving tables about. Cantankerous, yes. But a nut? More like a short, sharp thorn that Collins and Speck can't seem to get out of their sides. The seventy-three-year-old retired Simon Fraser University philosophy professor, who lives in a duplex midway between this market and the *North Shore News* offices, found out the hard way that A.J. Liebling was right—freedom of the press belongs to whoever owns one. Three years ago, Kenner took it on himself as a reader, a philosopher, and a Jew to challenge the *News* by complaining to the B.C. Press Council about Collins, in particular a column similar to "Hollywood Propaganda." It was called "The Story Keeps Changing," published August 18, 1993, and in it Collins mentioned the usual suspects—Irving, Rassinier, Faurisson, and Butz—to support his revisionist argument. Through rhetorical sleight of hand, he also managed to find support in Winston Churchill, the International Red Cross, and two of the world's most acclaimed Holocaust scholars, Raul Hilberg and Yehuda Bauer. "What difference does it make," Collins concluded, "whether the figure was six million, one million, or 300 000, as was stated by the Red Cross after the war?" It was an impressive argument, if you're what Deborah Lipstadt calls "the average person who is uninformed."

Kenner spent the better part of a year researching his complaint—becoming about as informed as a reader can be. He went to the original sources cited by Collins, contacted the International Red Cross in New York, even telephoned the office of the Chief Rabbi in London, then brought all his polemical skills to bear in a seventeen-page single-spaced statement of complaint. "Some people say the numbers are irrelevant—what does it matter whether the number of Jews deliberately killed was five million or six million or seven million?" wrote Kenner. "But the numbers do matter. As Hegel said, a sufficient difference in degree constitutes a difference in kind—keep enlarging a car and it ceases to be a car and what you then have is a bus. . . . A disagreement as to whether there were five or six million Jews deliberately killed does not constitute a disagreement as to whether the Holocaust occurred, but a disagreement as to whether the figure was six million Jews or, say, just twenty Jews who were deliberately murdered would constitute a disagreement as to whether the Holocaust occurred."

Lionel Kenner submitted his complaint to the Press Council because he subscribes to the "marketplace of ideas" theory of newspaper publishing, and in fact has become one of the *North Shore News*'s more regular letter writers. He hoped, in this case, all could be resolved on the printed page—in the form of an apology and correction.

The Press Council ruled that Collins and his publisher had, indeed, breached its Code of Practice by misleading readers and misquoting scholars. *The News* was obliged to run the half-page adjudication, but the Press Council did not mandate an apology or correction. "The Code's accuracy provisions must not be narrowly applied here because Mr. Collins was engaging in the expression of opinion, not writing a news story," wrote the Press Council's executive secretary Gerry Porter summarizing the adjudication. "Therein lies the most rigorous expression of this Council's deep commitment to freedom of speech." It would be inappropriate, Porter went on, "for Mr. Collins and the *News* to apologize for publishing opinion columns that the complainant does not like or approve of."

So Kenner's year of research was put down to a question of his own likes and dislikes. He was incensed by the ruling, as were many others who read it. Sparks flew in the letters sections of newspapers across the province, including this submission to the *Victoria Times-Colonist* from Sol Littman of the Simon Wiesenthal Centre in Toronto: "By its decision, the Press Council essentially says that none of the editorials in B.C. newspapers can be trusted since they are expressions of opinion and not necessarily based on fact. What a way to trivialize your own industry!"

The next Jewish complaint against Collins was taken to the provincial Human Rights Commission rather than to the Press Council. "That would have been pointless," says Dr. Michael Elterman, the CJC's Pacific Region chair. Using stacks of Kenner's research to bolster their case, the CJC launched their "Hollywood Propaganda" complaint in the fall of '95, putting the New Democrats' Human Rights Code amendment to its first serious test. Lionel Kenner sat in the front row of the public seating area almost every day of the hearing.

"What offends me mainly is the dishonesty of the thing," Kenner tells me as our waitress recedes in a funk. We've been discussing the famous Voltaire quote, comparing notes on all the ways we've seen it skewed in the last few months. The most original version appeared in a letter of response to Sol Littman by Gerry Porter, in *the Victoria Times Colonist*: "Perhaps he [Littman] should reflect on Voltaire's silly old notion that while 'I may hate to hear what you have to say, I will defend with my life your right to say it.'" This drives Kenner mad: "I may hate to hear" suggests to him that what is being said is the hurtful truth, as in, "Jews don't like to hear the possible truth that the Holocaust never occurred."

And then there's the *News*'s variation on the theme. If Speck and Renshaw are willing to defend their columnist's views as reasonable, says Kenner, "then it is false that they are publishing Collins because they believe in free speech—that we disagree with what he says but uphold his right to say it. They're saying that they are putting out what is in effect neo-Nazi propaganda, deliberately. That neo-Nazi propaganda is reasonable according to them."

"It's the end of rational discourse," says Kenner. "Obvious distortions become accepted as truths. You have to look at the words: he's not just saying the Holocaust didn't happen. He's saying it was manufactured for money-making reasons. So the community around here is being told, week in and week out, that the Jews are financial swindlers who make up a story like this just to line their own pockets, that there's a worldwide conspiracy."

But what's the remedy? Neither of these complaints has silenced Collins, I suggest, pointing to the steady howl of indignation emanating all summer long from page seven of the *News*. ("Taking on a powerful pressure group is bad for the health," he wrote in one column; "Criticizing Jewish organizations is not on," in another.) "No, but at least now the public is finding out what Collins has actually been saying," says Kenner. "Now everyone in Canada knows exactly what has been going on here. *The North Shore News* is in a panic, as they should be. Because the real crime here is that this hate propaganda has been coming out in what's supposed to be a community newspaper delivered free of charge to almost every door in the North Shore. If you want *International Historical Review* stuff, you have to send away for it. Or Aryan Nations stuff—send away for it. But up here, people are being force-fed the same stuff."

At least we were—up to the middle of September when Doug Collins retired. Martyred on the altar of free speech, say his supporters. But Collins won't have any of that: "All things come to an end, good, bad and indifferent," he told a *Vancouver Sun* reporter. (He refused to talk with me.) He had intended to retire years ago, he said, but when the complaints came in he felt obliged to stay and fight: "It would not have been proper to leave before the hearing. . . . I would not run out on the bravest publisher in the country." He added that he is not hopeful about the outcome of the tribunal (see www.bchrt.gov.bc.ca/abramsv1.htm for a summary of the B.C. Human Rights Tribunal decision) and he doesn't want to be seen "running out" after a negative decision. Collins does not run out. And anyway, he's got work to do, from home—putting out a collection of columns, and a book titled *Rights and Wrongs*, "even if I have to publish it myself. I may be retiring, but I am not quitting."

"He's quite a guy, you know, he really is," says Speck. "He has his principles."

GLOBAL COOPERATION IMPERATIVE TO CURB SPREAD OF INTERNET HATE

B'nai Brith Canada

The government of Canada should amend the Criminal Code to penalize the downloading and possession of hate propaganda with intent to promote hatred. This was one of dozens of recommendations presented at the International Symposium on Hate on the Internet, which concluded in Toronto this week [March 25, 1999]. The Symposium was sponsored by B'nai Brith Canada's Institute for International Affairs and League for Human Rights.

"This symposium underlines the urgency of our task," said conference co-chair, Marvin Kurz. "The Internet is without boundaries and, therefore, without limits in terms of its potential for spreading hateful and potentially dangerous mis-information" added Kurz, who is the League's national counsel intervening in the Zundel case of Hate on the Internet. Over the course of the four-day event, delegates heard from speakers in the legal, technical, educational, government and community service sectors. The overall message was loud and clear. "We can't just keep talking about Ontario and Canada" emphasized Kurz. "We must focus our attention on the world."

Prior to the closing session, representatives of each sector met in private to deliberate their findings. The dominant themes were Partnerships (cooperation and sharing of information and strategy both internationally and amongst concerned groups), Prevention (education), and Protection (policing and law). Symposium participants concluded that a strong base in domestic law is needed in order to develop international agreements. The following is a synopsis of the Symposium recommendations:

Education

- Anti-discrimination should be included in all curricula, and anti-racism/anti-bias policies should be implemented by all school boards.
- Both business and community organizations should support youth and community activity in the area of anti-hate.

B'nai Brith Canada. Global cooperation imperative to curb spread of Internet hate. Press release, Toronto, March 25, 1999.

- Public education campaigns and partnerships should adopt the techniques and principles of commercial advertisers in order to get their message across to the widest possible audience.

- Teachers should be trained in using the Internet and receive support in the form of strategies, tools and resource materials.

- Conference participants should work with youth to develop programs based on the findings of the Symposium.

Policing

- Police need technical education to understand what they are dealing with so they can, in turn, educate their peer trainers.

- A police Web site should be established to disseminate anti-hate information.

- Police should work in tandem with local Internet Service Providers (ISPs), schools and community groups, both nationally and internationally.

- Police departments should employ trained experts to monitor the Net.

- Clear-cut national guidelines should be established for police prosecutions.

Legal and Legislative

- Territorial limitations should be removed and hate offenses put under universal jurisdiction.

- Courts should be allowed to recognize any historically recognized act of genocide. The list of identifiable groups that may be targeted for hate activity should be expanded.

- The Canadian Human Rights Act should be amended to list explicitly those messages likely to arouse hatred spread via the Internet.

- Prosecutors and Attorneys General should more actively initiate investigations, and lay charges in cases of hate incitement on the Internet.

Technical

- All ISPs should require proper identification when issuing a new account. They should be required to belong to a national ISP governing body.

- ISPs should share information to develop an international Uniform Set of Standards.

- The industry should encourage global partnerships and sharing of information.

TEN FALLACIES OF INTERNET CENSORSHIP

Jeffrey Shallit

The Internet is growing—growing in the number of users, and growing in public perception. Although most Internet users are convinced of its general utility and positive benefits, the naive reader of the daily newspaper might well conclude that most Internet users pass their

Jeffrey Shallit. Ten fallacies of Internet censorship. 1995. gopher://insight. mcmaster.ca:70/0R0-19485-/org/efc/doc/ ten-fallacies.27apr94 time by pirating software or distributing child pornography. As the Internet grows, there are increasing calls for its regulation from many sides.

Those who call for more regulation or censorship often treat the Internet as if it were some terrible dragon that needs to be slain; they are often ignorant of the Internet culture and seem almost proud of their lack of techno-literacy. Many ignore obvious historical parallels with more familiar media and the guidance provided by analogies with them. The censors and regulators also frequently have no awareness that the issue has even been discussed.

The Ten Fallacies

Here are some of the arguments presented for censorship of the Internet and why they are defective.

1. "People frequently post offensive material to Usenet newsgroups and our organization (university, business, etc.) shouldn't be supporting that."

    Those unfamiliar with Usenet often picture racist propaganda and child pornography popping up, unbidden, on users' computer screens. But, of course, it's not like that at all. To read a particular Usenet newsgroup, one must explicitly "subscribe" to it by name and issue a command to read the messages posted to that newsgroup. It is difficult to feel much sympathy for someone who chooses to read a newsgroup named "alt.sex.bestiality" and then is shocked at what they find.

    Just as large cities contain seedy areas where one can find X-rated movie theaters and bookstores, so the virtual community of the Internet also has areas where people may discuss things you don't approve of. But, just as you can avoid the local X-rated movie theater simply by not going there, you can avoid Usenet newsgroups you don't like simply by not subscribing.

    To paraphrase US Justice Oliver Wendell Holmes, if freedom of speech means anything at all, it means protection for the thoughts we hate, not just for the thoughts we agree with.

    The mere fact that an organization provides access to material does not imply endorsement of the views contained therein. Your local public or university library, for example, may contain controversial books such as Arthur Butz's *Hoax of the Twentieth Century* (denies the existence of the Holocaust and blames a Jewish conspiracy); Adolf Hitler's *Mein Kampf*; Petronius' *Satyricon* (encourages sexual activity among small children); etc.

    As the American Library Association says, "Viewpoint-based discrimination has no place in publicly supported library collections or services; for the library to espouse partisan causes or favor particular viewpoints violates its mission . . . The fact of public sponsorship of a library in no way implies endorsement of any of the myriad viewpoints contained within a library's collection."

2. "We have to regulate use because we've had problems with obscene and/or harassing electronic mail."

    No doubt about it, harassing e-mail is a potential problem. But what many users don't seem to know is that it is relatively simple to change one's mailer to simply dump messages from users you don't want to communicate with. Individuals can also configure their own e-mail software to scan for words they find objectionable, and delete messages automatically on that basis, if they so choose.

Even without this facility, it is worthwhile to examine what is done with harassing regular mail or telephone calls. We don't deny access to these important services simply because some users abuse them. Rather, we provide methods for tracking use (such as Call Display) and penalties for abuse. The same methods can be used on the Internet under already existing laws. No new regulation is necessary.

3. "We've had problems with users displaying offensive images on workstations in public areas."

Again, this problem has arisen before in other media. Many organizations have guidelines about what material is inappropriate to display in public areas (such as Playboy centerfolds, or Nazi swastikas). Most likely, your organization has sexual harassment guidelines that can be applied without change to the case of material on computer screens.

4. "Computer pornography is illegal and harms women; therefore, it must be removed."

First, there is a common confusion between "pornography" (defined to be erotic depictions intended to provoke a sexual response) and "obscenity" or "child pornography." "Pornography," per se, is protected speech and is not generally illegal. The Canadian Supreme Court, in its February 1992 *Butler* decision, held the obscenity provision of the Canadian Criminal Code to be constitutional. In the decision, very specific tests were provided for determining whether or not material is obscene and hence contrary to the law. (Briefly, illegal material must combine both violence and explicit sex.) In the waning days of the Mulroney government, the Canadian Parliament passed a "child pornography" law that criminalizes many kinds of depictions of sex with minors or those "depicted" to be minors. This law has yet to be tested in the Supreme Court, and many believe it will not survive challenge.

The historical record shows clearly that laws against pornography have been used to stifle unpopular opinions and dissent [. . .]. Ironically, by denying access to "pornographic" newsgroups, organizations may be removing an effective route for combatting pornography by those who feel it needs combatting. Retaining the groups allows anti-pornography activists to post in response to pornographic stories, expressing their position and explaining their displeasure.

Despite what some might have you believe, there is no consensus about whether pornography can be demonstrated to be harmful to women. [Other writers] present a more skeptical view of the alleged harmful effects of pornography. Even Catharine MacKinnon, one of the leaders of the modern anti-pornography movement, advocates the decriminalization of pornography (she would prefer treating it as a civil matter).

Even if it were conclusively demonstrated that pornography had ill effects on society, that alone would not necessarily be enough to ban it. For example, [Varda Burstyn's, *Women Against Censorship*] a collection of essays by prominent Canadian feminists takes the view that pornography may be bad, but censorship is worse. Even the Dworkin-MacKinnon model pornography ordinance suggests that pornography in university libraries, even on open shelves, should be exempt from censorship.

5. "We have to ban some newsgroups because they are obscene and we might be prosecuted for publishing obscene material."

Essentially this rationale was used by University of Waterloo President James Downey to ban the following five newsgroups at the University of Waterloo: alt.sex.stories, alt.sex.stories.d, alt.sex.bestiality, alt.sex.bondage, and alt.tasteless.

There are several fallacies here. First, it is quite doubtful that the University can be held to be a "publisher" by having a Usenet feed, which passively receives and redistributes millions of bytes each day. Second, newsgroups themselves cannot be obscene: a newsgroup is simply a logical archive or a meeting place. It is conceivable that some individual postings to newsgroups might possibly contravene Canadian law, but this has never been demonstrated. The *Butler* decision is held by some observers to apply only to explicit pictorial depictions made for commercial gain, and has no applicability to non-commercial text. In any event, banning an entire newsgroup because once in a while an "obscene" posting might appear is, to use the words of US Supreme Court Justice Felix Frankfurter in an obscenity decision , a case of "burn[ing] the house to roast the pig." The vast majority of postings to newsgroups constitute legally protected legitimate expression. Third, the likelihood of criminal prosecution of universities is virtually non-existent. No Canadian university has even been charged with distributing obscene material.

Justice John Sopinka of the Supreme Court of Canada raised serious questions about this censorship in a speech given at the University of Waterloo on November 26, 1994. He said,

> First, one must ask whether it is not preferable to permit the expression and allow the criminal or civil law to deal with the individual who publishes obscene, defamatory or hateful messages rather than prevent speech before it can be expressed. Otherwise, individuals may be putting themselves in the positions of courts to determine what is obscene and what is acceptable.

6. "Most of the material posted to Usenet newsgroups is worthless trash; therefore we shouldn't provide access to it."

   Yes, a lot of what gets posted to Usenet is worthless trash, no doubt about it. But as Theodore Sturgeon has observed, "90 percent of everything is crap"—why should Usenet be exempt?

   Many Usenet newsgroups are like discussions at a bar—a lot of heat, and little light. Except, every once in a while, the world's expert on the subject walks in, and suddenly the discussion is transformed.

   It is unrealistic to expect the same standards of writing on Usenet as one would find in a newspaper, magazine, or book. After all, newspapers, magazines, and books are generally commercial productions prepared by professionals. People who post to Usenet, however, don't get paid for their efforts, and they're often devoted amateurs.

   Usenet is a communications medium, first and foremost. Does your organization have rules on what may be said over its public telephones?

   If you don't find the Internet useful for your purposes, fine. But don't deny access for those who find it extraordinarily useful, even vital, for their work. In a few years, not having a Usenet feed at a University will be like not having a library.

7. "The Internet is a broadcast medium; therefore, it should be regulated like radio and television."

   Part of this argument is a semantic trick which makes it look like something profound is being said. "Broadcast" has two definitions; one means "to distribute via radio or television." Now this does not yet apply to Internet, which is usually not distributed by radio or television. The other definition means "to distribute widely," which can be said to apply to Internet—but it also applies to magazines, newspapers, and books, none of which are regulated like radio and television.

But even if one rephrases this argument to read "The Internet is like radio and television; therefore it should be regulated like those media," the argument is a poor one.

Internet has little in common with broadcast radio and television. You can't just go to a store, buy a computer, bring it home, turn it on, and suddenly get newsgroups. You have to get the proper software, and you have to have a Usenet feed, or dial the right phone number on your modem. As the Chairman of the Electronic Frontier Foundation recently remarked, the Internet-broadcasting analogy is "a highly inappropriate mapping of one idea onto another."

You don't turn on your computer and get flooded with newsgroups—you have to explicitly ask for them. Once you're "tuned in," you don't get deluged with pictures and sound until you turn your computer off—you have to explicitly request each additional message. You can easily prevent access by children in your household simply by not telling them your password.

In any event, cable television (which is more analogous to Internet than traditional broadcast television) has a completely different (and weaker) set of content regulations. Before we regulate Internet to death, let's treat the case of radio and television content regulations as a cautionary tale.

8. "The newsgroup alt.fan.karla-homolka violates a Canadian publication ban; therefore, it must be removed."

Judge Francis Kovacs imposed a publication ban on the details of the trial of Karla Homolka in July 1993. Almost immediately a newsgroup called alt.fan.karla-homolka was created and an active discussion developed and continued for more than five months. It went largely unnoticed until one institution, McGill University, suddenly censored it because they did not want to violate the court order. Many organizations swiftly followed suit.

The main problem with this reasoning is that the newsgroup was *not* created with the intention of breaking the publication ban, but rather to discuss aspects of the trial that were *public knowledge*, rumours, the wisdom of Judge Kovacs' ban, and the wisdom of publication bans in general. Of the approximately 2000 messages posted to the newsgroup in the first few months, fewer than 1 percent might have contained banned trial details. Hence 99 percent of the messages constituted legally protected legitimate speech.

Even if all the messages contained banned trial details, the decision to remove the newsgroup was not justified. If you post a message to the Internet, it is you who are doing the publishing, not the organizations that passively transmit the message. Hence, you are the one who should be liable for breaking the law.

The alt.fan.karla-homolka newsgroup fiasco points to the need for "common carrier" status for the Internet. Awarding such status will allow organizations to carry all forms of speech, no matter how controversial, without fear of criminal charges. On the other hand, those who post can be held responsible for their postings.

9. "Users in other countries have an obligation to respect our laws."

This argument was heard most frequently in regard to the alt.fan.karla-homolka newsgroup. But it is fatally flawed.

As more and more countries become connected to the Internet, more and more forms of speech will become freely available. Do we have an obligation to restrict our speech so that it remains legal in *all* those countries, even Iran, Iraq, North Korea, China, etc.?

Of course not. Each individual country must decide for itself whether it will be connected to the Internet or not. Each individual country must decide how to handle postings that it deems illegal. There is no obligation for people around the world to self-censor their postings to ensure, for example, that no Iranian law is violated.

And now, for good measure, here is one fallacy from the anti-regulation camp.

10. "It's all just bytes. How can bytes sent over the Internet be an illegal act?"

This is a reductionist argument that is evidently invalid. By the same argument, death threats over the telephone are "just" sound waves and libel published in the daily newspaper is "just" molecules of ink on paper. But a claim this somehow decreases one's liability would be laughed out of any court.

Conclusions

It is beyond doubt that the Internet can be used as a tool to break the law in various ways (utter death threats, conduct mail fraud, break publication bans, etc.). Is it really surprising, when these laws can also be broken through traditional media?

What is remarkable is that, in a community estimated to be as large as 25 000 000 users, there have been so few incidents of this type. Let us not use them as an excuse to over-regulate a "technology of freedom." Let us instead work towards wise enforcement of already existing laws, and more uniform international laws.

DISCUSSION QUESTIONS

1. Given the nature of the Internet as a form of communication, discuss the problems associated with—and potential solutions to—the control and regulation of its content.

2. Discuss the B'Nai Brith proposals. Are there other ways to control hate on the Net that do not threaten freedom of speech in other areas?

3. Research the outcome of the Collins hearing. Was justice done?

4. Some argue that prosecution under existing anti-hate legislation merely provides a larger public forum for racists to express their views. Discuss the implication of this position with respect to the protection of minority group members from the consequences of hate speech.

5. Given that individuals are legally protected from various forms of negative expression (e.g. threat, libel, defamation), should identifiable social groups (e.g., women, ethnic and racial minorities, gays and lesbians, etc.) be similarly protected? If so, how may this be reconciled with a position favouring freedom of speech and opposition to censorship?

 **WEBLINKS**

The Canadian Civil Liberties Association
www.ccla.org/

The B'Nai Brith
www.bnaibrith.ca/

Electronic Frontier Canada (EFC)
insight.mcmaster.ca/org/efc/efc.html

Nizkor Project
www.almanac.bc.ca/

Information Highway Advisory Council (Canadian government)
strategis.ic.gc.ca/SSG/ih01015e_pr702.sgml

Media Awarness Network: Challenging Online Hate
www.media-awareness.ca/eng/issues/internet/hintro.htm

Hate on the Net
www.cariboo.bc.ca/ae/php/phil/OREILLY/COURSES/Library/hateonthenet.HTM

chapter twenty one

Advertising in Canada: Kidstuff

INTRODUCTION

Canadians have a love/hate relationship with advertising: while many feel that it is a necessary aspect of selling products, others argue that ads aimed at children and teenagers are particularly cynical and exploitative. The authors in this chapter express a high degree of discomfort with ads and marketing agencies that communicate consumerist values to children—particularly through the school system.

Heather Jane Robertson writes on a conference she attended on marketing to children, and she can barely contain her fury at attempts by marketers to exploit this innocent audience. Like Joyce Nelson in *Sultans of Sleaze*, she notes that companies, under the guise of education or other charitable stances, merely wish to exploit the considerable economic power of children—even very young children. Noting that advertisers openly discuss "the molding of the mind," she is alarmed by the number of companies who have penetrated the school system—at all levels—to reach the child and youth audience even when they are not in front of the television set.

Charlie Angus notes that in many places in Canada, school funding is inadequate, and thus impoverished school boards have looked to private industry for help. However, this help comes at a price—the increasing introduction of ads to the classroom. Everything is fair game, from using M&Ms to teach math to making children memorize lines with company names in them. Many educators worry about the creation of a "captive audience" of young children, given the complete absence of government guidelines on advertising in schools. In the end, Angus and others worry about blurring the distinction between education and advertising.

Anita Lahey argues that as governments slash school budgets, our expectations from the school system are escalating. What alternative do schools have, she asks, other than seeking corporate investment? She notes that businesses and schools do not play on a level field, because school boards who need money are forced to accept science projects like testing the thickness of Prego Spaghetti sauce! Here, advertising clearly masquerades as education. Lahey further argues that U.S. studies confirm that product exposure in schools has a significant impact on brand popularity, but that students tended to remember the commercials and not the news programs they were shown.

Many Canadian schools have rejected the advances of the Youth News Network, a Montreal-based company which produces programming for the classroom. Erika Shaker argues that YNN is based upon a U.S. model (Channel One) that promises advertisers access to a very hard-to-reach demographic by getting programming into the classroom. Noting that much of the content on YNN is politically driven—like the hosts of the "Student Bodies" series telling students that "the low Canadian dollar is a direct result of spending on social programs"—she worries that increasingly impoverished Canadian school boards are hard pressed not to accept YNN in the classroom.

MARKETING TO KIDS

Heather Jane Robertson (*Canadian Forum*)

Toronto, June 12, 1995

I'm attending "Kid Power: Creative Kid-Targeted Marketing Strategies" as a teacher unionist and a parent, predisposed to see 2- to 12-year-olds as citizens-in-training, students and children. The brochure promises that I'll: learn how to tap into 4.4 million Canadian kids with a spending power of $20 billion; discover how to ensure that "gatekeepers for kids" don't intercept messages intended for children; and find out "how and why you should use school-based programs to support your kid marketing activities." "Kid Power" has been promoted mainly to Canadian advertising and marketing firms, but the brochure has also made its way to local unions. As a result, a handful of teachers, labour leaders and parents have informed the media that they are planning a little nostalgic resistance: a protest and a press conference.

News of this embarrassing public scrutiny surfaces during conference registration. Candi Schwartz, managing director of the event's New Jersey sponsor, the International Quality and Productivity Centre, fields media calls with some bewilderment. "Canada is so conservative," she tells participants. "In the States, we've been doing this for absolutely years, and no one ever complained."

A few minutes later the keynote address, "Kids Marketing Goes International," begins. James McNeal, a marketing guru from Texas A&M University and author of *Kids as Consumers*, welcomes us to markets without borders and kids without cultures. We are told that children represent disposable income of almost $100 billion (U.S.), and that they influence

Heather Jane Robertson. Marketing to kids. *Canadian Forum* 74(845), December, 1995. 10-15.

approximately $1 trillion of their parents' spending. But most importantly, he says, children are consumers-in-training, imprinting constantly as they prepare to take their place as adult customers. Reverently, McNeal summarizes the findings of his life's work: because children constitute a global market, they deserve our respect.

The globalization of culture presents almost unlimited marketing opportunities, he continues, since now American-style consumerism can be cultivated anywhere. True, American children organize their thinking around brand names by 18 to 24 months, and this feat isn't matched by Chinese children until 36 to 48 months, but we are assured this developmental lag is just an artifact of socialism. To emphasize the inevitability of cultural convergence, McNeal projects slides of beautifully drawn Chinese children's self-portraits, set in markets and shops. We are told that through their drawings, children offer us "windows into their souls. You see, they see themselves as customers! Isn't it wonderful that when you're so young you can say it so clearly?"

McNeal then describes "the pester factor" and its ramifications around the world. North American children nag their parents to buy them something an average of 15 times during each shopping trip, but Mom gives in only half the time. But China's one child policy and comparatively high disposable adult incomes, he says, mean that Chinese parents—and descendant-deprived grandparents—are much more indulgent.

Marketers who get it right, adds McNeal, will realize that "kids are more giving—they'll give you more profits." But first, he tells us, you must come to know your customer. Children everywhere prefer "imported" (i.e. American) goods bearing brand names imprinted through movies, TV and advertising. To exploit this pre-sold market, high-demand products must be tailored to each setting. Although vestigial differences are receding, North American companies should be aware that, inexplicably, "learning, education and schooling" are much more important in many other countries, where children actually choose to spend their own money on school supplies.

According to McNeal, this is because Chinese kids identify with achievement, while North American kids prefer play. It is up to marketers to fuse achievement with the ownership of brand name products in the minds of those children who haven't yet made the connection. Imprinting brand names should be the pre-eminent goal of marketers. "What a wonderful way to communicate with kids as consumers," McNeal says. "We are talking about the moulding of the mind."

Next, Youth Marketing Systems Consulting, represented by the California team of Drs. Dan Acuff and Robert Reiher, take over the podium. The pair present a well-rehearsed précis of their post-conference one-day workshop, available to participants for an additional $379.35 (U.S.). "It's all about essence—getting to the essence of essence." What is essence? "Essence is what can be evoked in the consumer." We embark on a glib trip through "research" (Harvard is cited in passing) on multiple forms of intelligence, followed by a fast-forward version of Maslow's hierarchy of needs and Kohlberg's stages of moral development, with a little biological determinism thrown in for good measure. We are told that between the ages of 4 and 15, the right brain (affective, non-rational, emotive) predominates, and that personal identity becomes the key developmental task for adolescents. These are just two of the many developmental characteristics marketers must exploit if they are to cunningly position their product's essence. Regrettably, they say, we pay too little attention to nature's own marketing opportunities, such as the preconventional moral sense of 3- to 7-year-olds, the brain stem dominance of 0- to 2-year-olds and the sexual preoccupations of 13- to 15-year-olds.

We practise by completing a worksheet that helps us analyze the essence of Madonna. Can we apply developmental psychology to expand her appeal to children? We are reminded that children seem to be accelerating through the stages of development—or at least some of them are. The soft cartoon characters of the Peanuts gang may appeal to the preschool set, but by 6 or 7 kids (especially boys) want attitude, even in their cereal box characters. Clever Captain Crunch has an essence sufficiency bland to fool parents, but he has enough edge to appeal to wanna-be teens. He's also a guy. We are reminded that little girls can be wooed with soft characters longer than boys, and that of course while girls will identify with male characters, boys will never bond with anything feminine unless they are stuck in the preconventional stage. (I take it the conventional stage begins when bonding with Madonna comes naturally.)

After lunch, the inside story of how Nintendo orchestrated the revival of "Donkey Kong Country" through innovative marketing. Not content with T-shirts, sampling opportunities and pre-Christmas hype alone, Nintendo mailed 170,000 kids a 15-minute video "infomercial" promoting "Donkey Kong." Apparently, this "insider's" report was a stroke of genius: "Kids love to think they're getting the real goods." The clip we are shown features all-male, mostly black, street-talking cap-backwards players praising the game's awesome qualities. As well, Nintendo ensured that similar TV promotions dominated the pre-Christmas (oops— pre-"gift-giving") season. Several ads featured rapid-fire cuts of superlatives quoted from video game magazines—hardly surprising, since that's where Nintendo had already placed "advertorials," commercials in journalistic drag.

One of Nintendo's ongoing marketing problems is the high retail price of its products. At \$60–\$80 per game, not enough target customers (males 7–15) have that kind of pocket change. This means that parents, whose peculiar tastes can be safely ignored when marketing small-ticket items, have to be considered.

"We have to be careful not to be completely offensive," says Kirsty Henderson, Nintendo of Canada's marketing manager. "We have to position ourselves to be seen to respect parents, but not lose kids." The print ads for "Donkey Kong" placed in the TV magazines that parents see feature a gentle real gorilla, not the animated search-and-destroy version. Nintendo's ads in children's magazines drop the pretence. For instance, the copy for another hot game, "Kirby's Dreamland 2," reads: "Next one to call them 'cute' gets a fire ball in the butt. What's that smell? Oh, it's your butt. Sizzling, scorched and smoking . . . [K]neel before the hamster that coughs up white-hot spheres of justice. Cuddly? Hardly." Since "Kirby 2"'s game box is illustrated with just the kind of cute and cuddly characters that would appeal to adults trying to limit videoized violence, "Dreamland 2" is perfectly positioned to work both sides of the street.

Perhaps daunted by the size of Nintendo's \$2 million advertising investment in "Donkey Kong," participants seem ready for something a little closer to their budget lines. Phoneworks account executive Cybelle Snour moves to the podium. She tells us that the secret of relationship marketing on a budget is to "create positive experiences" for kids, since their experiential memory is more powerful than any other kind. "Let's think of your brands as the rides on the playground," she says. Monitor your customers' experiences diligently, to ensure "constant and real-time satisfaction surveillance."

How can you keep track of so many kids on so many swings? By using their favourite relationship device—the telephone. "Kids understand the telephone is key to dialoguing with Mom, Dad and Grandma," Snour explains. While this is sad comment on the quality of family life, at least these conversations are between real people. The ones Phoneworks promotes are between real children and prerecorded messages—virtual relationships on call. Apparently virtual relationships are better than none at all: 4.5 million calls were logged in 90 minutes during a YTV phone-in promotion last Halloween. YTV was "blast programming," running four back-to-back episodes of *Are You Afraid of the Dark?* featuring segments in which two preteen hosts assured each other that they weren't afraid, they could hack it, they were cool. Only the uncool resist their initiation into ghoul.

The next session is the first to show the effects of the protest just getting under way outside the hotel. I overhear Carole Green Long, President of Children's Creative Marketing, tell a colleague that she's "changed the examples" in her presentation. I'm disappointed. The agenda promised that she would tell us how to use "school-based programs to support your kid marketing activities" and how to "incorporate the school-based program with new product launches, promotions, special events, direct mail, kids clubs and advertising." I was eagerly anticipating private sector insights on "how new Canadian education developments will impact on marketing."

Long apologizes for having missed the last presentation. She's been giving media interviews, trying to dispel the misconception that marketers were somehow exploiting students. If that were the case, she said, people would have every right to be offended, but the parents and teachers outside just didn't understand. She was talking about "good" in-school programs, not the kind "with very little educational content." The programs she would be describing were "serious," endorsed enthusiastically by school boards and Ministries of Education.

Endorsation somewhat overstates the reaction of Canada's education gatekeepers; denial and avoidance better describe the institutional response to corporate materials in the classroom. This is in rather marked contrast to the attention this issue receives in the United States. "Captive Kids," a 1995 report on "commercial pressures on kids at school" published by Consumers Union Education Services, states that strict guidelines have been adopted by 14 state departments of education, and that almost all 21 national education organizations surveyed have taken cautious if not hostile positions on commercialism in schools. Not that it has made much difference: the report concludes that increasing commercialism "poses a significant and growing threat to the integrity of education in America."

In both countries, there is quite likely a considerable distance between the views of those outside and those inside the classroom. "Captive Kids" reports that some classroom teachers are among those most willing to trade a few principles for much-needed resources: "If it's free (and good) it's for me!" said one teacher. "Great, glossy, up-to-date, motivating materials . . . are a heck of a lot better than the 1966 text books that many teachers are refurbishing to pass out each September."

Long describes how some corporations have capitalized on the bind created by decreasing resources and increasing expectation. A nutrition unit sponsored by the Dole Food Company, Inc. reaches beyond eat your (Dole) fruits and vegetables; the free CD-ROM-based program includes access to a World Wide Web site, a kids' cookbook, fridge magnets and large characters for classroom display, including Barney Broccoli. Let's think cross-curricular integration! Lesson plans for use in social studies, language arts and mathematics can all be printed from Dole's master disk, although grocery store tours are the most important component of the "5-Day Adventure." During 1994, 1.5 million American children embarked on the Dole adventure, and sales of fruits and vegetables increased. "It's a win-win situation," says Long.

Long moves on to SchoolNet, education's on-ramp to the information highway. Currently managed by Industry Canada, SchoolNet is charged with linking 16 000 Canadian schools,

3400 libraries and 200 colleges and universities. It has also been told to find ways to become "self-sufficient" (i.e. private) by 1998. Long admits that in the past the "commercialization issue" has been contentious within SchoolNet's advisory committee, but she assures us that the climate is at last welcoming for "responsible" partners. In fact, that climate may still be a little chilly; the advisory committee recently trashed a strategic plan commissioned by Industry Canada that recommended bartering on-line advertising for corporate sponsorships. The few education voices on the committee won this round, but no alternative funding solution for SchoolNet has been found. The spectre of sponsored on-line math and history lessons is not about to disappear along with one set of chagrined consultants.

There are other hopeful developments, Long tells us. Citing Ontario's Royal Commission on Learning, Long explains that "the number and power of school boards are diminishing" as they are "replaced by parent councils." This is a stroke of luck because now neophyte parent councils, not seasoned bureaucrats, will have the power to decide whether corporate-sponsored programs will be welcome in their schools. Parent councils will be more easily tempted by promises of cash donations, free teacher materials, technology or, better yet, higher student achievement.

At this good news an extended coffee break is called—or, rather, an ice-cream break, sponsored by MIR Communications and *Kids World Magazine*. According to MIR, *Kids World* is distributed to more than 1600 large English-language elementary schools, close to 40 percent of the target school population, and it is used by 70 percent of classroom teachers as a "teaching aid." I pick up a copy of the bright purple media kit that announces "Kids World: Putting the Cool in School." Everything inside the folder is in hyper-colour, except for the plain white four-page fold-over insert called "Strategies: A Teachers' Guide to *Kids World Magazine*." The pitch to teachers is literacy. "The product will entice children to make the voluntary decision to read." It's also respectable: "Educator and reader input ensures that *Kids World Magazine* remains an exciting and responsible publication."

The pitch to advertisers drops the pretence of responsible literacy. The 13 pages begin:

> Kids spend forty percent of each day in the classroom where traditional advertising cannot reach them. Kids World Magazine is in class, too, and can provide your brand with an opportunity to stand out! . . . Competition and clutter can kill the chances of great advertising being noticed by kids. Kids World Magazine stands out from all the other kids' media because our publication is enjoyed in the non-cluttered, non-competitive and less commercial classroom environment. . . .

> An advertising oasis. Imagine a classroom of ten-year-olds using your brand in a class assignment. . . . Envision groups of children huddled over your ad trying to solve its puzzle. . . .

> Can it get any BETTER than this?

Apparently it can, if the services of MIR Communications are engaged by companies wishing "to maximize their in-school presence" through "product sampling, sponsored lesson plans, sponsored school/class activities, [and] individual and class contests."

My copy of the "advertising oasis" falls open at a two-page spread placed by the Bank of Montreal. A young reader wants to complain about the unfairness of different PST levels in different provinces. According to the Bank of Montreal, it's because Alberta is "very wealthy" and "Newfoundland has a higher unemployment rate." A column called "biz-words" has kids match important literary terms like GST and RRSP to their definitions.

During the break, a few participants carry their ice cream to the front doors to take a surreptitious look at the press conference going on outside. Jim Turk of the Ontario Federation of Labour is trying to explain that when they're at school, his members' kids deserve protection from the commercialism that surrounds them every other waking moment. Larry French, from the Ontario Secondary School Teachers' Federation, hands out leaflets that warn that the principles of Kid Power are perverted—the power isn't with the kids, but with the adults.

I talk with two Toronto Teachers' Federation members who've been attending the conference. One looks like she's about had it, but the other is as animated as he's been all day, raising his hand to ask polite questions, keen to call back "good morning" to each one of the parade of presenters. He tells me he's sceptical about some of it, but he has to admit that the space activity and the A&E project look pretty good. Later at the YTV wine and cheese reception, I try to restrain him from picking up yet another freebie—a YTV mouse pad. "But I need one," he pleads as he piles it on top of his hand outs. He does not return for day two.

Toronto, June 13, 1995

Candi Schwartz welcomes us to what she hopes will be a quiet day after yesterday's media attention, "which everyone handled really really well." Most participants had seen a one-minute clip of the protest, followed by a defence of the conference by its organizers, on last night's six o'clock news. *The Globe and Mail* ran a 250-word story. Hardly bold media scrutiny, but it was enough to discourage a couple of presenters who backed out of day two, including Gordon Cressy of "The Learning Partnership," a Toronto-based consortium founded by "education and business leaders who believe education is everyone's business."

Today's first presenter is Linda Magnall, President of Imagination Youth Marketing, on Proprietary Kids Magazines—"a reach on the rise." I discover a PKM is an extended advertisement in magazine format, owned and published by corporations with marketing savvy and deep pockets. According to Magnall, the number of PKMs has doubled in the last decade, as marketers capitalize on reading preferences. Sixty percent of kids find magazines more "hands on and personal" than books. Reading is believing: Magnall explains that over-exposure to TV has made even the youngest viewers cynical, but, luckily for PKM, kids still naively believe that if it's in print, it must be true.

Magnall claims that the most successful PKM is *McDonald's Fun Times*, honoured worldwide as an "overall company image-builder." *Fun Times* is a "pro-social effort to fight illiteracy," Magnall explains, and it's even endorsed by Frontier College and the Canadian Library Association (a representative of the latter denies this claim). Originally, *Fun Times* was designed for "pre-literates" (more conventionally known as pre-schoolers), and its goal was "to build character recognition" of Ronald McDonald et al. But in the mid-1980s, McDonald's underwent "a radical change in its marketing objectives." Environmentalists—led mainly by youth—made the connection between hamburger consumption and rain forest destruction. Protests over excessive packaging had an impact. Ever-sensitive to customer opinion, the new *Fun Times* would drop Ronald in favour of rain forests with its "very savvy" audience of 8- to 12-year-olds. They would be encouraged to reposition McDonald's as a friend of the environment; "facts" about eco-friendly McDonald's are now dropped into articles throughout the magazine.

This kind of success breeds imitators. Magnall speaks admiringly of "a major financial services" corporation that has established a PKM even though few children require investment advice; it knows that it is possible to "develop a solid relationship that will stay with kids through their decision-making years." Magnall urges PKM hopefuls to respect children's "cognitive levels," a point she illustrates, peculiarly, by observing that "pre-literates still have their parents involved." Subtlety is an issue, she says, but with care your corporate message can be inserted in such a way that the company will receive "absolutely no negative feedback."

Done right, a PKM doesn't just avoid criticism, it attracts public financing. What could be better than accessing tax dollars to help get your corporate message to kids? Let's hear it for the Junior Jays!

The Junior Jays success story is brought to us by Eric Conroy, President of Community Programs Group. Conroy explains that he "learned the philosophy" he applies to the Junior Jays at teachers' college, but that he knew elementary school teaching wasn't for him when his first principal discouraged him from moonlighting.

Teaching at the high school level turned out to better accommodate his ambitions, but, in the end, teaching just couldn't compete with "alternative methods . . . to reach young minds."

Conroy obviously relishes telling the convoluted history of the Junior Jays. We learn that this PKM began as the solution to a problem of political correctness. For many years, police officers had been visiting classrooms across Canada, preaching bicycle safety with varying levels of enthusiasm and indifferent results. The Canadian Association of Chiefs of Police wanted to spruce up the program by handing out comic books when officers visited schools. Naturally, just like real comics, the play safe version would have to include lots of advertising. A partnership was born: Marvel Comics handed over *Spiderman*, and, with McDonald's in the lead, "the conscience of corporate Canada opened" and $10.5 million was raised in no time flat. The Spiderman comic was an instant success with both kids and police officers.

"Then came the day the earth stood still," according to Conroy. He met with officials from what was then Health and Welfare Canada. The Feds were dealing with the perennial problem of how to get their messages to kids when education and health are both jealously guarded provincial turf. The government was interested in a vehicle, and Spiderman looked appealing.

Alas, Spiderman was about to fall victim to the strange illness of political correctness. Spidey was "white, male, Anglo-Saxon and middle class . . . just the kind of thing the people outside yesterday wouldn't appreciate," explains Conroy, with a smirk. What was worse, even though the comic claimed to be promoting literacy, someone noticed that kids who didn't speak English or French—"immigrant kids"—were being ignored. "Now who'd think of that?" Spiderman was banished; the Junior Jays were born. No longer redolent with "white Anglo-Saxon malism," members of the Junior Jays, a group of adventurous pre-teen baseball fans, portray several races and include one girl, one dog and one boy in a wheelchair, led by an octogenarian coach, Dr. Jay.

Conroy boasts that more than one million copies of the spring issue of the *Junior Jays Magazine* were handed out to children through elementary schools. This issue includes full-page ads from "Mighty Morphin Power Rangers," Cheesestrings and National Trust, but buried in the comic strip are an assortment of more subliminal messages: Dr. Jay's time machine is a Coke can, the kids eat at McDonald's and wear Warner Bros. T-shirts. The Junior Jays even adventure in the wetlands with Ducks Unlimited, another corporate sponsor.

The copy is unrelentingly pro-social: fitness, inclusiveness, tolerance, anti-bullying, fire prevention awareness, environmentalism and personal safety all find their place. It is obvious that advertisers are eager to associate themselves with such current causes. Presumably Hubba Bubba, Super Nintendo, Eggo and Esso are among those stalwart corporations toiling to support employment equity, fair corporate taxation, an end to child poverty and more strict environmental legislation. Both Health Canada and Heritage Canada must think so too, since their logos appear proudly throughout.

The conference planners have saved a hot topic for the post-luncheon session. Participants will hear how profits multiply from "marketing with licensed products." It's a gold mine: media characters from *The Lion King* to *The Mask* decorate kids, their lunch boxes and their bedrooms. Even ("I love you, you love me") "Barney" has been leveraged to contribute his share to $1.2 billion in licensed profits in 1994. Brian Stewart, President of "Canada's leading entertainment-based consumer promotion company," doesn't waste time convincing kid-marketers to use *Batman* and *Casper* to promote sales. His focus is how to choose the next hit, and how much to pay. To help us decide, he's brought video clips from the kid-targeted summer releases, but before he shows them he has some advice.

Marketers need to watch out for the zealous "vocal minority" that gets such an unfair amount of media attention. For example, all that fuss about "Power Rangers" meant that Canadian sales for "Mighty Morphin" products peaked at only $5 million, when by U.S. standards they should have reached $15 or $20 million. However, Stewart reassures us, unreasonable "historical" concerns about violence are not likely to surface around the new "Power Rangers" movie, since the Mighty Morphins have been rehabilitated into a kindlier, gentler species.

We watch a short clip from the movie in which this didactic dimension, whatever it might be, is not apparent. The kicks and body blows, imitated on playgrounds across the country, are. I try unsuccessfully to imagine wanna-be gangs of 6-year-old boys replacing playground violence with passionate pleas for cooperative conflict resolution. Perhaps it is easier to rehabilitate characters than kids, but repositioning still requires a deft hand. Stewart notes that the sad decline of the "Teenage Mutant Ninja Turtles" may have been precipitated by just this kind of taming. In the name of damage control, a new TMNT movie is in production, in which the "Ninja Turtles go bad" in an attempt to restore them in all their former repugnance.

The summer releases include films destined to be automatic hits among kids: we watch clips from *Batman*, *Casper*, *Pocahontas* and *Indian in the Cupboard*. Stewart admits that some early "posturing" about violent and suggestive content may prove problematic, but no doubt the sheer quantity of *Batman* hype will overcome any puritanical whining. *Batman* is actually rated PG-14—what was known as "mature" until the name of the category, but not the standard, was changed thanks to industry lobbying—but we should expect the movie to appeal to kids (i.e. boys) from age 6 up. The clip we are shown features a vampy Nicole Kidman trying to seduce a reluctant Batman: "What do I need? Skin tight vinyl and a whip?"

Unfortunately, it may be too late to link our products with *Batman*, but other opportunities present themselves every day. Stewart advises us to consider the marketing possibilities served up by the remake of *The Hunchback of Notre Dame*. We are told Burger King is investing heavily. (I try, without success, to imagine Hunchback action figures sold with hamburgers.) *Free Willy 2* may have some appeal, since it's "nice and safe," and "maybe you can exploit the environmental angle," suggests Stewart. The action figures pose fewer problems too.

We break for popcorn. I decide to skip the last session on marketing to kids by radio and instead sort through my handouts and my notes. I start to write, no laptop, scribbling everything I remember, session by session. I write until it's time to take the plane, and then again on the plane, and when I get home. I don't answer when I'm spoken to.

Finally, I show a first draft of this article to my husband. He reads it once, mostly during commercials. With uncharacteristic reserve, he tells me to put it away and come back to it in a few weeks. When I demand an explanation, he says it's beneath me—it's bitchy, it's sarcastic, and I'm too angry to write. Gentle critic he is not, but he is usually right. I put it aside.

On June 29, the media report that the Mounted Police Foundation has entered into a licensing agreement with Walt Disney Co. (Canada) Ltd. For several days, Canadians ooze outrage onto op-ed pages and talk shows, expressing shock, dismay, etc. that we would stoop to selling a national symbol. I decide it's time to get back to work on this article. Perhaps a few of the same people may be half as outraged that we've already sold our children.

THE KORPORATE KLASSROOM

Charlie Angus (*HighGrader Magazine*)

Schools across Canada are in a race to buy cornflakes. The school that collects the most box labels from a Kellogg's product gets $20 000 worth of computers (second place gets $10 000 and third $2500). This is the gist behind the Education is Tops program being floated by the cereal giant. One set of prizes will be awarded in Ontario, one in Quebec and one in western Canada. All the other schools who take part will be treated to educational supplements written by Kellogg's. The supplements deal with nutrition and the importance of having a well-balanced breakfast.

Jackie Nelson is a spokesperson for Kellogg's. She says the educational supplements are not simply an attempt to advertise to Kellogg's target market.

> Kellogg's' reputation is not worth risking on some hard brand sale in the schools. That's not what the children are there to learn about. They are there to learn about the 3 R's. Naturally, however, we hope that when they think of breakfast they think of Kellogg's.

Nelson says that it is important to have Kellogg's name on the supplements because "it will lend credibility" to what the children are learning.

The program is also good for business. Says Nelson, "Since they (the students) do have to collect UPC labels they will inadvertently be purchasing Kellogg's products. We are (after all) a business."

Heather Jane Robertson, the author of *No More Teachers No More Books: The Commercialization of Canada's Schools*, isn't impressed.

> It's absolutely foolish for us to think that Kellogg's is doing this for the welfare of the children. The private sector does not exist to serve the interests of children. That's not what it's there for.

Robertson says she is outraged that the education system is allowing the schools to become a vehicle for corporate advertising.

> Think about it. There's 25 000 schools in Canada. For about $3 a school they (Kellogg's) are getting God knows how many students, teachers and parents to buy their products. We're not just selling our students. We're selling them incredibly cheap.

The Great Bunny

The Kellogg's' program is just one of numerous forays by corporations into the classroom. The education "industry" is being tagged by marketers as having a value of $630 billion

Charlie Angus. The korporate klassroom. *HighGrader Magazine* 4(6), November/December, 1998. 9–11.

(U.S.) for all of North America and $57 billion (U.S.) for Canada. Among those getting in on the action are Campbell's Soup, Gillette, Coca-Cola and Proctor and Gamble. Each of these companies provide schools with programs and educational tools. Product placement is part and parcel of these educational efforts.

Cadbury Chocolate, for instance, has been working with schools to push the story of the "Great Bunny." Almost 35 percent of the students under the age of nine have been exposed to this campaign. Cadbury supplies the schools with posters, copies of the story for each student and lesson plans for teachers.

One of the suggested ways of integrating this tale of the true meaning of Easter in the classroom was for the teacher to read the story out loud and then have students memorize lines. "Let's call this wondrous chocolate world/The Land of Cadbury/For 'Cadbury' is a bunny word/For chocolate don't you see."

Not to be outdone, M&Ms has come forward with a math program. The teacher's kit advises the educator to first of all make sure they have bought enough packages of M&Ms for all the students. Then the teacher can use the chocolates to teach the principal of graphs (sorting the M&M's by colour). The graph even comes with its own slogan "melts in your mouth not on your graph."

Erika Shaker is with the Canadian Centre for Policy Alternatives. She has been tracking the growing "partnership" between corporations and Canadian schools. Shaker says that is has become difficult to keep track of all the initiatives because so many companies are getting in on the educational business.

> If you can pull back from this for a moment it's very interesting to look at the kind of techniques being used by these companies. But it's very hard to pull back because this is such an obvious abuse of the classroom. The marketing literature is quite open in describing classroom advertising as reaching a captive audience.

Shaker, in the booklet, *Education Limited: Corporate Content Inside and Outside the Schools*, points to the efforts to sell screen-savers on classroom computers to advertisers. According to ScreenAd, a company working the Ontario market, advertisers have the chance to "expose your brand identity to over 1.5 million students in Ontario's classrooms every 15 minutes of their school day."

The ScreenAd Mission statement includes the laudable goal of not letting advertising get in the way of the true meaning of education—"To become a truly broad based advertising medium and not allow our ideals or those of the Institutions we support to become influenced in any way by our Corporate Clients."

Those clients, however, are encouraged to buy advertising because "you grow your consumers from childhood."

Who's Minding the Store

Given the proliferation of corporate-based education initiatives, one would think that education officials are working overtime to separate the crass from the constructive. Apparently not.

Gerri Connelly is with the Ministry of Education and Training in Ontario. She says the Ministry doesn't have any guidelines on the use of corporate materials. According to Connelly, this is the responsibility of school boards.

In the case of the Kellogg's campaign, Bill Parent, of the North East Catholic Board (covering Cobalt to Kapuskasing), said that he hadn't heard of the program even though it was being used in area schools.

Parent says the decision about what corporate programs to adopt is a "function of the schools taking it on at a local level." He says the Board is, however, developing a policy to ensure that younger students do not take part in door-to-door fundraising.

Heather Jane Robertson says that the lack of protocol among School Boards and School Ministries regarding advertising in the classroom is common across Canada.

> Think of the size of the Education Act and the regulations that go with it. Add to it all the policy manuals of every school. I can't believe the lack of regulation (on classroom advertising) is an oversight. It's a purposeful decision that says "we'll duck the political consequences and download this to the level of the school."

When it comes to advertising programs, marketers simply by-pass the system and contact teachers and principals directly.

Robertson says that poorer schools are particularly susceptible to this direct marketing approach.

> Poor schools are more inclined to hold their nose and get into sponsorships with companies because they need supplies. They feel desperate and so you get schools doing things like naming a classroom the 'Pizza Hut' class.

Robertson says that she is concerned that Canadians aren't taking a stronger stand over the growing commodification of education.

> It's a much bigger deal in the United States. The consumer's union has taken it on. Ralph Nader has taken it on. Every national organization of principals, teachers and school boards have studied the issue and have taken very public stands in opposition to corporate curriculum. It's astounding that we have done nothing similar here.

She worries that Canadians are simply accepting the logic behind such advertising campaigns.

> I am concerned that we have become so brainwashed with the message that the market is synonymous with being alive that we don't even think there is anything wrong with blurring the difference between education and advertising.

In the case of the Kellogg's program, Jackie Nelson says she is very proud of the feedback the company has received. "We hope to renew the program (next year) because it is such a wonderful program."

OPEN DOOR POLICY

Anita Lahey (*Marketing Magazine*)

A decimal lesson based on judging Olympic figure skating. An Easter Bunny maze. An art assignment involving imagining what's inside a house before drawing it. A lesson on puberty. A physical education program involving various levels of achievement. A calculator math exercise. A health class on body care.

These are all examples of classroom activities, but there's something else they have in common. Each is part of a program sponsored by a corporation: the Stentor Alliance's Olympic Resource Kit; Cadbury's "Tale of the Great Bunny"; Crayola's "Dream-makers"; Procter & Gamble's "The Changing Program"; the Royal Bank Activ8 phys-ed program (which includes

Anita Lahey. Open door policy. *Marketing Magazine* 103(25), June 29, 1998. 13-14.

secondary sponsors like Gatorade, Nike P.L.A.Y., the Raptors Foundation, YTV and Zellers); Hewlett-Packard's "Calculator Connections"; and Gillette Canada's active living diary and workbook. These programs, some of which have made their way into thousands of schools across the country, are examples of how Canadian corporations are taking bolder steps into classrooms—and how cash-strapped educators seem to be welcoming them with open arms.

"We're cutting back financially at the same time the expectations of school systems are escalating," says John Gregory, a partner in Cunningham Gregory & Co., education consultants in Toronto. "Corporations are being asked to step in."

Opportunities for corporate sponsorship in schools are becoming so vast that the Conference Board of Canada's National Business Education Centre brought corporate members together last year to develop ethical guidelines and operating principals for school-business partnerships. NBEC also began compiling an idea booklet in 1996 entitled 100 Best Business-Education Partnerships. The Conference Board estimates there are at least 20 000 alliances across the country between schools and businesses.

The schoolhouse door seems to be wide open for marketers. This is a dramatic change from just a few years ago, when educators and parents barred the way to anything perceived to remotely suggest a corporate agenda.

The question is whether or not marketers should be charging through that door in the numbers that they are. Not only are there logistical issues—the impact is difficult to judge, the nature of the school system may make many initiatives costly and inefficient—there are ethical considerations as well: does a marketer really belong in a school?

Many companies are not shy about sharing their motives for school sponsorships. Bev Deeth, executive director of the Raptors Foundation, admits her organization is keen on getting its name in front of kids. "The youth of this province are the future of our sport, both playing as well as being fans," says Deeth. "Those are the kids who are spending the money, buying the Nike apparel. They see on the module right in front of them our logo. That logo is powerful. When they see the Raptor's face and teeth, they know we were part and parcel of the whole thing." The Raptors, in partnership with Nike P.L.A.Y., have put $50 000 toward sponsorship of fitness modules for Grades 7 to 9 in the Royal Bank Activ8 program, currently in 1500 Ontario schools and reaching 400 000 students.

It's no wonder schools are tempting for marketers. A recent YTV study, in association with *Chatelaine* magazine, put the annual spending power of "tweens" aged 9 to 14 at almost $1.4 billion.

Some marketers say it's not the kids they're after. Amalia Costa, manager of market development for the Royal Bank in Toronto, says youth are a key target for the bank's sponsorship initiatives because their well-being is a priority in the community at large. "Our marketing message is really a message of goodwill to all the stakeholders around young people: educators, parents and the community at large."

The mood, at least, appears to be conducive to such initiatives. A recent poll by Environics Research Group of Toronto showed a majority of Canadians believe businesses should be more involved with schools, through mentorships, co-op placements, even helping design program content.

But here is where things get murky, and where the first of many caveats to school sponsorship rears its head. The same poll shows 74 percent of Canadians are opposed to corporate advertising in classrooms, schoolyards and hallways, and 64 percent oppose advertising on school computer screens.

The issues are obvious: not only do you have a captive, impressionable audience, but the balance of power rests with the advertiser. As Erika Shaker, an education researcher at the Canadian Centre for Policy Alternatives in Ottawa, says: "The literature talks about a win-win situation, how schools benefit and how business benefits. It rests on the notion that both are on equal footing when in fact they're not. It's an enforced relationship."

Furthermore, it's often hard to differentiate advertising from legitimate educational support. "Sometimes the concerns are warranted," says education consultant John Gregory. "Campbell's Soup does a whole science thing on Prego sauce; students are supposed to see if it's thicker than other sauces. That's an abuse of the system." He says M&M candies have been given to schools to be used as manipulatives in math classes, and calls this nothing more than sampling: "These tend to give legitimate education programs a really bad name. It tars them with the same brush."

Yet here's just how foggy the line can be: Many of the activities in the 52 000 copies of Stentor's Olympic program distributed to classrooms across Canada—such as sending messages to athletes via e-mail or toll-free numbers—encourage kids to use those services the telcos offer. "We wanted youngsters to experience online learning through Web pages, e-mail and calling 800 numbers," says Linda Forestell, team leader for Olympic sponsorship. "That was the only product-specific focus we had on it."

Gregory's client, Hewlett-Packard (Canada) Ltd. of Mississauga, Ont., runs the $100 000, year-old "Calculator Connections" course in 130 schools. Carrie Rands, citizenship program manager at HP, says Calculator Connections was developed with teacher input, follows curriculum guidelines, and is primarily concerned with getting kids interested in math and technology. Couldn't appear more legit, right? But wait. The course is about teaching children to use a product that HP sells. It also comes with six HP-38Gs—fancy high-tech, bargraph calculators.

Might this be construed as sampling? Rands says no, because the calculators go to teachers, not students. "Students can do the graphing on paper."

Elio Antunes, executive director of the Foundation for Healthy Kids and the Ontario Physical and Health Education Association in Toronto, which developed and distributes Royal Bank Activ8, says a legitimate curriculum sponsorship can include sampling—if it's done carefully. P&G's Changing Program offers sample Always pads, but only on request. "Anything that involves corporate sponsorship and samples we don't blanketly distribute," says Antunes. "It's up to the schools or teachers to order them. Product sampling seems to be accepted when it has a direct link to the educational component." However, some companies attempt to avoid skepticism by steering clear of any tangible link to their products and services. That's one reason why a phys-ed program appealed to the Royal Bank. "This is an area not related to money management," says Costa. "It's allowed us to support in a way that people wouldn't be questioning."

To Shaker of the CCPA, even this sounds like a careful spin on a particularly insidious form of marketing. She says a truly ethical company would keep its name out of the school completely. "We're seeing more business sectors determining what an education should be composed of to prepare future workers and future consumers," she says. "It's very limiting and it benefits only one sector of society."

Certainly, when a bank ventures into a school, whether it's to sponsor a program that seems linked to banking, or one that's as far off as physical education, people will automatically try to sniff out an ulterior motive. "Some might call it indirect marketing, trying to build a reputation," says Gregory. "If you get a kid to bank with you for their first account, it's likely he'll stay with you for life."

Costa says the only way to convince people you aren't recruiting clients is simply not to. That means not putting products or anything about them in front of students. The bank considered using standard educational pamphlets with the program, but decided instead to produce new ones that don't mention specific banking services.

"At the beginning, I wasn't as acutely aware of the sensitivity as I am today," says Costa. "That's a skepticism people in the community have up front: are you here to sell something?"

Stentor's Forestell says the bottom line is to give schools something practical. "If it's not useful, they won't use it," she says. "If it's too corporate or too simple, or if it's inappropriate to the grade level, it just won't get used."

There are no hard and fast rules regarding what is and is not allowed in schools. Individual boards, and in some cases individual schools, have their own guidelines or policies on working with corporations. This makes national sponsorship rollouts nearly impossible. Most happen in phases. Hewlett-Packard, for example, implements in four large cities each fall.

Marketers say the only way around the inconsistent procedures—and perhaps the best way for a marketer to legitimize itself in a school's eyes—is to not go it alone. Thus, the Royal Bank teamed up with the well-known and respected Ontario Physical and Health Education Association, Stentor partnered with the Canadian Olympic Association and HP hired experienced education consultants. "To be linked with a reputable third party is critical to success," says Costa. "They're the experts on the school system."

Says Antunes of the OPHEA: "Alignment with a credible organization already in the system makes a difference in whether teachers order materials. Before they started working with us, P&G tried to go directly to schools. They got the doors closed."

With most school sponsorships still in their infancy, the biggest question remains unanswered: what impact do they have?

Shaker says the experience of Channel One in the U.S.—ad-sponsored news programming segments played in classrooms—shows school exposure has a significant impact on a brand's popularity. "Studies on Channel One showed students weren't any better aware of current events, but they did remember the commercials and were purchasing those products being shown to them everyday," she says.

While this may sound encouraging to some marketers, the overwhelming impact it can have is the reason why Shaker says advertising doesn't belong in schools. But not everyone agrees the effects are so blatant. "If a technique is new and different, there aren't established measures in place," says John Hulland, marketing professor at the Richard Ivey School of Business at the University of Western Ontario in London. "There's clearly some kind of justification for the investment, but it's not quantitative."

OPHEA has measured media exposure for Royal Bank Activ8: more than $200 000 worth, including 67 print articles and spots on shows like "Breakfast Television" on Citytv in Toronto. Beyond that, reports are gathered from branch managers who've participated at local schools.

"As far as how effective, how people see it, what kind of message is perceived, a lot of it is anecdotal," says Costa. "That's the real challenge when dealing with programs that involve schools. There's soft qualitative reasoning behind this, not hard facts."

Stentor and the COA, meanwhile, have conducted awareness surveys. Among educators, 95 percent of respondents were aware of Stentor's sponsorship. That figure fell to 8 percent in the rest of the community.

Even where there is awareness, the real effects remain tenuous. As Hulland says: "It's hard to measure the impact of getting your name and info into the hands of kids. It's a pretty subtle effect. You really take it on faith."

It may be a strange kind of faith to show in the school system, but it's one that marketers seem willing to pursue, for now.

MUST-SEE TV

Erika Shaker (*This Magazine*)

In 1992, the Montreal-based Youth News Network (YNN) approached Canadian high schools with a Faustian bargain. In exchange for the free loan of audio/video and computer equipment, schools would guarantee the attention of students as YNN piped in 10 minutes of current affairs programming (and 2.5 minutes of commercials) to classrooms every day.

After fierce resistance from parents, teachers, provincial governments and students, YNN retreated. It returned last year to a far more hospitable climate for corporate partnerships. This fall, YNN makes its public school debut—approximately 15 contracts have been signed thus far for the upcoming school year. That's less than YNN's original target of 400 schools and 800 000 students by September 1999, but if the U.S. experience is any indication, it's only a matter of time before the numbers increase.

So just what do students have to look forward to from their mandatory viewing? YNN's links with business and government offer some clues.

Rod MacDonald

The president of YNN is Rod MacDonald, former organizer of the Progressive Conservative party of Manitoba. Although mostly a high-profile spokesperson for YNN, he believes it's time the public accepted corporate presence in schools as a reality. "Technology is already changing the way in which students learn and the way that teachers teach," MacDonald told the *Toronto Star*. "To deny that the private sector must play a role in managing this change is tantamount to sticking one's head in the sand." MacDonald, who also points out that "Schools are no longer the hallowed halls of sacred public trust they used to be," is doing his part to help bring the overly "sheltered" classroom into the commercial domain.

Nicole Lyn (Emily) and Ross Hall (Chris)

In keeping with the dictates of synergy, the two YNN hosts also star in the popular Telescene-produced teen show, "Student Bodies"—providing a subtle product placement for Telescene. "Emily" and "Chris" help teach students that the low Canadian dollar is a direct result of spending on social programs and that genetic engineering is eliminating the need for pesticides.

Ministries of Education in British Columbia, Nova Scotia, New Brunswick, Prince Edward Island and Quebec have formally closed their doors to YNN. Other provinces have left the decision to sign contracts with YNN up to individual school boards, even though a deal with YNN potentially amounts to selling school time to a private corporation—and instruction time allotment is very much the ministry's jurisdiction.

Erika Shaker. Must-see TV. *This Magazine* 33(2), September/October, 2000. 9.

Athena Educational Partners Inc. (AEP)

YNN is a production of AEP, which is billed as a "partnership" between BKM Research and Development Inc., Cancom and Gage Educational Publishing. But these names may just provide a comfortable distance from AEP's owner, Montreal-based Telescene Film Group Inc., which is responsible for the content and the production of YNN. (Telescene and AEP share a mailing address, president and vice president.)

Channel One

YNN is modelled after the enormously profitable U.S. network Channel One, which reaches approximately 40 percent of U.S. schools, and is seen daily by over eight million students. The network, which promises advertisers access to the hardest-to-reach demographic, charges $200 000 per 30-second slot. While advertisers may enjoy Channel One, schools don't necessarily feel the same way. In 1993, a University of Massachusetts/Amherst study on the demographics of Channel One schools determined that poverty and a lack of resources is the mitigating factor in "choosing" Channel One—schools that can afford to say no, do.

Telescene Film Group Inc.

Telescene, a successful entertainment-based company specializing in teen entertainment, has absolutely no experience producing educational content and explains its $500 000 stake in YNN this way: "YNN will be a success, creating significant value relative to its investment; it will enable the company to test concepts for teenage programming; and it will develop closer relationships with advertisers." Eighty percent of YNN's revenue is expected to come from advertisers who find the company's "target demographic" notoriously difficult to reach though other media. AEP's presence allows Telescene to move into the production of educational content without the public being too nervous about the obvious commercial implications of this arrangement.

Meadowvale Secondary School, in Mississauga, Ont., is YNN's pilot site, although the contract appears to contravene the Peel Board of Education's guidelines regarding corporate partnerships. In spite of substantial opposition, school administrators have signed a six-month contract with Athena. Lindsay Porter, a student at Meadowvale, was threatened with suspension after she started an underground newspaper in opposition to YNN.

DISCUSSION QUESTIONS

1. Tape and analyze two commercials from Saturday morning children's programming. What is the strategy of address used to sell the products? How different is this approach from the one used to sell to adults?

2. Visit the Canadian Advertising Standards Web site and, bearing these guidelines in mind, analyze the marketing of a product currently popular with children (e.g., "Pokémon").

3. How visible is advertising in schools? How influential is it? Does it have a gendered aspect?

4. Analyze the possible harm to children of allowing a corporate sponsored curriculum in the classroom. Are there any benefits to using commercial television (like the Youth News Network) in the schools? Check out the Peel District School Board's Evaluation Report of YNN on the Web site below.

 WEBLINKS

YNN (Youth News Network)
www.ynn.ca/

Peel District School Board's Evaluation Report of YNN
www.peelschools.org/facts/ynnreport.htm

Media Awareness Network papers on YNN
www.reseau-medias.ca/eng/med/class/edissue/ynn.htm

Canadian Code of Advertising Standards
Cii2.cochran.com/mnet/eng/indus/advert/adcode.htm

The Broadcast Code of Advertising for Children
Cii2.cochran.com/ment/eng/indus/advert/thecode.htm

Institute of Canadian Advertising Links
www.ica-ad.com/links/index.html

Commercialization in the Classroom
www.screen.com/mnet/eng/med/class/edissue/commed2.htm

Adbusters
www.adbusters.org/main.html#1

Conference Board of Canada National Education Centre
www.conferenceboard.ca/nbec/

Canadian Centre for Policy Alternatives
www.policyalternatives.ca/

ScreenAd
www.screenad.com/

chapter twenty two

Corporate Sponsorship:
Something for Nothing?

INTRODUCTION

David Menzies begins this chapter by wondering how altruistic large corporations are when they contribute to charity. Occasionally slipping into a cynical frame of mind, Menzies tends to see corporate philanthropy as just another form of advertising: take a worthy cause (but make sure it is a popular one!) and promote it along with your company's name. On the other hand, large corporations often do considerable service to the community when they support good causes where no other funding is available (as long as they do not try to form "intrusive ties" within the school system, argues the Canadian Teachers Federation).

What happens when private corporations begin to drive the research initiatives of Canadian universities? asks Linda Pannozzo, an author who still values the endangered idea of the independent research institution. Like many Canadians, Pannozzo is concerned that pure research will become a casualty of government cuts to universities, with the result that research will only be valuable if it benefits corporations who use the skills and facilities of the universities to further their corporate interests and not necessarily the public good.

Charles Gordon laments the advent of corporate sponsorship of Girl Guide Cookies: is nothing sacred? We have even gone as far, he argues, as permitting corporate sponsorship for the Ministry of National Defense in a donut commercial for the Super Bowl. How far are we, then, from the Tim Horton's brigade? Fearing that corporate sponsorship has become the way of the world, all Gordon can muster is a sigh of resignation and the fervent hope that concerned parents will make their feelings known when corporate interests try to get into the classroom.

Andrew Cash takes a very dim view of large companies who sponsor rock groups. He argues that these companies inevitably influence the kind of music that gets made, and notes a few instances of companies which have harmed musician's careers. He argues that artists can survive without the kind of patronage that companies provide: if the art is good enough, it will prosper. He also feels that companies are cynical and that their support is not about the music; it is about getting the company name to the target audience—in this case to youth for whom music is a particularly important form of cultural expression. In the end, Cash prefers "public" support of the arts—that is, government support, because it gives the public a share in the art, and the artist a sense of accountability to the public.

THE MARKETER AS HELPING HAND

David Menzies (*Financial Post 500*)

It was 1987, and AIDS had been recognized for the scourge that it was. Among other fund-raising efforts, a group of Toronto-based volunteers came together to organize Dancers For Life, a performing-arts gala to raise money and awareness in the fight against AIDS. The evening would go on to become a large-scale annual event—it celebrated its 10th anniversary this March at Toronto's 3200-seat Hummingbird Centre for the Performing Arts—but its first production had comparatively humble beginnings in a theatre one-sixth the size. Still, as preparations mounted for the inaugural performance, the organizing committee hoped that maybe—just maybe—Dancers For Life could attract some much-needed support from the ranks of corporate Canada.

Alas, fear-mongering and prejudice against AIDS sufferers meant that enticing big business to join the fight against the disease was no easy sell. Even so, a volunteer practised her sales pitch, took a deep breath and placed a phone call to Molson Breweries to see if it might be interested in supplying the event's reception with a few cases of Export or Canadian.

In retrospect, Dancers For Life staffers will tell you they wouldn't have been surprised if Molson had flatly refused the request. It's not that the beer company has a reputation of being tight-fisted when it comes to sponsorship. On the contrary. Each year, Molson pours millions of marketing dollars into such sporting endeavors as professional car-racing and NHL hockey. However, notes Ann Rosenfield, director of development for the AIDS Committee of Toronto (a Dancers For Life beneficiary), "Historically, in terms of corporate philanthropy, major corporations have never been major risk-takers, and for Molson to come on board with us, they took an enormous corporate risk. Molson was being asked to fund a cause that the general public found difficult to accept or even talk about."

As it turned out, Dancers For Life was pleasantly jolted by the response it received. Not only did Molson agree to supply the show's reception with beer, but—astonishingly—company executives inquired if there were other, more meaningful ways they could lend a helping hand. By the third year of the gala, Molson was on board as a fully-fledged corporate

David Menzies. The marketer as helping hand. *Financial Post 500* (1997), 1997. 60-73.

sponsor, providing funding for the event as well as using its considerable marketing muscle to promote the evening more professionally. "Their presence has been huge," says Judy Harquail, co-chair of Dancers For Life. "In addition to all their support, it was almost as if they gave us credibility overnight."

In fact, after Molson signed on, other corporate sponsors followed, including CIBC, Rogers Communications, Air Canada, Bravo!, AT Canada and Discount Car and Truck Rentals, among others. The pay-off for Dancers For Life is clear: this year's production netted more than $200 000 in a single evening, with the proceeds going to the AIDS Committee of Toronto.

But if you think about it for a moment, what's a beer company doing enlisting itself in the war against AIDS in the first place? Much of Molson's carefully crafted and lavishly produced TV ad campaigns would have you believe that the company is all about frenzied house parties, rock music and co-ed beach volleyball. And at first glance, there would seem to be little commonality between the manufacture and marketing of bottled beer and a debilitating disease. Yet around the same time Dancers approached Molson, the brewer was conducting some research of its own. In an attempt to get a grasp on the social issues that mattered to its customers, Molson was visiting university campuses and running in-depth consumer focus groups. As they say in the polling business, AIDS registered "top of mind" awareness.

"What we found in our research was that young adults were saying AIDS was very important to them," says Marilyn McCrea, Molson Breweries' director, corporate affairs. "For example, single, young males—our most important target market—were telling us that because they were sexually active, AIDS very much affected their lifestyle and it would be seen as a positive for us to get involved."

Based on this kind of response, Molson's sponsorship of AIDS-related causes has grown to include not only Dancers For Life but such initiatives as the Kumbaya Festival, AIDS Walk Canada, the CANFAR Youth Awareness Program, the Eight Ball Gala, Laughing Matters and Fashion Cares. In total, Molson has helped raise more than $8 million for AIDS-related causes. But the brewer's involvement is not just behind-the-scenes, cheque-book altruism. As McCrea stresses: "Whatever the event, we make sure that our logo, the M-hexagon, is always visible."

Welcome to corporate philanthropy, '90s style. Fading fast are the days when a company would simply pop a cheque in the mail to a specific charity because it was the personal favourite of the chairman's wife. Today, firms are embracing a new kind of benevolence in which altruism is merged with marketing. And unlike yesteryear, more and more companies are wearing the causes they support on their corporate shirt sleeves.

There is, of course, a sound commercial reason for this public display of goodwill. As Mark Sarner, president of Toronto-based Manifest Communications Inc., points out, "Research indicates that consumers care very much about what a company does in terms of social responsibility." Manifest, Canada's oldest and largest agency devoted to social marketing, last fall surveyed 350 of Canada's top 1000 companies, conducting interviews with 175 senior executives in public affairs. The result? "Less than 25 percent of the companies we surveyed considered that this kind of marketing had nothing to do with them," says Sarner. As for the others: "Companies with programs already in place plan to expand them, and several companies without programs plan to start them in the next 24 months." Sarner says only 17 percent of the companies surveyed believed it wasn't appropriate for them to become involved in social issues, while just 16 percent said it was unethical or exploitive for a corporation to take credit for supporting a good cause.

On the other side of the philanthropic coin, Sarner says one of the motivating reasons for companies embracing social marketing is the realization that old marketing techniques just aren't working the way they used to. Be it Exxon or Shell, Coke or Pepsi, Molson or Labatt, in the eyes of jaded consumers, gas is gas, cola is cola and beer is beer. Marketers would like consumers to perceive an added value in a particular brand. But the truth is, more and more consumer products are simply looked upon as commodities, and are virtually indistinguishable from a price/value/quality standpoint.

But social marketing doesn't just help to differentiate one product from another; it's also what Canadians want from their corporations. According to a study conducted by Toronto-based Market Vision Group, people in this country have come to demand more from big business in terms of social issues. A solid 41 percent of Canadians said they expect companies to have more involvement in the community than they did a few years ago, while 44 percent said they expect the same amount of involvement.

The net result of these findings makes for something of a dichotomy. Says Market Vision president Gregory White: "An increasing number of Canadians are expecting more community and charitable involvement from the private sector when most companies are downsizing and don't have anywhere near the same resources they had five years ago."

Given this reality, many companies have made the decision to combine philanthropy with mass-marketing, thus benefitting all concerned. Sarner cites U.S. research that suggests a company seen to be supporting a favourable issue will influence 68 percent of consumers at the point of purchase. Conversely, the Market Vision 2000 study indicates that consumers won't think twice about voicing their displeasure with a company by boycotting it. The reasons for a boycott, it should be noted, can be due to such factors as, say, a corporation's environmental record or its labour-relations policy. As Market Vision's White points out: "A growing number of consumers aren't just looking at the price, value or quality of the offering any more—they're also looking at the record of the offerer."

Sarner says that he received a telling response to the question "What should be the main reason to get involved in social marketing?" One-third of respondents said the purpose was to "Benefit society generally," while another third opted for "Maximize profits and/or develop a positive company image." Interestingly, the remaining third refused to choose between the two, and instead said that both reasons were equally important.

A glance at the corporate philanthropic landscape reveals that many companies are pursuing social marketing in the hopes of realizing this two-pronged agenda. McDonald's Restaurants of Canada Ltd. is a case in point. Director of communications Maureen Shaughnessy Kitts likes to point out that McDonald's has always been big on social marketing. In 1968, when senior chairman George Cohon opened his first restaurant in London, Ont., he donated the entire day's sales to a local children's charity. By 1982, the Golden Arches had established Ronald McDonald Children's Charities of Canada. To date, more than $3 million has been granted to Canada's 13 Ronald McDonald Houses (each one a home away from home for families of seriously ill children being treated at hospitals), and an additional $9.5 million has been given to other Canadian children's charities. McDonald's still likes to get its customers involved in the fund-raising process. On McHappy Day, for example, McDonald's earmarks $1 from the sale of every Big Mac and pizza for Ronald McDonald Houses. The call to action works wonders: sales of the specified menu items soar on McHappy Day, as, of course, does the amount of money given to needy families.

Kitts labels McDonald's cause-marketing strategy a win-win scenario for both the fast-food chain and the charities it supports. The charitable causes receive much-needed funding and awareness, and as for McDonald's, says Kitts, "We'd like to think that if two competing stores were side by side, perhaps the programs we're involved with would give us that extra competitive edge."

Amex Canada Inc. also funds a number of causes through the American Express Foundation, with recipients ranging from the United Way of Canada to the Learning Centre at the National Gallery. But David Barnes, vice-president of public affairs and communications, says the company has moved away from "cheque-book charity" and is increasingly focusing more on "how we can better help causes with our marketing expertise and the volunteer efforts of our employees."

Thus, when Amex supports Taste of the Nation—a benefit staged in conjunction with the hospitality industry to raise money and awareness for food banks—Barnes says that in addition to providing funding, hundreds of Amex employees volunteer their own time to sort and package food at various Canadian food banks. "We are not just into 'buying' a good image," says Barnes.

Still, Market Vision's White notes that there are two important caveats linked to social and cause-related marketing. "It has to be perceived that the company is in it for the long term," he says. "And it has to be an issue that matters a great deal to the market they're trying to attract."

In regard to the second caveat, White points to another finding from his Market Vision 2000 study—the ranking of Canadians' personal priorities—which more or less helps explain why some corporations are throwing their weight behind those causes that have little or nothing to do with their core business. Some of the highest priorities, according to Market Vision, include job creation, crime prevention, affordable/accessible health care, the environment and programs to protect abused women. Languishing at the bottom of the list are support for community and recreational events, amateur sports, the arts and—much to the astonishment of a couple of breweries—support for professional sports, which ranked last in terms of importance. "It was this finding that had me referred to as a sports marketer's worst nightmare," jokes White.

If anything, White says, the ranking of consumer priorities makes for a cautionary tale. If a corporation is visibly and actively involved with an issue at the bottom of the agenda, not an issue that is high on the list, it runs the risk of doing well at those things that don't matter a great deal. That, says White, "is the very definition of irrelevance."

Dr. Alan Middleton, a lecturer in marketing at Toronto's York University, says that in addition to bolstering the corporate image in the eyes of the public and government regulators, yet another reason for companies getting involved in social and cause-related marketing is that such initiatives "allow them to amass a reserve of goodwill . . . with the idea being that if something negative happens, they can draw upon that reserve."

Given the record-breaking profits of Canada's Big Five banks—and the public's negative reaction to the news—Middleton predicts that the banks will become much more heavily involved in social and cause marketing in the years to come. "Public criticism of the banks is sufficiently vocal that they'll want to try to better manage their image," he says. "I can almost hear the PR agencies being called right now."

Then again, White contends that social and cause marketing isn't so much about a corporation throwing money at a problem as it is about getting consumers to realize the company is indeed actively involved. "If you asked the people at the Royal Bank, they'd tell you they're doing a great job in terms of corporate philanthropy," says White. "They have a huge foundation and they are giving a ton of money away. I'm just not so sure anybody knows about this."

As a cautionary note, observers say embracing social-marketing initiatives can sometimes prove to be a double-edged sword. Middleton attests that any company setting itself up as a social crusader "will invariably be more closely examined by pressure groups, media commentators and consumers." And as Sarner highlights in *Social Marketing For Business*, a book he co-wrote for his company with Janice Nathanson, if not managed properly, social issues can turn against a corporation. Example: when the U.S.-based Christian Coalition asked AT&T to deny support to Planned Parenthood, the corporation conceded. Planned Parenthood's response came in the form of a full-page advertisement in *The New York Times* protesting this turn of events—all of which resulted in deep embarrassment to AT&T.

Closer to home, not all social marketing initiatives have been embraced with open arms either. As Middleton notes, a common concern of companies considering social-marketing programs for the first time is that their support of a do-good campaign might be looked upon by the public as nothing more than pompous self-promotion. A business that wants to get into social marketing has to be able to tread the fine line separating a social-cause champion and a braggart.

Then there's the line that separates welcome support and meddlesome propaganda. Maureen Morris, president of the Canadian Teachers' Federation, bristles at the idea of corporations trying to forge intrusive ties with the public education system that involve promotion of their product. "The CTF feels very strongly that if business is using their product as part of the curriculum, that's not what we would call a partnership," she says. "We would call that a misuse of their ability to support schools. Schools are there to provide education for students, not propaganda."

Despite some criticism, the likes of Sarner and White contend that more companies will indeed become increasingly involved in social and cause marketing. For a start, most Canadians seem to expect big companies to get involved in issues unrelated to their core business. And from a self-serving standpoint, social marketing is one of the ways a company can set itself apart from the competition. "I don't think there is any research to prove that this kind of marketing helps us sell any more cases of beer," says Molson's McCrea. "But just as there are people with brand loyalties, there are those who are cause-loyal. And if all things are equal, our cause marketing might just break the tie."

Consumers with Conscience

While a growing number of Canadian consumers will seek out and support those companies they deem socially responsible, those same consumers are more than willing to punish firms perceived as socially irresponsible. That's just one of the findings uncovered by Market Vision 2000, a groundbreaking study that tracked consumer attitudes toward corporations operating in Canada.

Released by the Market Vision Group in 1995, the report "really shook up corporate Canada," says company president Gregory White. One thing the report revealed was that 26 percent of consumers (a staggering 5.5 million Canadians) were actively involved in boycotting goods or services for reasons that had nothing to do with price or quality—the traditional reasons for shunning a firm. Rather, various boycotts were being organized due to some companies being perceived as bad corporate citizens.

"What we were seeing," says White, "was a new breed of consumer who's saying, 'Mess with my agenda and I'm going to mess with your bottom line.'"

Topping the boycott list were tuna companies (for endangering dolphins) and cosmetic firms (for animal testing). Nestle was prominent on the hit list due to its ill-conceived move of selling baby formula to Third World countries. In this case, it's clear that some consumers never forget. The company apparently is still being punished for a marketing strategy that was initiated—and discontinued—years ago. Procter & Gamble and McDonald's made the boycott list for environmental reasons: P&G because of concerns about disposable diapers and McDonald's because of hostility to polystyrene packaging. If anything, the inclusion of McDonald's demonstrates that different consumers have radically different agendas. McDonald's is highly regarded by many for its support of numerous children's charities, but for some people, that's clearly not enough to offset concerns about the food packaging the Golden Arches once used.

In the final analysis, White says his statistics reveal a majority of Canadians would prefer to deal with a company that's considered to be a social-cause champion. But if a firm is perceived as being uncaring or harmful in any way—watch out. "A significant number of Canadians will simply walk away," says White. "They'll hurt those companies where it hurts them most—on the balance sheet."

PEPSI U

Linda Pannozzo (*HighGrader Magazine*)

> We are faced by a problem of conformity brought on by our corporate structures. While the Universities ought to be centres of active, independent public criticism, they tend instead to sit prudently under the protective veils of their own corporations. Universities, which ought to embody humanism, are instead obsessed by aligning themselves with specific market forces.
>
> –John Ralston Saul, *Unconscious Civilization*

Last year, the School of Journalism at the University of King's College in Halifax, had a tough choice to make. Like any other university program, they were faced with having to make do with fewer government dollars. The pressures to offer the best program with the latest and most up-to-date equipment are real, especially when students could choose to go elsewhere. So when the Sable Island Gas Project came calling they made a point of listening.

The multi-billion dollar project to tap into the natural gas reserves off the coast of Nova Scotia has been touted as the one-stop solution for the job-challenged province. So, why were they interested in the J-school?

The project promoters stated they felt there was a need for a course in Science Journalism and were willing to pay for it. What better way to teach students how to write about the field of science than to have them write about the Sable Island Gas Project—where the class of budding journalists could put out a weekly newsletter with articles answering all those touchy, controversial questions the pesky citizenry were raising. Oh, and of course there would be editorial independence.

See any potential conflict here? The J-school did and decided to reject the offer.

University-industry "partnerships" have become ubiquitous features of university campuses. Corporate advertising is everywhere. Food is provided by names like Tim Hortons, Pizza Pizza, Burger King, universities sign exclusive contracts with soft drink companies in

Linda Pannozzo. Pepsi U. *HighGrader Magazine* 5(4), Summer, 1999. 23-25.

exchange for cash (Dalhousie University in Halifax is a Pepsi university), and pressure is palpable to commercialize nearly everything—even the cheerleading team at Acadia University has buckled and goes by the name Pepsi Power.

The new alliances have also hatched numerous research projects in the fields of biotechnology and applied sciences raising a raft of concerns about whether universities are selling their souls. For instance, Novartis Pharmaceuticals Inc. recently funded the first chair worldwide in xenotransplantation (using animal organs/tissues in humans) at Western University in London, Ontario. The $1.5 million investment by Novartis gives them access to the university's facilities, equipment and expertise.

If the research bears fruit, Novartis will be reaping quite a harvest. The expected profits to be made by transforming animals into organ factories is astronomical. One estimate is that by the year 2010, there will be a need for more than 500 000 pig organs alone—a drug industry revenue of $10–12 billion.

In John Ralston Saul's book *The Doubter's Companion*, he says that the "aura of independent expertise" that is unique to universities is being sold to governments and corporations. He writes, "universities are now desperate for money and only too eager to prostitute themselves. Presidents and their boards accuse the departments, who do not bring in their share, of fleeing reality. But do they have the right to destroy an essential creation of modern civilization?"

Sam Scully is the Vice President of Academics and Research at Dalhousie University. He's heard questions like this before and says they are "serious and appropriate." He says it's important to discuss whether private sector research funding is shaping or dictating the research agendas of universities and to what degree it distorts the amount of "basic" or non-directed research that is funded.

Scully says there are definitely more research dollars coming from industry but he argues it tends to go to the applied fields where they end up benefiting the public.

But Dr. Jeff Hutchings disagrees. He teaches biology at Dalhousie University. According to Hutchings, basic research is seriously underfunded and, yet, this is the research that will in the long-run best serve society. Conversely, industry funded research, by way of contracts to professors, Industrial Research Chairs and research grants via partnerships, prepares the university as a training ground for industry or government.

He says that when this happens, important questions no longer get asked.

"It's important to be able to conduct research and not be constrained by it," he says. "If I had a Department of Fisheries and Oceans Chair at the university, how much would I be able to speak out against the DFO, or draw attention to problems?" Hutchings says these associations would make independent and unfettered critique impossible.

The Federal agency that provides funding for university research is the Natural Sciences and Engineering Research Council (NSERC). It reports to parliament through the Minister of Industry. Funding what they call Industrial Research Chairs (IRC) has increased. Since 1988 the amount of money put toward University-Industry projects has nearly doubled and presently there are 258 IRC's across the country. According to NSERC the whole point of IRC's is to "respond to industrial needs." These Chairs, funded jointly by industry, are appointed for a five-year period, and can be renewed for another five years if "satisfactory" and industrial support continues.

Dr. Peter Rans is the director of program policy at the Nova Scotia Council on Higher Education. He says it is true that the amount of private money injected into university research has increased. He adds that governments want this and encourage it by creating incentives—even making money available for those that do.

A recent example of this is the Stora Enso Chair at Dalhousie University in Population Genetics and Molecular Breeding of Forest Trees.

Bob Fournier, who initiated the project, is Vice President of research services. He and Dalhousie president, Tom Travis, were on a trip to Sweden where they approached the forestry giant at their head offices. "We showed them that some of our capabilities and expertise at Dal could help them. In addition, we could leverage the money they contributed—put it in a proposal to the Federal government and double it."

Eventually, Stora donated $600 000 to create the Chair and Dalhousie submitted a proposal to NSERC to match it—with taxpayer's money.

The goal of the research is to focus on mapping the genetic make-up of economically important trees such as pine and spruce so as to improve productivity, that is, to create stands of the tallest, straightest, fastest growing trees which will boost profit for the company's shareholders.

Dr. Kristoff Herbinger is the project's Junior Chair. He says that since a large part of the funding comes from the company, they want something they can use in the end. "It has to benefit them."

Fournier argues that if it benefits the sponsor it also benefits the public. "If the company makes money then they stay here and provide jobs." He dismisses out of hand that direct involvement of industry in research is a bad thing.

"If it was 100 percent of what we do, then it would be an abomination to the university." As it is, $55 million is spent in research per year at Dalhousie and about $10 million of that comes from industry.

Fournier has no problem with the fact that taxpayers are partially subsidizing industry research. In fact, some argue they are wholly subsidized since many of the most profitable corporations in Canada pay lower rates of income tax than their lowest paid employees. Fournier rejects the implication that corporate money changes the notion of what a university can be.

"Some people think that now that industry has its nose in the tent it will definitely occupy the tent—they have no faith in the people who run this place." He says there is no cause for alarm, at least not yet.

While no limit has been set for industry money—things are being monitored, says Fournier. "If the problem emerges, then we'll deal with it. There are a lot of intelligent people concerned that it could be dangerous and at some point we may have to quantify it."

In March of this year, the Irving family of New Brunswick, owners of Irving Oil and the forest giant J.D Irving, offered Acadia University in Wolfville, Nova Scotia an "extraordinary" gift. For an undisclosed amount of money Irving offered to build botanical gardens, a campus meeting place and an environmental research centre.

Elaine Benoit, spokesperson for Acadia's office of public affairs, insists this will have no bearing on the research conducted. "We will continue to conduct the same kind of research we have in the past. It's not a buy-out, we're not selling ourselves to the family."

Ralston Saul argues that as the power of learning grew back in the second millennium, "universities became places which those with power sought to control. Initially the churches assumed this task." To undo the corrupt system now in place may be as "complex as the 18th and 19th century battle to separate church and learning."

HAVE WE FORGOTTEN THE TROJAN HORSE?

Charles Gordon (*Maclean's*)

The commercialization of just about everything began the day the Berlin Wall came down. That event represented the triumph of capitalism over communism, which no one will dispute, and the right of corporations to do anything they please, which hardly anyone seems to dispute either.

At least not yet. The free market is in. Regulation is out. Taxation is discredited. Government spending is passe. And what corporations do, provided it is within the letter of the law, is OK, even putting advertising on boxes of Girl Guide cookies.

Is nothing sacred? *The Globe and Mail* felt constrained to comment. Here is its editorial: "The Girl Guides of Canada are going to solicit advertising sponsors for their cookies. Sigh." Although the Guides founder "would probably have harrumphed herself into a coronary over it, advertising isn't immoral," *The Globe* continues, "we are a culture as much defined by what we buy as what we believe. And thinking creatively, is it just possible that, in addition to badges in pet-keeping, fishing and canoe safety, future Girl Guides could receive awards for demonstrating mastery of the fine art of product placement? Still. Sigh."

Could there be a better illustration of our modern dilemma? *The Globe*, as demonstrated by all the sighing, clearly knows that something is not quite right. But it cannot bring itself to say so, because "advertising isn't immoral" and because the Girl Guides are responding to market forces that are, by definition, good. Still. Sigh. This is not the only example of cherished institutions entering into partnerships with the corporate world. There is the well-publicized relationship between the Royal Canadian Mounted Police and Walt Disney. There is the Walt Disney Co.'s involvement with Canada Post, which issued a series of stamps featuring a Disney character.

More recently, there is a peculiar relationship between a doughnut company, the Canadian armed forces and the minister of national defence, as illustrated by a Tim Hortons commercial aired during the Super Bowl game. It shows the minister's limousine pulling up beside a Canadian Forces ship and several cases of Tim Hortons coffee being unloaded from the trunk for the coffee-hungry crew. This is likely to become a trend. Explained a Forces public affairs officer: "Next time I want to put out a brochure on a navy ship, I'm going to try to track down some company that's willing to put its logo on the back and cover the cost."

No money seems to have changed hands here, but are we, the Canadian public, ready for the idea of our armed forces being sponsored? Well, we know how strapped the armed forces are, and how much demands are already being placed on the taxpayer. If a corporation wants to help out, where's the harm? That's the conventional logic. Still, sigh.

Further examples are all around. Some are almost too familiar, particularly in the world of sports, where corporations are able to attach their names to anything that moves, not to mention skis, skates or drives. We take for granted the advertising on the boards in hockey arenas, or on the uniforms worn by tennis players and race car drivers. Rare now is the tournament, stadium or big game that does not have some corporation's name on it. And now Girl Guide cookies. Next: the northern lights.

Can we do anything but sigh at this corporate invasion of our public and private spaces? Well, sigh. To legislate bans would be in violation of many fundamental human rights. And that's assuming that the political will to take such action existed, which it doesn't.

Charles Gordon. Have we forgotten the Trojan horse? *Maclean's* 112(9), March 1, 1999. 11.

The answer lies, as it usually does, with us as individuals. If we protest and make a noise, things can happen. The Nike corporation came to Ottawa last year to offer a free gymnasium floor, then withdrew its offer when city councillors asked questions about the corporation's record in the Third World.

Continuing attempts by corporations to get their names into schools have also met with resistance. The most recent example involves a school being offered a satellite dish and television monitors in classrooms, on which students are shown 12-minute news broadcasts that include 2 to 2 1/2 minutes of commercials.

It is funding cuts, of course, that increase the appeal of such proposals. The school (or the city, or the hospital, or the team) gets some equipment it would not otherwise be able to afford, virtually free. Only on rare occasions does someone dare to suggest that virtually free is too high a price. But, in the case of the schools, that has happened in the past, with groups of parents and educators being able to convince departments of education to look gift horses in the mouth. That could work again, and it wouldn't hurt either to do some serious lobbying against funding cuts.

More direct approaches can work, too. Corporations are sensitive about their public image (otherwise, why spend vast sums to be just above the elbow on the left sleeve of a race car driver's jacket?), and will respond to letters of protest. A smart corporation president is like a smart politician—able to recognize when the mail, be it snail or e-, represents a segment of public opinion that it would be risky to offend. The president of a company thinking of putting the company logo on either the vanilla creme or the chocolate mint, would certainly think again after receiving some personal letters urging him or her to take another advertising approach.

If we want to stop the commercialization of everything, if we want corporations to keep their names to themselves, then we have to let them know. A sigh is just a sigh.

REBELS WITH SPONSORS

Andrew Cash (*This Magazine*)

It is 1987. The singer is standing offstage on the grounds of the University of Toronto, waiting. Beyond the stage is a throng of university students. They are drunk. It's their first week of post-secondary education. The band is announced over the p.a. system. As the singer begins to climb the stairs to the stage, a strange man turns to him and says, "I'd like to change your mind about corporate sponsorship."

That singer was me. The man backstage was the rep for the brewery sponsoring the show. But wait a minute: If the show was already sponsored by a brewery, what did the singer need to be convinced of?

This is how it happens. Band books a show. Band and promoter make an agreement—in this case, the promoter is the University of Toronto. But when the band arrives at the show, it discovers that there has been a third party involved in the deal. The telltale signs being the huge beer banners across the stage, the inflatable beer cans on the stage, and other beer-promotion material scattered about including baseball hats, tote bags and plastic cups. The only beer available is the sponsor's beer. And perhaps worst of all, the band is constantly being pestered by the evangelical beer rep.

Andrew Cash. Rebels with sponsors. *This Magazine* 28(7), March/April, 1995. 32-37.

If the band had any ethical questions about corporate sponsorship, the journey up to the stage is not the time to hammer them out. It's too late to cancel the show or to rip down the signs. Instead, the band goes on and it looks like they have given the brewery permission to advertise at their show. In an instant, what is for virtually all musicians the most precious of things—the making and performing of music for others—has become a vehicle for the promotion of beer.

That event at U of T crystallized the vague feeling I was having about a phenomenon which, like the emergence of rock videos, took most young Canadian bands by surprise. At that time, musicians like me were finding more and more that at the end of the night, our gigs were paid for, either wholly or in part, by a brewery.

Today, corporate sponsorship has permeated the music business on all fronts, through live music, radio and television. Given this reality and the seeming indifference of music fans to it, why are we still wringing our hands?

It all started back in the mid-eighties.

That's when Molson and Labatt discovered that rock promotion was a unique marketing tool—not to mention a cash cow. One of the first big, sponsored Canadian rock tours was Labatt's promotion of Platinum Blonde. Remember them? The Blondes were on their way to becoming a Canadian phenomenon, eventually selling half-a-million albums in this country. While there was some concern in the music business over the ethics of pushing beer to young rock audiences, the success of that tour set the stage for a war between Molson and Labatt for the rock dollar.

What ensued was a spending spree. Between 1985 and 1990 there was virtually no summer outdoor music or community event that did not have some financial support and advertising presence from one of the two big breweries. Whenever young people gathered around rock music, they were chaperoned by a beer company. Over the years, the constant use of promotions like the Molson Rocks campaign has helped entrench the idea that beer is what rock music is all about.

Today, many mega-rock acts and medium concert draws are paid directly by a brewery. Take the recent Rolling Stones tour. Canadian rock promotion company CPI promoted the entire Voodoo Lounge tour, and CPI is owned by Labatt. CPI's rival MCA Concerts is owned by Molson. And wherever these two promoters are—and they are everywhere—you'll find their parent companies.

A new corporate player has recently entered the rock and roll sponsorship sweepstakes. Export A cigarettes began funding a program last year called the Export A Inc. Plugged New Music Series. According to John Donnelly, its creator and producer, the program works as a trust fund. Unlike the sponsorship programs of the past where the sponsor would approach bands or promoters, individual bands are encouraged to apply to Export A themselves. For a club show, the band will receive $500 and free print and radio ads which promote the show and mention the sponsor. If the venue's capacity is over 1000 people, the band gets $1000.

In real terms, this is what the deal means: a fledgling band is doing a 15-date tour from Montreal to Vancouver. At $200 a night, the tour will inevitably lose money. The math is simple: $200 will just barely cover the gas costs to travel this vast country in a van. Add to that the cost of van rental, meals on the road, agent costs, long-distance phone bills and someone is out a couple of grand.

If, on the other hand, the band applies to Export A, it receives an extra $500 a night. A tour that is only netting $3000 is now getting an extra $7500. And that's not the end of it.

Export A may also throw in the agent's 15 per cent fee. What would have been a money-losing tour is now netting the agent an extra $1125.

In return for the cash, the band has to hang a few innocuous banners on the walls of the venue (you have to look very hard to see the Export A Inc. Plugged logo). This is definitely not the hard sell of the Molson Rocks blow-up beer bottle variety. That's because Donnelly, himself a 25-year veteran musician of the Canadian club scene, has been careful to allow the bands to remain the focal point.

But despite Donnelly's sympathies, for Export A, this deal isn't about musicians—it's about getting their product's name into the bars and on the radio. That's why anyone who can book a club can get sponsored; to date Export A Inc. hasn't turned anyone down. Forty-five bands and $400 000 later, Export A has just announced that it will be extending its program for 1995. Its rumoured budget is $1-million, which will include two fully-loaded tour buses.

As I write these words, I am tempted to call up Export A and jump on board. This truly seems like a great deal for a band. The only problem is that both my parents died from cancer, linked to smoking cigarettes. Both of them grew up in an era where the health risks of tobacco use were unknown. In fact, cigarettes back then were sometimes marketed as having health benefits.

It isn't the purpose of this article to go into the costs of our culture's addiction to tobacco, but it does need to be mentioned. After all, can any real discussion of sponsorship take place without considering the nature of the products with which we are involved and the impact they may have on our fans?

While Export A has limited its sponsorship to shows with audiences 19 years and older, the print and radio ads will reach a much larger market. This market includes teenagers—the people most likely to take up smoking, particularly if it is associated with something as important to them as music.

There is every reason to expect that other cigarette companies will jump into the fray. In fact, Belvedere has its own regional sponsorship program for bands in eastern Canada. In an industry that has such limited avenues to market its product, John Donnelly's brainchild may ignite a new spending spree similar to the one by the breweries in the eighties.

I am aware that my career as a musician and songwriter has been buoyed by corporate involvement in rock. Once you have been written up in a magazine, been on MuchMusic or had any radio play, you have achieved wider exposure through an advertising vehicle. So if you are offered more money and more exposure by becoming more directly involved with a sponsor—especially if the promotional idea isn't tacky—then why not take it? Is there really a difference between taking money from Warner Music or Sony Music and taking it from Labatt?

I think there is. Involving your art with a corporate sponsor is not the same as doing the work involved in trying to sell your art. Nor is it the same as accepting public money in the form of arts grants. Public arts funding gives the work a sense of public ownership and public service. Ultimately, that should mean public accountability.

If the existence of rock and roll relied upon the largesse of the corporate culture, sponsorships would be easier to justify. But it doesn't. The Canadian music business is a $900-million industry—we are not talking about modern dance or avant garde music, arts which need financial assistance from both the public and private sectors to survive. Rock and roll would exist without the involvement of a corporate sponsor. It would exist in a somewhat different form, but it would still have a large audience.

Advertisers, particularly cigarette companies, need music more than music needs sponsors. But corporate reps like Export A's John Donnelly say that we need to piggyback on their steam in order to get our message (i.e. music) out. "Hey look, you are in the music business," he says. "Remember that there is a second word in the title of our industry. You want to reach millions of people. Here are these giant corporations that do reach millions, that have the clout to run ads in newspapers simultaneously in every market in the country. They do have the clout to buy radio. But they need something to put in the spot."

But the truth is that it is the sponsor that needs to reach the rock audience. Music is one of the few media that has the attention and fidelity of young people; the relationship could be described as sacred. To be able to tap into, even mediate, between this reverential bond is any advertising executive's dream. The presence and influence of pop music is the envy of anyone—like beer and cigarette companies—who wants to sell to the 15- to 40-year-old rock demographic. While legislation prevents cigarette manufacturers from advertising directly (and curtails beer companies, albeit to a lesser degree), rock music has free-flowing access to this fertile consumer group.

Desperate to "fill their spots" with rock, advertisers will throw money at bands notorious for being broke. Helping the band, however, is really incidental to the process, but if a band does well, the sponsor is quick to grab the credit. Donnelly claims that without Export A's involvement, for example, west-coast singer/songwriter Art Bergman's recent tour would never have made it to Toronto.

While the corporate sponsor loves to paint itself as a patron of the arts, the truth is that there have been many more failures than successes in the rocky world of corporate sponsorship. Ethics aside, it could be argued that it isn't a wise business move to be sponsored directly by a beer or tobacco company if one of your career goals is longevity. Where is Platinum Blonde today? Or Chalk Circle? How is Allanah Myles' career going? What happened to the Spoons, whose career seemed to nose-dive around the time they did a clothing commercial? The problems of some of these acts can't necessarily be blamed on sponsorships, but there is no denying that, time and again, the famed naïveté of rock musicians has turned us into corporate dupes.

This happens in part because, just as the products the sponsors sell are addictive, so is their sponsorship money. There was a time when a band was booked into a venue when there was demand for the band. If no one wanted to see the band or didn't know of their existence, you did what you could to create a buzz. You played a Monday, Tuesday and Wednesday for free until you started drawing an audience. This protocol for rising up through the ranks tested a band's mettle and resolve. Quickly the weak cut out. Soon the poseurs did too because they discovered that the myth of the rock and roll lifestyle is a lie—it is bloody hard work and humbling. The bands that were left were the ones with an over-riding passion and gift and a pretty intense work ethic.

Corporate sponsorship works on very different principles. It plays on the bands' short-sighted desperation for overnight success. It is drummed into a band's head from day one that if they don't "make it" now they will be replaced. And it is very hard to go back—once a band has a little taste of sponsorship money, it will be difficult to imagine life without it. Small wonder the average career of a recording artist is about two years.

There is one obstacle faced by sponsors wishing to use rock as an advertising vehicle—part of the allure of rock is its rebellious image, its alternative views and counter-cultural lifestyle. This is part of the attraction for people who become musicians and part of the reason music is so important to its fans. Today, many bands become well known through word-of-mouth and grass-roots support. The hard sell and the over-hype make the discerning fan suspicious. The advertising world, however, has taken note of this shift in the public's taste and like Export A's low-key push—adjusted its own strategies accordingly.

Take last summer's Labatt ad campaign. Four bands appeared in very stylized, grainy black-and-white commercials. None of the bands were hyping the beer. In fact, the spots I saw looked no different than a good rock video. In one commercial, the lead singer for Toronto band The Headstones appeared and simply said, "Who cares."

In exchange for the appearance, cases of Labatt's beer contained a free CD single from one of the four bands. From the musician's standpoint, they weren't selling beer—they were selling themselves. And it worked. Both Hugh Dillon of the Headstones and Tom Wilson of Junkhouse have said that their records sold much better during the length of the campaign.

For Wilson the issue is simple. Labatt included 125 000 copies of Junkhouse's single "Praying for Rain" in cases of beer, and Wilson, who is a respected 20-year veteran of the Canadian music scene, is finally enjoying some success. "We have an obligation to ourselves as artists but we also have an obligation to our kids who are looking for their next meal," Wilson says. "I put all my integrity into my music. My responsibility after I finish creating music is to sell it so I can continue doing this. If I have to put an Export A banner up that doesn't bother me at all. It has nothing to do with me, with creating music or the next song I am going to write."

Wilson's bottom line is that the promo must be tasteful. If the band appears simply as an addition to a corporate promotional event, then no thanks. As he puts it, "If you want to be involved in my show then fine, but I don't feel like being involved in yours."

But whose show is it really? Part of the unwritten terms of any agreement with a sponsor is a certain measure of self-censorship—even if the restriction simply means not bad-mouthing the sponsor. Toronto Celtic stomp band the Grievous Angels found out the hard way that their involvement with the Mariposa folk festival a few years ago had some strings attached. Mariposa had swung a deal with Molson, who underwrote the cost of the festival at Molson Park in exchange for a promotional presence at the event. Since the band had been hired by Mariposa, not Molson, they decided to speak out against the level of beer advertising at the legendary folk festival. The remark offended the brewery reps and Mariposa threatened to withhold the band's pay and cancel the Grievous Angels' remaining shows at the festival.

Chalk Circle had a similar experience when the late-eighties pop band was booked to play a show in Ottawa. The Labatt promotion was so intense (there was an inflatable beer can right in the middle of the room, blocking some of the sight lines) that lead singer Chris Tait thought it would be funny to thank rival company Molson for putting on the show. Unbeknownst to Tait, Labatt was having a convention in Ottawa that weekend and all of the regional reps and the president of Labatt were on hand. They didn't see the humour in Tait's joke. One week later, the band was notified that the brewery would like a written apology. Tait refused and what followed, according to him, was that the band's entire summer festival tour mysteriously "fell through." Tait estimates that the band lost between $15 000 and $20 000 worth of work.

What lingers from all of this is an after-taste of control. Far from being the independent purveyors of alternative culture—let alone the last line of defense against conformity and excessive consumption—the music community ends up beholden to corporate sponsors. Maybe rock and roll doesn't really matter that much anymore. One of its fundamental components, after all, is its disposability. Still, it's undeniable that in a culture that has virtually no credible institutional role models, rock and roll has become what John Lennon hinted it was over 25 years ago: more important than religion, politics or school.

The bottom line is that bands don't want to be seen as vehicles for advertisers. Those of us who long for a place free from the incessant noise of the great North American selling machine have come to expect music and, more specifically, rock and roll, to be that place. Music turns all the rules around. It communicates in so many ways at the same time. There is no substitute for it. It is inclusive of all people and gives voice to our fears, longing and happiness. Advertising in music is about something very different.

If, as musicians, we don't wish to dwell on the ramifications of our affiliations, that is one thing, but it is highly doubtful that at some level the corporate sponsor hasn't weighed its affiliation with the band. Advertising has its own agenda. It excludes those who can't afford their products and it defines the way the product is consumed for those who do consume it.

The great danger for all musicians is that we lose the most important power we have: to set the terms for what we do. We lose ownership of it. We think we are still free to say what we want but we generally don't test the boundaries of that freedom. Those who do, whether by accident, stupidity or sheer audacity, discover that there is a price.

What is the effect, then, of the sponsor's mediation between band and audience? In among the vague nuances of what is cool and what isn't in pop culture, the question is hard to answer. This isn't the first time and it won't be the last that the corporate world has raided the innovations of youth culture and attempted to harness it to sell beer, burgers, blue jeans and now cigarettes. What is clear, however, is that this intervention definitely puts the band-audience relationship at risk. On a fundamental level, the nature of corporate sponsorship seeks to define what is acceptable rock and roll, just as it seeks to define who is acceptable as a consumer. It would suit corporate sponsors very well if rock and roll only meant partying, but at its best, rock has never been just about that.

If rock and roll was never to mean anything other than those inane beer commercials, all those band sponsors would be delighted. The irony is that if rock and roll were only that, it would never have attracted the corporate community in the first place.

DISCUSSION QUESTIONS

1. How visible is advertising on your campus? Is it beneficial to students to allow large corporations to advertise to students or to have outlets on campus?

2. Should universities allow corporate interests to support faculty research? Does such support undermine academic freedom or the public good?

3. Should public funds be used to support the arts? Are artists in fact more accountable to the public when they are given government money? Are they more able to express their ideas freely?

 ## WEBLINKS

Boycott Pepsi
www.euroburma.com/asian/euro-burma/pepsi

Alberta Report: "In the Maw of the Mouse"
Albertareport.com/23arcopy/2332aro1.htm

Expert Panel on Commercialization of University Research
acst-ccst.gc.ca/acst/comm/home_e.html

The Commercialization of University Teaching and Research
www.mscs.dal.ca/~dilcher/Comm/

chapter twenty three

Public Relations:
The Canadian Spin

INTRODUCTION

"Flacks, shills and spin doctors" producing bafflegab, newspeak and "the latrine of parasitic misinformation"; these are just some of the unkind epithets used to describe PR people and the misinformation that they produce (see Joyce Nelson's *The Sultans of Sleaze,* Toronto: Between the Lines, 1989, for a sustained critique of PR and the media). Despite this negative view, public relations has become a major source of public communication, often underpinning corporate or government lobbying and cover-ups.

Richard Swift examines the oil industry in Alberta and environmental destruction that is undermining the health of both humans and animals in Alberta's rich farm country. With gigantic budgets for public relations, large corporations consistently overpower citizen activist groups concerned about public health and the environment. Accusing the international public relations industry of creating an "Orwellian nightmare," Swift worries about the ability of large corporations to "administer" democracy for us and the inability of individual citizens to make themselves heard at all.

Bruce Livesey is even less well disposed to PR than Swift. Livesey documents some scandalous incursions of PR into politics: large American and Canadian PR firms helping governments hide political murders and maintain racist practices. Noting how powerful PR machines actually are, he wonders how much of the daily news is news and how much is PR. He concludes with the mordant statement: "PR is highly dangerous" in a democratic society.

David Weiner argues that PR practitioners get a bad rap in the press. Finding a certain amount of paranoia in many claims about the Machiavellian nature of PR professionals, Weiner argues that public interest groups are a greater threat to democracy because they frequently represent narrow private concerns and are seldom held to the same standards of truth as large corporations. Weiner sees PR professionals as "the antenna and conscience" for their clients who in the end push corporations toward "social responsibility."

The chapter concludes with an article by Peter O'Malley, a member of the Canadian Public Relations Society. O'Malley compares public relations professionals to lawyers: their obligation is not in the end to morality or fair dealing, but to their clients. He notes that much public relations is concerned with "crisis avoidance and damage control" and giving out selective bits of information (called focussed messaging) to minimize corporate disasters like Bhopal or the Exxon *Valdez* oil spill. O'Malley suggests four basic propositions that he argues give PR its ethical foundations, and in the end he maintains that the main moral decision that a PR professional makes is whether or not to represent a particular client.

MINDGAMES

Richard Swift (*New Internationalist*)

Alberta's romance with cowboy capitalism has proved a resilient one. Oil-rich and staunchly conservative, it is hard to find a more corporate-friendly jurisdiction—certainly not in Canada, perhaps not in all of North America—than here, in the eastern shadow of the Rocky Mountains. The corporations, particularly in the oil and gas industry, are most grateful. To hear them tell the story, as their public-affairs flacks are only too happy to do, a prosperous partnership is based on responsible self-regulation and "freeing enterprise" for the good of all. And it's not just words. The PR people point to a corporate-led volunteerism which supports everything from local theatre and museums to large hospitals and universities. Oil men—they are, almost invariably, men—sit on Boards of Governors, organize charity drives. They have wiped the mud off their cowboy boots long ago to become polite corporate citizens. Some companies, like Shell, present themselves as great defenders of nature and endangered species. Others, like Syncrude—the first company to go into Alberta's vast oil-shale fields, where reserves exceed those of Saudi Arabia—champion native art and culture.

But trouble is brewing in paradise. Wayne Johnston's voice breaks frequently as he tells me the story of his dealings with Big Oil, an unwelcome guest on his ranch in the Alberta foothills for more years than he cares to remember. Johnston is a sturdy, self-reliant man now plainly agitated. He sits at one end of the kitchen table, his wife Ila at the other. Wayne reels off the names of all the companies he's had to deal with over the years. Some, such as Shell and Amoco, are major global players. Others I'd never even heard of. The number of them here has exploded from 70 to more than 1200 in the past decade. The pipeline leaks were bad enough—the Johnstons claim one of them killed 30 head of cattle. But what really bothers them is the air pollution. It's associated with the "flaring" of superfluous but deadly sul-

Richard Swift. Mindgames: It's just a short step from political propaganda to corporate public relations. *New Internationalist* (314), July, 1999. 7-10.

furic "sour" gas. The Johnstons have had a lot of health problems with their cattle, particularly with pregnancies and calving. They are also worried about their own health.

Ila can hardly speak. I ask her about her persistent pneumonia. She shakes her head: "My lungs just aren't what they used to be." As if on cue, the phone rings and she goes over to answer it. "That was them again. We'll be getting intermittent flaring from compressor number nine, which is just across the fence."

Rural Alberta is mostly farmland owned by people like the Johnstons. The province is at the heart of Canada's oil patch and is dotted with hundreds of thousands of oil installations. It has been drilled with more than 230 000 wells, plays host to some 760 gas plants and is crisscrossed by 300 000 kilometers of pipeline. Farmers simply have no choice. In return for financial compensation—for loss of land use, and sometimes intermittent work tending oil facilities—they have to let the companies in. After all, this is a $26-billion industry. It owns or leases subsurface rights, provides 20 percent of the provincial budget and is a big backer of Premier Ralph Klein's ruling Conservatives.

If the farmers fight back, as the Johnstons have done, they are quickly branded as "troublemakers" trying to ruin the productive partnership of industry and community that is the centrepiece of energy-industry public relations. Then the stick replaces the carrot. Companies refuse to pay compensation. Whispering campaigns isolate "troublemakers." According to Wayne: "There are some neighbours that just try and avoid me now. Most of them have the idea that you can't do nothing, so you might as well collect the couple of bucks they give you and forget it."

Martha Kostuch has learned first-hand how the industry plays hard ball. Martha is a vet in the town of Rocky Mountain House, known locally as "Rocky" because of its fabulous backdrop of snowcapped mountains. Kostuch is a persistent thorn in the industry's side. She has seen the effects of air pollution on the health of the cattle from nearby ranches, effects that are now being verified by scientific studies. She says that, despite the PR spin by Big Oil to appear friendly to farmers and nature alike, "their image has always been poor."

Kostuch has been involved in several lawsuits and studies about shoddy environmental practices or inadequate legal processes. One of these efforts led to an investigation of the Shell gas plant in Caroline following complaints about poor air quality. Kostuch approached some 25 experts in the province to help her study these effects, but no dice: "I was told, if they work for me they'll never work in this province again." Kostuch says that behind the companies' sunny "partnership" image lurks a strategy of "intimidating, blacklisting and threatening." She points to calls in the middle of the night, locks changed on the doors of meeting halls, out-of-court settlements with gag clauses to keep people quiet. Still Kostuch is optimistic. She feels industry has to listen more these days because "the public is simply less willing to accept impacts, and more willing to speak out."

Things have indeed gotten very lively in rural Alberta. In the Peace River district the Alberta Energy Company (AEC) is facing off with a farmer named Weibo Ludwig, a leader of the communal Trickle Creek Farm and an outspoken critic of Big Oil. "The Peace" has witnessed a spate of eco-sabotage—sometimes known as "monkey-wrenching"—of isolated oil-company facilities. Although nothing has been proved, the industry plainly believes that Ludwig is involved. He too has cause for complaint: his farm is surrounded by gas flares. Already there have been three miscarriages and one stillbirth amongst the dozen or so women at Trickle Creek.

Then, last fall, an AEC oil site was bombed. Six days later the company sponsored a tour of local communities by an "anti-terrorism" expert from the Mackenzie Institute in Toronto—

one of those "strategic studies" institutes that provide a haven for right-wing propagandists. According to Ludwig's Edmonton lawyer, Richard Secord: "Some of the locals were ready to go down the road and lynch Weibo from the nearest tree." The industry strategy of defaming and isolating critics reached a new level. Shortly after that, Ludwig and another Trickle Creek farmer were arrested on various "soft" conspiracy charges relating to sabotage.

When Richard Secord tried to get his clients out on bail, he told me, he was shocked to read the Crown's disclosure information—the bomb had been planted by the Royal Canadian Mounted Police (RCMP), in collaboration with the AEC. This had been done, they claimed, in an attempt to catch the saboteurs. The shit hit the fan. According to Secord: "The media were particularly annoyed, having chartered a plane and being toured around the bomb site by both the company and the cops." Oil pollution became the main story, rather than "ecological terrorists"—a "deniable" local problem turned into a Canada-wide issue. The spin strategy had gone badly off the rails and turned into a PR nightmare for the industry.

Things got even uglier. When I turned on the TV news, back in Toronto, I was confronted with the image of Ludwig's bombed-out truck in the parking lot of the Comfort Inn in downtown Edmonton. Apparently, persons unknown had planted a bomb in the truck and blown it up, with Ludwig only yards away.

Out in Alberta I had met with the Rimby and District Clean Air People, one of the growing number of groups that has sprung up in rural areas to address issues of oil pollution. I asked how they felt when the story of the RCMP/AEC bombing broke. Answers varied. For some it was outrage. Others were awed by the power of an industry that can enlist the police, the government or whoever in their cause. Some felt the industry as a whole would not condone such activities and had been embarrassed by them. None of them was in the least discouraged from carrying on their own activism. Their frustration focused as much on the under-funded government regulators as it did on the oil companies themselves. According to Gord Laxer of the Parkland Institute, a research centre at the University of Alberta, public-royalty rates on oil and gas are three times higher in Norway and 1.75 times higher in Alaska. Yet Alberta's right-wing Premier always insists: "We have no revenue problem, only a spending problem."

What, then, does the case of Alberta have to tell us about corporate PR? One lesson is that most PR strategies have two faces. While industry may prattle on about partnership and responsibility, come a challenge and the gloves are off. Dialogue dissolves. "Isolate and Intimidate" is the name of the game.

In a sense, we have all come to live in Alberta. The vast increase in corporate and government PR worldwide means that those with power are falling over themselves to let us in on the good things they are doing for us. They are also quick to disparage both the intelligence and the motives of their critics. Billions are spent each year on this effort. The New York-based O'Dwyer's Directory of Public Relations Firms lists hundreds of companies with offices around the world. Interspersed among the corporate profiles are ads promising the world to prospective clients—"Reach the press without stress" or "Your PR agency has an office in Cairo run by a guy named Al." Overheads are low—a computer bank, some telephones, a bit of high-priced "creative"—so profits are high. Over the past two decades, growth in this sector has run at three times the level in the overall economy. And the actual PR firms are just the tip of the proverbial iceberg. To get a complete picture, you have to include the PR departments inside every major corporation, and a growing industry of professional spin-doctors on whom most politicians with any cash pin their hopes. Then add a plethora of pollsters, tele-marketers, focus-group organizers, think tanks and related "policy consultants." It's an enterprise whose collective purpose is to "administer" democracy, eliminating risks for clients. The key "project" is not to reform reality, but to manage our perceptions of it.

All this adds up to a propaganda effort of major proportions, undermining the cherished democratic belief that each citizen has the right to make up their own mind. When George Orwell wrote *1984* back in the late 1940s he saw the major threat to democracy as a kind of sinister totalitarianism. Brainwashing was backed up by the fear of police jackboots on the stairs. This is the classic image of propaganda usually associated with the heavy hand of the state. But PR gurus have transformed the propaganda industry, making its two faces much more subtle and userfriendly. Positive images of home and family, a trusted public figure, the wisdom of your grandparents or the inevitable bounty of progress are used to convince. There are negative threats to our economic well-being, if we get too squeamish about downsizing, privatization, environmental problems or child labour in Southeast Asia.

The original Orwellian nightmare still holds true in parts of the South. In places like Burma and Sudan, pro-regime propaganda is of the classic variety; a tightly-controlled media, streets adorned with huge billboards setting out the parameters of acceptable thought. Yet even the fundamentalists who rule Sudan have adapted modern "image" techniques—like martyr programmes on TV—to "celebrate" those who have fallen in their endless war on the south of that unhappy country.

Unsavoury regimes these days hire the best talent available to spruce up their international image. Among countless others, the two PR giants Burson-Marsteller and Hill and Knowlton have done particularly well out of what has come to be known as "the torturers' lobby." Their job is to represent regimes such as Turkey, Indonesia, Nigeria, Kenya—or the military regime in Argentina during its Dirty War, when the "disappeared" were being snatched off the streets and dropped from helicopters over the Atlantic.(f.1) The PR technique is simple enough: minimize the human-rights abuses, talk about it as a "complex," two-sided story, play up efforts at reform, speak of all the positive "modernization" that is going on and—most of all—the crucial economic stake "we" all have in Nigerian oil or Indonesian markets. If possible, it is best to put these words in the mouth of some apparently "neutral" group of "concerned citizens," or a lofty institute with academic credentials.

A lot of this kind of PR is done directly by the major corporations that have a stake in the South. The recent decision of Shell Oil to spend $32 million cleaning up its image, after widespread environmental damage and complicity in human-rights abuses in the Niger Delta region of Nigeria, is a classic case. The alter-image-not-reality approach has lead to an international campaign by the Boycott Shell Organization which sends postcards to CEO Jack E. Little demanding: "Why is Shell spending $32 million to clean up its image, not its mess in Nigeria?"

Perhaps the biggest—and certainly the most expensive—PR effort on a Southern issue was the campaign undertaken by the Wexler Group for the ratification of the North American Free Trade Agreement (NAFTA) with Mexico in 1993. Wexler worked for a coalition of Fortune 500 companies to reassure a worried US public about job losses and environmental deterioration. NAFTA's broken promises were so under-reported that Project Censored named them "one of the top-ten censored stories of the year," just one year after Wexler's successful sales job.(f.2)

The Australian analyst of corporate propaganda, Alex Carey, divides it up into "grassroots" and "treetops" varieties.(f.3) The first—like that in the Alberta oil patch—is either aimed at local communities or broad public manipulation. The second is primarily aimed at elite decision-makers. Together they make up a huge amount of public discourse on major political issues. Corporations hold that this is a legitimate cost of doing business. But it is hardly a contest of equals. The massive resources at the disposal of the corporate elite hugely outweigh the voluntary effort of citizen-activists trying to put the opposite case. It's as if a public meeting to make an important decision were attended by two or three people who are allowed to shout at the top of their voices, while the rest are forced to communicate in a barely audible whisper. Democracy it ain't!

Carefully-crafted soundbites from the powerful are a poor substitute for the rough-and-tumble of real democratic dispute. The expensive techniques of corporate PR are now exercised at the cost of other people's right to free speech—the democratic dice are loaded. Little wonder that many are becoming cynical and apathetic, sinking into a tranquilized silence. Why bother voting? Why bother speaking up? Why bother having an interest in anything but private pleasures and worries? And it's not just ordinary folk. Contemporary theorists of democracy are preoccupied with what has gone wrong, and how to set it right. From Robert Dahl to Norberto Bobbio, they feel the democratic promise can only be revived when the public are encouraged to form and act on their own opinions—not just to parrot the company line.(f.4)

A democracy where the public conversation is managed—and often silenced—by PR professionals and their ilk must be resisted. Even in unlikely places like the Alberta oil patch, it is possible to outsmart them as they trip over their own arrogance. Perhaps corporations should be expelled from the political process entirely and restricted to the narrower business aims for which they were originally incorporated. But, however it is done, it has to be done. Included in the rich legacy left us by the cultural critic Raymond Williams are these words: "[We] must get rid of the idea that communication is the business of a minority talking to, instructing, leading on the majority... the false ideology of people who are interested in communications only as a way of controlling people, or of making money out of them."

Notes

f.1   John Stauber and Sheldon Rampton, *Toxic Sludge is Good for You*, Common Courage Press, Monroe, Maine 1995.

f.2   Nancy Snow, *Propaganda Inc*, Seven Stories Press, New York, 1998.

f.3   Alex Carey, *Taking the Risk Out of Democracy*, University of Illinois Press, 1997.

f.4   Stephen Coleman, *Stilled Tongues*, Porcupine Press, London, 1997.

PR WARS: HOW THE PR INDUSTRY FLACKS FOR BIG BUSINESS

Bruce Livesey

Beside me, Bob Heim was becoming rather agitated. After all, it was his job as a PR flack to make sure I didn't ask his boss any pointed questions. The problem was, I was doing just that.

It was October of 1994 and I was in the Bahamas interviewing the South African multi-millionaire and casino tycoon Sol Kerzner. Myself, Kerzner and Heim, the tycoon's PR point man, were sitting in a spartan basement office located in one of Kerzner's new casinos. But Heim was getting ticked off with my questions—ones like: "How did you feel about Sun City being associated with apartheid?"

It was a relevant query. After all, Kerzner is the hotelier who built Sun City in a black homeland just outside Pretoria in 1979. A Las Vegas-styled casino-resort that catered to affluent white South Africans who wanted to gamble, party, ogle topless dancers and bed prostitutes, Sun City was boycotted by the United Nations in the 1980s, even becoming the subject of an anti-apartheid song called "I Ain't Gonna Play Sun City."

This resort was singled out because Kerzner was getting rich from one of apartheid's most evil policies—the creation of the so-called "independent" homelands. Designed to segregate blacks and exploit them as cheap labour, the white regime installed corrupt puppet governments to run them and forcibly removed blacks to live in these arid, remote parcels of land. There, people subsisted in horrific squalor.

Kerzner built Sun City in Bophuthatswana, which was ruled by a dictator named Lucas Mangope, who was propped up by a gang of mercenaries from Ian Smith's Rhodesian regime and South Africa's intelligence service. The hotelier went on to establish casinos in other homelands, often using bribery to grease the wheels. In 1989, he publicly admitted he'd bribed the former prime minister of the Transkei to the tune of one million dollars to secure that homeland's gambling rights. To this day, Transkei has a warrant for Kerzner's arrest.

When I met Kerzner two years ago, his company, Sun International (UK) Ltd., had just bought three bankrupt casinos in Nassau to exploit the lucrative North American tourism market. Sun International is one of the world's largest casino-resort chains, controlling 33 mega-hotels and earning annual revenues of one billion dollars. To stir up press coverage for the reopening of the casinos, Kerzner was flying in journalists from all over the world by the planeload. As a freelancer, I was assigned to profile the South African businessman for the *Financial Post*.

What I didn't expect was such a well-oiled PR machine. Kerzner had hired a bevy of PR firms in the U.S. and Europe to shepherd journalists through his new resort. I was met at Nassau's airport by Bob Heim, a senior vice-president of M. Silver Associates Inc., a New York-based PR firm. Heim plied me with a bushel of press kits and video displays trumpeting Kerzner's business successes. None of this material mentioned the profits Kerzner had made from apartheid. We were put up in the casino's swanky suites for free. Heim wined and dined us at ritzy restaurants, and even gave money to one journalist who wanted to do some late-night gambling.

And, of course, Heim sat in on all the interviews with Kerzner, making sure nothing went awry. (Kerzner gave a disingenuous reply to my question about Sun City and apartheid, saying: "We never supported the system.")

Kerzner's use of PR to seduce journalists into writing puffery—and to overlook the stains of his past—is by no means unusual. Corporations that befoul the environment, sell shoddy and dangerous products, collude with Third World dictatorships, and seek to influence government policies to better their bottom lines are increasingly turning to the PR industry for assistance.

A Booming Industry

The PR industry—which Britain's *Guardian* newspaper once called the "latrine of parasitic misinformation"—has enormous impact on debates about a host of critical issues. PR firms furtively mobilize private detectives, lawyers, high technology and spies, influence editorial and news decisions, launch phoney "grassroots" campaigns—all to further right-wing and corporate causes.

According to Joyce Nelson—one of North America's foremost critics of the PR industry and author of the 1989 book *Sultans of Sleaze*—social justice groups seeking press coverage often find themselves up against PR firms with large war chests and powerful connections in the media. "It becomes PR wars," she says.

So popular is PR among corporations and governments that the PR industry is booming. Today, there are approximately 9000 PR firms in North America with a combined ten billion dollars a year bankroll. They employ 165 000 PR professionals—as compared with an estimated 140 000 journalists who work for newspapers, radio and TV stations. More alarmingly, this PR colossus is the primary source for at least 40 to 50 percent of all the "news" we read, hear and see in the mainstream media. It may be even more, given that newspapers and broadcasters have been laying off reporters in recent years. Indeed, Nelson estimates as much as 80 percent of the news we imbibe originates from PR people.

True, much of PR is benign, and some is even produced by unions, social justice and anti-corporate groups. But a great deal is downright insidious, designed to manufacture consent for neo-conservative policies. Produced by Canadian and U.S.-based firms that span the globe, PR has been used to whip up support for the 1991 Gulf War, hide the human rights abuses of Third World juntas, defame environmental groups fighting clearcut logging and lobby for free trade. Today, it's even helping to lay the groundwork for the privatization of Medicare and other government services.

Why is PR in such demand? Largely because the chemical, nuclear, oil, tobacco, pharmaceutical, food processing, mining, arms, forestry and other industries with poor environmental and public health records have realized it's cheaper to change people's minds rather than their own manufacturing practices. As media critic Morris Wolfe once said: "It is easier and less costly to change the way people think about reality than it is to change reality."

Just how powerful is PR?

Take the Gulf War as an example. After Iraqi dictator Saddam Hussein invaded neighbouring Kuwait in August of 1990, it was apparent that very few North Americans knew where Kuwait was, and most really didn't care less that it had been overrun.

Thus the deposed Kuwaiti ruling oligarchy realized it needed to manufacture support for an armed intervention to get back its oil-rich fiefdom. As documented by the CBC's "the fifth estate" in its award-winning 1992 broadcast, "To Sell A War," a temporary coalition of Kuwaiti citizens and government officials—called Citizens For A Free Kuwait—was established.

This coalition paid $10.7-million to America's second-largest PR company, Hill & Knowlton Inc., to generate public and Congressional backing for a war against Iraq. One of Hill & Knowlton's tactics was to produce video news releases designed to portray Hussein as evil incarnate. The most effective one they made featured a 15-year-old Kuwaiti schoolgirl tearfully testifying before a Congressional caucus. She said she'd seen Iraqi soldiers enter a Kuwaiti hospital, take 22 babies out of incubators, and leave them to die on the "cold floor." Hill & Knowlton used the incubator story to push the U.S. government and United Nations into declaring war on Iraq.

But as "the fifth estate" revealed, the incubator story was a complete fabrication. Moreover, the 15-year-old girl turned out to be the daughter of Kuwaiti's U.S. ambassador and was unlikely to be anywhere near a hospital after Iraq's invasion. As the publisher of

Harper's magazine, John MacArthur—who wrote a book about propaganda and the Gulf War—said: "(It's) an incredible subversion of democracy when you begin allowing PR firms . . . to make the decision on whether or not we're going to war."

If PR firms are not manufacturing atrocities, they are covering up real ones. Indeed, dictatorships in Guatemala, pre-revolutionary Nicaragua, Indonesia and Franco's Spain used PR firms to hide human rights abuses.

Jorge Garcia Orgales, 44, a good-humoured labour activist who lives in Toronto, knows how effective such PR can be. In the summer of 1975, he was working as a young labour lawyer in Buenos Aires, Argentina's capital city. Back then, Argentina had a militant trade union movement and a tiny left-wing guerrilla force numbering about 1000. Yet the government was slowly falling under the sway of the military. Late one night, a group of non-uniformed soldiers burst into Orgales' apartment, stripped him and his wife naked, assaulted and interrogated them for two hours, even threatening to torture their baby boy before their eyes. Finally, the couple was dragged off to prison and charged with possessing left-wing literature.

In March of 1976, while Orgales was locked up awaiting trial, Argentina's army generals staged a coup d'etat, closing down the country's parliament. On the day of the coup, Orgales and other political prisoners were placed in solitary confinement. Immediately the army went on a killing spree against Argentina's left. During the five years of this so-called "dirty war," 35 000 Argentinians "disappeared." Military death squads kidnapped, tortured and executed them. In many cases, the bodies were dumped into the Atlantic Ocean by helicopter. Countless thousands were imprisoned and tortured.

During his two years in solitary confinement, Orgales was regularly taken out of his cell, stripped naked, hosed with ice-cold water for 45 minutes, and then beaten by soldiers. "They would sometimes burn me with cigarettes," he recalls.

Yet such stories were not reported outside Argentina: Indeed, in the West there was a virtual media blackout about the military's atrocities. A survey of 60 American newspapers revealed that only 10 items about Argentina mentioning the words "torture," "death squads" and "disappeared" appeared in all of 1978. Why? One reason is because shortly after the 1976 coup, the generals hired the largest PR firm in the world, Burson-Marsteller Ltd.

Based in New York, and with 62 offices in 29 countries and annual billings of $192 million (U.S.), B-M specializes in flacking for corporate and right-wing interests. On behalf of Argentina's generals, B-M ensured that only favourable press coverage—and no mention of death squads—made its way into the international media. In one memo, B-M said the aim of its PR campaign was "to generate a sensation of confidence in Argentina among the ranks of the target audiences in eight countries around the world, through projecting an aura of stability for the nation, its government and its economy."

By chance, Orgales was released from prison during the 1978 soccer World Cup, which was being staged in Argentina that year. Usually when a political prisoner was let out, he says, they were met by a death squad at the gates and never seen again. When Orgales came out, he was greeted by a gaggle of foreign journalists who were covering the World Cup. Twenty-four hours later, the labour lawyer was on a plane to Holland.

Orgales observes that when he moved to Canada in 1982, "most people knew of Argentina because of the Falklands War. Some progressives knew about the death squads, but most other people did not." For this, Argentina's military junta could thank B-M's five-year PR campaign.

How They Do It

PR is not new, having been invented in the U.S. at the turn of the century. From its early origins, though, PR was designed to protect the rich and powerful from public scrutiny, and to justify and downplay the misery chasmic inequities of wealth inevitably create.

To this end, PR companies embrace methods that are sophisticated and scientific, utilizing polling firms, lobbyists, focus groups and the latest in video and communications technology. Such firms even boast of their ability to manipulate. One Burson-Marsteller sales pitch says it can "manage issues by influencing—in the right combination—public attitudes, public perceptions, public behaviour and public policy." Last year, the CEO of Toronto-based Burson-Marsteller Canada, Sheila Rathke, was quoted as saying that where "traditional" communications seek to clarify or explain, her firm's goal is to "impact behaviour."

One reason PR firms are effective is because they often employ former journalists. Indeed, many of Canada's leading journalists have been, or are now, PR flacks. They are often enticed to quit newspapers and television stations by better pay and less frenetic working conditions. While the starting salary at a newspaper like *The Globe and Mail* is $672 a week, a starting salary for an Ontario government PR position is $819 per week.

Yet some believe that journalism and PR are inherently inimical. "The difference between journalism and PR is that journalism tries to show centres of power, how they work and the effects of how they work," says Loren Lind, a journalism professor at Ryerson Polytechnic University. "PR tries to cover them up and disguise the actual workings of centres of power."

This was William Burrill's experience. In the early '80s, Burrill, 42, was a *Toronto Star* columnist and assistant features editor. But in 1985, after having a falling-out with the newspaper's top brass, he quit and became a PR officer with Ontario's Ministry of Environment. There he saw how PR people manipulate the press. "There was a pecking order of favoured journalists," recalls Burrill. The favoured ones would receive the ministry's press releases via courier, while those who were out of favour would get them by third-class mail. This practice often affected reporters' careers, Burrill relates, because if they were late in getting a breaking story, they would catch hell from their editors. "(The ministry) could more or less control the fate of reporters," says Burrill. "The government got people replaced."

Burrill's bosses told him to always use diminishing metaphors when describing pollution problems to the media. "If there was 100 parts per million of dioxin in water, we were told to say that this is like one inch to the moon, or one drop in a lake," he remembers. "We were told to diminish everything, to indicate that (dioxin) was of no environmental concern. We were told to tell people that it had always been there and the only reason it was showing up was because of advanced technology."

Nineteen months after taking the job, Burrill resigned his PR post to return to journalism.

Pressuring the media is a time-honoured tradition in the PR trade. An editor I know at the *Financial Post* recently told me that of the 60-odd phone calls he fields every day, one-third are from PR firms following up on press releases. Such pressure can be effective, as the case of the *Vancouver Sun* and its coverage of the forest industry reveals.

By the late '80s, B.C.'s forest industry had an international reputation for being the "Brazil of the North" as a result of its habit of clearcutting rainforests. Moreover, environmental groups like Greenpeace were making strides in pressuring European countries to stop buying B.C. pulp and paper. The forest industry fought back with PR blitzes. "There's a term called 'greenwash' to label the propaganda MacMillan Bloedel puts out," explains Dan

McDermott, executive director of the Toronto-based environmental group Earthroots Coalition. "(This PR) says how good deforestation is. (One forest industry flack) often says forests are improved through logging, and that a clearcut is not the loss of a forest but the creation of a meadow."

Initially, many of these PR campaigns were ineffective. So, in 1990, the Council of Forest Industries of B.C.—the forest companies' main lobby group—secretly went shopping around for a PR firm. Eventually it hired Burson-Marsteller. B-M suggested that a separate, arm's-length organization, called the B.C. Forest Alliance, be set up. Its purpose would be to stimulate public support for the forest industry.

With a two million dollar annual budget culled mostly from sixteen forest companies, the Alliance declared war on environmentalists and the press. It sent delegations to Europe to persuade customers to continue buying B.C. wood, disrupted Greenpeace meetings and ran ads in newspapers.

The Alliance would also frequently meet with the editorial board of the *Vancouver Sun* to complain about its coverage. Soon *Sun* journalists were feeling the heat. One was even asked into his editor's office, where he was interrogated by a logging company official. Eventually, the number of reporters covering B.C.'s natural resources industry was chopped from five down to two.

Moreover, polls showed public support for government intervention in the forestry industry was plummeting, from 73 percent in 1990, down to 40 percent three years later. Today, Joyce Nelson says forestry practices remain as destructive as ever, yet "basically, (the forest industry) has worn down people. People get tired of the issue—and that works in (the industry's) favour."

Burson-Marsteller is active not only in Lotusland, though. Nelson has revealed its presence elsewhere, notably:

- In Mexico, where the Mexican government hired the PR firm in 1990 to promote the country's position at the NAFTA talks. B-M received eight million dollars (U.S.) for this contract.

- Colluding with the Trilateral Commission (TC), the world's most powerful corporate-government planning body. The commission has close ties to B-M. Indeed, from 1992 to mid-1995, former Canadian ambassador to the U.S., Allan E. Gotlieb, was the North American deputy chairman of the TC, as well as chairman of Toronto-based Burson-Marsteller Canada. In conjunction with the PR firm, the TC successfully lobbied for the passage of NAFTA, which came into effect in 1994. (During the 1988 federal election, 56 million dollars was spent by the Mulroney government and corporations on a PR campaign to persuade the Canadian public to support free trade. Much of this money came from U.S.-based multinationals.)

- In the debate about Medicare's future, the Trilateral Commission and B-M, in collusion with a powerful cabal of government, banking and think-tank officials, are now pressing to have Canada's health care system privatized. American health-care and insurance companies are hoping to grab the spoils.

In the States, PR is even more intrusive. There, PR firms have developed sophisticated means to undermine the efforts of community and social-justice movements. One of the most effective ways is to set up competing groups. Known in the trade as "astroturf," this tactic is designed to garner public support for corporate causes at the grassroots level. PR firms have successfully been used to counter NIMBY (Not In My Backyard) groups that protest the dumping of toxic wastes.

Ultimately, the PR industry's encroachment into, and influence on, the media—combined with its take-no-prisoners tactics—means that Canadians are poorly informed about numerous important political, economic, health and environmental issues that directly affect them. This is truly alarming. Indeed, as Nelson maintains, "if we believe in upholding the principles of democracy—and to do so depends on an informed consent—PR is highly dangerous." Much more than most people realize.

A PR PRO FIRES BACK

David Weiner (*Marketing Magazine*)

A number of recent media reports have vilified public relations consultants ("Flack Attack," *The Globe and Mail*, Oct. 31, 1998; "The Public Relations Industry has a PR Problem," *Report on Business Magazine*, November 1998; and "Truth Merchants," "Witness," CBC-TV, Nov. 5, 1998) accusing them of thwarting the role of the media as a "public forum for democratic discourse."

In suggesting public relations consultants use Orwellian tactics to deceive and mislead the public, these media have put a "spin" on the facts beyond the imagination of any communications practitioner.

The democratic discourse so cherished by industry critics must provide freedom for corporations, government or citizens' groups to contribute to public dialogue through advocacy. Companies have a right and an obligation to shareholders and employees to explain and defend their positions.

Critics see only conspiracy, deceit and manipulation in the workings of public relations consultants. Do they believe that media alone should serve as police, judge and jury on public issues? As in the judicial process, are individuals and companies not also entitled to the best counsel in the court of public opinion?

Public relations advisors are not saints. But neither are the journalists so quick to attack them. That's probably why public distrust of the media has never been higher. Are self righteous "media hacks" who don't let truth get in the way of a good story any less a threat than so-called "PR flacks"?

Spin is no substitute for truth. The role of the free press, as brokers of public opinion, is to separate fact from fiction—to interpret, assess and report news. Just how well do they meet this test? The public relations industry did not create "Geraldo" or "Jerry Springer." Nor did it invent the 10-second "sound bite" that reduces complex issues and encourages nanosecond attention spans. The media makes no contribution to public dialogue when it panders to the lowest common denominator, whether it's O.J., Diana, or Lewinsky.

It takes two to tango. There are bad journalists and bad PR types. When "Dateline NBC" publicly admitted it staged an explosion of a GM truck to make its point, it was more guilty of "spin" than anything the PR industry could be accused of.

Conspiracy theorists see cloak-and-daggers in corporations that support advocates for their cause. Is an industry expert speaking for a company to be denounced as a "paid shill" while a dilettante from a "public interest" group is acknowledged as a "credible source"?

David Weiner. A PR pro fires back. *Marketing Magazine*, 103(45), November 30, 1998. 70.

Why is a letter-writing campaign orchestrated by an interest group accepted as free expression, but condemned as a manipulation if done by a corporation?

In fact, one of the most insidious threats to democracy may lie in the activities of public interest groups, which are often little more than creations of media. Increasingly, social activism has become a caricature of itself. Assemble a handful of friends, get some placards and alert the media. A sure fire formula for getting on the nightly news no matter the cause. Bring the kids along to march as well. Better television visuals. More sympathy.

The "public" interest that such groups claim to represent is often just the "private" interest of its members. Would these groups be judged by the same standard as the companies they denounce, or submit to the same level of mandatory disclosure?

Did Michael Shapcott disclose his political aspirations when his "Bread not Circuses" coalition killed Toronto's last Olympic or Expo bids? (He emerged as an NDP candidate in the next provincial election.) Did media analyze the impact of the city losing billions of dollars of economic development as a result?

When Greenpeace confessed to the international community that it had used bad science to denounce Royal Dutch Shell's Brent Spar project in the North Sea, did media question their actions and behaviours?

Those critics who rant against the PR industry overlook its indispensable two-way role. In addition to speaking, the second, equally vital, role of public relations is listening. As the antenna and conscience for their organizations, public relations professionals have been important agents of change, driving much of what we now call corporate social responsibility.

In dismissing the role of the public relations counsellor as bridge-builder, critics would reduce democratic discourse to adversarial confrontation.

Small wonder the general public has become disillusioned with the political process and national institutions. Society becomes increasingly ungovernable as values diminish and truth becomes a question of whose truth. Can the demise of tolerance, civility and social order be far behind?

The lesson for all: As a society, each of us has an obligation to better seek and discern the truth, or pay the consequences for not doing so.

IN PRAISE OF SECRECY: THE ETHICAL FOUNDATIONS OF PUBLIC RELATIONS

Peter O'Malley (*Vox*)

When pondering ethical matters in the abstract, there is a natural and powerful human tendency to want to reach personally comforting, and perhaps truly inspiring, conclusions, even if it requires that we overlook the obvious.

Such appears to be the case with the Canadian Public Relations Society (CPRS) Code of Professional Conduct, which preaches that ethical professional conduct for public relations practitioners has something to do with promoting "honesty, accuracy, integrity and truth" in public communications. While this notion might be truly inspiring, it nonetheless fails to adequately grasp what public relations is centrally all about—namely, the advocacy and dissemination of the partisan viewpoints of those who engage our services.

Peter O'Malley. In praise of secrecy: The ethical foundations of public relations. 1998. www.cprs.ca/cprspraise.html (Originally published in the October 1976 issue of *Vox*, The Newsletter of the Ottawa Chapter of the Canadian Public Relations Society. Revised by the author May 1998.)

Contrary to what the CPRS Code says, the real basis for defining how we serve the public good, and for our ethical professional behaviour, is not found in any set of transcendent values, however inspiring they may be. Rather, our ethics are stated in the terms of the contracts we freely enter into with the clients we choose to serve. As with lawyers, the deal is not complicated. We agree to use our expertise to promote the interests of the client—as ultimately defined by the client—within the parameters of the law, in exchange for which they compensate us, usually in the form of cashable cheques.

In some specific instances, a client's true interest may lie in complete openness, transparency and disclosure in their public communications, and even in tub thumping to draw attention to their story and message. In such situations, we have every reason to be candid, open and forthcoming. We may even get to hire brass bands, barkers and clowns, balloons and airships to get the client's message out, thus fulfilling our abiding ambition to be enlighteners of the public, perhaps with a mark-up.

In many instances, however, the client's interest lies in seeing that a particular fact, or set of facts, never see the light of day, and if they do, to minimize the impact, duration and even the clarity of any resulting reporting and public communications. This is crisis avoidance and damage control. As we all know, it constitutes a large part of what we do for a living. It is also what many clients most value in our work.

In crisis situations where a client's real or perceived culpability in a matter is low, damage control can be, and usually should be, approached in a manner that may happily promote "honesty, accuracy, integrity and truth." (Example: the Tylenol crisis, where the company was seen to be a victim.) In situations where the client's perceived or real culpability is high, however, damage control almost always means being highly selective in what is said publicly, and very careful about when and where anything at all is said. (Example: Bhopal, or the Exxon *Valdez* crisis.)

In all instances, on both practical and legal grounds, effective public relations means not lying or defaming. But when perceived or real culpability is high, damage control inherently requires that engaged PR practitioners not volunteer facts they may know which are true and relevant—maybe even important to getting at the "truth" of the matter—but the disclosure of which would be harmful to the client's interests. And it frequently requires being steadfast in characterizing a "nearly empty" bottle as being "almost full." We may like to call all this "focused messaging," but in plain language, it means being selective in the presentation of information, and being secretive. It may also mean being disingenuously muleheaded. All of this may serve the client's interests, but none of it serves to enlighten the public.

If it is true that, as a profession, we are not, fundamentally and at all times, in the "honesty, accuracy, integrity and truth" business, does it then follow that there is no ethical foundation for what we do? Not at all. There are, I believe, a set of important, societally sanctioned propositions around which to anchor our professional conduct, once we move beyond the silly idea that we are really journalists, once removed from the news copy.

I offer the following four propositions which gives public relations an ethical foundation.

1. We live in a society which espouses and values "freedom of the press," which in practice means that the only people who can "control" what is reported are those who own media, and who assign and pay the reporters.

2. Reporters in our society operate according to a standard set of reporting protocols and formulae which, in general, shape and determine the reporting outcome—namely, the published news report.

3. Through study and experience, one can develop expert knowledge of these standard reporting formulae. Using this expert knowledge, it is possible to intervene in the reporting process in a manner that has a reasonable chance of influencing the reporting outcome in known ways. This is what public relations professionals do.

4. Finally, our society affords people the right to manage their self-defined interests in the reporting process as they see fit, within the parameters of the law, and to avail themselves, by financial or other inducements, of the services of those who are expert in doing this.

Thus seen, public relations is a product of our societal commitment to freedom of the press, and to the freedom of citizens to look after their interests in dealing with the press. (This explains why totalitarian regimes need propagandists, who disseminate information through controlled media, but have no domestic need for PR professionals, who influence reporting outcomes through media they do not control.)

From this it follows that the "public good" served by public relations lies in its ability to promote the rightful and lawfully pursued interests of those we serve, ultimately as they define their interests. It means that the main ethical decision to be made by a public relations professional is whether or not to undertake a particular assignment, and to cash a particular cheque. Further, it means that unethical professional conduct is any conduct which deliberately undermines the interests of the client, in breach of our contract with them.

Thus seen, it is apparent that it is the practitioner's personal view of the ethics of the client's interests that circumscribes their ethical conduct. Ethics are not defined by the tactics used in a public relations intervention (such as the determination of what to disclose and not to disclose, to whom, when and how). Nor are our ethics rooted in any transcendent set of values (such as honesty, accuracy, integrity and truth in public communications). If we are ethical, we choose to serve clients whose self-defined lawful interests are, in our view, ethical. Or we clear out. Period.

So where does "public enlightenment" come into public relations?

Theoretically, in a free society with a free press, it should go like this: the responsibility of the newsmaker (or their PR agent) is to advance only those facts and advocate only those views that they want the public to receive; reporters have a responsibility to report all the facts and viewpoints they hear from a variety of sources which they deem relevant, so as to provide a fair and "balanced" account of the matter being reported; "public enlightenment" should be the end result of this process.

In practice, needless to say, this dynamic process never works perfectly, but in the long run, it works reasonably well, at least better than any apparent alternative, provided that everyone does their job. However, confounding the role of the public relations professional in this process with that of the journalist, as happens in the CPRS Code, serves neither the process, the profession, our clients, or the public interest. It is, at best, muddle-headed self-deception. It ultimately makes us look foolish, or dishonest, or both.

Time for a Code rethink, I'd say.

DISCUSSION QUESTIONS

1. Research the news reporting around logging in British Columbia, the Alberta oil industry, the Bhopal disaster, or the Exxon *Valdez* oil spill. How is PR at work in statements from company officials?

2. Find some examples of newspeak (our favourite is an airline company that called a crash an "involuntary conversion") and discuss how such language functions to manage a particular crisis.

3. Contrast O'Malley's four propositions with the Canadian Public Relations Society's Code of Professional Standards.

4. Look around campus for evidence of corporate public relations. Is this PR beneficial or problematic in your view?

WEBLINKS

Canadian Public Relations Society Code of Professional Standards
www.cprs.ca/mstwo.htm

Public Relations Society of America
www.prsa.org/

Public Relations Society of America: Tips for crisis management
www.prsa.org/ppc/68001.html

The Center for Media & Democracy (investigative reporting on the public relations industry)
www.prwatch.org/

chapter twenty four

History for Sale:
Let the Buyer Beware

INTRODUCTION

What are the Heritage Minutes and the Historica project: propaganda, a dose of American-style patriotism, or revisionist corporate bafflegab? The articles in this chapter try to answer these questions when dealing with nationalistic commercials on television and new media versions of Canadian history. Two of the articles deal directly with the Heritage Minutes, those short, snappy "commercials for Canada" which many thought were created by the Canadian government. In fact the Heritage Minutes were made by the Charles Bronfman Foundation (CRB) and, according to Elspeth Cameron and Janice Dickin McGinnis, their mission was to make Canadian history "something exciting and inspirational" rather than stereotypically "dull and boring."

Cameron and Dickin McGinnis express mixed feelings about the Heritage Minutes. While they admire their high, American-style production values, they note their similarity to Trivial Pursuit, and later their ambivalence is clear when they wonder about the Minutes' propaganda value. Perhaps their most serious question is reserved for the way in which the Minutes reveal the very myths they seek to propagate—will this "discomfit" viewers, or does this very process of "demystification" promote a healthy nationalism?

Katarzyna Rukszto is concerned with whose stories get told in the Heritage Minutes. Arguing that the Minutes collapse "heritage, nation and culture" into a homogenized "whiteness," she notes that 42 out of 52 of the Minutes deal with white heroism. She also argues that the makers of the Minutes are very selective about what they choose as signifi- cant moments in Canadian history, and she asks if some of the "troublesome" aspects of Canadian society are omitted because they undermine the project of national unity that those who finance the Minutes support.

Paul Webster is concerned by the new-found interest of media moguls (and other kinds of moguls as well) in retelling Canadian history. He sees the creation of both the Dominion Institute and the Historica project as disturbing attempts to revive an old-fashioned, exclusionist brand of historical narrative. Webster notes the self-serving nature of these media history pro- jects—in the end, they sell a very conservative brand of history and they are also commodi- ties that return handsome profits to the very moguls who created them. A win-win situation?

AMBUSHED BY PATRIOTISM: THE WIT, WISDOM AND WIMPS OF HERITAGE MINUTES

Elspeth Cameron and Janice Dickin McGinnis (*Canadian Forum*)

The experience of viewing Heritage Minutes—those one-minute commercials for Canada shown since 1991 on television and in Odeon theatres—bears an eerie resemblance to a cam- era zooming in, panning out, zooming in again. Drawn at first to the imagery, we immedi- ately stepped back like the trained Canadianists we are, to a position of sceptical detachment. Anything that makes anyone feel that good about being Canadian must be suspect. In the end, however, we found the Minutes (now numbering more than 40) too compelling to ignore.

Admittedly, one of the reasons the Minutes succeed is their use of slick techniques associ- ated with American high-tech production values: they are calculated to reach out and grab us by our patriotic throats. Another fascination is their resemblance to Trivial Pursuit—a Canadian game, after all, only this time with all-Canadian content. But the Minutes can also be read at a deeper level. Closer examination reveals that the imagery made accessible by the Minutes touches many of the themes and ideas scholars endeavour to analyze in inaccessible prose.

The Minutes succeed because they function as "cues"—to use Lévi Strauss's term—acti- vating convictions that Canadians hold dear. This was never clearer than at a screening of the Minutes to an American audience. Bewildered by what they saw, the viewers had to have not only the historical content explained but the cultural context as well.

To give but one example of how Canadian audiences are destined to read the Minutes in a culturally conditioned manner, take the truism that Canadian heroes differ fundamen- tally from American heroes. While "theirs" is the larger-than-life aggressive individualist, "ours" is more appropriately dubbed a protagonist and is as likely as not to be a member of either a group or a collectivité, and to be a wimp or a woman.

Of Wimps and Women

"Heroes in Groups" Minutes include "Saguenay Fire" (showing a family saving itself from catastrophe), "Underground Railroad" (about the Quaker network that shuttled slaves north to "freedom") and even "Rural School Teacher" (where a young woman wins her point

Elspeth Cameron and Janice Dickin McGinnis. Ambushed by patriotism: The wit, wisdom and wimps of Heritage Minutes. *Canadian Forum* 73(837), March, 1995. 12-15.

through nurturing consensus). All validate team or group efforts. The urge to do this is so strong, in fact, that "groups" are sometimes manufactured to fill the need. An example is the Minute on the Victoria Cross, wherein separate vignettes about three men who distinguished themselves in quite separate events during the Great War are interwoven into a whole. It is not just their bravery that is being celebrated here; it is also the fact that they had all lived at one point on Pine Street in Winnipeg, renamed, in their honour, Valour Road.

The most interesting example of the wimp hero is James Naismith, the quintessential self-effacing Canadian Superman (the subject of another Minute). In "Basketball," rather than leap tall buildings at a single bound, he sends the janitor up to poke balls out of peach baskets. The treatment of his invention of basketball makes a virtue of ineptitude; it's referred to by an American in the Minute as "some kind of Canadian joke." A similar wimp is Jacques Plante, celebrated for the invention of the hockey mask—i.e., for refusing to take yet another puck in the face.

Women heroes include not only the nameless protagonists in "Rural School Teacher" and "Midwife" but also historical figures whose stories have been retold here to fit the purpose. Nellie McClung and Emily Murphy fight for women's rights, Jennie Trout contributes to the medical education of women by ripping off a fig leaf, la Bolduc triumphs by keeping faith with her right to express herself in song. And Laura Secord once again saves the country, albeit sans cow.

This last Minute also demonstrates the use the series makes of the keen anti-Americanism that has always informed Canadian ideology. It shows up in several of the Minutes. "Underground Railroad" compares Canada favourably to a racist U.S., as does the Ruddick episode (about the Springhill mine explosion) set a century later. Anti-Americanism is central to "Steele of the Mounties," in which an officer uses only firm self-control in deporting a gun-wielding Yankee prospector who doesn't even realize the Yukon is part of Canada.

To be fair, stirrings of Canadian patriotism are not always bought at American expense, but the way that the Minutes "retrieve" some of our stories have a feeling of comparison about them. For example, a good deal of the thrill to such episodes as "Basketball," "Superman," "Bombardier" and "Sir Sandford Fleming (Standard Time)" is the surprise information that these are stories of Canadian invention rather than someone else's. And of course there is the satisfaction of seeing Marconi finally get his kite up on Signal Hill.

The Minutes even strive for quintessential Canadianness in the manner in which they seek to cushion us from any unaccustomed surges of patriotism they may engender in us. Many are told with self-deprecatory humour. "Marconi," "Basketball," "Superman," "Nellie McClung," "Jennie Trout" and "Steele of the Mounties" are all, well, funny. "The Naming of Canada" is presented as a joke in one Minute, the discoverer Nicollet as an idiot in another. The episode on Frontenac is a broad burlesque and, perhaps most outrageously, Victoria's granting of Responsible Government parodies Red Rose Tea ads.

In other words, contrary to what Marshall McLuhan says in his Minute, the medium is not the message. Skilful manipulation of imagery engages us in these Canadian concepts and subliminally suggests other patterns that we espouse. The idea that evolution is better than revolution, for example, is implicit in the trial-and-error methods of surgeon Wilder Penfield, the development of Jacques Plante's hockey mask, the movement from blacksmith to organ builder in Casavant and of course James Naismith's invention of basketball. The notion of making peace instead of war shows up in the Native legend of "Peacemaker," the creation of the United Nations Peace Force in Cyprus and the confrontation between Chief and Officer in the episode on Sitting Bull now in production.

The Sizzle and the Steak

First released at a time when the country perceived itself in national peril, the Minutes were labelled as, among other things, "feel-good agit-prop." Some people assumed them to be federal government propaganda. Instead, they are private initiatives, sponsored by the CRB (Charles R. Bronfman) Foundation. In 1986, Bronfman decided to act on a desire to celebrate extraordinary Canadians. He invested part of the proceeds from his sale of the Montreal Expos in an effort to transform the teaching of Canadian history from something dull and boring into something exciting and inspirational.

It is important to understand that the propagandistic Heritage Minutes are, according to Deborah Morrisson, spokesperson for their creators, only the "sizzle." The "steak" it promises is being cooked up in the kitchen of the Heritage Project, which has its headquarters in the Foundation offices in Montreal and connections with Queen's and Simon Fraser universities. The Project is working to develop a complex range of teaching aids for use in classrooms, but also for such popular venues as airports and shopping malls.

Still, many people will see only the commercials. To argue that simplification of complex ideas and situations is excusable because the Minutes are only meant to create a demand, not sell a product, is disingenuous. They attract our attention through excitement and inspiration, things Canadians are generally suspicious of in themselves and others. Is it ever safe to traffic in propaganda? Is dissemination of visceral imagery always innately dangerous?

We would argue that much depends on whose images are being disseminated. No matter how slickly they are produced, the images in the Heritage Minutes are ours, mainly because Bronfman's Heritage Project has consulted widely with Canadian experts from both the scholarly community and the media—and has responsibly polled the public. For example, it sought and received special participation on the part of the B.C. Chinese community for the final version of the "Nitro" Minute. On a broader level, three television programs based on the quiz format openly invited viewer participation in further development of the Project.

Perhaps the most unsettling thing about the Heritage Minutes is that they confront us with feelings and myths about our country. They make palpable what for many are deeply buried convictions. While such exposure can be intensely discomfiting, it is our duty as Canadians to confront it. In facing and debating basic tenets of our heritage, we have the opportunity to articulate and shape our identity, an exercise that has become increasingly pressing in this era of so-called global culture.

UP FOR SALE: THE COMMODIFICATION OF CANADIAN CULTURE

Katarzyna Rukszto (*FUSE Magazine*)

McDonald's, the fast food chain, is the new player on Canada's arts and culture scene. The company has agreed to distribute and subsidize True North comics, a series of historical comics produced by McClelland and Stewart and the CRB Foundation. The first comic in the series, with a new comic due to be distributed every three months, is "The Halifax Explosion," which depicts the 1917 collision of two ships in the Halifax Harbour. The dis-

Katarzyna Rukszto. Up for sale: The commodification of Canadian culture. *FUSE Magazine* 20(4), 1997. 7. (The research and writing of this article was generously assisted by a grant from Toronto Arts Council.)

aster resulted in over 2000 deaths. Upcoming comics will depict the discovery of dinosaur remains in Canada, the building of the Canadian railways and the story of the hockey mask.

The comics are based on the Heritage Minutes, also produced by the CRB Foundation and shown on television and in movie theatres. Largely hailed as an innovative way to attract kids and teenagers to Canadian history, this collaboration raises questions about the impact of market prerogatives on Canadian art and culture. One of these questions is, what sells?

Selling at Home

Barbara Godard argues that the establishment of the Canada Council has produced a home-grown cultural community, where "no longer dependent on the market place of the metropole, artists could create more freely for the Canadian public."[1] But forsaking international fame in the name of artistic integrity may soon be left without much reward. As more and more artists turn to fundraising to weather the storm of cuts to Canadian arts organizations, different strings get attached to their work on the domestic front. Unlike Canada Council, with its arms-length policy, funding from private foundations and financiers often comes with specific criteria for the artists' work based on the mandate of the organization. The artists, still producing for the Canadian public, are bound by the representational limits that such mandates impose. While the objective of selling Canada abroad is not omnipresent, in the case of organizations or agencies mandated to promote national unity the objective of selling Canada to Canadians can be as limiting. The question becomes, which stories will be told, which aspects of Canadian collective memory get financed?

The Heritage Minutes that gave rise to the True North comics distributed at McDonald's are one example of work produced by artists guided by the objectives of private financiers of "Canadian culture." The CRB Foundation developed its Heritage Project in order "to increase young people's sense of Canadian pride and identity by stimulating greater interest in Canada's past." The Minutes, high quality "mini-movies" about notable Canadian events and persons, form the centrepiece of this project. Clearly then, while the Minutes were not designed as export material, they are in the business of selling Canada to Canadians. The writers, directors and actors involved in the creation of the Minutes were guided by the objectives of the CRB Foundation Heritage Project, dedicated as it is to promoting Canadian heritage.

On the surface, the Heritage Minutes offer an assortment of diverse moments in Canadian history, from Ukrainian migration to the Prairies to Canadian inventions of such highly Americanized symbols as the basketball hoop and Superman. They certainly do feature, as the Project's promotional literature boasts, "such diverse subjects as political rights, heroism, achievements in sports and entertainment, women's issues, and medical breakthroughs." But what I would like to know is, would Andrew Moodie's potential film based on *Riot* have better luck getting funded by the Foundation?

Selling Abroad

The debate about the marketability of Canadian culture (and, conversely, whether such a thing is desirable) has been raised to a new pitch on the heels of comments by Trade Minister Art Eggleton about the viability of protectionist cultural policies. Eggleton suggested that the policies that protect Canadian cultural ownership and control may in fact hinder the export of Canadian cultural products. These latest comments provided more ammunition to publishers, arts groups, TV producers and writers who have consistently criticized the federal and provincial governments' lack or withdrawal of commitment to the arts. But the fury was also directed (at least by some) at the prejudicial interest of Eggleton in commercial artistic ventures, in fostering the link between artists and private enterprise. Again, if selling Canada is the objective of institutions providing financial support to artists, what will be on the market? Remember the criticism of the CRTC for rendering its decision that Bryan Adams' record did not have enough Canadian content? How do commercially successful Canadian superstars—Celine Dion, Shania Twain, Bryan Adams—differ from their American counterparts?

The debate clearly recognizes two markets, the domestic and the export. The problems with exporting cultural products anchored in Canadian politics and cultures has been well documented. Andrew Moodie, the author of the award-winning *Riot*, has recently reported on the seemingly insurmountable difficulties of turning his play into a movie without sacrificing recognizable Canadian content.[2] American cultural invasion notwithstanding, *Riot* is about a group of young Black Canadians living in Toronto during the riot sparked by the Rodney King verdict. Moodie writes of the seeming incongruity in the movie industry between, in the words of a Canadian producer he quotes, "producing for Canada and producing for the world." Moodie's lament against the metamorphosis of the Kensington Market stuffed pepper into a Big Mac is shared by many others (witness such domestically successful, but internationally unknown artists as Luba, The Parachute Club, Jane Siberry and The Tragically Hip).

Advertising Heritage

The CRB Foundation Heritage Project is explicitly devoted to promoting Canadian heritage. This it does by sponsoring educational forums and fairs about Canadian heritage, by funding the creation of learning resources about Canadian heritage, and by producing the Heritage Minutes. Since their first arrival on our television screens, the Minutes have become a recognizable reference in Canadian pop culture. One would be hard pressed to find anyone with a TV set who has not seen some of the Minutes, and a spoof of the Minutes has even made it into the repertoire of "This Hour Has 22 Minutes."

The Heritage Minutes are a rather curious product(ion). They are promoted as mini-movies, but are shown in the advertising space of television and cinema. The series' mandate (and it does have one) is, at times, excruciatingly obvious: its objective is to foster national identification among Canadian citizens by raising awareness of and interest in Canadian heritage and history. The pathos and solemnity of the Minutes emphasize the sacredness of their subject, and the seriousness of their address. Whether the focus is on the famous Saguenay Fire or Nellie McClung's activism, the Minutes tell us, one after another, that we have much to be proud of. Our heritage is rich and adventurous, full of heroes and inventors; in the words of Michael Valpy, it is "our cultural DNA." If they were exportable, the Minutes would fit the criteria for funding from External Affairs. The recently published set of guidelines by that department for artists applying for travel grants specified that artists who promote "respect for Canadian unity and Canadian sovereignty" will be eligible.[3] A number of Heritage Minutes focus explicitly on the relations between the English and the French in Canada. The Heritage Minute titled "Baldwin and Lafontaine" is exemplary in its depiction of the "two politicians from Upper and Lower Canada [who] demonstrate an early example of French/English cooperation when Lafontaine seeks election in Toronto and goes on to help shape democratic reforms of all Canada."[4] The hopeful possibility of brotherly love is carried through all of the Minutes depicting French-English relations. National unity is the emblem of the series.

The nationalist address of the Minutes promotes "the role of art in nation-building as civilizing to unify."[5] The narrative of heritable belonging is silently couched against the forces of plural narratives and critiques of the nation. The discourse of these representations is one that is shared by many believers in the panacea of "cross-communication": we don't see ourselves/each other as Canadians because we are ignorant of our history/heritage. The role of the minutes, as one vehicle of communication, is to infuse patriotism into the everyday of Canadians. That great Canadian pastime, the game of "what is a Canadian," will be more entertaining with answers in the positive.

Truth in Advertising

What are the representational limits that organize the work of artists in such an enterprise? What aspects of the Canadian imaginary sell, and which cannot be "consumed" as heritage? It is quite clear that national unity is the over-riding theme of the CRB Foundation series. But the Minutes do represent moments of crisis, diverse populations and political conflicts. When read casually (like an ad) the Minutes can be seen as participants in a larger pedagogical discourse of multiculturalism as a sort of history lesson from a liberal educational perspective. But the impetus behind this lesson in cross-cultural understanding of Canadians' different experiences is to homogenize them as "heritage." Although diverse, the heritage traits that Canadians are deemed to share are those of adventure, survival and cooperation in the joint project of nation-building. That's our cultural DNA.

The theme of national unity creates enormous strains on artists interested in those histories best known for their challenges to and survival against the Canadian nation-state. The minute "Underground Railroad" fully embodies the contradictions of telling a story of struggle against racist oppression within the framework of homogenizing nationalism. In this minute, a distraught Black woman is awaiting her loved one who is journeying to freedom in Canada. A white woman saves the day by restraining the hysterical Black woman. Black people are the grateful recipients of the organization of good white folks on their behalf, shouting praises for Canada as the land of freedom. While it is commendable that the story of Black presence in Canada is included in this popular rendition of Canadian heritage, it is done so only by removing all hints of the mistreatment that awaited Black people here. It is just a hunch, but I doubt that a minute about the return to the United States during and after the American Civil War of the majority of African Americans who fled to Canada is in the making.[6] Could a minute be made about the infamous razing of Africville, or about the police shootings of young Black men?

The framework of national unity necessarily homogenizes the subject of its address. Heritage, nation and culture are collapsed into one, presupposing the homogeneous "Canadian." At the same time, there is a tension between this generic Canadian and the actual histories and presence of voices intent on making their particularity within the Canadian nation-state known. This brings us back to the questions of "our" culture's genes.

The DNA of Nationalist Discourse

For an artist who is commissioned/hired to participate in such a venture as the Heritage Minutes, the question of what will sell as Canadian heritage can be a troublesome one. Often it seems to have been answered in the traditional mode of heritage discourse, that is by showcasing great men and women and their contributions to the project of nation-building. Not surprisingly, this approach resulted in the overwhelming whitening of the Canadian "mosaic." While diversity—of gender, ethnic origins, political persuasion, religious belonging, hobbies—organizes the series, it is contained within a mostly white populace. It is this racial grammar that literally enhances the metaphor of genes to describe the representations of Canadian identity. Out of fifty-two Minutes, forty-two are stories of white heroism, adventure and contributions to the nation.

The homogenizing effect of the Heritage Minutes reminds me of another display of the Canadian imaginary, the "Oh! Canada Project" presentation at the AGO, "starring" the Group of Seven. That exhibit also struggled with the contradictions between the myth of national identity (represented by the Group of Seven) and the actuality of multiple differences (represented by the "community-based arts groups" included in the exhibit). The spatial arrangement of the various segments of the show naturalized the dominant/subordinate relations in the larger society. The result, as argued by Rinaldo Walcott, was that "the very people who a colonizing discourse of nation must relegate to the margins of national space (both real and imagined) are housed on the margins of 'The Group of Seven: Art for a Nation' exhibit."[7]

The DNA of Canadian culture and heritage presented in the Minutes is a highly racialized one. As the most dominant presence in the Minutes, whiteness is produced as a heritable trait of the nation. Visually, the Minutes establish European presence and culture as the founding principle of Canada. Now this should not be read as some kind of conspiracy on the part of the producers of the series to purposely render Canada white. For all we know, each minute may have been conceptualized and produced quite independently of the others, and the selection of concepts for the Minutes may have to do with such things as regional representation, ratio of historical figures to events and so on. Regardless of the process, the result is quite extraordinary. Whiteness is the dominant gene in the Canadian body politic.

However, the Minutes, like the Oh! Canada Project, consciously display its awareness of the existence of multiple ways of belonging. It can be said that the series is responsive to the crisis in representation that is being felt in all areas of cultural and political life in Canada. Dionne Brand has called it a certain panic:

> . . . the panic of the "white" intellectual elite. It now hears other opinions and experiences of the people of colour in the country who challenge its definitions of what the country is and what it looks like.[8]

This means that some gestures that reference the unequal ways of belonging to the nation must now be made. The specific processes of Canadian nation-building have been made known through marginalized artists' art and literature. The Heritage Minutes, unable to deny difference within the body politic, attempt to neutralize them through the narrative of common heritage. Because difference can interrupt the seamlessness of a nationalist address, it is stripped of all oppositional traits. The minute "Nitro" admits that Chinese railway workers were oppressed, but that's ancient history now (embodied through the figure of a Chinese elder telling the story to his grandchildren); similarly, aboriginal communities are imagined in the Minutes as relics of the past, Canadian heritage itself.

Selling Canada, both abroad and at home, is a difficult task. The troublesome events that continue to occur simply don't construct a glossy story of Canada "the good." Would Eli Langer's interrogation of child sexuality ever become a part of a Canadian conversation about ourselves in popular media, rather than an excuse for tabloid scandal-mongering? Can troublesome people, particular acts and art be sellable as Canadian heritage? As we enter an era when government officials argue for a "national" culture that sells, will cultural producers be forced deeper into poverty, or will they have to capitulate to private financiers' dictates on representational strategies?

Notes

1.   Barbara Godard "Writing on the Wall," *Border/Lines* 38-39, 1995, p. 101.

2.   Andrew Moodie, "The King and I: Al Waxman (almost) makes a movie about young black Canadians," *This Magazine* 30, no. 5, 1997.

3.   Lysiane Gagnon, "Effort to Boost Unity Through Artists is Wrong-Headed," *The Globe and Mail*, 22 February 1997, p. D3.

4.   CRB Foundation Heritage Project, promotional materials.

5.   Godard, op. cit., p. 102.

6.   Bruce R. Shepard, *Deemed Unsuitable* (Toronto: Umbrella Press, 1997), p. 10.

7.   Rinaldo Walcott, "Lament for a Nation: The Racial Geography of 'The Oh! Canada Project,'" *FUSE Magazine* 19, no. 4, 1996, p.16.

8.   Quoted in Scott McFarlane, "The Haunt of Race: Canada's Multiculturalism Act, the Politics of Incorporation and Writing Thru Race," *FUSE Magazine* 18, no. 3, 1995, p. 20.

WHO STOLE CANADIAN HISTORY?

Paul Webster (*This Magazine*)

Canadian history used to be merely yesterday's news. It is now today's hot national concern. Just why are Canada's corporate giants, from Charles Bronfman to "Red" Wilson, pouring money into foundations and projects promoting the subject?

When the Toronto Four Seasons Hotel opened in Yorkville in 1971, the ghosts of the rebels of 1837, who used to ride through the area on their way to Montgomery's tavern, were thought to be displeased with the not-so-subtle scenery change. It was a building that utterly defied local history. The 32 storeys of guest-swaddling concrete in brutally basic skyscraper style didn't endear themselves to local antiquarians either. Plush synthetic Persian rugs, paper-thin hardwood veneers, plate brass and pseudo antique chandeliers do lend a certain aerosol colonial charm to the place, but even so, few can deny it is an unanswerable statement of contemporary corporate convictions.

It was thus a significant venue for the launch of the largest initiative in Canadian History by Lynton "Red" Wilson, chairman of Bell Canada Enterprises. "As citizens, we need to take the initiative and get involved," Wilson told a gathering of history-minded businessmen and reporters at the launch of his new foundation last fall. "And that is why we are asking leaders of the business community to join us in creating Historica." Details on the foundation are still in development, but Wilson says the main plan is for Historica to focus on building Canadian history's presence on the Internet and on TV. With a picture of a computer on every other page of its brochure, Historica wants to build the cyber-venue where educators will find "a truly Canadian community on the Internet . . . providing multi-layered information

Paul Webster. Who stole Canadian history? *This Magazine* 33(5), March/April, 2000. 28-31 on Canadian historical events and placing them in a pan-Canadian, chronological context. . . . Celebrating the future of our past, Historica is a lasting gift to Canadians."

When Wilson pledged $500 000 for the foundation, people were impressed. Next, Imasco, Royal Bank, Toronto-Dominion Bank, the Bank of Nova Scotia, McCain, Weston, McClelland & Stewart, CanWest Global, Maritime Broadcasting and a bunch of other memory-minded brands pledged a further $10 million. Then Charles Bronfman said he would match their money. If the federal government answers their call to match that total, Wilson's foundation will have $50 million. Historica is not the only foundation of its kind. Bronfman has his own foundation, the Charles R. Bronfman Foundation, which funds various history projects. Then there's the Dominion Institute, also dedicated to reviving history. Cleo herself must be impressed. Canadian history is getting its very own millennial dust-off.

In a field where news is archived for at least a decade or two, then retrieved on microfilm, these are strange days. History, it seems, has become an issue for the chauffeur-driven crowd, an urgent cultural concern, just like split-run magazines, cable TV, the NHL and the CBC. That's true south of the border, too: if you take a taxi from New York's La Guardia airport into Manhattan these days, you'll get a glimpse of why history matters. Towering over a significant chunk of Queens is an enormous golden "H." Below it, an inscription urges commuters to watch History TV. Look up as you pass Columbus Circle, and you'll see a giant neon sign flashing an ad for Biography TV. History makes great fodder for low-budget, high-ratings TV, and network executives are making money off it in, well, historical proportions.

For Canada's newfound corporate history buffs, public relations is key: an interest in history is considered a noble pursuit. Giving money to it soothes the conscience. Charles Bronfman's personal foundation has been pumping out Heritage Minutes for years (though cynics would say he's needed a bigger PR boost since his multibillion-dollar family trust slid out of the country, tax free.)

So Historica seems to be born of a pretty typical mix: ratings, rewards and redemption. But there's more to it than that. History is about ideology, not just industry. "Education in the history of Canada is essential preparation for responsible citizenship," Red Wilson said at a conference of Canadian historians at McGill University last winter. Wilson says he's "profoundly concerned as a Canadian" about historians' success in "encouraging reasonable loyalty, national pride and citizenship."

Parsing that statement should be relatively easy. When Toronto patricians start talking about loyalty and citizenship, they're usually worried about one of two things: Quebec or the monarchy. In this case, some historians fear it's both. "History is the latest cultural tool favoured by the financial elite to calm their national unity fears," says Dalhousie University historian Michael Cross. "We're back at an argument that began in the 1960s. Back then, the idea of Canadian history was painfully reinvented to overcome the limitations of the approach Bronfman and Wilson now seem to be again promoting. I worry the clock is being turned back."

To understand Cross's concern, you need to remember some history. Up until the 1960s, Canadian history was barely credited as a worthy scholarly field. Underfunded and isolated, scholars such as George Wrong, Frank Underhill, Harold Innis, Arthur Lower and Donald Creighton struggled to develop a national history. Their most abiding success came with the publication of Creighton's 1944 synthesis, *The Dominion of the North*. Creighton's vision of a unified—and unifying—national history promoted Canada as a story of conflict resolved: two nations, fused into a modern power on the world stage.

Not surprisingly, this tidy vision proved serviceable for only a brief period. There's a film archived somewhere deep in the bowels of the CBC that was telecast in 1972 as *The Craft of History*. In it, the new social historian Ramsay Cook interviews Arthur Lower, Donald Creighton and Michel Brunet, a Quebec historian with a strong nationalist orientation. The film is a relic of the days before History TV, of a time when historians were allowed to appear on TV as themselves, rather than as the disembodied sources of heavily edited ideas voiced by actors as cover script for video sequences.

The producers were bold in their own quaint way (remember, this is before the CBC went commercial). They had Cook interview Lower in his boat out in Lake Ontario. It was one of those small, quiet, epochal events. One of the great proponents of the old history was out on a lake with one of the new historians, and the whole thing was being recorded by the (now old) new media. It was show biz, but Lower stuck to his script: The history of the French-Canadian identity starts with the Conquest. Confederation and Conquest are of the "first importance" in our history. When Cook pressed Lower about Canadians' "colonial mentality," Lower switched on the motor and changed the topic. "I think we're uncomfortably close to the shore there, Ramsay," he said. "No danger of going on the rocks."

But the Creighton-and-Lower vision grew stale. With a flood of new money for Canadian universities in the 1960s, and a popular surge of interest in Centennial themes in 1967, Canadian history was blossoming. And it wasn't the same old Canadian history. According to University of Toronto historian Carl Berger, the number of historians in Canada expanded sixfold through the 1970s. The new historians successfully focused on social themes: women, labour, the environment, minorities, immigrants and aboriginal people—narratives that had gone mostly untouched by older historians. While promoting a more diverse understanding of Canada's past, they began downgrading some of their predecessors' ideas. Unifying notions such as the two founding nations, the concept of a classless society, the country where slavery never existed and where the wars were fought in noble ways for noble causes began to crumble. Confederation was no longer the cure for Conquest and colonialism.

The new social historians measured their success not only in academic terms. They've been astonishingly effective in conveying their results to film, TV and literature. The CBC—which is currently producing a 30-hour "people's history"—has been especially receptive to a broadened, diversified history encompassing the issues that, in truth, divide as well as unite.

People anxious about national unity were bound to take offence. It was the precarious result of the October 30, 1995, Quebec referendum on separation that finally triggered decisive counteraction. But the backlash didn't come from within Canadian history departments. It came from the financial community. Quite a few powerful businessmen must have woken up on the morning after the referendum thinking Canadian history looked less like a big snowy map sprinkled with obscure dates and places and much more like a blood-stained spreadsheet. Before long, heavyweights such as Imasco, Consumers Gas, Alliance Communications, RBC-Dominion Securities, History TV and the right-wing Donner Foundation were backing a new lobby organization dedicated to redirecting history. They called it the Dominion Institute. If you think the name sounds like a throwback to the monarchy, you're on the right track.

The Dominion Institute spent most of its start-up capital in 1997 on a series of Angus Reid polls that purported to demonstrate that Canadians don't know their history. Once that chasm of need was created, the results were turned over to Jack Granatstein, a retired York University historian. Granatstein is a Dominion Institute director—along with Mike Harris's adviser, Allister Campbell, and Conrad Black's closest business associate, Peter White. Granatstein used the Dominion polls as the basis for a 1998 book titled *Who killed Canadian History?*, which argues that the post-Creighton generation of Canadian historians shirked its cultural responsibilities by shifting "to victimization and blame-seeking on the fringes." The message was businesslike: "We pay vast sums for education," complained Canada's favourite gradgrind, "and we are simply not getting the returns we should."

This bottom-line theme went down well with the corporations behind the Dominion Institute, which regularly calls for a national history curriculum focused on the wars, the prime ministers, the constitution and the economy. Why teach all the divisive stuff, Granatstein asks, and why promote multicultural examinations of our past? "The aim of every Canadian and of all levels of government should be to welcome immigrants and turn them into Canadian citizens as quickly as possible," Granatstein wrote. "Not one cent of federal, provincial, or municipal government money should be devoted to fostering retention of their cultures."

Granatstein proposed action. He called for "clear, measurable standards" for teaching history: "Courses must be grounded solidly in chronology, and must treat both the political and the social history of the nation," he wrote. He recommended that the federal government intervene (as, of course, it already does) with cash for television and radio history programs, and the establishment of a Centre for Canadian History, located "near, but not at, a major university."

Then, less than two years later, along came Historica. Not surprisingly, Red Wilson says he consulted extensively with Granatstein concerning the plan for the rich new foundation. There will be foundation money for staid stuff like Canada's National History Society and *The Dictionary of Canadian Biography* (as editor of the dictionary, Ramsey Cook, one of the stars of that 1972 CBC documentary, will be getting a little help from Historica). But the first priority will be the Internet. The Historica board (which brings together tobacco, energy, banking, telephone, TV and publishing executives with former politicians Frank McKenna and Peter Lougheed, three Bronfman representatives, several corporate lawyers and former Chief Justice of Canada Antonio Lamer, all in the absence of a single historian or teacher) met for the first time in early February and voted to back five Web-based projects, more Heritage Minutes and a TV series, produced in partnership with History Television. Historica also plans to back several grassroots projects directly aimed at school kids and teachers.

The e-and-TV emphasis here comes as no surprise: Wilson and the others behind Historica own a good chunk of our airwaves and cyberspace. Business development is always better when it's tax-deductible.

This is not the first time Canadian business has tackled history. In the 1950s, businessmen took education very seriously. An Industrial Foundation on Education, set up by the president of the A.V. Roe Company in 1956, promoted education in all fields, including history. But in those days business wanted a more complex and cosmopolitan history. An editorial in the Bank of Montreal's "Monthly Letter" of August 1960 reveals this concern. "It is a fatal mistake," wrote the Bank's editors, "to believe that democratic education consists of teaching children some of the facts about our government and making them learn the provisions of the British North America Act." Now, the banks seem to want this approach back.

It's of course important that business leaders take an interest in education. But the notion that the financial elite can step in to direct scholarship and schoolteachers to serve national unity (or any other political concern) is so obviously dubious as to seem self-satirical. Scholars and patrons with the Maple Leaf in their eyes should do some quick background reading. Historical approaches designed for specific utilitarian purposes such as national unity or citizen loyalty (or the monarchy, for that matter) seldom age well. Herodotus may be celebrated as the fourth century BC father of history, but much of his work long ago fell into partisan disrepute. Edmund Burke's attack on revolutionary French democracy soured in the same way. More recently, historiography scripted to serve both sides of the Cold War has been junked.

"They're not going to be able to leverage history into a force for national unity," says Michael Cross, "no matter how many millions they say they'll spend." Teachers need to make independent curriculum decisions based on independent scholarship and input from students and parents, says Cross. Besides, scholars and educators are fiercely territorial. They're not about to let a telephone executive, a beverage billionaire, a business lobby group or even Jack Granatstein dictate new terms.

"History must be defended against attempts to abuse it in the cause of change. We should constantly be on our guard against theories which either dismiss the past or give it a drastically new interpretation." When Donald Creighton said these words in a speech at Trent University in November 1965, he had the new social historians' radicalism in his sights. "Such theories are likely to abound in an age of doubt and uncertainty about the future," Creighton continued, "and most of them, whether consciously or unconsciously, have been developed to serve the radical program of the moment." One wonders what Creighton would think of Granatstein's project now, were he alive. Might he display the same distaste?

"An understanding of the historical context of any society is the only way to make sense of the motivations that drive behaviour, including the behaviour of business counter-parts and customers," says Wilson in the Historica brochure. Utilitarian thinking from a util-ity boss is fine. But he's not talking telecom strategy. Among other things, he's talking about the rebels of 1837. You can just imagine what they're thinking: first they build the Four Seasons, now this.

The new social historians taught us that we are more than the sum of our wars, our prime ministers, our constitution, our economy, our unity and our disunity. Canada has always been a complicated country. Paradox is our strongest cultural condition. In the words of Donald Creighton, "A nation that repudiates or distorts its past runs a grave danger of forfeiting its future."

DISCUSSION QUESTIONS

1. Cameron and Dickin McGinnis argue that the Heritage Minutes "unsettle" the audience because they confront viewers with "feelings and myths" about Canada. Discuss some of these Canadian myths and the way Heritage Minutes handle them.

2. Discuss the Heritage Minutes as propaganda, and respond to Cameron and Dickin McGinnis's query about the safety of the "dissemination of visceral imagery" on television.

3. Discuss the concern expressed in the Rukszto and Webster articles about the power of private, foreign, or domestic financiers over the "representational strategies" used to sell Canadian culture.

4. Have a look at the Historica or Schoolnet Web sites. Discuss their interpretations of Canadian history.

WEBLINKS

CRB Foundation
heritage.excite.sfu.ca/

Dominion Institute
www.schoolnet.ca/greatquestions/e/about_di.html

Historica
www.historica.ca/

"The Canadians—Biography of a Nation"
www.histori.ca/historica/eng_site/resources/the_cdns/intro.html

The History Channel
www.historychannel.com

Heritage Post Interactive
heritage.excite.sfu.ca/hpost_e/defaultlsh1.html

"Canada: A People's History"
cbc.ca/history/

List of Contributors

Charlie Angus is a journalist and editor of *HighGrader Magazine*. He is also a singer, songwriter, and guitarist with the Grievous Angels.

Ian Austen is a freelance writer based in Ottawa.

Brenda Austin-Smith is an assistant professor of English at the University of Manitoba.

Maude Barlow is the national volunteer chairperson of the Council of Canadians and the co-chair of Action Canada Network. She is the author of four best-selling books, including *Class Warfare: The Assault on Canada's Schools* (with Heather Jane Robertson) and *Straight Through the Heart* (with Bruce Campell).

Cheryl Binning is a freelance writer specializing in film and television, and based in Winnipeg. She has written for various industry publications including *Playback Magazine*, *Real Screen*, *Take One*, *Montage Magazine*, and *The Hollywood Reporter*. She was formerly associate editor at *Playback Magazine*.

Alan Borovoy is General Counsel of the Canadian Civil Liberties Association and author of *The New Anti-Liberals*.

Paula Brook is a Vancouver-based journalist and author.

Elspeth Cameron is a professor of English at the University of Toronto.

Andrew Cash is a musician and writer based in Toronto.

Joe Chidley is a journalist with *Maclean's*.

Andrew Clark is a writer for *Maclean's* magazine.

Tony Clarke now heads the Polaris Institute and is author of *Silent Coup, Confronting the Big Business Takeover of Canada* (Canadian Centre for Policy Alternatives and James Lorimer & Co., Ltd.).

Lynn Coady is a writer and essayist. Her work includes a novel, *Strange Heaven* (Goose Lane Editions, 1998), and a collection of short stories, *Play the Monster Blind* (Doubleday Canada, 2000). A second novel, as yet untitled, is due to be published by Doubleday Canada and Houghton Mifflin (USA) in the spring of 2002.

Ronald I. Cohen is National Chair, Canadian Broadcast Standards Council.

Christy Ann Conlin is a writer and crew member of a lobster boat in Nova Scotia.

Ray Conlogue is *The Globe and Mail*'s Quebec Arts Correspondent and the author of *Impossible Nation: The Longing For Homeland in Quebec and Canada* (Mercury Press).

Andrew Coyne is formerly a columnist for *The Ottawa Citizen*, and is now with *The National Post*.

Janice Dickin McGinnis is a professor of General Studies at the University of Calgary.

Greig Dymond is a Toronto-based television and radio producer, and co-author of *Mondo Canuck: A Canadian Pop Culture Odyssey* (Prentice Hall).

Sarah Elton is a Toronto-based writer.

John Fraser is the Master of Massey College at the University of Toronto and former editor of *Saturday Night* magazine.

Robert Fulford is a Toronto author, journalist, broadcaster, and editor. He writes a weekly column *for The National Post* and is a frequent contributor to *Toronto Life*, *Canadian Art*, and CBC radio and television. His books include *Best Seat in the House: Memoirs of a Lucky Man* (1988), *Accidental City: The Transformation of Toronto* (1995), and *Toronto Discovered* (1998).

Samir Gandesha is a Toronto-based writer and professor in the Department of Arts and Science at Centennial College.

Rachel Giese writes a regular column for *The Toronto Star*.

Sky Gilbert is a writer, theatre director and drag queen extraordinaire. His memoir of his years as the artistic director of Buddies in Bad Times Theatre, *Ejaculations From The Charm Factory*, was recently published by ECW Press. ECW will publish his next novel, *I Am Kasper Klotz* (an AIDS dissident novel), in 2001.

Don Gillmor is a freelance writer based in Toronto.

Terry Glavin is a Mayne Island, B.C. writer whose most recent book, *This Ragged Place—Travels Across the Landscape* (New Star Books) was nominated for a Governor General's Literary Award 1997 in non-fiction.

Noreen Golfman teaches English and film studies at Memorial University of Newfoundland.

Marina Gonick teaches sociology at O.I.S.E., University of Toronto.

Charles Gordon is a columnist for *The Ottawa Citizen* and *Maclean's* magazine.

Taras Grescoe is a Montreal-based writer and author of *Sacre Blues: An Unsentimental Journey through Quebec*.

The Hon. Henry (Hal) Jackman is currently Chancellor of the University of Toronto.

Anita Lahey is a freelance writer based in Ottawa.

Bruce Livesey is a Toronto-based journalist and staff reporter with the newspaper *Eye Weekly*.

David MacFarlane is the author of *Summer Gone* and *The Danger Tree*. He writes a weekly column for *The Globe and Mail*.

Thelma McCormack is Professor Emerita: Research Associate at the Institute for Social Research, York University.

Brian McKenna is a film and television producer.

Martin Melhuish is a Toronto-based author, freelance writer, and entrepreneur. He has authored several books and written for North America's top music publications.

David Menzies is a freelance writer based in Toronto.

John Miller is director of newspaper journalism at Ryerson Polytechnic University and founding editor of *The Crier*. Earlier in his career he was deputy managing editor of *The Toronto Star.*

William Morgan is a former CBC Ombudsman.

Vincent Mosco is a professor of communication, sociology and political economy at Carleton University. He is the author of *The Political Economy of Communication: Rethinking and Renewal.*

Nicole Nolan is a freelance writer formerly based in Toronto, currently in New York.

Peter O'Malley is an Ottawa-based consultant who has been a member of Canadian Public Relations Society for 15 years, and has served on the Board of Directors of the Ottawa Society.

Linda Pannozzo is a freelance journalist and researcher living on Nova Scotia's south shore.

Geoff Pevere is the co-author of *Mondo Canuck: A Canadian Pop Culture Odyssey*. His new book, *Team Spirit: A Field Guide to Roots Culture*, will be published by Doubleday this fall.

Dr. Victor Rabinovitch is the head of Canada's largest museum, the Canadian Museum of Civilization, in Hull-Ottawa. He was formerly the Assistant Deputy Minister of Cultural Development in the federal Department of Canadian Heritage. He has an extensive background in both public policy and program administration.

Krishna Rau is a freelance writer based in Toronto.

Jake Reichert is a Winnipeg teacher and writer.

Gail Robertson is a journalist at *The Windsor Star* and a lecturer in Communications Studies at The University of Windsor. She is currently on leave from her job at the newspaper and living on Pelee Island.

Heather Jane Robertson is director of professional development for the Canadian Teachers' Federation, an executive member of the Canadian Centre for Policy Alternatives, and co-author (with Maude Barlow) of the best-selling book, *Class Warfare*.

Katarzyna Rukszto is in the Sociology Department at York University.

Douglas Rushkoff is the author of *Coersion, Media Virus!* and *Ecstacy Club.*

Rick Salutin is a journalist, writer, and a regular columnist in *The Globe and Mail* on Canadian media, politics, and cultural issues.

Doug Saunders is a features journalist at *The Globe and Mail.*

Erika Shaker is a researcher and Director of the Canadian Centre for Policy Alternatives' Education Project.

Jeffrey Shallit is an associate professor of Computer Science at the University of Waterloo and a founding member of Electronic Frontier Canada.

David C. Smith is a professor of education in the Department of Values and Culture at McGill University.

Philip Sullivan teaches at the Institute for Aerospace Studies, University of Toronto, and was a member of the Board of the Society for Academic Freedom and Scholarship.

Richard Swift is a writer and frequent contributor to the *New Internationalist.*

Maurice Switzer is a member of the Mississaugas of Rice Lake First Nation at Alderville, Ontario, and Director of Communications for the Assembly of First Nations.

Clive Thompson is an editor at *Shift* magazine and a writer for publications including *Report on Business Magazine, The New York Times, This Magazine*, and *Newsday.*

Maria Tippett is a Senior Research Fellow at Churchill College and member of the Faculty of History, Cambridge University, as well as a Fellow of the Royal Society of Canada. She has written biographies on Emily Carr, for which she won the Governor General's Award and the John A. Macdonald Prize, and F.H. Varley. She has also written studies of Canadian culture—Canadian art and the Great War, a history of cultural institutions in the twentieth century, Canadian women and the visual arts, and British Columbia landscape painting—in addition to a memoir and a collection of short stories. She is currently writing a biography of Bill Reid.

Bruce Wallace is a journalist with *Maclean's Magazine*.

Patrick Watson is a journalist, filmmaker, producer, and former Chair of the CBC.

Paul Webster is a documentary producer for the CBC. He is currently on leave from the CBC and is living in Russia, where he is writing a book on Russia's environmental crisis.

David Weiner is a Senior Partner at NATIONAL Public Relations, specializing in corporate communications and issues management.

Dwayne Winseck is an associate professor at Carleton University's School of Journalism and Communication. His most recent book is *Reconvergence: A political economy of telecommunications in Canada*.

James Winter is a professor of communications at the University of Windsor. He is the author of four books, including *Democracy's Oxygen*, on corporate concentration in the news media, and *Common Cents: Media Portrayal of the Gulf War and Other Events*.

Chris Wood writes for *Maclean's Magazine*.

Maxwell Yalden was Chief Commissioner of the Canadian Human Rights Commission from November 1987 to December 1996.